日本生物武器作战调查资料

〔日〕近藤昭二　王　选／主编

第四册

社会科学文献出版社
SOCIAL SCIENCES ACADEMIC PRESS (CHINA)

目 录

7 日本细菌部队人员向美国提供的人体实验解剖报告

7　日本细菌部队人员向美国提供的人体实验解剖报告

7.1 The Report of “A”

资料出处： Technical Library, Dugway Proving Grounds, Utah, US.

内容点评： 战后，日军细菌部队石井四郎等以免于追究其战争犯罪责任为交换条件，向美国提供日本细菌武器研究资料，包括人体实验解剖报告，其中目前公开的有“A”报告、“G”报告及“Q”报告三种。

本资料为人体实验解剖报告“A”报告，即“炭疽”报告。根据实验对象的号码，共 33 人，经皮下注射感染 1 例、口入感染 6 例、口腔散布感染 12 例、鼻腔感染 4 例。为实验对象感染后人体器官病理变化记录报告。全体均有睾丸解剖，为 25 ~ 37 岁男性。感染至死亡时间：2 ~ 4 日。

[redacted]

549275

XChE REP

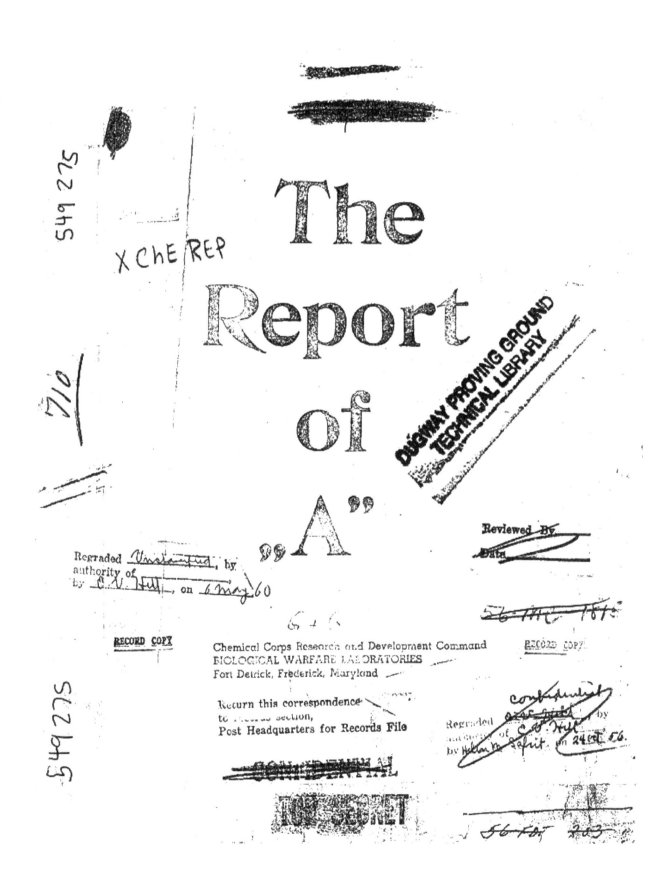

The Report of "A"

710

Reviewed By
Date

Regraded Unclassified, by
authority of
by C. V. Hill, on 6 May 60

56 MC 1815

RECORD COPY

Chemical Corps Research and Development Command
BIOLOGICAL WARFARE LABORATORIES
Fort Detrick, Frederick, Maryland

RECORD COPY

549275

Return this correspondence
to Records section,
Post Headquarters for Records File

Regraded confidential, by
authority of C. V. Hill
by Helen M. Safrit, on 24 Oct 56.

~~CONFIDENTIAL~~

TOP SECRET

~~56 FDr 203~~

[redacted]

CONTENT.

[redacted]

~~56-F875-203~~

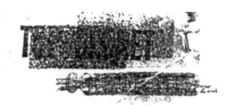

[redacted]

[redacted]

I have investigatéd 30 cases of anthrax disease, which could be classified into 3 groups:

a) Percutaneous infection: Í case.

b) Peroral infection: 9 cases.

c) Pernasal infection: 20 cases.

a) Percutaneous infection: 1 case.

	Case	Days of Course	Main Pathological changes
1.	No 54.	7 days.	Localised cutaneous ulcers and perifocal phlegmons (r-thigh) Some parenchymatous degeneration: Heart: Intense degeneration and interstitial edema. Liver: Hepatitis serosa III, accompanied with some hemorrhagic changes. Kidney: Glomerulo/nephrosis, with vacuolar degeneration of epithliums. Spleen: Splenitis infectiosa

b) Peroral infection:

9 cases were infected perorally with some food stuffs, which contain some quantity of anthrax bacillus and all patients died definitely after several days by acute abdominal symptoms and severe hemorrhagic ascites.

In alimentary canals: occured no remarkable changes in stomach and extraordianary severe hemorrhagic changes (fungous swelling of mucous

[redacted] 36-CATS-203

[redacted]

[redacted]

54

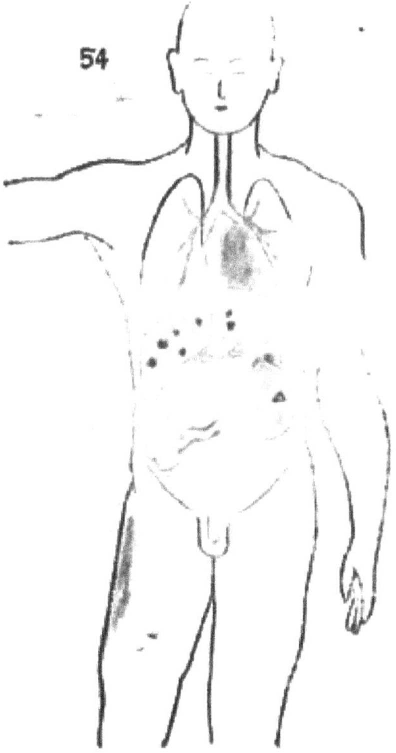

[redacted]

[redacted]

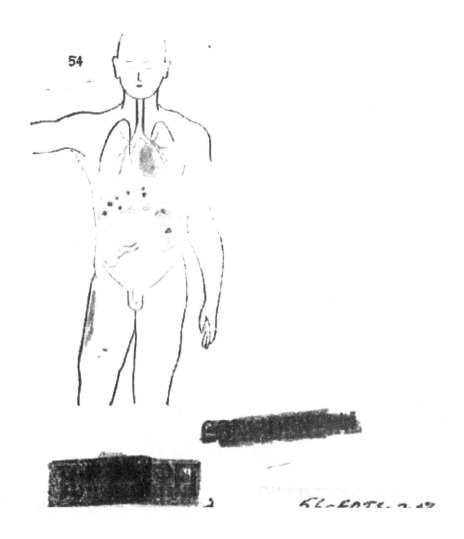

[redacted]

[redacted]

membrane with hemorrhagic leucocytic reactions) of intestines, especially at ileocoecal portoions, lower parts of ileum or sometimes all over the intestinal tracts (upper parts of ileum, duedenoum, jejunum or large intestine), accompanied with intense gelatinous (exudative) swelling of mesentenial fatty tissues and following severe hemorrhagic ascites, which caused the death.

Representive records of 6 cases:

Case	Dys of counse	Main Pathological changes
1. No. 318.	3 days.	Primary abdominal symptoms: Intense hemorrhagic exudative changes of intestines, accompanied with intense hemorrhagic ascites. Secondary metastatic changes: Lung with slight Alveolitis and some bacterial dissemination. Liver with Hepatitis serosa IV and some hemorrhagic reactions (hemorrhages in central zone of acinus). Heart with some parenchymatous degeneration and partial hemorrhages. Kidney with some parenchymatous degeneration and some exudative changes. Supra-renal with diffuse hemorrhages in cortical tissues. [redacted] Thyreoid in floocular collapze.

[redacted]

[redacted]

[redacted]

Spleen: Splenitis infectiosa.

2. No. 26. 3days. Primary abdominal symptoms:

Intense hemorrhagic-exudative changes of intestines, accompanæd with intense hemorrhagic ascites.

Secondary metastatic symtoms:

Liver with Hepatitis serosa III and partial hemorrhages in central zone and multiple miliary necrosis.

Heart with no remarkable changes.

Kidney with some Clomerulo-nephrosis and intense interstitial edema.

Lung with some pulmonal congestion and some metastatic bacterial dissemination.

Spleen: Spænitis infectiosa.

3. 320. 2 days. Primary abdominal symptoms:

Intense hemorrhagic exudative swelling of intestines. accompanied with intense hemorrhagic ascites.

Secondary metastatic changes:

Liver with slight Hepatitis.

Heart with some interstitial edema.

Kidney with Considerable Glomerulo-nephrosis and slight interstitial edema.

Pancreas with moderate congestion and some peri vascular round cell in iltration. L

[redacted] 4 [redacted]

[redacted]

[redacted]

Supra-renal gland withvacuolar degeneration and multiple hemorrhages in cortifal tissues. Spleen Spelenitis infectiosa.

4. 328. ca. 2 days.

Primary abdominal symptoms:

Intense hemorrhagic exudative changes of intestines, accompanied with intense hemorrhagic ascites.

Socundary metastatic changes:

Heart with intense degeneration intense capillary congestion and some hemorrhagic reactions.

Liver with Hepatitis serosa III.

Kidney with parenchymatous degeneration and some interstitial edema.

Lung with no remarkable changes.

Pancreas with some parenchymatous degeneration.

Supra-renal gland with partial hemorrhages and some parenchymatous degeneration.

Thyreoid in intense follicular collapse.

5. 325. ca. 2 days.

Primary abdominal symptoms:

Intense hemorrhagic exudative changes of intestines, accompanied with intense hemorrhagic ascites.

[redacted]

[redacted] 5

[redacted] [redacted]

Secondary metastatic changes:
Heart with intese degenetation and intense interstitial edema.
Liver with Hepatitis serosa II.
Lung with moderate diffuse Alveolitis and some bacterial dissemination.
Kidney with moderate Glomerulo-nephrosis and intense interstitial edema.
Supra-renal gland with intense vacuolar degeneration.
Spleen: Splenitis infectiosa.

6. I7. ca 2 days. Primary abdominal symptoms:
Intense hemorrhagic exudative changes of intestines, accompanied with intense hemorrhagic a scites.
Secondary metastatic changes:
Heart with moderate degeneration.
Liver with Hepatitis serosa II and intense fatty degeneration.
Kidney with moderate Glomerulo-nephrosis and some exudative hemorrhagic reactions in interstitiums.
Supra-renal gland with so me bionecrotic places.
Thyreoid in sl ightly activated state.
Spleen: Splenitis infectiosa.

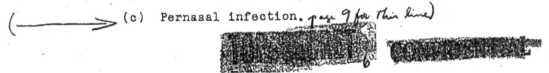

(——> (c) Pernasal infection. page 9 for this line)

[redacted] 6 [redacted]

TOP SECRET

[redacted]

318

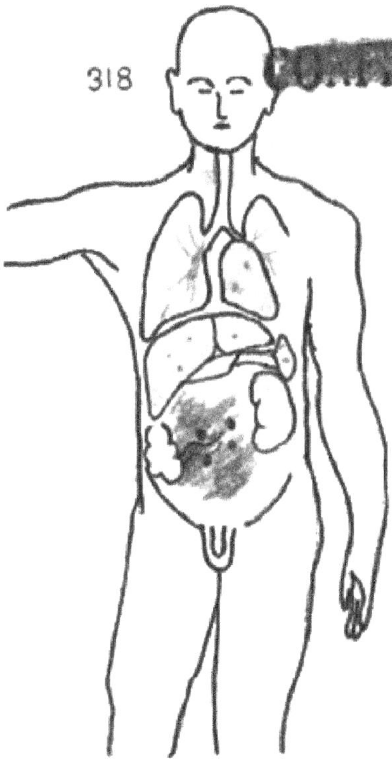

320

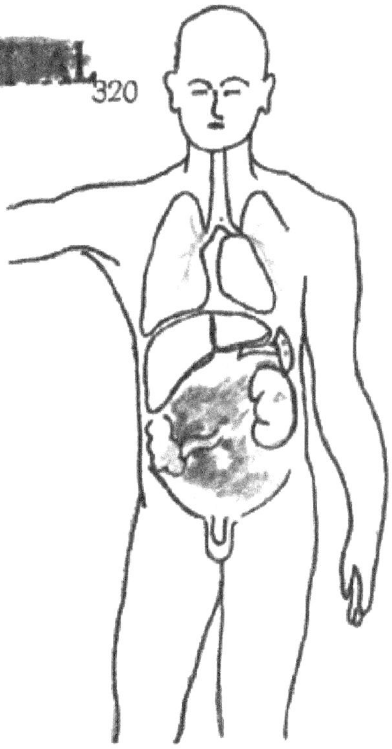

328

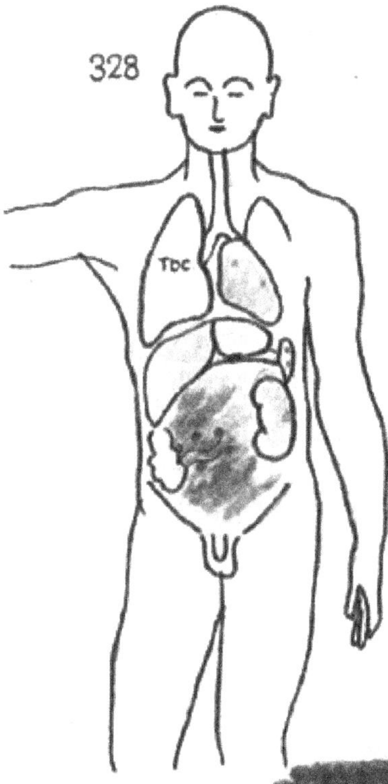

26

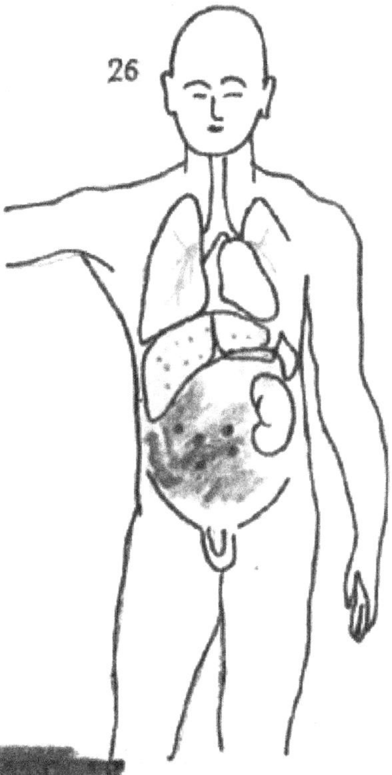

[redacted]

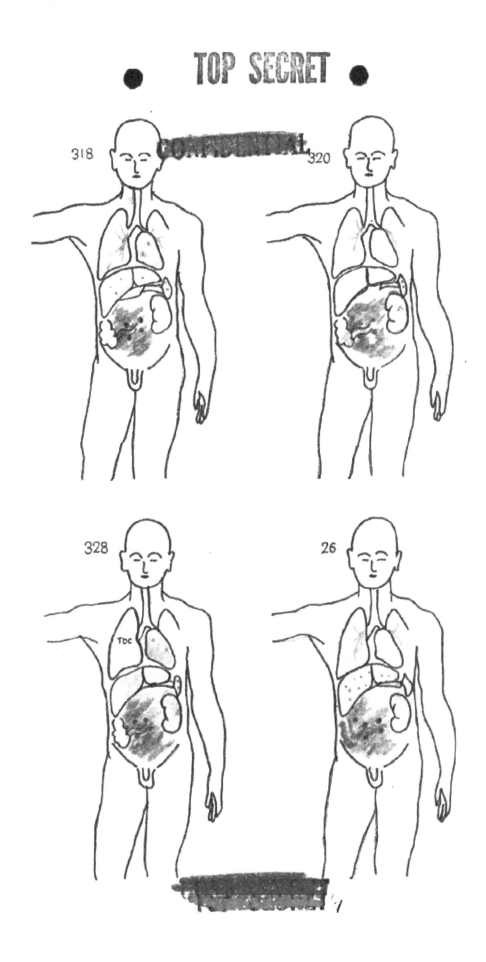

TOP SECRET

[redacted]

325

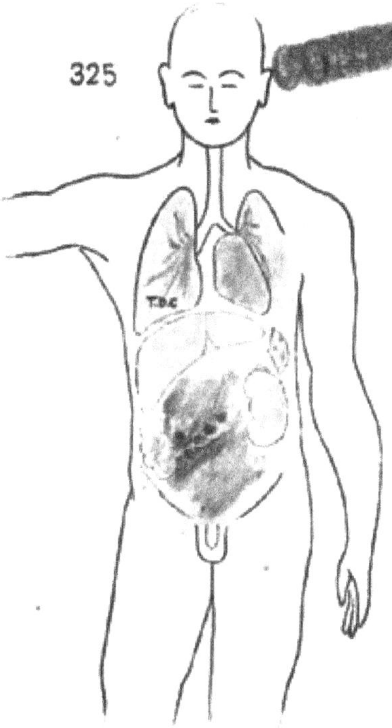

17

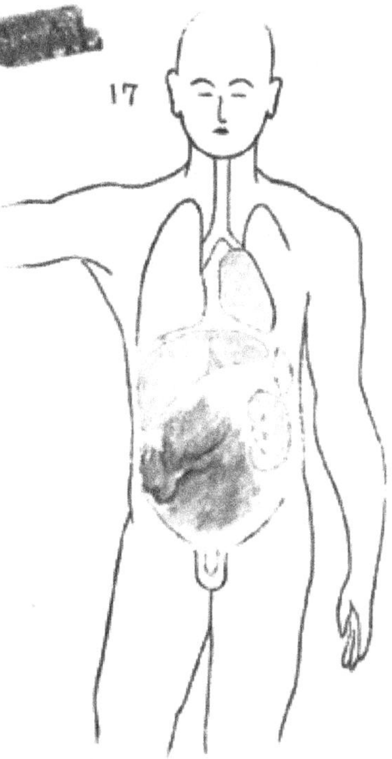

225

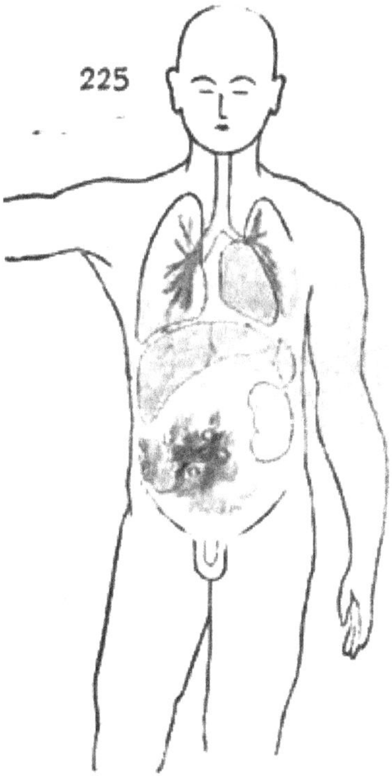

18

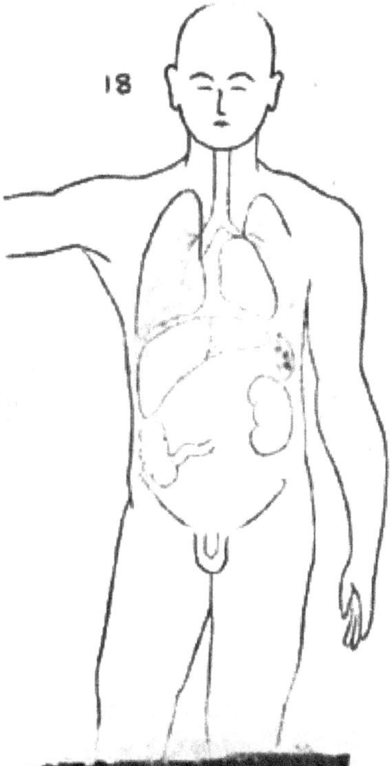

383

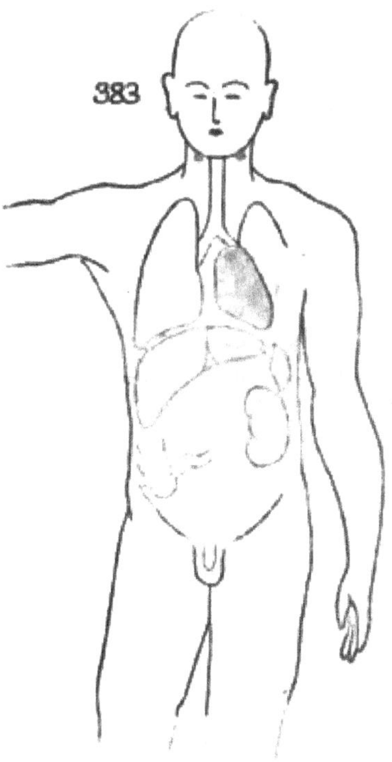

[redacted]

TOP SECRET C

It occured suddenly an epidemie of anthrax disease in some prison.
About 20 men in the prison were affected succesbively with soiled air, who which contained some quantity of anthrax bacillus and died all of them definitely after several days by severe thoracal or abdominal symptoms.

At first they complained of acute Tonsillitis:
tonsil was the main entrance-port.

Then intense hemorrhagic changes, due to anthrax infection spreaded in 2 manners: a) perbronchially and b) sometimes perorally.

a) Perbronchial spread.

Acute tonsillitis caused then acute hemorrhagic Perbronchitis and Mediastinitis, accompanied with intense hemorrhagic exudation in perbronchial and mediastinal tissues, which could be investigated easily by X-ray test clinically.

a) Perbronchial spread.

In some cases Peribronchitis caused severe Peribronchiolitis and furtermore in some cases of them intease hemorrhagic leucocytic changes at peribronchiolar pulmonal tissues (lobular multifocal lobular pneumonia).

---

1. 380. ca. 3 days.

Primary thoracal symptoms:

Acute hemorrhagic exudative Mediastinitis and.
Acute hemorrhagic Peribronchitis (Lgmphadenitis haemorrhagica peribronchiale) and Perirbonchiolitis.
Moderate diffuse Alveolitis

9

TOP SECRET

[redacted]

2. 396. ca. 3 days.

Prmary thocracal symptoms:

Acute Tonslplitis.

Acute hemorrhagic Mediastinitis.

Acte hemorrhagic Peribronchitis and Peribronchi-olitis. (Lymphadenifis haemorrhagica peri bronch-icals).

Diffuse moderate Alveolitis and reactive hemorrha-gic exudative Pleuritis.

Secondary metastatic changes:

Heart with moderate degeneration and intense interstitialedema.

Liver with Hepatitis serosa III and some perica-pillary leucocytes accumulation.

Kidney withmoderate Glomerulo-nephrosis and modera-te interstitial edema.

Supra-renal gland with intense degeneration and moderate inter-renal gland with intense degenerat-tion and some locplised hemorrhages.

Thyreoid in follicular collapse, accmmpanied with some bacterial metstasis,

Spleen: Splemitis infectionsa.

3. 412. ca. 3 days.

Primary thoracal symptoms:

Acute Tonsillitis.

[redacted] 10

TOP SECRET

[redacted]

Lymphadenitis jaemorrhagboa peribronchiale.

Diffuse Alveolitis and multiple hemorrhagic pneumonic places.

Secondary merastatic changes:

Heart with moderate cegeneration and slight mesen-chymal reaction.

Kidney with slight Glomerulo-nephrosis and intense interstitialedema.

Large intestine withmoder te submucous congestion andn slight perivascular leucocytes accumulation.

Pnacreaswith moderate degenerqtion and so me edema.

Liver csn not be investigated microscopically.

....

....

In one case(No. 405) acute Tonsillitis anusedintenseEnodbronchitis and succesively mulitple bronchogenous pneumonia.

4. No. 405. ca. 3 days.

Primary thoracal symptoms:

Acute Tonsillitis.

Multiple acunous lobular hemorrhagic exudative pneumonia.

Secondary matastatic changes:

Herat with intense degeneration and so me intersttial edema.

Liver with Hepatitis serosaIII.

Kidney withslight glomerulo-nephrosis and intense interstitial edema.

Large intesine with moderate subnucous congestion

[redacted]

[redacted]

[redacted]

and some peeivascular leucocytes accumulation.
Supra-renal gland with intense degeneration(vacuolar or honeycombed degeneration) and diffuse hemorrhages in cortical tissues.
Thyreoid in statical state.
spleen: splenitic infectionsa.

[redacted]

12

[redacted]

[redacted]

b) Peroral spread.

In some cases Anthrax bacillu intruded into alimentary canals and caused intense hemorrhagic changew ofintestine , so as decreibedin chapter(a),peroral infection.

Case	Coruse.	Main Pathological changes
1. 411.	4 days.	Primary thorqcal symptoms: Acute hemorrhagic Mediastinitis. Acute hemorrhagic Peribronchitis and Peribronchiolitis. Lymphadenitis haemorrhagica peribrochiale. Acino.lobular hemorrhagic leucocytic pneumonia. Reactive hemorrhagic pleuritis. Primary abdominal symptoms.: Acute hemorrhagic fungous swelling of intestinal walls. Acute jemorrhagic ascites. Secondary metqstatic changes.: Herat with mederate degenerqtion and some mesenchymal reactions. Liber with hepatitis serosa III. Kidney with slight Glomerulo-nephrosis and moderate inyerstitial edema. Pancreas with moderqte deganeration and slight periv[redacted] infiltrationl.

[redacted] 18

[redacted]

[redacted]

Supra-renal gland with intense (vacuolar) degeneration and some diffuse hemorrhages in cortical tissues.

Thyreoid withacute disfuguring (follicular collapse).

Brain with moderage congestion and slight hemorhhges. in menigs.

.... Spleen: Splenitis infectiosa.

....

2. 407. ca 3 days,

Primery thorqcal symptoms:

Tonsillitis acuta haemorrhagica.

Acute hemorrhagic Mediastinitis.

Acute hemorrhagic Peribronchitis and Peribronchiolitis

Lymphademitis haemorraghica peribrochiale.

Moderate pulmonal congestion(or Alveolitis).

Primary abdominal symptoms:

~~Tons-illitis-acuta-haemorrhagica~~.

Duodenitis haemorrhagica.

Enteritis haemorrhagica with some fungous swelling of mucousmembrane.

Acute hemorrhagic assites.

Secondary metastqtic changes :

Heart with intense degenerqtion and moderqte interstitial edema.

Liver with Hepatitis sersa III , mulitple miliary necrosis and so-called net-necrosis like degeneration.

Kidney with slight Glojerulo.nephrosis and moderate interstitial edmma.

[redacted] 14

[redacted]

[redacted]

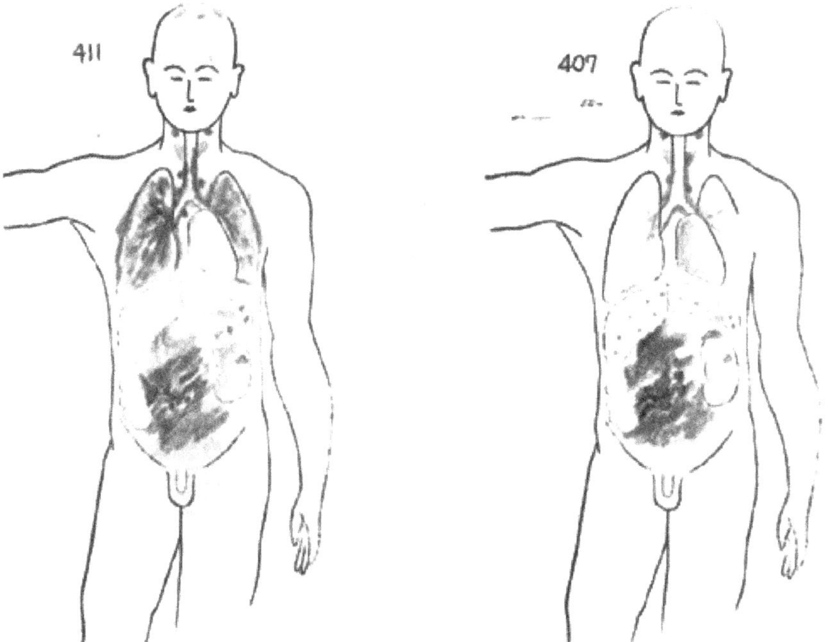

[redacted] 15

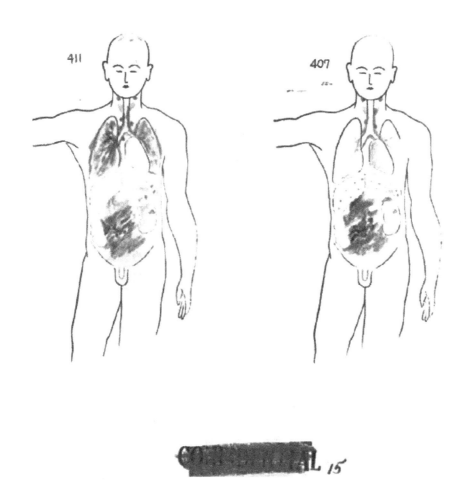

[redacted]

[redacted]

Pancreas withvacuolar degeneration of parenchymatous cells.

Supra-renal gland with intense (honeycombbed) degeneration of parenchymatous cells and some licalised hemorrhgges in cortical tissues.

Intense hemorrhagic changes of interstil walls, accompanied with fugous swelling , so as decribedin cas No, 411 and No,407, could not be determined exactly in the following cases,since I have not recieved the microscipical slices at issue nor autopsic nodululs, causing sometimes severe intestinal symptoms or sometimes not.

....

Case Corse Main pathological changes.

....

1.401. 2 days.

Primary-~~abdominal~~ thoracal symptoms:

Acute ~~thoracal-sv~~ hemorrhagic Mediastinitis.

Acute hemorrhagic Peribronchitis and Peribronchiolitis.

Lymphadenitis haemorrhagica peribronchiale.

Primary abdominal symptoms:

Lymphadenitis acuta haemorrhagica.

Acute hemorrhagic ascites.

Acute hemorrhagic Enteritis, accompanied with intense fugous swelling of intestinal walls.

Secondary metastatic symptoms:

Herat with moderate degenerqtion and some mesenchymal reaction. [redacted]

16

[redacted]

[redacted]

Liver ,not investigated microscopically.

Thyreoid in follicular collapse.

Spleen: Splemitis infectiosa.

....

2 400 3 days.

Primary thoracal symptoms:

Acute hemorrhagic Mediastinitis.

Acute hemorrhagic Peribronchitis nad Peribronchiolitis.

Lymphadenitis haemorrhagica peribronchiale.

Acute intense Endobronchitis.

Multiple hemorrhagic acinous pneumonic placrs.

Primary abdominal symptoms:

Lymphadenitis haemorrhagica acuta mesneteriaae.

Acute hemorrhagic ascites.

Intestines, can not investigated microscopically.

Secondary metastatic changes:

Herat with moderate degeneration and some mesenchymal reaction.

Liver with Hepatitis serosa II.

Surpra-renal gland with intese parenchymatous degeneration.

Spleen: Splenitis infectiosa.

....

3.404 3 days.

Primary thoracal symptoms:

Acute hemorrhagic Mediastinitis.

Acute hemorrhagic Peribronchitis

[redacted] 17

[redacted]

[redacted]

(Lymphadenitis haemorrhagica peribronchiale).

Diffues slight Alveolitis.

Primary abdomiaal symptoms:

Lymphadenitis haemorrhagica acuta mesentericae.

Acute hemorrhagic ascites.

Moderate subnucoud congestion of small intestine.

Moderate subnucoux bongestion and some perivascular leucocytes accumulation of large intestine.

Secondary metastatic chagnes:

Herat withmoderate degeneration , intense edema and some mesenchymal reaction.

Liver with Hepatitis derosa IV .

Kidney with moderate Glomerulo-nephrosis and so me interstitial edema.

Spleen: Splenitis infectiosa.

4.417 ca 3 days.

Primary thoracla symptoms:

Tonsillitis acuta.

Acute hemorrhagic Mediastinitis.

Acute hemorrhagic Peribronchitis and Peribronchiolits.

(Lymphadenitis haemorrhagica peribronchiale).

Acute slighr pulmonal congestion.

Primary abdomiaal cymptoms:

Lymphadenitis acuta with slight exdative changes(congestion and some leucocytes dissemiantion).

[redacted] 18

[redacted]

No remarkable ascites. [redacted]

Small intestine:some inflammatory changes in submucous tissue with edema, slight hemorrhages and some perivascularroud cell accumulation.

Secondary metstatic changes:

Herat with intense degenerqtion and moderate interstitial edema.

Liver with Hepatitis serosa III.

Kidney withslight Glomerulo-nephrosis and medrate interstitial edema.

Supra-renal gland with diffues hemorrhages in cortical tissues and intense degeneration(bionecrotic changes) of cortical cells.

Thyreoid infollicular collapse.

Pancreas withvacuolar degenertion of parenchymatous cells.

Spleen: Splenitis infectiosa.

....

5 399 3 days.

Primary thoracal symptoms:

Tonsillitis acuta.

Acute hemorrhagic Mediastinitis.

Acute hemorrhagic Peribronchitis.

(Lymphadenitis haemorrhagica peribronchiale).

Slight pulmonal congestion.

Primary abdominal symptoms:

Lymphadenitis acuta haemorrhagica mesentericae.

[redacted] 19

[redacted]

[redacted]

Acute hemorrhagic ascites.

Intestines:notinvestigate microscopically.

Secondary merastatic changes:

Heart with moderate degeneration and sme hemorrhagic changes.

Liver with Hepatitis serosa III-IV.

Kidney with slight Glomerulo-nephrosis and moderate interstitial edema.

Supra-renal gland with intense parenchymatousdegeneration and intense hemorrhages in Z. reticulatis].

Thyreoid in follicular collapse.

Spleen: Splenitis infectiosa.

....

....

6. 393 ca 4 days.

Primary thoracal symptoms:

Acute hemorrhagic Mediastinitis.

Acute hemorrhagic Peribronchitis

(Lymphadenitis haemorrhagica peribronchiale).

Slight diffues Alveolitis.

Pleuritis exdudative tuberculosa.

Primary abdominal symptoms:

Lymphadenitis haemorrhagico-necroticans mesentericae.

Acute hemorrhagic ascites.

Ontestines, can not be investigated microscopically.

Secondary metastatic changes:

[redacted]

20

[redacted]

[redacted]

Heart with intense degeneration, intense congestion adn slight hemorrhages.

Liver with Hepatitis serosa III.

Kidney with meddrate Glomerulo-nephrosis and moderate interstitial edema.

Pancreas with ~~moderate Glomerulo~~ some parenchymatous degeneration.

Supra-renal gland with intense degeneration.

Thyreoid in follicular collapse.

Spleen: Splenitis infectiosa.

....

....

7. 390 ca 3 days.

Primary thoracal symptoms:

Tomsillitis acuta haemorrhagica.

Acute hemorrhagic Mediastinitis.

Acute hemorrhagic Peribronchitis and Peribronchiolitis.

(Lymphadenits haemorrhagica peribronchialte).

~~Moderate su~~

Diffuse Alveolitis withhemorrhagic necrotic changes at some places.

Primary abdominal symptoms:

Lymphadenitis haemorrhagico-necroticans mesentericae.

Acute hemorrhagic ascites.

Moderate submucous congestion of intestines.

Secondary metastatic changes.:

Heart with intense [redacted] 21

[redacted]

[redacted]

Liver,not investigated microscopically.

Kidney, not investigatedmicroscopically.

Supra-remal gland with multiple miliary necrosis.

---

8 403 3 days:

Primary thoracàà sgmptims:

Tonsillitis acuta.

Acute hemorrhagic Mediastinitis.

Acute hemorrhagic Peribronchitis.

(Lympahdenitis haemorrhagica peribronchiale).

Acimo-lobular pneumonia(hemorrhagic leucocytic).

Primary abdominal symptoms:

Lymphadenitis haemorrhagico-necroticans mesentericae.

Acute hemorrhagic ascites.

Moderate catarrh of intestines.

Secondary metastatic changes:

Heart with moderate degeneration and some Endoarteritis of blood-vessels, accompanied with some round cell adcumulation.

Liver with Hepatitis serosa III, accomapanied with some bacillus in capillaries.

Kideney withslight Glomerulo-nephrosis and mederate interstitial edema.

Pancreas withmoderate degeneration.

Thyreoid in follicular collapse.

....

9 409 ca 2 days.

[redacted] : 22

[redacted]

Primary thoracal symptoms: [redacted]

Tonsillits acuta.

Acute hemorrhagic Mediastinitis.

Lymphadenitis haemorragica peribronchiale.

Peribronchiolitis acuta haemorrhagica.

Severe Alveolitis and some bacterial dissemination.

Primary abdominal symptoms:

Lymphadenitis haemorrhagica mesanterica.

Acute hemorrhagic ascites.

Hemorrhagic fungous swelling of interstitial walls ?

Secondary metastatic chamges:

Heart with moderate degeneration and edema.

Liver with Hepatitis serosa III and some bacterial dêssemiantion.

Kidney with slight Glomerulo-nephrosis and some interstitials edema.

:Pancreas with moderate degeneration.

Supra-renal gland with moderate congestion and diffuse hemorrhges in Z. reticularis.

Skin(r-thigh) with intense congestion, localised hemorrhages and diffuse wandering cells dissemination in subcutaneous tissues.

10-388 3 days-

Primary thoracal symptoms;

Tonsillitis haemorrhagico-catarrhalis acuta.

Acute hemorrhagic Mediastinitis.

Lymphadenitis haemorrh gica peribronchalis.

Endobronchiolitis and Peribronchiolitis gravis.

[redacted] 23

[redacted]

[redacted]

Slight diffuse Alveolitis.

Primary abdominal symptoms:

Lymphadenitis haemorrhagico-necroticand.

by

Acute hemorrhagic ascites.

No remarkable changes of intestines.

Secondary metastatic changes.:

Heart with intense degenerqtion

Liver with Hepatitis serosa II.

Kidney with slight glomerulo-nephrosis and slight interstitial edema.

Supra-renal gland with intense parnechymatous degenrqtion and diffuse hemorrhages in cortical tissues.

Brain with slight hemorrhages in meniges.

Skin with intense congestion, some .localised hemorrhages and some round cell infiltration in subsutaneous tissues (r-upper arm).

Accordingly, the primary changes of pernasal infection are thoracal and abdominal symptoms.

Thoracal: Acute hemorrhagic exudative Mediastinitis.

Acute hemorrahgic inflammation of peribronchial lymphnodulus.

Acute hemorrhagic Peribronchitis and Peribronchiolitis.

Hemorrhagic(-leucocytic) pneumonia,acino-lobular.

Some times reagtive hemorrhagic Pleuritis.

[redacted] 24

[redacted]

[redacted]

401

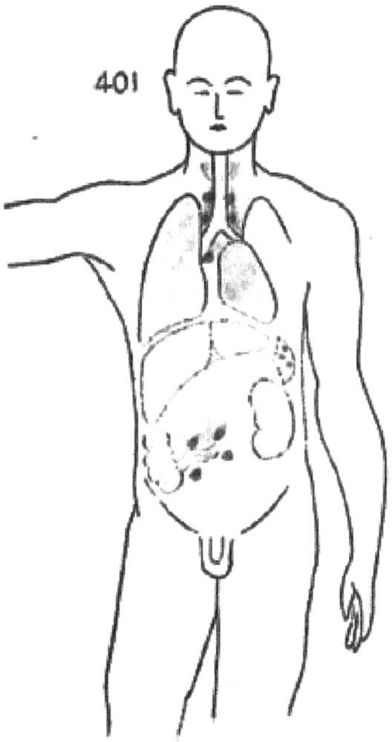

400

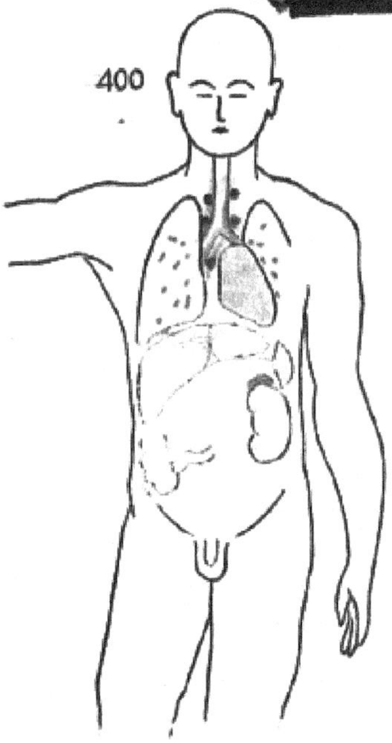

404

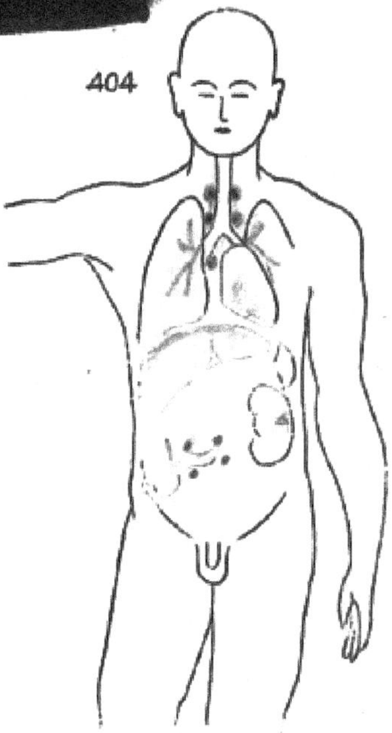

417

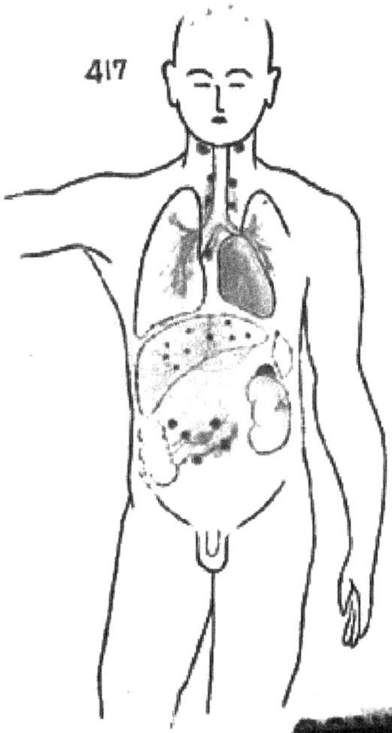

399

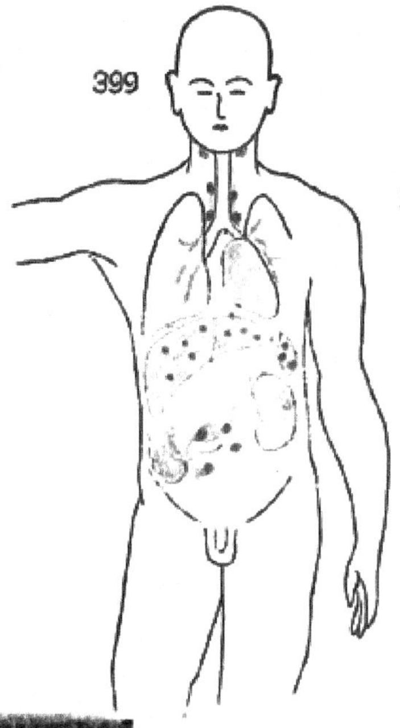

[redacted]

25

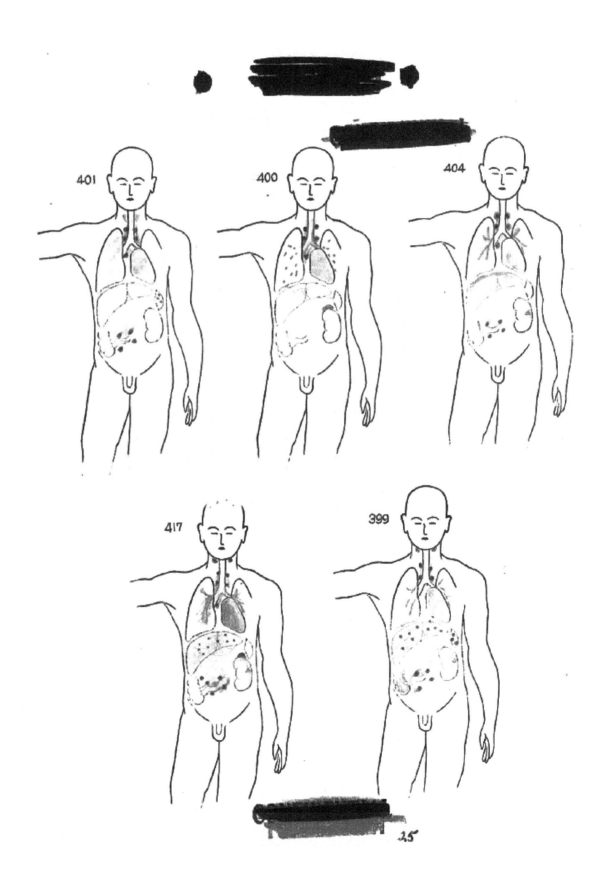

[redacted]

CONFIDENTIAL

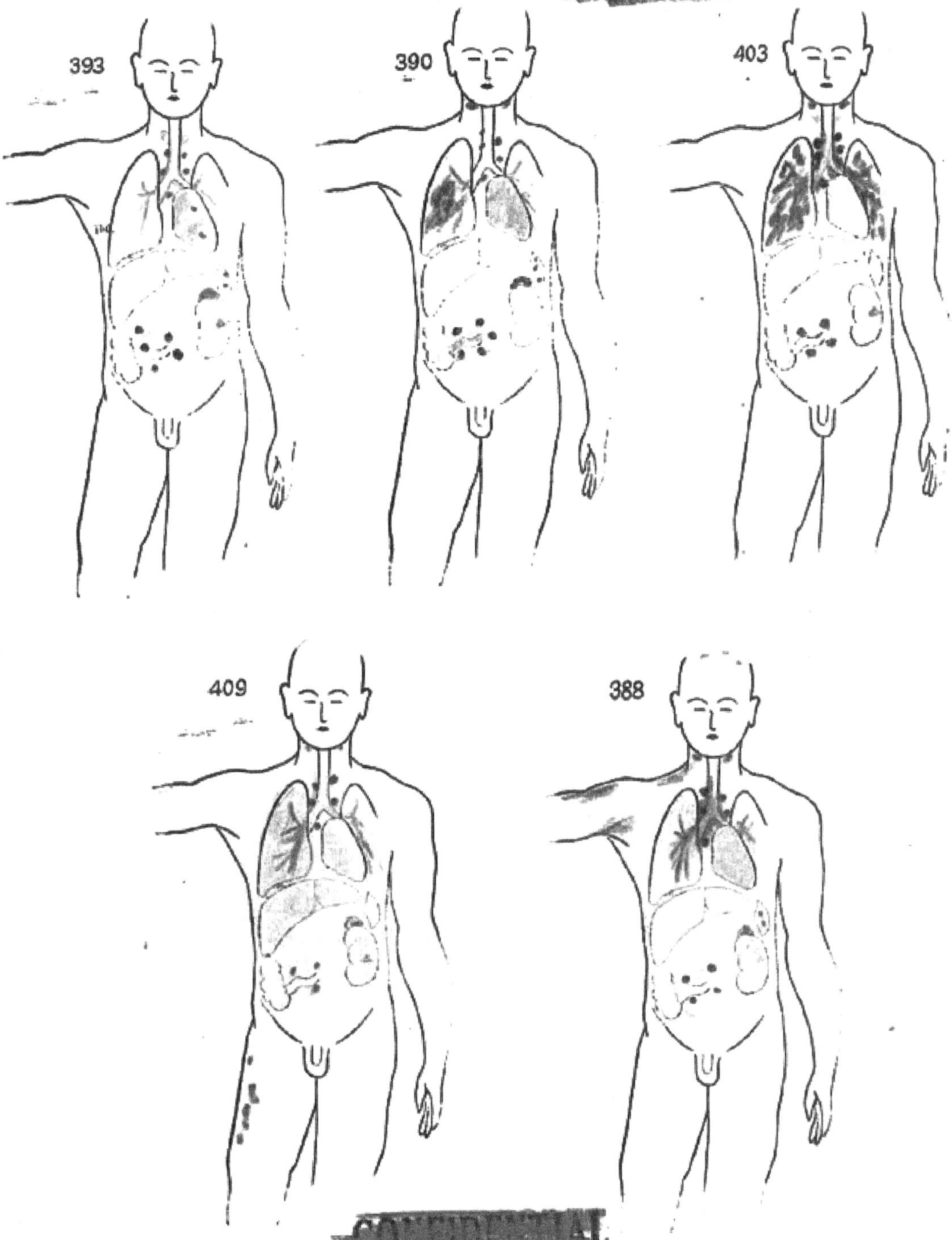

CONFIDENTIAL

26

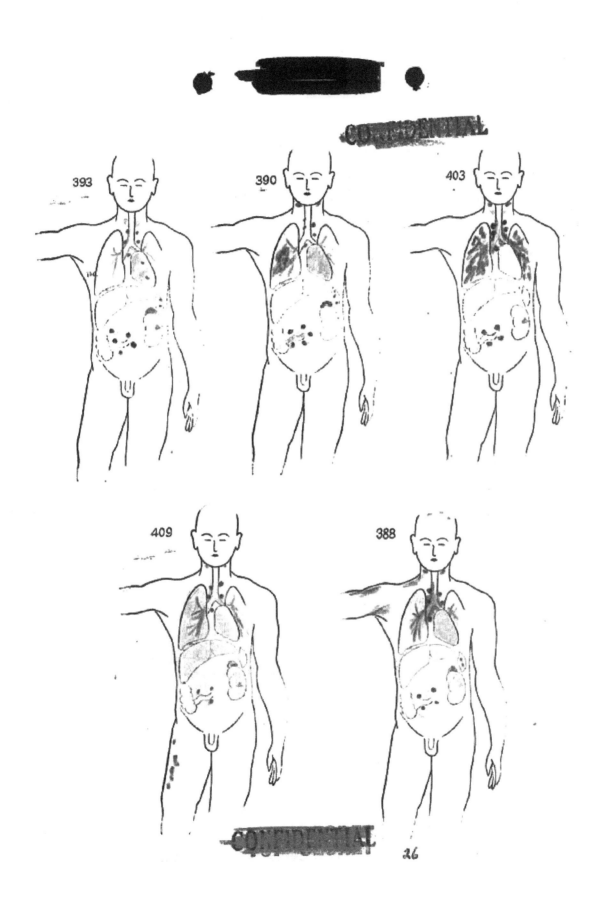

[redacted]

[redacted]

Abdominal:

Acute hemorrhagic inflammation of intestines, accompanied with fungous swelling of intestinal walls.

Acute hemorrhgic inflammation of mesenterial lymph-nodulus.

Acute hemorrhagic ascites.

Then Anthrax bacillus, intruded metastatically into various organs, espeially liver, spleen, lung or some cutaneous tisses etc.

The most particular second-ry symptoms ate as follows:

Heart withintense degeneration, sometimes accompanied with some hemorrhagic reaction or interstitial edema.

Liver with intense Hepatitis serosa, sometimes accompanied with some hemorrhagic changes (hemorrhages in central zone of acunuses) or multiple miliary mecrosis (or knots) formation.

Kidney with intense parenchymatous degeneration, dometimes accompanied interstitial edema.

Spleen with splenitis infectiosa, namely our so-called

Angio-folliculitis haemorrhagico-exsudativa. and

Fasciculitis haemorrhagico-exsudativa.

Cutaneous tissues: I have investigated some metastatic localised erythema in 2 cases of all examined 10 cases.

[redacted]

[redacted]

CO[redacted]

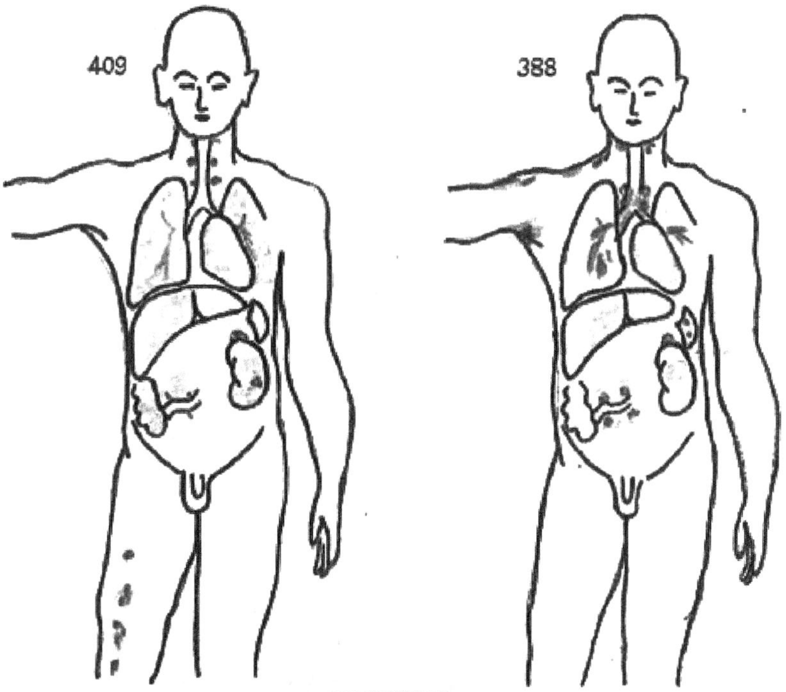

CO[redacted] 28

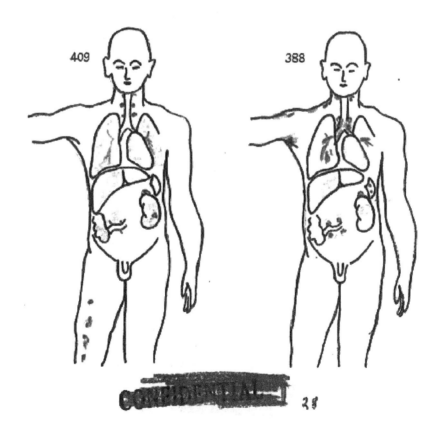

[redacted]

17. [redacted]

38 years old. 6

Entrance-port.	Peroral infection.
Days of course.	Ca 2 days.

Heart.	Degeneratio myodardii.
Aorta.	No remarkable changes, macroscopically.

Tonsil.	Slight submucous congestion.
Pharynx.	No remarkable changes, macroscopically.
Bronchus.	No remarkable changes.
Lung.	No remarkable changes.

Liver.	Hepatitis serosa II, with intense fatty degeneration.
Stomach.	No remarkable changes.
Small-Intest.	Intense hemorrhagic-leucocytic inflammation with fungous swelling of mucous membrane, due to Anthrax-infection.
Large-Intest.	Intense hemorrhagic-leucocytic inflammation with fungous swelling of mucous membrane, due to Anthrax-Infection.

Kidney.	Considerable Glomerulo-nephrosis (glomenuli in degenerative form), with some polar changes. Nephrosis I (at some places III), with interstitial edema and some localised

[redacted] 29

[redacted]

[redacted]

hemorrhages.

Spleen.	Angio-folliculitis exsudativa.
	Spleno-Fasciculitis exsudativa.
Lymph-node, Mesenterial :	Intense follicular congestion and Lymphadenitis caseosa tuberculsa.
Pancreas.	missed.
Supra-renal.	Considerable atrophia.
	Ruining processes of Z. reticularis with some leucocytes in capillaries and some round cell infiltration in Z. reticularis.
Thyreoid.	Struma colloides nodosa levis and slight activated state.
Pituitary B.	
Testicles	Atrophia testis III.
Brain.	Not invetigated.
Skin.	-
Muscles.	No remarkable changes.

[redacted] 30

[redacted]

[redacted]

18

---

29 years old. ♂

Entrance port. Peroral infection.

Days of course. ca 2 days.

Bronchus. No remarkable changes.

Lung. Stasis pulmonum with slight Bronchiolitis.

Spleen. Angio-Folliculitis haemorrhagico-exsudativa.

Spleno-Fasciculitis exsudativa

Other organs. Can not be invetigated, microscopically.

[redacted] 31

[redacted]

26. CONFIDENTIAL

25 years old. ♂

Entrance port. Per-oral infection.

Days of course. ca 3 days.

Heart.	No remarkable changes.
Aorta.	No remarkable changes, macroscopically.

Tonsil	No remarkable changes, macroscopically.
Bronchus.	Slight edema and slight hemorrhages in submucous tissues.
Bronchilolus.	Slight catarrh.
Lung.	Stasis pulmonum with some metastatic bacterial dissemination.

Liver.	Hepatitis serosa III, with partial hemorrhages in central zone and multiple miliary necrosis (some lymphocytes-accumulation).
Stomach.	No remarkable changes, macroscopically.
Small-Intest.	Intense hemorrhagic-leucocytic inflammtion with fungous swelling of mucous memebrane, due to Anthrax-infection.
Large-Intest.	Intense hemorrhagic-leucocytic inflammation with fungous swelling of mucous membrane, due to Anthrax-iafection.

CONFIDENTIAL

[redacted] 32

[redacted]

[redacted]

Kidney. Slight Glomerulo-nephrosis (glomeruli in acute congestion with some degenerative changes).
Nephrosis I with slight or intense interstitial edema.

Spleen. Sngio-Folliculitis hemorrhagico-exsudativa.
Spleno-Fasciculitis. exsudativa.

Lymph-node.
Mesenterial : Lymphadenitis haemorrhagico-necroticans.

Perbronccial: Considerable follicular congestion.

Pancreas. Intense degeneration of parenchymatous cells. (some of them, vacuolar).
Considerable congestion.
Vacuolar degeneration of island-cells.

Supra-renal. -

Thyreoid. -

Pituitary B. -

Testicles. Can not be investigated microscopically.

Brain. Can not be investigatd microscopically.

Skin.

Muscles. No remarkable changes, macroscopically.

[redacted] 33

[redacted]

[redacted]

54.

ca 25 years old. ♂

Entrance-port.	Per-cutaneous infection.
Days of course.	ca 7 (pag. 1) days.
Heart.	Intense dgeneration. Atrophia and some interstitial edema.
Aorta.	No remarkable changes.
Tonsil.	No remarkable changes, macroscopically.
Pharynx.	Slight catarrh with some congestion and some round cell infiltration in submucous tissues.
Bronchus.	Slight edema in mucous and submucous tissues.
Lung .	Slight congestion, macroscopically.
Licer.	Hepatitis serosa II-III, with some partial hemorrhages in central zone of acinuses.
Stomach.	Slight catarrh.
Small-Intest.	Slight catarrh-macroscopically.
Large-Intest.	Almost normal.
Kidney.	Slight Glomerulo-nephrosis (glomeruli in degenerative form), with slight polar changes. Nephrosis I with rather atrophic tubular epitheliuns and at some places some vacuolar degeneration.

[redacted] 34

[redacted]

[redacted]

Spleen.	Missed.
Lymph-nodes.	Not investitigated microscopically.
Pancreas.	Slight congestion and slight degeneration of parenchymatous cells and island-cells.
Supra-renal.	Considerable congestion and slight some hemorrhages in cotical tissues. Vacuolar or honeycombed degenertion of cortical cells, some ruining process of Z. reticularis.
Thyreoid.	Slight activated state. Struma celloides diffusa.
Pituitary B.	-
Teticles.	Atrophia testis III.
Brains.	Not invetstigated, microacopically.
Skin.	Diffuse phlegmonous.

[redacted] 33

[redacted]

225. [redacted]

---

35 years old. ♂

Entrance-port. Per-oral infection.

Days of course. 2 days.

Heart.	Considerable degeneration.
Aorat.	No remarkable changes, macroscopically.

Tonsil.	No remarkable changes. macroscopically.
Pharynx.	Considerable congestion and some round cell infiltrat.
Bronchus.	Considerable congestion (some leucocytes in capillaries) and slight edema in submucous tissues.
Lung.	Bronchiolitis catarrhalis. Edema et stasis pulmonum.

Liver.	Hepatisis serosa III.
Stomach.	Considerable congetion in submuocous tissues.
Small-Intest.	Fungsus swelling of mucous membrane, with intense hemorrhagic-leucocytic reaction.
Large-Intest.	Considerable catarrh.

[redacted] 36

[redacted]

[redacted]

Spleen. Angio-Folliculitis haemorrhagico-exsudation.
Spleno-Fascioulitis exsudativa.

Lymph-node.

Mesenterial. Pericapsulitis hiaemorrhagica and considerable follicular congestion.

Pancreas. Considerable congestion and slight edema.
Considerable degeneration and some atrophia of parenchymatous cells.
Considerable degeneration of island-cells.

Supra-renal. Considerable congestion and diffuse hemorrhages in cortical tissues with considerable degeneration.

Thyreoid. In slight activated atated.
Struma colloides diffusa levis.

Pituitary B. -

T sticles. Atrophia testis Ⅲ.

Brain. Considerable congestion (some leucocytes in capillaries) and slight edema.

Skin. No remarkable changes.

[redacted] 37

[redacted]

318. [redacted]

---

ca 30 years old. ♂

Entrance-port. Per-oral infection.

Days of course. 2 Days.

Heart.	Degeneratio myocardii. Considerable congestion and some partial hemorrhages.
Aorta.	No remarkable changes, macroscopically.

Tonsil.	No remarkable changes, macroscopically.
Pharynx.	Intense congestion and some hemorrhages in submucous tissues.
	Slight round cell(some of them, leucocytic)-accumulation in submucosttissues.
Bronchus.	No remarkable changes, macroscopically,
Lung.	Bronchilolitis catarrhalis.
	Stasis levis and some bacterial dissemination.

Liver.	Hepatitis serosa III-IV, with slight hemorrhages in central gone of acinuses.
Stomach.	Slight cotarrha and congiderable congestion in submucous tissues.
Small-Intest.	Intense hemorrhagic-leucocytic inflammation, due to Anthrax-infection.
Large-Intest.	Slight congestion (can not be investigated macroscopically)

CONFIDENTIAL 38

[redacted]

------------------------------[redacted]------------------------

Kidney. Slight Glomerulo-nephrosis (glomeruli in acute congestion. Some of them in hyaline cirrhsosis.). Nephrosis I (or III at some places), with considdrable interstitial edema and some round cell accumulation.

Spleen. Angio-folliculitis haemorrhagico-exsudativa. Spleno-fasciculitis exaudativa.

Lymph-node.
Mesenterial. Lymphadenitis haemorrhagico-necroticans and Periadenitis haemorrhagica.

Peribronchial : Lymphadentis tuberculosa obsoleta.

Pancreas. Slight congestion and some slight hemorrhages. Slight degeneration of parenchymatous cells and island -cells.

Supra-renal. Partial hemorrhages in Z. glomrulosa and Z. fasciculartas. Intense degeneration (ruining process) of Z. reticularis, accomapanied with diffuse hemorrhages.

Thyreoid. Acute disfiguring (follicular collapse).

Testicles. Atrophia testis Ⅲ .

Pituitary B. -

Brain. -

Skin. No remarkable changes.

-

[redacted] 39

[redacted]

[redacted]

320.

ca. 30 years old. ♂

Entrance-port. Per-oral infection.

Days of course. 2 days.

Heart. Slight degeneration Considerable atrophia and some interstitial edema.

Aorta. No remarkable changes, with some stasis of peri-adventitial tissues.

Tonsil. No remarkable changes, macroscopically.

Pharynx. Slight congestion and slight edema. Diffuse round cell (mainly plasma cells) accumulation and slight hyperplasia of lynphatic apparatus in submucous tissues.

Bronchus. No remarkable changes.

Lung. Slight Congestion, macroscopically.

Liver. Hepatistis serosa I-II.

Stomach. Slight catarrh and considerable congestion in submucous tissues.

Small-Intest. Intense hemorrhagic-leucocytic inflammation with fungous swelling of mucous memebrane, due to Anthrax-infertion.

Large-Intest. Considerable catarrh.

[redacted] 40

[redacted]

[redacted]

Kidney.	Considerable Glomerulo-nephrosis (glomeruli in acute exudation), with considerable polar changes. Kephrosis I, with slight (at some places intense) interstitial edema (Nephritis serosa).
Spleen.	Angio-Folliculitis haemorrhagico-exsudativa. Spleno-Fusciculitis exsudativa.
Lymph-node.	
Mesenterial.	Lymphadenitis haemorrhagica. macroscopically.
Peribronchial:	Considerable follicular congestion.
Pancreas.	Considerable congestion and some perivascular round cell (some of them, leucocytic) infiltration and some edema. Cloudy swelling of parenchymatous cells. Intense congestion and considerable hyperplasia of capillary endothel-cells in island.
Supra-renal.	Atrophia. Vacuolar degeneration of parenchymatous cells. Multiple hemorrhages (with bionecroic changes of adjacent parenchym. cells). Some round cell accumlation in Z. reticularis.
Thyreoid.	Statical stats. Strume colloides non-proliferativa.
Pituitary B.	-
Testicles.	Atrophia testis II .

[redacted] 41

[redacted]

CONFIDENTIAL

Brain.   No remarkable changes.

Skin.   No remarkable changes.

CONFIDENTIAL 42

[redacted]

325 [redacted]

about 25 years old. ♂

Entrance-port.	Per-oral infection.
Days of course.	about 8 days.

Heart.	Intense degeneration and consididerable strophy. intense interstitial edema and some myocytes.
Aorta.	No remarkable changes.

Tonsil.	No remarkable changes.
Pharynx.	No remarkable changes.
Bronchus.	Slight congestion and some leucocytes-dissemination in submucous tissues.
Lung.	Bronchiolitis catarrhalsis. Stasis et edema pulmonum and some bacterial dissemination. Acinous-nodese tuberculosis.

Liver.	Hepatitis serosa II.
Stomach.	No remarkable changes.
Small-Intest.	Intense hemorrhagic-leucocytic inflammation with fungous swelling of mucous membrane, due to Anthrax-infection, Macroscopically.
Large-Intest.	Catarrh and considerable congestion in submucous tissues.

[redacted] 43

[redacted]

[redacted]

Kidney.	Considesble Glomerulo-nephrosis (glomeruli in acute stimulised state with some degenerative changes). Nephrosis I, with intense interstitial edema with slight polsr changes.

Spleen.	Angio-Folliculitis haemorrhagico-exudativa. Spleno-Fasciculitis exaudativa.
Lymph-node.	
Mesenterial :	Lymphadentis haemorhagico-necroticans.

Pancreas.	-
Supra-renal.	Intense vacuolar degneration of cortical cells.
Thyreoid.	-
Pituitary B.	-
Testicle.	Atrophia testis II.

Brain.	Slight stasis of meninges. Slight edema of brain.
Cerebellum. -	Considerable congestion, slight hemorrhages and some edema in meninges and cerebellum.

Skin.	No remarkable changes.

[redacted] 44

[redacted]

CO[redacted]AL

328.

32. years old. δ

Entrance-port. Per-oral infection.

Days of course. ca 2 days.

Heart. intense degeneration and intense congestion, accompanied with slight hemorrhages. (many leucocytes in capillaries).

Aorta. No remarkable changes.

Tonsil. No remarkable change.

Pharynx. No remarkable changes, macroscopically.

Bronchiolus. No remarkable changes.

Lung. Acinous-nodose tuberculosis and no remarkable changes else.

Liver. Hepatits serosa III.

Stomach. No remarkable changes, macroscopically.

Small-Intest. Intense hemorrhagic-leucocytic inflammation with fungous swelling of mucous membrane, due to Anthrax-infection.

Darge-Intest. Catarrh and considerable congestion in submucous tissues.

Kidney. Slight Glomerulo-nephrosis (glomeruli in acute

CO[redacted]T 45

[redacted]

CONFIDENTIAL

congestion with some degenerative changes), with slight polar changes.

Nephrosis I, with considerable interstitial edema and slight cirrhosis of capillary walls in medullary tissues.

Spleen.	Angio-Folliculitis haemorrhatico-exsudativa. Spleno-Fasciculitis exsudativa.
Lymph-node. mesenterial.	Lymphadenitis haemorrhagico-neccoticans.
Pancreas.	Considerable congestion and some edema. Atrophia and slight degeneration of parenchymatous cells. Considerable degeneration of island-cells.
Supra-renal.	Partial hemorrhages and some degeneration of cortical tissues. Vacuolar degeneration of medullary cells.
thyreoid.	Acute disfiguring (follicular collapse).
Pituitary B.	-
Testicle.	Atrophia testis I.

Brain.	No remarkable changes, macroscopically.

Skin.	No remarkable changes, macroscopically.

CONFIDENTIAL

[redacted] 46

[redacted]

383. [redacted]

---

ca. 40 years old. ♂

Entrance-port.	Per-oral infection.
Days of course.	ca. 3 days.

Heart.	Intense degeneration and intense edema.
Aorta.	No remarkable changes.

Tonsil.	Tonsillitis catarrhalis acuta, with slight superficial ulcers and some swollen germinative centres of lymph-nodulus. Slight congestion (some bacterial masses in capillaries in follicular tissues. Considerable congestion in submucous tissues.

Other organs.	Cannot be invetstigated microscopically.

[redacted] 47

[redacted]

CONFIDENTIAL

388.

27 years old. ♂

Entrance-port. Per-nasal infection.

Days of course. about 2 days.

Heart.	Intense degeneration.
Aorta.	No remarkable changes and slight congestion of peri-adventitial tissues.

Tonsil.	Tonsilitis haemorrhagico-catarrhalis acuta. Ctarrh and some superficial ulcers. Remarkable swelling of germinative centres with some swollen reticulum cells and plenty leucocytes. Considerable congestion, edema, multiple hemorrhages and some leucocytes-dissemination in follicular and submucous tissues.
Pharynx.	
Bronchus.	Intense disturbances of mucous tissues with considerable congestion and some round cell infiltration.
Bronchiolus.	Endobronchiolitis and Peribronchiolitis gragis with Lymphadenitis acuta in peribronchiolar tissues.
Lung.	Slight Alveolitis and alveolar congestion.

Liver.	Bepatitis serosa I-I^I.
Stomach.	No remarkable changes, macroscopically.

[redacted] 48

[redacted]

CONFIDENTIAL

Small-Intest. Atrophic glandular cells. No remarkable changes esle.

Large-Intest. No remarkable changes, macroscooplically.

Spleen. Angio-Folliculitis haemorrhagico-exsudativa.
Spleno-Fasciculitis. exsudativa.

Lymph-node.
Mesenterial: Lymphadenitis haemorrhagico-necroticans.
Peribroonhial: Lymphadentis haemorrhagico-necroticans.

Kidney. Slight Glomerulo-nephrosis (glomeruli in acute stimulised form).
Nephrosis I, with slight pinterstitial edèma.

Pnacreas. -

Supra-renal. Considerable congestion and some diffuse hemorrhages.
Honeycombed degeneration in Z. fasciculata.
Round cell accumulation in Z. glomerulosa.

Supra-renal.(2). Considerable atrophia.
Intense vacuolar degeneration in Z. reticularis.
Considerable edema and diffuse hemorrhages in cortical tissues.
Vacuolar degeneration of medullary cells.

Thyreoid. -

Pituitary B. -

Testicle. Atrophia testis 1.

CONFIDENTIAL 49

[redacted]

[redacted]

Brain.	Slight congestion.
Cerebellum.	Considerable congestion, slight pericapillar hemorrhages and edema in meninges and cerebellum.

Skin.	upper arm (r) : Intense congestion, neccotic ruins of capillary walls, some localised hemorrhages and some round cell(some of them, leucocytic) infiltration in submucous tissues.

[redacted] 50

[redacted]

389. [redacted]

ca 25 years old. ♂

Entrance-port.	Per-nasal infection.
Days of course.	3 days.
Heart.	Considerable degeneration.
Aorta.	No remarkable changes.
Tonsil.	No remarkable changes, macroscopically.
Pharynx.	Can not be invetstigated macroscopically.
Bronchus and Bronchiolus.	Bronchitis and Bronchiolitis catarrhalis, with intense Peribronchiolitis.
Lung.	Slight Alveolitis or Slight pulmonal edema.
Liver.	(can not be investigated microscopically.)
Stomach.	No remarkable changes, macroscopically.
Small-intest.	Considerable catarrh.
Large-Intest.	Catarrh and considerable congestion in bubmucous tissues.
Kidney.	(can not be investigated minroscopically).
Spleen.	måssed.
Lyph-nodulus. Mesenterial :	Considerable congestion and some hemorrhages in follicular tissues.

[redacted] 51

[redacted]

[redacted]

Peribronchial : Lymphadentis haemorrhagico-necroticans gravis totialis.

Pancreas. -

Suprarenal. Considerablw atrophia and severe degeneration of parenchymatous cells.
Considerable edema and diffuse hemorrhages in Z. reticularis.

Thyreoid. -

Pituitary B. -

Testicule. Atrophia testis ll.

Brain. -

Cerebellum. -

Skin. -

[redacted] 52

[redacted]

25 years old. ♂

Entrance-port. Per-nasal infection.

Days of course. 3 days.

Heart.	Intense degeneration and some congestion.
Aorts.	No remarkable changes and slight congestion of peri-adventitial tissues.

Tonsil.	Tonsillitis acuta haemorrhagica. Bio-necrotic swelling of mucous membrane. Intense congestion in follicular and perifollicular tissues. Some hemorrhages in perifollicular tissues. Remarkable swelling of germinative centres with some localised hemorrhagic places. Intense congestion in submucous tissues.
Bronchiolus.	Bronchiolitis acuta catarrhalis.
Lung.	Slight Alveolitis and slight Stasis et edema pulmonum. Hemorrhagic-necrotic changes at some places.

Leber.	can not be investigated microscopically.
Stomach.	No remarkable changes.
Small-Intest.	Considerable catarrh.
Large. Intest.	Catarrh and considerable congestion in submucous tissues.

[redacted] 53

[redacted]

CONFIDENTIAL

Kidney. can not be investigated microscopically.

Spleen. Angio-Folliculitis haemorrhagico-exsudativa.

Spleno-Fasciclutis exsudativa.

Lymph-node.
Mesenterial. Lymphadenitis haemorrhagico-necroticans.

Peribronchial : Lymphadenitis haemorrhagica-gravis.

Pancreas. -

Supra-renal. Multiple miliary absesses.

Diffuse necrosis in Z. fasciculata and Z. reticularis.

Edema in medullary tissues.

Thyreoid. -

Pituitary B. -

Testicle. ~~Atrophia testes.~~ -

Brain. -

Skin. No remarkable changes.

CONFIDENTIAL 54

[redacted]

393. [redacted]

34 years old. ♂

Entrance-port. Per-nasal infection.

Days of course. 4 days.

Heart. Intense Hegeneration and considerable atrophiy.

Intense congestion, slight hemorrhages and edema.

Aorta. Slight congestion of vasa vasorum in media.

Tonsil. can not be invetstigated micorocaopically.

Pharynx. "

Bronchiolus. Bronchiolitis catarrhalis.

Lung. Stasis, edema and slight Alvëolitis.

Pleuritis exsudativa tuberculosa.

Liver. Hepatitis serosa II-III.

Stomach. No remarkable changes.

Small-Intestin. --

Large-Intest. --

Kidney. Considerable Glomerulo-nephrosis (glomeruli in acute atimulised state), with slight polar changes.

Nephrosis I with (or III at someplaces), with considerable interstitial edema.

[redacted] 55

[redacted]

Spleen. Angio-Folliculitis. haemorrhagico-exsudativa.

Spleno-Fasciсluitis exsuda[redacted]

L. mph-node.
Mesenterial: Lymphandentis haemorrhagico-necrotic ans.

Peribronchial: Lymphadenitis haemorrhagica.

Pancreas. Considerable congestion.

Cloudy swolling of parenchymatous cells and islandcells.

Supra-renal. Intense degeneration (desolative decay) of parenchymatous cells. esp. bionecotic changes in Z. fascicoulta.

Honeycombed degeneration or vacuclar degeneration of medullary cells.

Intense edema of capillary walls in medullary tissues.

Thyreoid. Acute disfiguring (follcular collapse).

Pituitary B. -

Testicles. Atrophia testis Ⅲ.

Brains. No hemarkable changes.

Skin. No remarkable changes.

[redacted] 56

[redacted] C

396. [redacted]

29 years old. ♂

Entrance-port. Per-nasal infection.

Days of course. 3 days.

Heart. Considerable degeneration and intense atrophy. Intense edema and some leucocytes in capillaries.

Aorta. No remarkable changes.

Liver. Hepatitisserosa II-III, with some pericapillary leucocytes-accumulation (initial stage of miliary necrosis).

Stomach. Slight edema.

Small-Intest. Atrophic glandular cells(microscopically).

Large-Intest. Almost normal(microscopically).

Kidney. Slight Glomeurlo-nophrosis (glomeruli in degenerative form), with slight polar changes. Nephrosis I (or at some places III), with considerable edema and some leucocytes in capillaries.

Spleen. missed.

Lymph-node.
Mesenterial : No remarkable changes.

Peribronchial: Lymphadonitis haemorrhagico gravis.

[redacted] 57

[redacted]

CO[redacted]

Tonsil.	Tonsillits acuta.
	Intense edema, localised superficial ulcers and catarrh of mucous membrane.
	Intense congestion (some bacterial masses) and intense edema in follicular tissues.
	Swollen gerinative centres.
Bronchiolus.	Bronchilioliti s catarrhalis.
Lung.	Diffuse Alveolitis. Atelectasis at someplaces.
	subpleural localised exudative -hemorrhagic places.
Pancreas.	-
Supra-renal.	Intense atrophy.
	Intense Degeneration and partial necrosis in Z. fasciculata.
Thyreoid.	Acute disfiguring(follicular collapse).
	Some bacterial masses in capillaries.
Pituitary B.	-
Testicle.	Atrophia testis 111.

Brain.	No remarkable changes.

Skin.	No remarkable changes.

CO[redacted] 58

[redacted]

[redacted]

397.

27 years old.♂

Entrance-port. Per-nasal infection.

Days of course. 4 days.

Heart. Slight degeneration.
Considerable interstitial edema and considerable hemorrhages in epicardial tissues.

Aorta. No remarkable changes.

Tonsil. Tonsillitis acuta.
Considerable congesti on and edema in follicular tissues.
Remarkable swelling of germinative centres.
Considerable congestion and slight hemorrhages in submucous tissues.

Pharynx. No remarkable changes.

Bronchus. Considerable edema in submucous tissues.

Lung. Bronchiolitis catarrhalis.
Slight stasis pulmonum and diffuse Alveolitis.

Liver. Hepatitis serosa III. with multiple submilary kno'ts with plenty of lymphocytes.

Stomach. No remarkable changes.

Small-Intest, Slight congestion, microscopically.

Large-Intest. Catarrh and considerable congestion.

[redacted] 59

[redacted]

CO[redacted]

Kidney. Can not be investigated microscopically.

Spleen. Angio-Folliculitis exsudativa.

Spleno-Fnsciculitis exsudativa.

Lymphnodes.
Mesenterial: Lymphadenitis catarrhalis.

Peribronchiala: Lymphadenitis haemorrhagico-necroeticans totalis.

Pancreas. -

Supra-renal. Vacuolar or honeycombed degeneration, esp, in Z. fasciculata.

Intense edema, slight perivascular leucocytes-accumulation and diffuse hemorrhages in Z. reticularis.

Considerable edema in medullary tissues.

Thyreoid. -

Pituitary B. -

Testicle. Atrophia testis.

Brains. No remarkable changes.

Skin. No remarkable changes.

CO[redacted] 60

[redacted]

CONFIDENTIAL

399.

26 years old. ♂

Entrance-port. Per-nasal infection.

Days of course. 3 days.

Heart. Considerable degeneration.

Considerable edema and some hemorrhages.

Some Myocytes.

Aorta. No remarkable changes, macroscopically.

Tonsil. Tonsillitis acuta.

Intese congestion in follicular and perifollicular tissues.

Swelling of germinative centras with some leucocytes and someplasma-cells.

Intense congestion and some plasma cell dissemination in submucous tisues.

Bronchiolus. No remarkable changes.

Lung. Patial slight congestion and partial ateloctasis.

Liver. Hepatitis serosa III-IV.

Remarkable congestion, remarkable exudative change and multiple hemorrhages in acinus.

Stomach. Almost normal. ~~remarble chages.~~

CONFIDENTIAL 61

[redacted]

[redacted]

Small intestine.	Atrophic glandular cells(microscopically).
Large intestine.	Catarrh and considerable congestion in submucous tissues.

Kidney.	Slight Glomerulo-nephrosis (glomeruli in acute stimulised state with some bacterial and fibrinous masses in gromerular loops),with slight polar changes.
	Nephrosis 1,with considerable interstitial edema and some erythrocytes-cylinders in tublar spaces.

Spleen.	Angio-Folliculitis haemorrhagico-exsudativa.
	Spleno-Fasciculitis haemorrhagico-exsudativa.
Lymphnode.	
Mesenterial:	Lymphadenitis acutea haemorrhagica.
Peribronchial:	Lymphadenitis haemorrhagico-necroticans.

[redacted] 62

[redacted]

[redacted]

Pancreas.	-
Supra-reanl.	Considerable vacuolar degeneration, and at some places honeycombed edegeneration (in Z. reticulfis). Intesne hemorrhages in Z. reticularis.
Thyreoid.	Acute disfiguring (follicular colapsea).
Pituitary B.	-
Festicles.	Atrophia testisⅡ.

Brain.	-

Skin.	No remarkable changes.

[redacted] 63

[redacted]

CONFIDENTIAL

400.

32. years old. ♂

Entrance-port. Pernasal infection.

Days of course. 3 days.

Heart.	Considerable degeneration and some mesenchymal reactions.
Aorta.	No remarkable changes, macroscopically.

Tosill.	--
Pharynx.	--
Bronchus.	Consideable congestion and somė edema in submucous tissies. Some leucocytes in capillaries.
Bronchus.	Intese Bronchiloitis catarralis.
Lung.	Mulliple acinous hemorrhagic places. Atelectasis at some places.

Liver.	Hepatitis serosa II, with intense congestion at Glisson's capsules.
Stomach.	Can not be investigated, microscopically.
Small-Intest.	"
Large-Intest.	"

Kidney.	"

CO[redacted] 64

[redacted]

CONFIDENTIAL

Spleen.		Angio-Folliculitis exsudativa.
		Spleno-Fasciculitis exsudativa.
Lymph-node.	Mesenterial:	Periadenitis haemorrhagica.
		Follicuclar congestion.
	Peribronchial:	Lymphadenitis haemorrhagico-necrosticans.
Pancreas.		Stasia and slight degeneration of parenchym, cells.
Supra-renal.		Considerable clouding, vacuolar or honeycombed degeneration of cortical cells.
		Intense edema and diffuse hemorrhages in Z. reticularis.
Thyreoid.		--
Pituitary B.		--
Testicles.		--
Brain.		--
Skin.		No remarkable changes.

[redacted] 65

[redacted]

CON[redacted]AL

401.

37 years old. ♂

Entrance-potr. Per-nasal infedtion.

Days of course. 2 days.

Heart. Considerable degeneration (some places with basophilic degeneration).

Some mesenchymal reations.

Aorta. No remarkable changes.

Bronchiolus. No remarkable changes.

Lung. Slight diffuse Alveolitis.

Liver. Can not be investigated microscopically.

Stomach. No remarkable changes.

Small-Intest. Slight catarrh, microscopically.

Larga-Intest. Slight catarrh, microscopically.

Spleen. Angio-Folliculitis haemorrhagico-exsudativa.

Spleno-Fasciculitis exsudativa.

Lymph-node.

Mesenterial : Lymphadeniis haemorrhagico-purulenta.

Peribronchial ; Lymphadenitis haemorrhagico-necroticans.

Thyreoid. Follicular collapse with Struma parenchymatoaa Levis.

CO[redacted] 66

[redacted]

403. [redacted]

34 years old. ♂

Entrance-port. Per-nassl infection.

Days of course. 3 days.

Heart. Some degeneration. Some Endoarteritis with some round cell accumulation in intima.

Aorta. No remarkable changes.

Tonsil. Tonsillitis acuta, with

Intense bionecrotic swelling and multiple diffuse superficial ulcers.

Intense congestion and edematous swelling of follicular tissues with bionecrotic swelling of germinative centres.

Intense congestion and edemátous swelling of sub-mucous tissues.

Pharynx. --

Bronchus. Intense congestion (with some leucocytes in capillaries) and intense edema in submuous tissues.

Peribronchiolitis with some congestion and some hemorrhages.

Lung. Bronchiolitis catarrhalis.

Acino-lobular pneumonia (hemorrhagic-leucocytic)

[redacted] 67

[redacted]

CONFIDENTIAL

Liver. Hepatitis serosa II-III, with some bacillus in capillaries.

Stomach. No remarkanle changes, macroscopically,

Small-Intest. Atrophic glandular cells.

Large-Intest. Catarrh and considerable congestion in submucous tissues.

Kidney. Slight Glomerulo-nephrosis (glomeruli in stimulised state with some bacterial and fibroious masses in glomerular loops), with slight polar changes.

Nephrosis I (or III at some places) with considerable interstitial edema.

Spleen. ~~Angio-Folliculitis~~

~~Spleno-Fasciculitis~~

Lymph-node.

Mesenterial : Lymphadenitis haemorrhagico-necroticans.

Peri-bronchial : Lymphaadenetis haemorrhagicoo-necroticans.

Pancreas. Considerable congestion and edema.

Considerable degeneration of parenchymatous cells and island-cells.

Supra-renal. -

Thyreoid. Acute disfi guring (follicular collapse).

Pituitary B. -

Testicles. Atrophia testis III.

Brain. -

CO[redacted] 68

[redacted]

CONFIDENTIAL

Skin.   No remarkable changes.

[redacted]

[redacted]

C[redacted]

404.

27 years old. ♂

Entrance-port. Per-nasal infection.

Days of course. 3 days.

Heart.	Some degaeration and intesne edema. Some Histiocytes.
Aorta.	No remarkable changes.
Tonsil.	-
Bronchiolus.	No remarkable changes.
Lung.	Stasis pumonum, Slight Alveolitis and atelectasis.
Liver.	Hepatitis serosa III-IV.
Stomach.	No remarkable changes, macroscopically
Small-Intest.	Considerable congestion and edema in submuceres.tissues, microscopically.
Large-Intest.	Considerable congestion and edema in submuocus tissues. some perivascular leucocytes accumulation.
Kidney.	Slight Glomerulo-nephrosis with slight polar changes. Nephrosis I (or III at some places), with considerable edema and some round cell infiltration.

C[redacted] 70

[redacted]

CONFIDENTIAL

Spleen. missed.

Lymph-node.

Mesenterial: Lymphadenitis haemorrhagica.

Perinronchial: Lymphadenitis catarrhalis levis and Peri-adenitis gravis, with intense congestion , hemorrhages and edema.

CONFIDENTIAL 71

[redacted]

405. [redacted]

27 years old. ♂

Entrance-port.	Per-nasal infection.
Days of course.	3 days.

Heart.	Intense degeneration, intense atrophy and some edema.
Aorta.	No remarkable changes.

Tonsil.	Tonsillistis catarrhalis acuta. Catarrh, slight superficial ulcers. Slight congestion and edema of follicular tissues. Intense serlling of germinative centres and slight congestion in submucous tissues.
Lung.	Multifocal acino-lobular exudative-hemorrhagic pneumonia with intense atelectasis at some places.

Liver.	Hepatitis serosa II-III.
Stomach.	No remarkable changes, macroscopically.
Small-Intest.	Can not be investigated, microscopically.
Large-Intest.	Considerable congestion and edema. Slightperivasculat leucocytes accumulation

---

Spleen.	Angio-Folliculitis. haemorrhagico-exsudativa. Spleno-Fasciculitis. exsudativa.

[redacted] 72

[redacted]

[redacted]

Lymph-node.	
Mesenterial:	Lymphadentis catarrhalis acuta with slight pericapsular hemorrhages.
Peribronchial:	Lymphadenitis catarrhalis.
Kidney.	Slight Glomeruol-nephrosis with slight polar changes. Nephrosis I, with intense vacuolar degeneration of some tubular epitheliuma and intense edema.
Pancreas.	-
Supra-renal.	Vacuolar or honeycombed degeneration, esp. in Z. fasciculata. Diffuse hemorrhages in cortical tissues.
Thyreoid.	In statical state.
Pituitary B.	-
Testicle.	Atrophia testis II.
Brain.	-
Skin.	No remarkable changes.

[redacted] 73

[redacted]

406. [redacted]

---

31 Years old.

Entrance port. Per-nasal infection.

Days of course. ca 2 days.

Lung. Slight congestion and edema.

Liver. Hepatitis serosa ll-lll.

Stomach. No remarkable changes.

Large intest. No remarkable changes.

Thyreoid. In slight activated state.

Testicle. Atrophia lll.

Othererorgans . Can not be investigated, microscopically.

[redacted] 74

[redacted]

407. [redacted]

28 years old. ♂

Entrance-port. Per-nasal infection.

Days of course. 3 days.

Heart. Intense degeneration and atrophiy.

Some interstitial edema.

Aorta. No remarkable changes and stasis of periadventitial tissues.

Tonsil. Tonsillitis haemorrhagica acuta.

Intense congestion in follcicular and perifollicular tissues and slight hyperplasia of geriminative centres with some swollen reticulum fibres.

Intense congestion and diffuse hemorhages in submucous tissues.

Bronchiolus. Bronchiolitis catarrhalis.

Lung. Stasis pulmonum.

Liver. Hepatitis serosa III, with multiple miliary necrosis and so-called net-necrosis-like changes.

Duodenam. Duodenitis haemorrhagica with diffuse hemorrhages in submucous tissues and some hemorrhages in submucous tissues.

Small-Intest. Enteritis haemorrhagico-exsudativa with some

[redacted] 75

[redacted]

	fungous swelling of mucous membrane.
	Macroscopically. [redacted]
Large-Intest.	Almost normal, macroscopically.
Spleen.	Angio-Folliculitis haemorrhagico-exsudativa.
	Spleno-Fasciculitis exsudativa.
Lymph-node. Mesenterial :	Lymphadenitis haemorrhagico-purulenta and
	Periadenitis haemorrhagico-purulenta.
Peribronchial :	Lymphadenitis haemorrhagica.
Kidney.	Slight Glomerulo-nephrosis with slight polar
	changes.
	Nephrosis I with considerable edema.
Pancreas.	Considerable congestion and edema.
	Atrophia and cloudy swelling (sometimes
	vacuolar) degeneration of parenchymatous cells.
Supra-renal.	Honeycombed degeneration, esp. in Z. fasciculalta.
	Some localised hemorrhages and perifocal
	leucocytes accumulation in Z. reticularis.
Thyreoid.	Acute disfiguring (follicular collapse).
Pituitary B.	-
Testicle.	Atrophia testis III.

[redacted] 76

[redacted]

Brain. -

---------------------------------------[redacted]--------------

Skin. No remarkable changes.

[redacted] 71

[redacted]

409. [redacted]

32 years old. ♂

Entrance port.	Per-nasal infection.
Days of course.	2 days.

Heart.	Considerable degeneration, some atrophia and edema.
Aorta.	No remarkable changes. Slight congestion of periadventitial tissues.

Torsil	Tonsillitis acuta. Intense edema and some leucocytes-accumulation in mucous epitheliums. Intense congestion and edema in follicular and perifollicular tissues. Some swollen germinative centres. Intense congestion and edema and some round cell accumulation in submucous tissues.
Bronchus.	Intense congestion (some bacterial masses in capillaries), considerable edema and some leucocytes dissemination in submucous tissues. Intense congstion and edema in peribronchial tissues.
Lung.	Bronchiolitis catarralis. Severe Alveolitis and edematous swelling of pleura. Some bacterial dissemination in alveoli.

[redacted] 78

[redacted]

[redacted]

Liver. Hepatitis serosa II-III, with some bacterial masses in capillaries.

Stomach. No remarkable changes.

Small-Intest. No remarkable changes, microscopically.

Large-Intest. Catarrh.

Kidney. Slight Glomerulo-nephrosis with slight polar changes.
Nephrosis I with considerable edema and some round cell accumulation.
Miliary cirrhotic portion in cortical tissues.

Spleen. Angio-folliculitis exsudativa.
Spleno-Fasciculitis exsudativa.

lymph-nodes.
Mesenterial: Lymphadenitis haemorrhagica.
Peribronchial: Lymphadenitits haemorrhagico-purulenta.

Pancreas. Edema. Parenchymatous degeneration.
Vacuolar degneration of island-cells.

Supra-renal. Considerable congestion and diffuse hemorrhages in Z. reticularis. Some atrophy.
Intense edema and desolative degeneration of parenchymatou cells.

Thyreoid. In activated state.

Pituitary B. -

[redacted] 79

[redacted]

Testicles. Atrophia testis Ⅱ.

---[redacted]-----

Brain.

Skin. Intense congestion, localised hemorrhages and diffuse wandering cells (some of them, leucocytic)-dissemination in subcutaneoud tissues.

[redacted] 80

[redacted]

410.

27. years old. [redacted]

Entrance-port. Por-nasal infection.

Days of course. 3 days.

Heart.	Considerable degeneration. Atrophia and interstitial edema. Some Myocytes.
Aorta.	No remarkable changes, macroscopically.

Tonsil.	Can not be investigated micrescopically.
Bronchiolus.	Bronchiolitis catarrhalis.
Lung.	Slight aiffuse Alveolitis.

Liver.	Hepatitis serosa II-III, with partial hemorrhages in central zone of acinuses.
Stomach.	Some lymphocytes in Glisson's capsule. Paeudo-biliary tract. Considerale congestion in submucoaus tissues.
Small-Intest.	Can not be investigated microscopically.
Darge-Intest.	Slight catarrh.

Kidney.	-

Spleen.	Angio-Folliculitis haemorrhagico-exsudativa. Spleno-Fasciculitis exsudativa.
Lymph-node.	Can not be investigated microscopically.

CO[redacted] 81

[redacted]

[redacted]

Supra-renal.　　Vacuolar degeneration and pabial necrosis in Z. reticularis. Plenty loucocytes in capillaries (with some myelocytes and some bacillus).

[redacted] 82

[redacted]

411. [redacted]

---

28 years old. ♂

Entrance-pert. Pernasal infection.

Days of course. 4 days.

Heart.	Considerable degeneration and atrophia. Some mesenchymal reactions. Some Myocytes.
Aorta.	No remarkable changes, macroscopically,

Liver.	Hepatitis serosa II-III.
Stomach.	No remarkable changes, macroscopically.
~~Small-Intest.~~	~~Can not be investigated, microscopically~~.
Duodenal parts.	Slight catarrh. Considerable congestion and edema in submucous tissues.
Small-intest.	Intense hemorrhagic-loucocytic inflammation with fungous swelling of mucous membrane, due to Anthrax-infection.
Large-Intest.	No remarkable changes, macroscopically.

Kidney.	Slight Glomerulo-nephrosis with slight polar changes. Nephrosis I, with considerable interstitial edema and intense vacuolar degeneration of tubular epitheliums at subcapsular pertions.

[redacted] 83

[redacted]

[redacted]

Spleen. Angio-Folliculitis haemorrhagico-exsudativa.

Spleno-Fasciculitis haemorrhagico-exsudativa.

Lymph-node.
Mesenterial: Lymphadenitis haemorrhagica.

Peribronchial: Lymphadenitis haemorrhagica gravis.

Tonsil. Tonsillitis catarrhalis acuta.

Intense congestion and edema in follicular and peri-follicular tissues, accom panied with multiple hemorrhages and some leucocytes-emigration.

Bronchus. Considerable congestion and some hemorrhages in sub-mucous tissues.

[redacted] 84

[redacted]

[redacted]

Bronchiolus.	Bronchiolitis necroticans and Peribronchiolitis.
Lung.	Acino-lobular catarrhalic-necrotic pneumonia with Pleuritis haemorrhagica.

Pancreas.	Considerable degeneration of parenchymatous cells and some atrophia.
	Considerable congestion and slight perivascular round cell accumulation.
	Intense vacuolar degeneration of island-cells.
Supra-renal.	Vacuolar degeneration of cortical cells.
	Considerable congestion, some diffuse hemorrhages in Z. reticularis and intense edematous swelling of cortical tissues.
	Vacuolar degeneration of wedullary cells.
Thyreoid.	In acute disfiguring. (follicular collapse).
Pituitary B.	-
Testicle.	Atrophia testis II.

Brain.	Slight congestion of meninges.
	Considerable congestion, slight hemorrhages and some edema in brain.
Cerebellum.	Slight congestion and slight edema.

Skin.	No remarkable changes.

[redacted]

85

[redacted]

412. [redacted]

---

27 years old.♂

Entrance-ports.	Per-nasal infection.
Days of course.	3 days.

Heart.	Considerable degeneration. Slight congestion (some leucocytes in capillaries) and slight edema. Some histiocytes.
Aorta.	No remarkable changes.

Tonsil.	Tonsillitis catarrhalis acuta. Intense bionecrotic swelling of mucous epitheliums. (bacterial intbrusion in epitheliums). Intense congestion and edema in folliculab tissues. Remarkable swelling of germinative centers with some bacterial accumulations. Intense congestion and edema (some leucocytes in Submucous tissues.
Bronchus.	Intense congestion in submucous tissues. Peribronchitis with congestion and some hemorrhages.
Bronchilous.	Bronchiolitis catarrhalis gravis and peribronchiolitis.
Lung.	Diffuse Alveolitis and some lacinous hemorrhagic places.

[redacted] 86

[redacted]

Liver. Can not be investigated, microscopically.

Stomach. Slight catarrh. [redacted]

Small-Intest. Considerable catarrh.

Large-Intest. Slight catarrh, considerable congestion and slight perivascular leucocytes-accumulation.

Kidney. Slight Glomerulo-nephrosis with slight polar changes. Nephrosis I (or III at some places), with intense interstitial edema.

Spleen. -

Lymph-node.
Mesenterial: Slight catarrh.

Peribronchial: Lymphadenitis haemorrhagica gravis.

Pancreas. Considerable degeneration of parenchymatous cells and island-cells. Some edema.

Supra-renal. -

Thyreoid. -

Pituitary B. -

Testicle. ~~Atrophia testis~~.

Brain. -

Skin. No remarkable changes.

[redacted]

87

[redacted]

413. [redacted]

---

37 years old.

Entrance-port. Pernasal infection.

Days of course. 3 days.

Heart.	Considerable degeneration. Some atrophia.
Aorta.	No remarkable changes.

Tonsil.	Tonsillitis catarrhalis acuta. Considerable congestion and edema in follicular and perifollicular tissues. Considerable swelling of germinative centres. Considerable congestion in submucous tissues.
Bronchus.	Peribronchitis with some hemorrhagic places.
Bronchiolus.	Bronchiolitis catarrhalis.
Lung.	No remarkable changes.

Liver.	Hepatitis serosa II.
Stomach.	Slight catarrh and considerable congestion in submucous tissues.
Small-Intest.	Considerable catarrh.
Large-Intest.	No remarkable change, macroscopically.

[redacted] 88

[redacted]

[redacted]

Kidney.	Slight Glomerulo-nephrosis with slight polar changes. Nephrosis I (or III at some places) and Nephritis interstitialis at some places, with some round cell accumulation, considerable edema and considerable hyperplasia of connective tissues.

Spleen. ~~Angio-Folliculitis~~. —

Lymphnode. ~~Spleno-Fasciculitis~~.
Mesenterial. Missed.

Peribronchial : Lymphadenitis haemorrhagica.

Thyreoid. In acute disfiguring(follicular collapse).

[redacted]

89

[redacted]

[redacted]

414.

---

29 years old.

Entrance port. **Pernasal infection.**

Days of course. ca.2days.

Heart. Considerable degeneration and interstitial edema.

Liver. Hepatitis serosa ll.with remarkable exudation and congestion.

Stomach. No remarkable changes.

Large intest.No remarkable changes.

Testicle. Atrophia testis ll.

Other organs.Can not be investigated,microscopically.

[redacted] 90

[redacted]

416. ~~CONFIDENTIAL~~

31. years old.

Entrance-port.	Pernasal infection.
Days of course.	4 days.

Heart.	Considerable degeneration and some atrophia. Some edema and some mesenchymal reations.
Aorta.	No remarkable changes.

Tonsil.	-
Pharynx.	-
Bronchus.	Some bacterial masses in bronchilolus.
Lung.	Stasis and edema pulmonum, with numerous bacterial masses in alveoli.

Liver.	Hepatitis serosa II-III.
Stomach.	No remarkable changes, macroscopically.
Small-Intest.	Considerable congestion in mucous and submucous tissues, microscopically.
Large-Intest.	Slight congestion.

Spleen.	~~Angio-Folliculitis~~. —. ~~Spleno-Fasciculitis~~.

~~CONFIDENTIAL~~

91

[redacted]

[redacted]

Lymph-node.
Mesenterial. Follicular congestion

Peribronchial : Lymphadenitis haemorrhagica with considerable follicular congestion.

Supra-renal. Vacuolar degeneration of cortical cells. Some edema and intense diffuse hemorrhages in Z. reticularis.

Brain. -

Skin. No remarkable changes.

[redacted] 92

[redacted]

417. [redacted]

Years and sex.	27.
Entrance-port.	Pernasal infeection.
Days of courses.	3 days.

Heart.	Intense degeneration. Considerable edema and Atrophia.
Aorta.	No remarkable changes.

Tonsil-	Tonsillitis acuta with bionecrotic swelling of mucous epitheliums, intense congestion and edema in follicular and peri-follicular tissues, intense hemorrhages and some bacterial accumu-lation in perifollicular tissues, bionecrotic swellingof germinative centred and intense congestion in submucous tissues.
Bronchus.	Considerable congestion adn edema in submucous tissues.
Bronchiolus.	Bronchiolitis catarrhalis.
Lung.	Slight congestion and at some places atelectasis.

Liver.	Hepatitis serosa II-III.with multiplemiliary necrosis(some leucocytes, a few histiocytes and a few lymphocytes , and decayed masses).
Stomach.	Slight edema and considerable congestion in mucous

[redacted] 93

[redacted]

[redacted]

tissues.

Small-Intest. Catarrh and edema in mucous tissues.
Some inflammatory changes in submucous tissues with edema, slight hemorrhages and some perivascular wandering cell accumulations.

Lasge-Intest. No remarkable chamges.

Kidney. Slight Glomerlulo-nephrosis with slight polar changes.
Nephrosis I (or III at some places), with considerable interstitial edema.

Spleen. ~~Angio-folliculitis.~~ —.
~~Fasciculitis.~~

Lymph-node
Mesentrial: Lymphadenitis acuta with slight exudative reactions(congestion and some leucocytes).
Peribronchial L. haemorrhagica.

Pancreas In autolysis. Vacuolar degeneration of parenchymatous cells.

Supra-renal. Partial hemorrhages in cortical tissues and intense edema and diffuse hemorrhages in Z, reticularis.
Vacuolar or intense degeneration of cortical tissues (ruining processes of cortical cells),with some round cell accumulation in Z.fasciculata and

CO[redacted] 94

[redacted]

[redacted]

Z. reticularis.
Remarkable atrophia of cortical cells.
Edema in medullary tissues.

Thyreoid. In acute disfigurring (follicular collapse), with some bacterial masses in capillaries.

Pituitary B. -

Testicles Atrophia testisⅡ.

Brain. Considerable congestion ans slight perivascular hemorrhages.

Skin. No remarkable changes.

[redacted] 95

[redacted]

CO[redacted]

Heart

CO[redacted] 96

[redacted]

[redacted]

H E A R T

(A) Microcopical Investigation.

I6.

Considerable parenchymatous degeneration and edema.

26.

No remarkable changes.

53.

Basophilic degeneration of some muscular cells. Slight mesenchymal reactions.

54.

Severe parenchymatous degeneration and atrophia. Edema in interstitium.

225.

Considerable parenchymatous degeneration.

3I8.

Considerable parenchymatous degeneration and atrophia. Partial hemorrhages in interstitium and desolative decay of the neighbouring muscular fibres. Considerable venous congestion.

320.

Slight parenchymatous degeneration and considerable atrophia. Interstitial edema.

325.

Severe parenchymatous degeneration and considerable atrophia. Remarkable perivascular edema and some myocytes-accumulation.

[redacted] 97

[redacted]

328. -C[redacted]L

Severe parenchymatous degeneration. Severe venous congestion and slight hemorrhages in interstitium. Many leucocytes in blood-vessels.

383.

Severe parenchymatous degeneration and considerable edema.

388.

Severe parenchymatous degeneration.

389.

Condiderable parenchymatous degeneration.

390.

Severe parenchymatous degeneration and congestion.

393.

Severe parenchymatous degeneration and considerable atrophia. Severe venous congestion and considerable edema. Slight hemorrhages in interstitium.

396.

Severe atropia and considerable parenchymatous degeneration. Severe edema and accumulation of leucocytes in blood-vessels.

397.

Slight parenchymatous degeneration. Considerable edema and hemorrhages in interstitium and epicardial tissues.

CO[redacted] 98

[redacted]

399. [redacted]

Considerable parenchymatous degeneration, edema and hemorrhage in interstitium. Appearance of some myocytes.

400.

Considerable parenchymatous degeneration with slight mesenchymal reactions.

401.

Considerable parenchymatous degeneration and basophilic degeneration of some muscular cells. Some mesenchymal reactions and slight infiltration of lymphocytes at some places of interstitium.

403.

Some parenchymatous degeneration and edema. Endoarteritis of some arteries (with small round-cell-infiltration in intima).

404.

Some parenchymatous degeneration and edema. Remarkable perivasculare edema around some blood-vessels, with histiocytes-accumulation at some places.

405.

Severe parenchymatous degeneration, atrophia and interstitial edema.

407.

Severe parenchymatous degeneration, atrophia and interstitial edema.

409.

Considerable parenchymatous degeneration, atrophia and interstitial edema.

[redacted] 99

[redacted]

410. [redacted]

Considerable parenchymatous degeneration, atrophia and interstitial edema. Some myocytes around blood-vessels.

4II.

Considerable parenchymatous degeneration and atrophia. Some mesenchymal reactions. Accumulation of many myocytes.

4I2.

Some parenchymatous degeneration, atrophia and edema. Leucocytes in blood-vessels. Accumulation of histiocytes around blood-vessels.

4I3.

Considerable parenchymatous degeneration and atrophia.

4I4.

Considerable parenchymatous degeneration, atrophia and inter-stitial edema.

4I6.

Considerable parenchymatous degeneration, atrophia and inter-stitial edema. Slight mesenchymal reactions.

4I7.

Severe parenchymatous degeneration, considerable atrophia and interstitial edema.

[redacted] 100

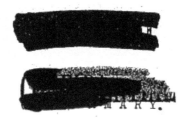

[redacted]

[redacted]

Investigation on 3I micro-slices.

a) Epicardium with severe edema. Generally no remarkable changes else. In I specimen, some mesenchymal reactions with leucocytes-infiltration.

b) Myocardium: In many cases, muscular fibres are atrophic with plenty of lipofuscin-deposits. Generally with severe cloudy swelling and occasionally with slight hyaline degeneration. Slight vacuolar degeneration in 6 cases and basophilic degeneration of some muscular cells in 3 cases. Severe edematous swelling in interstitial tissues and frequently slight exposed perivascular hemorrhages (4 cases of them in severe degree).

In one-third of all cases, intense congestion, and occasionally leucocytes accumulate in blood-vessels with more or less intense perivascular edema.

Increase of adventitial cells in some cases. Rarely round-cell accumulate in interstitium. 4 specimens have many myocytes, which in 1 specimen accumulate as glanulom.

c) Epicardium with edema and round-cell-infiltrations.

~~CONFIDENTIAL~~

104

[redacted]

[redacted]

HEART

		17	26	53	54	225	318	320	325	328	383	388	389	390	393	396	397
Parenchyma of Myocardium	Fragmentation	−	+	−	−	++	÷	−	−	−	−	−	−	−	∸	+	−
	Brown Pigment	+++	++	++	++	++	++	++	++	+	÷	(+)	(++)	++	+	÷	+
	Atrophia	+	∸	+	++	(+)	(++)	++	+++	+	(++)	−	÷	÷	++	(+++)	+
	Hypertrophia	÷	−	−	−	÷	−	−	−	−	−	−	−	−	−	−	−
	Disappearance of Striations	++	∸	∸	++	(++)	(+)	+	(+++)	++	++	++	++	++	++	(++)	+
	Cloudy Swelling	++	÷	÷	++	(++)	(+)	+	++	(+++)	+++	+++	++	+++	+++	++	+
	Vacuolar Degeneration	−	−	−	−	(+)	−	−	(+)	−	(+)	÷	÷	−	∸	∸	−
	Hyaline Degeneration	−	−	−	÷	−	−	−	∸	∸	∸	(÷)	−	−	(∸)	−	−
	Waxy Necrosis	−	−	−	−	−	−	−	−	−	−	−	−	−	−	−	−
	Changes of Nuclei: Pyknosis	∸	−	÷	∸	÷	+	∸	÷	−	+	++	++	+	++	++	++
	Changes of Nuclei: Swelling	∸	∸	∸	∸	∸	∸	∸	∸	∸	∸	÷	∸	∸	∸	−	∸
	Changes of Nuclei: Karyolysis	÷	∸	∸	+	÷	÷	÷	+	∸	+	++	+	+	+	÷	÷
	Changes of Nuclei: Disappearance	÷	−	−	+	÷	÷	÷	÷	÷	+	+	+	+	+	+	÷
Interstice of Myocardium	Edema	++	∸	∸	++	+	+	++	++	÷	(++)	+	+	(+)	++	(+++)	(++)
	Hemorrhage	∸	−	−	−	∸	++	∸	∸	(+)	÷	÷	∸	÷	(+)	−	(+)
	Contents of Blood vessels: Erythrocytes	+	++	++	++	+	(+++)	++	++	+++	++	++	+	+++	+++	+	+
	Contents of Blood vessels: Leucocytes	−	÷	∸	÷	−	−	∸	−	++	+	∸	−	÷	+	++	÷
	Contents of Blood vessels: Lymphocytes	∸	÷	∸	÷	−	−	−	−	∸	∸	∸	−	−	÷	∸	−
	Contents of Blood vessels: Monocytes	∸	∸	−	∸	−	−	−	−	∸	∸	−	−	−	∸	∸	∸
	Infiltration of Leucocytes	−	−	−	(+)	−	−	−	−	−	−	∸	−	−	−	∸	∸
	Infiltration of Lymphocytes	∸	−	−	∸	−	∸	÷	÷	∸	÷	∸	÷	∸	∸	÷	∸
	Proliferation of Histiocytes	∸	−	∸	∸	∸	∸	∸	÷	÷	+	÷	∸	∸	∸	∸	−
	Proliferation of Myocytes	−	−	−	−	−	−	−	+	−	−	−	−	−	−	−	−
	Changes of Vessel walls: Thickening	−	−	−	−	∸	−	−	−	−	−	−	−	−	−	−	−
	Changes of Vessel walls: Edema	∸	−	∸	+	++	÷	÷	÷	−	÷	÷	∸	÷	∸	+	÷
	Changes of Vessel walls: Adventitial cells	−	∸	(+)	−	∸	∸	(÷)	−	+	+	÷	÷	∸	(÷)	÷	∸
	Perivascular Edema	++	+	+	++	++	++	+++	++	(÷)	++	+	++	++	++	++	++
Endocard.	Edema	|	∸	∸	++	++	÷	++	|	∸	++	÷	+	++	++	(+++)	++
	Infiltration: Erythrocytes	|	−	−	−	÷	(÷)	−	|	÷	−	−	−	−	∸	−	−
	Infiltration: Leucocytes	|	−	−	(∸)	−	−	−	|	(+)	−	−	−	−	∸	−	−
	Infiltration: Lymphocytes	|	−	−	∸	∸	−	−	|	÷	∸	∸	∸	−	∸	−	−
Epicardium	Proliferation of Mesenchym cells	−	÷	∸	∸	−	−	−	−	(+)	÷	÷	∸	∸	÷	∸	−
	Edema	+	∸	÷	+	+	++	++	++	∸	+	+	+	+	++	++	++
	Congestion	++	+	+	+	+	+	÷	++	+++	+	+	+	++	++	+	∸
	Infiltration: Erythrocytes	−	−	∸	−	∸	÷	÷	÷	∸	∸	∸	∸	÷	−	∸	+
	Infiltration: Leucocytes	−	−	−	∸	−	−	−	−	−	−	−	−	∸	−	∸	−
	Infiltration: Lymphocytes	∸	++	÷	∸	−	∸	+	∸	+	÷	+	(∸)	∸	(÷)	+	+
	Proliferation of Histiocytes	÷	÷	∸	∸	∸	∸	÷	÷	−	∸	÷	(∸)	+	∸	∸	÷

[redacted] 102

[redacted]

[redacted]

HEART

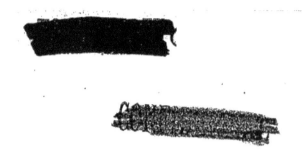

			399	400	401	403	404	405	407	409	410	411	412	413	414	418	417
Parenchyma of Myocardium	Fragmentation		−	∸	−	∸	÷	−	−	∸	+	−	++	+	÷	+	−
	Brown Pigment		+	+	+	(+++)	(++)	+	++:	(++:)	++	++:	+	∸	+	++	+
	Atrophia		(++)	(++:)	(++)	(++)	÷	++	++	(+++)	+	++	∸	++	++	∸	(++)
	Hypertrophia		∸	÷	−	÷	−	−	(∸)	∸	÷	−	÷	−	−	∸	∸
	Disappearance of Striations		(++)	++	(++)	+	+	++:	++	++	++	++	+	++	++:	+	+:
	Cloudy Swelling		(+++)	++	(+++)	++	+:	++:	++	++	++	++	+:	++	++	++:	++:
	Vacuolar Degeneration		∸	(+)	−	(∸)	−	−	∸	∸	∸	−	∸	−	∸	−	−
	Hyaline Degeneration		∸	−	−	∸	−	÷	−	−	−	−	−	−	−	−	(÷)
	Waxy Necrosis		∸	−	−	−	−	−	−	−	−	−	−	−	−	−	−
	Changes of Nuclei	Pyknosis	÷	∸	(++:)	∸	+	++	+	÷	÷	+	∸	÷	÷	∸	+:
		Swelling	÷	÷	(÷)	÷	÷	−	∸	+	÷	∸	÷	−	∸	÷	∸
		Karyolysis	+	+	÷	÷	÷	+	÷	+	+	÷	÷	∸	+	∸	÷
		Disappearance	+	∸	÷	∸	∸	÷	∸	÷	÷	∸	∸	÷	∸	∸	∸
Interstice of Myocardium	Edema		(++)	+:	(++)	(+++)	+:	++	(++)	++	(++)	(++)	+	÷	++	(++)	++
	Hemorrhage		(∸)	−	÷	∸	−	−	÷	−	∸	∸	−	(∸)	−	∸	∸
	Contents of Blood vessels	Erythrocytes	+	+	÷	+	∸	+	÷	÷	(+:)	++	÷	∸	÷	+:	+
		Leucocytes	−	÷	∸	+	(∸)	−	∸	∸	(+)	−	++:	∸	−	∸	−
		Lymphocytes	∸	÷	∸	∸	(÷)	∸	∸	∸	∸	∸	(∸)	∸	−	∸	∸
		Monocytes	−	∸	−	−	∸	−	∸	−	−	−	−	−	∸	∸	−
	Infiltration of Leucocytes		−	÷	−	−	−	−	−	−	(∸)	−	−	−	−	−	−
	Infiltration of Lymphocytes		∸	÷	(+:)	(÷)	(÷)	∸	∸	∸	(÷)	−	+	−	∸	−	−
	Proliferation of Histiocytes		∸	÷	(+)	∸	(+)	∸	∸	∸	∸	+	+:	∸	∸	∸	∸
	Proliferation of Myocytes		+	−	−	−	−	−	−	−	+	+	−	−	−	−	−
	Changes of Vessel walls	Thickening	−	−	−	−	−	−	−	−	−	−	−	−	−	∸	−
		Edema	∸	∸	−	∸	÷	−	∸	÷	÷	−	÷	∸	∸	÷	+
		Adventitial Cells	÷	+	(++:)	+	∸	÷	∸	÷	(÷)	+:	+	÷	÷	+	∸
	Perivascular Edema		(+++)	+	+:	+	++:	+	++	++	(++)	(++)	+	+	++	+:	++
Endocard.	Edema		÷	÷	(÷)	++	+:	+	|	+:	÷	++	++	|	+	+	+:
	Infiltration	Erythrocytes	−	−	−	−	−	−	|	−	−	−	−	|	−	−	−
		Leucocytes	−	−	−	−	−	−	|	−	−	−	−	|	−	−	−
		Lymphocytes	∸	∸	−	∸	−	∸	|	−	∸	−	−	|	∸	−	−
	Proliferation of Mesenchym cells		∸	÷	÷	÷	−	∸	|	∸	÷	÷	∸	|	∸	−	−
Epicardium	Edema		+:	++	|	++	|	++	++	+	+	+	+	+	+	+	++
	Congestion		+	÷	|	÷	|	+	+	÷	÷	+:	÷	+	+:	÷	+
	Infiltration	Erythrocytes	÷	−	|	−	|	÷	∸	−	÷	∸	−	∸	−	÷	∸
		Leucocytes	−	−	|	−	|	−	−	∸	−	−	−	−	−	−	−
		Lymphocytes	+	+:	|	÷	|	++	+	(++)	++	(+++)	÷	∸	∸	+	+
	Proliferation of Histiocytes		÷	÷	|	÷	|	+	÷	+	+	∸	÷	÷	÷	∸	∸

[redacted]

103

[redacted]

CONFIDENTIAL

Degeneratio et Atrophia myocardii [illegible]
gravis.

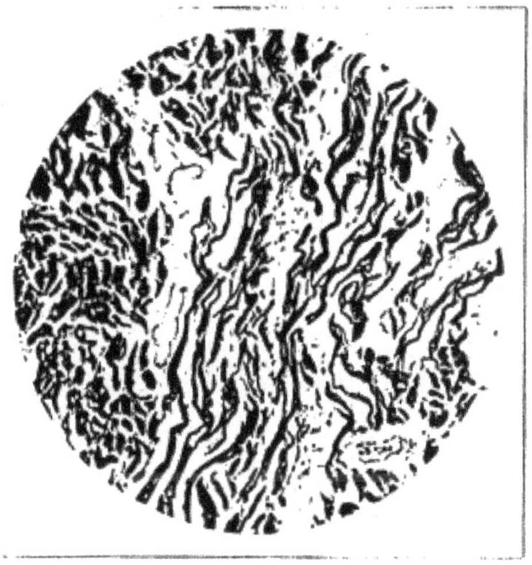

Degeneratio et Atrophia myocardii
gravis, in high power.

CONFIDENTIAL

[redacted]

Hemorrhages in intermuscular tissues.

[redacted]

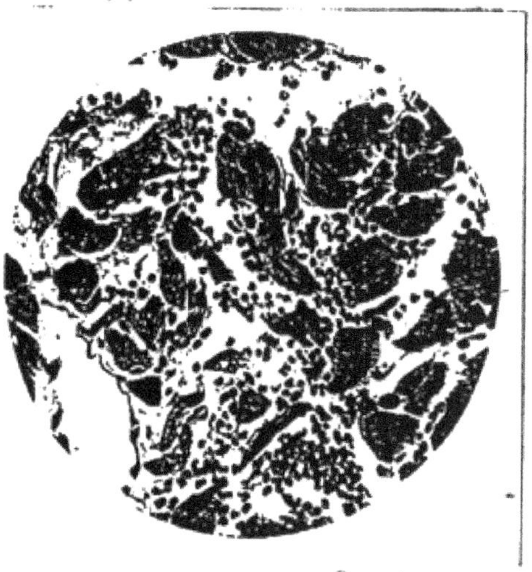

Myocytes-granulom.

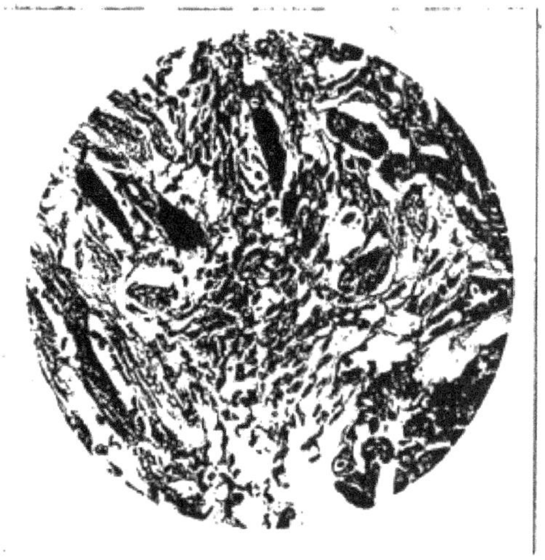

[redacted]

105

[redacted]

Some endocard-reaction.

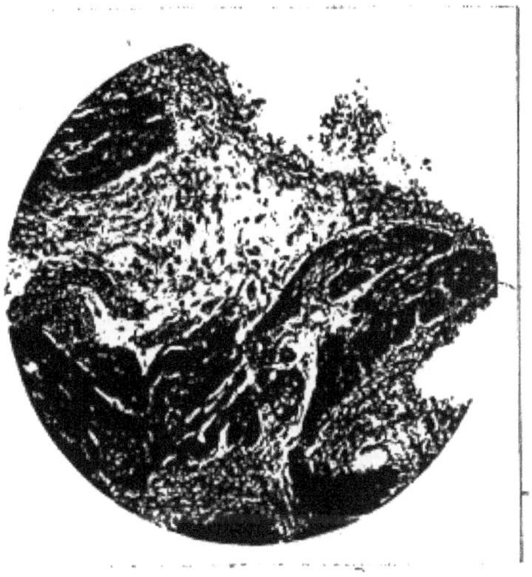

[redacted] 106

[redacted]

Lung

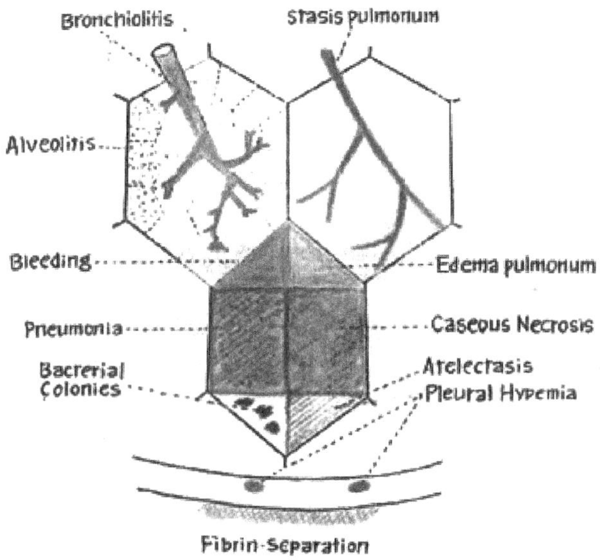

CONFIDENTIAL 107

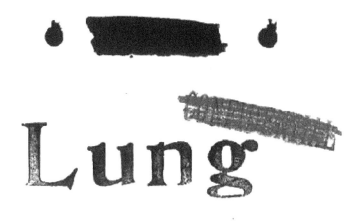

[redacted]

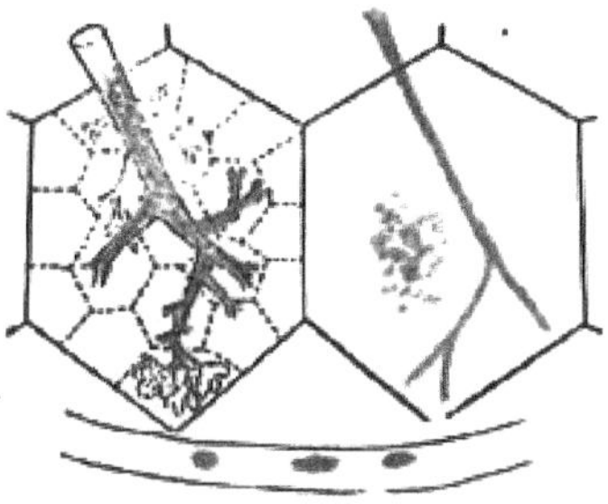

18.

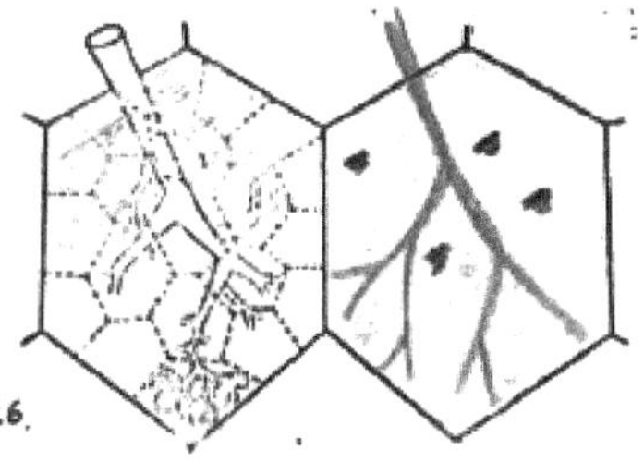

26.

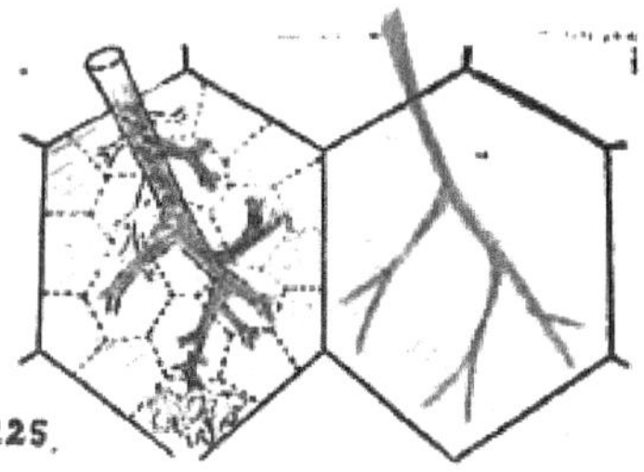

225.

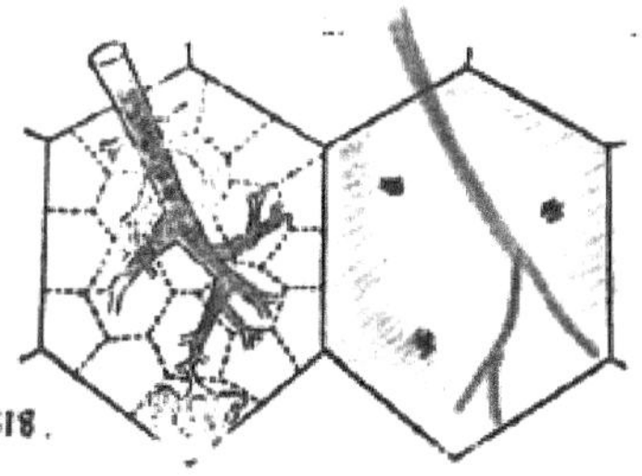

318.

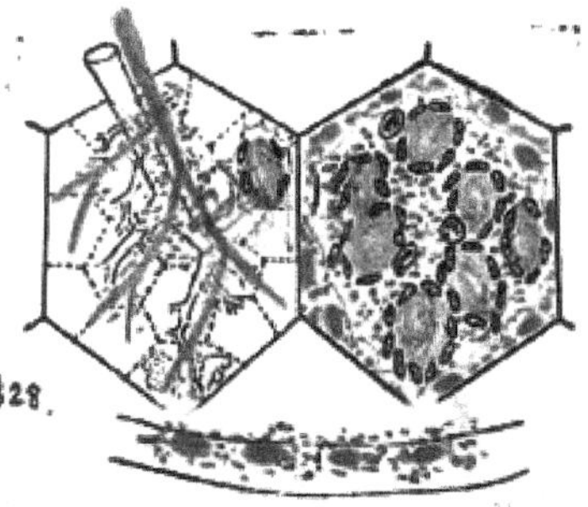

328.

LUNG.

(A) Microscop.Investigation.

17.

Almost normal .

18.

Almost normal. Edema et. stasis pulmonum levis. Bronchiolitis catarrhalis levis. Pleural hyperaemia.

26.

Edema et stasis pulmonum gravis. Bacterial colonies in alveoli.

225.

Edema et stasis pulmonum. Bronchiolis.

318.

Bronchiolitis catarrhalis. Slight congestion of alveolar capillaries, and slight edema. Bacterial colonies in alveoli.

325.

Acinous-nodose lung-tuberculosis. (conglomerat-tubercles-formation) No remarkable changes else.

328.

Acino-lobular lung-tuberculosis in productive, somewhat exudative form. The focal parts of tubercles are caseous with cavern and perifocal parts rather proliferative with epitheloid cells

[redacted] 108

[redacted]

[redacted]

and giant cells.

These are surrounded with moderate lymphocytic-hemorrhagic reactive zones.

No remarkable changes else.

388. (r. sup.)

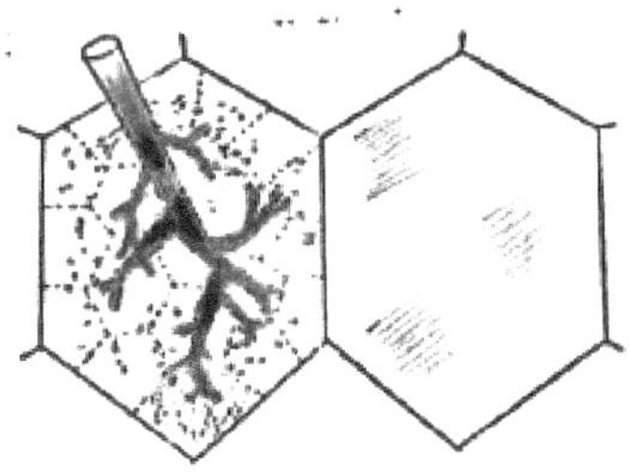

388. (right superior).

Bronchiolitis catarrhalis, slight emphysema and atelectasis.

388. (right median).

388. (r. med.)

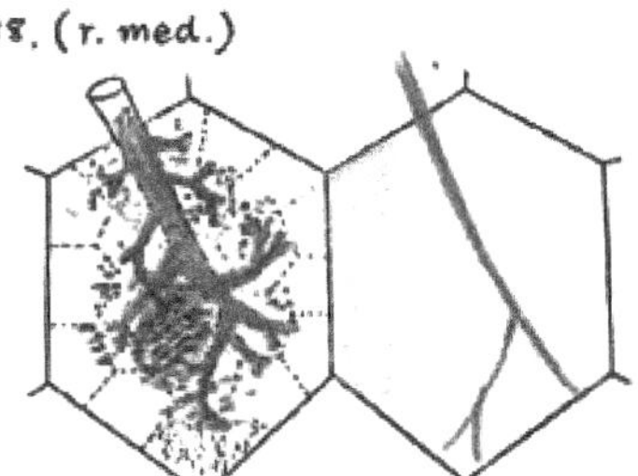

Endobronchiolitis catarrhalis and Peribronchiolitis acuta with inflammatory swelling of peribronchial lymphodulus, which fall into totally hemorrhagic and partially necrotic state and bacterial accumulations in peribronchial lymph-vessels or -nodulus.

Generally slight inflammatory swelling and congestion in peribronchial tissues.

Slight congestion and slight edema of alveoli.

389. (r. sup.)

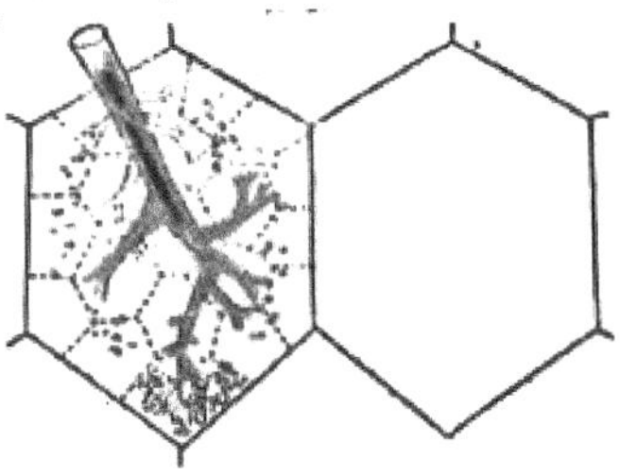

389. (right superior).

Bronchiolitis catarrhalis and slight Alveolitis (congestion and slight emigrations of lymphocytes and leucocytes in alveolar-walls).

389. (right inferior).

389 (r. inf.)

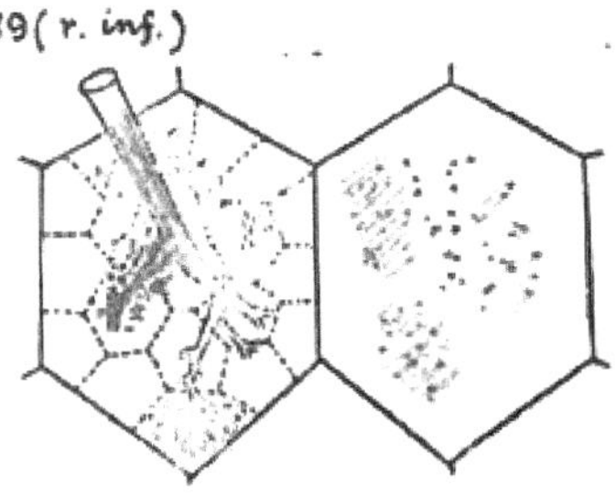

Moderate Alveolitis (congestion, moderate emigrations of leucocytes in alveolar-walls) and edema pulmonum.

[redacted] 409

[redacted]

[redacted]

389. (l. sup.)

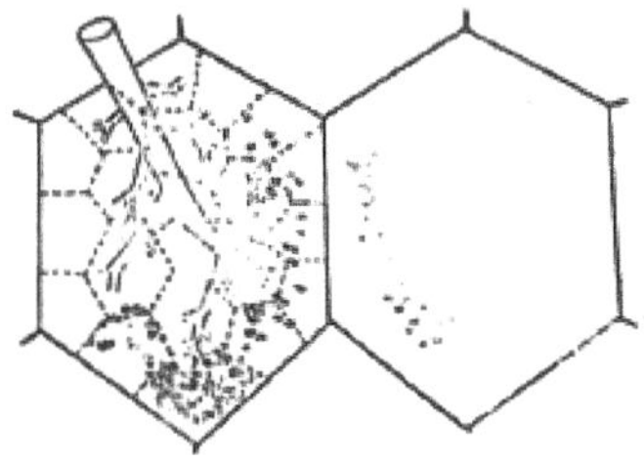

Slight leucocytes-accumulation in peribronchial lymph-nodulus and Bronchiolitis catarrhalis.

Slight reactive Pleuritis (congestion and edematous swelling of pleural tissues).

389 (left, superior).

slight lymphocytes-emigration in alveolar walls.

389 (left inferior).

389. (l. inf.)

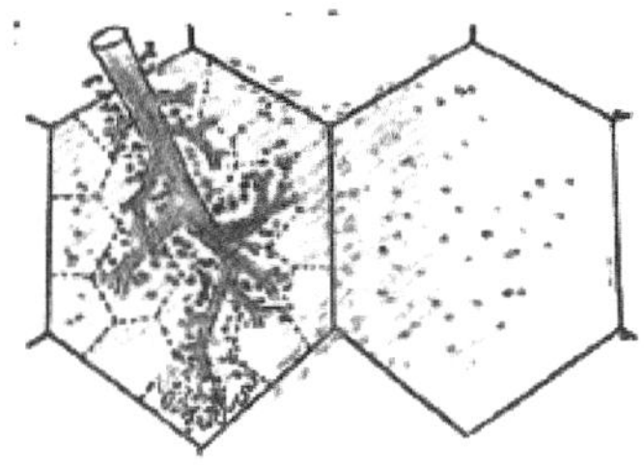

Endobronchiolitis catarrhalis and Peribronchiolitis.

Slight lymphadenitis acuta of peribronchiolar lymph-nodulus (inflammatory swelling and leucocytic accumulation in lymphodulus) and slight leucocytic -infiltration of peribronchiolar tissues.

Slight plumonal odema and slight leucocytic emigration in some acinus of catchment-area to attacked bronchiolitis.

390. (l. inf.)

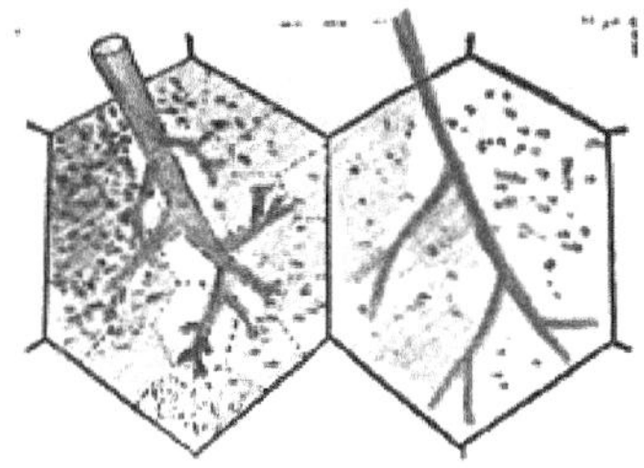

Edematous swelling and slight diffuse bleeding of interlobular connective tissues.

390 (left ~~superior~~ inf).

Diffuse Alveolitis and localised miliary hemorrhagic pneumonia.

Edematous swelling, considerable congestion, and leucocytes-emigration at alveolar walls and

[redacted] 110

[redacted]

CONFIDENTIAL

furthermore at some places multiple miliary hemorrhagic pneumonia : most parts of them are strongly hemorrhagic (bleeding and separation of fibrinous masses) and fall into partiall necrosis with many leucocytes-fragments.

These inflammatory changes spread with severe exudative reactions (cell-infiltration and hemorrhages) to the neighbouring tissues (= diffuse Alveolitis).

393. (r. sup.)

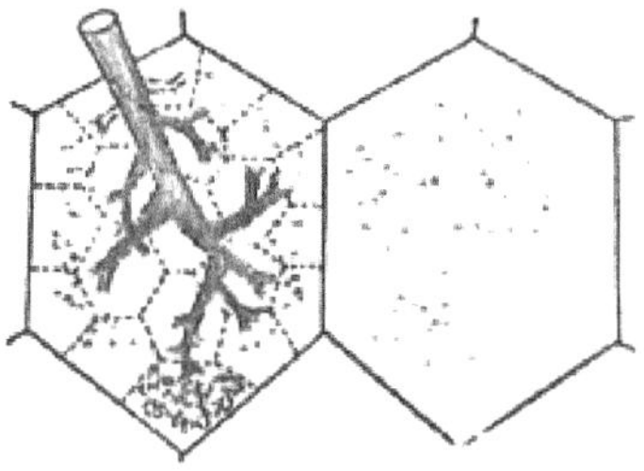

Bronchiolitis catarrhalis in high degree and considerable congestion, slight cell-infiltration and edematous swelling of peribronchial connective tissues (Peribronchiolitis).

393(right superior).

Bronchiolitis catarrhalis and slight diffuse Alveolitis with partial slight emphysema.

393. (r. inf.)

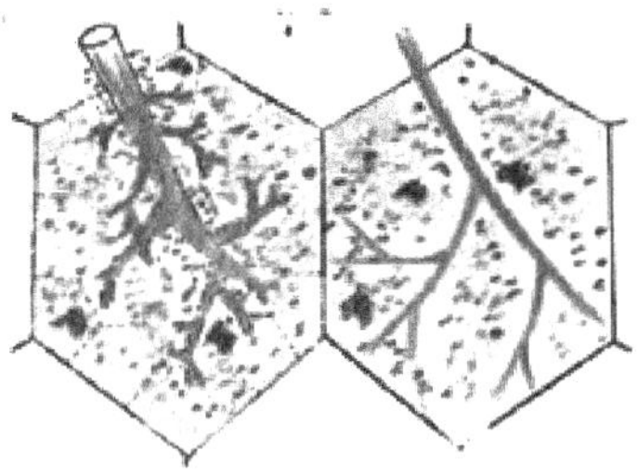

393(right inferior).

Endobronchiolitis catarrhalis in high degree and diffuse Alveolitis : odematous swelling, congestion and leucocytesemigration at alveolar walls with odema and slight erythrocytes-leakage in alveoli. Bacterial colonies in some alveoli.

CONFIDENTIAL,,,

[redacted]

[redacted]

Edematous swelling, slight round-cell-infiltration and congestion of peribronchial connective tissues (Peribronchiolitis).

393. (L. sup.)

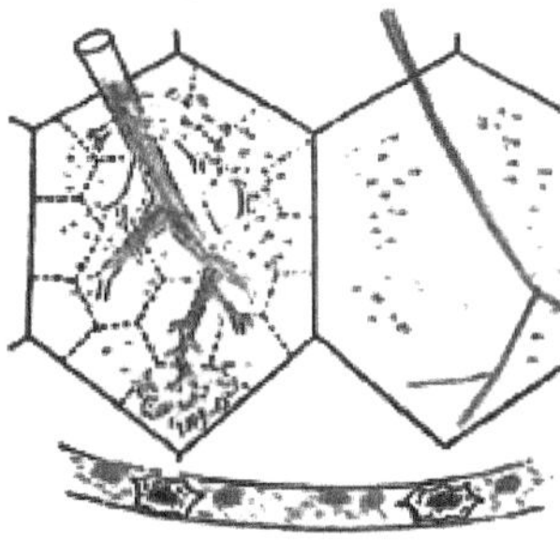

393(left superior).

Bronchiolitis and Congestion pulmonum: slight congestion and slight cell-infiltration at alveolar walls (slight Alveolitis).

In pleural tissues, considerable congestion and edematous swelling with many productive miliary tubercles. (Pleuritis tuberculosa productiva and reactive inflammatory changes, due to Congestion pulmonum).

393. (l. inf.)

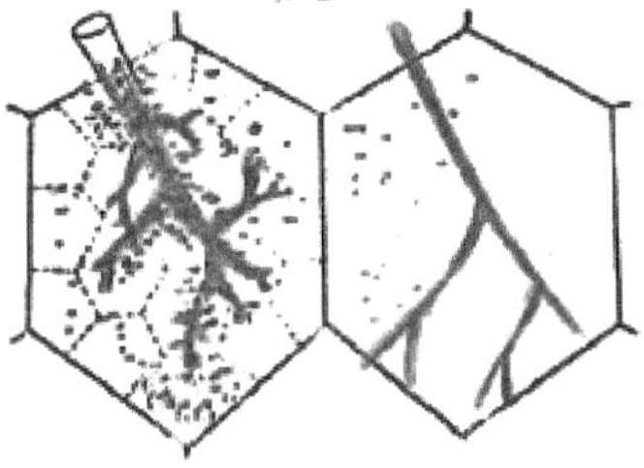

393(left Inferior).

Bronchiolitis catarrhalis and diffuse Alveolitis: congestion and leucocytes-emigration at alveolar walls.

Slight round-cell-infiltration of peribronchiolar tissues (slight Peribronchiolitis) and slight hemorrhages and edematous swelling of pleural tisses. (reactive inflammatory changes of pleural tissues).

396. (r. inf.)

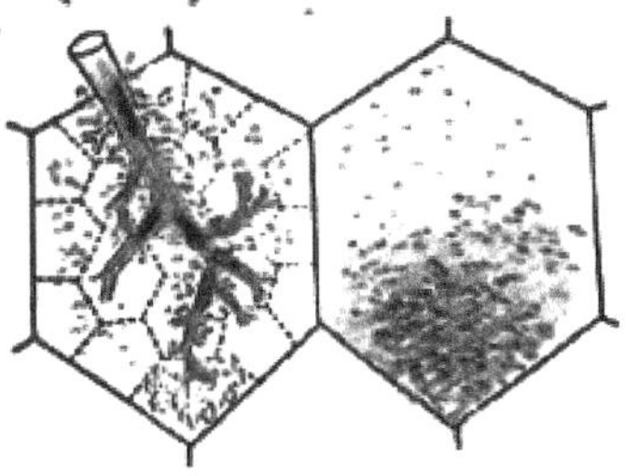

396 (right inferior).

Bronchiolitis catarrhalis gravis (bacterial colonies as contents) and diffuse Alveolitis : leucocytes-infiltration at alveolar walls, slight edema and some heart-disease-cells in alveoli.

[redacted] 112

• [redacted] •

[redacted]

396. (l. sup. & inf.)

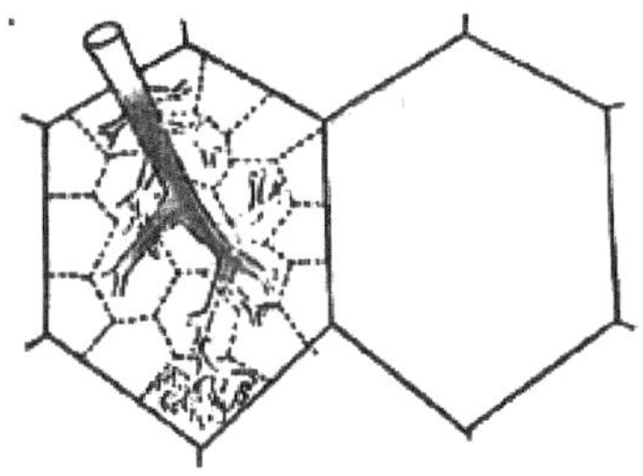

397. (r. sup.)

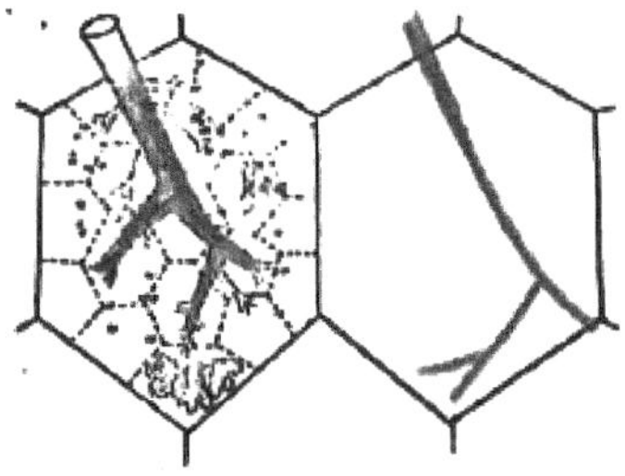

399. (l. sup.)

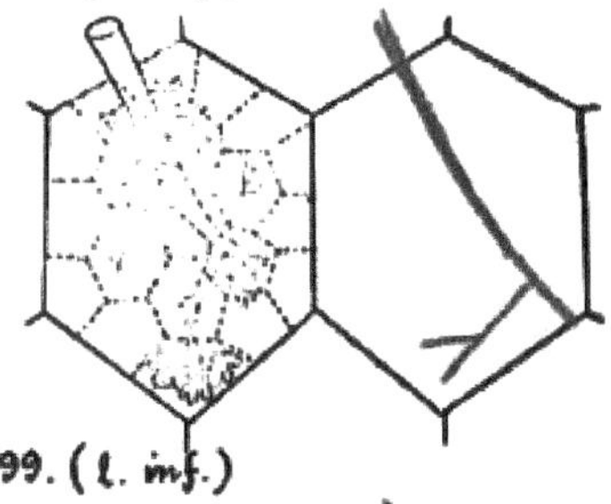

399. (l. inf.)

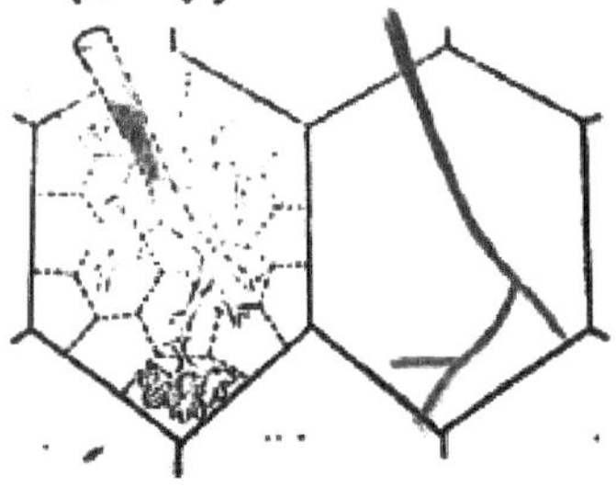

These diffuse Alveolitis develop at some subpleural tissues to acinous hemorrhagic pneumonia (severe congestion, hemorrhage, edema, desquamation of alveolar epitheliums and bacterial accumulation in some alveoli).

Bacterial colonies accumulated at some places, esp. in alveoli, in pleural tissues and in bronchioli.

396(left superior and inferior).

Bronchiolitis catar halis levis.

Slight edema. No remarkable changes else.

397(right superior).

Bronchiolitis catarrhalis and diffuse Alveolitis levis: slight cell-infiltration at alveolar walls.

Slight pulmonal congestion and slight edema.

399 (left superior).

Partial slight pulmonal congestion.

No remarkable changes else.

399 (left inferior). Slight congestion. Heart desease cells in bronchiolus.

No particular changes else.

[redacted] 113

[redacted]

[redacted]

400.

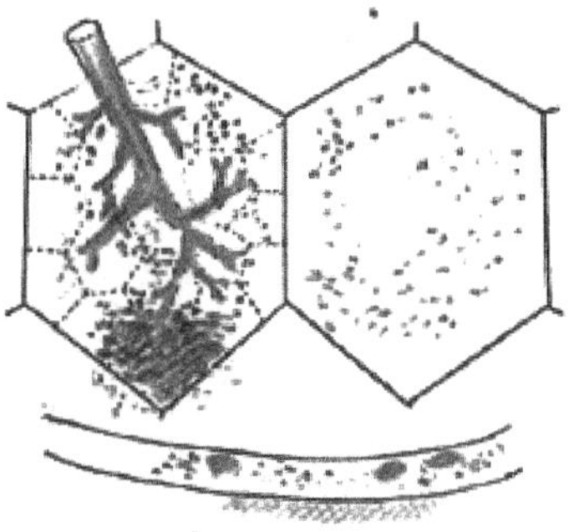

400.

Bronchiolitis catarrhalis gravis and diffuse Alveolitis : edematous swelling and leucocytes--emigration at alveolar walls and at some places in severe degree. These inflammatory changes develop at some places (peribronchial and subpleural tissues) to acino-lobular hemorrhagic pneumonia (severe Alveolitis, leakage of leucocytes and severe bleeding in some alveolar spaces, attached to catarrhalic bronchioli).

Subpleural severe congestion and sero-fibrinous Pleuritis at adjacent parts.

401.

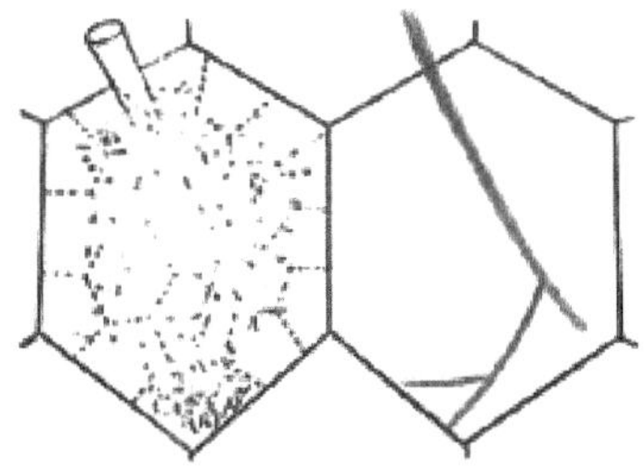

401.

Slight stasis and slight cell-infiltration at alveolar walls.

No remarkable changes else.

403.

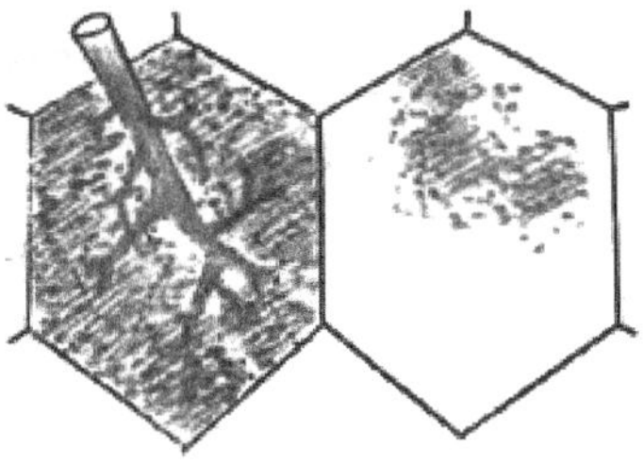

403.

Bronchiolitis catarrhalis and acino-lobular pneumonia with diffuse Alveolitis: remarkable leucocytes-emigration at alveolar walls and leakage of leucocytes in alveolar spaces to form multifocal acinolobular pneumonic places.

In peribronchiolar tissues, edematous swelling and slight cell infiltrations. (Peribronchiolitis levis).

[redacted] 714

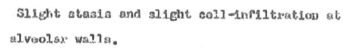

[redacted]

[redacted]

405. (r. sup.)

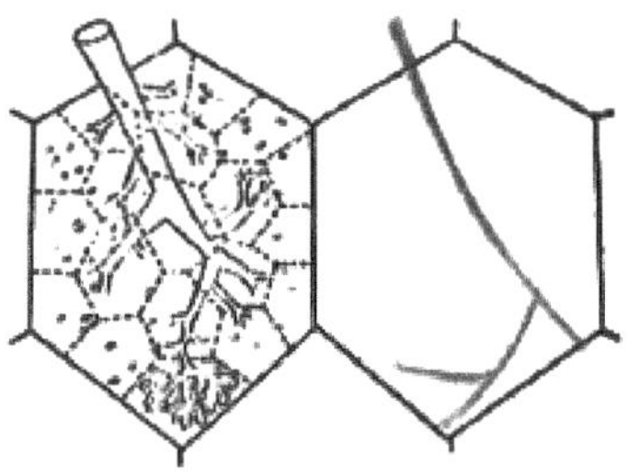

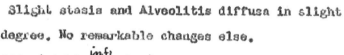

405. (right superior).

Slight stasis and Alveolitis diffusa in slight degree. No remarkable changes else.

405. (right ~~sup~~*inf*erior).

Multiple acino-lobular pneumonia with diffuse Alveolitis and following intense reactive changes :remarkable congestion and remarkable leucocytes--emigration at alveolar walls and inflammatory edema, leakage of leucocytes and hemorrhages in alveoli, which develop at some places to multifocal acino-lobular hemorrhagic leucocytic pneumonia.

405. (r. inf.)

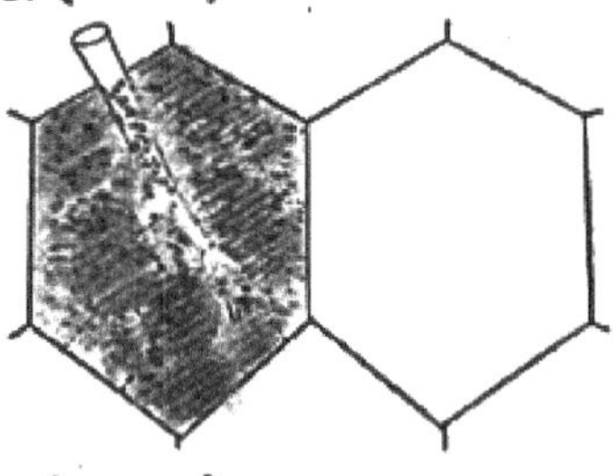

405. (l. sup.)

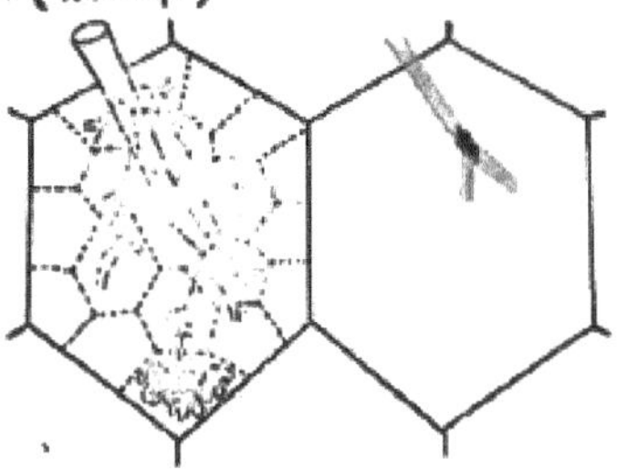

405. (left superior).

Bacterial colonies in blood-vessels. No particular changes else.

405.(left inferior).

Multifocal acinous hemorrhagic exudative pneumonia Diffuse Alveolitis : considerable congestion and leucocytes-emigration at alveolar walls. At some places leakage of leucocytes in alveolar spaces to form multifocal acino-lobular pneumonic places, accompanied with severe hemorrhages and leucocyter--infiltrations.

405. (l. inf.)

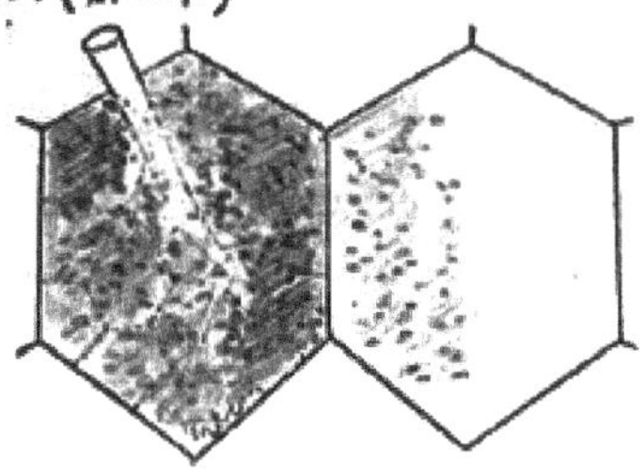

406.

Pulmonal congestion and slight edema. No remarkable changes else.

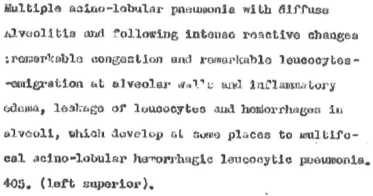

[redacted] /115

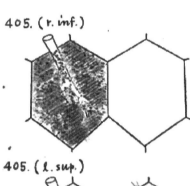

[redacted]

[redacted]

407.

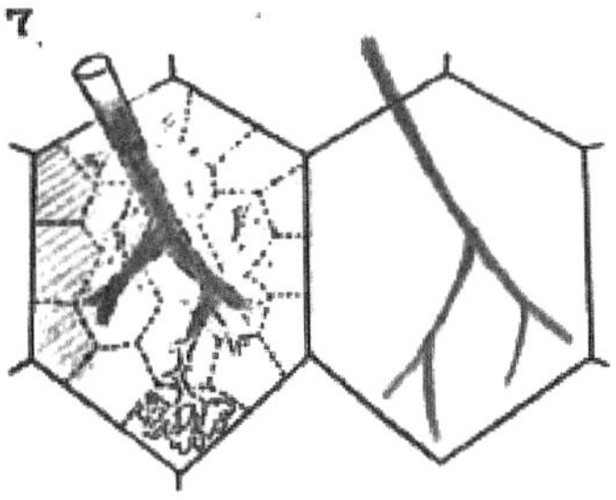

407.

Bronchiolitis catarrhalis levis. Considerable congestion and edematous swelling , of alveolar walls to form at some places atelectasis of alveolar spaces. No remarkable changes else.

409.

409.

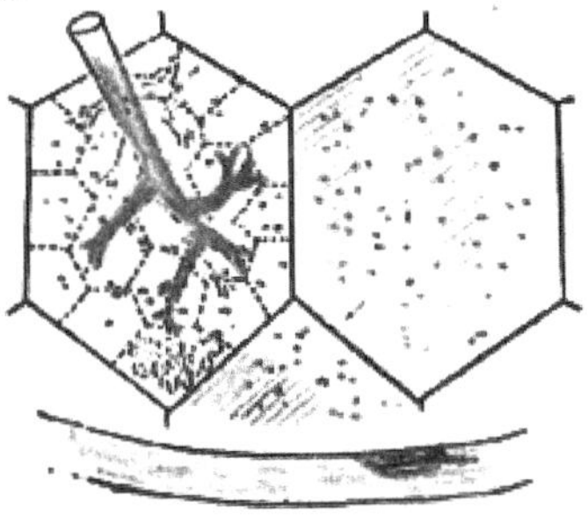

Bronchiolitis catarrhalis lavis and diffuse slight Alveolitis: considerable congestion, edematous swelling of alveolar walls and leucocytes-emigration at alveolar walls and at some places remarkable atelectasis of alveolar spaces, due to edematous swelling of alveolar walls.

Edematous swelling and bacterial dissemination in adjacent pleural tisses.

410.

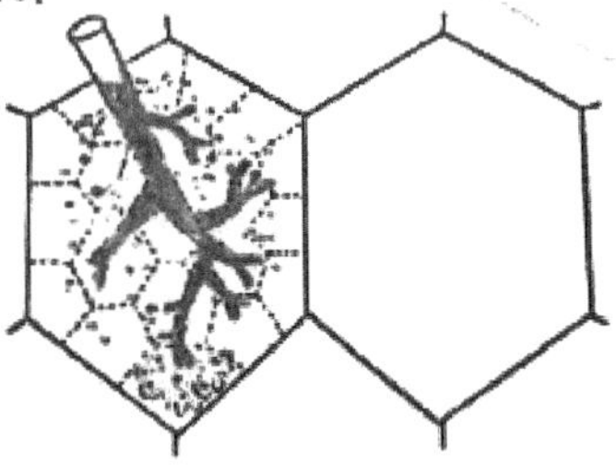

410.

Bronchiolitis catarrhalis and diffuse Alveolitis : slight edematous swelling, slight congestion and slight leucocytes- infiltraion at alveolar walls with desquamation of alveolar epitheliums and slight ödema in alveoli.

411.

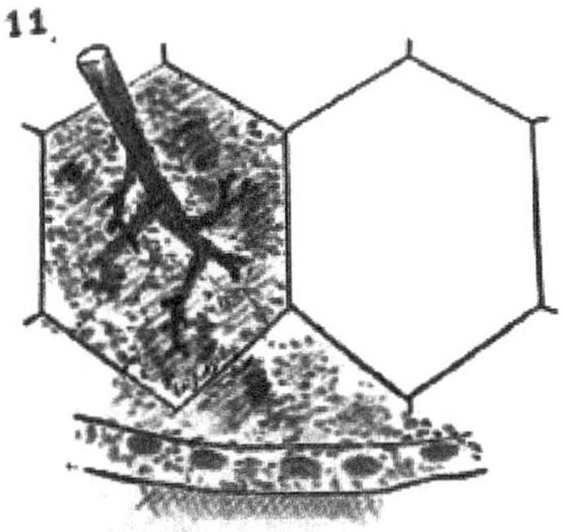

411.

Broncho-Bronchiolitis necroticans, acino-lobular catarrhalic-leucocytic pneumonie and Pleuritis haemorrhagico-fibrinosa.

[redacted] 116

[redacted]

[redacted]

A large quantity of decayed masses and bacterial colonies in bronchiolus.
N-Necrotic ruins of bronchiolar walls and edematous and inflammatory swelling of peribronchiolar tissues in high degree.
These bronchogenous inflammation spread to multifocal acinous or acino-lobular pneumonic changes in attachment-areas : leucocytic-hemorrhagic infiltration and at some places necrotic ruins of alveolar walls.
These inflammatory processes spread to the neighbouring tissues with more or less considerable exudative reactions:severe Alveolitis, namely considerable congestion and leucocytes-emigrations at alveolar walls and at some places with inflammatory édema, with hemorrhages and leucocytic infiltration in alveolar spaces.
Remarkable congestion, diffuse hemorrhages and separation of fibrinous masses in adjacent pleural tissues (Pleuritis haemorrhagico-fibrinosa) and multifocal acinous hemorrhagic-exudative pneumonia of subpleural lung-tissues : severe congestion, bleeding, leucocytes-emigration, decayed masses of alveolar epitheliums and bacterial deposits in

[redacted] /117

[redacted]

[redacted]

pneumonic places.

412 (a).

Broncho-Bronchiolitis gravis and Peribroncho-Bronchiolitis gravis with remarkable diffuse Alveolitis.

Catarrh of bronchus in severe degree : a large quantity of catarrhalic masses, hemorrhages, desquamation of alveolar or bronchial epitheliums and bacterial colonies as contents. Severe exudative changes of bronchial walls and severe oedematous swelling, severe congestion and diffuse hemorrhages in peribronchial tissues.

These inflammatory processes spread to the adjacent bronchioles, to peribronchiolar tissues, and moreover to lung-tissues in catchmentareas. Namely in lung-tissues of attachment-areas, multifocal acinous hemorrhagic-leucocytic pneumonia with diffuse more or less remarkable Alveolitis in the neighbouring general lung-tissues (considerable congestion, leucocytes-emigration of alveolar walls and at some places leakage of leucocytes and hemorrhages in alveolar spaces).

412.(b).

Bronchiolitis catarrhalis, slight diffuse

412 (a).

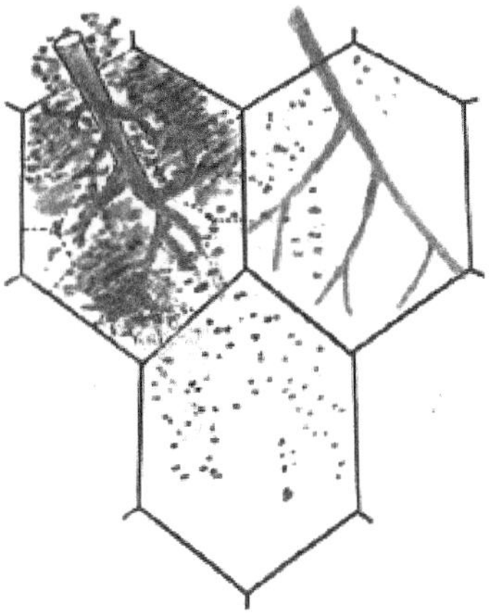

412 (b).

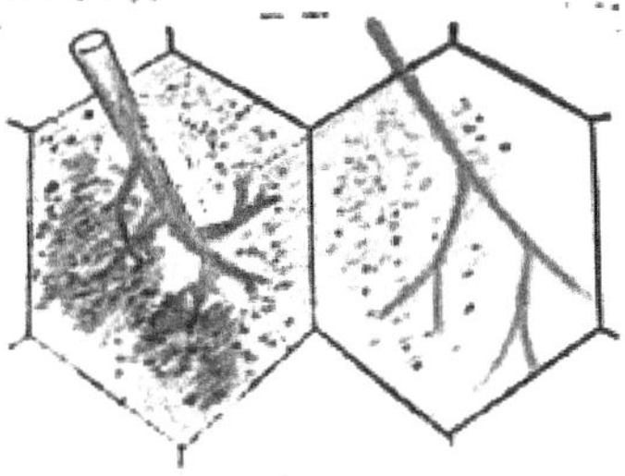

[redacted] 118

[redacted]

[redacted]

413. (r. inf.)

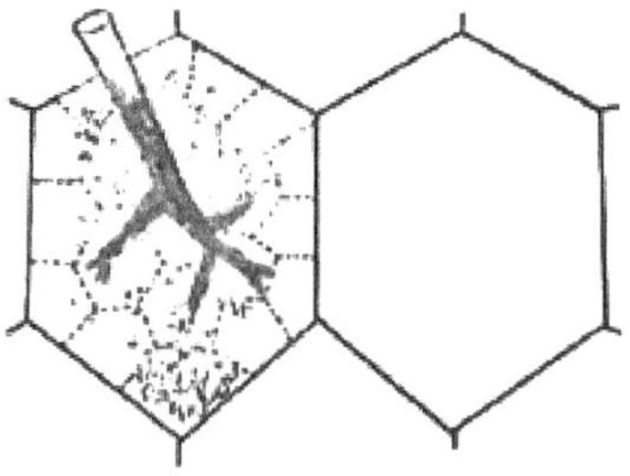

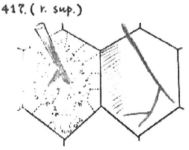

Alveolitis and multiple acino-lobular hemorrhagic pneumonia in peribronchiolar pulmonal tissues.
: considerable congestion, leucocytes -emigration at alveolar walls with edema or slight hemorrhages in alveoli. These hemorrhagic processes develop at some places, esp. at peribronchiolar tissues, to acinolobular hemorrhagic pneumonic changes.

413. (l. inf.)

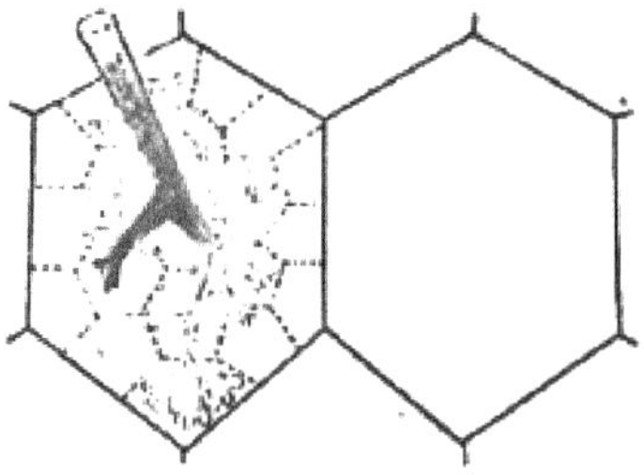

413. (right inferior)

Bronchiolitis catarrhalis levis and very slight cell-infiltration at alveolar walls. No remarkable changes else.

413 (left inferior).

Bronchiolitis catarrhalis levis.
No remarkable changes else.

416.

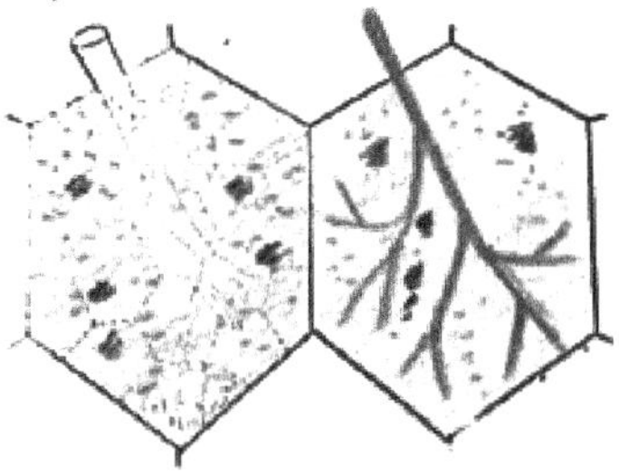

416.

Congestion et edema pulmonum in high degree.
Remarkable edematous swelling and severe congestion of alveolar walls with inflammatory edema and slight hemorrhages in alveoli.
Bacterial masses in some alveoli and bronchiolus.

417. (r. sup.)

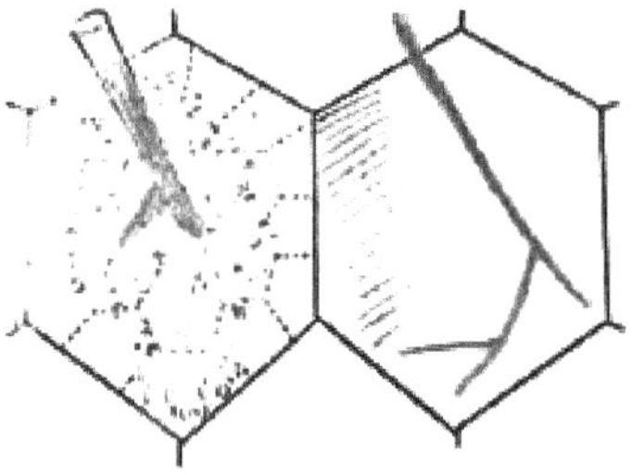

417 (right superior).

Bronchiolitis catarrhalis. Edematous swelling and slight leucocytes-emigration at alveolar walls, to form at some places atelectasis of alveolar spaces.

[redacted] 119

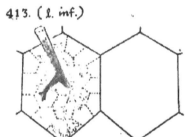

[redacted]

[redacted]

417. (r. inf.)

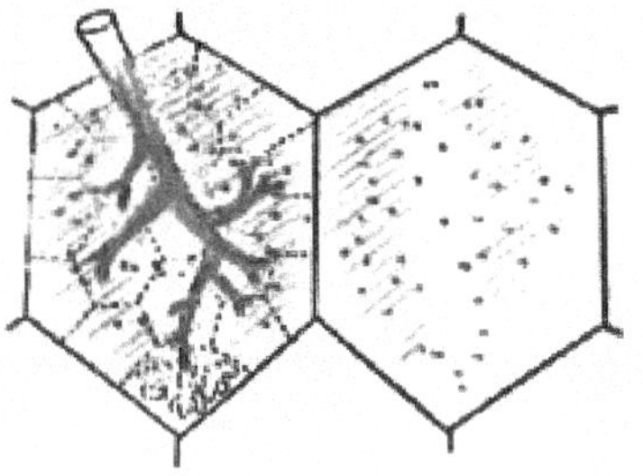

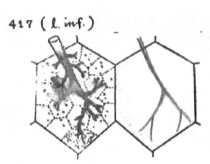

417. (right inferior).

Bronchiolitis catarrhalis. Edematous swelling and slight cell-infiltrations at alveolar walls, to form severe atelectasis of alveolar spaces.

417(left inferior).

Bronchiolitis catarrhalis gravis and diffuse Alveolitis : edematous swelling, considerable congestion and cell-infiltration at alveolar walls with severe atelectasis of alveolar spaces.

417 (l. inf.)

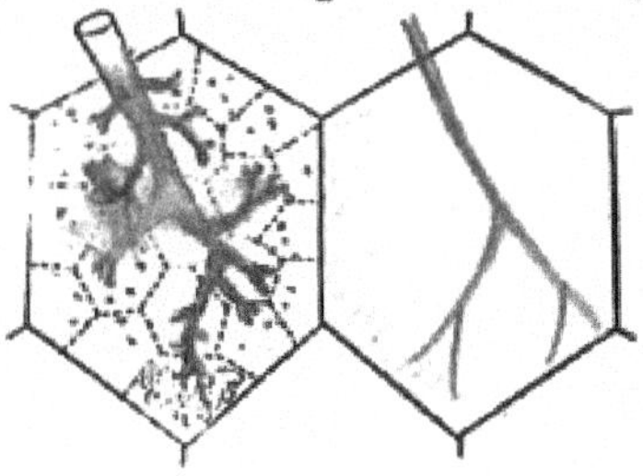

[redacted] 120

[redacted]

[redacted]

(B). SUMMARY.

(I)

The bird's eye-view of all investigated cases.

---

17. Almost normal.

18. Edema et stais pulmonum levis and Bronchitis catarrhalis levis.

26. Elema et stasis pulmonum in high degree, with some bacterial dissemination in alveoli.

225. Edema et stasis pulmonum.
Bronchitis catarrhalis.

318. Bronchitis catarrhalis.
Edema et stasis pulmonum levis, with some bacterial dissemination in alveoli.

325. Acino-lobular tuberculosis.
No significant changes, due to Anthrax-infection.

328. Acino-lobular tuberculosis in productive, somewhat exudative form.
No significant changes, due to Anthrax-infection.

388. (right, superior).
Bronchitis catarrhalis.
Slight emphysema and considerable atelectasis at some places, due to edematous swelling of alveolar walls.

388. (right,median).
Bronchitis and Peribronchitis acuta with intense hemorrhagic-necrotic changes of peribronchial lymph-nodulus.
Edema et stasis pulmonum levis.

389. (right'superior).
Bronchitis catarrhalis and slight Alveolitis diffusa.

[redacted] 121

[redacted]

[redacted]

389. (right,inferior).
Bronchitis and Peribronchitis acuta, with some leucocytes-dissemination.
Alveolitis diffusa in medium degree and Edema pulmonum inflammtorium in slight degree.
Some pleural congestion.

389. (left,superior).
Alveolitis diffusa in slight degree, with some lymphocytes-emigration in alveolar walls.

389. (left, inferior).
Bronchitis catarrhalis and Peribronchitis acuta with some congestion and some inflammtory changes of peribronchial lymph-nodulus.
Slight edema and some leucocytes-dissemination in some acinous places.
Slight hemorrhages in inter-lobular tissues.

390. (left, superior).
Diffuse Alveolitis with some localised hemorrhagic pneumonic places.
Edema pulmonum in medium degree in the neighbouring pulmonal tissues.
Bronchitis and Peribronchitis acuta with some inflammtory changes.

393. (right, superior).
Bronchitis and slight diffuse Alveolitis.

393.(right, incerior).
Bronchitis catarrhalis and Peribronchitis with some congestion and edema.
Diffuse Alveolitis with slight hemorrhagic changes and some bacterial dissemination in some acinous areas.

393. (left, superior).
Bronchitis and some pulmonal congestion.
Some pleural congestion and Pleuritis tuberculosa productiva.

393. (left, inferior).
Bronchitis and Peribronchitis acuta with slight round-cell-infiltration.
Some congestion and some hemorrhages in pleural tissues.

396. (right,inferior).
Bronchitis catarrhalis gravis.
Diffuse Alveolitis with some hemorrhagic pneumonic places in subpleural tissues.

[redacted] 122

[redacted]

[redacted]

396. (left, gsuperior).
Bronchitis catarrhalis and slight edema.
No remarkable changes else.

396. (left, inferior).
Bronchitis catarrhalis and slight edema.

397. (right, superior).
Bronchitis catarrhalis and slight diffuse Alveolitis.

399. (left, inferior).
Slight pulmonal congestion.

400. Bronchitis catarrhalis gravis and Peribronchitis acuta with some hemorrhages.
Diffuse Alveolitis and some acino-lobular, hemorrhagic pneumonia.
Pleuritis sero-fibrinosa with intense pleural congestion.

401. Slight Alveolitis and slight pulmonal congestion.

403. Bronchitis catarrhalis and Peribronchitis acuta.
Diffuse Alveolitis and multiple acino-lobular pneumonia.

405. (right, superior).
Diffuse Alveolitis and multiple acino-lobular, leucocytic-hemorrhagic pneumonia.

405. (left, superior).
Some bacterial masses in blood-vessels.
No remarkable changes else.

405. (left, inferior).
Diffuse Alveolitis and
multiple acinous hemorrhagic-exudative pneumonia.

406. Pulmonal congestion and slight edema.

407. Bronchitis catarrhalis levis.
Slight edematous swelling of alveolar walls.
Rather atelectatic alveolar spaces , due to edematous swelling and congestion of alveolar walls.
No remarkable changes else.

409. Bronchitis catarrhalis levis.
Slight diffuse Alveotlitis.
Remarkable atelectasis, due to edematous swelling of alveolar walls.
Edematous swelling and some bacterial dissemination in pleural tissues.

[redacted] 123

[redacted]

[redacted]

410. Bronchitis catarrhalis and diffuse Alveolitis.

411. Broncho-Bronchiolitis necroticans.
Acino-lobular,catarrhalic-leucocytic pneumonia.
Pleuritis haemorrhagico-fibrinosa, with
multiple acinous hemorrhagic-exudative pneumonia in subpleural tissues.

412. Broncho-Bronchiolitis in intense degree and Peribronchitis in intense degree.
Intense diffuse Alveolitis with some inflammtory edema.

412. Bronchitis catarrhalis and Peribronchitis with some congestion and some hemorrhages.
Slight diffuse Alveolitis and
multiple acino-lobular, hemorrhagic pneumonia in peribronchiolar pulmonal tissues.

413. Bronchitis catarrhalis levis and very slight Alveolitis.
No remarkable changes else.

413.(left, inferior).
Bronchitis catarrhalis levis and no remarkable changes else.

416. Edema pulmonum inflammatorium and Stasis pulmonum in high degree, with some hemorrhages and some bacterial dissemination in some alveolit and bronchioli.

417. (right, superior).
Bronchitis catarrhalis.
Remarkable atelectasis, due to intense edematous swelling and slight cell-infiltration at alveolar walls.

417. (left, inferior).
Bronchitis catarrhalis gravis.
Diffuse Alveolitis.
Remarkable atelectasis, due to edematous swelling, congestion and some cell-infiltration at alveolar walls.

[redacted]

124

[redacted]

[redacted]

(2).

I divide all cases in to 2 groups : a)peroral infection and
b)pernasal infection.

(a). On peroral infection.

Peroral infection caused sometimes no particular changes.

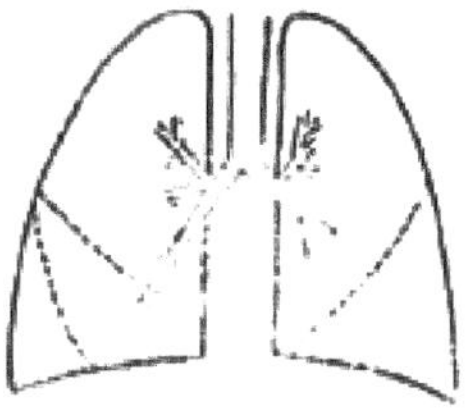

17.

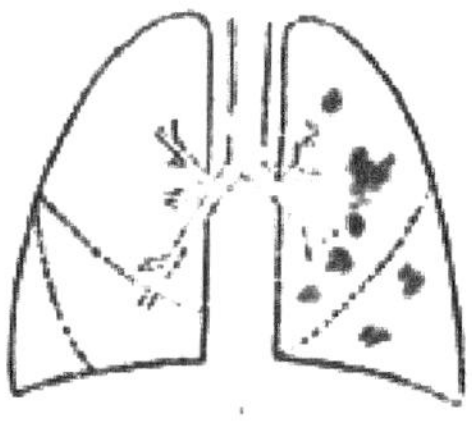

325.

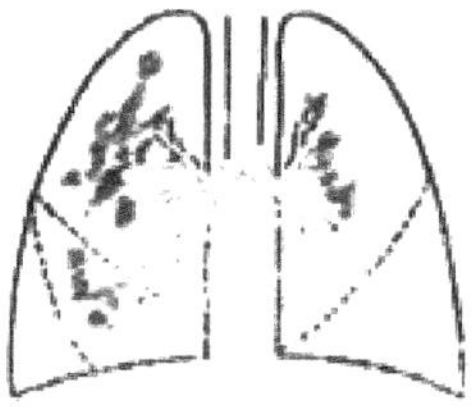

328.

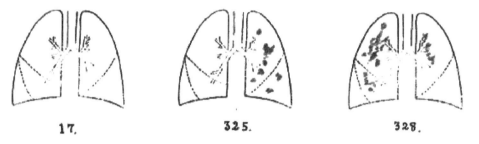

Sometimes slight pulmonal congestion (initial stage of diffuse Alveolitis).

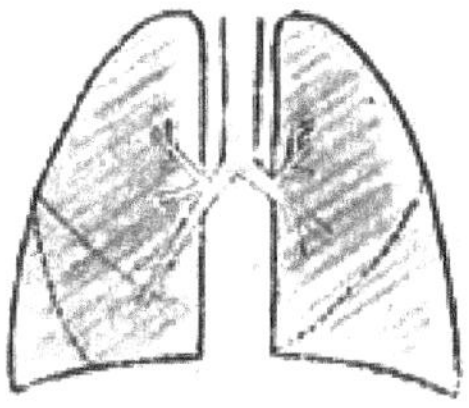

18.

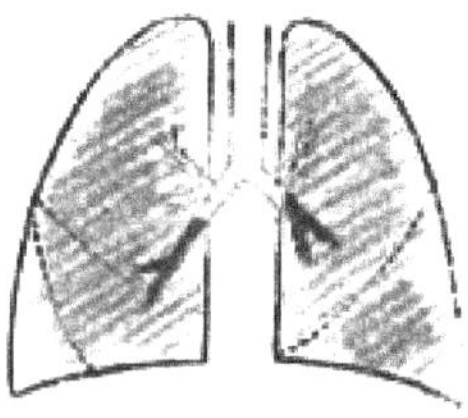

225.

Sometimes caused slight or intense diffuse Alveolitis,accompanied with some bacterial dissemination in pulmonal tissues (secondary metastatic pneumonic changes).

[redacted]

125

[redacted]

[redacted]

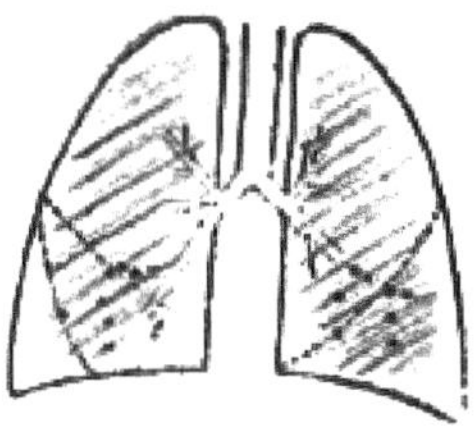
318.

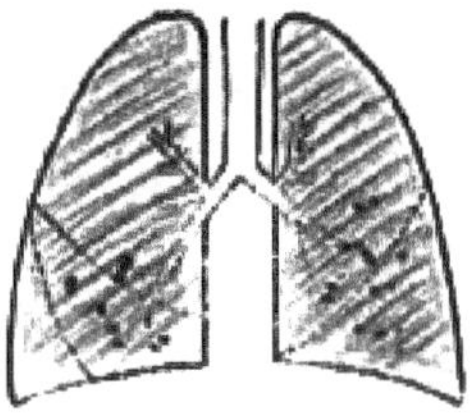
26.

(5). On pernasal infection.

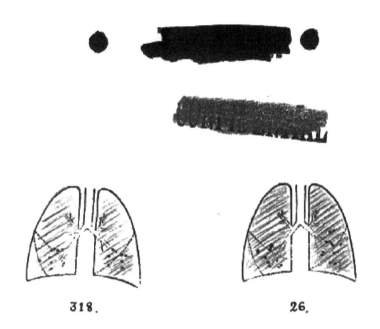

All patients, affected with pernasal infection, died difinitely after several (2 - 5) days course.

I have investigated 2 0 cases of them.

•) 10 cases of them died in slight or intense diffuse Alveolitis, which were caused mainly by Peribronchitis and Bronchitis, following sings of pernasal infection.

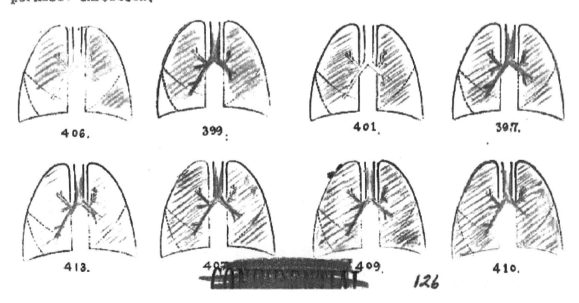

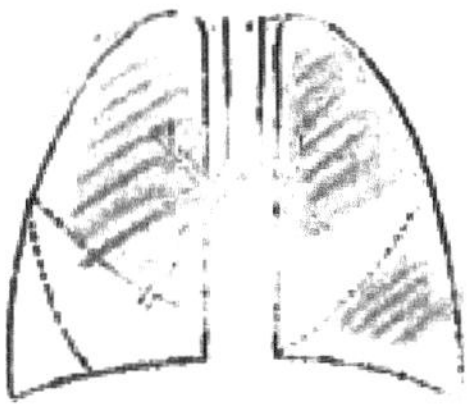
406.

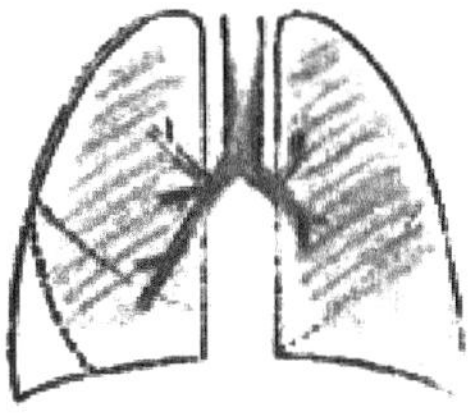
399.

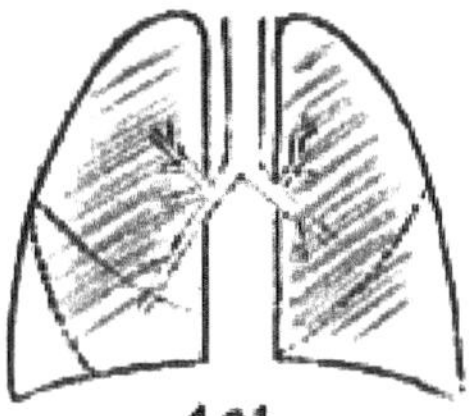
401.

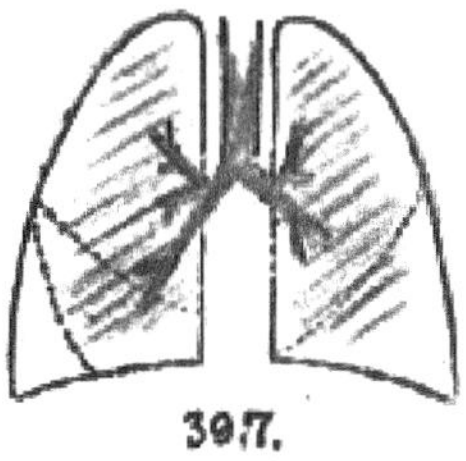
397.

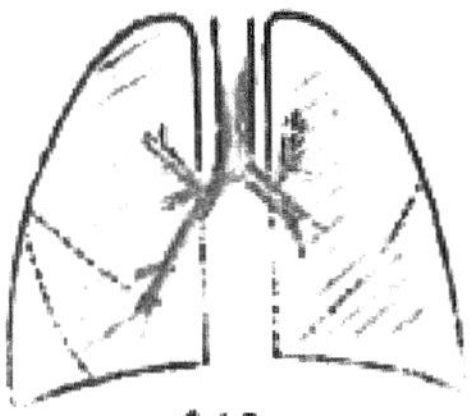
413.

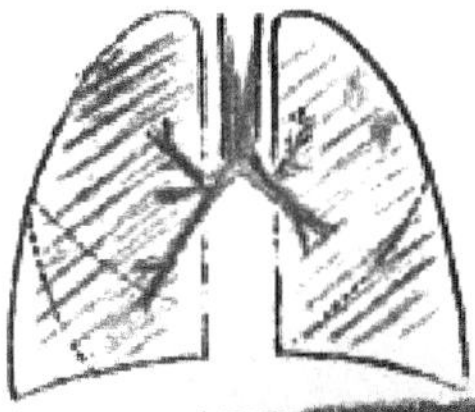
[redacted]

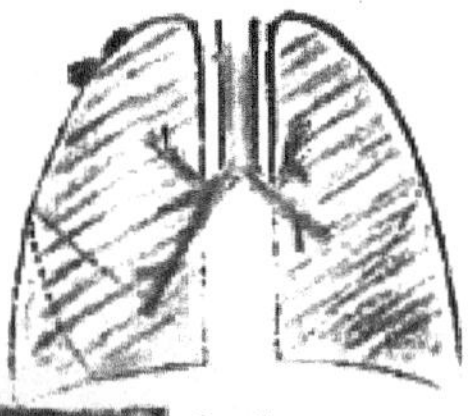
409.

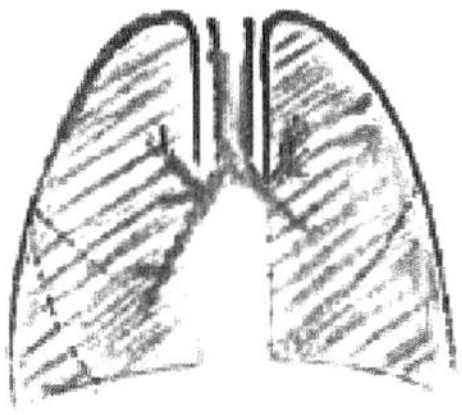
410.

126

• [redacted] •

[redacted]

I case of them, in intense inflammatory edema, accompanied with some hemorrhagic and bacterial dissemination in some alveoli.

And I case of them, in intense inflammatory congestion.

Intense congestion or intense edema of alveolar walls caused frequently remarkable atelectatic changes. Atelectasis, due to pulmonal congestion or edema, is one of the main pathelogical changes of this disease.

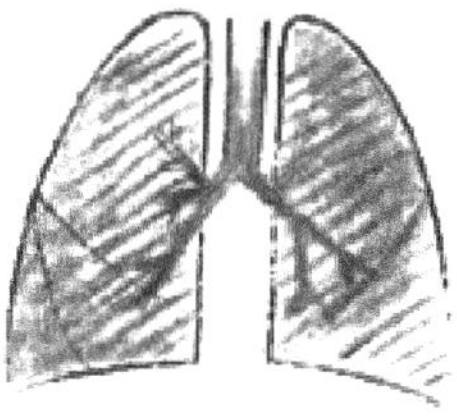

417.

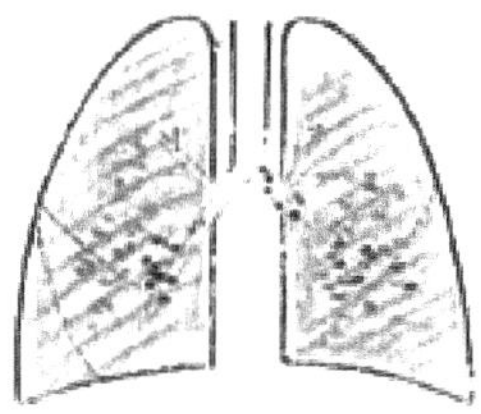

416.

(..) In 10 cases of them, developed these Alveolitis into the more intense pulmonal changes : (intense diffuse Alveolitis, Bronchitis and Peribronchitis), accompanied with some hemorrhagic and leucocytic changes in multifocal acinous or acino-lobular areas.

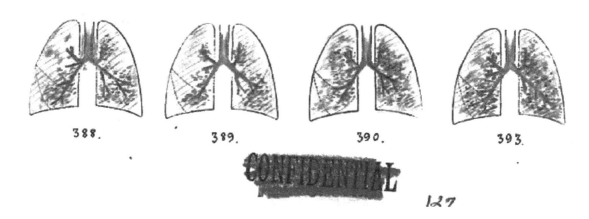

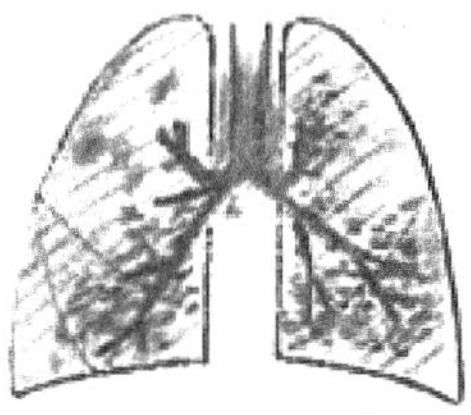

388.

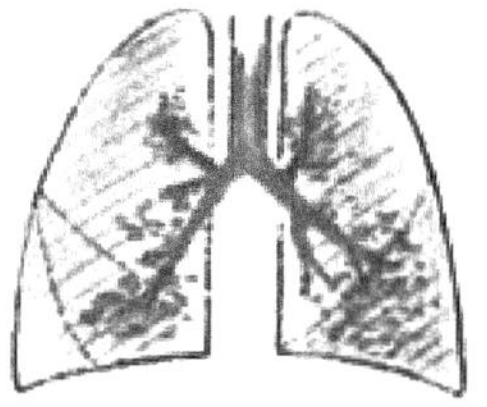

389.

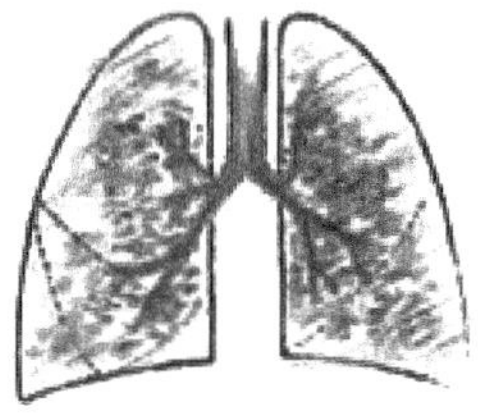

390.

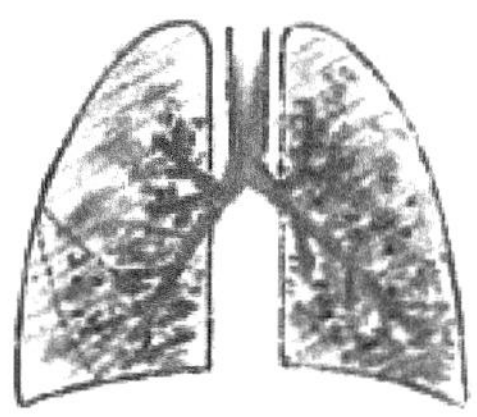

393.

CONFIDENTIAL

127

• [redacted] •

[redacted]

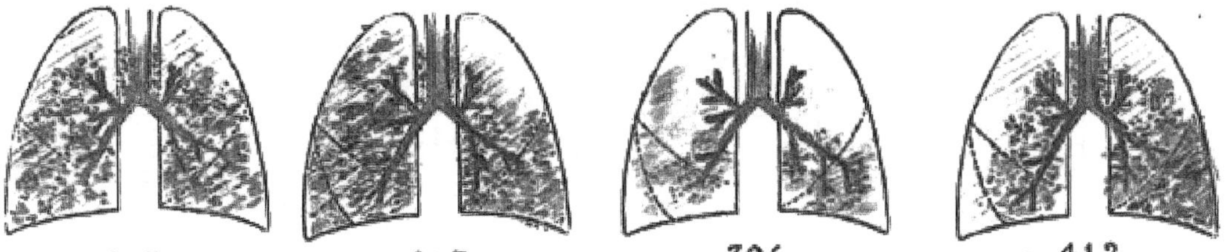

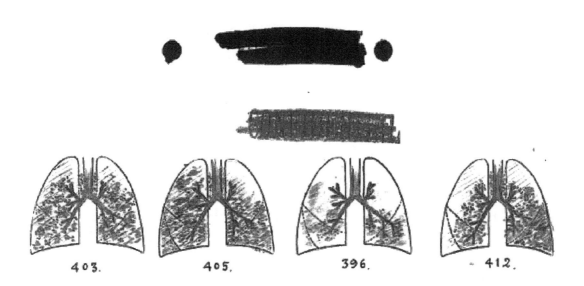

403.   405.   396.   412.

2 cases with intense hemorrhagic-leucocytic pneumonia all over the pulmonal tissues, caused furthermore some intense pleural reaction with Pleuritis sero-haemorrhagico-fibrinosa.

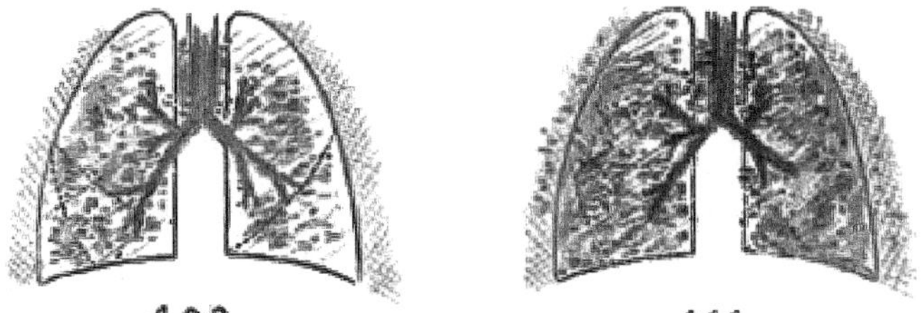

400.   411.

[redacted]   128

[redacted]

LUNG

[redacted]

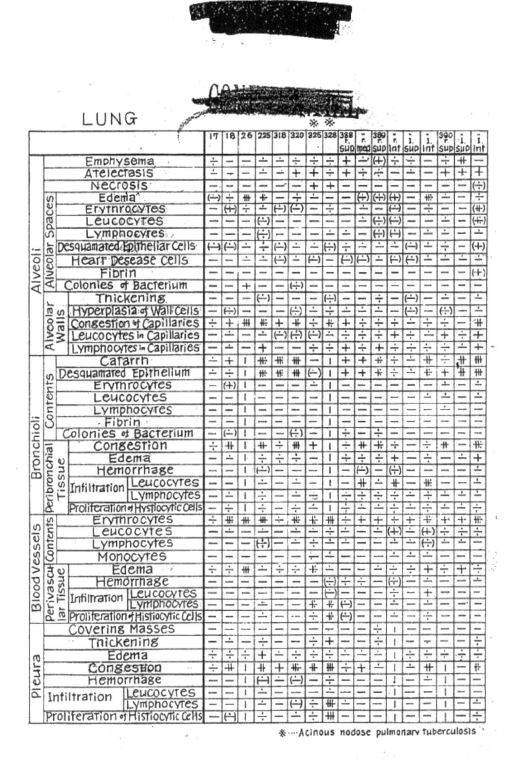

			17	18	26	225	318	320	225 ※	328 ※	388 r. sup	〃 r. med	389 r. sup	〃 r. int	〃 l. sup	〃 l. int	390 r. sup	〃 l. sup	〃 l. int
Alveoli		Emphysema	÷	−	−	÷	÷	÷	÷	÷	+	÷	(+)	÷	÷	−	÷	#	−
Alveoli		Atelectasis	÷	−	−	÷	÷	+	+	÷	+	÷	÷	−	÷	−	+	+	+
Alveoli		Necrosis	−	−	−	−	−	−	+	+	−	−	−	−	−	−	−	−	(÷)
Alveoli	Alveolar Spaces	Edema	(÷)	÷	卌	+	−	÷	÷	−	−	(÷)	(÷)	(+)	−	#	÷	−	÷
Alveoli	Alveolar Spaces	Erythrocytes	−	(+)	÷	÷	(÷)	(÷)	−	÷	−	÷	−	(÷)	−	÷	−	−	(#)
Alveoli	Alveolar Spaces	Leucocytes	−	−	−	(÷)	−	−	−	−	−	÷	(÷)	(÷)	−	−	÷	−	(#)
Alveoli	Alveolar Spaces	Lymphocytes	−	−	−	(÷)	−	−	−	÷	÷	−	(÷)	(÷)	−	÷	÷	−	÷
Alveoli	Alveolar Spaces	Desquamated Epitheliar Cells	(÷)	(÷)	÷	÷	(÷)	÷	÷	(÷)	÷	÷	÷	÷	(÷)	÷	÷	−	(+)
Alveoli	Alveolar Spaces	Heart Desease Cells	−	−	÷	÷	(÷)	÷	(÷)	−	(÷)	(÷)	÷	(÷)	(÷)	÷	÷	÷	÷
Alveoli	Alveolar Spaces	Fibrin	−	−	−	−	−	−	−	−	−	−	−	−	−	−	−	−	(+)
Alveoli	Alveolar Spaces	Colonies of Bacterium	−	−	+	−	−	(÷)	−	−	−	−	−	÷	−	−	−	−	−
Alveoli	Alveolar Walls	Thickening	−	−	−	(÷)	−	−	−	(÷)	−	−	÷	−	(÷)	−	÷	−	÷
Alveoli	Alveolar Walls	Hyperplasia of Wall Cells	−	(÷)	−	−	−	(÷)	÷	÷	÷	÷	÷	−	(÷)	−	(÷)	−	÷
Alveoli	Alveolar Walls	Congestion of Capillaries	÷	+	卌	#	+	#	÷	#	+	÷	÷	÷	÷	÷	÷	−	#
Alveoli	Alveolar Walls	Leucocytes in Capillaries	−	÷	−	÷	(÷)	(÷)	(÷)	÷	÷	÷	÷	+	÷	÷	+	÷	+
Alveoli	Alveolar Walls	Lymphocytes in Capillaries	−	÷	−	+	−	−	÷	÷	+	÷	+	÷	÷	÷	÷	÷	+
Bronchioli	Contents	Catarrh	÷	+	|	#	#	卌	−	|	+	+	#	÷	÷	#	÷	#	卌
Bronchioli	Contents	Desquamated Epithelium	÷	÷	|	#	#	卌	(÷)	|	+	+	#	÷	÷	#	+	#	卌
Bronchioli	Contents	Erythrocytes	−	(+)	|	−	−	−	÷	|	−	−	−	−	−	−	÷	−	÷
Bronchioli	Contents	Leucocytes	−	−	|	−	−	−	−	|	−	−	−	−	−	÷	÷	−	÷
Bronchioli	Contents	Lymphocytes	−	−	|	−	−	−	−	|	−	−	−	−	−	−	÷	−	−
Bronchioli	Contents	Fibrin	−	−	|	−	−	−	−	|	−	−	−	−	−	−	−	−	−
Bronchioli	Contents	Colonies of Bacterium	−	(÷)	|	−	−	(÷)	−	|	÷	−	÷	−	−	−	−	−	−
Bronchioli	Peribronchial Tissue	Congestion	÷	#	|	#	÷	卌	+	|	÷	#	#	÷	−	÷	#	−	#
Bronchioli	Peribronchial Tissue	Edema	−	÷	|	÷	÷	÷	−	|	÷	÷	÷	+	−	÷	−	÷	+
Bronchioli	Peribronchial Tissue	Hemorrhage	−	−	|	(÷)	−	−	−	|	−	(÷)	−	(÷)	−	−	−	−	÷
Bronchioli	Peribronchial Tissue	Infiltration: Leucocytes	−	−	|	÷	−	÷	−	|	−	#	÷	#	−	#	−	−	÷
Bronchioli	Peribronchial Tissue	Infiltration: Lymphocytes	−	÷	|	÷	−	÷	÷	|	÷	÷	÷	÷	÷	÷	÷	÷	÷
Bronchioli	Peribronchial Tissue	Proliferation of Hystiocytic Cells	−	÷	|	÷	−	÷	÷	|	÷	÷	÷	÷	÷	÷	÷	÷	÷
Blood Vessels	Contents	Erythrocytes	÷	#	卌	卌	÷	#	#	卌	÷	+	+	÷	+	#	+	+	#
Blood Vessels	Contents	Leucocytes	−	÷	−	÷	−	÷	÷	÷	÷	−	÷	(+)	÷	(+)	÷	÷	÷
Blood Vessels	Contents	Lymphocytes	−	−	−	(÷)	−	÷	÷	÷	÷	−	−	÷	÷	(÷)	÷	÷	−
Blood Vessels	Contents	Monocytes	−	−	−	−	−	−	÷	÷	−	−	−	÷	÷	÷	−	−	−
Blood Vessels	Perivascular Tissue	Edema	÷	÷	卌	÷	÷	÷	#	÷	−	−	÷	÷	÷	+	÷	+	÷
Blood Vessels	Perivascular Tissue	Hemorrhage	−	−	−	−	−	−	−	(÷)	÷	÷	−	(÷)	−	÷	−	−	÷
Blood Vessels	Perivascular Tissue	Infiltration: Leucocytes	−	−	−	−	−	−	−	(÷)	−	−	−	÷	−	+	−	−	−
Blood Vessels	Perivascular Tissue	Infiltration: Lymphocytes	−	−	−	÷	−	−	#	#	(÷)	−	−	÷	−	÷	−	−	−
Blood Vessels	Perivascular Tissue	Proliferation of Histiocytic Cells	−	−	−	÷	−	−	÷	#	(÷)	−	−	÷	−	÷	−	−	−
Pleura		Covering Masses	−	−	−	−	−	−	−	÷	−	−	÷	|	−	−	−	−	−
Pleura		Thickening	−	÷	−	÷	−	−	÷	+	−	−	÷	|	−	÷	−	−	÷
Pleura		Edema	÷	÷	÷	+	÷	÷	÷	÷	÷	÷	÷	|	÷	÷	÷	÷	÷
Pleura		Congestion	÷	#	|	#	+	#	#	卌	÷	+	÷	|	÷	#	|	−	#
Pleura		Hemorrhage	−	−	|	(÷)	÷	(÷)	−	÷	−	−	−	|	−	÷	|	−	−
Pleura	Infiltration	Leucocytes	−	−	|	÷	−	−	−	÷	−	−	−	|	−	−	|	−	−
Pleura	Infiltration	Lymphocytes	−	−	|	÷	−	(÷)	÷	卌	÷	−	−	|	−	−	|	−	÷
Pleura		Proliferation of Histiocytic Cells	−	(÷)	|	÷	−	÷	÷	卌	−	−	−	|	−	−	|	−	÷

※…Acinous nodose pulmonary tuberculosis

[redacted] 129

[redacted]

[redacted]

LUNG

			393 r sup	″ r int	″ l sup	″ l int	398 r int	″ l sup	″ l int	397 r sup	″ r int	399 l sup	″ l int	400	401	403	404
Alveoli		Emphysema	+	−	−	−	−	−	−	∸	−	∸	(∸)	−	÷	−	−
Alveoli		Atelectasis	÷÷	÷	÷	÷	++	+	÷	∸	−	÷	+	(+++)	÷	(++)	÷÷
Alveoli		Necrosis	−	−	−	−	−	−	−	−	−	−	−	−	−	−	−
Alveoli	Alveolar Spaces	Edema	∸	++	(∸)	÷	÷	−	(∸)	∸	−	(∸)	−	÷(÷÷)	−	÷÷	∸
Alveoli	Alveolar Spaces	Erythrocytes	−	(+)	∸	−	+	−	−	(÷)	−	(∸)	−	(+++)	−	+	(∸)
Alveoli	Alveolar Spaces	Leucocytes	÷	(+)	∸	÷	(÷)	∸	(∸)	(∸)	−	−	(∸)	−	−	++	∸
Alveoli	Alveolar Spaces	Lymphocytes	−	∸	∸	−	−	−	−	−	−	−	−	−	−	∸	−
Alveoli	Alveolar Spaces	Desquamated Epitherial Cells	∸	+	∸	∸	÷÷	∸	(∸)	∸	(∸)	(∸)	(∸)	(+)	−	+	÷
Alveoli	Alveolar Spaces	Heart Desease Cells	−	÷	∸	∸	∸	∸	−	∸	−	(∸)	(∸)	÷	(∸)	÷	(÷)
Alveoli	Alveolar Spaces	Fibrin	−	−	−	−	−	−	−	−	−	−	−	−	−	−	−
Alveoli	Alveolar Spaces	Colonies of Bacterium	−	÷	−	−	(+)	−	−	−	−	−	−	−	−	÷	−
Alveoli	Alveolar Walls	Thickening	(−)	−	−	(∸)	−	−	−	(∸)	−	−	−	−	−	÷	÷
Alveoli	Alveolar Walls	Hyperplasia of Wall Cells	(÷)	−	−	(∸)	−	−	−	(∸)	−	(∸)	−	−	−	÷	÷
Alveoli	Alveolar Walls	Congestion of Capillaries	+	++	+++	++	+	÷	∸	+	÷	÷÷	(+)	+	÷	++	++
Alveoli	Alveolar Walls	Leucocytes in Capillaries	(+)	÷	÷	+	÷	+	∸	÷	(∸)	∸	÷	+	(+)	÷÷	÷
Alveoli	Alveolar Walls	Lymphocytes in Capillaries	∸	−	∸	+	∸	÷	∸	÷	(∸)	−	−	∸	÷	÷	∸
Bronchioli	Contents	Catarrh	÷	++	÷	÷	−	−	−	−	−	−	−	−	−	−	−
Bronchioli	Contents	Desquamated Epithelium	+	++	÷	÷	+	÷	÷	÷÷	(∸)	∸	÷	+++	∸	+++	(∸)
Bronchioli	Contents	Erythrocytes	−	−	−	−	−	−	−	−	−	−	−	−	−	∸	−
Bronchioli	Contents	Leucocytes	−	∸	−	∸	−	−	−	−	−	−	−	÷	−	∸	−
Bronchioli	Contents	Lymphocytes	−	∸	−	−	−	−	−	−	−	−	−	÷	−	∸	−
Bronchioli	Contents	Fibrin	−	−	−	−	−	−	−	−	−	−	−	−	−	−	−
Bronchioli	Contents	Colonies of Bacterium	−	−	−	−	(+)	−	−	−	−	−	−	−	−	−	−
Bronchioli	Peribronchial Tissue	Congestion	∸	+	÷	+	+	−	−	÷	−	−	−	÷	−	+	÷
Bronchioli	Peribronchial Tissue	Edema	∸	÷	∸	∸	+	∸	÷	÷	÷	(∸)	−	(∸)	∸	∸	−
Bronchioli	Peribronchial Tissue	Hemorrhage	−	−	−	−	−	−	−	−	−	−	−	−	−	(∸)	−
Bronchioli	Peribronchial Tissue	Infiltration Leucocytes	−	∸	−	−	−	−	−	−	−	(∸)	−	(÷)	−	÷	−
Bronchioli	Peribronchial Tissue	Infiltration Lymphocytes	∸	∸	−	∸	−	−	−	−	−	∸	−	∸	−	∸	∸
Bronchioli	Peribronchial Tissue	Proliferation of Histiocytic Cells	−	−	−	∸	−	−	−	∸	−	∸	−	∸	−	÷	÷
Blood Vessels	Contents	Erythrocytes	÷	÷÷	++	++	++	÷	÷÷	÷÷	+++	÷÷	+	++	++	+++	(++)
Blood Vessels	Contents	Leucocytes	(+)	÷	÷	÷	÷	+	÷	÷	÷	∸	÷	÷	÷	∸	−
Blood Vessels	Contents	Lymphocytes	÷	∸	∸	∸	∸	∸	−	∸	∸	−	−	∸	÷	−	−
Blood Vessels	Contents	Monocytes	∸	−	−	∸	−	−	−	−	∸	−	∸	−	∸	−	−
Blood Vessels	Perivascular Tissue	Edema	÷	(+++)	÷	∸	÷	÷	÷	+	∸	∸	÷	∸	(+)	∸	−
Blood Vessels	Perivascular Tissue	Hemorrhage	−	−	(∸)	−	−	−	−	−	−	−	−	−	−	−	−
Blood Vessels	Perivascular Tissue	Infiltration Leucocytes	−	−	−	(+)	−	−	−	−	−	−	−	−	−	−	−
Blood Vessels	Perivascular Tissue	Infiltration Lymphocytes	−	−	−	(++)	−	−	−	−	−	−	−	−	−	−	−
Blood Vessels	Perivascular Tissue	Proliferation of Histiocytic Cells	∸	∸	∸	∸	−	−	−	−	−	−	−	−	−	−	−
Pleura		Covering Masses	−	−	−	−	−	−	−	−	−	|	−	÷	−	−	−
Pleura		Thickening	−	−	÷	÷	−	−	−	−	−	|	−	+	−	∸	÷
Pleura		Edema	+	+	++	+	+	÷	+	+	÷	|	+	+	+	÷	∸
Pleura		Congestion	÷÷	÷	÷÷	+++	−	(∸)	−	++	÷	|	∸	++	−	÷	÷÷
Pleura		Hemorrhage	−	∸	(+)	−	−	−	−	−	−	|	−	÷	−	∸	−
Pleura		Infiltration Leucocytes	∸	−	∸	−	−	−	−	−	−	|	−	−	−	−	−
Pleura		Infiltration Lymphocytes	∸	∸	(+)	∸	−	−	−	∸	−	|	−	−	−	−	−
Pleura		Proliferation of Histiocytic Cells	∸	∸	÷	÷	−	−	−	−	−	|	−	−	(∸)	÷	∸

[redacted] 130

[redacted]

[redacted]

LUNG

			405 r. sup	r. int	l. sup	l. int	406	407	409	410	411	412	:·	413 r. int	l. int	416	417 r. sup	r. int	l. sup
Alveoli		Emphysema	÷	—	—	—	—	—	—	—	—	—	—	—	—	—	—	÷	—
		Atelectasis	÷	+	+	÷	÷	++	++	—	÷	÷	(+)	—	+	÷	+	+++	÷
		Necrosis	—	—	—	—	—	—	—	—	+	—	—	—	—	—	—	—	—
	Alveolar Spaces	Edema	—	++	—	÷	÷	(÷)	—	(÷)	+	+	÷(++)	÷	—	+++	÷	÷	÷
		Erythrocytes	—	+++	—	(+)	÷	—	—	—	++	—	(++)	—	—	+	—	—	÷
		Leucocytes	—	÷	—	(÷)	÷	—	—	—	++	(÷)	(÷)	—	—	÷	—	—	÷
		Lymphocytes	—	+	—	(+)	—	—	—	—	—	—	(÷)	—	—	(÷)	—	—	÷
		Desquamated Epitherial Cells	—	++	÷	(++)	÷	÷	(÷)	++	++	÷	(÷)	—	÷	÷	÷	÷	÷
		Heart Desease Cells	—	÷	(÷)	—	(÷)	(+)	+	+	—	(÷)	—	—	—	(÷)	÷	÷	÷
		Fibrin	—	(÷)	—	—	—	—	—	—	(÷)	—	—	—	—	—	—	—	—
		Colonies of Bacterium	—	÷	—	—	—	—	(÷)	—	+	—	—	—	—	++	—	—	—
	Alveolar Walls	Thickening	—	—	—	—	—	—	(÷)	(÷)	—	÷	—	—	—	—	÷	÷	(÷)
		Hyperplasia of Wall Cells	÷	÷	(÷)	(÷)	—	—	(÷)	÷	—	÷	—	—	—	—	—	÷	÷
		Congestion of Capillaries	+	++	+	++	++	+	÷	÷	+	++	+	÷	÷	+++	÷	—	++
		Leucocytes in Capillaries	÷	÷	÷	÷	÷	÷	÷	÷	÷	—	÷	(÷)	÷	÷	÷	÷	+
		Lymphocytes in Capillaries	—	÷	÷	÷	÷	÷	÷	÷	—	—	—	(÷)	÷	÷	÷	÷	÷
Bronchioli	Contents	Catarrh	(÷)	(÷)	—	÷	÷	+	+	++	+++	÷	(+++)	+	++	÷	++	++	++
		Desquamated Epithelium	(÷)	(÷)	—	÷	÷	+	+	++	|	÷	(++)	÷	++	÷	+++	++	+++
		Erythrocytes	—	(÷)	(÷)	(÷)	—	÷	—	—	|	—	(+)	—	—	—	—	÷	—
		Leucocytes	—	(÷)	—	(÷)	—	—	—	—	+++	—	(÷)	—	—	—	—	—	÷
		Lymphocyte	—	—	—	(÷)	—	—	—	—	|	—	—	—	—	—	—	—	÷
		Fibrin	—	—	—	—	—	—	—	—	|	—	—	—	—	—	—	—	—
		Colonies of Bacterium	—	—	—	—	—	—	÷	—	+++	—	—	—	—	(+)	—	—	—
	Peribronchial Tissue	Congestion	—	++	—	÷	+	÷	÷	+	|	÷	+	—	÷	÷	++	÷	÷
		Edema	(÷)	+	—	÷	÷	÷	÷	—	|	÷	÷	÷	÷	+	+	÷	÷
		Hemorrhage	—	+	—	—	—	—	—	—	|	—	—	—	—	—	—	—	—
		Infiltration Leucocytes	(÷)	÷	—	—	—	—	—	—	|	—	—	—	—	—	÷	—	—
		Infiltration Lymphocytes	(÷)	÷	—	—	—	÷	—	÷	|	—	—	—	÷	÷	÷	÷	÷
		Proliferation of Histiocytic Cells	÷	÷	—	—	÷	—	÷	÷	|	÷	—	—	—	—	÷	÷	÷
Blood Vessels	Contents	Erythrocytes	++	++	+	++	++	+	÷	÷	+++	+++	++	+	÷	++	÷	+	++
		Leucocytes	—	÷	(÷)	÷	—	—	÷	÷	÷	÷	÷	÷	(+)	—	—	÷	÷
		Lymphocytes	—	—	—	—	—	—	—	—	—	÷	—	—	—	—	—	—	—
		Monocytes	—	—	—	—	—	—	—	—	—	—	—	—	—	—	—	—	—
	Perivascular Tissue	Edema	÷	+	÷	÷	÷	÷	+	÷	++	+	÷	÷	+	÷	++	+	÷
		Hemorrhage	—	÷	—	—	—	—	—	—	—	—	—	—	—	—	—	÷	—
		Infiltration Leucocytes	—	—	—	—	—	—	—	—	÷	—	—	—	—	—	—	—	—
		Infiltration Lymphocytes	—	—	—	—	—	—	—	—	—	—	—	—	—	—	—	—	—
		Proliferation of Histiocytic Cells	—	—	—	—	÷	—	—	÷	÷	÷	—	—	—	—	—	—	—
Pleura		Covering Masses	—	|	—	—	|	|	—	—	÷	|	—	—	|	—	|	|	|
		Thickening	÷	|	—	—	|	|	÷	÷	—	|	÷	—	|	—	|	|	|
		Edema	÷	|	(+)	÷	|	|	+	÷	+	|	÷	+	|	÷	|	|	|
		Congestion	÷	|	÷	÷	|	|	÷	÷	+++	|	+	÷	|	÷	|	|	|
		Hemorrhage	—	|	—	—	|	|	—	—	+++	|	—	—	|	(÷)	|	|	|
		Infiltration Leucocytes	—	|	—	—	|	|	—	—	+	|	÷	—	|	—	|	|	|
		Infiltration Lymphocytes	—	|	—	—	|	|	÷	÷	÷	|	÷	—	|	—	|	|	|
		Proliferation of Histiocytic Cells	—	|	—	—	|	|	÷	÷	—	|	÷	—	|	—	|	|	|

[redacted] 131

[redacted]

Endobronchitis necroticans and
Peribronchitis with intense swelling. [redacted]

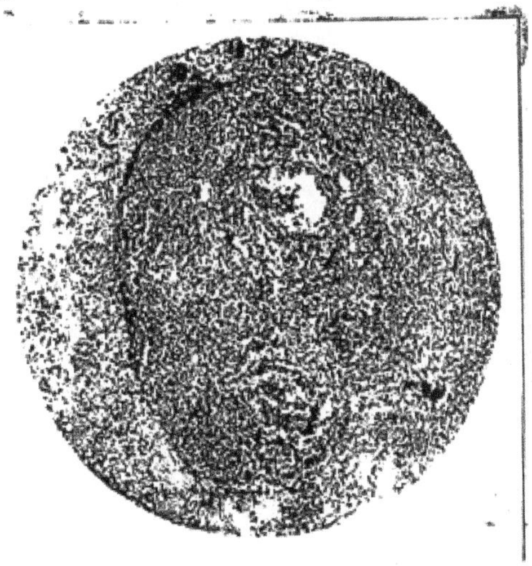

No. 389. x60
(left inferior.)

Intense inflammtory changes of peribronchial lymph-nodulus.

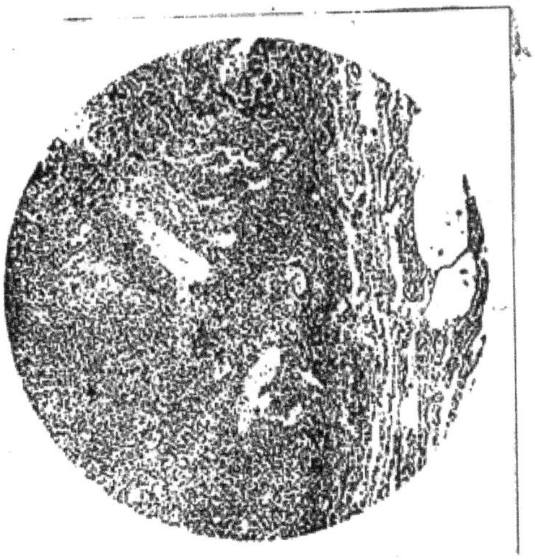

No 388 x60.
(right median.)

[redacted] 132

[redacted]

Acino-lobular,hemorrhagic-exudative pneumonia. [redacted]

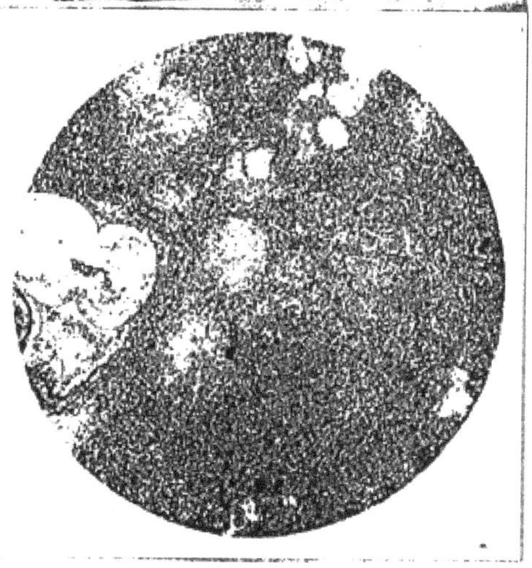

(x 60)

No. 405 (right inferior.)

Eobular pneumonia, hemorrhagic-exudative.

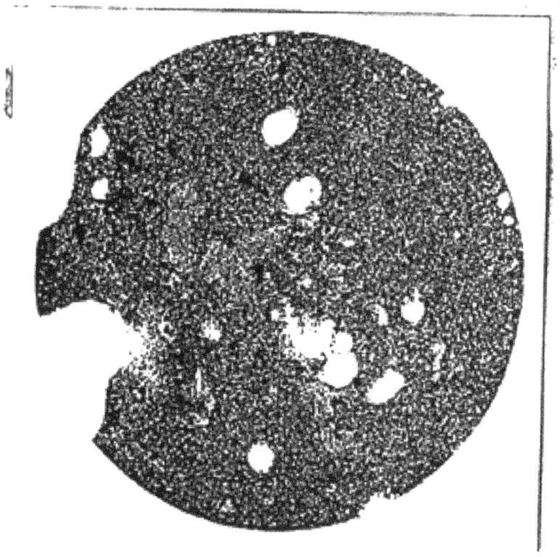

No 403 X 60.

[redacted] 133

[redacted]

Bronchitis and Bronchiolitis catarrhalis gravis.

CONFIDENTIAL

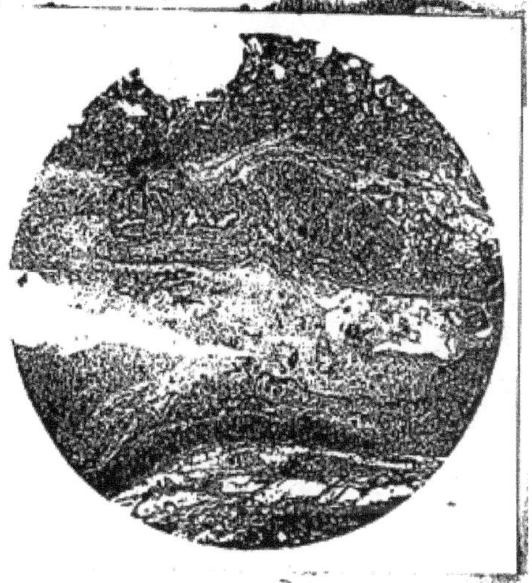

No. 412 (a) X 20

Bronchitis catarrhalis gravis, with massive desquamated epitheliums.

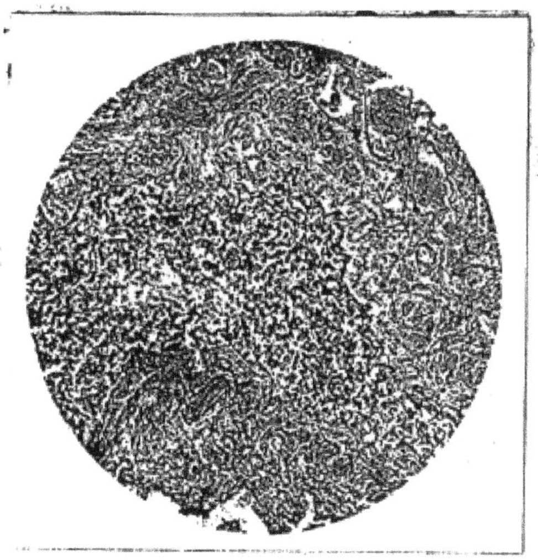

No. 390 X 60
(left inferior)

CONFIDENTIAL 134

[redacted]

Endobronchitis necroticans with
massive decayed masses. [redacted]

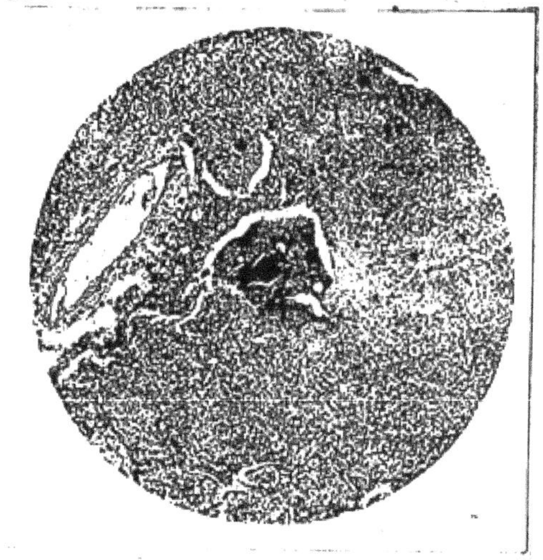

No. 411. X60

Endobronchitis necroticans with
massive decayed masses.

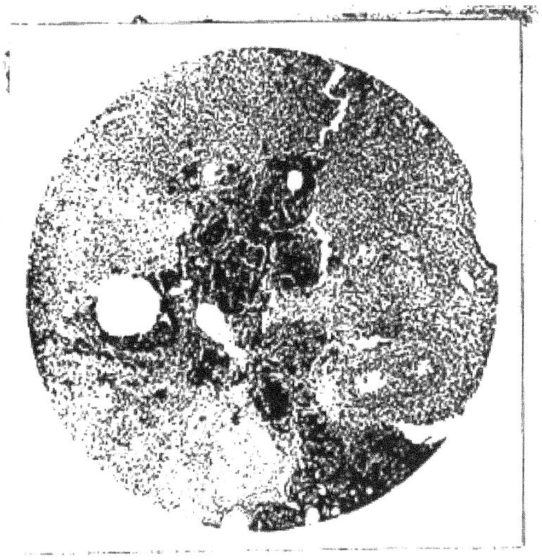

No. 411. X60.

[redacted] 135

[redacted]

CONFIDENTIAL

Pleuritis haemorrhagica and

Subpleural acuno-lobular pneumonia.

No. 411.

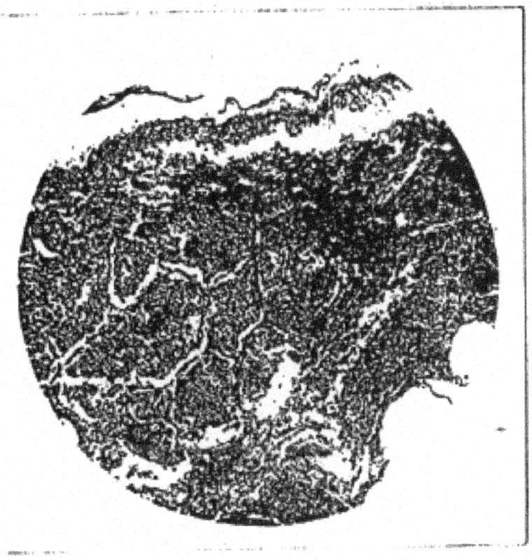

(X64)

CONFIDENTIAL 136

[redacted]

CONFIDENTIAL

Bronchitis catarrhalis gravis
(with massive desquamated epitheliums)
and Alveolitis of peribronchial tissues.

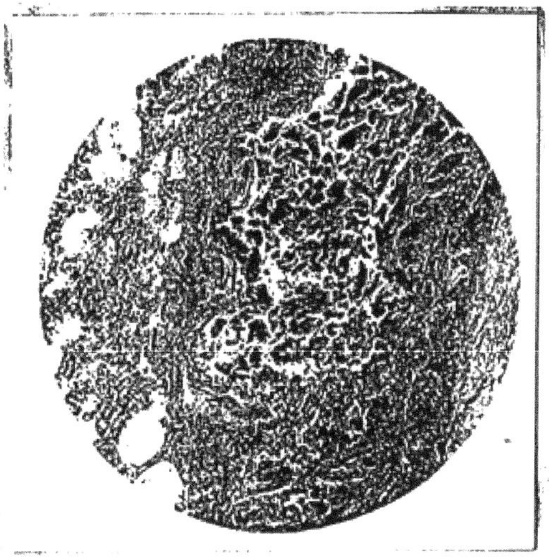

No. 417. X 60.
(left superior.)

Edematous swelling and congestion
of alveolar walls and some
atelectatic alveolar spaces.

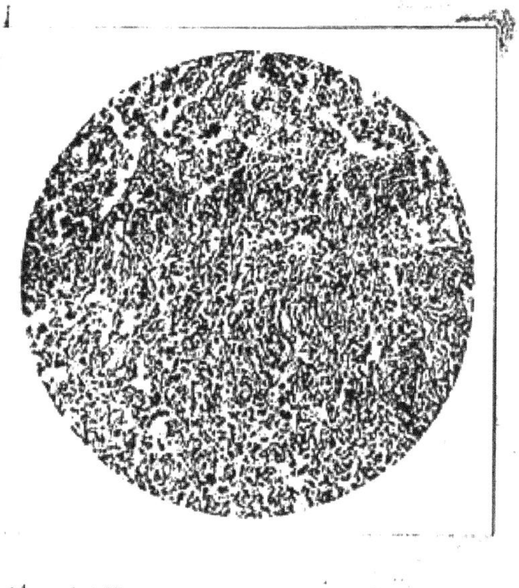

No. 417. X 120
(right superior.)

[redacted]

137

[redacted]

[redacted]

Tonsil

[redacted]

138

[redacted]

CONFIDENTIAL

T O N S I L.

(A) Microscop. Investigation.

I7.

Slight submucous congestion and no remarkable changes else.

380.

In crypts, some desquamated masses (fibrinous separations, serous fluids, some leucocytes, some decayed cells and some bacterial masses) with slight localised superficial ulcers and severe cloudy or bionecrotic swelling of mucous epithelial cells.

Considerable swollen follicles with some slightly hyperplasieal germinative centres, which have some swellen reticulum cells and some karyorhextic masses.

Slight congestion (especially remarkable congestion, edematous swelling and some bacterial masses in subepitheliar tissues) and considerable hyperplasia of endothelial cells of capillaries. considerable congestion of other submucous tissues with some round-cell-accumulation (some hitiocytes and some plasma-cells).

388.

In crypts, a large quantity of desquamated masses (fibrinous masses decayed cells, some leucocytes and some bacterial masses) with some localised superficial ulcers and severe edematous or cloudy swelling of mucous epithelial cells.

Considerably swollen follicular tissues with some hyperplasied germinative centres, which have plenty of leucocytes, bionecrotically swollen reticulum cells and some karyorrhextic cells.

Considerable congestion, severe edematous swelling, multiple remar-

CONFIDENTIAL 189

[redacted]

[redacted]

kable hemorrhages and some leucoytes-emigration in follicular and submucous tissues.

399.

A large quantity of desquamated masses and severe bionecrotic or necrotic swelling of mucous epithelial cells.

Remarkable congestion of subepitheliar, peri- and intra-follicular tissues and remarkable leucocytes-emigration in subepitheliar tissues and others.

Considerable hyperplasia and swelling of germinative centres with intensely swollen reticulum-cells, -fibers, and partial slight hemorrhages, accompanied with considerable hemorrhages in perifollicular tissues.

Remarkable congestion and remarkable edematous swelling of submucous tissues.

396.

Remarkable edematous swelling and localised superficial ulcers of mucous layers with some desquamated masses (fibrinous separation, some leuco- and lymphocytes, massive decayed cells).

Remarkable congestion with some bacterial masses as capillaries contensts) and remarkable edematous swelling of follicular tissues with slightly swollen derminative centres.

Remarkable congestions (with some bacterial masses), remarkable edematous swelling and slight increase of histiocytic cells in other submucous tissues.

397.

Considorable edematous swelling of mucous tissues with some

[redacted] 140

[redacted]

[redacted]

desquamated masses.

Considerable congestion and edematous swelling of follicular tissues with remarkabl increased, but remarkably swollen germinative centres, which have some increased, cloudy sowllen reticulum-cells and karyorrhextic masses.

Considerable congestion, slight localised hemorrhages and edematous swelling of other submucous tissues.

399.

Some desquamated masses (fibrinous separations, some leucocytes, erythrocytes and some bacterial masses) and edematous swelling of mucous tissues.

Remarkable congestion (with some lymphocytes as capillary contents) in subepitheliar, peri- and intra-follicular tissues and considerable hyperplasia of germinative centres with some increased, but cloudy swollen reticulum-cells, some lymphocytes and some leucocytes (and plasma-cells).

Some plasma-cell-accumulations at perivascular parts of submucous tissues, with remarkable congestion.

403.

Remarkable bionecrotic swelling and multiple diffuse superficial ulcers of mucous layers with massive desquamated decayed cells.

The most intense congestion and edematous swelling of follicular tissues with rather atrophic germinative centres, which have some bionecrotically swollen reticulum-cells and karyolytic masses.

Remarkable congestion and edema of submucous tissues.

405.

Some desquamated masses [redacted] ons, some leucocytes,

141

[redacted]

[redacted]

and some decayed epithelial cells) and slight localised superficial ulcers.
Slight congestion and edematous swelling of follicular tissues with some swollen germinative centres, which have some increased, but remarkably cloudy swollen reticulum-cells and some karyorrhextic masses.
Slight congestion in other submucous tissues.
407.
Without significant desquamations and ulcers-formations.
Remarkable congestion and edematous swelling in subepitheliar, peri- and intra- follicular tissues with some hyperplasied, but edematously swellen germinative centres.
Remarkable congestion and diffuse hemorrhages of perifollicular tissues.
409.
Cystic dilatation of lacunal spaces with a large quantity of serous fluids, some leucocytes and decayed cells and severe edematous swelling of mucous tissues.
The most intense congestion and edematous swelling of subepitheliar capillary-plexus, peri- and intra-follicular tissues with some hyperplasied and swollen germinative centres, which have some swollen feticulum-cells and some karyolytic masses.
Remarkable congestion and edematous swelling of submucous tissues with slight perivascular round-cell-infiltrations.
4II.
Severe desquamation with a large quantity of decayed epithelial cells,

[redacted] 142

[redacted]

[redacted]

serous fluids, some leucocytes and some bacterial masses.
Remarkable congestion and edematous swelling of subepitheliar, peri- and intra-follicular tissues with some leucocytes- emigrations, esp. in subepitheliar tissues and multiple diffuse remarkable hemorrhages.
Lymph-nodulus in solid-form (with slightly swollen germinative centres) and some plasma-cells in subepitheliar tissues.

4I2.
The most intense, bionecrotic swelling of mucous cells and some bacterial accumulations (intrusions) in intercellular spaces of mucous epithelial cells and in lymph-capillaries of attached subepitheliar tissues.

4I2.
The most intense, bionecrotic swelling of mucous cells and some bacterial accumulations (intrusions) in intercellular spaces of mucous epithelial cells and in lymph-capillaries of attached subepitheliar tissues.
Massive decayed masses (some leucocytes, severe serous exudation, fibrinous separations and some decayed epithelial cells) and the most intense congestion and remarkable edematous swelling of follicular tissues with some hyperplasied germinative centres, which have some bionecrotically swollen reticulum-cells and some karyorrhextic masses and at some places some bacterial accumulations.
Remarkable congestion and remarkable edematous swelling of follicular tissues with some leucocytes-emigrations.

4I3.
Slight desquamation and [redacted] swelling of mucous tissues.

[redacted] 143

[redacted]

[redacted]

Considerable congestion and edematous swelling of subepitheliar, peri-and intrafollicular tissues with some hyperplasied and swollen germinative centres, which have some swollen reticulum-cells (and -fibres) and some karyorrhextic masses.

Considerable congestion of perifollicular and submucous tissues.

4I7.

Some desquamated masses in crypts and bionecrotic swelling of mucous epithel cells. The most intense congestion and edematous swelling of subepitheliar, peri- and intrafollicular tissues.

Remarkable perifollicular diffuse hemorrhages (with edematous swelling) and remarkable reduction of follicular tissues with some bacterial accumlations at some places.

Slight hyperplasia and swelling of germinative centres with some bionecrotically swollen reticulum-cells and some karyorrhextic masses, accompanied with considerable congestion of capillaries in germinative centres and remarkable deminution of lymphocytes with some leucocytes-accumulations.

[redacted] 144

[redacted]

(B [redacted] Y.

(I)

Accordingly the common changes in all cases are as follows:

In crypt:

Massive desquamated masses in all cases, except in I case. (serous fluids, fibrinous separations, some leucocytes, some decayed epithelial cells and some bacterial masses. Sometimes some erythrocytes).

In mucous epithelium:

With atrophy	in 6 cases.
With remarkable or considerable congestion and edema.	in all cases.
With bionecrotic swelling.	in 4 cases.
With superficial ulcers.	in 5 cases.

In I cases (4I2 cases), I have investigated an intrusions of bacterial masses in interepithelial spaces: tonsilla as entrance-port of bacteria.

In germinative centres:

Generally with reactive hyperplasia.	in almost cases.
(Sometimes disappeared) only remained karyolyticcells.	4 cases.
The border of follicles indis tenctly	5 cases.
hyalinois smuling	4 cases.
Sometimes with bionecrotic swelling of slightly increased reticulum-cells.	in 4 cases.
With some leucocytes-emigrations.	in 3 cases.

In follicular tissues:

[redacted] 145

[redacted]

[redacted]

Reactive considerable or remarkable congestion and edema.
in all cases.

In perifollicular tissus:

Reactive considerable or remarkable congestion and edema.
in all cases.

With some hemorrhages.	in 6 cases.
With some bacterial accumulations.	in 2 cases.
With some bacterial accumulations.	in 2 cases.

In submucous tissues:

Sometimes inflammatory changes spread to the neighbouring submucous tissues intensely.

With considerable or remarkable congestion, edema and haemosshoge
in all cases.

With some hemorrhages.	in 2 cases.
remarkably haemorrhage	in 3 cases.
With some leucocytes-emigrations.	in I case.
remarkably leucocyte-emiyuration.	in 3 cases.
With some round cell disseminations.	in 4 cases.
With distributed bacteria.	in 3 cases.

Accordingly the main pathological pindings of tonsils are as follows: Remarkable swelling and sometimes bionecrotic swelling (intrusion of bacterial masses). accompanied with multiple necrotic ruins or ulcers-formation of mucous epitheliums and following some inflammatory changes in the follicular tissues with reactive hyperplasia of

[redacted] 146

[redacted]

[redacted]

germinative centres (sometimes bionecrotic swelling of hyperplasied reticulum cells).

These inflammatory changes spread into the perifòllicular of subepithelíar tissues with severe congestion and sometimes leucocytes-emigrations and propagate themselves furthermore to the neighbouring submucous tissues with some inflammatory signs.

Therefore tonsil is one of the main entrance ports of bacteria.

[redacted] 147

[redacted]

[redacted]

Intense congestion and intense
edematous swelling of follicular
tissues. In high power.
With some bacterial masses in
capillaries.

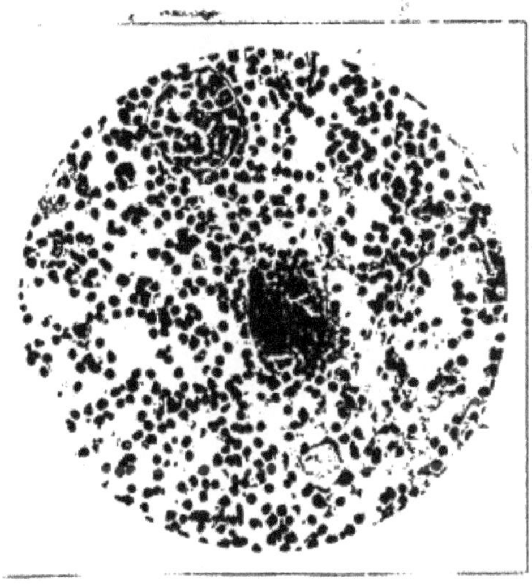

M. 417

[redacted] 148

[redacted]

~~CONFIDENTIAL~~

Intese congestion and some hemorrhages in follicular tissues.

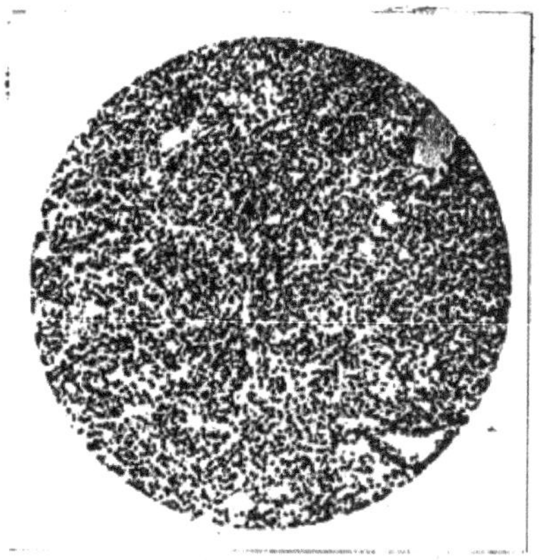

Intese congestion and diffuse hemorrhages in follicular tissues.

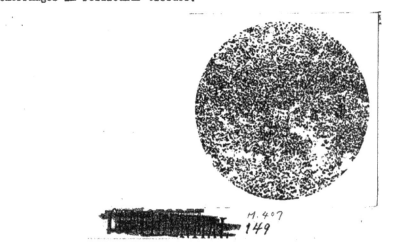

[redacted] M.407
149

[redacted]

CONFIDENTIAL

Intense necrosis of epitheliar layers.

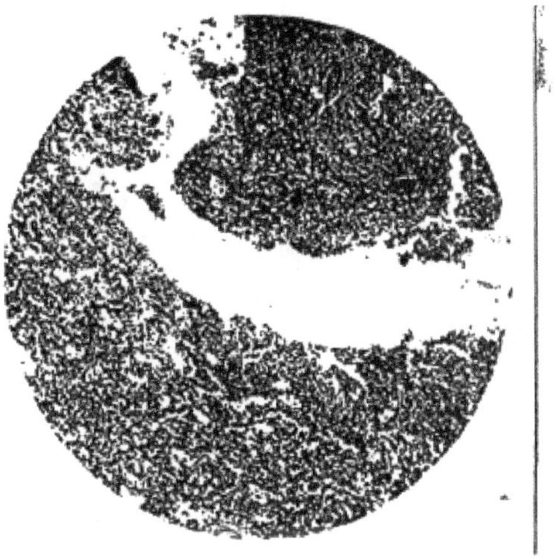

Necrosis of epitheliums.

CONFIDENTIAL 150

[redacted]

CONFIDENTIAL

Bronchus

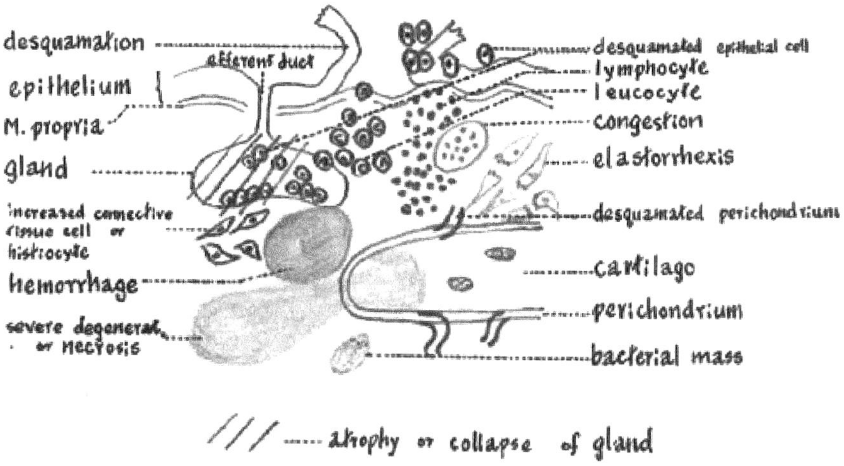

[redacted]

CONFIDENTIAL 151

[redacted]

CONFIDENTIAL

BRONCHUS.

A) Microscop Investigation .

54

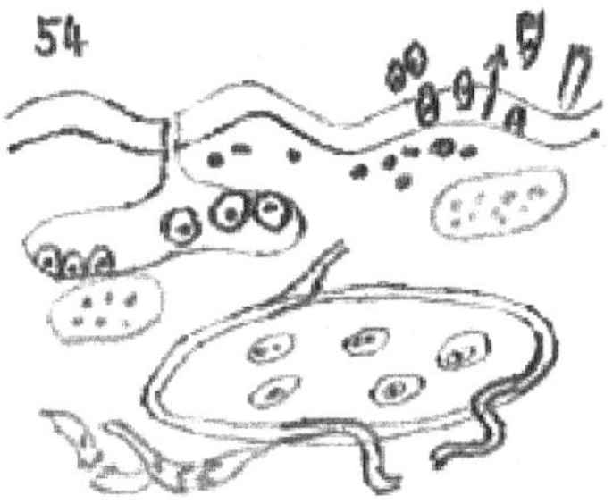

54.

Slight edema in mucous and submucous (at perivascular portions) tissues and slight congestion with slight degeneration of mucous epithelial cells.

325

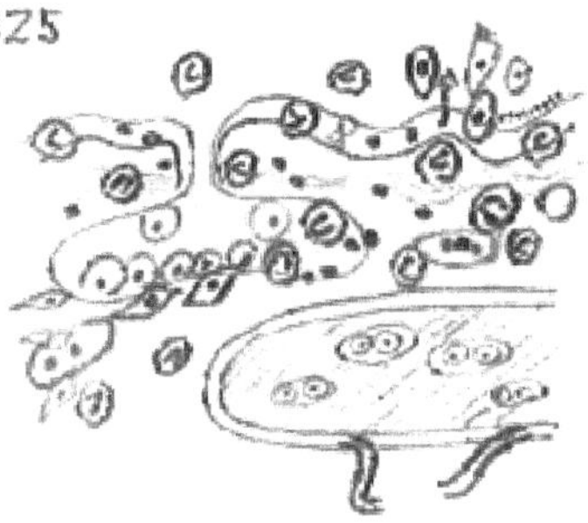

325.

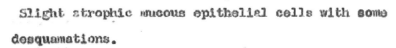

Slight atrophic mucous epithelial cells with some desquamations.

Considerable leucocytes-and lymphocytes-emigration in all layers. esp. in submucous and inter-glandular tissues. Slight congestion.

388

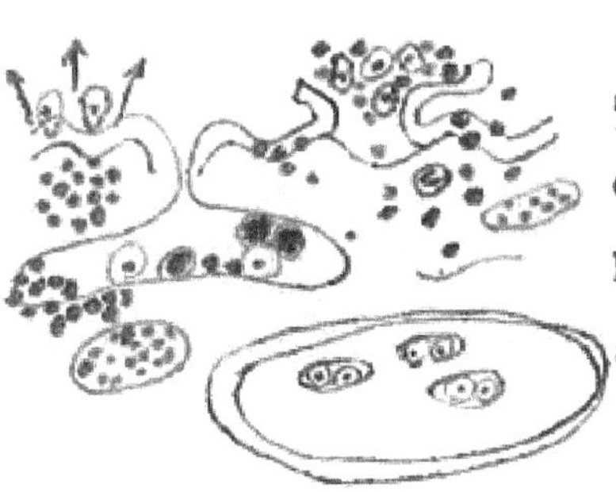

388.

Some degenerative changes of mucous epithel cells and some sero-mucous secrets with desquamated epithelial cells : Epithelial cells with pycnosis, karyorrhexis and infiltrated with some round-cells and some erythrocytes or their fragments.

Slight round-cell-infiltration ins submucous or interglendular tissues (atrophic glanduler cells) and considerable congestion.

[redacted] 152

[redacted]

[redacted]

393

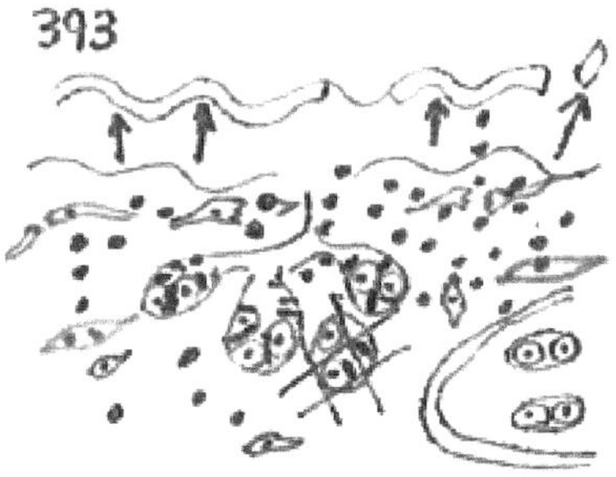

393.

Intense edematous swelling (elastorrhexis) of mucous and submucous tissues with some round-cells (mainly lymphocytes)-emigration in submucous or interglandular tissues.

397

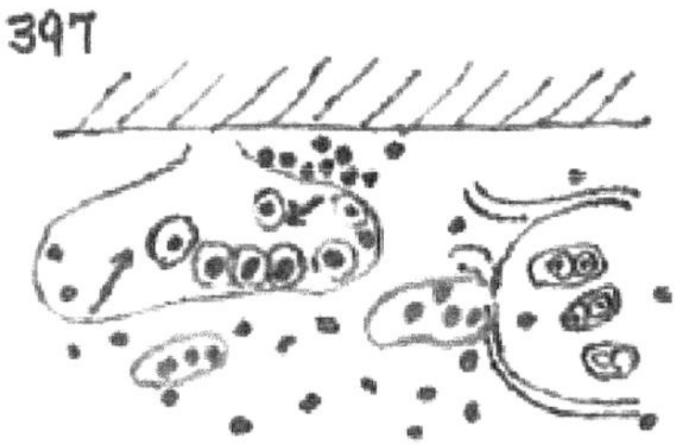

Collaese of glands : epithelial cells with somewhat phenosis and karyorrhexis and infiltrated with some round-cells (mainly lymphocytes), due to hyperplasia of lymphatic nodulus.

397.

400

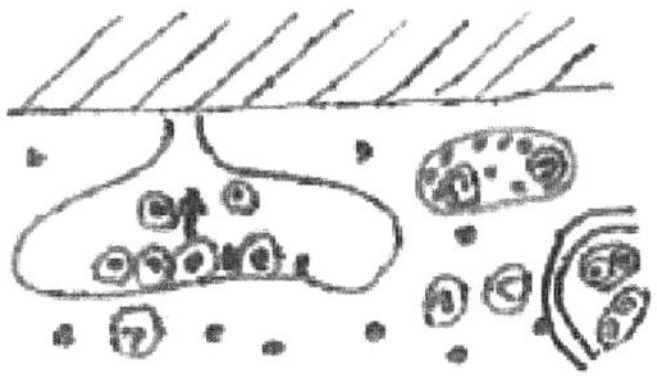

Considerable edema and slight round-cell-infiltration in subepitheliar or submucous tissues. Dissociation of cellular arrangements of glands. Slight peribronchial hyperaemia.

400.

403

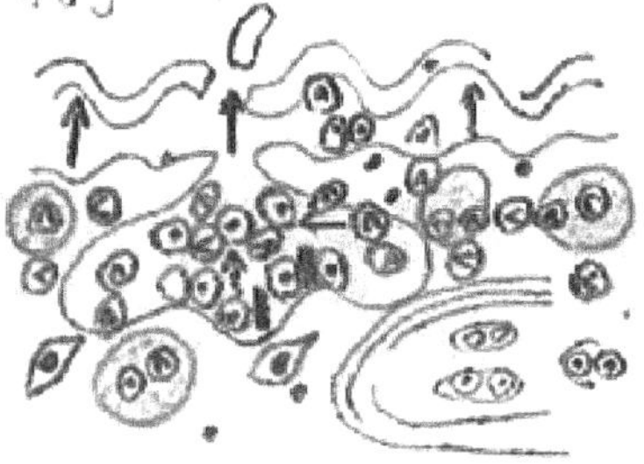

Considerable congestion (with some leucocytes as capillary contents) and considerable edematous swelling of mucous or submucous tissues. Some round-cell-dissemination in these tissues.

403.

Intense desquamation of epithelial cells, due to remarkable edema in mucous tissues. Remarkable congestion and intense edema in submucous tissues with slight round-cell-disseminations.

Glandular cells are dissociated, due to edematous

[redacted] 153

[redacted]

swelling and infiltration of some leucocytes. Peribronchial tissues with considerable congestion and some localised hemorrhages.

405.

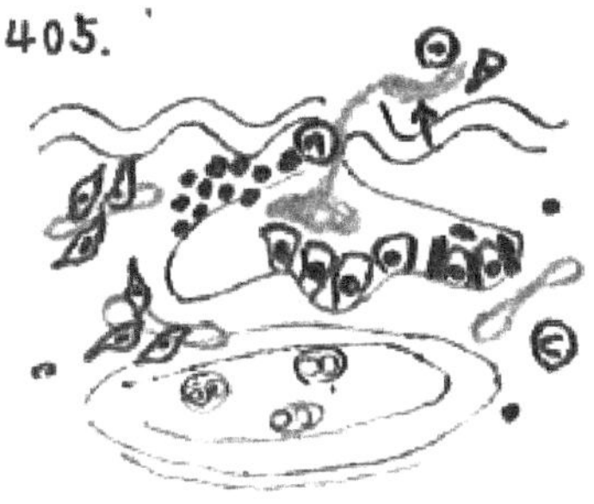

405.

Rather anemic, and no significant changes in mucous tissues.

Diffuse lymphocytes-infiltration (hyperplasia of lymphatic nodulus) and some hypersecretion of the glands.

409.

Considerable desquamation of epithelial cells and edematous swelling of mucous tissues. Remarkable congestion and considerable edema, accompanied with some leucocytes-emigration in mucous or submucous tissues. Some atrophic glandular cells and some lymphatic nodulus in glands.

Peribronchial tissues with remarkable edema and considerable congestion.

409

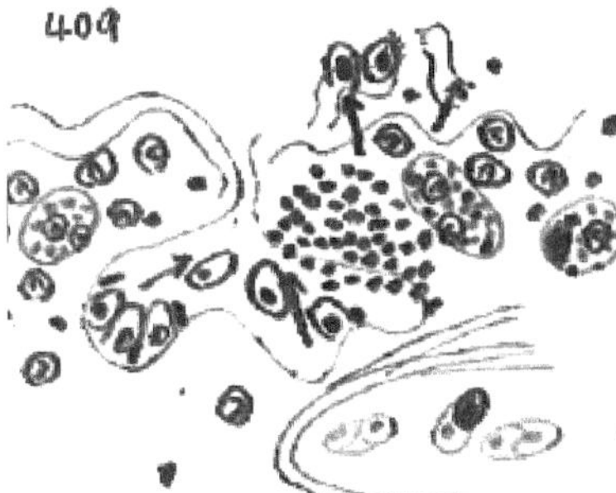

409.

Considerable desquamation of epithelial cells and severe edema of mucous tissues. Remarkable congestion (with some bacterial masses as capillary-contents) and considerable edema, accompanied with some leucocytes-emigration in mucous and submucous tissues.

[redacted] 154

[redacted]

CONFIDENTIAL

411

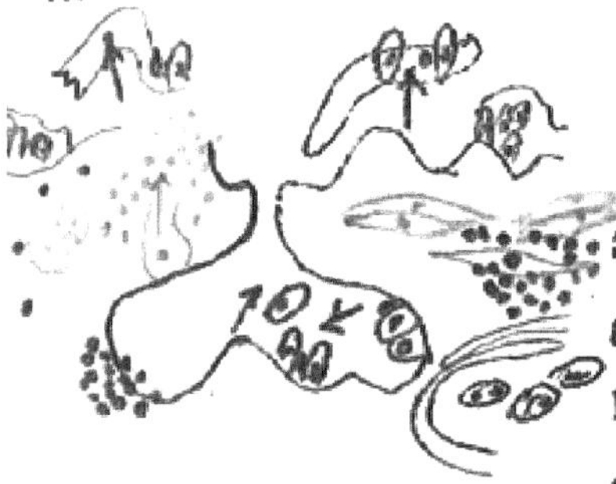

Some atrophic glands and some lymphatic nodulus in glands.

Peribronchial tissues with remarkable edema and considerable congestion.

4II.

412

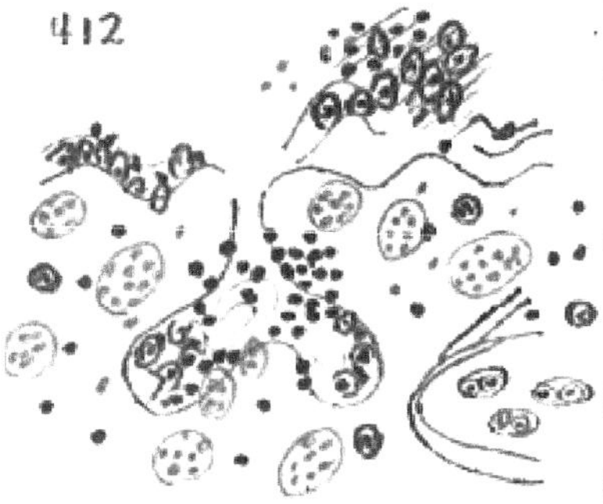

Desquamation of epithelial cells and considerable edema of mucous tissues. Considerable congestion (with some edema) and some localised hemorrhages in submucous and periglandular tissues. Atrophic glands.

4I2.

413

Some desquamated masse (serous secreta, some desquamated epithelial cells, some lymphocytes etc.) and considerable edema of mucous tissues. Remarkable congestion in all layers, esp. in submucous and periglandular tissues. Peribronchial tissues with some hemorrhagic-exudative changes.

4I3.

417

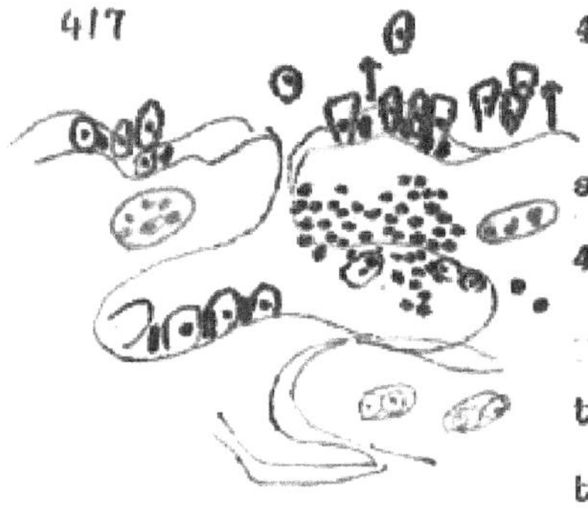

Peribronchial tissues with considerable congestion and some edema.

4I7.

Some desquamated epitheliums. Considerable congestion and edematous swelling of mucous and submucous tissues. Some lymphatic nodulus among the glands.

CONFIDENTIAL 155

[redacted]

CONFIDENTIAL

3). S U M M A R Y .

(I)

The bird's-eye-view of pathological changes in all cases.

---

54. Slight edema in mucous and submucous tissues.

325. Slight congestion and considerable leucocytes-dissemination.

388. Remarkable disturbances of mucous tissues and considerable congestion in submucous tissues, accompanied with some round-cell dissemination.

393. Intense edematous swelling of mucous and submucous tissues with hypofunction of glands.

397. Considerable edema in submucous tissues. Slight peribronchial congestion.

400. Considerable congestion (with some leucocytes) and edema in submucous tissues.

403. Remarkable edema of mucous tissues and remarkable congestion and intense edema of submucous tissues. Some leucocytes-emigration in interglandular tissues.
Peribronchial tissues with considerable congestion and hemorrhages.

405. No significant changes.

409. Remarkable congestion (some bacterial masses in capillaries), considerable edema and some leucocytes-dissemination in submucous tissues.
Peribronchial tissues with remarkable edema and some congestion.

4II. Considerable congestion and some hemorrhages in submucous tissues.

4I2. Remarkable congestion in submucous and periglandular tissues.
Peribronchial tissues with some exudative-hemorrhagic changes.

4I3. Peribronchial tissues with some hemorrhages.

4I7. Considerable congestion and some edematous swelling of submucous tissues.

[redacted] 156

[redacted]

[redacted]

(2)

I divide all cases into 2 groups : a) group of peroral infection and b) pernasal infection.

a) Peroral infection with no significant bronchial and peribronchial changes. (for examples, No. 54 and No. 325).

b) Pernasal infection, investigated all cases.

These are accompanied with some exudative changes.

Considerable acute congestion and edema. in all cases.

Items :

with slight exudative changes.	2 cases.
with considerable exud. changes.	3 cases.
with remarkable exud. changes.	3 cases.
with slight hemorrhages.	4 cases.
with some leucocytes-emigrations.	6 cases.
with bacterial masses as capillary contents.	I case.

(!)with some peribronchial exudative changes (not investivgated in all cases).

some cases.

In all autopsical cases, intense diffuse mediastianal hemorrhagic-exudative changes are recognized (also by X-ray tests, clinically). These autopsical cases are nor investigated microscopically in all casses, while I have nor recieved all microscopical materials.

[redacted] 157

[redacted]

[redacted]

Some bronchial and peribronchial changes with congestion and odema in submucous tissues are complications of these main pathological fidings.

Therefore the main pathological changes are Medistinitis and Peribronchitis haemorrhagico-exsudativa.

(3)

Accordingly the general sketches of pathological changes are as follows :

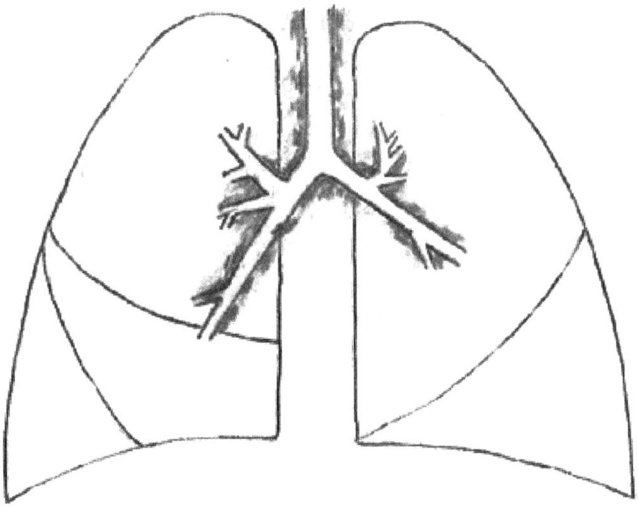

CONFIDENTIAL

158

[redacted]

M-412 Leucocytid hemorrhagic changes in submucous tissues.

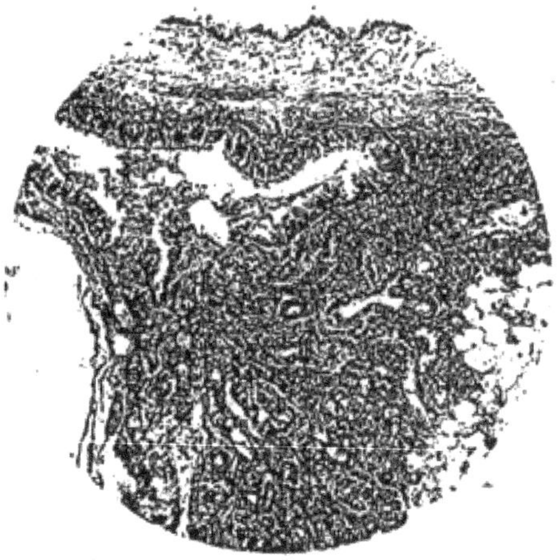

M.385 Leucocytes infiltration in submucous tissues.

x 80

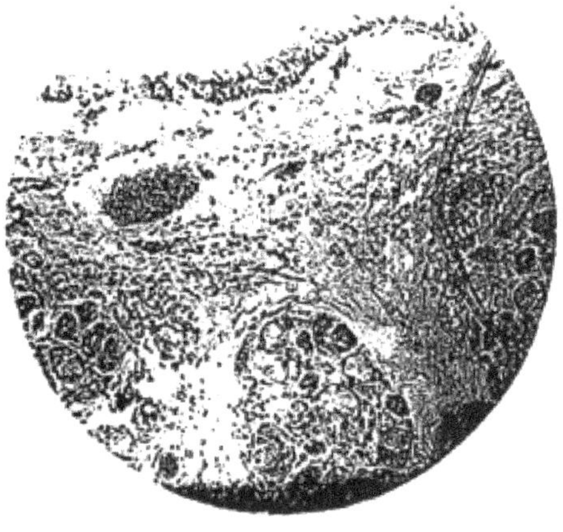

[redacted]

159

[redacted]

[redacted]

M-411 Multiple localised hemorrhages in submucous tissues.

× 100

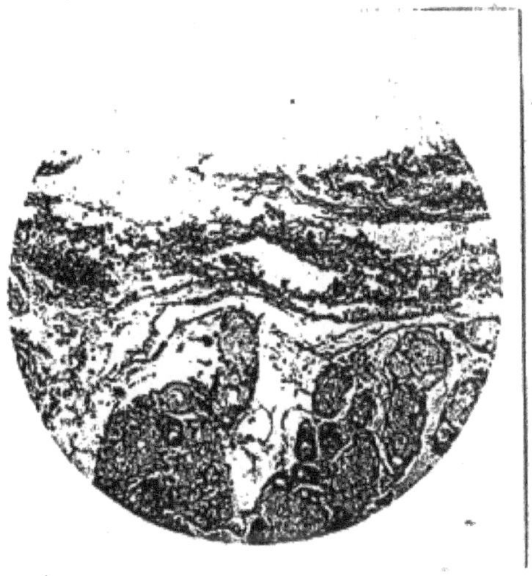

M-343 Necrotic ruius of lymphatic apparatus in submucous tissues.

× 15

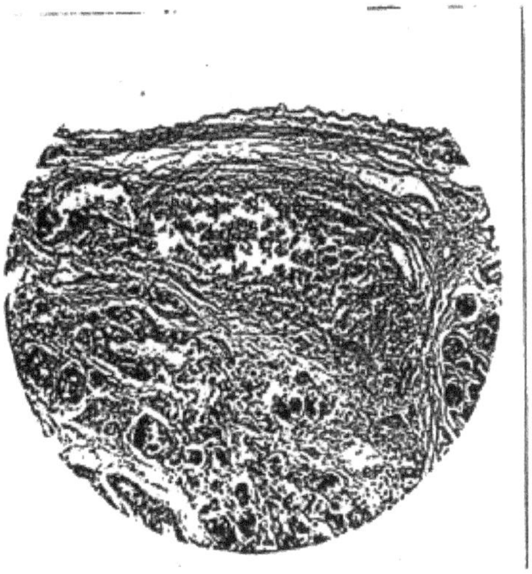

[redacted] 160

[redacted]

[redacted]

M-409 Leucocytes infiltration in high power.
Leucocyted infiltration around the outer tube of gland.

X235

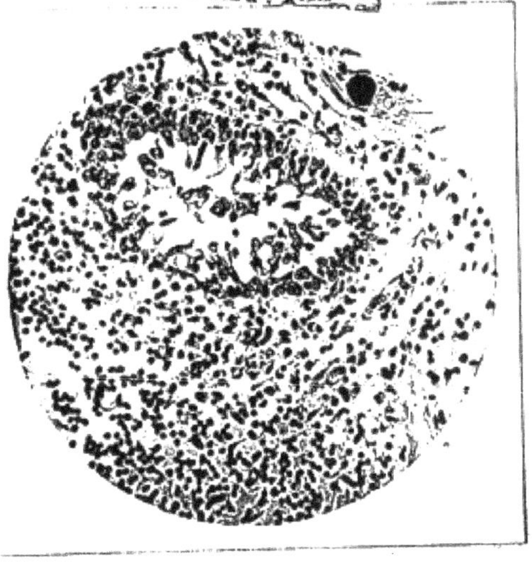

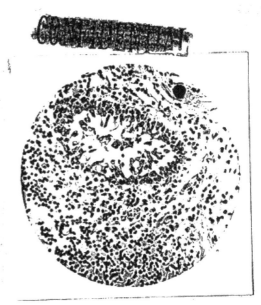

M-325 Slight cat rrh and some leucocytes infiltr tion in subnucous tissues.

X24

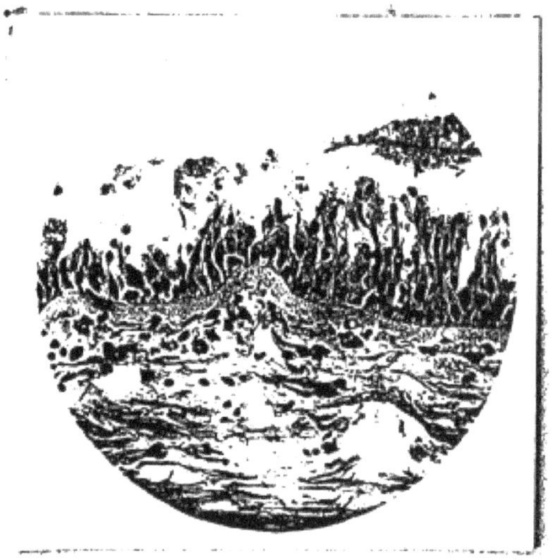

[redacted] 1.61

[redacted]

[redacted]

Liver

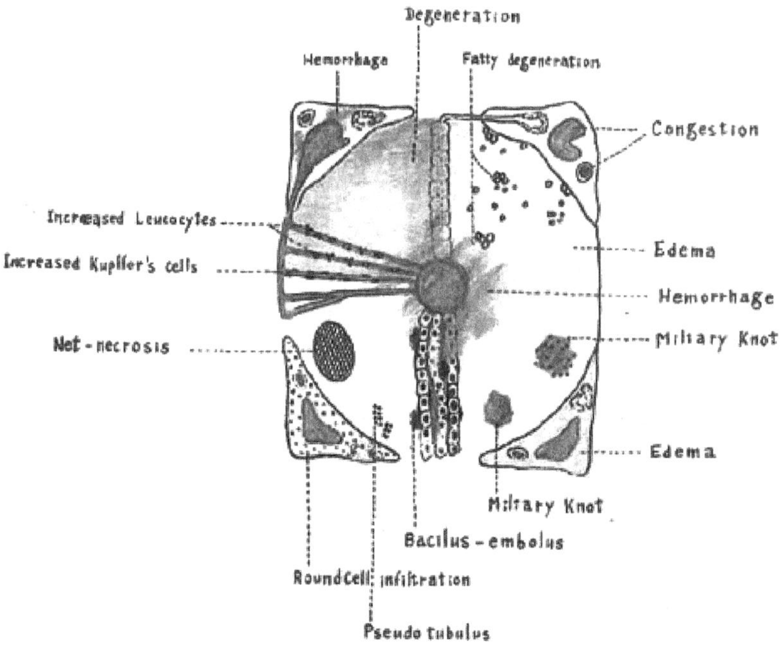

[redacted] 162

[redacted]

17.

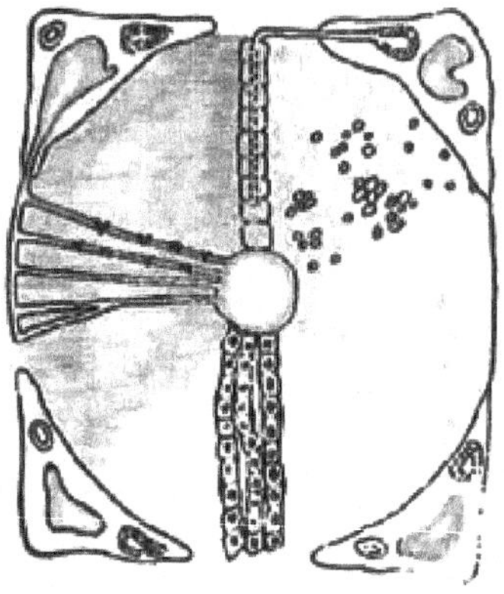

[redacted]

LIVER

(A) Microscop. Investigation.

17.

Hepatitis serosa II,. with considerable exsudative changes in Disse's spaces and considerable diffuse fatty degeneration of parenchymatous cells.

26.

Hepatitis serosa III.

Parenchymatous degeneration and atrophia, caused by extremly severe congestion with partial hemorrhages, esp. in the central zone of acinuses (severe congestion, exudative changes in Disse's spaces, partial hemorrhage and increased lymphocytes as capillary contents).

26.

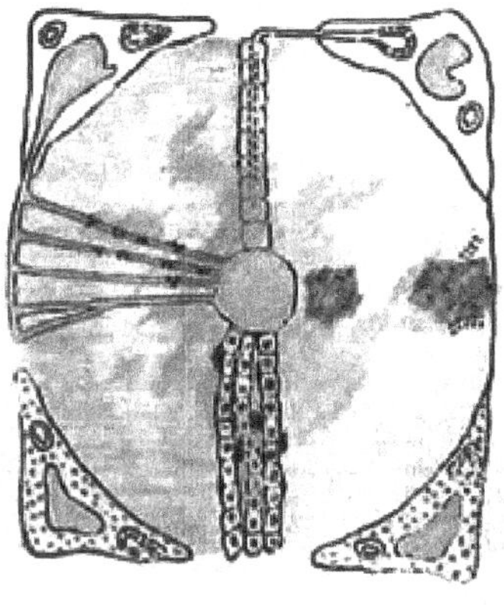

And multiple miliary knots in acinuses, which are formed at partial hemorrhagic places with wandering-cell-accumulations. In the focus of knots exist plenty of lymphocytes, some residual masses of decayed parenchymarous cells and more or less increased histiocytic cells, with remarkable pseudo-tubulus formations. These seats are bounded not sharply and spread with exudative changes arborescently to the perifocal tissues.

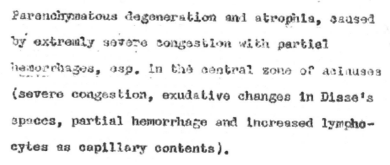

[redacted] 163

[redacted]

53.

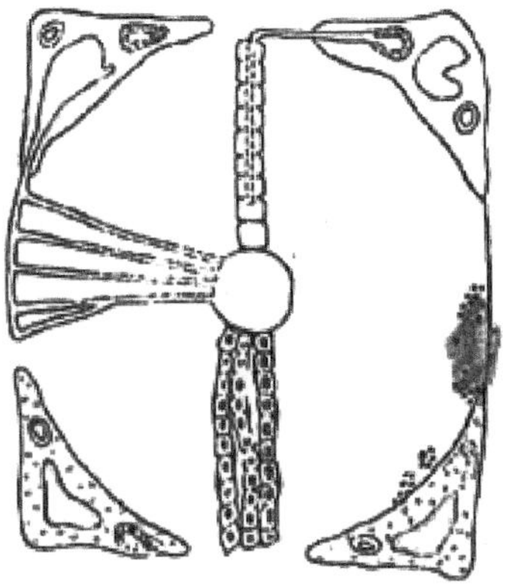

54.

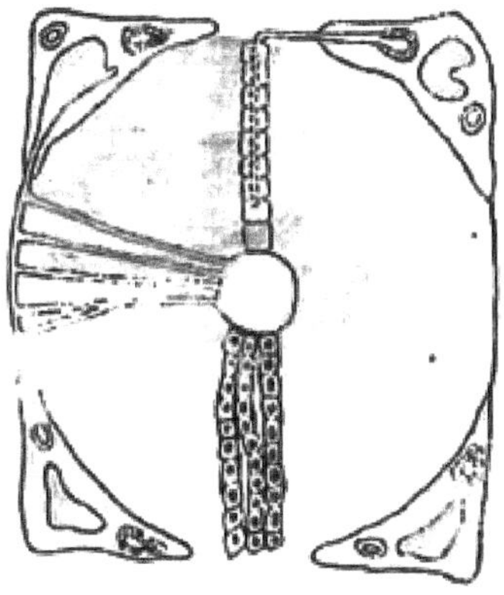

~~318~~.225.

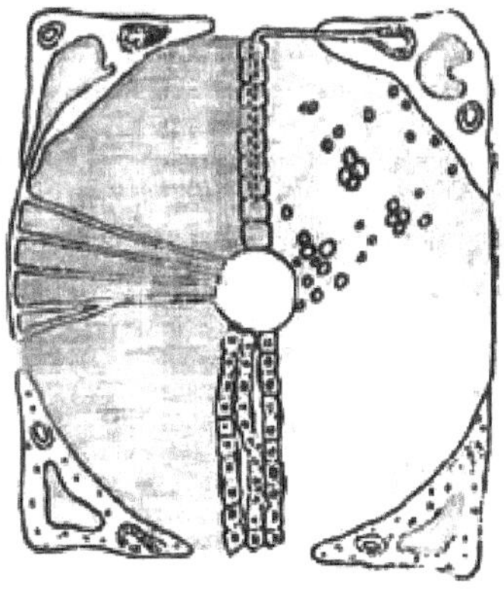

53.

Hepatitis serosa II.

Parenchymatous degeneration with more or less considerable congestion and multiple submiliary portions of acinuses, which are formed by some lymphocytes and slightly histiocytic cells, accompanied with pseude-tubulus-formation in slight degree.

54.

Hepatitis serosa. II,--III.

Parenchymatous degeneration with considerable congestion and slight partial hemorrhages, esp. in the central zone of acinuses.

225. Hepatitis serosa. III.

More or less cloudy and fatty degeneration of parenchymatous cells.

Dissociation of cell-arrangements, which are caused by congestion with slightly increased lymphocytes as capillary contents.

318.

Hepatitis serosa. III-IV.

More or less remarkable cloudy and fatty degeneration of parenchymatous cells and dissociation of

[redacted] 164

[redacted]

[redacted]AL

318.

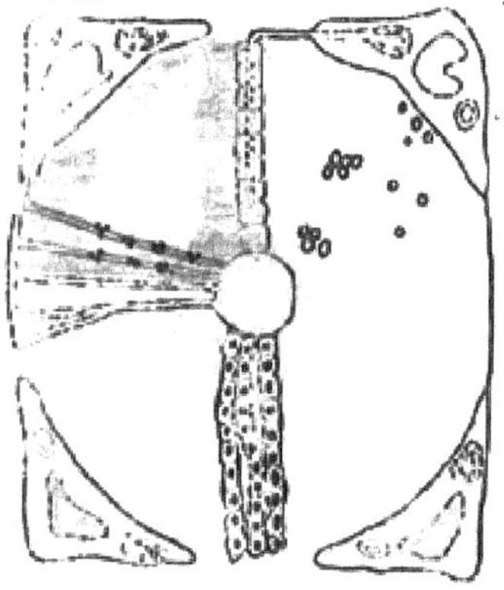

320.

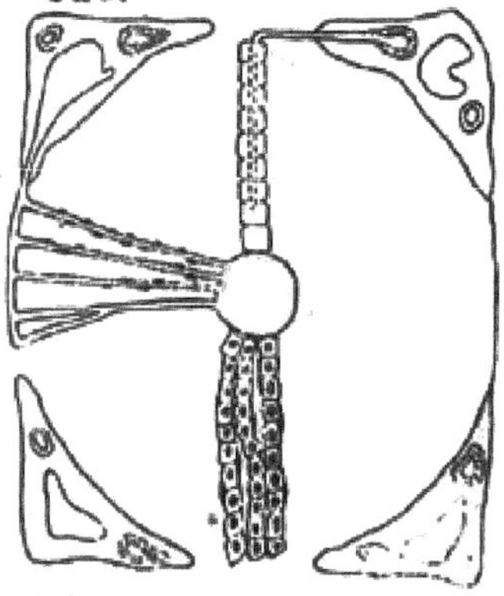

325.

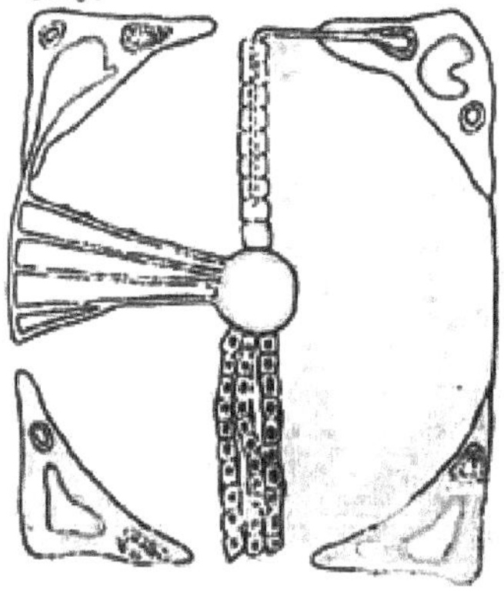

cellular arrangements which are caused by severe congestion (and increased wandering cells as capillary contents) with slight partial hemorrhages, (esp. in central zone of acinuses.)

320.

Hepatitis serosa I-II.

Parenchymatous degeneration with slight congestion, exudative changes in Disse's spaces, slightly increased lymphocytes as capillary contentss and more or less remarkable increase of Kupfer's cells. Slight bilous stagnation in acinuses and Glissons capsules.

325.

Hepatitis serosa II.

Parenchymatous degeneration with slight congestion hemorrhagic-exudative changes in Disse's spaces and slightly increased Kupfer's cells.

383.

Hepatitis seresa III. Severer exudative changes than 325-case.

388.

Hepatitis serosa II.

389.

Hepatitis serosa III.

Remark[redacted]tous degeneration with

[redacted]AL 165

388.

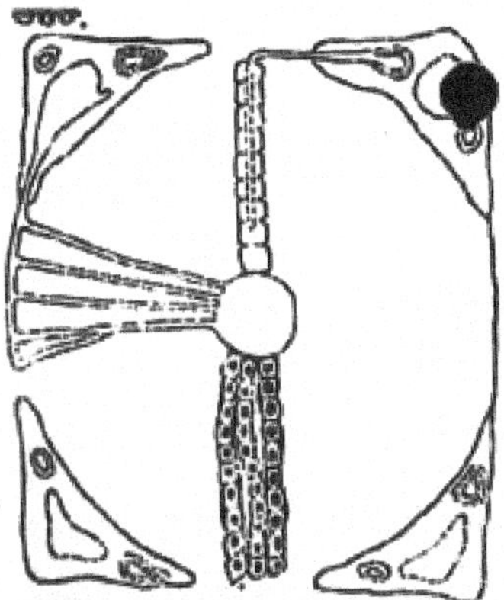

389.

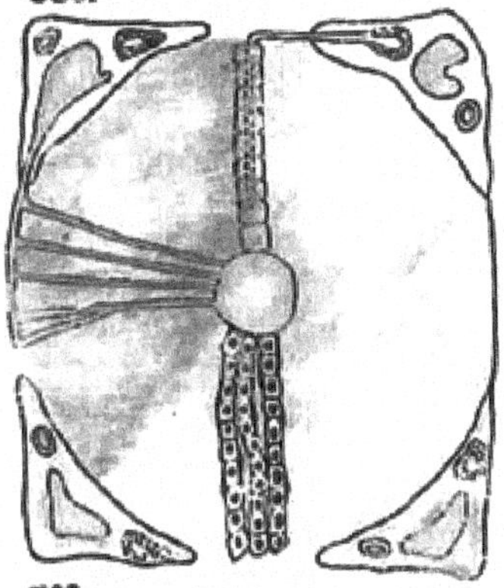

396.

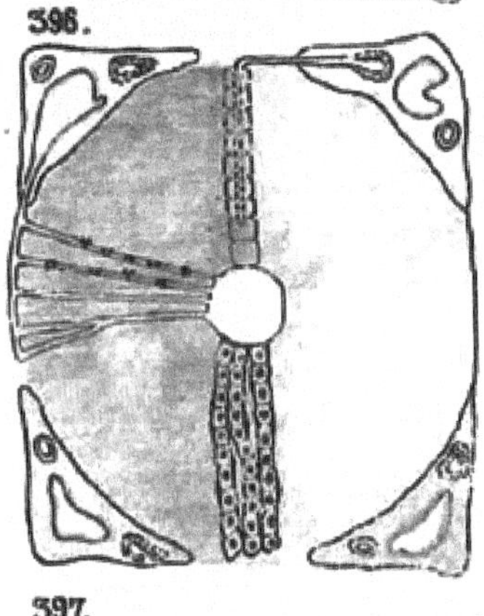

397.

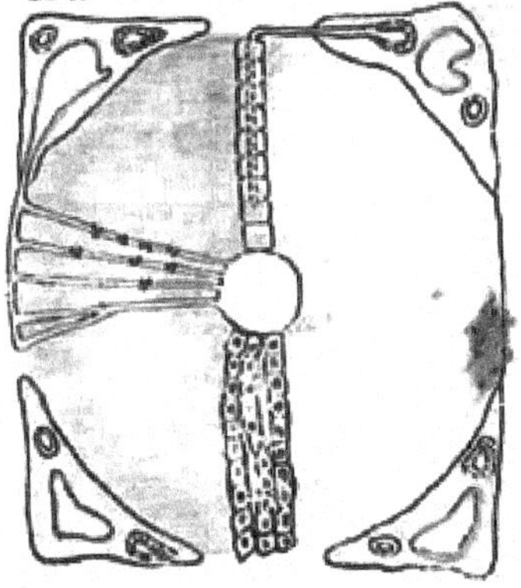

[redacted]

[redacted]

with severe congestion and severe hemorrhagic-exudative changes (remarkable hemorrhages in central zone of acinuses, increased lympho-or leucocytes as capillary contents, edematous swelling of capillary-walls and serous exudation).

393.

Hepatitis serosa II-III.

396.

Hepatitis serosa II-III. with slight pericapillar leucocytic cell accumulations in peripheral or marginal parts of acinuses (proportionated to the initial stage of submiliary knots-formation in No. 397-case).

Post mortal change in this specimen.

397.

Hepatitis serosa III. with multiple submiliary knots, mainly in peripheral zone of acinuses, which are formed by slight accumulation of lymphocytes and some decayed masses of parenchymatous cells at hemorrhagic places. Post mortal change in this specimen.

399.

Hepatitis serosa III-IV.

Remarkable congestion and remarkable exudative

CONFIDENTIAL 166

399.

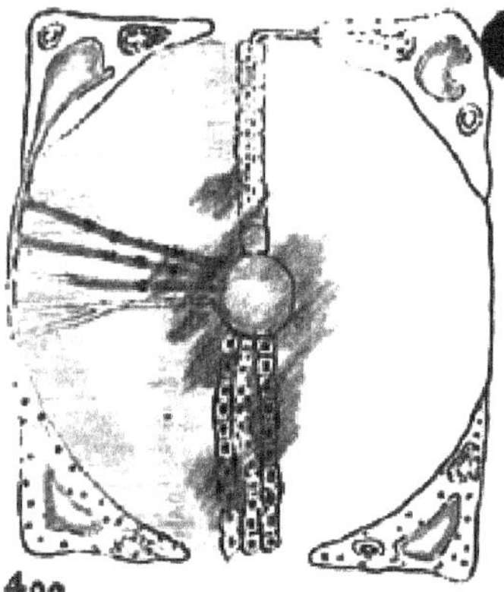

[redacted]

changes in Disse's spaces, with some wandering cells in capillary-nets and multiple hemorrhages in acinuses (where fall into necrosis).

400.

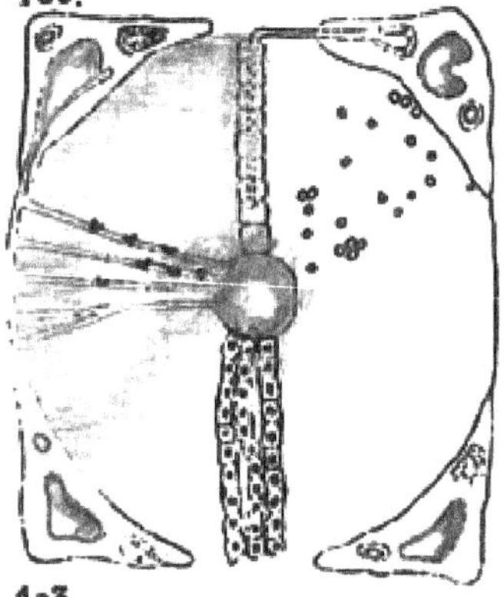

400.

Hepatitis serosa II.

Slight congestion and slight exudative changes in Disse's spaces, with considerable cloudy swelling and slight fatty degeneration of parenchymatous cells.

Intense congestion in Glisson's capsules.

403.

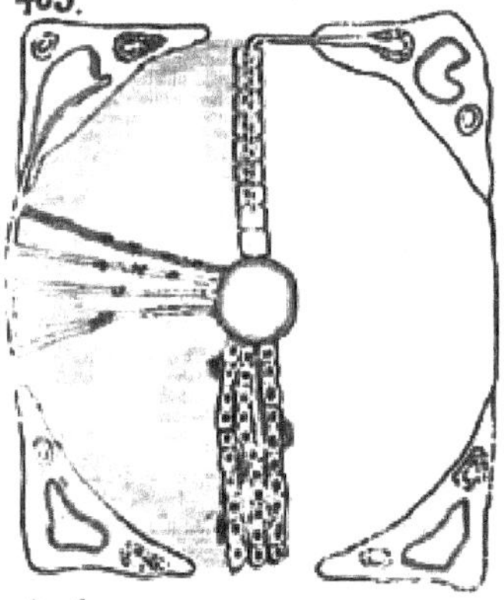

403.

Hepatitis serosa II-III. with bacterial emigration in capillary-nets in acinuses.

404.

Hepatitis serosa III-IV.

Intense exudative changes in Disse's spaces with intense dissociation and some cloudy degeneration of parenchymatous cells.

404.

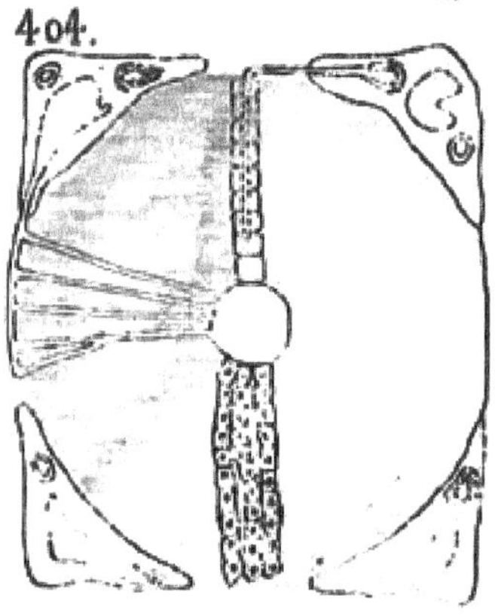

406.

Hepatitis serosa II-III.

407.

In acinuses occured so-called some net-necrosis with are produced by falling into the multiple localised miliary or submiliary knots, exsisting mainly in peripheral zone of acinuses.

[redacted] 167

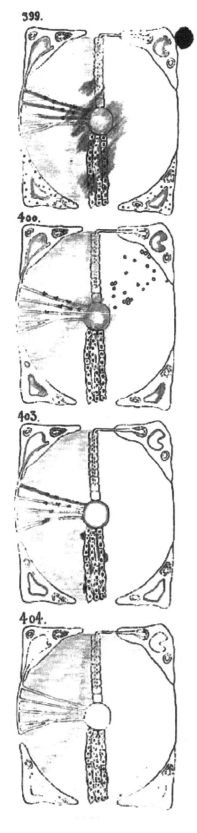

[redacted]

[redacted]

These net-necrosis are formed by some degenerated parenchymatous cells with net-likely clarified glassy protoplasma and their decayed fragments, accompanied with slight bile-pigments.
Situated at the hemorrhagic places.
In other general tissues of liver : cloudy serlling of parenchymatous cells with more or less exudative changes in Disse's spaces (Hepatitis serosa III.) and slightly increased histiocytic cells.

407.

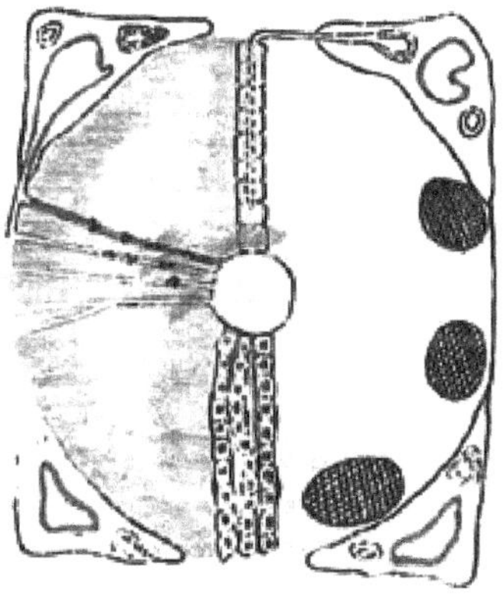

409.

Hepatitis serosa II-III. with bacterial deposits in capillary-net in acinus.

410.

Hepatitis serosa II-III. with severe congestion and partial hemorrhages in central zone of acinuses. Cloudy swelling or fatty degeneration of parenchymatous cells, esp. at hemorrhagic parts. Edematous swelling of Glisson's capsule with slight round-cell-infiltration and pseudo-biliary-tract formations.

4o 41o.

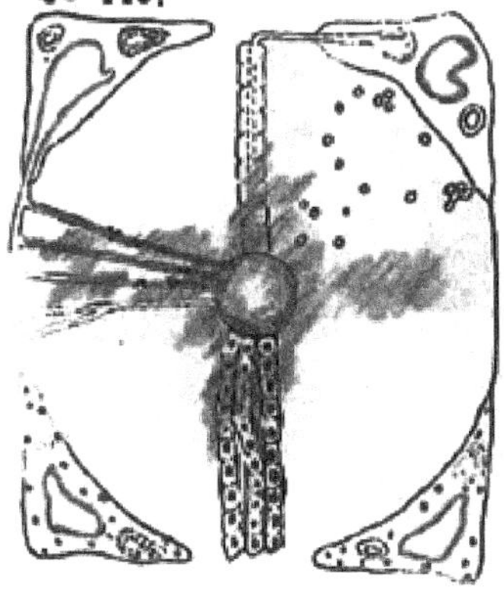

411.

Hepatitis serosa II-III.

[redacted] 168

[redacted]

414.

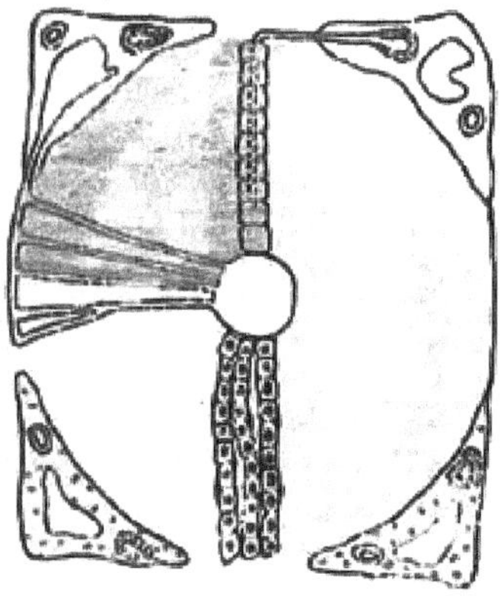

414.

Hepatitis serosa II, with remarkable exudative changes and considerable congestion.

416.

Hepatitis serosa II.-III.

417.

417.

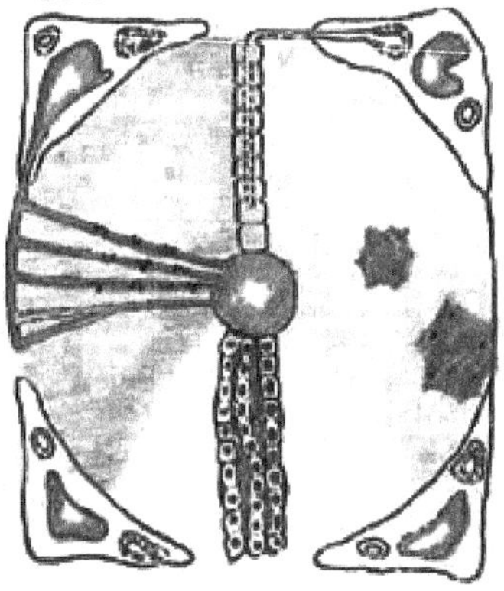

Hepatitis serosa II.-III. with severe congestion and exudative changes in Disse's spaces. Multiple submiliary knots in acinuses, which are formed by accumulation of some leucocytes, a little lymphocytes and histiocytic cells and decayed masses of parenchymatous cells.

CONFIDENTIAL 769

[redacted]

[redacted]

(B) S U M M A R Y

The bird's-eye-view of pathological changes of liver-tissues in all cases as following:

A) Acinus :

I) According to these results I classified the parenchymatous disturbances of liver tissues by Anthrax-disease as followed :

Hepatitis serosa	I.	1	cases.
"	II.	15	cases.
"	III.	9	cases.
"	IV.	0	cases.

with hemorrhages (esp. in central zone of acinus). ca. 9 cases

with miliary knots. 5 cases

2) Generally more or less considerable congestion.

In medium degree.	7	in cases of them.
In severe degree.	3	in cases of them.
with hemorrhages in central zone.	9	in cases of them.

3) And more or less remarkable exudative changes in Disse's spaces.

In slight degree.	8	cases.
In medium degree.	5	cases.
In severe degree.	3	cases.

[redacted] 170

[redacted]

[redacted]

4) In proportion to exudative-hemorrhagic processes, occured more or less considerable parenchymatous degeneration and dissociation of cell-arrangements.

Generally with cloudy swelling, esp. at hemorrhagic places.
With remarkable fatty degeneration in 5 cases.

And I case (No. 407) is accompanied with so-called net-necrosis in peripheral zone of acinus.
These necrosis are formed at hemorrhagic places by cell-groups of some degenerated parenchymatous cells with net-likely clarified protoplasma or their decayed masses, accompanied with slight deposits of bile-pigments.

Occaisionally emigration of some lymphocytes or leucocytes as capillarycontents and furthermore formation of multiple miliary knots, caused by accumulation of wandering cells, esp. in the peripheral zone or intercalary portion of acinuses.

With remarkable increased wandering cells as capillary contents.	5 cases.
Slight pericapillary leucocytes-accumulation in peripheral zone of acinuses. (initial stage of miliary-knot-formation).	2 cases.
Multiple miliary knots.	5 cases.

[redacted] 171

[redacted]

[redacted]

Remarkably increased wandering cells in capillary-nets gathered to form pericapillar accumulation, esp. in the peripheral zone of acinuses.

And frequently These changes into multiple miliary necrosis, which are formed by some hemorrhagic masses, some leuco-or lymphocytes and some residual masses of decayed parenchymatous cells
and occaisionally spread moreover with hemorrhagic-exudative changes to the perifocal tissues.

With the lapse of time, in some rather proliferative cases (No. 26, 53, 410 and 417), these are accompanied with slightly increased histiocytic cells and frequently pseudo-tubulus-formations.

B) Glisson's capsule. :
Generally slight edema, 12 cases of them in more or less considerable degree and slight round-cell-infiltration, 3 of them in more or less severe degree.
Occaisionally slight diffuse hemorrhages.

[redacted] 172

[redacted]

CONFIDENTIAL

LIVER

		17	26	53	54	225	318	320	325	383	388	389	393	396
Cell Cord	Irregular Arrangement	÷	++÷	÷	+	++	+++	−	÷	++÷	÷	(+++)	++	+++
	Dissociation	−	+++÷	−	(+)	+++	+++	(÷)	÷	+++	÷	++	(+++)	+++
Liver Cells	Clouding	+÷	++	÷	+	++	+	÷	÷	+÷	(+)	+÷	++	++
	Atrophia	÷	(+++)	+	+	++	+÷	÷	÷	++	(+÷)	++	+÷	+++
	Hypertrophia	−	−	÷	−	−	−	−	−	−	−	÷	÷	−
	Fatty Degeneration: central	+	−	−	−	+	÷	÷	−	÷	÷	−	−	÷
	Fatty Degeneration: intermediary	(++)	−	−	−	+	÷	÷	−	÷	(÷)	−	−	÷
	Fatty Degeneration: peripheral	÷	−	−	−	÷	÷	÷	−	÷	÷	−	−	÷
	Brown Pigment	÷	+÷	÷	÷	+	+	÷	÷	÷	+	(÷)	÷	+
Blood Vessels	V. centralis: Dilatation	÷	++	÷	÷	−	÷	−	++	÷	+÷	÷	−	+÷
	V. centralis: Congestion	+	+++	÷	+	÷	++	+	+	÷	÷	+÷	+	÷
	Capillaries: Dilatation	(+)	++	(++)	+	+	÷	+	(++)	++	(++)	++	+÷	++
	Capillaries: Congestion	(+)	+++	÷	+÷	÷	+	+	÷	+	÷	(++÷)	(+÷)	÷
	Capillaries: Leucocytes	+	+	(+)	−	÷	+÷	÷	÷	÷	÷	÷	÷	+÷
	Capillaries: Lymphocytes	+	÷	+	÷	+	÷	÷	+	+÷	÷	+	+÷	÷
	Capillaries: Monocytes	÷	÷	−	÷	−	÷	÷	÷	÷	÷	÷	−	÷
	Edema	(+÷)	++	+÷	+÷	++	+	(+)	(++)	++	+	++	++	+++
	Hemorrhage	÷	++	÷	÷	÷	++	−	(÷)	++	÷	++÷	+	+
	Kupffer's Cells: Proliferation	÷	÷	÷	−	÷	−	+÷	÷	÷	−	÷	÷	−
	Kupffer's Cells: Swelling	+	÷	÷	÷	−	−	÷	÷	÷	÷	÷	÷	−
	Kupffer's Cells: Hemosiderin	−	−	−	−	−	−	(÷)	−	÷	−	−	÷	−
	Bacterium	−	+	−	−	−	−	−	−	÷	−	−	−	−
	Congestion of V. hepatica	++	+++	+	+÷	+	++÷	÷	+	+	+	++	++	÷
Glisson's Capsule	Production of Connective Tissue	−	÷	÷	−	−	−	−	−	−	÷	−	−	−
	Pseudobiliary Tract	−	+	÷	÷	−	−	−	−	−	−	−	−	−
	Edema	÷	÷	÷	+÷	÷	+	+	+	÷	+	+	+	+
	Hemorrhage	(÷)	÷	−	÷	−	÷	÷	÷	−	−	÷	÷	−
	Round Cell Infiltration	÷	++	++	÷	+	÷	÷	÷	(+)	÷	÷	++	÷
	Leucocyte Infiltration	−	−	−	−	−	−	−	−	−	−	−	−	−
	Congestion of A. hepatica	÷	÷	÷	÷	÷	÷	÷	÷	÷	÷	++	÷	+
	Congestion of V. pforte	++÷	+++	+	+÷	+÷	++÷	÷	+	++	+	++÷	++	+
Miliary Necrosis	Necrosis	|	−	÷	|	|	|	|	|	|	|	|	|	|
	Lymphocytes	|	+	÷	|	|	|	|	|	|	|	|	|	|
	Leucocytes	|	−	÷	|	|	|	|	|	|	|	|	|	|
	Histiocytic Cells	|	÷	÷	|	|	|	|	|	|	|	|	|	|
	Erythrocytes	|	+	−	|	|	|	|	|	|	|	|	|	|

CONFIDENTIAL 173

[redacted]

[redacted]

LIVER

			397	399	400	403	404	406	407	409	410	411	414	416	417
Cell Cord		Irregular Arrangement	+	(+)	∸	++	+++	(+++)	++	++	+	+	÷	++	(++)
		Dissociation	÷	(÷)	(∸)	++	+++	÷	++	(+++)	+	∸	∸	(++)	∸
Liver Cells		Clouding	++	(++)	++:	++	+:	+	++	+	÷	+:	+	+	++:
		Atrophia	+++	(++)	(÷)	++	+++:	(++)	(+++)	(++)	+	+	÷	+	++
		Hypertrophia	−	÷	−	÷	−	−	−	∸	÷	∸	−	∸	÷
	Fatty Degeneration	central	∸	−	+	−	−	−	−	∸	∸	∸	−	−	−
		intermediary	∸	−	÷	−	−	−	−	∸	∸	∸	−	−	−
		peripheral	∸	−	÷	−	−	−	−	∸	+	÷	−	−	−
		Brown Pigment	+	∸	÷	÷	++	÷	+	∸	+:	+	÷	∸	+
Blood Vessels	V. centralis	Dilatation	++	÷	÷	+	÷:	−	÷	+	+	∸	∸	∸	÷
		Congestion	∸	++	+:	+	|	÷	∸	+	++	÷	÷	÷	++
	Capillaries	Dilatation	++	+	+	++:	+	+:	++	(+++)	+	+	(+:)	+:	(++:)
		Congestion	+	++	÷	++:	|	++	+	÷	(++)	++	÷	++	++:
		Leucocytes	+	+:	+:	++:	÷	∸	+	+	∸	∸	÷	∸	+
		Lymphocytes	÷	+	÷	∸	÷	+	+	÷	+	÷	÷	∸	÷
		Monocytes	∸	∸	∸	∸	∸	÷	∸	∸	∸	∸	∸	∸	−
		Edema	++	+	++	++:	+++	+	++	+	(+)	+	++:	+:	+:
		Hemorrhage	+	(++)	∸	−	|	÷	÷	∸	++	÷	÷	÷	÷
	Kupffer's Cells	Proliferation	−	÷	(∸)	÷	−	÷	∸	÷	÷	÷	∸	∸	−
		Swelling	−	÷	−	−	−	÷	÷	÷	+	+	−	+	∸
		Hemosiderin	−	∸	(+)	−	∸	−	∸	−	−	−	−	−	∸
		Bacterium	−	∸	÷	+	−	−	−	÷	−	−	−	−	−
		Congestion of V. hepatica	+	+:	++	+	|	+	+:	+	+	+	|	++	+:
Glisson's Capsule		Production of Connectiv Tissue	(∸)	−	−	−	−	−	−	−	−	−	−	−	−
		Pseudobiliary Tract	−	−	−	−	−	−	−	−	∸	−	−	−	−
		Edema	+	÷	+:	+	+	+	÷	÷	÷	÷	+:	+	(÷)
		Hemorrhage	÷	−	(÷)	÷	+:	−	−	−	∸	∸	−	∸	−
		Round Cell Infiltration	∸	(+)	÷	∸	÷	∸	÷	∸	+	÷	(+)	∸	∸
		Leucocyte Infiltration	−	−	−	−	−	−	−	−	−	−	∸	−	−
		Congestion of A. hepatica	∸	÷	+	∸	|	−	÷	∸	∸	÷	|	÷	∸
		Congestion of V. pforte	+	+:	++	+	|	+	+	+	+	+	|	++	+:
Miliary Necrosis		Necrosis	÷	|	|	|	|	|	|	|	|	|	|	|	÷
		Lymphocytes	÷	|	|	|	|	|	|	|	|	|	|	|	÷
		Leucocytes	−	|	|	|	|	|	|	|	|	|	|	|	÷
		Histiocytic Cells	∸	|	|	|	|	|	|	|	|	|	|	|	∸
		Erythrocytes	−	|	|	|	|	|	|	|	|	|	|	|	∸

[redacted] 174

[redacted]

[redacted]

Intense congestion and remarkable exudative reaction in Disse's spaces.

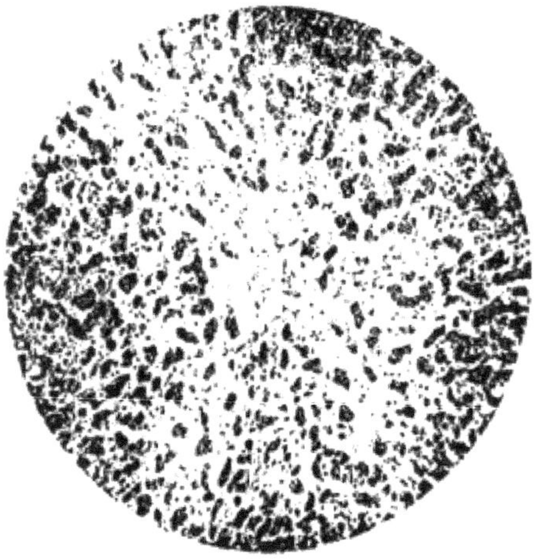

Intense congestion and some hemorrhages in the central zone of acinus.

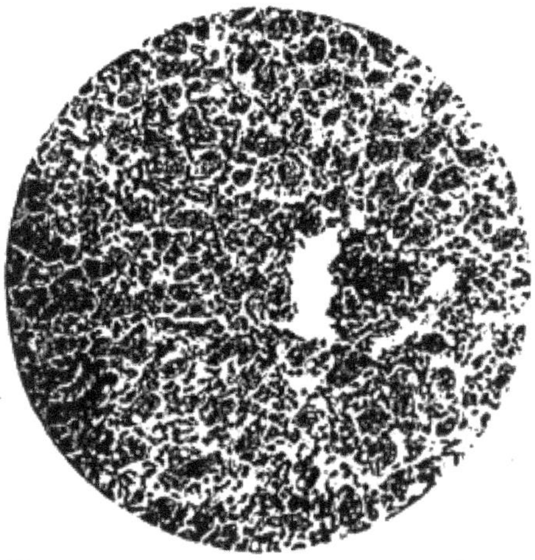

M419 X210

[redacted] 175

[redacted]

[redacted]

Hepatitis serosa with intense exudation in Disse's spaces and intanse parenchym. degeneration.

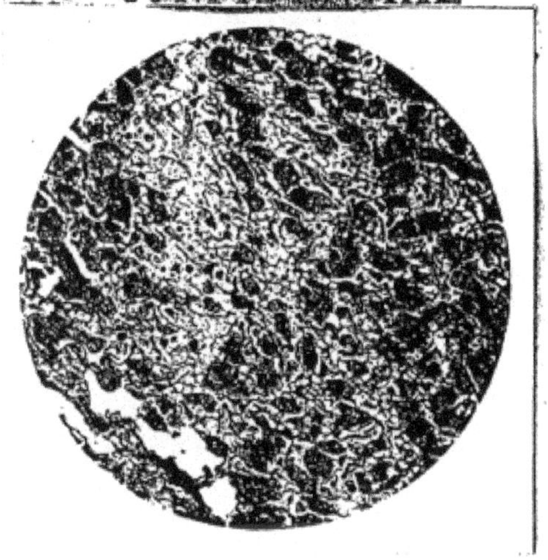

N 375 ×210

Hepatitis serosa with intense exudation in Disse's spaces and intense parenchymatous degeneration.

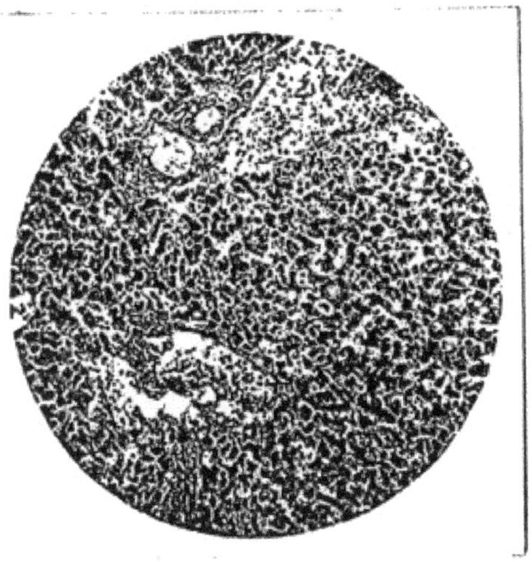

[redacted] 176

[redacted]

[redacted]

Hemorrhagic necrosis.

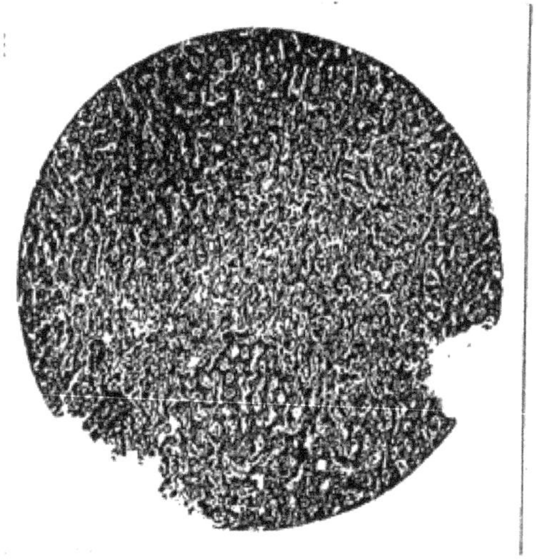

Hepatitis serosa in severe degree, in high power.

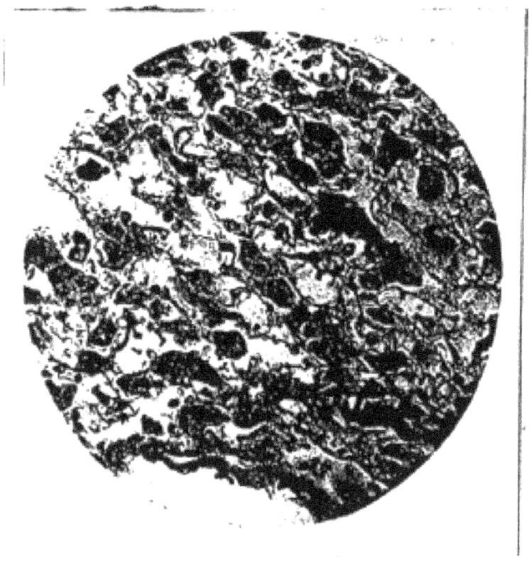

[redacted] 177

[redacted]

[redacted]

Our so-called net-like necrosis in acinus.

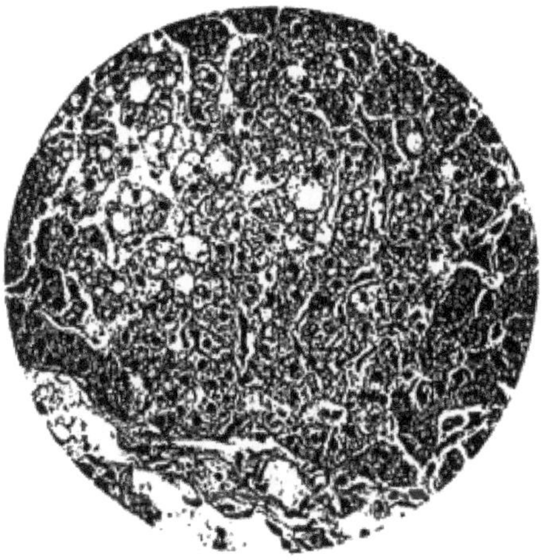

Our so-called net-like necrosis in acinus.

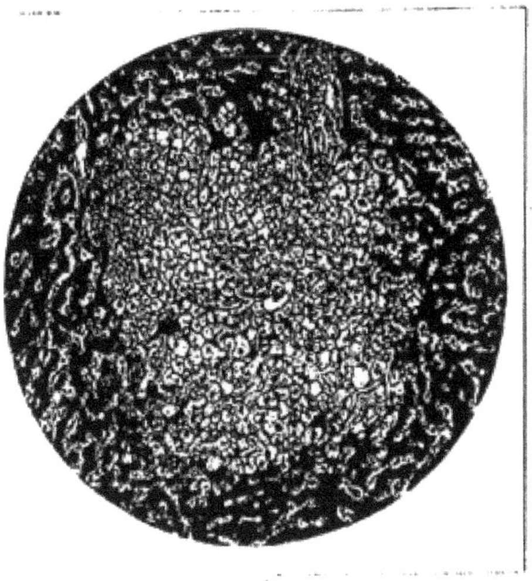

[redacted] 178

[redacted]

[redacted]

Diffuse wandering cells dissemination.

[redacted] 179

[redacted]

~~CONFIDENTIAL~~

Submiliary necrosis, with some lymphocytes accumulations.

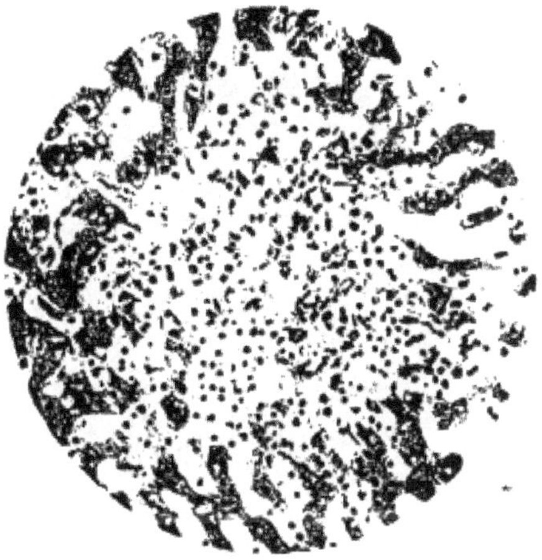

M 417 x220

Hepatitis serosaIII, with some exudative chagnes in Disse's spaces.

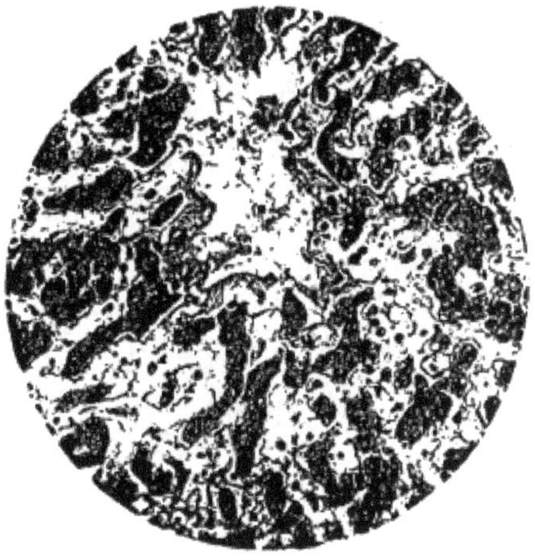

[redacted] M. 403 180 X240

[redacted]

[redacted]

Submiliary knot.

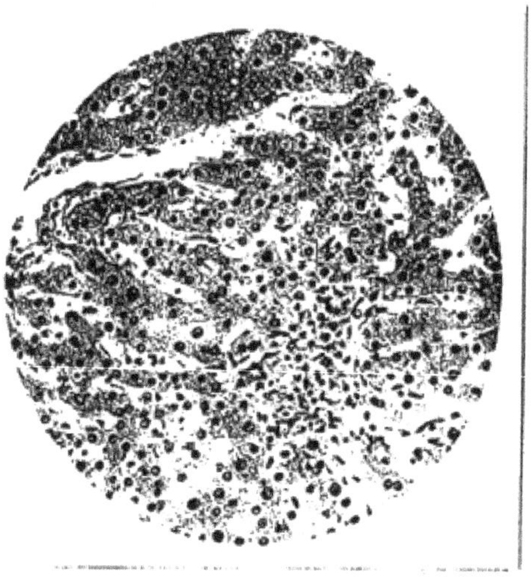

58 [illegible]

Submiliary knot.

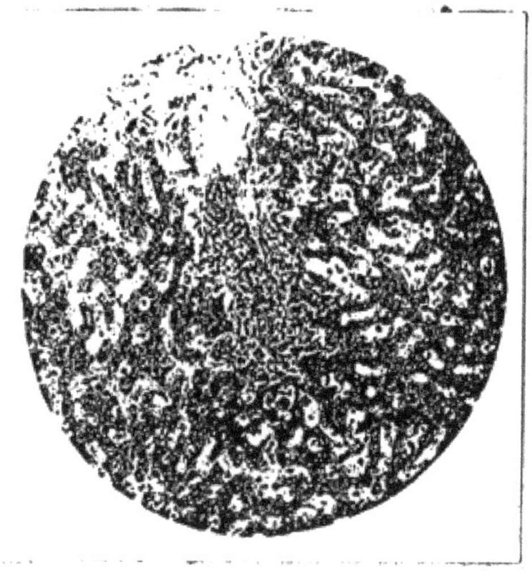

397 x 140

[redacted] 181

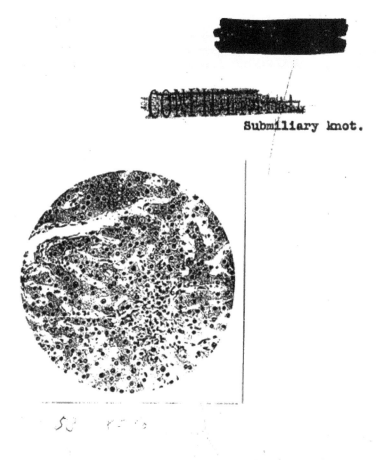

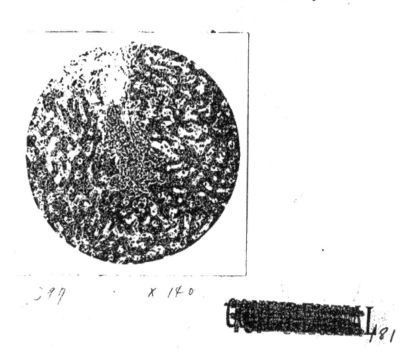

[redacted]

CONFIDENTIAL

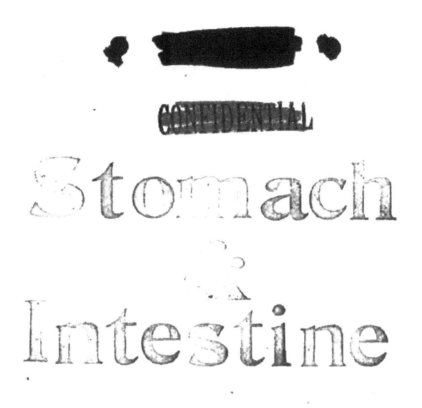

Stomach & Intestine

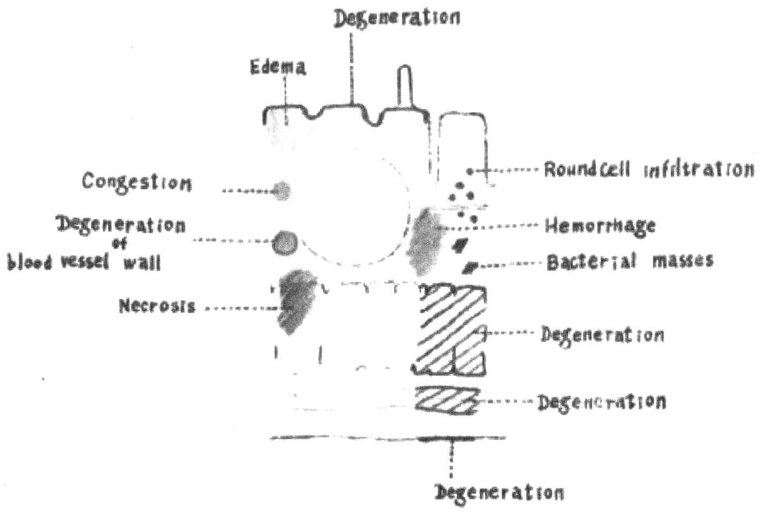

[redacted]

182

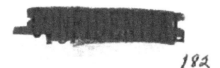

[redacted]

CONFIDENTIAL

STOMACH.

(A) Microscopical Investigation.

I7. Slight submucous hyperaemia and separation of decayed epitheliums cells.

54. Slight catarrh.

225. Considerable stasis in T. propria and T. submucosa.

318. Slight catarrh of mucous membrane and considerable congestion in T. submucosa.

320. Slight catarrh and considerable congestion in T. propria and T.submucosa.

390. Gastritis catarrhalis hypertrophicans levis.

396. Slight edema of mucous membrane.

397. Slight edema and slight stasis in T. propria.

399. Almost normal.

400. Considerable catarrh.

40I. Slight catarrh.

403. No remarkable changes.

406. No remarkable changes.

409. Slight stasis in T. propria.

410. Slight stasis and slight catarrh of mucous membrane and considerable stasis of T. submucosa.

4I2. Slight catarrh of mucous membrane.

4I3. Slight catarrh and slight hyperplasia of mucous membrane and

[redacted]

183

[redacted]

CONFIDENTIAL

4I4. No remarkable changes.

4I7. Slight edema and considerable stasis of mucous membrane and slight stasis of submucosa.

(B) SUMMARY.

Generally without any significant changes in all cases.

All observed 19 cases.

with slight catarrh, perhaps due to peroral infection. 10 cases.

with slight congestion. 5 cases.

with considerable congestion. 14 cases.

with no remarkable changes. 3 cases.

with rather atrophic glandular cells. 0 cases.

[redacted] 184

[redacted]

CONFIDENTIAL

M 17

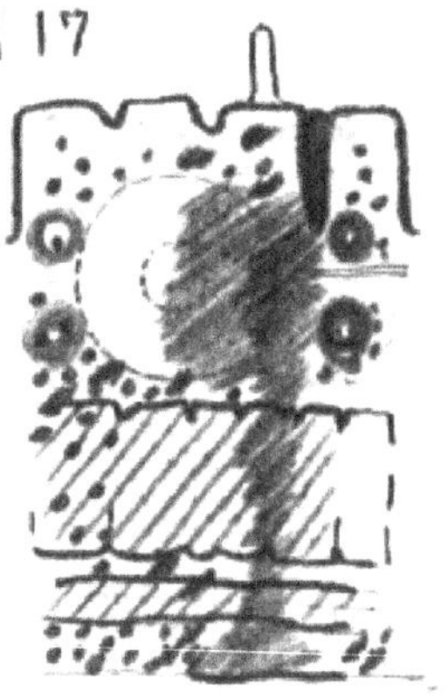

M.20

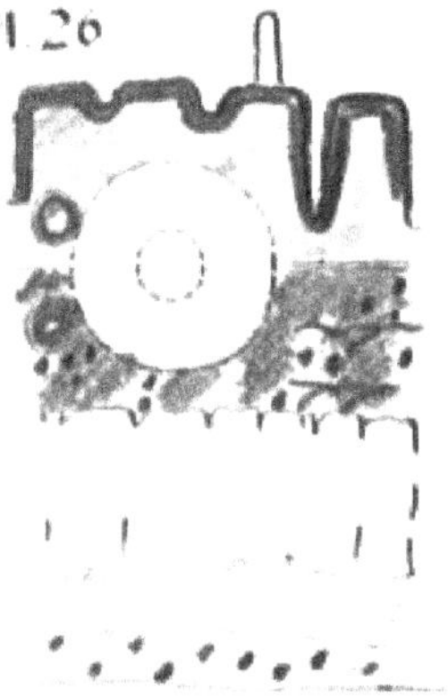

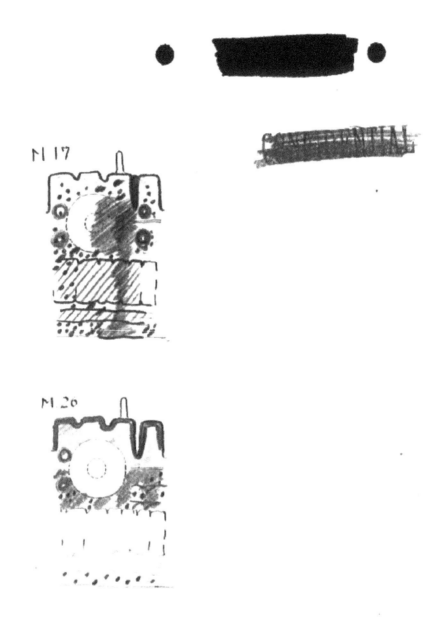

CONFIDENTIAL

[redacted]

[redacted]

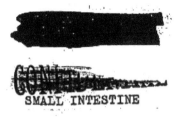

SMALL INTESTINE

(A) Microscopical Investigation.

I7.

Extraordinary severe marrowy swelling of mucous membrane with the severest perifocal haemorrhagic exudative reactions.

In the areas of swelling exist the severest edematous swelling, severest congestion (bacterial masses in blood-vessel and severe edematous swelling of capillary-walls), more or less remarkable hemorrhages and numerous leucocytes-emigrations. Glandular cells at these parts fall into decayed masses or disappeared totally, and at the surfaces of these parts exist in a large quantitiy of separated masses of desquamated epithelial cells, bacterial masses, leucocytes-fragments and exudative-hemorrahgic masses.

These leucocytic-hemorrhagic inflammations propagate themselves all over the neighbouring tissues (T. submucosa and perifocal mucous tissues) with severe exudative-hemorrhagic processes.

Perifocal mucous membrane in severe edematous swelling, severe congestion and more or less remarkable hemorrhages with severe catarrhalic masses.

T. submucosa in diffuse edematous swelling in high degree, severe congestion (bacterial masses in blood-vessels) and perivascular leucocytes infiltrations.

(53.)

Catarrh in medium degree and stasis of mucous membrane and considerable congestion of T. submucosa.

[redacted] 786

[redacted]

225. [redacted]

Slight catarrh and slight edema in mucous membrane.

318.

More or less remarkable diffuse hemorrhages in T. submucosa in extremely severe degree and these hemorrhagic processes propagate themselves to T. propria.

More or less remarkable diffuse hemorrhages and considerable leucocytes-infiltration with some bacterial masses in capillaries of T. submucosa. These hemorrahgic exudative changes spread to neighbouring mucous membrane, which fall into severe congestion and diffuse hemorrhages with atrophic glandular cells.

320.

Main Pathological changes exist in T. submucosa and serous membrane.

In T. submucosa: Considerable congestion and diffuse hemorrhages in extremely high degree. These hemorrhagic and exudative processes propagated themselves to serous membrane.

Serous membrane swelled extremely edematously with severe congestion with more or less remarkable hemorrhages and at other hands some proliferative reactions with some histiocytes, plasma cells, fibroplasts and fibrocytes. Namely, Serositis haemorrhagico-suprativa.

328.

Main pathological changes exist in T. submucosa.

T. submucosa swelled extremely edematously with severe congestion, severe diffuse hemorrhages, severe leucocytes emigration and bacterial

[redacted] 187

[redacted]

[redacted]

disseminations. These exudative-hemorhagic processes propagated themselves to the adjacent mucous membrane with severe congestion, severe hemorrhages and slight plasma cell-infiltration and to serous membrane with congestion, diffuse hemorrhages in high degree with hemorragic-fibrinous masses and slight plasma cell infiltrations.

388.

Atrophic mucous membrane with hyperplasia of Peyer's lymphnodulus (congenital) and slight congestion. No remarkable changes else.

390.

Catarrh in medium degree (separation of decayed desquamated epithelial cells and catarrahlic masses), slight congestion and no remarkable changes else.

393.

Atrophic mucous membranes and congenital hyperplasia of Peyer's lymphnodulus, considerable congestion in T. submucosa and no remarkable changes else.

396.

Atrophic mucous membrane and no remarkable changes else.

399.

Atrophic mucous membrane and no remarkable changes else.

40I.

Slight catarrh and congenital hyperplasia of Peyer's lymphnodulus. Slight congestion in T. submucosa and no remarkable changes else.

[redacted] 188

[redacted]

[redacted]

403.

Atrophic mucous membrane and congenital hyperplasia of Peyer's lymphnodulus. Slight congestion in T. submucosa and no remarkable changes else.

407.

Duodenal parts.

Main pathological changes exist in T. propria and T. submucosa.

T. propria swelled extremely hemorrhagic-edematously with severe congestion, severe diffuse hemorrhages with some bacterial masses in capillaries and considerable leucocytes infiltrations.

Atrophic glandular cells and separation of fibrinous-hemorrhagic masses on the surfaces of mucous membrane.

T. submucosa in severe congestion and diffuse hemorrhages. These hemorrhagic and exudative inflammatory processes propagate themselves to adjacent serous membranes with severe congestion, edematous swelling and considerable leucocytes infiltrations.

409.

Duodenal parts.

Catarrh in medeium degree, slight edematous swelling and congestion in T. submucosa.

4IO.

Slight catarrh, atrophic mucous membrane and slight congenital hyperplasia of Peyre's lymphnodulus. No remarkable changes else.

4II. Duodenal parts.

Considerable congestion and edematous swelling of mucous membrane.

[redacted] 189

[redacted]

Slight catarrh with some desquamative epithelial cells. Congestion of T. submucosa in high degree. [redacted]

4II.

At some places extremely severe fungous swelling of mucous membrane. The most parts of them falled into hemorrhagic-necrotic inflammatory changes with severe congestion, some vessels in Endophlebitis necroticans, severe diffuse hemorrhages with edematous swelling, fibrinous separations and more or less considerable leucocytes infiltrations. At the adjacent parts, the glandular cells and others fall into bionecrosis or severe degeneration with decayed masses of desquamated cells and some bacterial masses on the surfaces of mucous membrane. These inflammatory processes spread to neighbouring tissues with more or less remarkable hemorrhages and leucocytes-infiltration.

4I2.

Catarrh in medium degree with numerous desquamated epithelial cells and catarrhalic masses. Slight congestion in T. submucosa and no remarkable changes else.

4I3.

Catarrh in medium degree with numerous desquamated epithelial cells and catarrhalic masses. Slight congestion in T. submucosa and no remarkable changes else.

4I6.

Considerable congestion and catarrh in medium degree with slight atrophic glandular cells. Considerable congestion of T. submucosa and no remarkable changes else.

[redacted] 190

[redacted]

CONFIDENTIAL

417.

Catarrh and edematous swelling in T. propria in medium degree. Congenital hyperplasia of Peyer's lymphnodulus and no remarkable changes else.

T. submucosa at adjacent parts are attacked with some inflammatory reactions (edematous swelling, fibrinous separation, slight hemorrhages and perivascular leucocytes-infiltrations).

CONFIDENTIAL

191

[redacted]

[redacted] (B) S U M M A R Y .

I divide all cases into 2 groups: a) group of peroral infection and b) group of pernasal infection.

A) Cases in peroral infection with some large quantity of bacterial All patients died difenitely a few days after infection with severe intestinal symptoms.

In abdominal spaces, abandon (ca. I liter) hemorrhagic-serous ascites with extremly, severe edematous-gallertic swelling of mesenterial fatty tissues and severe hemorrhagic serous inflammation of serous membrane of intestine (mainly at lower parts of ileum or ileocoecal part and sometimes scattered at duodenal, jejunal or upper parts of ileum). Extraordinary severe microscopical changes can be appreciated repre-sentively in No. I7-case, with severe hemorrhagic-leucocytic changes all over the all layers of intestinal walls: fungous or marrowy swelling of mucous membrane, which fall into extremly severe hemorrha-gic-leucocytic changes with some ruined capillary-plexus: .) Primary affection of capillary-plexus in mucous tissues (esp. in lymphatic nodulus).

.) Then the intense and diffuse hemorrhagic-leucocytic infil-trations at perivascular tissues, are accompanied with fungous or marrowy swelling of mucous tissues.

.) These severe hemorrhagic-leucocytic inflammation propagate themselves to neighbouring perifocal mucous tissues and hematogenou-sly (some bacterial masses in blood-vessels) all over the all layers

[redacted] 192

[redacted]

[redacted]

of intestinal walls (T. submucosa and T. serosa).

Serous membrane swelled also extraordinary edematously with severe congestion and more or less remarkable hemorrhages and at sometimes slightly increased some histiocytic cells.

Some hemorrhagic-fibrinous masses on the surfaces of serous membranes.

. The some changes of duodenal parts are described in chapter A).

B). Cases in pernasal infection:

At these occasions, a smaller quantity of Anthrax-B can ride into alimentary canals and sometimes cause severe hemorrhagic-leucocytic changes in duodenal or ileocoecal parts, so as above mentioned in A).

.) Representive records of duodenal changes in No. 407-case.

Extraordinary severe hemorrhagic-edematous swelling of mucous tissues with severe congestion, necrotic ruins of capillary walls with some bacterial masses in capillaries and more or less remarkable leucocytes-emigrations. Separation of some hemorrhagicfibrinous masses on the surfaces of mucous tissues.

These inflammatory processes propagated themselves furthermore to the neighbouring tissues (T. submucosa and T. serosa) with severe perifocal hemorrhagic-leucocytic changes.

Serous membrane with severe congestion, severe edematous swelling and some leucocytes-disseminations.

oooo oooo oooo oooo oooo oooo

Frequency of pathological changes after pernasal infection:

[redacted] 193

[redacted]

[redacted]

Frequency of pathological changes after pernasal infection:

All microscopically observed 26 cases. (except No. 53)

with severe hemorrhagic-leucocytic infiltration. 2 cases.

with slight or considerable congestion. 14 ~~15~~ cases.

with slight catarrh, due to other factors. 4 cases.

with no remarkable changes. 0 cases.

with rather atrophic glandular cells. 2 cases.

Note). I have judged, according to the investigation of the some remained microscopical slices, while I have not recieved all microscopical slices and adjacent macroscopical autopsy-records. Accordingly the hemorrhagic-leucocytic inflammations should be occured more frequently than these 3 case, so I think.

[redacted] 194

[redacted]

CONFIDENTIAL

M.17

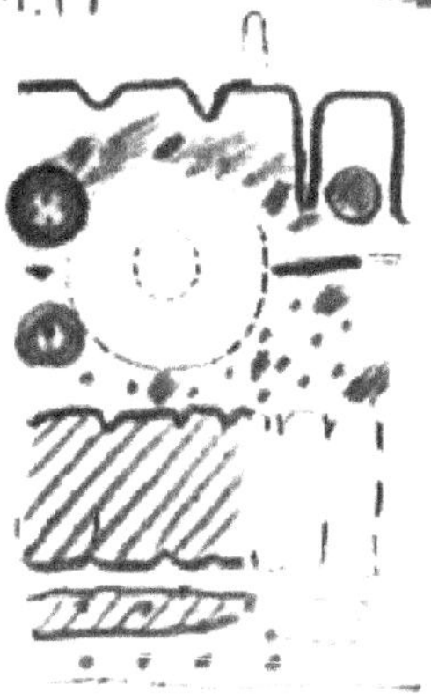

M 328

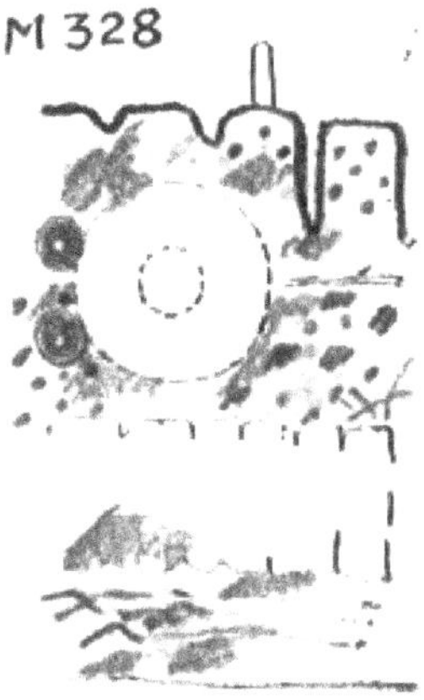

M.318

M.407

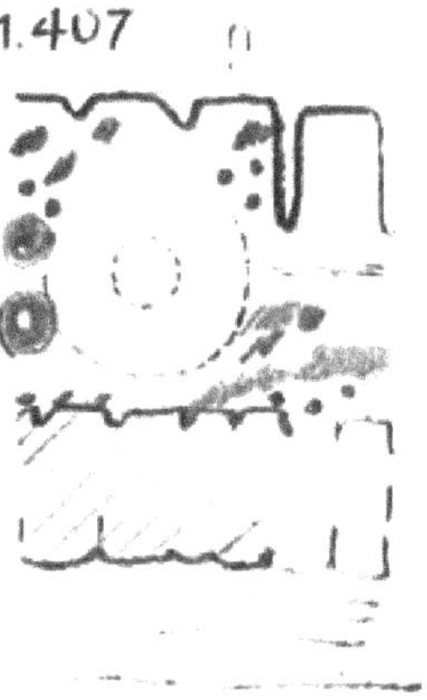

M.320

M.411

CONFIDENTIAL

195

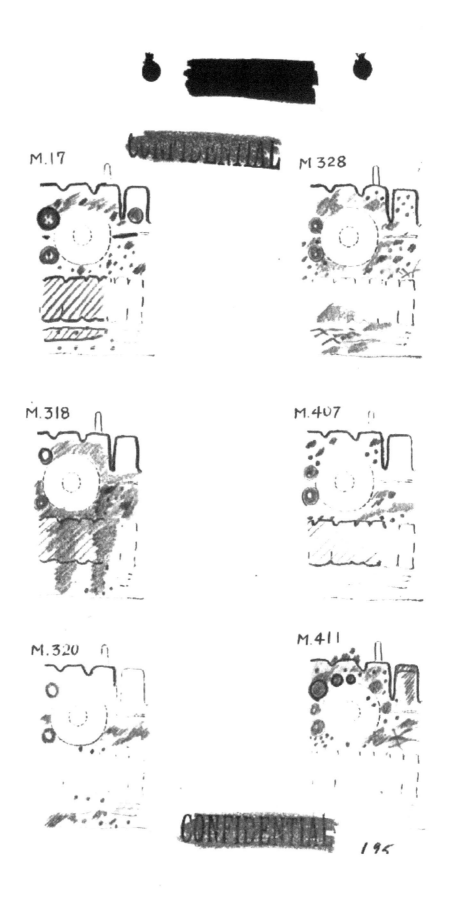

[redacted]

CONFIDENTIAL

Marrowy swelling of mucous membrane and intense congestion, diffuse hemorrhages and intense edema of mucous tissues.

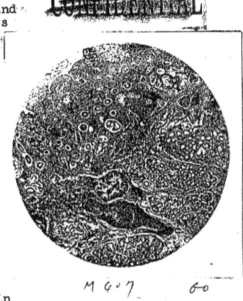

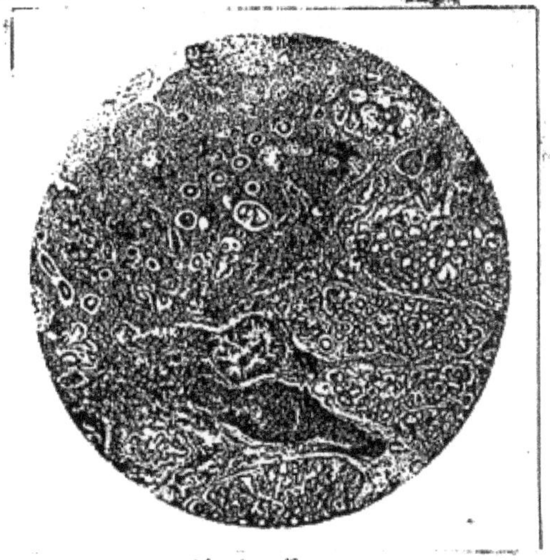

M 407 60

Marrowy swelling of mucous membrane in high power.
Diffuse hemorrhages and leucocytes-dissemination.

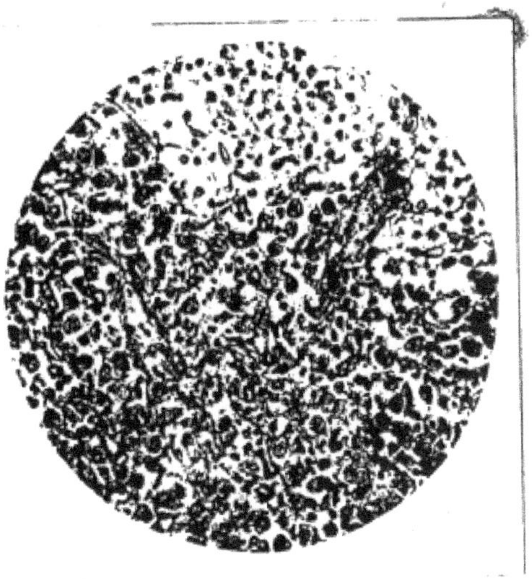

M. 17 270

[redacted]

196

[redacted]

Marrowy swelling of mucous membrane, accompanied with intense edema and diffuse leucocytes-dissemination in submucous tissues.

CONFIDENTIAL

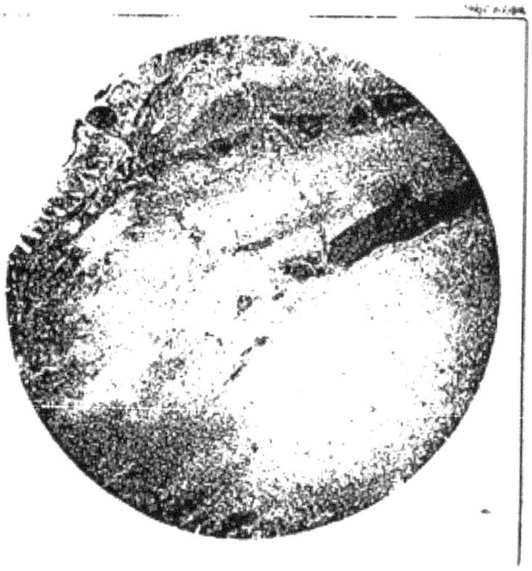

Intense ,diffuse leucocytes dissemination in submucous tissues, in high power.

M-328 ×20

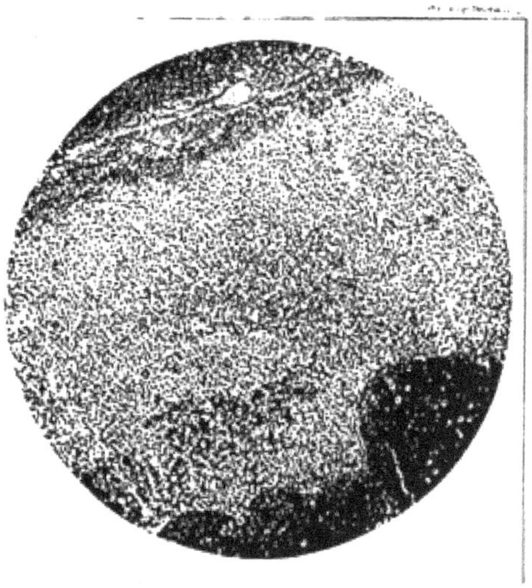

M-328 ×80

CONFIDENTIAL

197

[redacted]

Marrowy swelling of mucous membrane and diffuse hemorrhages.

[redacted]

M 318　　20.

Marrowy swelling of mucous membrane and intense hemorrhages(so-called blood-sea in mucous tissues).

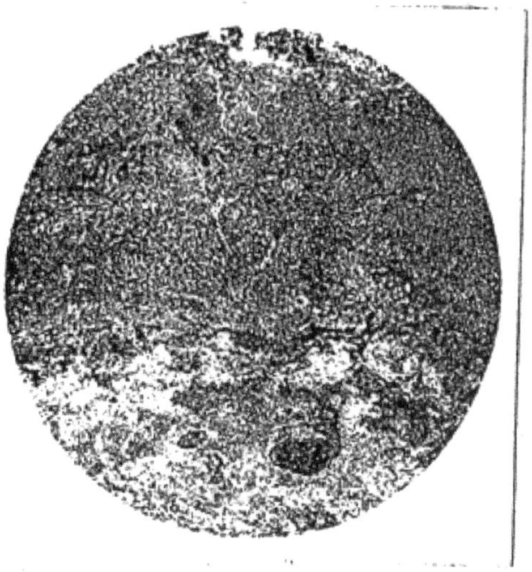

M. 17　　40

[redacted]

198

[redacted]

Fungous swelling of mucous membrane, [redacted]
accompanied with intense hemorrhagic
changes.
In low power.

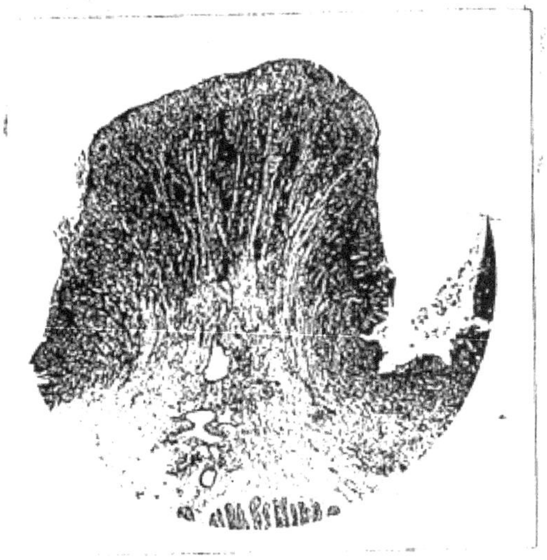

M 411 ×9

[redacted] 199

[redacted]

Intense hemorrhages and leuso-
cytes dissemination, in high power. [redacted]

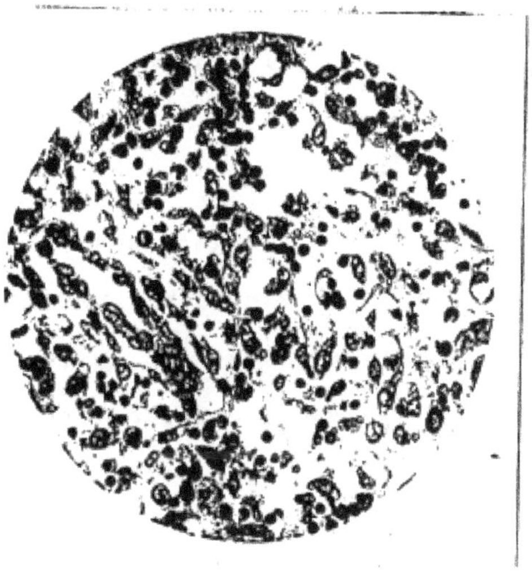

320 y 350

[redacted] 200

[redacted]

[redacted]

LARGE INTESTINE (M).

(A) Microscopical Investigation .

I7.

Main patholagical changes in T. submucosa.

In T. submucosa-:- venous plexus with intense Endophlebitis necroticans (the most intense congestion, a large quantity of leucocytes as contents and necrotic ruins of vessel-walls) and perivascular extraordinary intense exsudative-hemorrhagic-leucocytic reactions (edematous swelling, hemorrhages and leucocytes-infiltration in extremly high degree). These hemorrhagic-leucocytic processes propagated themselves all over the adjacent submucous tissues and furthermore to T. propria and serous membrane.

T. propria in edematous swelling and remarkable congestion with considerable leucocytes-emigration and bacterial disseminations in extraordinary high degree.

Some places with these hemorrhagic-leucocytic swelling falled into ruins and formed partial ulcers of mucous membrane in proceeding stage.

Serous membrane in severe inflammatory edema with considerable leucocytes-emigrations.

26.

Main pathological findings exist in T.submucosa.

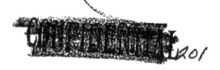

[redacted] 201

[redacted]

[redacted]

In T. submucosa : extraordinary intense congestion with intense exsudative-hemorrhagic processes: edematous swelling, diffuse hemorrhage, separation of fibrinous masses in extraordinary high degree with more or less considerable leucocytes-emigrations all over the submucous layers. These inflammatory procesesses propagated themselves to T. propria and serous membrane.

In T. propria : Considerable edema and congestion with atrophic, degenerative glandular cells.

(53.)

Considerable edematous swelling and congestion of mucous membrane. Slight atrophic glandular cells. Considerable congestion in T. submucosa.

54. Almost normal.

225.

Catarrh in medium degree. No remarkable changes else.

318.

Considerable catarrh and no remarkable changes else.

320.

Catarrh in medium degree with some desquamated epitheliums. Slight congestion in T. submucosa. No remarkable changes else.

325.

Slight catarrh and considerable congestion in T. submucosa.

328.

Catarrh in medium degree with sěparative masses of desquamated epitheliums and serous catarrhalic masses. Considerable congestion in

[redacted] 202

[redacted]

CONFIDENTIAL

T. submucosa.

388.

Slight catarrh, slight swelling, slight hyperplasia of lymphatic nodulus in mucous membrane.

Slight congestion in submucous tissues.

390.

Catarrh in medium degree, considerable congestion of mucous membrane with some separative masses and desquamated epithel. cells and catarrhalic masses. Slight congestion in T. submucosa.

396.

Almost normal, Slight catarrh.

397.

Catarrh in medium degree, considerable congestion of mucous membrane with some separative masses, desquamated epithel. cells and catarrhalic masses. Slight congestion in T. submucosa.

399.

Catarrh in medium degree with numerous separative masses of desquamated epithel. cells and catarrhalic masses. Considerable congestion in T. submucosa.

401.

Slight catarrh with desquamated epithel. cells and catarrhalic masses.

403.

Slight catarrh.

[redacted] 203

[redacted]

404.

Catarrh in medium degree [redacted]itheliums and catarrhalic masses, Considerable congestion in mucous [redacted]rane and T. submucosa. No remarkable changes else.

405.

Considerable congestion, slight perivascular leucocytes emigration and edematous swelling of T. submucosa.

Considerable congestion, edematous swelling and slight perivascular round -cell-accumulation in mucous membrane.

406.

Slight swelling and slight hyperplasia of lymphocytes in mucous membrame.

409.

Catarrh in medium degree with desquamated epithel cells and catarrhalic fluids. Slight congestion in T. submucosa and no remarkable changes else.

4I0.

Slight catarrh and slight congestion in T. submucosa.

4I2.

Slight catarrh with desquamated epithel. cells. Considerable congestion and slight edematous swelling of T. propria.

Considerable congestion, slight perivascular leucocytes-emigration and slight edematous swelling of T. submucosa.

4I4.

No significant changes.

4I6.

Slight congestion of T. submucosa.

[redacted] 204

[redacted]

[redacted]

(B) S U M M A R Y .

I devide all cases into 2 groups : a) group of peroral infection and b) group of pernasal infection.

A). Peroral infection with some large quantity of Anthrax-bac.
Peroral infection cause severe hemorrhagic-leucocytic inflammation of alimentary canals : at first in small intestines of all cases and furthermore in large intestines of some cases.
Representively the record of pathological changes in large intestine of No. 17-case:
Severe changes in mucous tissues with venous plexus, which fall into severe congestion and necrotic ruins of capillary-walls, accompanied with intense and propagating perivascular inflammatory changes.
These processes propagated themselves to the neighbouring tissues and all over the all layers of intestinal walls ; namely, Mucous tissues in the most severe hemorrhagic swelling and at some places partial superficial ulcers and
serous membrano in intense inflammatory edema with some leucocytes-disseminations.

oooooooo oooooooo oooooooo oooooooo

All microscopically investigated 8 cases.

[redacted] 205

[redacted]

[redacted]

with severe hemorrhagic-leucocytic infiltration.	4	cases.
with reactive considerable catarrh.	4	cases.
with reactive considerable congestion.	5	cases.
with no considerable changes.	3	cases.

I have found the same hemorrhagic-leucocytic inflammation in large intestines of some cases, so as above described in the chapter of small intestine.

B) Pernasal infection.

Even by pernasal infection with a small quantity, Anthrax-B can ride into alimentary canal occasionally and cause the hemorrhagic inflammation of small intestine in some cases. But, I can't the same hemmorrhagic changes of large intestine in the remained and preserved microscopical slices.

All microscopically investigated cases, 12 cases.

with considerable congestion.	6	cases.
with slight congestion.	4	cases.
with considerable catarrh.	2	cases.

(For example, in No. 405-case, considerable congestion with slight perivascular leucocytic [redacted] accumulations.)

[redacted] 206

[redacted]

[redacted]

with no considerable changes. 3 cases.

oooooooooooooooooooooooooooo oooooooooooooooooooooooooo

Riding of a large quantity of Anthrax-B into alimentary canals can acuse severe hemorrhagic-leucocytic inflammation in small intestine of all cases and also in large intestine of some cases of them.

By pernasal infection with a smaller quantity. can not cause intense hemorrhagic changes in large intestines.

But I can not investigate large intestines of some cases, which microscopical slices I have not received.

[redacted] 207

[redacted]

Diffuse hemorrhages and leucocytes dissemination in subserous tissues, in high power.

[redacted]

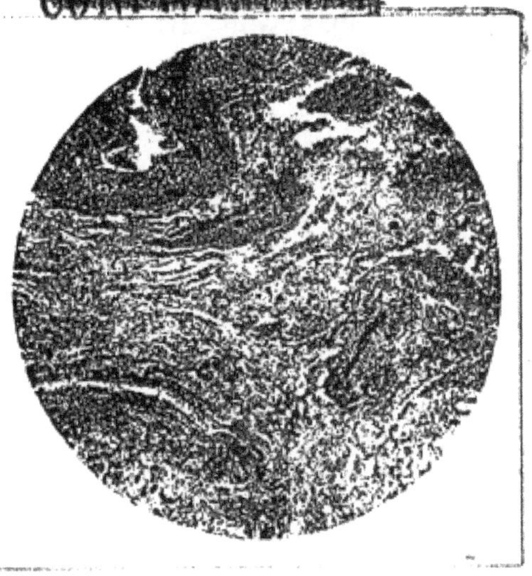

17 x 40

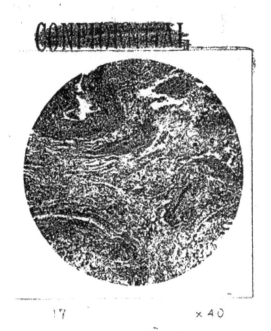

Diffuse hemorrhages in subserous tissues, in high power, accompanied with remarkable bacterial dissemination.

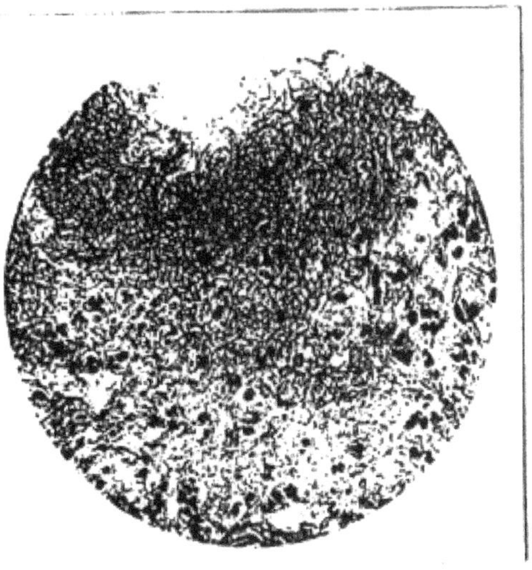

17 x 350

[redacted] 208

[redacted]

CONFIDENTIAL

Marrowy swelling of mucous membrane. Intense congestion, diffuse hemorrhages and intense edema.

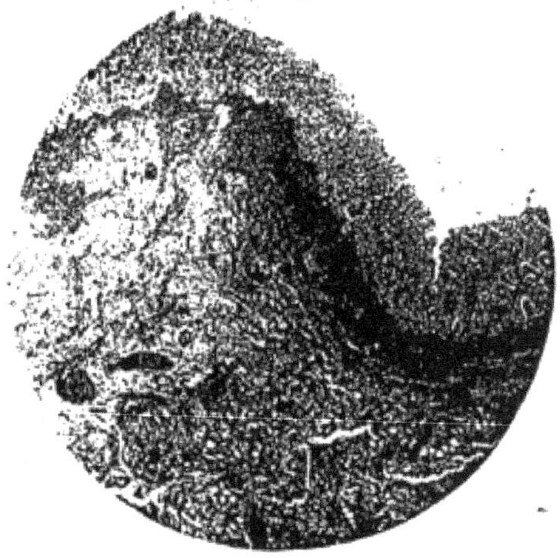

K.D M-26 30

Marrowy swelling of mucous membrane. Intense congestion, diffuse hemorrhages and intense edema.

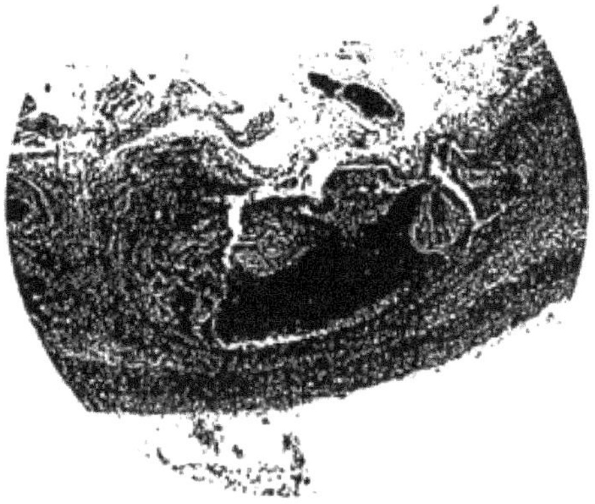

K.D. M-17 30

[redacted] 209

[redacted]

[redacted]

Diffuse hemorrhages and leucocytes dissemination in subserous tissues.

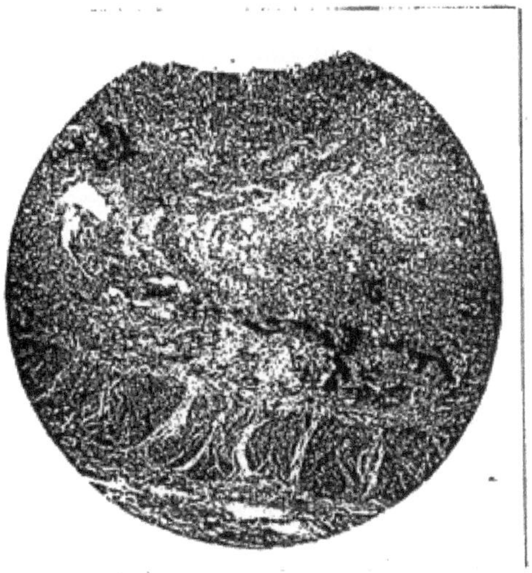

320 ×20

Endophlebitis necroticans and intense inflammatory changes of perivascular tissues.

×40

[redacted] 210

[redacted]

Marrowy swelling of mucous membrane.
Intese congestion, diffuse hemorrhages
and intense edema.

[redacted]

K.L M.26 20

Marrowy swelling of mucous membrane.
Intense congestion, diffuse hemorrhages
and intense edema.

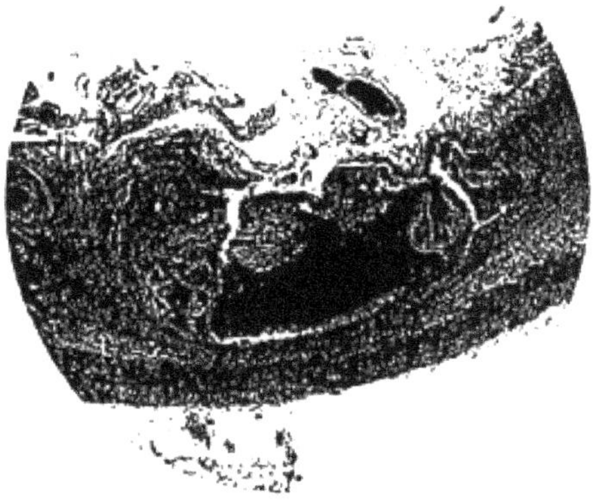

K.D. M.17. 20

[redacted] 211

[redacted]

Endophlebitis necroticans and intense inflammatory changes of perivascular tissues.

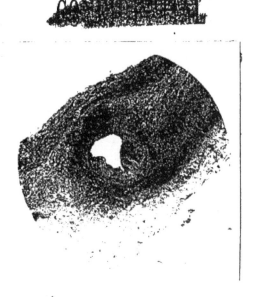

[redacted]

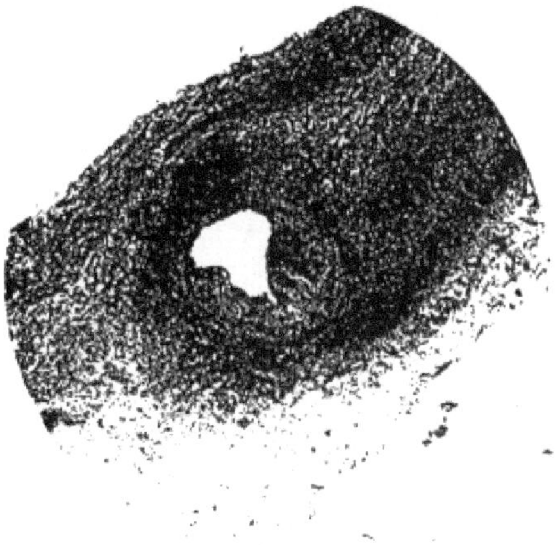

K-O.　M-17　x60

[redacted] · 212

[redacted]

[redacted]

Spleen

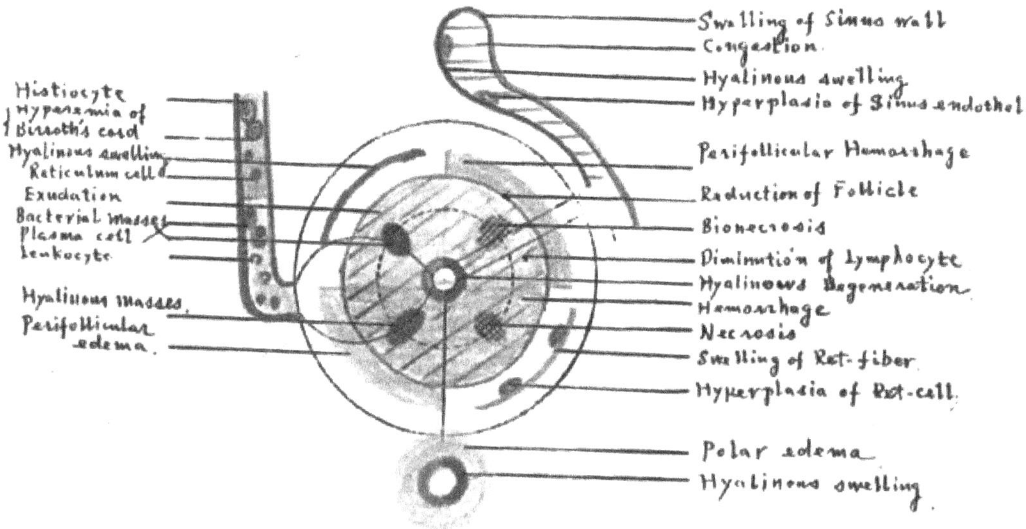
Histiocyte
Hyperaemia of Billroth's cord
Hyalinous swelling
Reticulum cell
Exudation
Bacterial masses
Plasma cell
Leukocyte
Hyalinous masses.
Perifollicular edema.
Swelling of Sinus wall
Congestion
Hyalinous swelling
Hyperplasia of Sinus endothel
Perifollicular Hemorrhage
Reduction of Follicle
Bionecrosis
Diminution of Lymphocyte
Hyalinous Degeneration
Hemorrhage
Necrosis
Swelling of Ret-fiber
Hyperplasia of Ret-cell.
Polar edema
Hyalinous swelling.

[redacted] 213

[redacted]

[redacted]

S P L E E N

17 (A) Microscopical Investigation.

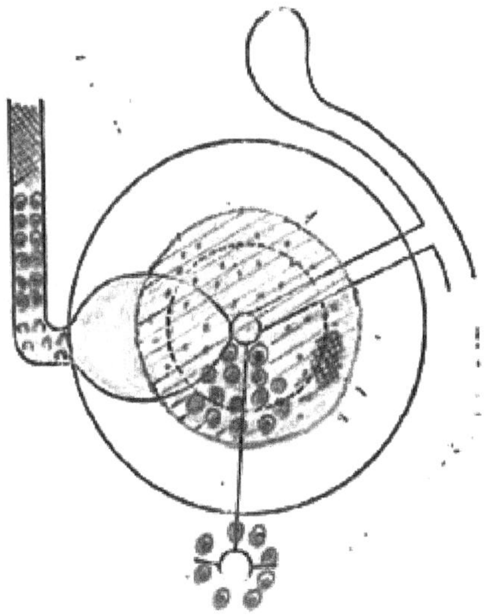

17.

Follicles: Diminution of follicles and hyalinous swelling of central arterie with more or less considerable perivascular edema, which caused edematous swelling of follicular tissues, slight hemorrhages, diminution of lymphocytes in follicular tissues and at some places subciliary exudative necrotic knots.

Beside these exudative changes, slight hypeer-plesia of histiocytes, esp.

at perivascular and our so-called polar portions.

Pulpa-meshes : Slight congestion in sinuses, slight edematous swelling of reticulum-fibres and more or less remarkable hyperplasia of histiocytes (or splenocytes) and endothelial cells of sinus-walls,

esp. with our so-called " polar proliferation" of histiocytes at polar portions of follicles.

Angio-folliculitis

Fasciculitis

26.

Follicles : Remarkable diminution of follicles

[redacted]

214

[redacted]

26

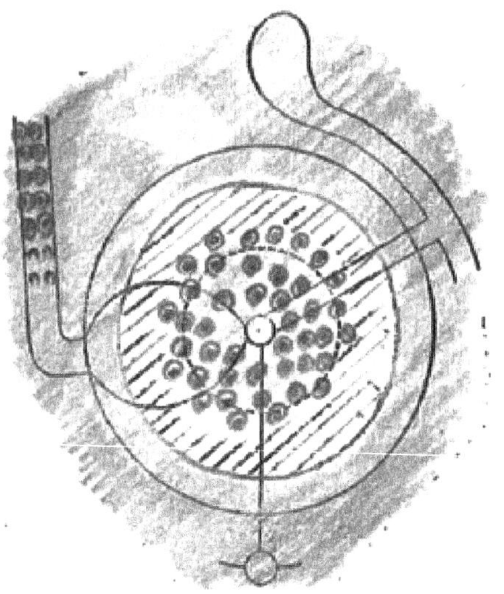

CONFIDENTIAL

and hyalinous swelling of walls of central arterie in high degree. Perivascular edema and edematous swelling of follicular tissues in high degree with considerable hemorrhages.

Beside these hemorrhagic-exudative changes, remarkable hyperplasia of histiocytes or macrophagens in follicular tissues.

Pulpa-meshes : Intense congestion and so-called blood-sea with intense swelling of reticulum-fibres.

Angio-folliculitis

Fasciculitis

225

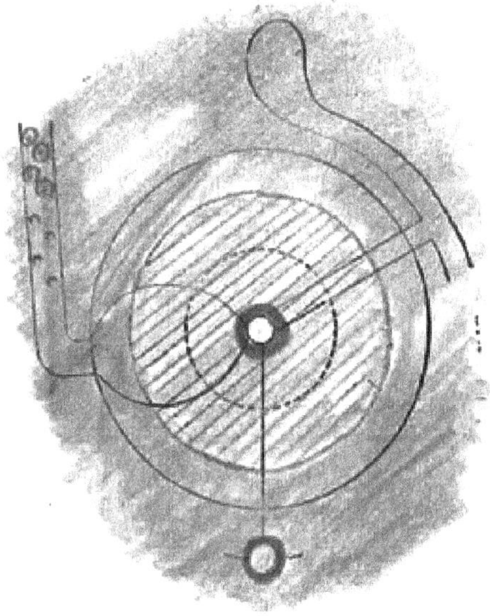

225. (a).

Folliceles : Slight diminution of follicles and hyalinous swelling of walls of central and penicillar arteries in more or less remarkable degree. Edematous swelling of follicular tissues with considerable diminution of follicular lymphocytes, severe exudation and slight hemorrhages in follicular tissues.

Slight hyperplasia of histiocytes with hemosiderin-phagocytosis.

Pulpa-meshes : Remarkable perifollicular hemorrhages and severe congestion in sinuses (so-called blood-sea) with edematous swelling

[redacted] 215

[redacted]

225

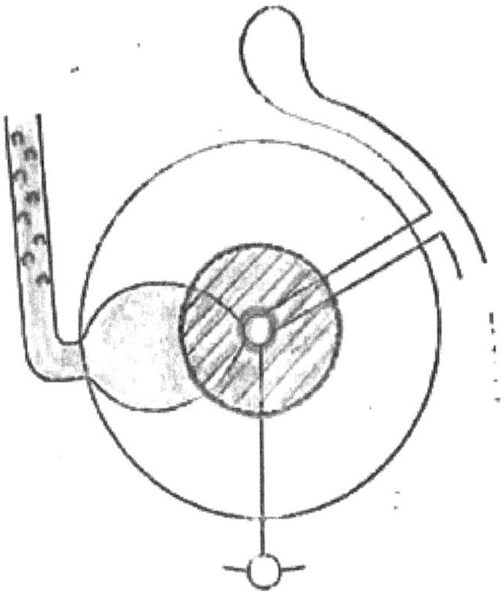

CONFIDENTIAL

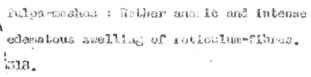

of reticulum-fibres in high degree.

Angio-folliculitis hemorrhagico-exsudativa

Fasciculitis hemorrhagico-exsudativa.

225. b.

Follicles : Intense diminution of follicles with intense edematous swelling of walls of central and penicilliar arteries. Severe perivascular edema with fibrinous separation and intense diminution of follicular lymphocytes and emigration of plenty of leucocytes. (plenty of leucocytes in follicular capillaries, some of them eosinophilic leucocytes or myelocytes).

Pulpa-meshes : Rather anemic and intense edematous swelling of reticulum-fibres.

318

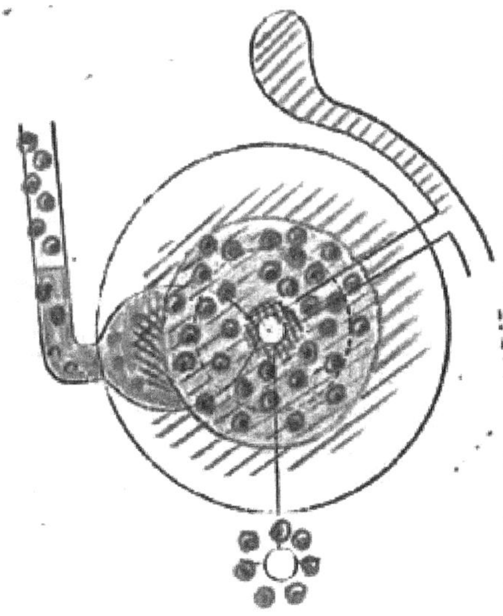

318.

Follicles : Intense diminution of follicles with severe edematous swelling of walls of central and penicilliar arterie and perivascular edematous swelling of follicular tissues, which caused some degenerative changes and on the other hand slight proliferative changes in germinative centres. Namely it occured in follicles, esp. at germinative centres some exudative

CONFIDENTIAL 216

[redacted]

CONFIDENTIAL

320

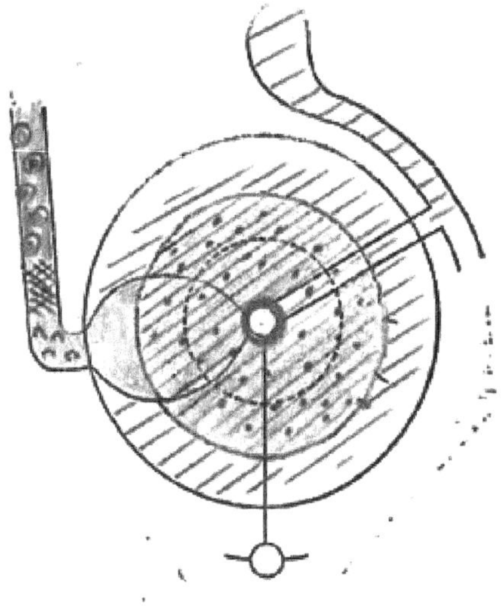

centres some exudative or degenerative changes (intense diminution of follicular lymphocytes, exudation in follicular tissues and decayed ruins of epitheloidial cells and their nuclear fragments) and other slight proliferative changes (considerable hyperplasia of histiocytes or macrophagens).

Pulpa-meshes : perifollicular hemorrhages and more or less considerable so-called blood-sea in pulpa-meshes with slight edematous swelling of reticulum-fibres and hemosiderin-deposits. More or less slight hyperplasia of histiocytes and endothel. cells of sinus-walls.

320.

Follicles: Intense diminution of follicles and hyalinous or edematous swelling of central and penicilliar arteries with intense exudative-hemorrhagic changes in follicular tissues (intense diminution of follicular lymphocytes, intense swelling of follicular tissues and more or less remarkable hemorrhages) and slight hyperplasia of histiocytes or macrophagens.

Pulpa-meshes : typical perifollicular hemorrhages and intense odematous swelling of reticulum-fibres, which are degenerated into structureless

CONFIDENTIAL 217

[redacted]

CONFIDENTIAL

fibrinous bionecrotic masses. Diminution of lymphocytes in pulpa-meshes.

393.

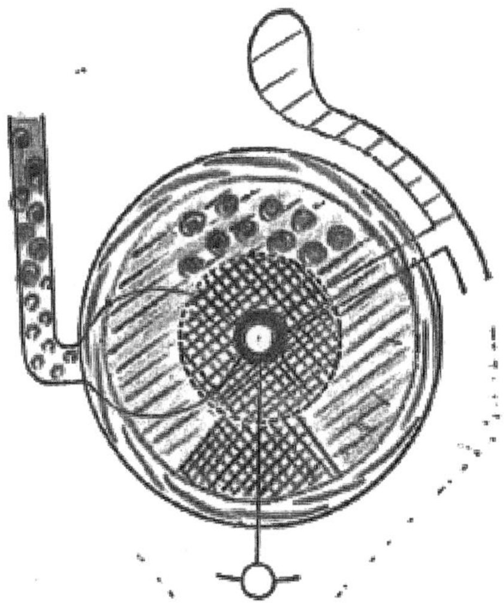

393.

Follicles : Intense diminution of follicles, which are in intense hemorrhagic and necortic processes : severe disturbances of walls of central and penicillier arteries with intense perivascular reactions (necrotic changes in germinative centres:severe edema, severe diffuse hemorrhages, leucocytes-emigrations and accumulations of decayed cellular masses or nuclear fragments).

Beside these degenerative changes, it shows some proliferative changes : slight or more or less considerable hyperplasia of histiocytic cells, which fell into intense cloudy swelling. These bionecrotic follicles are bounded with slightly increased and edematously swollen bundles of perifollicular reticulum-fibres.

Pulpa-meshes : More or less considerable congestion in sinuses and haemosiderin-deposits with edematously swollen reticulum-fibres, and more or less slightly increased, but cloudy degenerated histocytic cells and some leucocytes

CONFIDENTIAL 218

[redacted]

CONFIDENTIAL

397

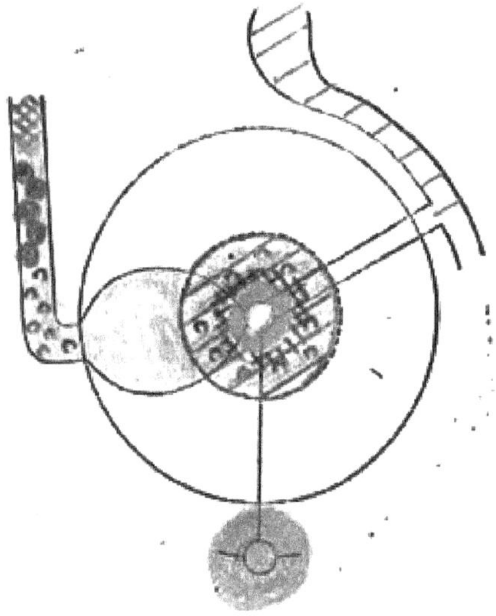

Remarkable diminution of lymphcytes in pulpa--meshes.

Angio-folliculitis

Spleno-fasciculitis

397. Follicles : intense diminution of follicles which are in intense exudative-necrotic changes: disturbances of blood-vessels, exudative-necrotic changes in germinative centres and slight hyperplasia of histiocytic cells.

Pulpa-meshes : also in degenerative-necrotic changes : severe edematous swelling, serous exudations, plenty of leucocytes-emigrations with eosinophilic cells, diminution of lymphocytes in severe degree and edematous swelling of reticular-fibres.

Angio-folliculitis

Spleno-fasciculitis

400

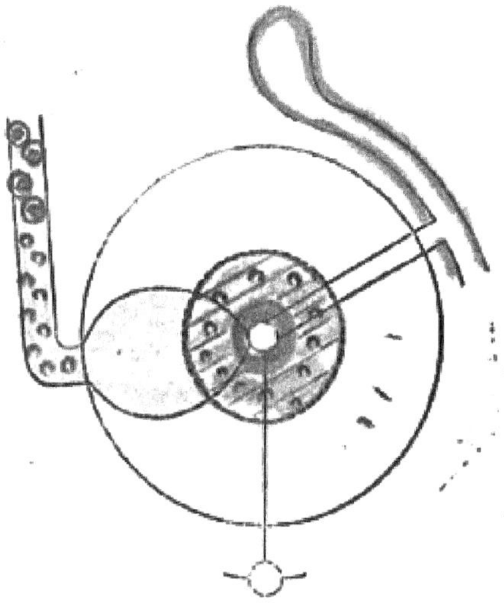

400

-Intense diminution of follicles. Follicles in intense exudative-necrotic changes : disturbances of walls of central and penicillier arteries, edematous swelling of perivascular tissues, intense diminutions of follicular lymphocytes etc.

Pulpa-meshes : also in intense exudative

[redacted] 219

[redacted]

CONFIDENTIAL

reaction: leucocytes-emigrations in high degree with eosinophilic leucocytes and myelocytes, intense edematous swelling of reticulumfibres which degenerate furthermore into structureless masses and more or less considerable congestion of sinuses with hemosiderin-deposits.
Angio-folliculitis
Spleno-fasciculitis.

403

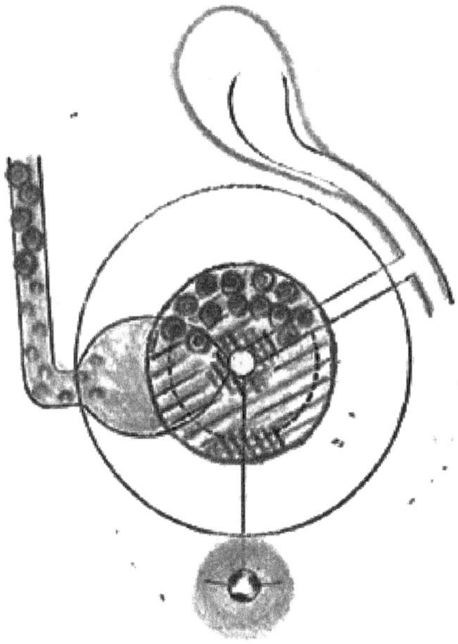

403.
Follicles : intenanse diminution and intense exudative changes of follicles:severe disturbances of central and penicilliar arteries, severe perivascular edema, bionecrotic processes in germinative centres, accumulation of decayed cellular masses and their nuclear fragments, leucocytes-emigrations and intense diminution of follicular lymphocytes.
Beside these degenerative reactions, more or les. remarkable hyperplasia of histiocytic cells which fall into considerable cloudy swelling.
pulpa-meshes : also in intense exudative changes:remarkable congestion, intense edematous swelling of reticulum-fibres and plenty of leucocytes-emigrations.

CONFIDENTIAL 220

[redacted]

[redacted]

Angio-folliculitis

Spleno-fasciculitis

404.

404

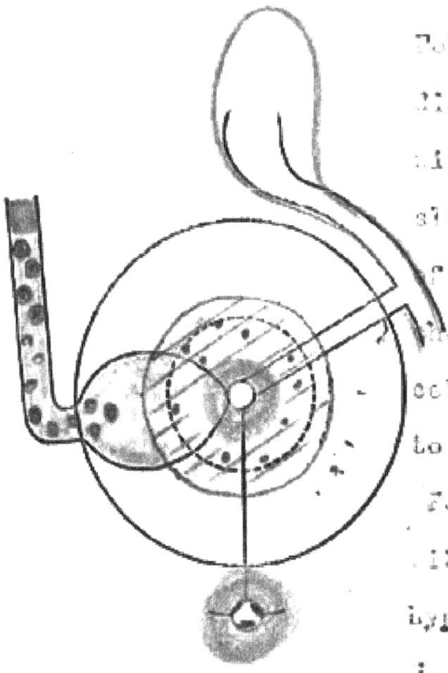

Follicles : Slight distention of follicles. [illegible] disturbances of central and penicillar arteries with perivascular exudative [illegible], slight diffuse haemorrhages and slight diminution of follicular lymphocytes. Beside these degenerative changes, it shows slight hyperplasia of histiocytic cells in germinative centres with a slight tendency to proliferation of perivascular fibres.

Pulpa-meshes : [illegible] congestion in sinuses with [illegible]. More or less slight hyperplasia of [illegible] histiocytic cells [illegible] in this case, shows it rather proliferative change, instead of acute [illegible] haemorrhagic or necrotic reactions.

Angio-folliculitis

Spleno-fasciculitis

405.

Follicles : slight distention of follicles with slight disturbances of central and penicillar arteries with [illegible] perivascular [illegible] changes, esp. in germinative centres, namely bionecrotic

~~TOP SECRET~~ CONFIDENTIAL 221

[redacted]

405

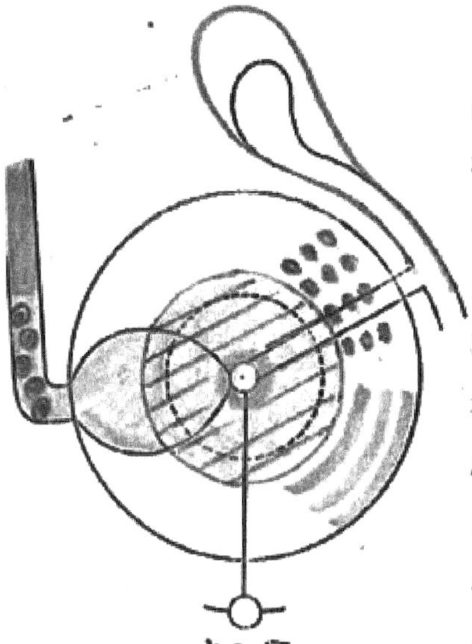

40 17

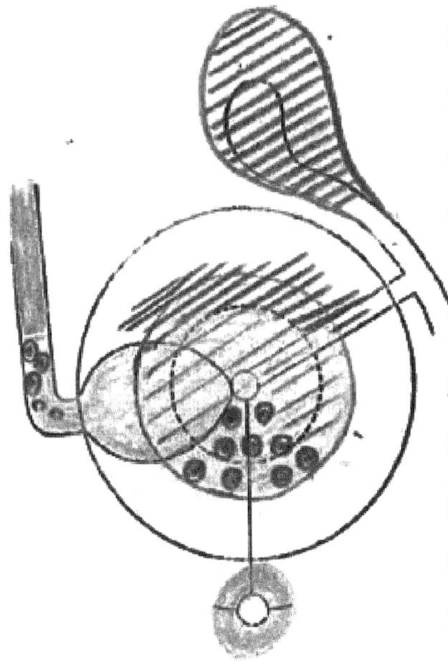

processes in germinative centres (some decayed masses of their nuclear fragments), slight edematous swelling of follicular tissues, with slight hyperplasia of histiocytic cells.

Pulpa-meshes : Considerable congestion in sinuses and hemosiderosis with some leucocytes-emigrations. Slight hyperplasia of reticulumfibres and histiocytic cells or endothelial cells of sinus-walls (some of them in erythrocytes-phagocytosis).

407.

Folicles:Remarkable diminution of follicles with more or less considerable hemorrhagic and exudative changes in germinative centres:disturbances of walls of central arteries. Perivascular edema, slight diffuse hemorrhages, slight diminution of follicular lymphocytes and cloudy swelling of follicular cells.

Beside these degenerative processes, remarkable hyperplasia of histiocytic cells in germinative centres.

Pulpa-meshes : In more or less considerable exudative changes:severe edematous swelling (e.g. our so-called [illegible]), [illegible] swelling of [illegible]-fibres, some leucocytes emigrations (containing eosinophilic

[redacted] 222

[redacted]

[redacted]

leucocytes and myelocytes) and slight hyperplasia
of histiocytic cells.

[illegible]-folliculitis

Splen[illegible]-[illegible]itis

409

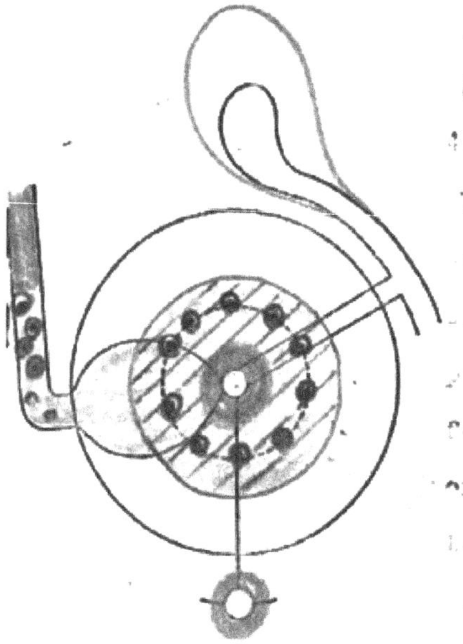

4[illegible].

Follicles : [illegible] follicles which [illegible] remarkable [illegible] changes : [illegible] swelling of follicular [illegible], slight [illegible] and more or less intense [illegible] of follicular lymphocytes.

[illegible] cells in germinative centres.

Pulpa-[illegible] : in remarkable exudative changes with anergic cellular reactions : intense oedematous swelling esp. [illegible] so-called polar [illegible], bacterial [illegible] in sinuses with some leucocytes-emigrations, without any [illegible] processes (no considerable hyperplastic [illegible] of histiocytic cells [illegible]).

4[illegible].

Follicles : intense [illegible] of follicles.

[redacted] 223

[redacted]

[redacted]

411

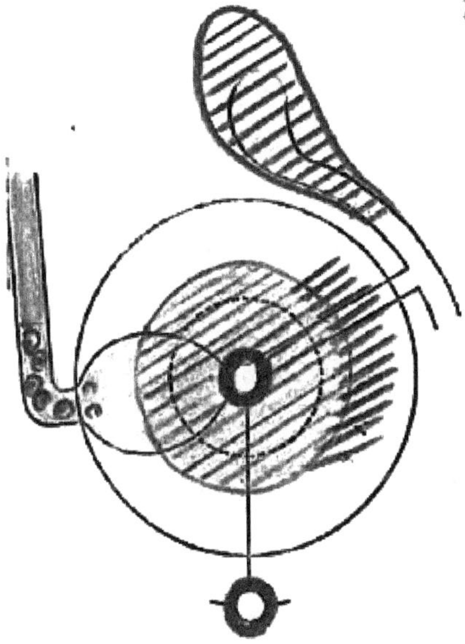

Hyalinous degeneration or hyalinous swelling of central arteries with slight perivascular edema, slight diffuse hemorrhages and a little leucocytes emigrations.

Intense diminution of follicular lymphocytes.

Pulpa-meshes : Intense perifollicular hemorrhages and so-called blood-sea with some leucocytes-emigrations Intense diminution of lymphocytes in pulpa-meshes. Without any remarkable proliferative reactions. Histiocytic cells are not increased and more or less degenerative.

[redacted] 224

[redacted]

[redacted]

18

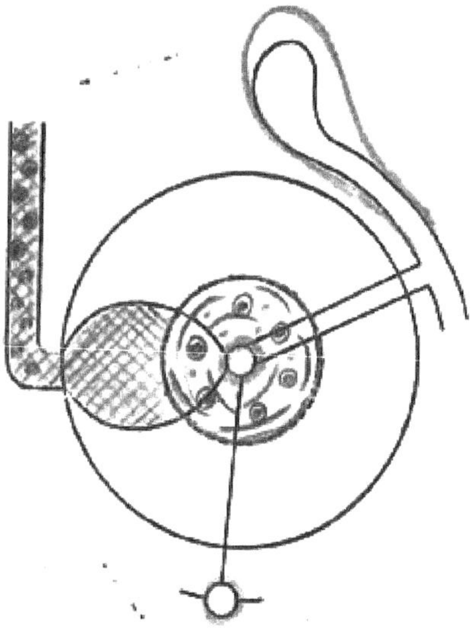

S P L E E N (S U P P L E M E N T).

18.

Extraordinary remarkable reduction of follicles and intense edematous swelling of central artery and penicillar artery-walls.

In follicles : intense roughness of basal fibres (intense edematous swelling), intense diminution of follicular lymphocytes, slight hemorrhages and slightly increased reticulum cells (some of them, in histiocytes-like form).

At polar portions : intense edematous swelling of penicillar artery-walls and considerable polar exudative changes (intense edema, congestion and some leakage of erythrocytes, in fascicular cords).

In sinuses : rather anemic and more or less remarkable swelling of reticulum-fibres with some leucocytes disseminations. Intensively degenerated reticulum-cells.

328.

Considerable reduction of follicles and intense hyalinous degeneration and somewhat edematous swelling of central and penicillar artery-wal[redacted]

[redacted] 225

[redacted]

328

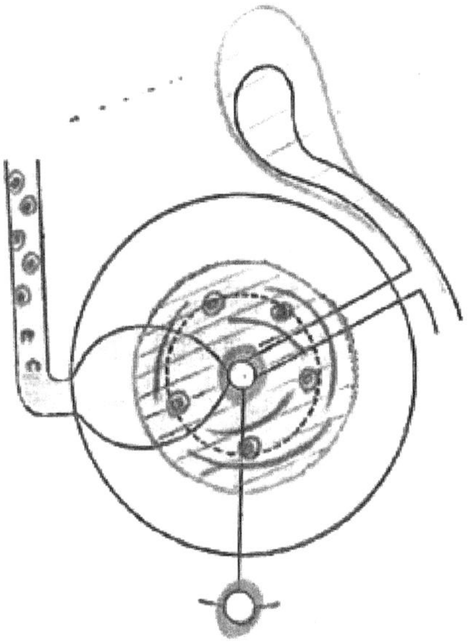

[redacted]

In follicles : slight swelling of basal fibres, deposits of some hyalinous masses, remarkable hyperplasia of reticulum-cells (some of them in histiocytes-like form), considerable hyerplasia of reticulum-fibres, esp. at perifollicular portions(some of them in hyalinisation) and intense diminution of follicular lymphocytes.

At polar portions : edematous swelling and some hyalinisation of penicillar arteries and c considerable perifolliclar congestion with some leakage of erythrocytes in fascicular cords.

In sinuses : slight or considerable congestior and some edematous swelling of walls.

In fascicular cords : slight congestion with a little leucocytes.

some (not increased) reticulum-cells in considerable cloudy swelling.

399.

Considerable reduction of follicles and intense edematous swelling (with some hyalinisation) of central artery-walls.

In follicles : intense edematous swelling (and some hyalinisation) of reticulum-cells

[redacted] 226

[redacted]

CONFIDENTIAL

399

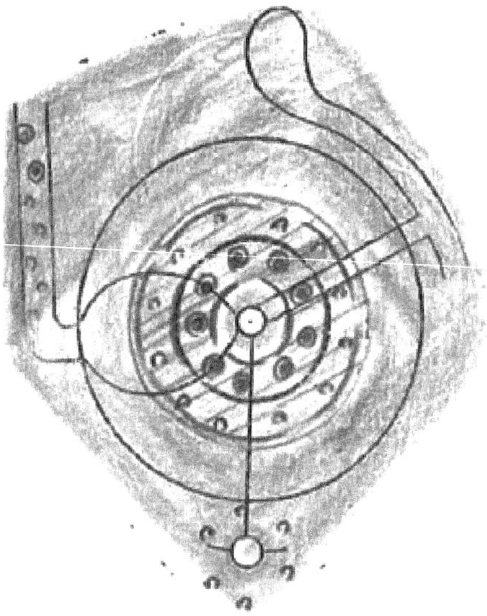

and-fibres with deposits of some hyalinous masses.

Some leucocytes-emigration in follicles with intensively swollen reticulum-cells (some of them, in macrophagen-like form).

At polar portion : intense edematous swelling of penicillar artery-walls and considerable peripolar exudative changes and some leucocytes -emigration.

In sinuses : remarkable congestion and some serous exudation with intense swelling of reticulum-fibres and sinus walls.

In fascicular cords : massive serous exudation , considerable leucocytes-emigration (with some myelocytes) and some degenerated swollen ratioulum-cells.

401.

Intense reduction of follicles with intense roughness or edematous swelling of central artery-walls.

In follicles : considerable hyalinous roughness of basal fibres, deposits of some hyalinous masses, some hemorrhages, some edema, some leucocytes-emigration, some considerable

CONFIDENTIAL 327

[redacted]

[redacted]

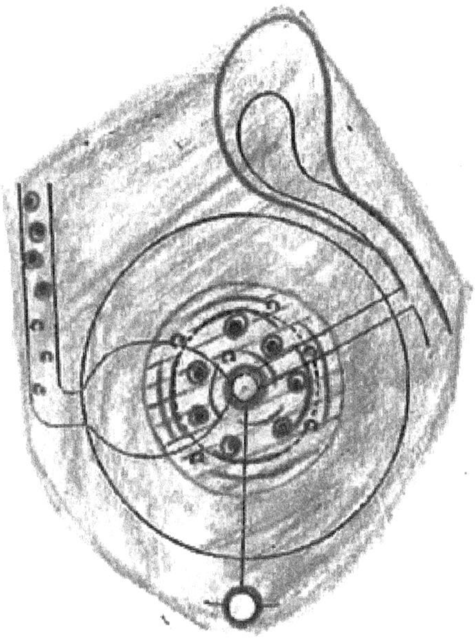

401

increased reticulum-cells (most of them, in histiocytes-like form) and considerable diminution of follicular lymphocytes.

Slight hyalinous degeneration and edematous roughness of penicillar artery-walls and some polar edema.

In sinuses : some congestion and some serous exudation with intense edematous swelling of reticulum-fibres.

In fascicular cords : some leucocytes-emigration (with a few myelocytes), with remarkable edematous swelling of reticulum-fibres and some degenerated (not increased), swollen reticulm-cells.

410.

Considerable reduction of follicles and intense edematous swelling (and some hyalinisation) of central artery-walls.

In follicles : intense edematous roughness of basal fibres, deposits of some hyalinous masses, considerable hemorrhages and some slightly hyperplasied, intensively degenerated reticulum-cells.

CON[redacted]IAL 228

[redacted]

410

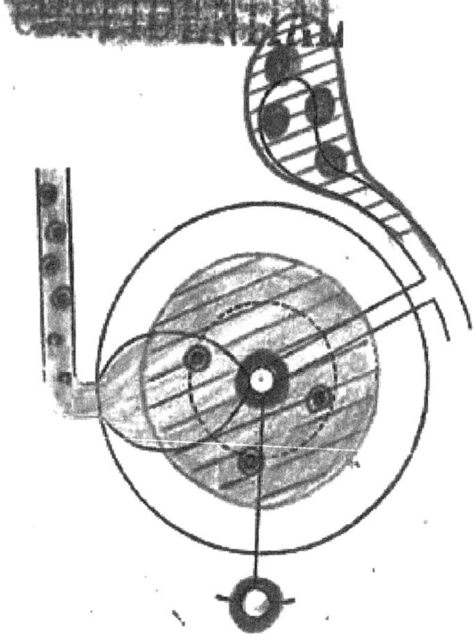

At polar portions : considerable edematous swelling or some hyalinisation of penicillar arteries and exudative changes.

In sinuses : remarkable congestion, massive serous fluids (some of them, in hyalinously coagulated masses) and considerable edematous swelling of sinus walls and reticulum-fibres.

In fascicular cords : massive serous fluids and remarkable congestion (leakage of erythrocytes), some leucocytes and some (not so hyperplasied) reticulum-cells in intense degeneration (some of them in erythrophagy).

[redacted]. 229

[redacted]

[redacted]

(B) S U M M A R Y

(I)

The birds-eye-view of all splenal changes of our materials are as follows:

[redacted] 230

[redacted]

The bird's eye view of all investigated cases.

[redacted]

---

17. Angio-Folliculitis exsudativa. Exudative changes in severe degree.
with miliary necrosis.
with some polar edema.
with slight proliferative tendency.

Fasciculitis exsudative. Exudative changes in severe degree.
with miliary necrosis in rather exudative form.
with some leucocytes dissemination.

---

18. Angio-Folliculitis haemorrhagico-exsudativa. Hemorrhagic changes in slight degree.
Exudative changes in medium degree.
with slight proliferative tendency.

Fasciculitis exsudativa. Exudative changes in severe degree.
with leucocytes dissemination in medium degree.
with some bionecrotic changes in exudative form.

---

26. Angio-Folliculitis haemorrhagico-exsudativa. Hemorrhagic changes in medium degree.
Exudative changes in medium degree.
with slight proliferative tendency.

Fasciculitis haemorrhagico-exsudativa. Hemorrhagic changes in severe degree.
Exudative changes in medium degree.
with slight proliferative tendency.
with some leucocytes dissemination.

---

225. Angio-Folliculitis haemorrhagico-exsuafativa. Exudative changes in severe degree.
with some leucocyted dissemination.
with some polar hemorrhages.

Fasciculitis exsuadativa. Exudative changes in severe degree.
with leucocytes dissemination in medium degree.
with some myeloic metaplasia.

[redacted] 231

[redacted]

[redacted]

225. Angio-Folliculitis exsudativa. Exudative changes in severe degree.
with polar edema.
with slight leucocytes dissemination.

Fasciculitis exsudativa. Exudative changes in severe degree.
with leucocytes dissemination in medium degree.

---

318. Angio-Folliculitis haemorrhagico-exsudativa. Hemorrhagic changes in slighy degree.
Exudative changes in severe degree.
with polar hemorrhages.
with some miliary necrosis.

Fasciculitis exsudativa. Exudative changes in severe degree.
with slight leucocytes dissemination.

---

320. Angio-Folliculitis haemorrhagico-exsudativa. Hemorrhagic changes in severe degree.
Exudative changes in severe degree.
with slight leucocytes dissemination.
with some polar hemorrhages.

Fassiculitis exsudativa. Exudative changes in severe degree.
with some leucocytes dissemination.

---

325. Angio-Folliculitis haemorrhagico-exsudativa. Hemorrhagic changes in slight degree.
Exudative changes in severe degree.
with polar edema.
with slight proliferative tendency.

Fasciculitis exsudativa. Exudative changes in severe degree.
with some leucocytes dissemination.

---

328. Angio-Folliculitis haemorrhagico-exsudativa. Hemorrhagic changes in slight degree.
Exudative changes in medium degree.
with some polar edema.

Fasciculitis exsudativa. Exudative changes in medium degree.
with slight leucocytes dissemination.

[redacted]L 232

[redacted]

[redacted]

388. Angio-Folliculitis haemorrhagico-exsudativa.
Hemorrhagic changes in severe degree.
Exudative changes in severe degree.
with intense leucocytes dissemination.
with some polar edema and hemorrhages.
with some polar miliary necrosis and some milairy bionecrosis in foll cular tissues.

Fasciculitis exsudativa.
Exudative changes in severe degree.
with leucocytes dissemination in medium degree.

---

390. Angio-Folliculitis haemorrhagico-exsudativa.
Hemorrhagic changes in severe degree.
Exudative changes in severe degree.
with some polar hemorrhages.
with some leucocytes dissemination. in medium degree.

Fascicnlitis haemorrhagico-exsudativa.
Hemorrhagic changes in medium degree.
Exudative changes in severe degree.
with leucocytes dissemination in medium degree.

---

393. Angio-Folliculitis haemorrhagico-exsudativa.
Hemorrhagic changes in slight degree.
Exudative changes in severe degree.
with some bionecrotic chages.
with leucocytes disseminat on in medium degree.

Fasciculitis exsudativa.
Exudative changes in medium degree.
with intense leucocytes disseminat on

---

397. Angio-Folliculitis exsudativa.
Exudative changes in severe degree.
with some polar edema.
with some bionecrotic changes.
with some polar miliary bionecrosis.

Easciculitis-exsudativa.
Exudative changes in severe degree.
with some leucocytes dissemination.

[redacted] 233

[redacted]

[redacted]

399. Angio-Folliculitis haemorrhagico-exsudativa.
Hemorrhagic changes in severe degree.
Exudative changes in severe degree.
with some leucocytes dissemination.

Fasciculitis haemorrhagico-exsudativa.
Hemorrhagic changes in severe degree.
Exudative changes in severe degree.
with intense leucocytes dissemination.
with some myeloic metaplasia.

---

400. Angio-Folliculitis exsudativa.
Exudative changes in severe degree.
with some polar edema.
with slight leucocytes dissemination.

Fasciculitis exsudativa.
Exudative changes in severe degree.
with intense leucocytes dissemination.
with some mueloic metaplasia.

---

401. Angio-Folliculitis haemorrhagico-exsudativa.
Hemorrhagic changes in medium degree.
Exudative changes in severe degree.
with slight proliferative tendency.

Fasciculitis exsudativa.
Exudative changes in medium degree.
with slight proliferative tendency.

---

403. Angio-Folliculitis haemorrhagico-exsudativa.
Hemorrhagic changes in dedium degree.
Exudative changes in severe degree.
with slight pro,iferative tendency.
with some polar edema.
with slight leucocytes dissemination.
with some necrosid and bionecrosis.

Fasciculitis exsudativa.
Exudative changes in severe degree.
with some leucocytes dissemination.

---

405. Angio-Folliculitis haemorrhagico-exsudativa.
Hemorrhagic changes in slight degree.
Exudative changes in severe degree.
with somebionecrosis.
with some polar edema.
with some polar hemorrhages.

[redacted] 234

[redacted]

[redacted]

	Fasciculitis exsudativa.	Exudative changes in severe degree. with slight proliferative tendency.
407.	Angio-Folliculitis haemorrhagico-exsudativa.	Hemorrhagic changes in slight degree. Exudative changes in severe degree. with some polar edema. with slight proliferative tendency.
	Fasculitis exsudativa.	Exudative changes in severe degree. with slight proliferative tendency.
409.	Angio-Folliculitis exsudativa.	Exudative changes in severed degree. with some polar edema. with slight proliferative tendency.
	Fasculitis exsudativa.	Exudative changes in severed degree. with some leucocytes dissemination. with some myeloic metaplasia.
410.	Angio-Folliculitis haemorrhagico-exsudativa.	Hemorrhagic changes in medium degree. Exudative changes in severe degree.
	Fasculitis exsudativa.	Exudative changes in severe degree.
411.	Angio-Folliculitis haemorrhagico-exsudativa.	Hemorrhagic changes in slight degree. Exudative changes in medium degree.
	Fasculitis haemorrhagico-exsudativa.	Hemorrhagic changes in slight degree. Exudative changes in medium degree.

[redacted] 235

[redacted]

(2) [redacted]

A). Disturbances of follicles.

I). Disturbances of A. centralis.

Hyalinous or edematous swelling of walls of A. centralis.

in slight degree. 0 cases.
in medium degree. 5 cases.
in severe degree. 18
(necrotic swelling). cases.

2) Disturbances of perivascular and follicular tissues.

Angio-folliculitis exsudativa. 23 cases.

in slight degree. 0 cases.
(Edema in perivascular tissues).
in medium degree. 3 cases.
in severe degree. 20 cases.
(Diffuse edema in follicular tissues).

Angio-folliculitis haemorrhagico-exsudativa.

(Angio-folliculitis exsudativa with hemorrhages).

17 cases.

in slight degree. 9 cases.
in medium degree. 5 cases.
in severe degree. 3 cases.

[illegible]

[redacted] 236

[redacted]

[redacted]

Angio-folliculitis exsudativa with leucocytes-emigrations.
11 cases.

in slight degree.	8	cases.
in medium degree.	2	cases.
in severe degree.	1	cases.
with myeloic metaplasia.	0	cases.

Angio-folliculitis cum necrosis milliaris.
7 cases.

in exudative form.	1	cases.
in exudative-hemorrhagic form.	5	cases.
in exudative form but with slight proliferative tendency.	1	cases.

Angio-folliculitis with remarkable our so-called "polar changes". 20 cases.

with remarkable polar edema.	12	cases.
with remarkable polar hemorrhages.	6	cases.
with some polar miliary necrosis.	2	cases.
with considerable polar plasma-cell-reactions.	0	cases.

Angio-folliculitis exsudativa with slight proliferative tendency. 8 cases.

[redacted] 237

[redacted]

[redacted]

B). Disturbances of Billoth's cords.

3) Disturbances of Pulpa-mesh.

Fasciculitis exsudativa. 23 cases.

in slight degree.	0	cases.
in medium degree.	5	cases.
in severe degree.	18	cases.

Fasciculitis exsudativa with so-called "blood-sea".
(Fasciculitis haemorrhagico-exsudativa).
4 cases.

in slight degree.	1	cases.
in medium degree.	1	cases.
in severe degree.	2	cases.
with myeloic metaplasia.	6	cases.

Fasciculitis exsudativa with leucocytes-disseminations.
(Fasciculitis sero-purulenta or haemorrhagico-purulenta). 18 cases.

in slight degree.	8	cases.
in medium degree.	6	cases.
in severe degree.	4	cases.
with myeloic metaplasia.	6	cases.

[redacted] 238

([redacted]

[redacted]

Fasciculitis exsudativa with multiple miliary necrosis.

2 cases.

in slight exudative form.	~~2~~0	cases.
in considerable exudative form.	0	cases.
in severe exudative form.	2	cases.
in exudative-hemorrhagic form.	0	cases.
in exudative, but with slight proliferaitve tendency.	0	cases.

Fasciculitis exsudativa with slight proliferative tendency.

4 cases.

C) Classification of splenal changes, according to "Folliculo-Fasciculitis"-concept, so as "Glomerulo-Nephrosis" in Kidney.

4) Disturbances of splenon, as functional-anatominical unit of spleen.

Folliculo-Fasciculitis exsudativa.

23 cases.

in slight degree.	0	cases.
in medial degree.	3	cases.
in severe degree.	20	cases.

[redacted] 239

[redacted]

[redacted]

Folliculo-Fasciculitis haemorrhagico-exsudativa.

17 cases.		
in slight degree.	9	cases.
in medial degree.	5	cases.
in severe degree.	3	cases.

Folliculo-Fasciculitis sero-purulenta or haemorrhagico-purulenta. (with leucocytes-disseminations).

18 cases.		
in slight degree.	8	cases.
in medium degree.	5	cases.
in severe degree.	5	cases.
with myeloic metaplasia.	6	cases.

Folliculo-Fasciculitis cum necrosis milliaris.

8 cases.		
in slight exudative form.	0	cases.
in medium exudative form.	0	cases.
in severe exudative form.	2	cases.
in hemorrhagico-exud ative form.	5	cases.
in exudative form, but with slight proliferative tendency.	1	cases.

[redacted] 240

[redacted]

[redacted]

Folliculo-Fasciculitis exsudativa with slight proliferative tendency: 9 cases.

oooo oooo oooo oooo oooo

Distributions and frequencies of pathological changes in every sections of splenon are as above described.

The main pathological findings are severe exudative or hemorrhagic-exudative changes, accompanied sometimes with remarkable Anthrax-knots formations.

[redacted] 241

[redacted]

SPLEEN

[redacted]

	17	18	26	A 225	B 225	318	320	325	328	388	390	393	397	399	400	401	403	404	405	407	409	410	411
Capsule – Thickness	↑+÷	↑÷	N	↑+	↓+++	↓+÷	↑++	↑+÷	↑++	↓++	|	↑÷	↓(+++)	↑+	↓÷	↑+÷	↓÷	↑+÷	↑++	↑+÷	↑++	↑−	↑÷
Capsule – Curve	÷	∸	+	+	∸	−	∸	+	÷	∸	|	∸	+	+	+	−	−	+÷	−	∸	∸	÷	÷
Trabeculae – Thickness	↑+÷	↓+	↓÷	↑+	↓+++	↓+	↑++	↑÷	↑+↓	↓++	↑÷	↑÷	↓+	↑+	↑+	↓∸	↓(+++)	↑++	↑÷	↑+÷	↑++÷	↑∸	↑−
Trabeculae – Blood Vessels – Congestion	÷	∸	+++	++÷	++	++	++	+	∸	++	+÷	++	++	+++	|	+++	+	++	++	+÷	∸	+	+÷
Trabeculae – Blood Vessels – Swelling of Walls	++	+	+	+	++	+÷	+	+	++	+	÷	++	+++	++	+++	++	+÷	+÷	+÷	+++	+++	+	+÷
Trabeculae – Blood Vessels – Loosening of Walls	+÷	+	+÷	+	++	++	+	+	∸	÷	÷	++	++	++	+++	++	++	+	+	++	++	+	++
Trabeculae – Blood Vessels – Hyaline Degeneration	÷	+	+	+÷	+	÷	++	÷	+++	∸	+÷	+	+÷	+÷	−	+	+	−	∸	−	−	+	+÷
Reticulum – Hyperplasia	−	÷	−	÷	÷	∸	+÷	+	−	+÷	−	+÷	+÷	−	−	∸	++	+÷	++	+÷	+	−	÷
Reticulum – Swelling	|	+	|	(+++)	+	+	++	÷	+	++	+	+	++÷	+	+++	+	++	++	+÷	+÷	+	+÷	÷
Reticulum – Hyaline Degeneration	−	+	−	∸	∸	∸	+	−	÷	−	++	++	−	+	−	+	−	−	∸	∸	−	+÷	+
Reticulum – Hyperplasia of Reticular Cells – in Follicles	|	∸	−	÷	∸	∸	÷	÷	∸	∸	∸	∸	∸	∸	++	+	+	++	++	∸	∸	−	∸
Reticulum – Hyperplasia of Reticular Cells – perifollicular	|	∸	∸	∸	∸	÷	∸	∸	∸	+	∸	÷	+	∸	÷	∸	+	++	++	+÷	+	−	∸
Reticulum – Hyperplasia of Reticular Cells – peritrabecular	|	∸	∸	∸	÷	÷	÷	∸	∸	÷	∸	∸	÷	∸	÷	∸	÷	+	+÷	+÷	÷	−	∸
Follicles – Size	↓(+++)	↓+++	↓(++)	↓(++)	↓(+++)	↓(+++)	↓++	↓(+++)	↓(++)	↓+÷	↓+++	↓(+)	↓+++	↓(++)	↓(+++)	↓+++	↓+++	↓+++	↓+++	↓(++)	↓(++)	↓÷	↓(++)
Follicles – Number	↓+++	↓+++	↓+÷	↓+÷	↓+++	↓++	↓+++	↓+++	↓+÷	↓+÷	↓+++	↓+	↓+++	↓++	↓+++	↓++	↓++	↓+++	↓++	↓+++	↓+++	↓++	↓++
Follicles – Decrease of Lymphocytes	(+++)	+++	+	+	(+++)	++	+÷	+++	++÷	++÷	++	++	+++	++	++÷	++	+÷	++	+++	++÷	(+++)	(++)	+
Follicles – Edema – in Follicles	++	+÷	+÷	++	++	++	++	++÷	+++	+++	++	++	+++	+÷	+++	++	++	++	+++	++	+++	++	+
Follicles – Edema – perifollicular	++	+÷	+	++	+++	++	++	++	+++	+++	++	++	+++	+÷	+++	++	++	++	++	++	++	++	+÷
Follicles – Hemorrhage – in Follicles	÷	÷	+÷	∸	∸	∸	(+÷)	÷	∸	+++	++	+	÷	÷	−	+	+	÷	+	(+)	∸	++	+
Follicles – Hemorrhage – perifollicular	+	÷	+++	∸	(+)	+++	+÷	+	∸	+++	++	|	÷	÷	−	+	+	÷	+÷	+÷	÷	++	+++
Follicles – Histiocytes – in Follicles	+	+	+++	÷	÷	++	+	+÷	∸	++	÷	+	∸	+	∸	÷	++	∸	÷	++	+÷	∸	÷
Follicles – Histiocytes – perifollicular	+÷	+	++	÷	÷	++	+	÷	÷	++	÷	|	+	+	÷	÷	+	∸	÷	+	+	∸	÷
Follicles – Central Artery – Congestion	÷	∸	++	÷	+	∸	∸	∸	∸	∸	∸	∸	−	÷	∸	∸	∸	−	−	∸	−	∸	∸
Follicles – Central Artery – Endothelium – Swelling	∸	+÷	÷	÷	∸	+	+	++	−	++	+	∸	++	+	++	++	+	+	+÷	+	÷	++	+÷
Follicles – Central Artery – Endothelium – Hyperplasia	−	−	−	−	∸	−	−	−	−	÷	−	−	−	−	−	−	−	÷	÷	∸	−	−	∸
Follicles – Central Artery – Endothelium – Desquamation	+	+	+	÷	÷	+	+	+÷	∸	(++)	∸	+	++	∸	++	+	+	∸	∸	+÷	÷	+	++
Follicles – Central Artery – Walls – Swelling	++	+÷	+÷	+++	++	+++	+÷	+++	++	++	++	+	(+++)	++	(+++)	++	+	+++	++	++	++	+++	+÷
Follicles – Central Artery – Walls – Loosening	++	++	+	+++	++	+++	+÷	+++	÷	+÷	+÷	++	(+++)	+	+++	++	+	+÷	+	+	+	÷	+++
Follicles – Central Artery – Walls – Hyaline Degeneration	(+)	+	∸	÷	+++	∸	+÷	÷	++	∸	++	++	++	++	−	+	+	−	∸	∸	−	+++	+++
Follicles – Exist of Germinating Center	−	−	−	−	−	−	−	−	−	−	−	−	−	−	−	−	−	−	−	−	−	−	−
Follicles – Necrosis – central	∸	−	−	−	−	−	−	+	−	(+)	−	+	(+)	−	−	−	(+)	−	(÷)	−	−	−	−
Follicles – Necrosis – peripheral	∸	−	−	−	−	−	−	−	−	(+)	−	−	(+)	−	−	−	+	−	−	−	∸	−	−
Venous Sinuses – Width	↑++	↑+	|	↑+	↑+÷	↑+	↑++	↑+	↑+÷	↑+	↑+÷	↑++	↑+++	↑+÷	↑++	↑+÷	↑++	↑+++	↑+++	↑++	↑+÷	↑++	↑+÷
Venous Sinuses – Cavernous Sinuses	÷	|	++	÷	+	∸	÷	∸	|	∸	+	∸	÷	|	|	+	+	÷	÷	∸	÷	+	+
Venous Sinuses – Congestion	÷	∸	+++	(+)	+++	(+++)	+÷	÷	÷	++	++	∸	∸	+++	|	++	÷	÷	+	++	∸	++	++
Venous Sinuses – Cellular Inclusion – Leucocytes	∸	−	|	÷	÷	∸	∸	|	−	+	+	+	+	−	+	∸	+	−	−	÷	∸	−	∸
Venous Sinuses – Cellular Inclusion – Lymphocytes	÷	∸	|	÷	+	+÷	+÷	|	∸	+	+	+÷	∸	∸	∸	∸	∸	+	∸	÷	∸	∸	∸
Venous Sinuses – Cellular Inclusion – Histiocytic Cells	÷	∸	|	÷	÷	+	+	|	∸	÷	∸	+	÷	∸	∸	∸	∸	÷	÷	∸	÷	÷	÷
Venous Sinuses – Endothelium – Swelling	∸	÷	|	∸	÷	+	+	(+)	∸	++	+	÷	+÷	+	+++	÷	++	+	+÷	+	÷	÷	÷
Venous Sinuses – Endothelium – Resolution	+++	+	|	÷	÷	∸	++	÷	÷	++	++	+÷	++	∸	++	÷	+	+	÷	∸	+	∸	∸
Venous Sinuses – Endothelium – Phagocytosis	+	+	|	÷	++	∸	++	∸	+	∸	+	+÷	÷	+	|	+	+	−	+	∸	∸	+	+÷
Billroth's Cord – Edema	++	++	|	+++	++	++	+++	++	++	++÷	++	+	+++	++	+++	++	+++	++	++	++	++	+++	+
Billroth's Cord – Hemorrhage	++	∸	+++	÷	(+++)	++	++	∸	+	+÷	++	∸	∸	+++	−	++	÷	÷	+÷	++	+	+	++
Billroth's Cord – Necrosis	+	|	−	−	∸	∸	÷	−	−	−	−	−	+	−	−	−	−	−	−	−	−	−	−
Billroth's Cord – Lymphocytes	↓+÷	↓+++	↓+	↓+++	↓++	↓+÷	↓+÷	↓++	↓+	↓+÷	↓++	↓+÷	↓÷	↓+÷	↓+	↓+	↓+÷	↓+	↓÷	↓+	↓÷	↓−	↑++
Billroth's Cord – Leucocytes	÷	+	÷	++	÷	+	÷	÷	∸	+÷	+÷	++	+÷	++	++	÷	++	÷	∸	∸	∸	∸	∸
Billroth's Cord – Plasma Cells	|	−	−	+	−	+	−	−	−	−	−	∸	−	−	−	−	−	−	−	−	−	−	∸
Billroth's Cord – Splenocytes	+÷	+	++	÷	+	+÷	+	+	∸	+	÷	+÷	+	∸	÷	+	+	+	+	÷	+	÷	+
Billroth's Cord – Reticular Cells	|	|	|	÷	∸	÷	+	÷	∸	+	∸	∸	÷	÷	÷	÷	+	+÷	+÷	+÷	+	−	∸
Hemosiderosis	∸	+	++	++	÷	+	+	+	÷	−	−	+÷	+÷	∸	∸	∸	+	÷	++	−	∸	−	∸

[redacted] 242

[redacted]

[redacted]

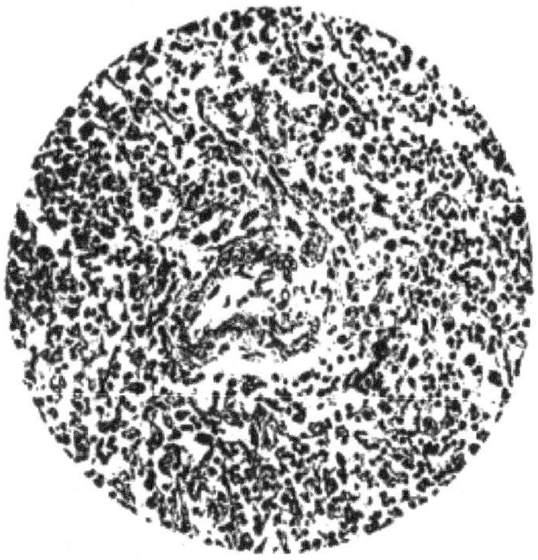

M 325 210

Angio-folliculitis exsudativa .
Edematous swelling of central artery wall.
Some leucocytes dissemination, some edematous swelling and some increased reticulum cells (in histiocytes-form)..

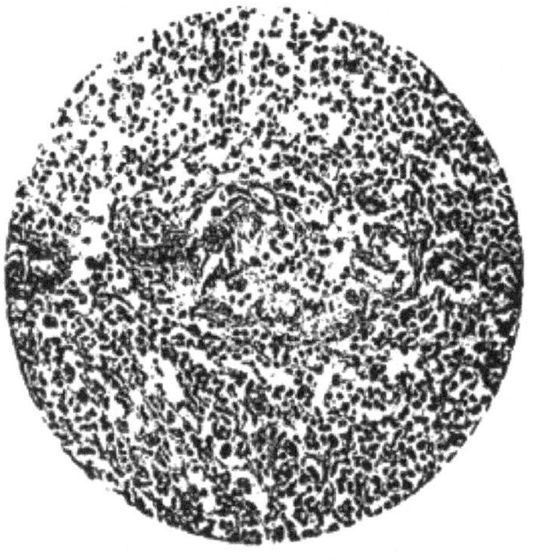

M 325 210

Angio-folliculitis exsudativa.
Edematous swelling of central artery wall.
Some edema, some leucocytes and some increased reticulum cells (in ~~macrophagen~~-form).
Histiocytes

[redacted] 243

[redacted]

Folliculitis exsudativa, with hyalinous swelling of central artery and intense edematous swelling of follicular tissues.

[redacted]

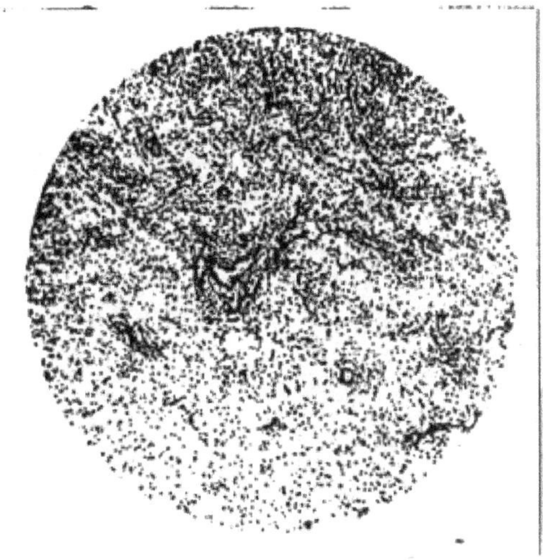

Follicultis exsudativa, with intense bionecrotic changes all over the follicular tissues and intense edematous swelling of central artery walls.

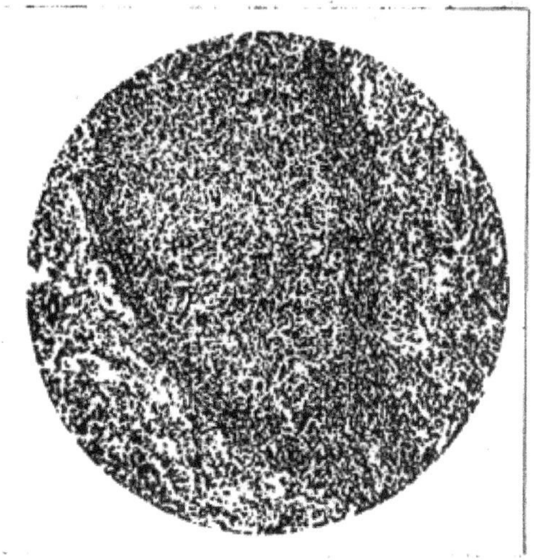

M 393　　×100

[redacted] 244

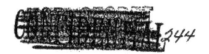

[redacted]

Hyaline droplets in sinuses.

[redacted]

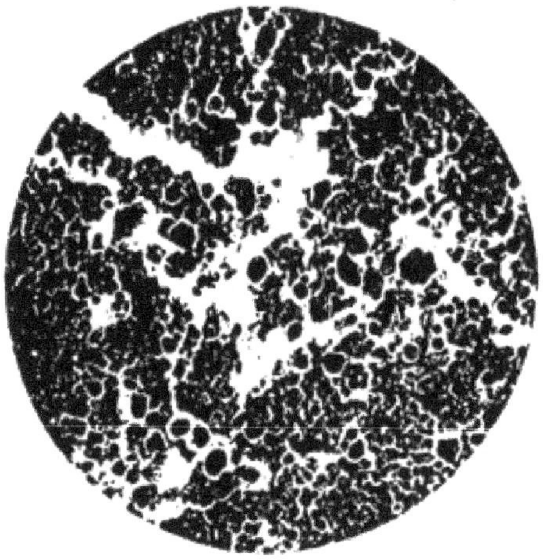

M 410 270

Hyaline droplets in sinuses.

M 407 300.

[redacted] 245

[redacted]

Hyalinous swelling of central artery wall.

[redacted]

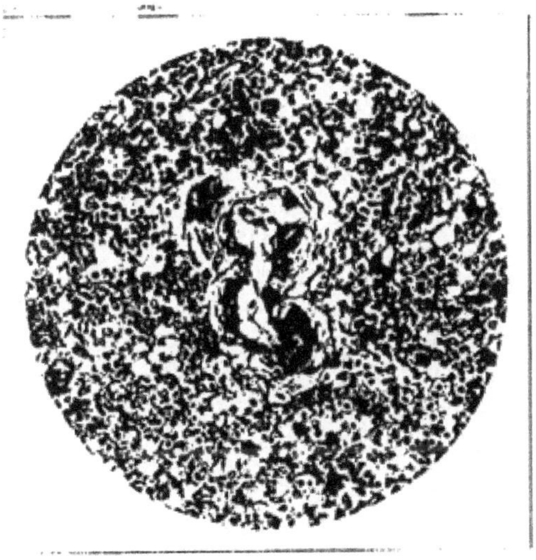

M4-11 x263

Hyalinous swelling of central and penicillar arteries wall.

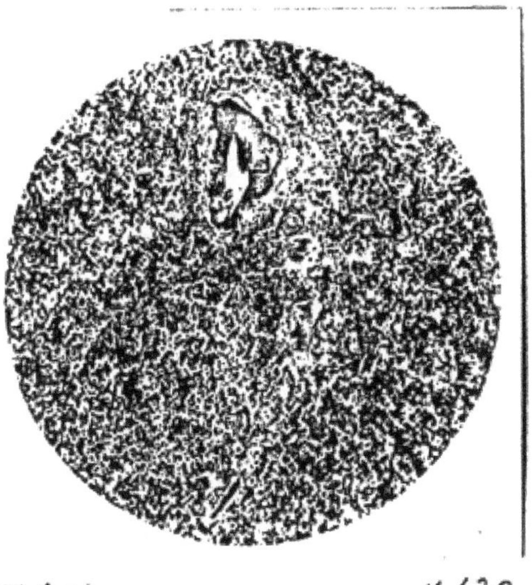

M4-11 x130

[redacted] 246

[redacted]

Folliculitiw haemorrhagica,
with some hemorrhagic changes
om follicles and some hemorrhages
at perifollicular portion.

[redacted]

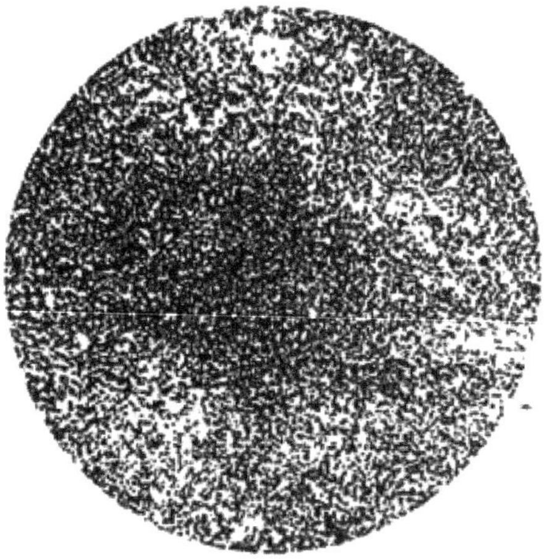

X170

Folliculitis haemorrhagica,
with some hemorrhages in follicle
and perifollicular tissues.

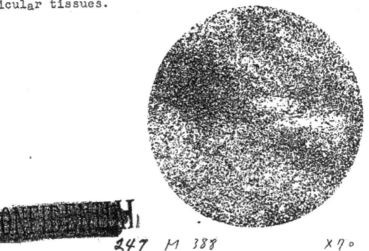

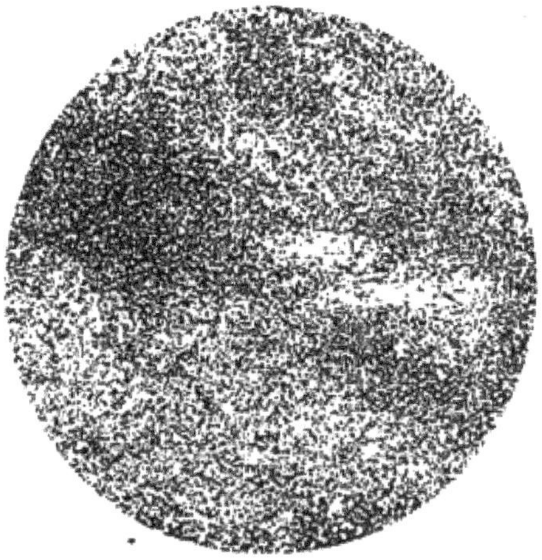

[redacted]

247 M 388 X70

[redacted]

Our so-called Angio-folliculitis haemorrhagico-exsudativa, with diffuse edema and hemorrhages in germinative center.

[redacted]

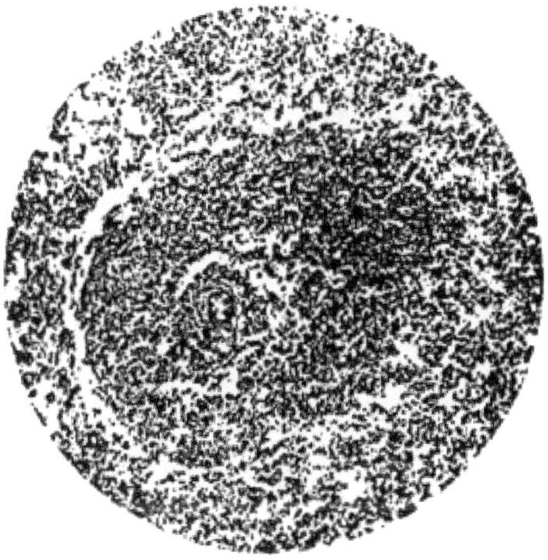

M 393. 100

Edematous swelling of wall of penicillar artery.
Intense edematous swelling and necrotic changes in follicular tissues, esp. around penicillar artery.

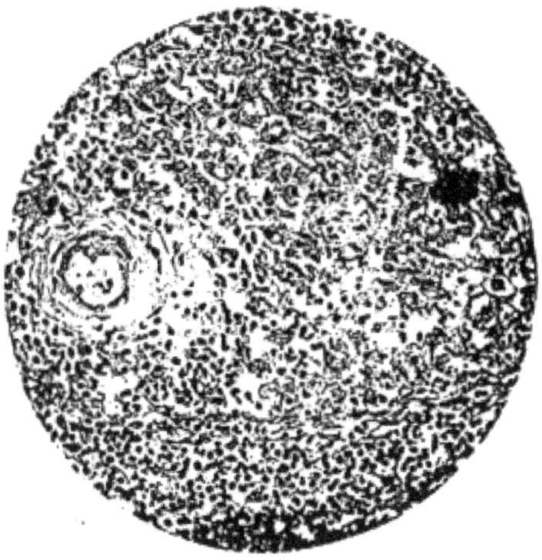

M 318. 200

[redacted]

248

[redacted]

Angio-folliculitis exsudativa with
some increased reticulum cells
(in macrophagen-form).

[redacted]

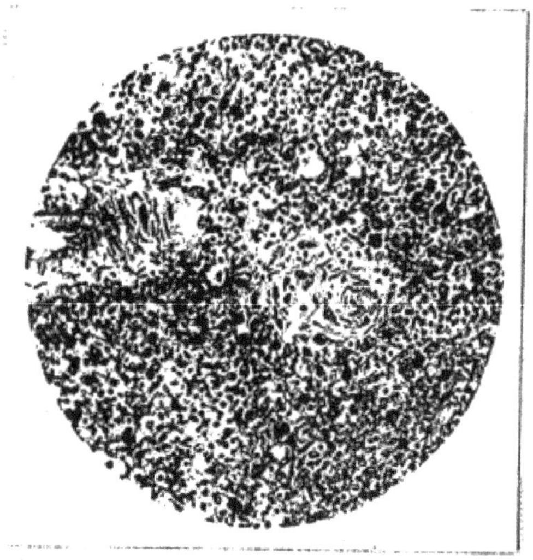

M.26 X210

[redacted]

249

[redacted]

Proliferative reaction at polar portion.
Some increased reticulum cells.

[redacted]

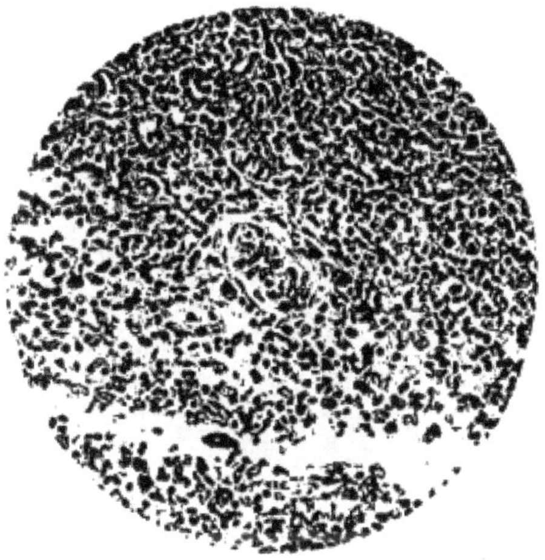

M 388 260

[redacted]

[redacted] 250

[redacted]

Swelling and slight hyperplasia
of reticulum fibres at perifollicular portion. [redacted]

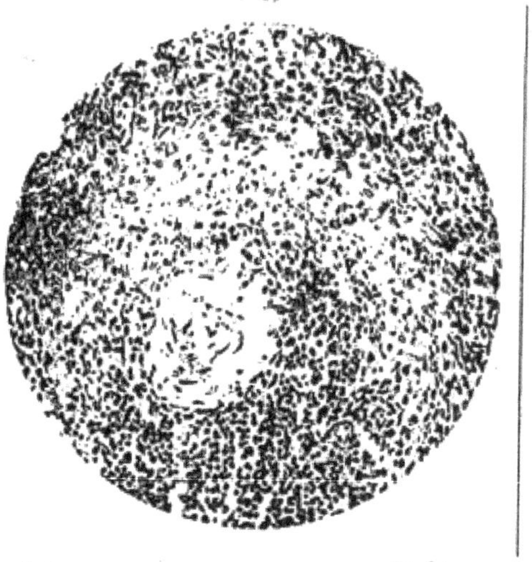

M 405 × 200

Proliferation of reticulum cells
at perifollicular portion.

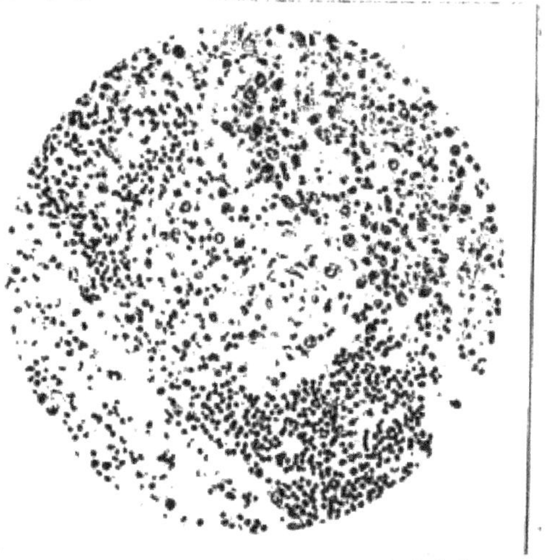

M 407 × 210

[redacted] 251

[redacted]

Our so-called Angio-folliculitis exsudativa, accompanied with many increased reticulum cells(in macrophagen-form). ([redacted]

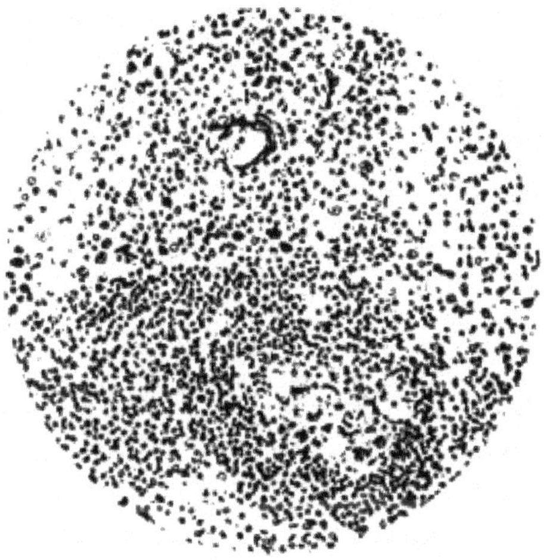

M 403 X200

Our so-called Angio-folliculitis exsudativa, accompanied with many increased reticulum cells.
Edematous swelling of central artery walls.
Edematous swelling, some leucocytes dissemination and some increased reticulum cells in follicular tissues.

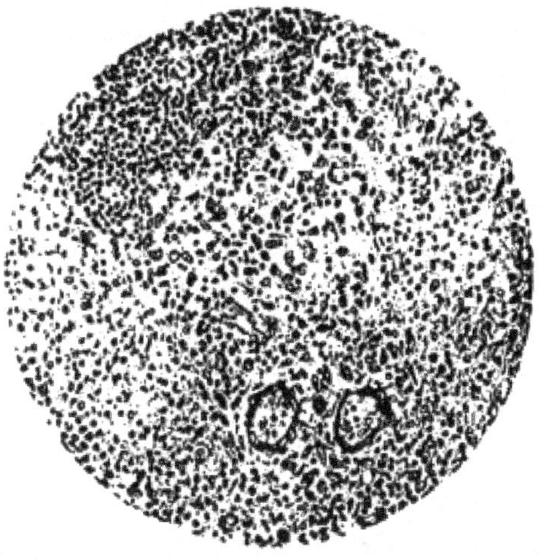

M. 403 X200

[redacted]

252

[redacted]

[redacted]

Kidney

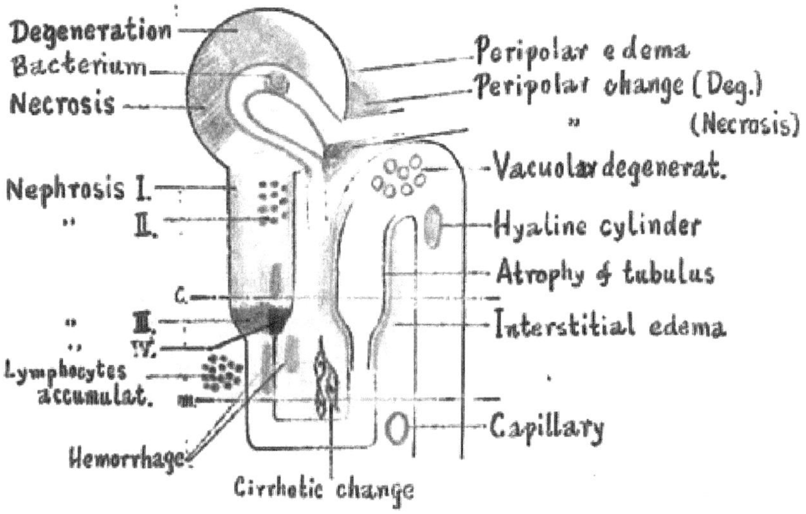

[redacted] 253

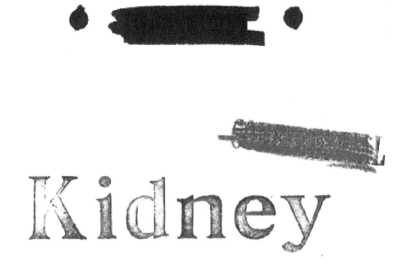

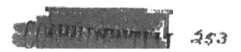

[redacted]

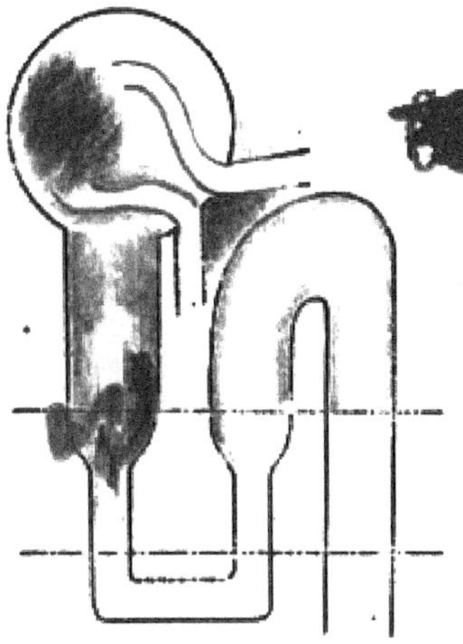

[redacted]

K I D N E Y.

(A) Microscop. Investigation.

17.

Considerable glo[illegible]lo-nephrosis (glomerulus mainly in rather degenerative form), with slight our so-called peripolar changes and Nephrosis in I. stage, at some places in III. stage with hemo-rrhages.

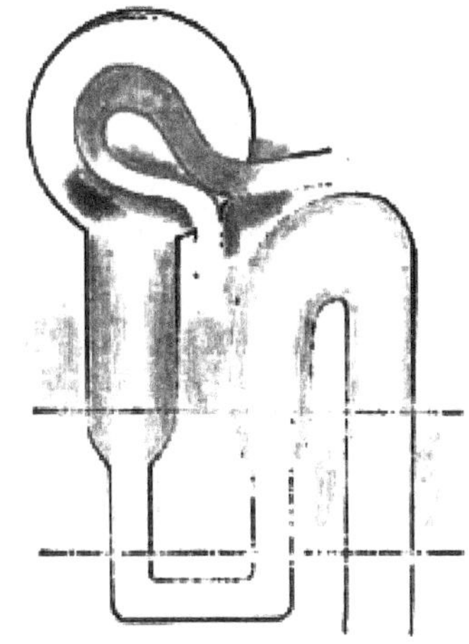

[illegible].

Slight Glomerulo-nephrosis (mainly in acute hyp[illegible] form, some in degenerative form) with slight our so-called peripolar changes and Nephrosis in [illegible] stage with slight, at some places remarkable interstitial edema.

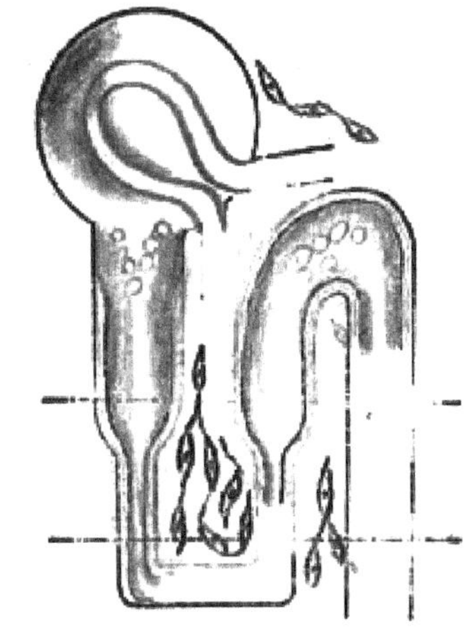

5[illegible].

Slight Glomerulo-nephrosis (mainly in degenera-tive form) with slight peripolar changes and Ne-phrosis in I. stage with rather atrophic glandular cells, and at some places remarkable vacuolar degeneration of glandular cells.

Considerable interstitial edema and slight atrophic changes with slight increase of connective tissues at subcapsular portions.

[redacted] R64

[redacted]

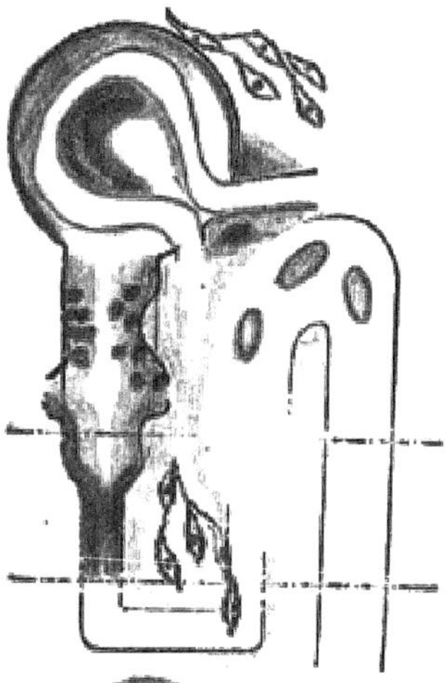

225. [redacted]

Considerable Glomerulo-nephrosis (mainly in rather degenerative form). Some glomerular loops and Bowman's capsules in hyaline degeneration, with considerable our so-called peripolar changes.

Nephrosis in I. stage and at some places in III. stage with some hyaline-droplets-degenerations. Considerable interstitial edema and slight cirrhotic changes of interstitial tissues with some large hyaline cylinders at some places, and some necrotic desolation of tubular epitheliums at some places.

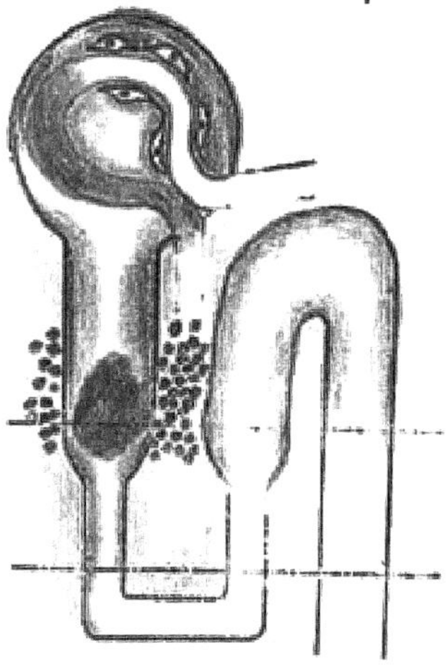

312.

Slight Glomerulo-nephritis (mainly in acute hyperemic form, some glomeruli in hyaline cirrhosis) and Nephrosis in I. stage, at some places in III. stage with some round-cell-accumulations and considerable edema in interstitial tissues.

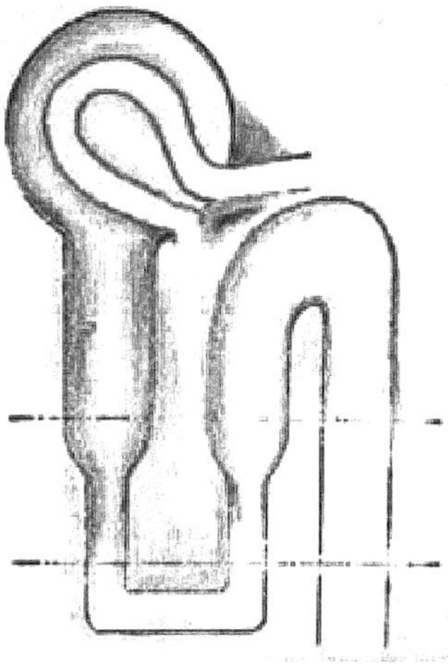

320.

Considerable Glomerulo-nephrosis (mainly in acute exudative form) with slight our so-called peripolar changes and Nephrosis in I. stage with considerable, at some places remarkable interstitial edema (Nephritis serosa).

[redacted] 265

[redacted]

325
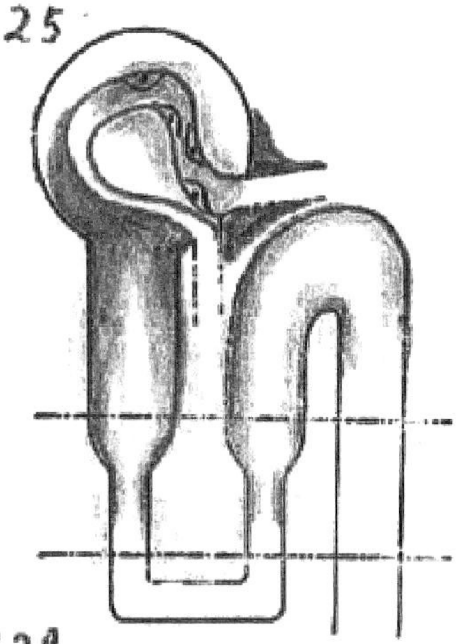

328
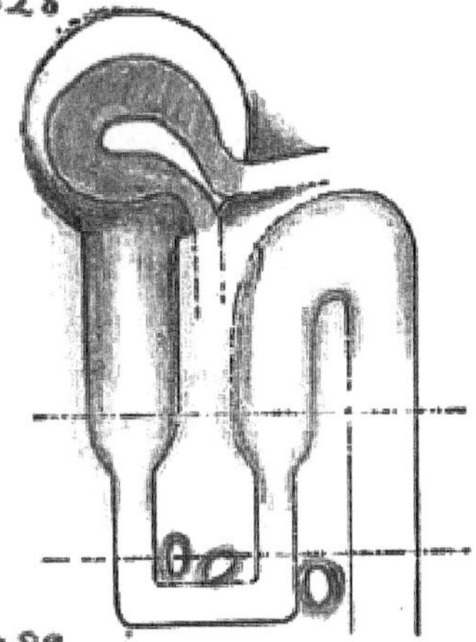

389
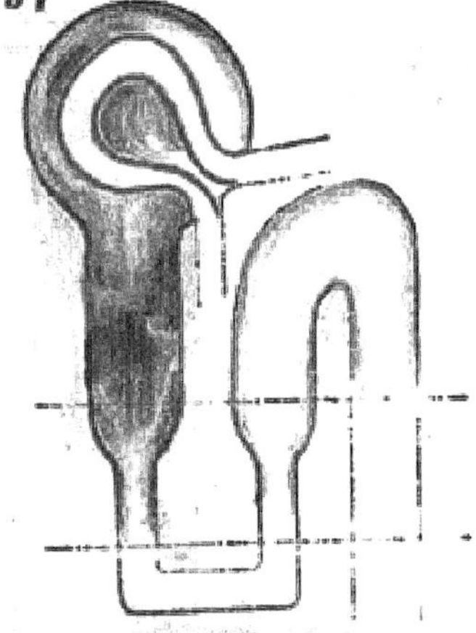

325. [redacted]

Considerable Glomerulo-[redacted] (mainly in acute stimulised form and some glomeruli in degenerative form) with slight our so-called peripolar changes and Nephrosis in I. stage with considerble interstitial edema.

328.

Slight Glomerulo-nephrosis (mainly in acute hyperemic fo. , some in degenerative form), with slight peripolar changes and Nephrosis in I. stage with considerable interstitial edema and slight necrotic changens of medullar capillary walls.

389.

Slight Glomerulo-nephrosis (mainly in degenerative form) with slight peripolar changes and Nephrosis in I. stage and at some places in III. stage with considerable, interstitial edema and hyaline-necrotic changes of tubulus contortus I.

393.

Considerable or slight Glomerulo-nephrosis (mainly in acute stimulised form) with slight peripolar changes and Nephrosis in I. stage, at some places in III. stage with considerable interstitial edema.[redacted]

[redacted]

[redacted]

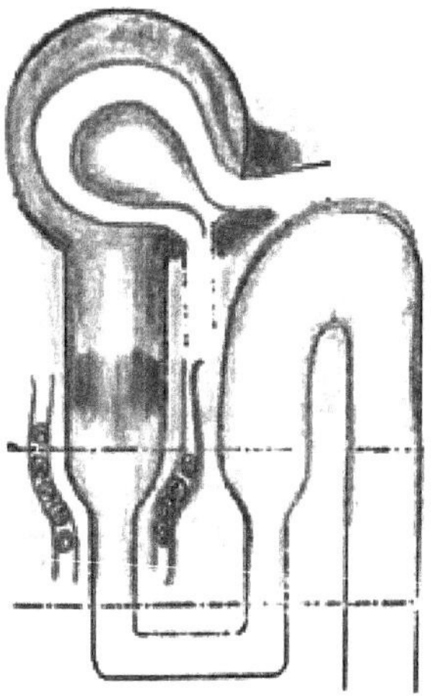
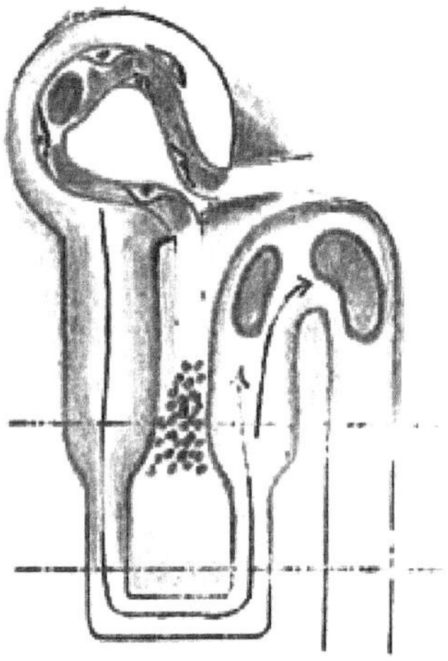
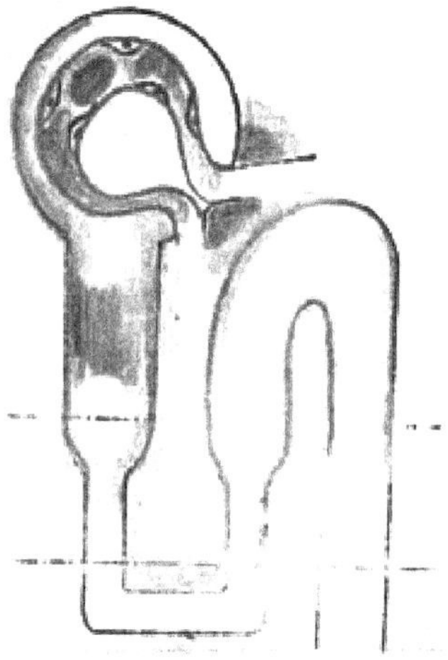

396.

Slight Glomerulo-nephrosis (mainly in degerative form) with slight peripolar change and Nephrosis in I. stage, at some places in III. stage with considerable interstitial edema, accompanied with some leucocytes as capillaries contents.

399.

Slight Glomerulo-nephrosis in acute stimalised form with some bacterial and fibrinous masses in glomerular loops and slight peripolar changes.
Nephrosis in I st stage with considerable interstitial edema and some round cell-accumulation in interstitial tissues.
Glomerulogenous erythrocytic cylinders in tubular spaces.

403.

Slight Glomerulo-nephrosis (in stimulided form) with bacterial and fibrinous masses in glomerular loops and slight peripolar changes.
Nephrosis in I st stage, at some places in III rd stage with considerable interstitial edema.

[redacted]

257

[redacted]

404

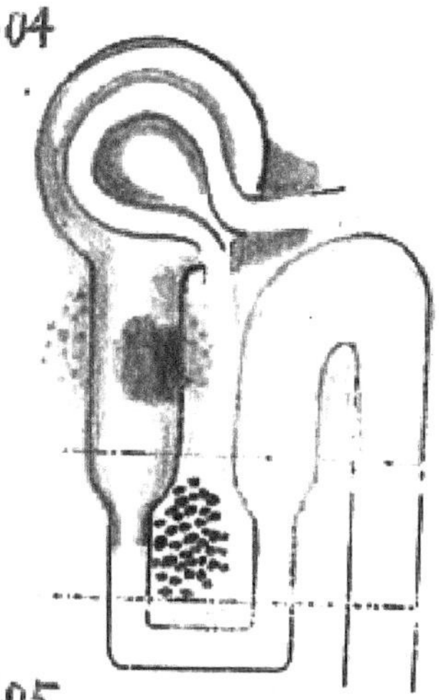

405

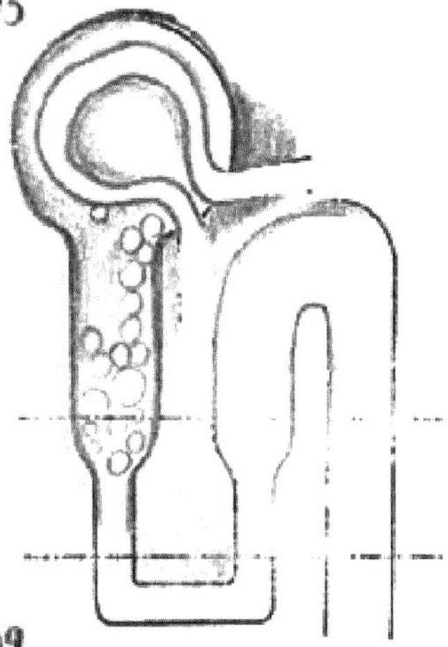

409

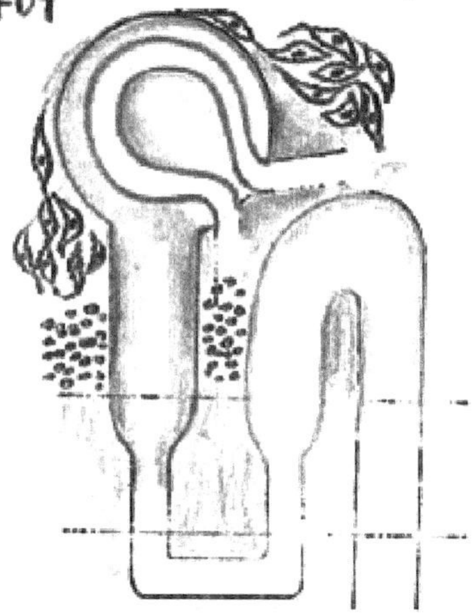

[redacted]

404.

Slight Glomerulo-nephrosis with slight peripolar changes and Nephrosis in I st or at some places in III rd stage with considerable interstitial edema and some round-cell-accumulations at cortico-medullar boundary.

405.

Slight glomerulo-nephrosis with slight peripolar changes and Nephrosis in I st stage with extremly severe vacuolar degenerations of tubulus contortus I. and considerable interstitial edema.

407.

Slight Glomerulo-nephrosis with slight peripolar changes and Nephrosis in I st stage with considerable interstitial edema.

409.

Slight Glomerulo-nephrosis with slight peripolar changes and Nephrosis in I st stage with considerable interstitial edema, some round-cell-accumulations at some places and miliary cirrhotic portions in cortex.

411.

Slight Glomerulo-nephrosis with slight peripolar changes and Nephrosis in I st stage with considerable interstitial edema and extremly severe vacuolar

[redacted] 258

[redacted]

[redacted]

412

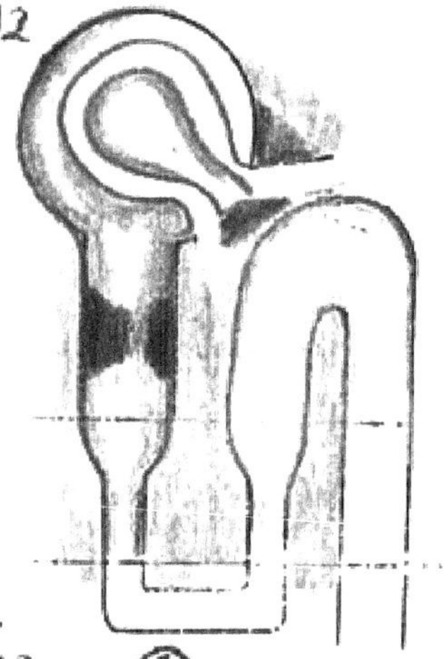

413

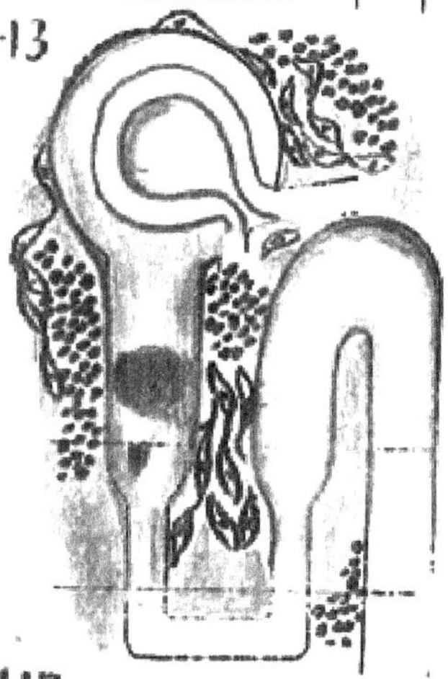

417

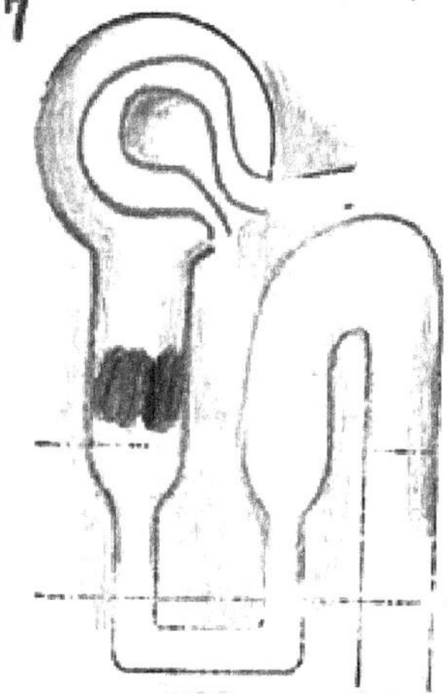

degeneration of tubular epitheliums at subcapsular portions.

412.

Slight Glomerulo-nephrosis with slight peripolar changes and Nephrosis in I st or at some places in III rd stage with considerable or remarkable interstitial edema.

413.

Slight Glomerulo-nephrosis with slight peripolar changes and Nephrosis in I st stage or at some places in III rd stage.

At some places, Nephritis interstitialis subacuta with massive round-cell-accumulations, considerable edema and considerable hyperplasia of connective tissues in interstitiums.

417.

Slight Glomerulo-nephrosis with slight peripolar changes and Nephrosis in I st stage or at some places III rd stage with considerable interstitial edema.

[redacted]

259

[redacted]

S U M M A R Y

[redacted]

A7 Tubular changes:

Generally occured more or less intense cloudy swelling of tubular epitheliums with some various cylinders in tubular spaces.

Nephrosis	in I. degree.	24 cases.
	in II. degree.	5 cases.
	in III. degree.	
	with some bionecrotic swelling,	2 cases.
	with some necrotic changes,	3 cases.
All investigated		34 cases.

Tubular contents:

	Protein-masses.	Hyaline subst.
in slight degree	8	0
in medium degree	15	18
in severe degree	I	I

B) Glomerular changes :

Generally occured some glomerular changes : Glomerulo-nephrosis, Randerath's, with some edematous swelling of capillary walls of

[redacted] 260

[redacted]

glomerular loops, swelling or slight increase of [redacted] and some serous exsudation in Bowmann's spaces.

Glomerulo-nephrosis

in very slight degree	( ).	19 cases.
in slight degree	( ).	4 cases.
in medium degree	( ).	I cases.

Polar changes :

in very slight degree:	10 cases:
in slight degree.	13 cases.
in medium degree.	1 cases.

C) Interstitium.

Generally with more or less intense edema, sometimes with some heemorrhages and sometimes with some round cell accumulation in interstiums.

A few cases with some signs of Nephritis interstitialis subchronica.

Haemorrhages.	cortical	medullary tissues.
in slight degree	2	0
in medium degree,	0	0
in severe degree.	0	0

[redacted] 261

[redacted]

On polar changes :

[redacted]

Our so-called polar portions of kidney fall within like periglomerular areas at afferent portions of blood-vessels, bounded with 2 blood-vessels (V.afferens and defferens) and intercalary portion of tubulus and equipped with special cellular arraggements with neuro-myo-angio-epitheliar segments, which belong to so-called diffuse endocrinic system.

These areas are very chemoreceptoric, and able to regulate blood-quantity in glomeruli and furthermore favorite-seats of various inflammatory changes.

Noxae, advanced hemotogenously to kidney, aause inflammatory changes firstly at afferent portions, due to their chemoreceptoric properties, then at glomeruli and sometimes at V. defferens.

Thus occrued inflammatory changes angio-vasculally at perivascular portions in Δ -areas.

These noxae are filtrated at glomerular loops, then excreted in tubulus with nephrosis and some of them absorbed again mainly at intercalary portions of tubulus, accompanied with considerable degeneration of tubular epitheliar cells and some peritubular inflammatory changes in neighbouring Δ -areas.

Thus occured inflammatory changes epitheliogenously at peritubular portions in Δ -areas.

Δ -areas are very sensitive to inflammatory changes, which occured in 2 manners, a) angiovasculally at perivascular portions with mesenchymal reactions and b) epitheliogenously at peritubular portions with epitheliogenous reactions and accompanied with various complicated changes, due to chemoreceptoric and regenerative properties of these

[redacted] 262

[redacted]

intercalary portions. [redacted]

In -areas, inflammatory changes apt to be occured and if occured, in 2 manners, not only with mesenchymal reactions, but also with epitheliogenous reactions.

Such special cellular arragements with mesenchymal and epitheliar segments which belong to diffuse endocrinic system, are expected to exist in each organs(for example, dicovery of "lung-island" by us) and inflammatory changes of these portions are named by us "polar changes" of each organs.

[redacted] 263

[redacted]

KIDNEY [redacted]

	17	26	54	225	318	320	325	328	389	390	393	396	399	401	403	404	405	407	409	411	412	413	416	417
Gromeruli – Glomerular Loop – Dilatation	+	+	+·	+·	+	+·	+·	+	+	+	+·	+	+·	+·	+	+·	+	+·	+·	+	+·	+·	+·	+·
Gromeruli – Glomerular Loop – Capillary-Walls – Swelling	+·	÷	+	+·	+	+	+	+·	+	+	+	+	+	+	÷	÷	+	÷	+	÷	+	+	+	+
Gromeruli – Glomerular Loop – Capillary-Walls – Deposition of Hyaline or Albuminoid Substance	+·	+	+	+·	+	+	+	+	+·	+	+	+	+	÷	÷	÷	÷	÷	÷	÷	+	÷	÷	÷
Gromeruli – Glomerular Loop – Changes of Nuclei – Increase of Nuclei	∸	÷	÷	+	÷	÷	+	÷	∸	÷	÷	−	÷	÷	∸	÷	+	∸	÷	∸	∸	∸	÷	∸
Gromeruli – Glomerular Loop – Changes of Nuclei – Swelling	+	+	+	+	+	+·	++	+·	÷	+	++	÷	++	++	÷	+·	++	+	++	+	+	+	+	+
Gromeruli – Glomerular Loop – Changes of Nuclei – Pyknosis	÷	÷	(+)	÷	∸	÷	∸	∸	+·	∸	∸	+	∸	∸	+·	∸	−	+·	∸	÷	÷	+	÷	+
Gromeruli – Glomerular Loop – Contents of Capillaries – Erythrocytes	(+)	+++	+·	+·	++	+·	++	+·	+·	++	+·	(+·)	++	++	++	+·	++	++	+·	++	+·	+·	+·	++
Gromeruli – Glomerular Loop – Contents of Capillaries – Round Cells	∸	∸	∸	∸	∸	∸	∸	∸	∸	∸	∸	∸	∸	∸	∸	∸	∸	∸	∸	∸	∸	∸	∸	∸
Gromeruli – Bowman's Lumen – Dilatation	∸	[illegible]	÷	[illegible]	∸	∸	∸	∸	∸	÷	∸	∸	−	∸	÷	÷	∸	∸	∸	∸	÷	∸	∸	∸
Gromeruli – Bowman's Lumen – Hyaline or Albuminoid Casts	÷	÷	∸	÷	÷	(+++)	÷	÷	+	÷	÷	÷	÷	+	∸	÷	+	÷	÷	∸	+	÷	∸	+
Gromeruli – Bowman's Lumen – Penetrative Fluid	÷	∸	∸	÷	÷	+	÷	∸	+	+	+·	+	÷	÷	÷	÷	÷	÷	÷	÷	÷	÷	+	÷
Gromeruli – Epithelium of Bowman's Capsules – Cloudy Swelling	∸	+	÷	÷	÷	∸	÷	÷	÷	÷	+	÷	÷	∸	∸	∸	÷	∸	÷	∸	∸	∸	∸	÷
Gromeruli – Epithelium of Bowman's Capsules – Proliferation	∸	−	∸	∸	∸	∸	÷	∸	∸	∸	÷	∸	÷	∸	∸	∸	÷	∸	∸	∸	∸	÷	∸	∸
Gromeruli – Bowman's Capsules – Swelling	÷	÷	∸	+	÷	÷	∸	∸	÷	÷	÷	÷	÷	÷	÷	÷	÷	∸	∸	∸	÷	÷	÷	÷
Gromeruli – Bowman's Capsules – Hyaline Degeneration	∸	∸	∸	+	∸	÷	∸	∸	÷	∸	∸	∸	∸	∸	∸	∸	∸	∸	∸	∸	∸	∸	∸	∸
Gromeruli – Vasa afferentia – Congestion	(+)	++	+	+	+·	+·	+·	+	+	++	+	+	+·	+·	+·	+·	+·	+·	+·	+·	+	+	+	+·
Gromeruli – Vasa afferentia – Endothelial Cells – Swelling	∸	∸	∸	÷	÷	÷	÷	÷	÷	÷	÷	÷	÷	÷	∸	÷	÷	(+)	÷	÷	÷	÷	÷	÷
Gromeruli – Vasa afferentia – Endothelial Cells – Proliferation	∸	∸	∸	∸	÷	(÷)	∸	∸	∸	∸	∸	∸	∸	∸	∸	∸	∸	(÷)	∸	∸	∸	∸	∸	∸
Gromeruli – Vasa afferentia – Endothelial Cells – Desquamation	∸	∸	∸	∸	∸	∸	∸	∸	∸	−	∸	−	∸	∸	∸	−	∸	∸	∸	∸	∸	−	∸	∸
Gromeruli – Vasa afferentia – Media – Swelling	÷	÷	+	+	÷	÷	÷	+	÷	÷	÷	÷	÷	÷	÷	÷	÷	÷	÷	÷	÷	÷	÷	÷
Gromeruli – Vasa afferentia – Media – Hyaline Degeneration	÷	∸	∸	(+)	∸	∸	∸	∸	∸	∸	∸	÷	∸	∸	∸	∸	∸	∸	∸	÷	∸	∸	∸	∸
Gromeruli – Vasa afferentia – Media – Tendency to Necrosis	∸	−	∸	÷	−	−	∸	∸	∸	∸	−	(÷)	−	−	−	−	−	−	−	∸	−	−	−	∸
Gromeruli – Vasa afferentia – Adventitial Cells – Swelling	÷	∸	÷	÷	÷	÷	÷	÷	÷	+	+	÷	(+)	÷	÷	÷	÷	(÷)	÷	÷	÷	÷	÷	÷
Gromeruli – Vasa afferentia – Adventitial Cells – Proliferation	∸	∸	∸	÷	÷	(÷)	∸	∸	∸	÷	÷	∸	(+)	∸	∸	∸	∸	÷	∸	÷	∸	∸	∸	÷
Gromeruli – Vasa afferentia – Adjoining Portion – Peripolar Edema	+·	÷	÷	+·	+	+	(+)	+	+	+	+	+·	+	+	+	+·	+	+	+	+	+·	+·	+·	+·
Gromeruli – Vasa afferentia – Adjoining Portion – Appearance of "Polkissen"	∸	(÷)	∸	÷	÷	÷	÷	(÷)	∸	÷	÷	∸	+	÷	(÷)	÷	(+)	(÷)	(÷)	÷	÷	∸	∸	÷
Gromeruli – Vasa afferentia – Adjoining Portion – Macula densa	∸	∸	∸	∸	÷	÷	∸	(÷)	∸	÷	÷	∸	÷	∸	∸	(÷)	÷	∸	∸	∸	∸	∸	∸	∸
Parenchyma – Tubules – Epithelium – Cloudy Swelling	++	++	+·	+++	++	++	++	+·	+·	++	++	++	+·	+·	+·	++	+·	+·	++	+·	++	++	++	++
Parenchyma – Tubules – Epithelium – Hyaline Droplet Degeneration	−	−	−	(∸)	−	−	−	−	−	−	−	−	−	−	−	−	−	−	−	−	−	−	−	−
Parenchyma – Tubules – Epithelium – Vacuolar Degeneration	∸	∸	÷	(+++)	+	÷	+	÷	÷	∸	∸	∸	(+)	÷	÷	÷	++	÷	(+)	(+)	÷	÷	÷	÷
Parenchyma – Tubules – Epithelium – Fatty Degeneration	∸	−	∸	+	÷	÷	∸	∸	∸	−	∸	−	÷	∸	−	∸	+	∸	÷	÷	∸	∸	∸	∸
Parenchyma – Tubules – Epithelium – Necrosis	+	−	∸	(+++)	÷	∸	∸	∸	∸	++	+	++	∸	−	(÷)	÷	−	∸	∸	−	(÷)	(∸)	(÷)	÷
Parenchyma – Tubules – Epithelium – Degenerations of Nuclei	+·	+	+	++	+	÷	÷	÷	÷	+	+	++	÷	÷	+	+	÷	÷	+	÷	+	÷	+	+
Parenchyma – Tubules – Contents – Cloudy or Massive Albuminoid Substance	÷	÷	÷	+	+	++	÷	+	+	+	+·	+	÷	+·	+	+	+	÷	+	÷	+	÷	+	+
Parenchyma – Tubules – Contents – Fibrinous Substance	−	−	−	(÷)	∸	∸	−	−	−	−	−	−	−	(+)	−	−	−	−	−	−	−	−	−	−
Parenchyma – Tubules – Contents – Hyaline or Colloid Cylinder	(+)	−	−	(+++)	+	(++)	(++)	(++)	(++)	(+)	−	(+)	−	+	(+)	(++)	(++)	(++)	(+)	+	(+)	(+)	+	−
Parenchyma – Tubules – Contents – Various Calcium Casts	−	−	+	÷	−	−	−	−	−	−	−	−	(+)	−	−	−	−	−	(+)	−	−	−	−	−
Parenchyma – Tubules – Contents – Erythrocytes	−	−	−	∸	∸	−	−	∸	−	−	−	−	−	(++)	−	−	−	−	∸	−	−	−	(++)	−
Interstitium – Congestion – Cortex	(+++)	+++	+·	+++	++	++	+	+·	+	++	(+)	(++)	+·	+·	+·	+·	+·	+·	+·	++	+·	+·	++	++
Interstitium – Congestion – Medulla	+	++·	(++·)	(+·)	++	(++)	+·	++·	++	+·	+	(++)	++	+·	+·	++	(++)	+·	+·	+	+·	+·	+++	++·
Interstitium – Edema – Cortex	++	÷	+	(++)	÷	++	+	+	+	+	+	+·	+	(+)	+	+·	+	+	+	+	+·	+·	+·	+·
Interstitium – Edema – Medulla	++·	++	+·	+	+·	+·	+·	+·	+·	+·	+·	(+·)	+	+	+·	+·	+	+·	+·	+·	+·	+·	+·	+·
Interstitium – Hemorrhage – Cortex	(÷)	−	−	(∸)	−	−	−	−	−	−	−	−	−	−	−	−	−	−	−	−	−	−	−	−
Interstitium – Hemorrhage – Medulla	−	∸	−	−	−	−	−	−	−	−	−	−	−	−	−	−	−	−	−	−	−	−	−	−
Interstitium – Round-Cell Infiltration – Cortex	−	∸	(+)	÷	(+)	∸	∸	(÷)	∸	−	∸	∸	∸	(+)	∸	−	∸	−	÷	−	−	−	++	−
Interstitium – Round-Cell Infiltration – Medulla	−	−	∸	∸	∸	∸	−	∸	−	−	−	−	−	−	−	−	−	−	∸	−	−	−	++	−
Interstitium – Vessel Walls – Hyaline Degeneration	÷	∸	∸	+	∸	+	÷	∸	÷	÷	∸	∸	∸	∸	∸	∸	∸	∸	∸	∸	∸	∸	∸	÷
Interstitium – Vessel Walls – Tendency to Necrosis	∸	−	∸	÷	∸	−	(÷)	∸	∸	(∸)	∸	∸	∸	−	−	∸	−	−	−	−	−	−	−	−
Interstitium – Vessel Walls – Proliferation of Adventitial Cells	÷	∸	∸	÷	∸	+	∸	÷	∸	∸	∸	+	∸	(+)	∸	(+)	+	÷	∸	∸	∸	∸	+	÷
Colonies of Bacterium	−	−	+?	÷?	−	−	−	−	−	−	−	−	+?	+	−	−	−	−	−	−	−	−	−	−

[redacted] 264

[redacted]

Intense exudation in Bowmann's spaces.
Our so-called serous apoplexy of glomeruli.

[redacted]

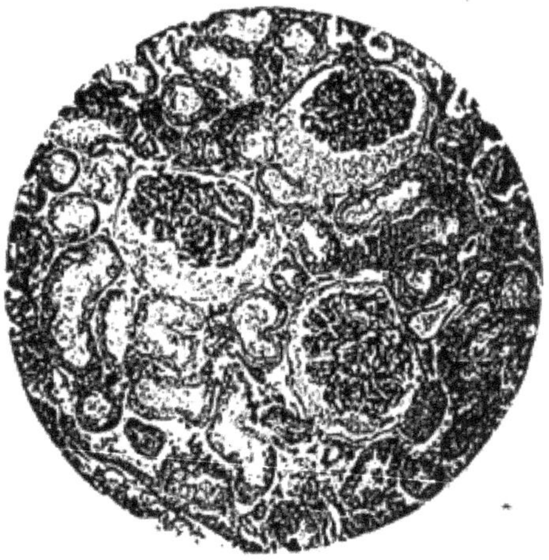

M 320 x120

Fibrinous masses in glomerular loops.

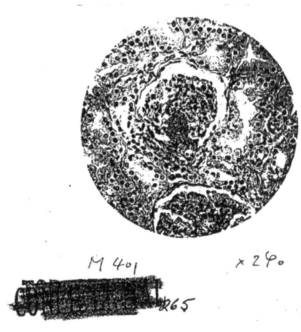

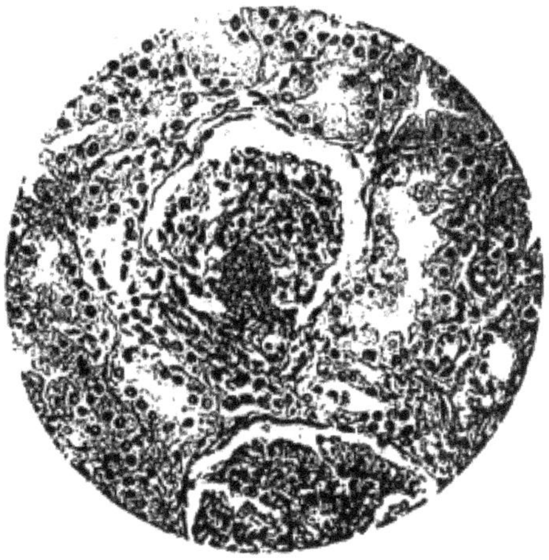

M 401 x240

[redacted] 265

[redacted]

Intese Glomerulo-nephrosis with erythtocytes-cylinders in tubulus.

[redacted]

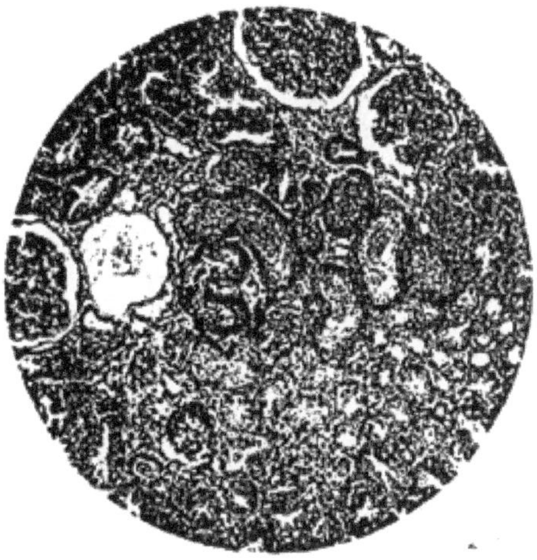

M-421 x70

Intese nephrosis with bionecrotic changes of tubular epitheliums.

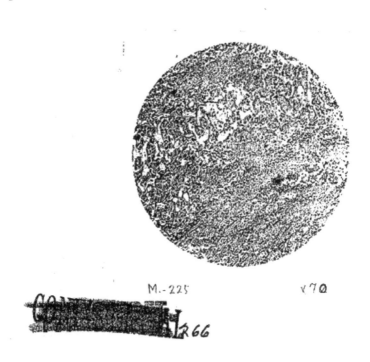

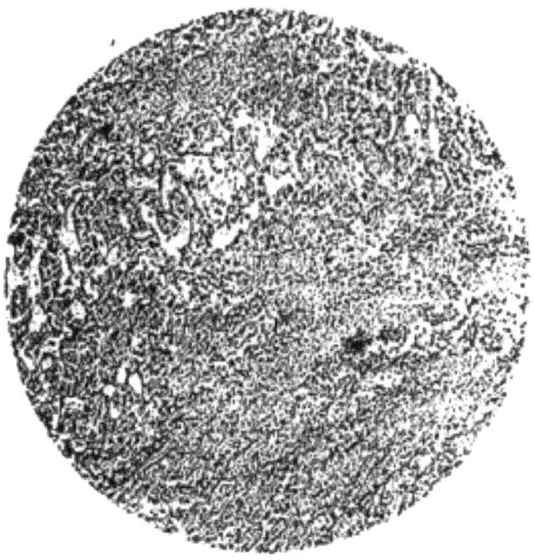

M.-225 x70

[redacted] 266

[redacted]

Nephritis interstitialis sub-acuta with some leucocytes accumulation.

[redacted]

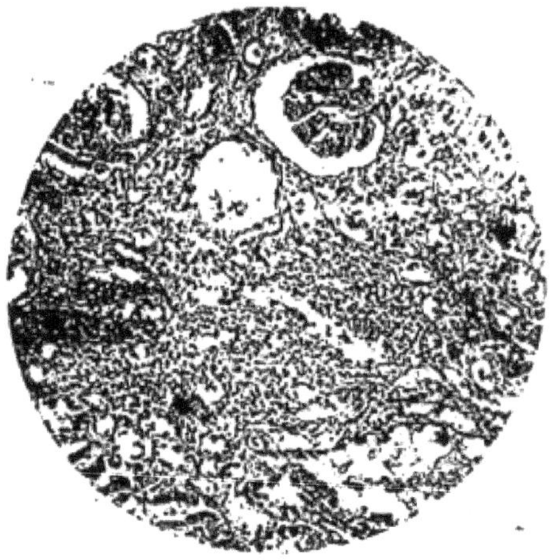

[redacted] R 67

[redacted]

CONFIDENTIAL

Pancreas

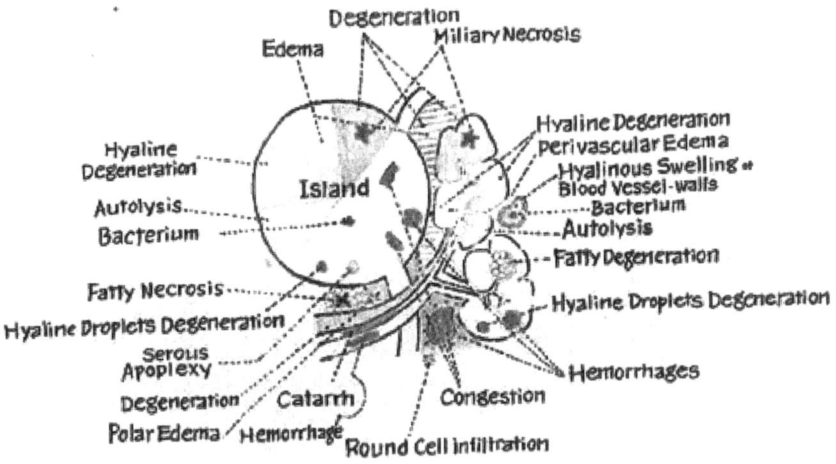

CONFIDENTIAL
[redacted]

268

[redacted]

PANCREAS.

[redacted] (A) Microscopical Investigations.

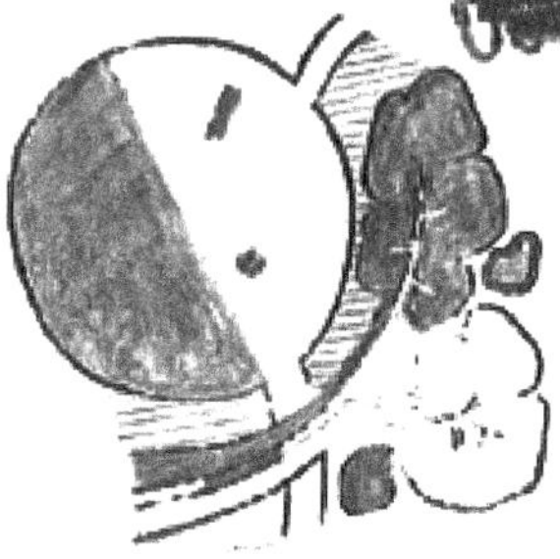

26.

Venous congestion and edematouls swelling of blood-vessels-walls. Remarkable parenchymatous degeneration, some of them in v-acuolar degeneration. Considerable vacuolar degeneration of island-cells.

53.

Slight venous congestion, slight degeneration of parenchymatous cells and island-cells. Hyalinous degeneration of blood-vessels-walls in slight degree.

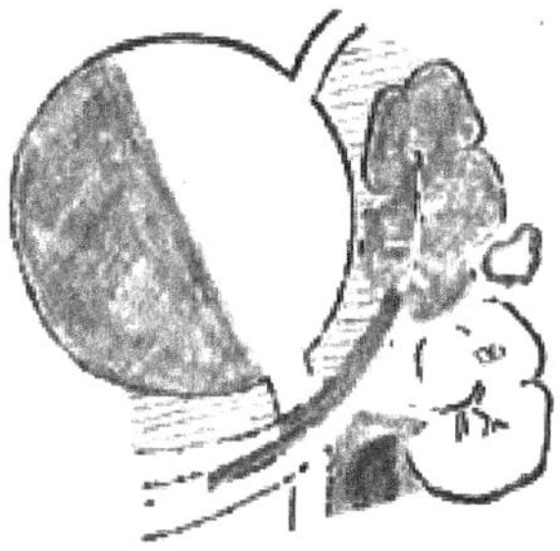

225.

Considerable venous congestion and slight edematous swelling of connective tissues. Atrophia of parenchymatous cells and slight dissociation of cell-arrangements. Considerable degeneration of parenchym. cells and island-cells.

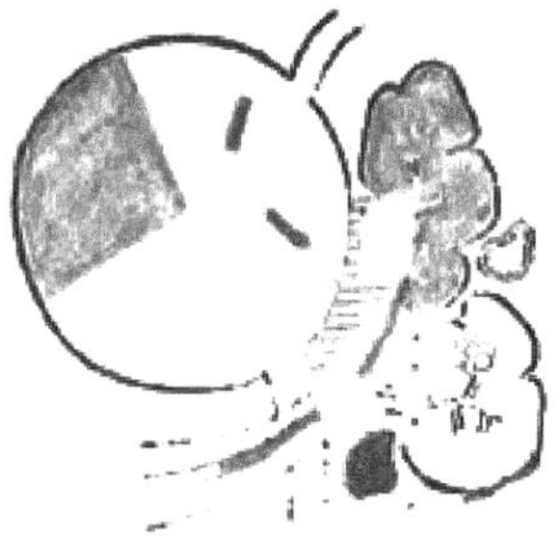

318.

Slight venous congestion and slight hemorrhages in connective tissues. Slight degeneration of parenchym. cells and island-cells. Slight catarrh of efferent ducts.

[redacted] 269

[redacted]

CONFIDENTIAL

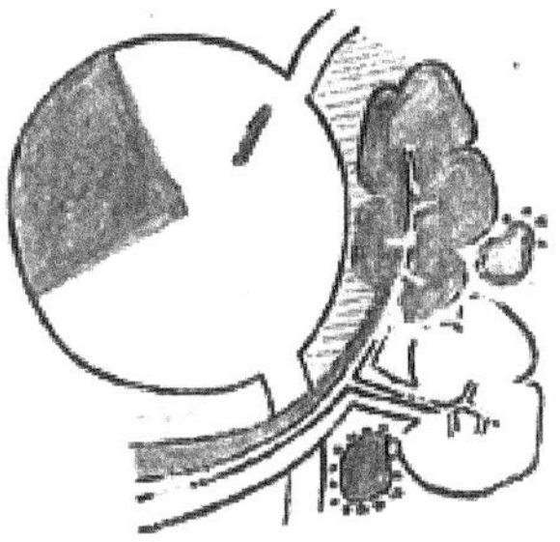

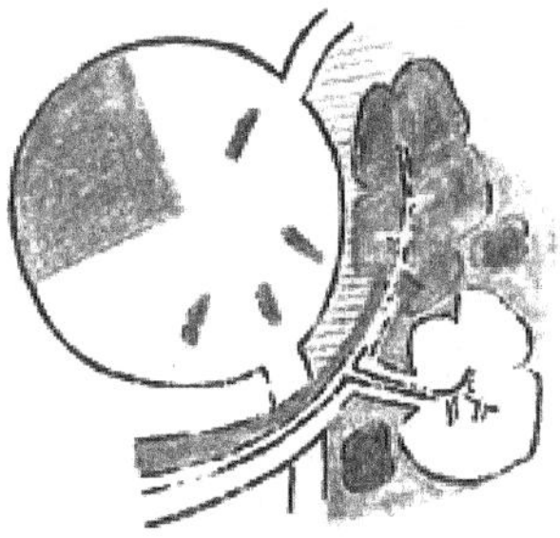

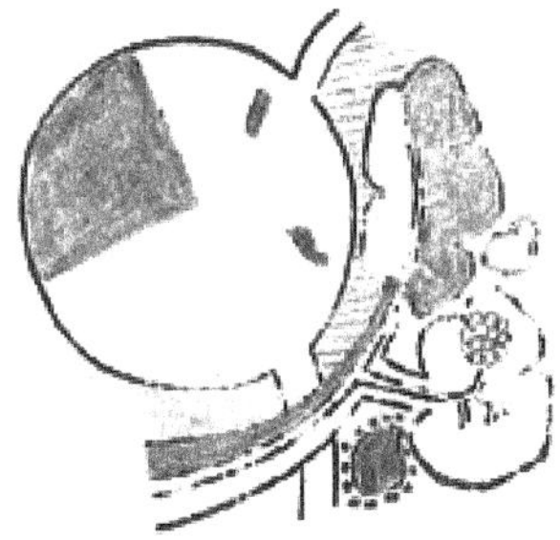

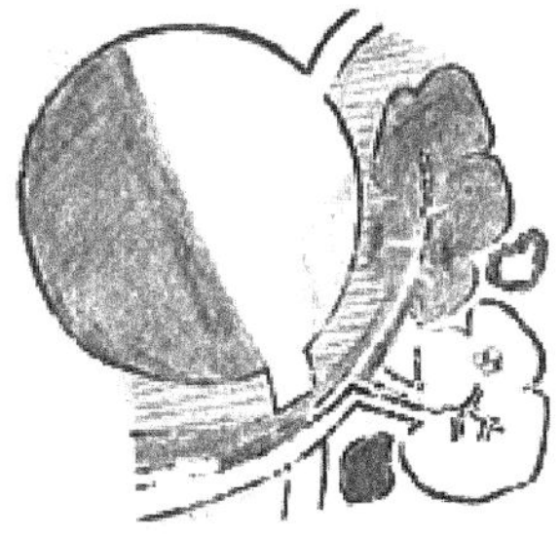

320.

Considerable venous congestion, perivascular round-cell-infiltration(some leucocytes, lymphocytes, plasma-cells and histiocytes) and perivascular edematous swelling.

Cloudy swelling of parenchymatous cells and island-cells.

Remarkable stasis of island-capillaries and considerable hyperplasia of capillary-walls-cells.

328.

Consid. venous congestion and edmatous swelling of connective tissues. Edematous swelling of blood-vessel-walls and slight dissociation of parenchym. cell-arrangements.

Atrophia of parenchymatous cells and slight degeneration of parenchym. cells, esp. at perivascular portions. Consid, degeneration of island-cells.

393.

Venius congestion and edematous swelling of connective tissues. Slight dissociation of cell-arrange-ments and cloudy swelling of parenchym. cells and island-cells.

406.

Stasis and slight degeneration of parenchymatous cells.

CONFIDENTIAL

270

[redacted]

[redacted]

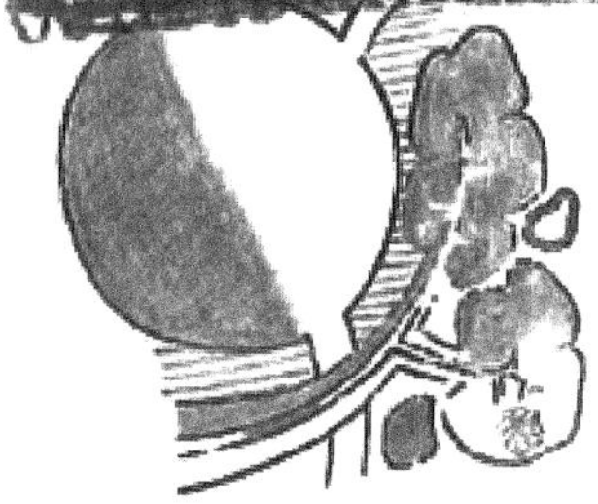

403.

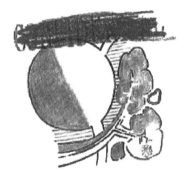

Considerable venous congestion, slight edematous swelling of connective tissues and slight hyalinous degeneration of bloodvessel-walls.

Dissociation of cell-arrangements and considerable degeneration of parenchym. cells and island-cells. Catarrh of efferent ducts.

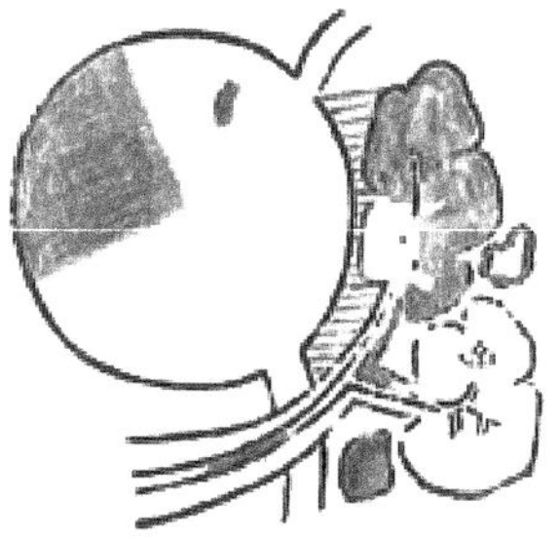

407.

Venous congestion and hyalinous degeneration of blood-vessels-walls. Atrophia and cloudy swelling of parenchym. cells and vacuolar degeneration of island-cells.

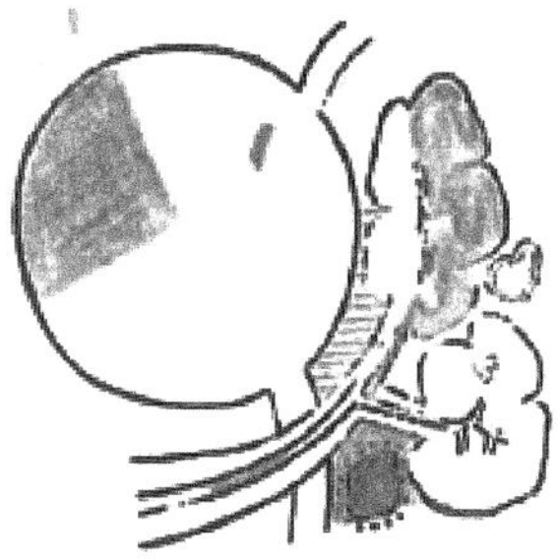

409.

Edematous swelling of connective tissues and dissociation of cell-arrangements. Cloudy swelling of parenchym. cells and vacuolar degeration of island-cells.

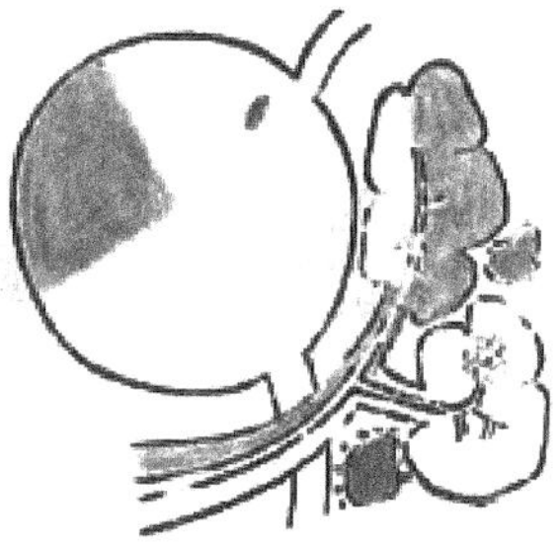

4II.

Considerable venous congestion, swelling of connective tissues and slight perivascular round-cell-infiltration.

Atrophia and cloudy swelling of parenchym. cells and remarkable vacuolar degeneration of island-cells.

[redacted] 271

● [redacted] ●

412. [redacted]

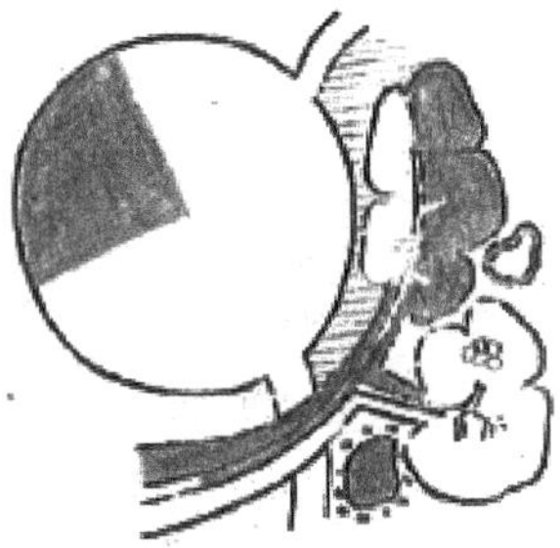

Swelling of connective tissues and dissociation of cell-arrangements. Considerable degeneration of parenchymatous cells and considerable swelling or cloudy degeneration of island-cells.

417.

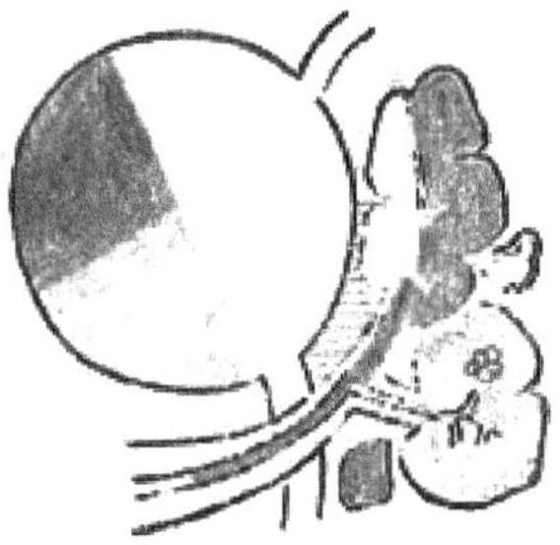

In autolysis. Vacuolar degeneration of parenchym. cells.

[redacted]

272

[redacted]

[redacted]

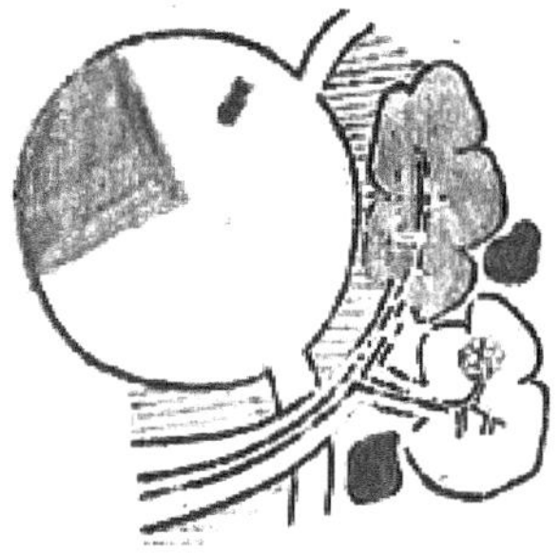

17.

Remarkable congestion with edematous swelling and hyalinous degeneration of blood-vessel-walls. Atrophia and remarkable cloudy swelling of parenchymatous cells. ; considerable vacuolar degeneration of parenchymatous cells and island-cells. Edematous swelling of connective tissiues.

Slight fatty degeneration of parenchymatous cells.

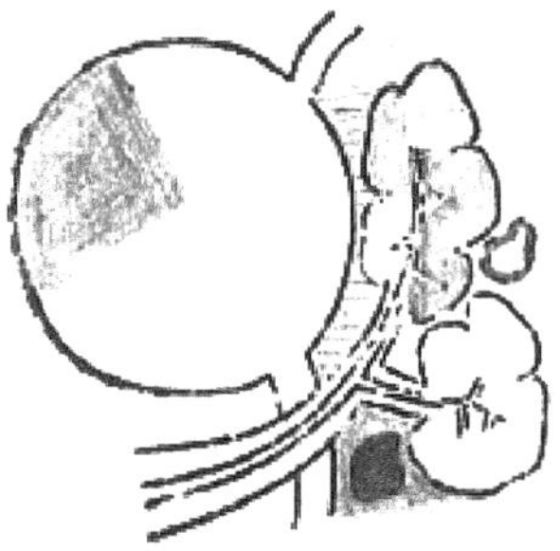

54.

Slight congestion with edematous swelling and hyalinous degeneration of blood-vesel-walls.

Slight cloudy swelling and atrophia of parenchymatous cells.

Considerable vacuolar degeneration of parenchymatous cells and island-cells.

Slight hemorrhages in interstitial tissues.

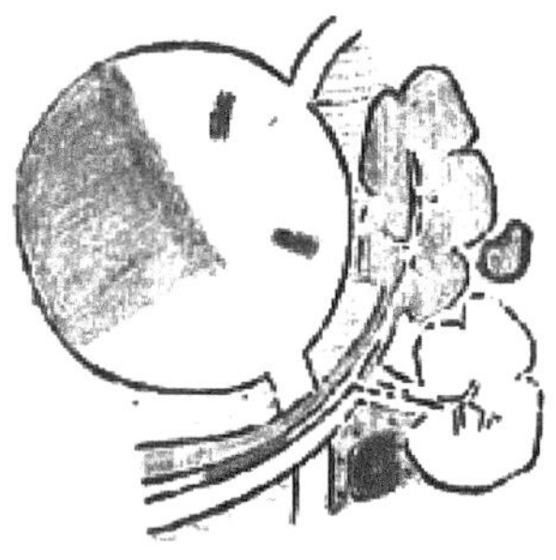

325.

Considerable congestion, perivascular round-cell-infiltration (some leucocytes, lymphocytes, plasmacells and histiocytes),

[redacted] 273

• [redacted] •

[redacted]

Slight edematous swelling and slight hyalinous degeneration of blood-vessel-walls, and perivascular edema.

Remarkable cloudy swelling of parenchymatous cells and island-cells. Slight swelling of connective tissues.

Catarrh of efferent ducts.

388.

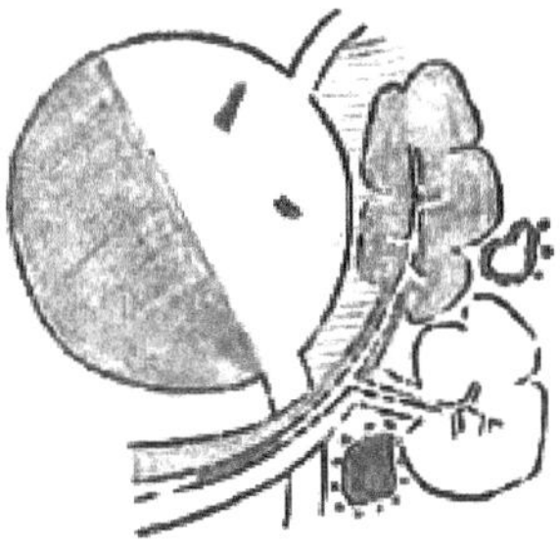

Slight congestion, perivascular round-cell-infiltration (some leucocytes, lymphocytes, plasmacells and histiocytes).

Slight edematous swelling and slight hyalinous degeneration of blood-vessel-walls.

Considerable cloudy swelling of parenchymatous cells and island-cells.

389.

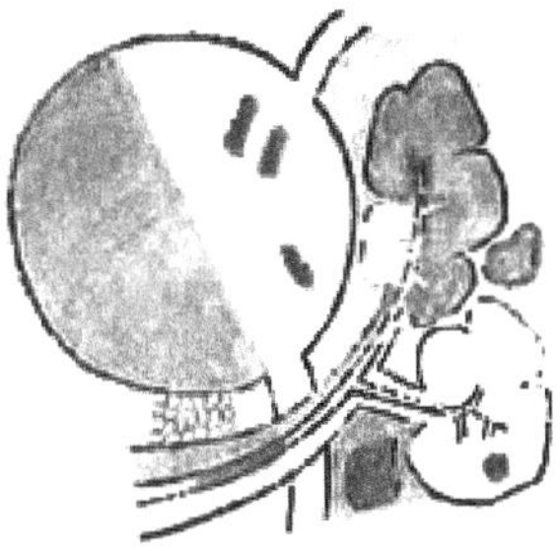

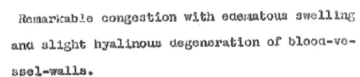

Remarkable congestion with edematous swelling and slight hyalinous degeneration of blood-vessel-walls.

Slight cloudy swelling of parenchymatous cells and island-cells ; considerable vacuolar degeneration of parenchymatous cells and island-cells.

Slight hemorrhages in acinous cells.

Catarrh of efferent ducts.

[redacted] 274

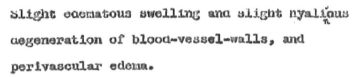

• [redacted] •

[redacted]

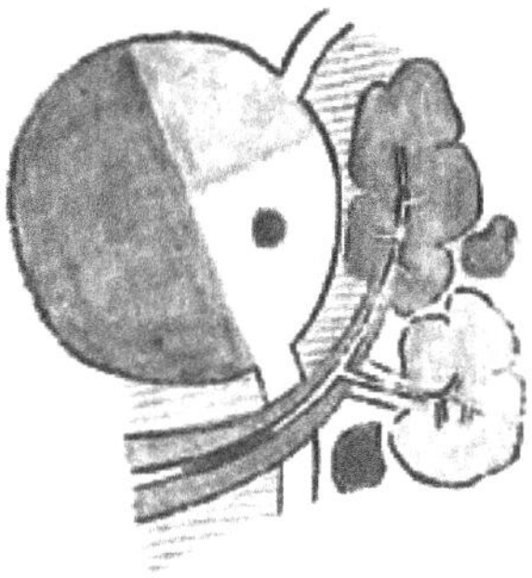

390.

In autolysis. Remarkable congestion with hyalinous degeneration and edematous swelling of blood-vesel-walls.

Perivascular edema. Remarkable swelling of connective tissusees. Remarkable cloudy swelling of parenchymatous cells and island-cells.

Hemorrahges in island-cells.

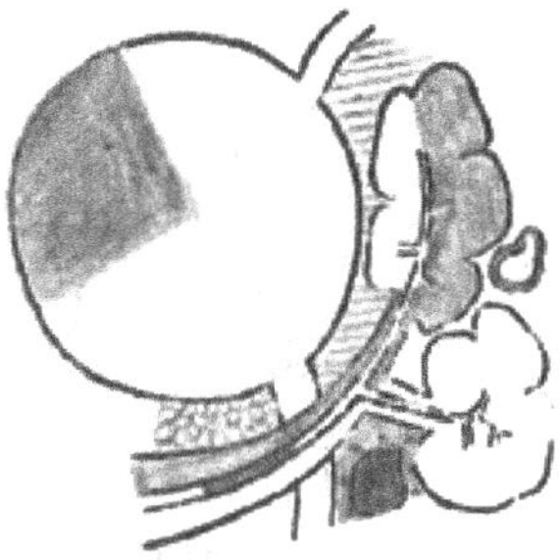

397.

Slight congestion with edematous swelling and hyalinous degeneration of blood-vesel-walls. Perivascular edema.

Slight cloudy swelling of parenchymatous cells and island-cells. Conciderable vacuolar degeneration of parenchymatous cells and island-cells. Dissociation and atrophia of parenchymatous cells.

Fatty degeneration and diffuse hemorrahges in interstitial tissues.

Remarkable pyknosis of island-cells.

[redacted] 275

[redacted]

399.

[redacted]

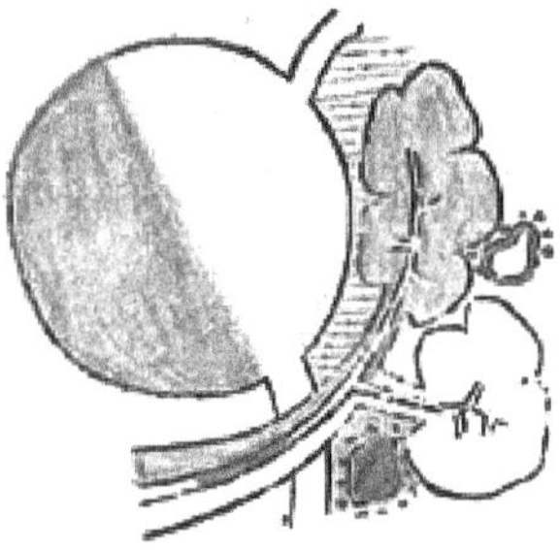

Slight congestion with edematous swelling and hyalinous degeneration of blood-vessel-walls.

Perivascular round-cell-infiltration, (some leucocytes,lymphocytes, plasma-cells and histiocytes).

Considerable cloudy swelling of parenchymatous cells and island-cells. Remarkable vacuolar degeneration of parenchymatous cells and island-cells.

Slight swelling of connective tissues.

Catarrh of efferent ducts.

401.

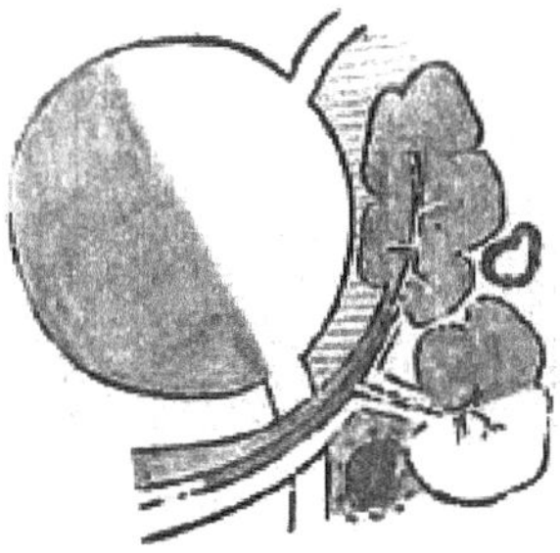

Slight congestion with edematous swelling and hyalinous degeneration of blood-vessel-walls.

Perivascular round-cell-immfiltration, (some leucocytes, lymphocytes,plasma-cells and histiocytes). Considerable cloudy swelling of parenchymatous cells and island cells.

Considerable vacuolar degeneration of parenchymatous cells and island-cells.

Arophia of parenchymatous cells.

Slight swelling of connective tissues. Catarrh of efferernt ducts.

[redacted] 276

[redacted]

[redacted]

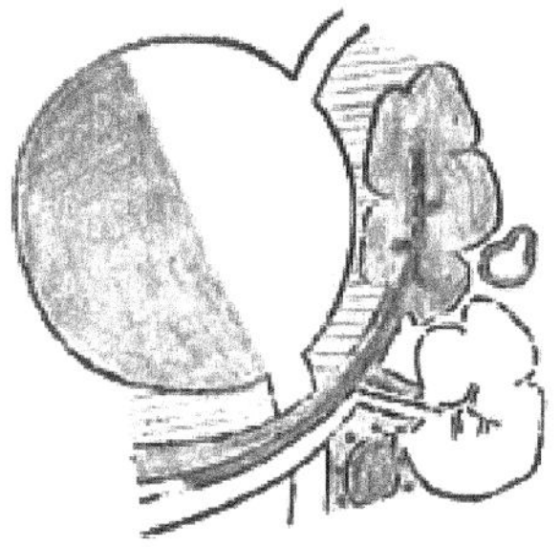

404.

Slight congestion with hyalinous degeneration of blood-vessel-walls. Considerable cloudy swelling of parenchymatous cells and island-cells. Remarkable vacuolar degeneration of parenchymatous cells and island-cells.
Dissociation and atrophia of parenchymatous cells.
Remarkable pyonosis of island-cells.

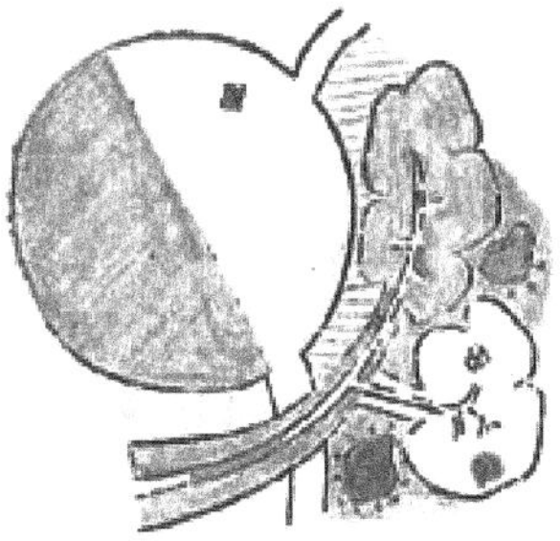

405.

Remarkable congestion with edematous swelling and hyalinous degeneration of blood-vessel-walls.
Perivascular round-cell-infiltration (some leucocytes, lymphocytes, plasmacells and hystiocytes).
Considerable cloudy swelling of parenchymatous cells and island-cells. Remarkable vacuolar degeneration of parenchymatous cells and island-cells.
Arophia and dissociation of parenchymatous cells.
Hemorrahges in acinous cells. Diffuse hemorrhagia per diapedisin in interstitial tissues.

[redacted] 77

[redacted]

[redacted]

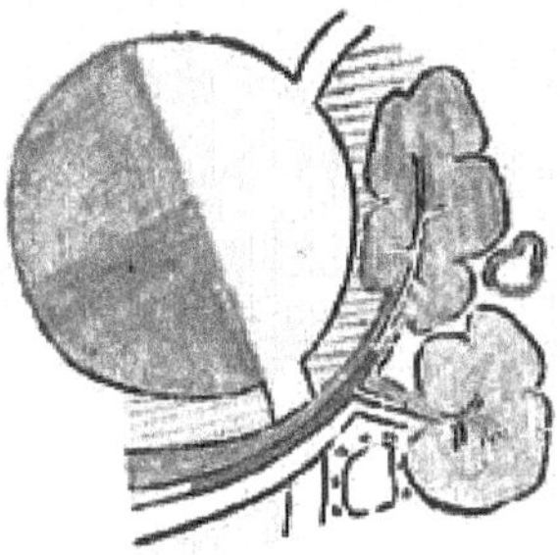

413.

In autolysis, Hyalinous degeneration of blood-vessel-walls.

Remarkable cloudy swelling of parenchymatous cells and island-cells. Vacuolar degeneration of island-cells.

Remarkable edema of interstitial tissues.

Dissociation of parenchymatous cells.

[redacted] 278

[redacted]

(B) SUMMARY.

[redacted]istological observation on 26 micro-slices, I case with severe post mortal changes.

A). Acinus.

I) In the most cases, with some congestion of inter- and intra-acinous capillaries.

Congestion in slight degree. 4 cases.

Congestion in medium degree. 12 cases.

Congestion in severe degree. 9 cases.

Congestion with hyalinous swelling or degeneration of capillary-walls. 17 cases.

Congestion, accompanied with considerable perivascular hemorrhages. 11 cases.

Congestion, accompanied with some perivascular round-cell-accumulations (some leucocytes, lymphocytes, plasma-cells and histiocytes) 13 cases.

Accordingly the main pathological changes are following:

Congestion (often, remarkable) ____ Edematous swelling of capillary walls ____ Perivascular edema, hemorrhages and some round-cell-accumulations (sometimes leucocytes-disseminations in interstitial tissues).

[redacted] 279

[redacted]

2) After that, occured some degenerative changes of parenchymatous cells esp. at pericapillar por-
[redacted] tions.

With cloudy swelling of parenchym cells

in slight degree. 11 cases.

in medium degree. 25 case.

in severe degree. 0 cases.

with hyalinous degeneration.

0 case.

With hyaline-droplets formation.

0 case.

Accordingly, it shows generally some considerable parenchymatous degeneration and sometimes, some remarkable changes without hyalinous degeneration or hyaline-droplets formation in acinus.

B). Islands.

I) Sometimes, with considerable congestion of islands-capillaries.

Congestion in considerable degree.

2 cases.

Congestion in remarkable degree, accompanied with edematous swelling of capillary-walls.

I case.

Congestion with our so-called "polar edema".

0 case.

[redacted] 280

[redacted]

[redacted]

Congestion with our so-called "serous apoplexy of island".

0 case.

Congestion with our so-called (hemorrhagic) apoplexy of islands.

1 case.

2. Sometimes, some degenerative changes of island-cells.

With rather atrophic cells.

4 case.

With cloudy swelling. 24 cases.

With (slight) vacuolar degeneration.

16 cases.

[redacted] 281

[redacted]

[redacted]

PANCREAS

			17	26	53	54	225	318	320	325	328	388	389	390	393	397
Acinus	Size		↓	↓	↓	↓	↓	↓	↓	↓	↓	↓	↓	↓	↓	↓
	Dissociation		−	−	−	−	−	−	−	−	−	−	−	−	−	−
	Necrosis		−	−	−	−	−	−	−	−	−	−	−	−	−	−
Parenchyma	Clouding		++	++	+	+̈	++	+̈	++	++	++	++	+̈	++	+	+
	Swelling		+̈	++	−	+̈	++	+̈	++	+̈	++	++	+̈	+	+	+
	Zymogen Granules		+	÷	+̈	−	−	++	+	−	−	−	÷	++	−	−
	Honeycombed Degeneration		+	÷	−	÷	÷	(++̈)	÷	++	−	÷	++	÷	+	++̈
	Changes of Nuclei	Swelling	−	−	−	−	−	−	−	−	−	−	−	−	−	−
		Pyknosis	÷	+	÷	÷	++̈	−	÷	+	+̈	÷	÷	÷	+	+̈
		Karyolysis	÷	−	−	−	++	−	−	−	−	÷	−	−	+	+
	Hyperplasia of Centroacinar Cells		−	−	−	−	−	−	−	−	−	−	−	−	−	−
	Dsq. of Epithelium of Efferent Ducts		−	÷	−	−	+̈	−	−	÷	−	−	−	÷	−	÷
Interstitium	Edema		+̈	÷	÷	÷	÷	÷	+̈	+	−	+̈	+̈	+̈	+̈	++
	Contents of Capillaries	Erythrocytes	++̈	++	++	+̈	+	+̈	++	++	+++	+̈	++	++	+̈	+̈
		Leucocytes	+̈	÷	−	−	−	−	+̈	−	+	+̈	÷	÷	÷	÷
		Lymphocytes	+	÷	−	÷	−	−	−	−	+	÷	÷	÷	÷	÷
	Hemorrhage		−	−	−	+	÷	÷	−	÷	(+++)	−	(++)	−	−	÷
	Infiltration	Leucocytes	−	−	−	−	−	−	−	−	−	−	−	−	−	−
		Lymphocytes	−	−	−	−	−	−	+̈	÷	−	÷	−	−	−	÷
	Proliferation	Plasma Cells	−	−	−	−	−	−	÷	−	÷	÷	−	−	÷	−
		Histiocytes	−	−	−	−	−	−	+̈	−	÷	÷	−	−	+	÷
		Capillary Wall-Cells	−	−	−	−	−	−	−	−	−	−	−	−	−	−
Langerhans's Island	Number		N	↓÷	N	N	↓+̈	↓−	N	↓÷	N	↓+++	N	↓+	↓÷	↓+̈
	Atrophia		÷	÷	−	÷	++	÷	−	÷	÷	+̈	÷	÷	−	+̈
	Necrosis		−	−	−	−	−	−	−	−	−	−	−	−	−	−
	Parenchymal Cells	Size	↓÷	↓÷	N	N	↓+	↓÷	↑÷	↓÷	N	↓+	↓÷	↓÷	N	↓÷
		Clouding	+	++	+̈	+	++	+	+	+̈	+	++	++	++	+	+̈
		Swelling	+	++	+̈	+	++	+	+	+̈	+	++	+	++	+	+
		Honeycombed Degeneration	÷	÷	−	÷	+	÷	−	−	−	−	+	÷	−	−
		Changes of Nuclei: Swelling	÷	−	−	−	−	−	−	−	+̈	−	−	−	−	÷
		Changes of Nuclei: Pyknosis	÷	++	+	÷	+	(+̈)	+	÷	−	÷	(+̈)	÷	++	++
		Changes of Nuclei: Karyolysis	÷	−	−	÷	+̈	÷	−	−	−	−	−	−	−	−
	Congestion of Capillaries		÷	÷	+	−	−	+	÷	+	++	÷	+	+̈	+	−
	Hemorrhage		−	÷	−	−	−	−	−	−	−	−	−	+	−	−
	Hyperplasia of Capillary Wall-Cells		÷	÷	−	−	−	+̈	+	−	−	−	÷	−	÷	−

[redacted] 282

[redacted]

[redacted]

PANCREAS

			399	400	401	403	404	405	407	409	411	412	413	417
Acinus	Size		↓	↓	↓	↓	↓	↓	↓	↓	↓	↓	↓	↓
	Dissociation		−	−	−	−	−	−	−	−	−	−	−	−
	Necrosis		−	−	−	−	−	−	−	−	−	−	−	−
Parenchyma	Clouding		#	#	#	#	#	#	+	+	+	+	#	+
	Swelling		#	#	#	#	#	+	+	+	+	+	#	+
	Zymogen Granules		+	−	#	−	−	+	−	−	÷	−	−	−
	Honeycombed Degeneration		#	+	#	−	#	#	÷	+	−	−	÷	−
	Changes of Nuclei	Swelling	−	−	−	−	−	−	−	−	−	−	−	−
		Pyknosis	+	+	+	+	+	÷	+	+	+	+	÷	#
		Karyolysis	÷	÷	÷	÷	÷	−	−	+	−	+	÷	÷
	Hyperplasia of Centroacinar Cells		−	−	−	−	−	−	−	−	−	−	−	÷
	Dsq. of Epithelium of Efferent Ducts		÷	−	−	÷	#	÷	÷	÷	−	+	+	#
Interstitium	Edema		÷	+	÷	#	#	+	+	+	÷	#	#	+
	Contents of Capillaries	Erythrocytes	+	+	+	+	÷	#	+	+	#	+	−	÷
		Leucocytes	÷	÷	−	÷	−	+	÷	÷	−	−	−	−
		Lymphocytes	÷	÷	[illegible]	÷	−	÷	÷	÷	÷	÷	−	−
	Hemorrhage		÷	−	[illegible]	−	−	#	−	÷	+	−	−	−
	Infiltration	Leucocytes	−	−	÷	−	÷	+	−	÷	−	−	÷	−
		Lymphocytes	÷	−	÷	−	÷	÷	−	÷	−	+	÷	−
	Proliferation	Plasma Cells	÷	−	−	−	−	−	−	−	÷	−	−	−
		Histiocytes	+	−	÷	−	−	−	−	−	÷	−	−	−
		Capillary Wall Cells	−	(÷)	−	−	−	−	−	−	−	−	−	−
Langerhans's Island	Number		↓÷	↓+	↓÷	↓÷	↓+	N	↓÷	↓÷	N	↓÷	↓÷	↓+
	Atrophia		−	+	+	÷	÷	÷	−	−	−	−	−	−
	Necrosis		−	−	−	−	−	−	−	−	−	−	−	−
	Parenchymal Cells	Size	N	↓÷	↓÷	N	↓+	↓÷	N	N	N	N	N	N
		Clouding	#	#	#	#	+	#	+	+	+	+	#	+
		Swelling	+	#	#	+	+	+	+	÷	÷	÷	#	÷
		Honeycombed Degeneration	+	÷	÷	−	+	+	+	+	÷	−	−	−
		Changes of Nuclei: Swelling	−	−	−	−	−	−	−	−	−	−	−	−
		Changes of Nuclei: Pyknosis	÷	+	÷	#	#	÷	+	+	+	#	÷	+
		Changes of Nuclei: Karyolysis	−	÷	−	−	−	−	−	÷	−	−	−	−
	Congestion of Capillaries		÷	−	÷	−	−	÷	÷	÷	÷	−	−	−
	Hemorrhage		−	−	−	−	−	−	−	−	−	−	−	−
	Hyperplasia of Capillary Wall Cells		÷	÷	÷	−	−	−	−	÷	−	−	−	−

N = normal or the slightest Decrease

[redacted] 283

[redacted]

Atrophy and intense
parenchymatous degeneration. [redacted]

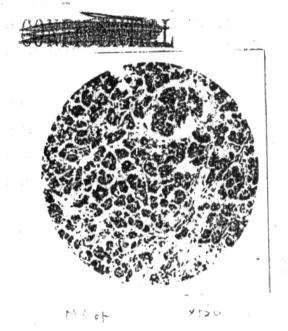

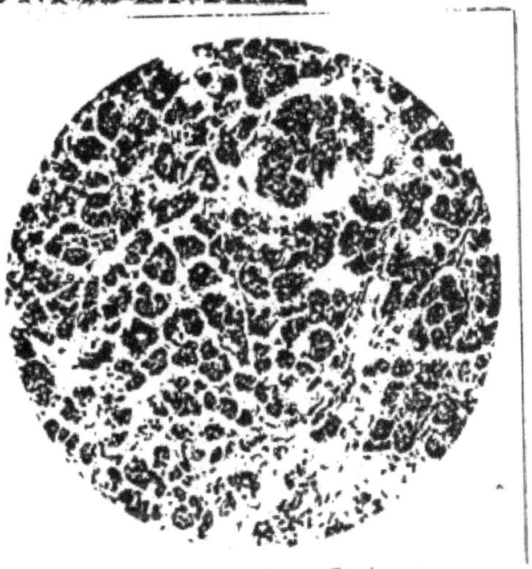

[redacted] 284

[redacted]

[redacted]

Parenchymatous degeneration, accompanied with some cirrhotic intersttial tissues.

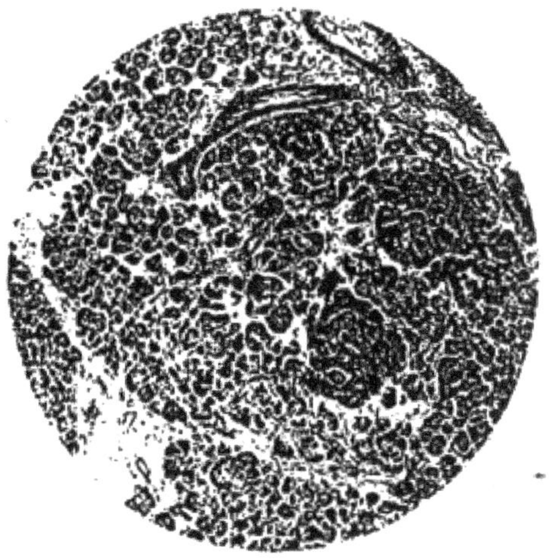

Increase of fatty tissues (not so significant changes).

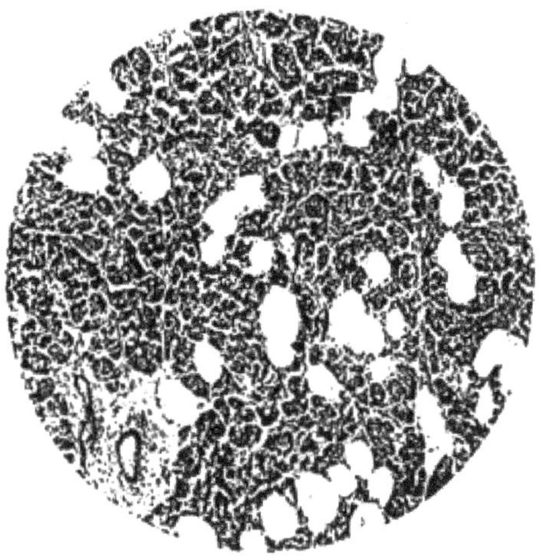

[redacted] 285

[redacted]

Parenchymatous degeneration.

[redacted]

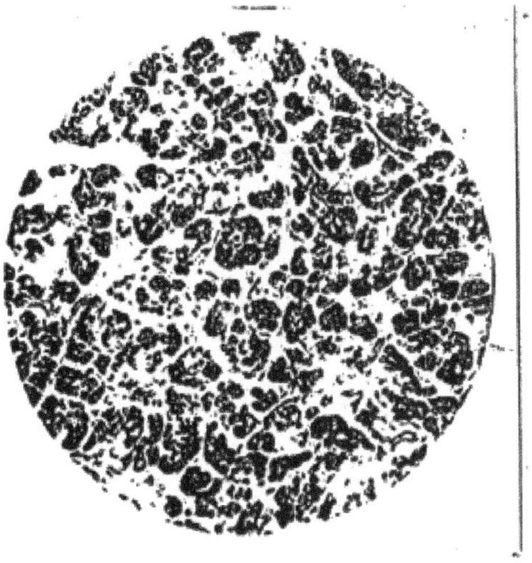

Parenchymatous degeneration.

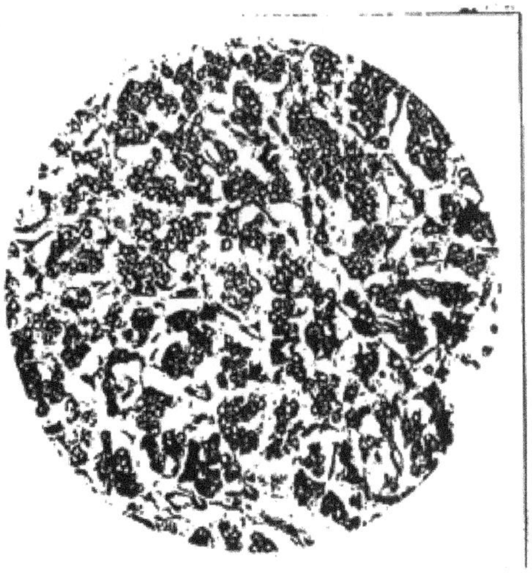

[redacted] 286

([redacted] (

Hemorrhages in inter-acinous tissues.

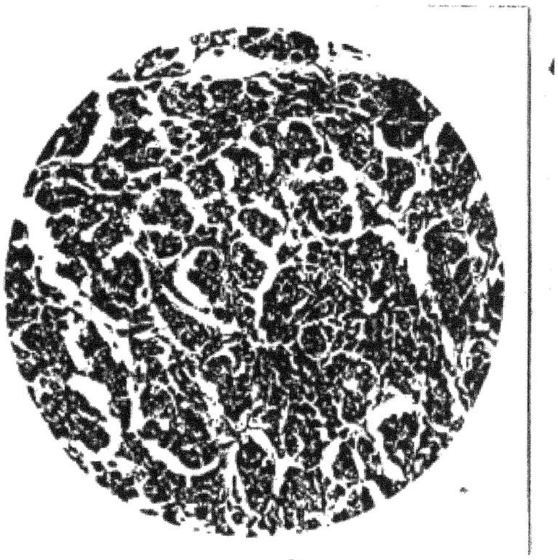

Exudative changes(edema and hemorrhages)
and parenchymatous degeneration.

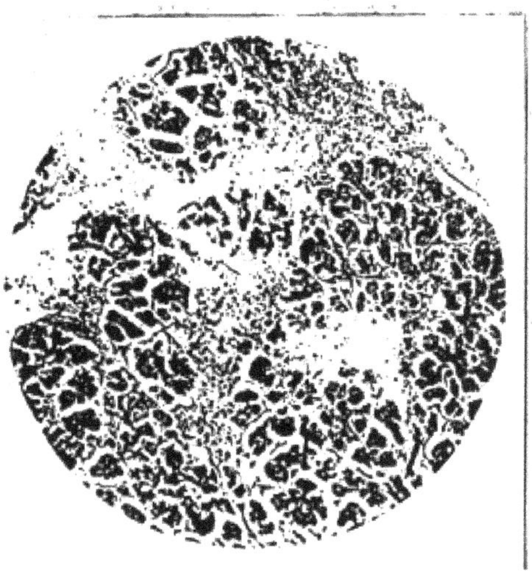

M 405 x 110

287

[redacted]

Vacuolar degeneration
of island.

[redacted]

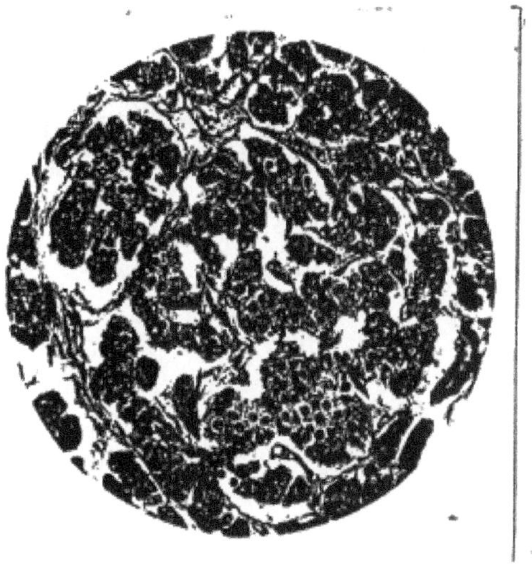

×250

Hyaline droplets degeneration
of island.

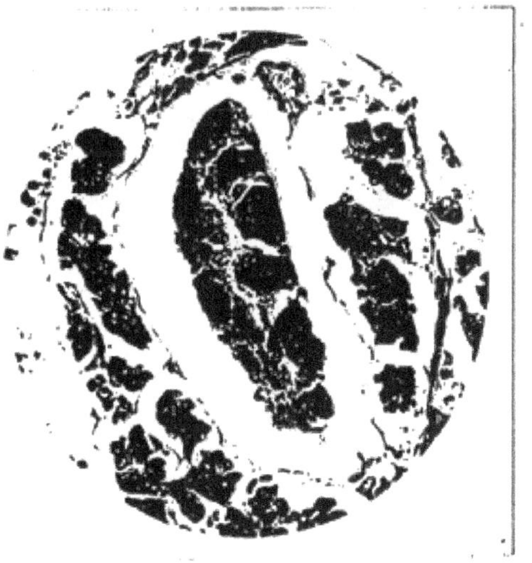

×350

[redacted] 288

[redacted]

Intense cloudyn
de generation of island.

[redacted]

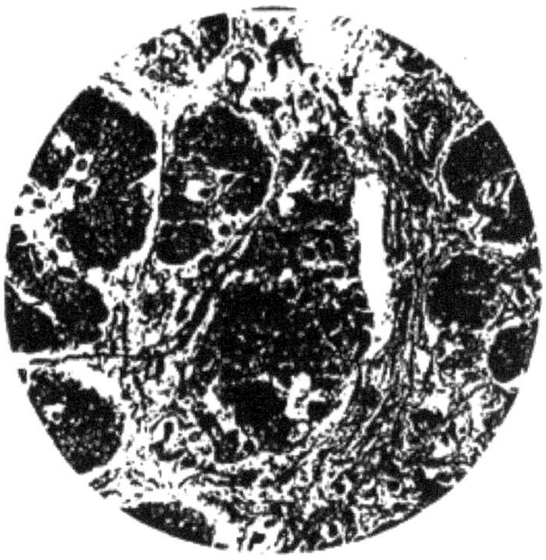

Apoplexy of island.
He morrhages in island.

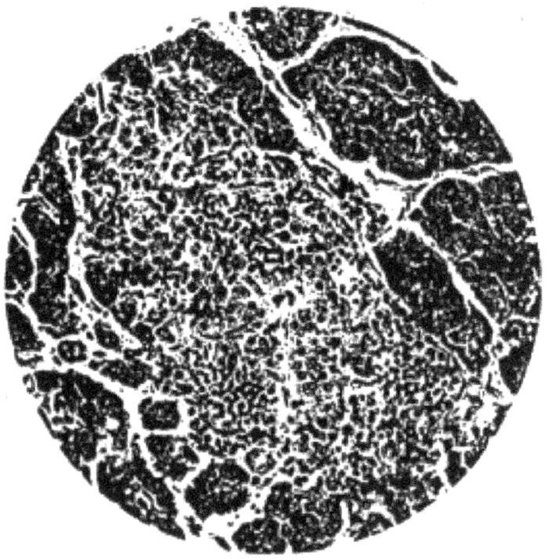

[redacted] 289

[redacted]

Edematous swelling at our so-called polar portion of island.

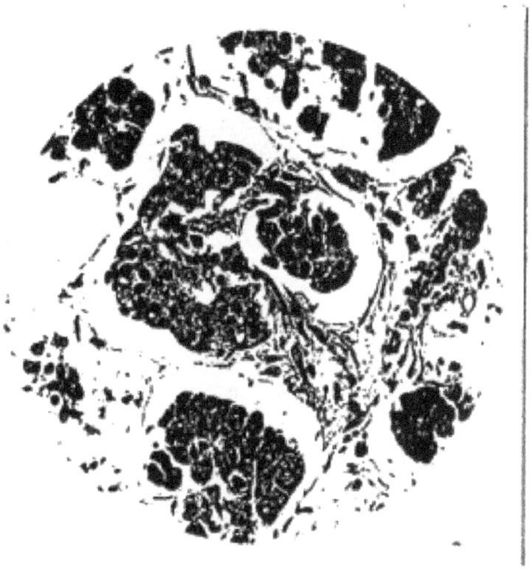

x 220

Edematous swelling at our so-called polar portion of island, in high power.

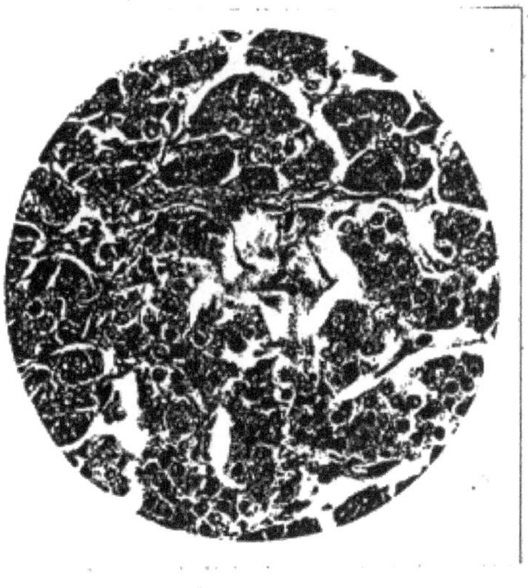

x 220

[redacted] 290

[redacted]

Intese congestion and
some hemorrhages in
island(socalled apoplexy
of island.)

[redacted]

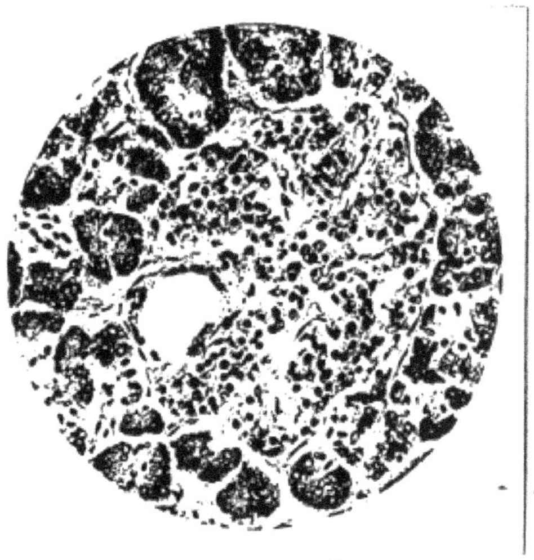

M1.26.　　×260

Edematpud swelling at so-called
polar portion of island and
slight hemorrhages in island.

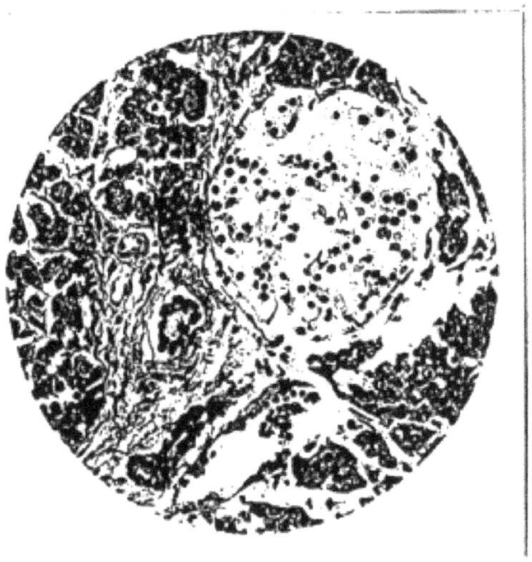

M1320.　　250.

[redacted] 291

[redacted]

[redacted]

Suprarenal

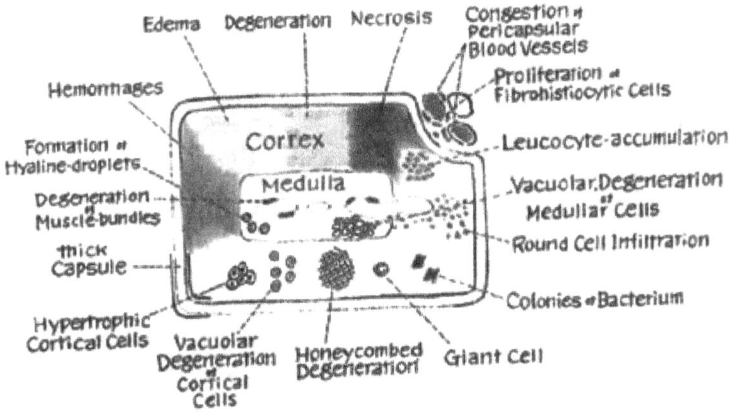

[redacted]

292

[redacted]

CONFIDENTIAL

( ) SUPRA-RENAL GLAND.

(A) Microscopical Investigation.

17.

Considerable atrophia, degeneration and dissociation of parenchymatous cells, esp. in Z. reticularis which are in ruining process.

Many polynuclear leucocytes (containing age-locytes) in capillaries of Z. reticularis.

Small round-cell-infiltration in Z. reticularis (around the central veins).

Some medullar cells with large nuclei and karyokinesis.

54.

Considerable congestion and slight partial hemorrhages in capsule. Cortical cells in more or less vacuolar degeneration. Z. faciculata with some cell-groups in honey-combed degeneration and Z. reticularis in ruining process.

Considerable edema and partial or diffuse hemorrhages mainly in Z. reticualris.

CONFIDENTIAL

293

[redacted]

[redacted]

225.

Considerable congestion in subcapsular capillaries and diffuse hemorrhages in Z. reticularis. Z. fasciculata with some cell-groups in hypertrophia and in adenous cell-arrangements.

Some medullar cells with large-nuclei (I7μ in dimeter as longest) and karyokinesis.

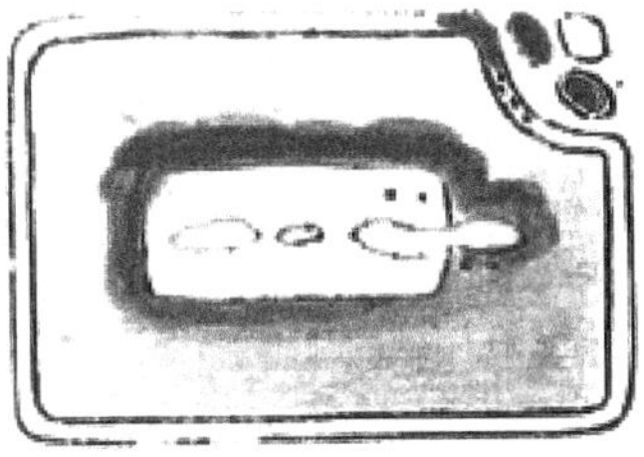

3I8.

Partial hemorrhages in capsule. Considerable atrophia and dissociation of parenchymatous cells. Z. reticularis in ruining process and in diffuse hemorrhages.

Some medullar cells with large nuclei.

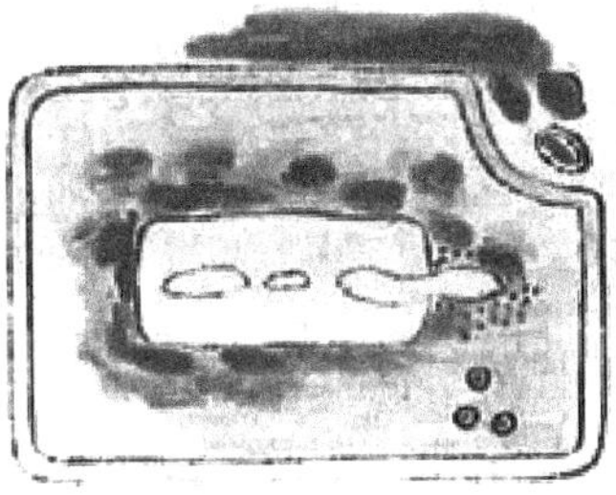

320.

Cortical cells in considerable dissociation, more or less considerable atrophia and vacuolar degeneration. Considerable edematous swelling of capillary-walls and multiple hemorrhagic places in Z. reticularis, which fall into necrobiosis (karyorhexis and disappearance of nuclei, etc) in adjacent parts. Considerable small round-cell-infiltration in Z. reticularis (around the central veins).

[redacted] 294

[redacted]

CONFIDENTIAL

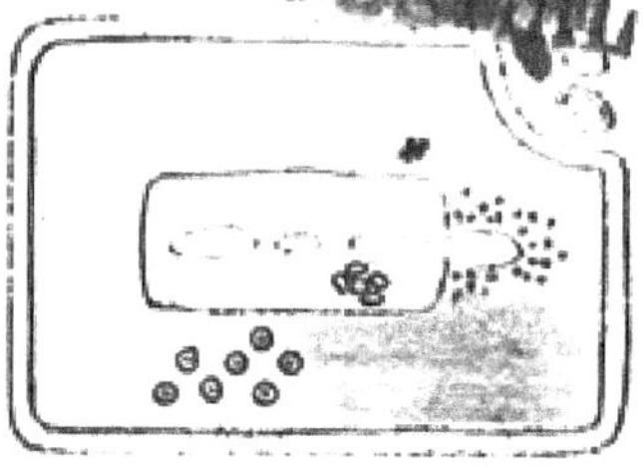

325.

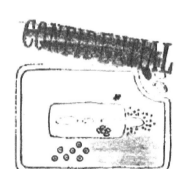

Remarkable vacuolar degeneration of cortical cells. Cortical cells in 2 types: a) with bright and more or less swollen protoplasma and bright nuclei and b) with eosinophilic and more or less smaller protoplasma and chromatin-rich or frequently phycnotic nuclei.

Bactorial masses in capillaries of Z. fasciculata. Cousiderable odema and diffuse hemorrhages in Z. reticularis.

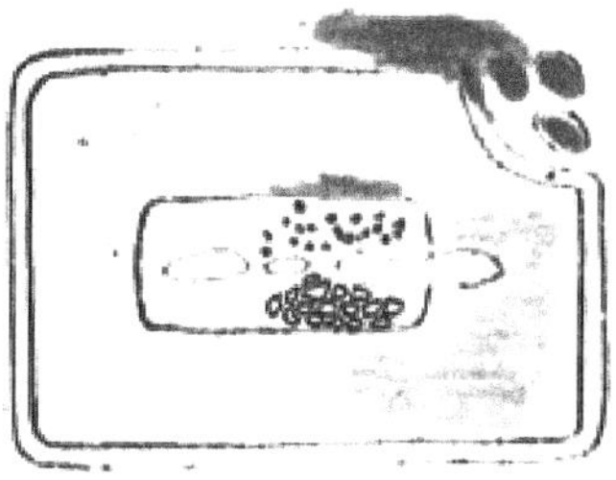

Small roud-cell-infiltration in Z. reticularis (around the central veins).

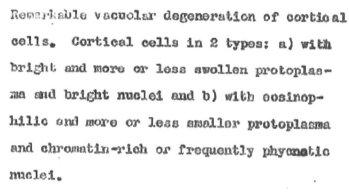

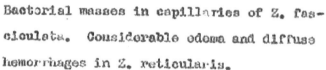

328.

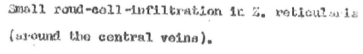

Partial hemorrhages in capsule and considerable congestion in [illegible].

Cortical cells in 2 types, as above mentioned and Z. fasciculata in more or less adenous cell-arrangements.

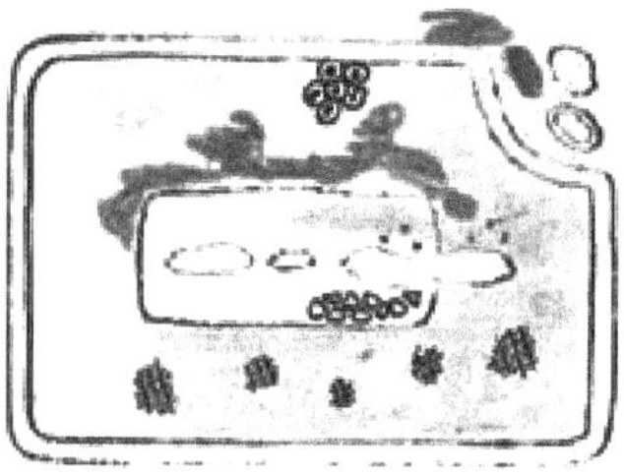

Medullar cells with more or less remarkable vacuolar degeneration.

388.

Some cortical cells with honeycombed degeneration in Z. fasciculata.

Some cell-groups with hypertrophic cells in Z. glomerulosa etc.

CONFIDENTIAL 295

● [redacted] ●

[redacted]

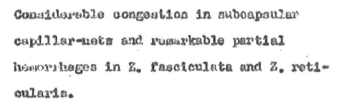

Considerable congestion in subcapsular capillar-nets and remarkable partial hemorrhages in Z. fasciculata and Z. reti-cularis.

Some medullar cells with large nuclei and more or less degenerative protoplasma.

389.

Considerable atrophia and desolative decays of parenchymatous cells (cortical cells in remarkable vacuolar degeneration or in partial bionecrosis).

Considerable edema and diffuse hemorrhages in Z. reticularis.

More or less remarkable vacuolar degeneration of medullar cells.

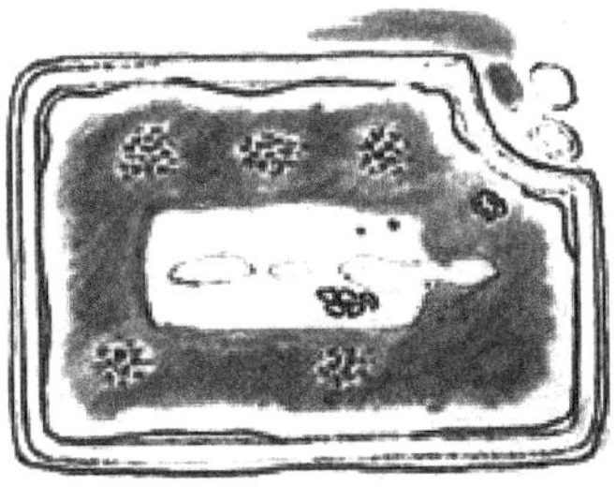

390.

Thick capsule with slight hyperplasia of Z. glomerulosa and multiple miliary abcesses in cortical tissues with total necrosis of Z. fasciculata and Z. reticularis.

At some places, slight hyperplasia of inter-stitial connective tissues with giant-cell (Langhans's type)-formation.

Some medullar cells with large nuclei.

[redacted] 391

[redacted]

[redacted]

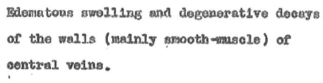

Edematous swelling and degenerative decays of the walls (mainly smooth-muscle) of central veins.

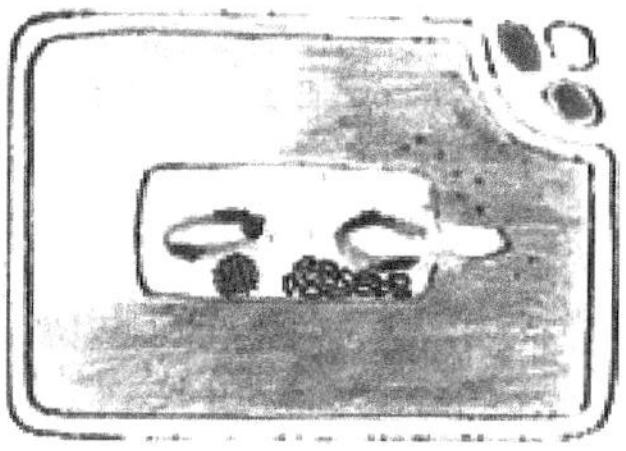

393.

Degeneration and desolative decays of parenchymatous cells in severe degree, esp. in Z. fasciculata with partial bionecrosis. Slight hyperplasia of Z. glomerulosa.

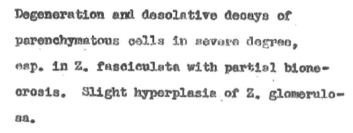

Honeycombed or vacuolar degeneration of medullar cells. Remarkable edematous swelling and degeneration of the walls of central veins.

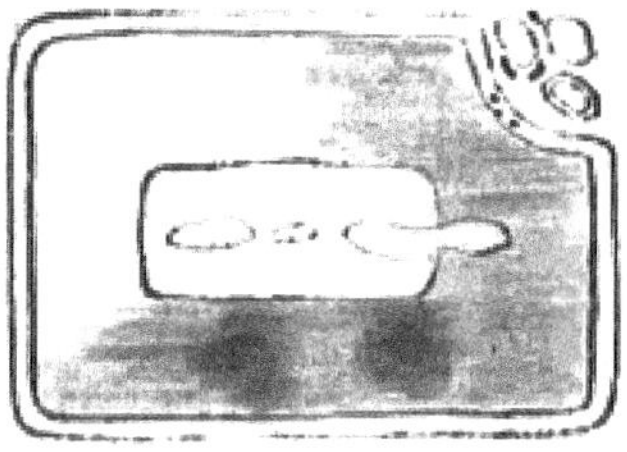

396.

Remarkable atrophia and desolative degeneration of parenchymatous cells, esp. in Z. fasciculata with partial necrosis.

397.

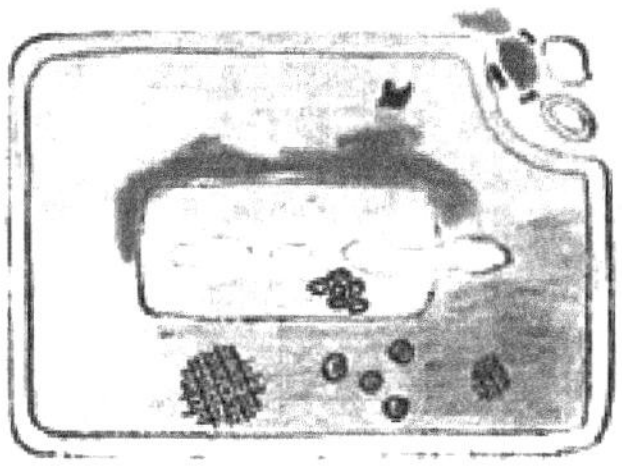

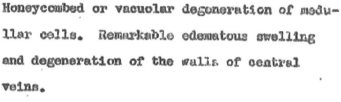

Vacuolar or honeycombed degeneration, esp. in Z. fasciculata.

More or less remarkable edema. Bacterial masses in capillar-nets and slight perivasculer leucocytes infiltration. More or less considerable diffuse hemorrages in Z. reticularis.

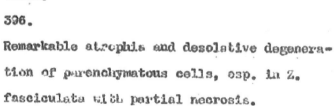

Some medullar cells with large nuclei and edematous swelling of medullar tissues.

[redacted]

297

[redacted]

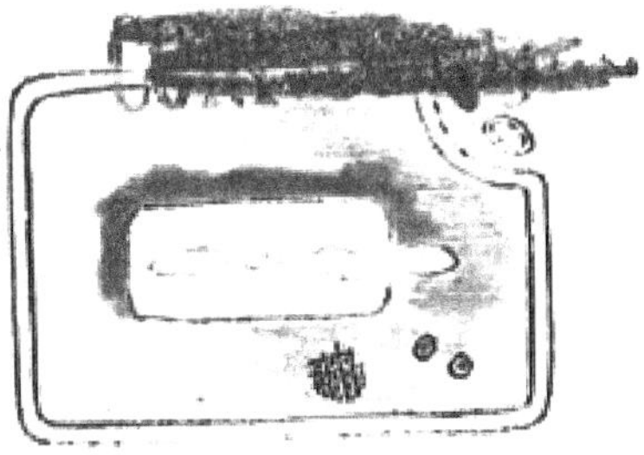

399.

Considerable vacuolar or honeycombed degeneration of parenchymatous cells (scattered in reticular tissues) with remarkable hemorrhages in Z. reticularis.

400.

Considerable vacuolar or honeycombed degeneration. More or less intense edema with diffuse hemorrhages in Z. reticularis.

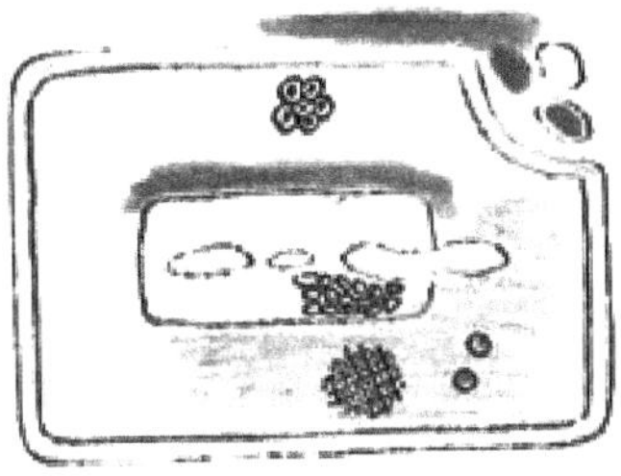

405.

Vacuolar or honeycombed degeneration of parenchymatous cells, esp. in Z. fasciculata. With diffuse hemorrhages in Z. reticularis.

Some medullar cells with large nuclei.

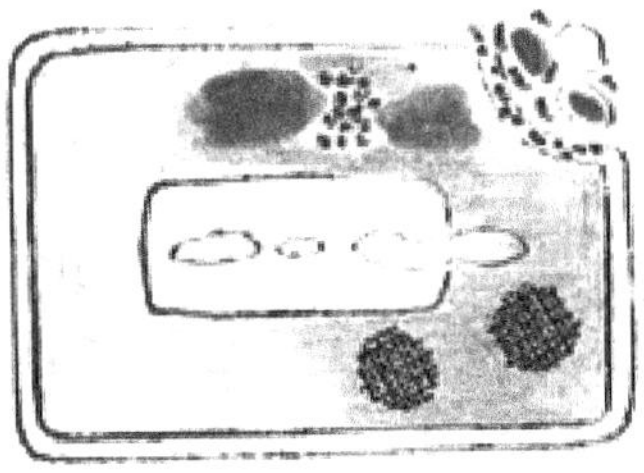

407.

Honeycombed degeneration of parenchymatous cells, esp. in Z. fasciculata with submiliary abscess-like changes (localised hemorrhagic parts and perifocal leucocyties accumulation).

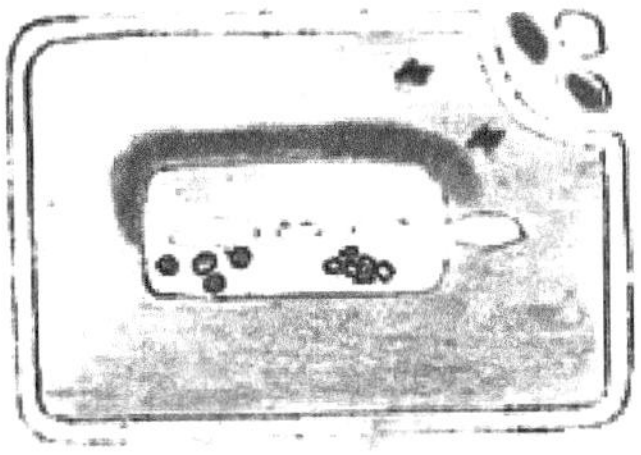

409.

Considerable atrophia and desolative degeneration of parenchymatous cells. More or less remarkable edema. Considerable subcapsular congestion and diffuse hemorrha-

[redacted]

[redacted]

ges in Z. reticularis. Bacterial masses in capillar-nets. [redacted]

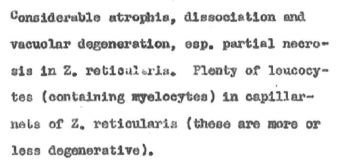

410.

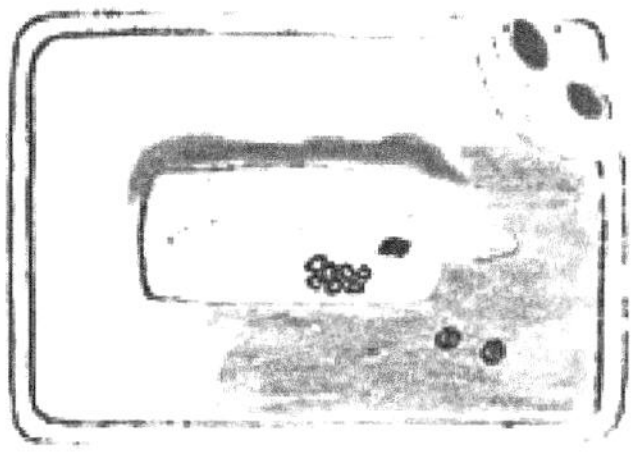

Considerable atrophia, dissociation and vacuolar degeneration, esp. partial necrosis in Z. reticularis. Plenty of leucocytes (containing myelocytes) in capillar-nets of Z. reticularis (these are more or less degenerative).

Some medullar cells with large nuclei and karyokinesis.

Bacterial masses in the central veins.

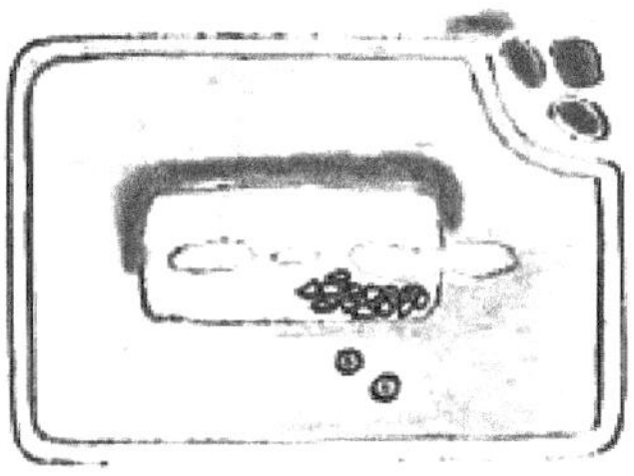

411.

Considerable vacuolar degeneration with more or less remarkable edema. Medium subcapsular congestion and intense diffuse hemorrhages in Z. reticualris.

Considerable vacuolar degeneration of medullar cells.

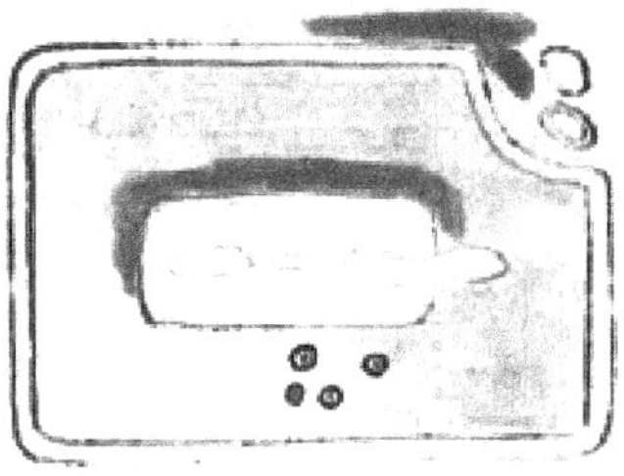

416.

Considerable vacuolar degneration and edema. Intense diffuse hemorrhages in Z. reticularis.

[redacted]. 249

[redacted]

[redacted]

417.

Partial hemorrhages in Z. reticularis.
Remarkable atrophia, intense desolative decays or vacuolar degeneration of cortical cells (cortical cells are ruining).
Intense odema and intense diffuse hemorrhages in Z. reticularis. Small round-cell-infiltration in Z. fasciculata and reticularis.
Considerable odema of medullar tissues.

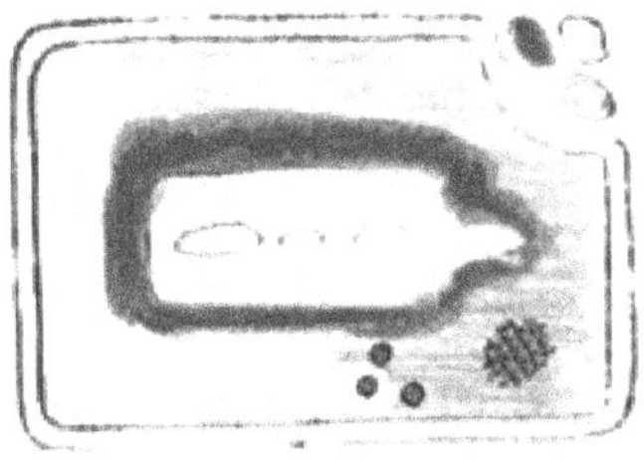

401. (post entry)

Vacuolar or honey-combed degeneration of parenchymatous cells with diffuse hemorrhages in Z. reticularis.

[redacted] 300

[redacted]

[redacted]

(B) S U M M A R Y.

Histological observation on 22 micro-slices.

a) Pericapsular tissues:

Intense congestion in IO cases.

Hemorrhage in I7 cases, 7 of them in more or less severe degree.

Remarkable desquamation of endothelial cells of capillaries, in 3 cases.

Generally slight perivascular lymphocytic or leucocytic cell infiltration.

b) Capsular tissues:

Edmatous swel?ing in II cases, 7 of them in severe degree.

Remarkable hemorrhage in 4 cases.

Congentially think capsule in 5 cases and localised cortical cellgroups in capsule in 5 cases.

c) Parenchymatous cells of cortex:

I) Z. glomeruosa.

Atrophia in 8 cases.

Slight hyperplasia in 2 cases, I of them with compensatory hyperplasia, due to total necrosis of Z. reticulalis and Z. fasciculata.

Glomerular cells with large nuclei or karyokinesis in 4 cases.

[redacted] B01

[redacted]

[redacted]

2) Z. fasciculata.

Generally in all cases, cortical cells are in more or less degenerative with various and intense nuclear changes (pycnosis, karyolysis and karyorrhexis).

In the most cases, more or less decrease of fatty contents in protoplasma (splitting of fatty drops and protoplasma with dark and homogenous tone. Some cases have localised seats of residual fatty masses).

Vacuolar degeneration (according to Dietrich's concept), in I5 cases. I of them in a severe degree.

Honeycombed degeneration (according to Dietrich), in I0 cases.

Formation of adenous lumina in fascicular cords, in I7 cases. I5 of them slightly and 2 of them in severe degree with decayed masses of desquamated cortical cells and some erythrocytes in lumina.

Remarkable atrophia of fascicular cells, in I3 cases.

8 cases with hypertrophic cortical cell-groups.

Dissociation of cell-arrangements in I3 cases. 9 of them in severe degree.

[redacted] 3 02

[redacted]

[redacted]

Parenchymatous disturbances with intense ruining changes, in 9 cases. 4 of them with some localised partial necrosis and I of them with diffuse intense necrosis, (multiple miliary abcesses fused each other), in Z. fasciculata and Z. glomerulosa.
Their glomerular cells are in compensatory hypertrophia, as above mentioned.
Accordingly in this disease, parenchymatous disturbances of cortical cells are more or less intense.
Note: In some case, cortical tisses are in confusion of 2 typed cellular attagements: a) with bright protoplasma and bright or swollen nuclei and b) with eosinophilic protoplasma and chromatinrich or pycnotic nuclei.

d) Interstice of cortex:
Generally with remarkable edema, I2 of them in a severe degree.
Frequently with remarkable congestion in capillar-nets of Z. reticularis and sub-capsular tissues.
Generally with more or less considerable leucocytes as capillary contents. In 8 cases of [redacted]arkable and in 2 cases

[redacted] 803

[redacted]

[redacted]

of them, containing myelocytes.
More or less remarkable localised small round-cell-infiltration (generally in Z. reticularis, around the central veins) in 8 cases. In the other cases, more slightly or scarcely.
With some hemorrhages in 2I cases (I7 cases of them in a severe degree). Generally in Z. reticularis partial or diffuse hemorrhages, and occasionally in Z. fasciculata partial hemorrhages.
We advocate the concept" Epinephritis serosa", refered to Hepatitis serosa as Eppinger's meaning and classify cortical changes of this disease as followed:

Epinephritis serosa I degree.
in I3 cases
Epinephritis serosa II degree.
in 7 cases.

We can find in so many cases (I6 cases), leucocytes-infiltration in cortical tissues and in 2 cases miliary abscess-like changes. These facts are unusual in the other diseases.
e) Medulla: Generally with edematous swelling, esp. 7 cases of them in a severe degree. In all cases with more or less

[redacted] 304

[redacted]

[redacted]

remarkable vacuolar degeneration and in 4 cases with hyaline-droplets-formation.
Medullar cells with anisonuclei in 7 cases and some of them with karyokinesis.
These facts signify the initial stage of medullar hypertrophia.
Generally with slight hemorrhages and small round-cell-infiltration in medullar tissues and 2 of them with intense edematous swelling of smooth-muscle-bundles of the central-vein-walls.
Ganglion cells in all cases, with more or less tygrolysis, karyolysis or vacuolar degeneration of protoplasma.

[redacted] 305

[redacted]

[redacted]

SUPRARENAL

		17	54	225	318	320	325	328	388	389	390	393	396	397	399	400	401	405	407	409	410	411	416	417
Serous Inflammation		II	I	-	I	I	I	I	I	II	-	II	II	I	I	I	I	-	I	II	II	I	I	II
Pericapsular tissue	Congestion	+	+	+++	++	++	+	+++	+	+	+	++	∸	+	+	+	+	++	++	++	++	+++	+	÷
	Hemorrhage	−	+	++	−	++	÷	+	÷	∸	+	−	−	÷	÷	÷	∸	++	∸	−	−	÷	+	÷
	Infiltration of Leucocytes	∸	∸	−	−	∸	−	∸	−	∸	∸	−	+	∸	∸	∸	∸	∸	∸	÷	∸	∸	∸	∸
	Infiltration of Lymphocytes	∸	∸	÷	÷	÷	∸	÷	÷	+	∸	+	÷	÷	÷	∸	÷	∸	∸	÷	÷	∸	∸	+
	Proliferation of Histiocytes	+	∸	÷	÷	÷	÷	÷	÷	÷	÷	÷	+	+	÷	∸	÷	∸	++	÷	÷	∸	∸	∸
Capsule	Edema	÷	++	÷	÷	++	÷	−	−	+	÷	+	+	++	÷	++	∸	+++	∸	∸	∸	++	∸	+++
	Hemorrhage	−	+	−	+	∸	−	+	−	−	−	−	−	÷	∸	−	−	∸	−	÷	∸	∸	∸	+
	Cellular Infiltration	∸	∸	÷	+	÷	−	∸	−	∸	−	−	÷	÷	−	∸	−	−	++	−	÷	−	−	÷
Parenchyma of Cortex	Decrease of Lipoid	+	++	+	++	++	++	++	++	++	++	+	++	++	+	++	+	++	+	+	+	++	+	++
	Dissociation	++	+	÷	++	++	÷	−	−	++	+++	+++	+++	+	÷	+	÷	∸	÷	++	++	÷	−	++
	Atrophia	+++	÷	∸	−	+	∸	−	−	++	+	++	++	+	−	+	∸	÷	+	+	++	÷	+	+++
	Hypertrophia	−	∸	+	−	−	−	∸	+	−	−	−	−	−	−	−	−	+	∸	−	−	÷	−	÷
	Splitting of Lipoid-drops	++	+++	+	++	+++	+++	+++	+++	++	++	+++	++	+++	++	+++	+++	+++	+++	++	++	+++	+	++
	Vacuolar Degeneration (Dietrich)	−	÷	−	−	+	++	−	÷	+	−	−	−	+	÷	+	÷	÷	∸	−	÷	÷	+	+
	Honeycombed Degeneration (〃)	−	+++	−	−	−	÷	−	++	−	−	−	−	++	+	+	+	+	++	−	−	−	−	∸
	Formation of Lumina	∸	∸	+	÷	∸	÷	+	÷	−	−	−	−	÷	÷	÷	∸	−	÷	÷	∸	∸	−	÷
	Brown Pigment	+	÷	++	+	++	+	∸	∸	+	+	+	∸	÷	∸	÷	−	∸	÷	++	∸	∸	−	+
	Changes of Nuclei: Pyknosis	+	++	−	∸	+	++	+	++	+	−	∸	∸	÷	÷	∸	∸	++	++	+	+	÷	÷	+
	Changes of Nuclei: Karyolysis	++	++	∸	+	+	+	∸	++	++	++	++	÷	+	+	+	÷	+	+	++	++	++	+	++
	Changes of Nuclei: Disappearance	+	++	÷	++	++	+	+	+	++	+++	++	+++	++	−	+	∸	÷	+	+	++	÷	+	+
Interstice of Cortex	Congestion of Subcapsular Blood v's	÷	++	++	+	÷	÷	++	++	∸	+	−	−	+	∸	∸	∸	+	+	++	÷	++	+	+
	Edema	++	++	∸	+	++	++	+	÷	++	∸	+	+	++	÷	++	+	÷	++	++	+	++	++	+++
	Contents of Capillaries: Erythrocytes	+	+	++	++	÷	++	++	++	+	+	−	∸	++	+	÷	+	+	÷	+	÷	+	÷	÷
	Contents of Capillaries: Leucocytes	++	∸	∸	∸	−	∸	÷	÷	∸	++	∸	+	÷	+	+	∸	∸	+	+	++	÷	∸	+
	Contents of Capillaries: Lymphocytes	÷	∸	∸	+	∸	÷	∸	∸	÷	∸	+	÷	∸	∸	∸	∸	∸	+	∸	∸	∸	÷	+
	Contents of Capillaries: Monocytes	∸	−	−	−	∸	∸	÷	−	∸	−	∸	÷	∸	∸	∸	∸	−	∸	∸	∸	∸	−	−
	Hemorrhage	+	+++	++	+++	+++	++	÷	++	++	++	−	−	++	++	+++	+++	+	++	++	+	++	++	+++
	Infiltration of Leucocytes	++	∸	∸	−	−	−	−	−	−	+++	−	−	∸	÷	+	∸	∸	+++	∸	+	∸	∸	∸
	Infiltration of Lymphocytes	+	∸	÷	÷	++	++	−	+	∸	+	+	÷	∸	÷	∸	÷	∸	÷	∸	+	∸	∸	++
	Hyperplasia of Capillarywall cells	−	−	÷	∸	∸	−	∸	−	−	−	−	−	−	−	−	−	∸	−	∸	−	∸	−	−
Medulla	Parenchyma: Hyalin-drops	+	−	−	∸	|	∸	−	÷	∸	−	−	|	∸	|	−	|	−	|	+	−	÷	|	∸
	Parenchyma: Vacuolar Degener.	∸	∸	−	∸	|	−	−	−	++	+	++	|	+	|	+	|	++	|	+	+	++	|	+
	Edema	++	++	÷	÷	|	++	÷	∸	++	÷	+	|	+++	|	+	|	∸	|	+	+	+	|	+++
	Congestion	∸	÷	−	∸	|	÷	++	÷	+	+	++	|	++	|	÷	|	−	|	÷	∸	++	|	÷
	Hemorrhage	−	∸	−	∸	|	∸	∸	∸	−	∸	∸	|	∸	|	÷	|	−	|	÷	∸	÷	|	∸
	Circumscribed Round cell infiltration	−	∸	÷	÷	|	÷	++	÷	+	÷	+	|	÷	|	∸	|	∸	|	÷	∸	∸	|	÷

[redacted] 306

[redacted]

[redacted]

Leucocytes-accumulation in cortical tissues, accompanied with intense bionecrotic changes of parenchymatous cells.

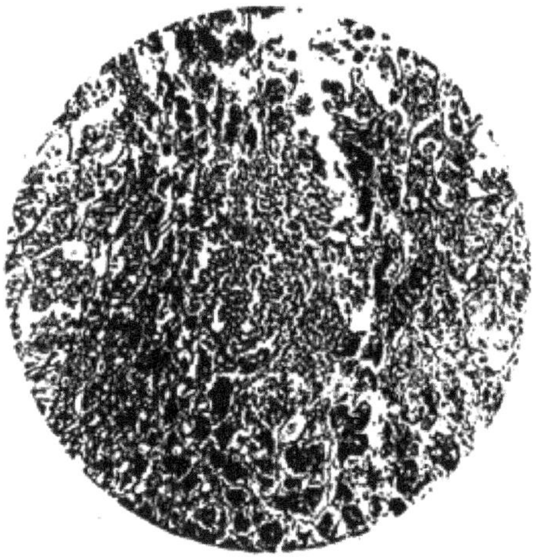

Intense bionecrotic changes of cortical cells.

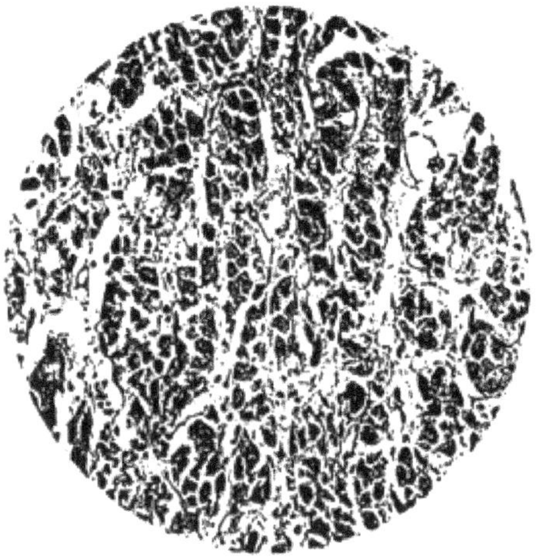

380 ×210

[redacted] 307

[redacted]

Vacuolar degenmaqation(Dietrich) of [redacted]
cortival cells.

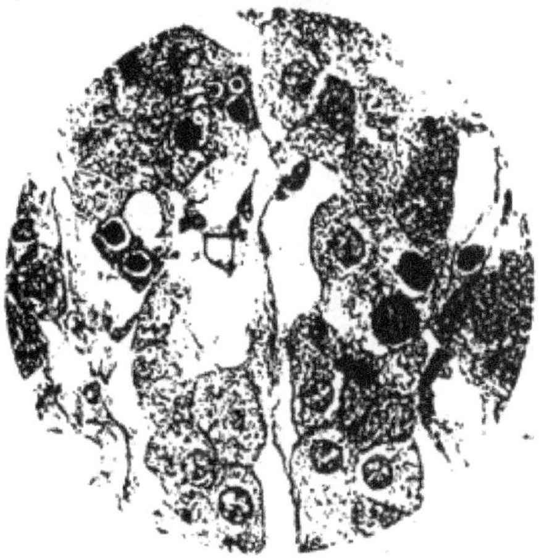

M 325 X520

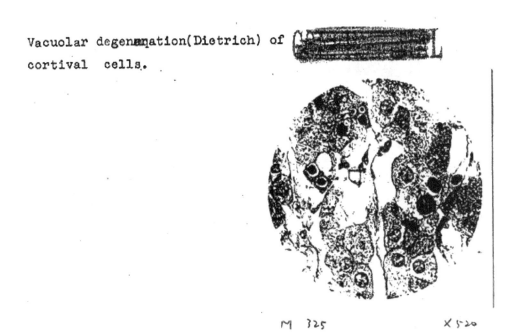

Honeycombed degenerqtion(Dietrich) of
cortical cells.

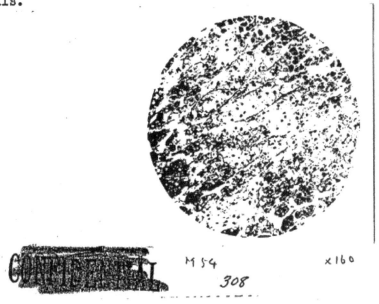

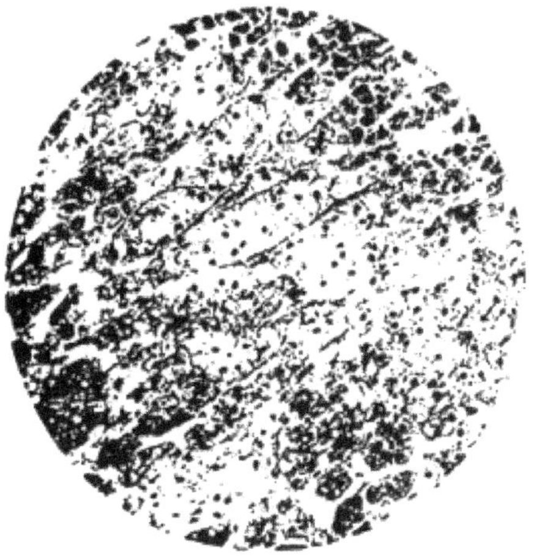

[redacted] M 54 x160

308

[redacted]

Hypertrophic cortical cell group.

[redacted]

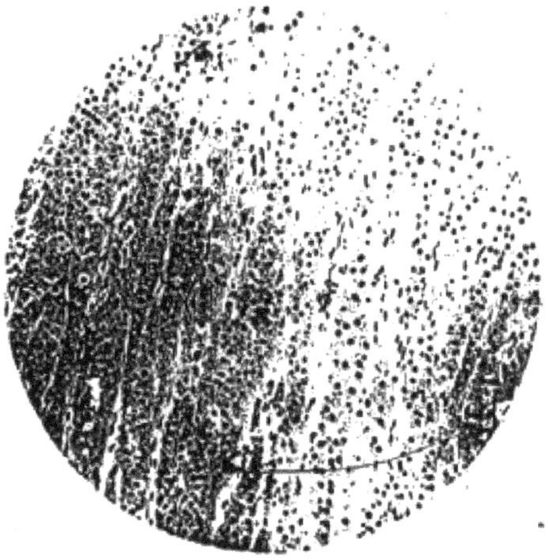

M 338 - x 110

Degenerated cortical cells in 2 types:a)bright and more or less swollen protoplasma withbright nuclei

b) eosinophilic and more or less smaller protoplasma with chrdmatin-rich or pycnotic nuclei.

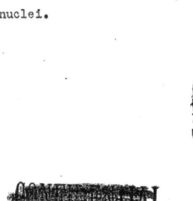

M 325 x 330

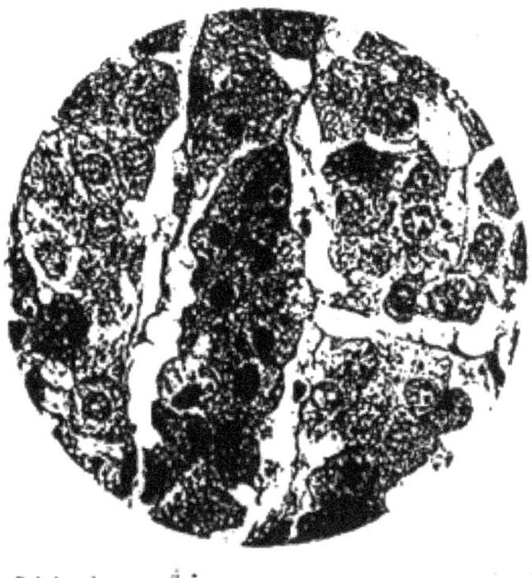

[redacted]

309

[redacted]

[redacted]

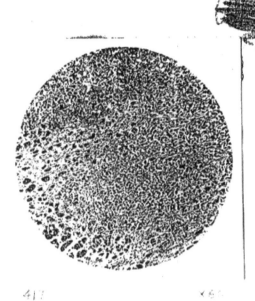

Diffuse hemorrhages in Z.reticularis round cell dissemination in Z.fasticulata, accompanied with intense degeneration of parenchymatous cells.

417 ×60

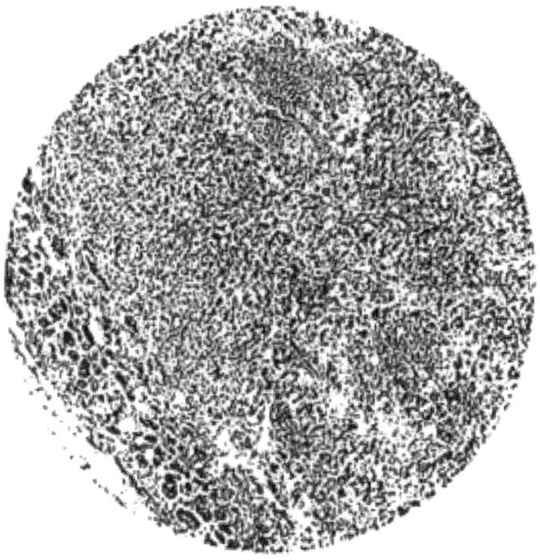

Intense total necrosis of Z.fasticulata and Z.reticularis.

Compensatory hyperplasia of Z.glomerulosa.

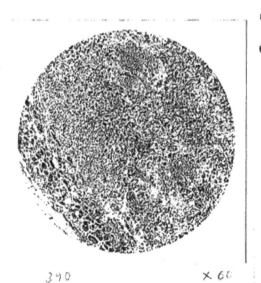

390 ×60

[redacted]

[redacted]

CONFIDENTIAL

Giant cells in cortical tissues.

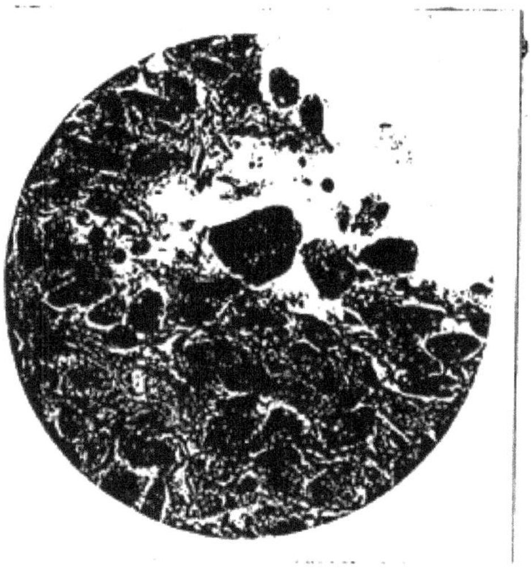

390

CONFIDENTIAL 311

[redacted]

[redacted]

Thyroid

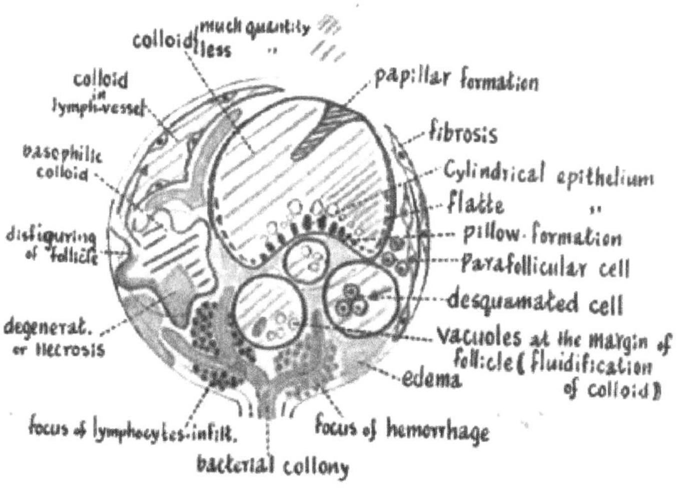

[redacted]

312

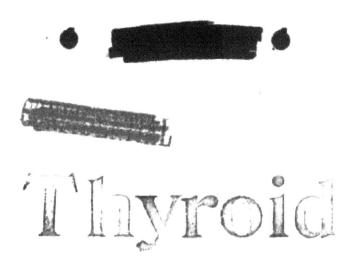

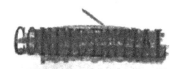

[redacted]

[redacted] THYREOID

(A) Microscopical Investigations.

17
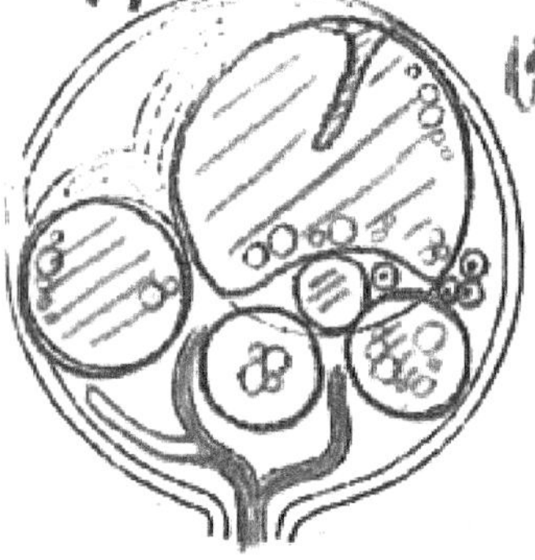

17. Struma colloides nodosa levis.

Slight activated state of thyreoid-tissues with slight hyperaemia, pillow-like or papillar increase of epithelial cells and some parafollicular cells. Vacuole-formation in colloidal masses at the margin of follicles.

53
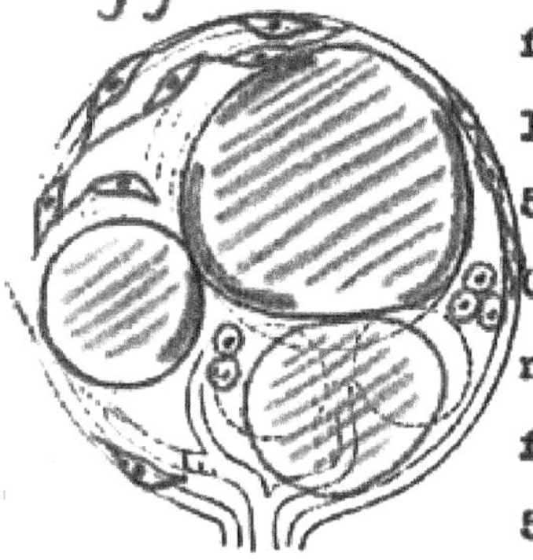

53. Slight fibrosis.

Condensation of colloidal masses and a slight degeneration of follicular epithel cells, and some parafollicular cells.

54. Struma colloides diffusa levis.

54
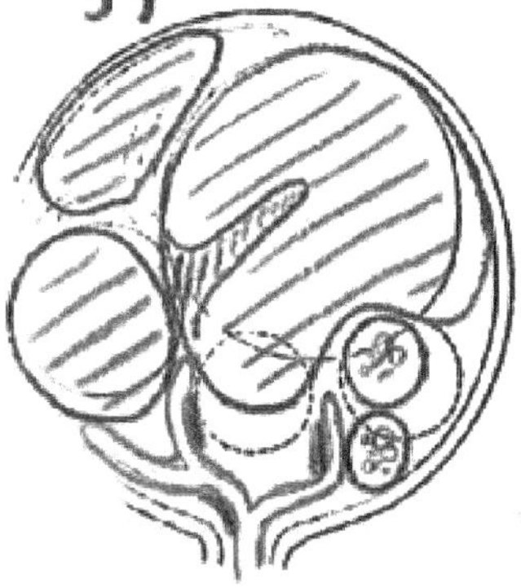

Slight hyperaemia and pillow-like or papillar increase of follicular epithelial cells with some microfollicles-formations. Slight hyaline degeneration of arteriole-walls.

225. Struma colleides diffusa levis

Slight heperaemia and pillow-like or papillar increase of follicular epithelial cells with some microfollicles-formations. Slight hyaline degeneration
cles-formations. Slight hyaline degeneration of arteriole-walls.

225
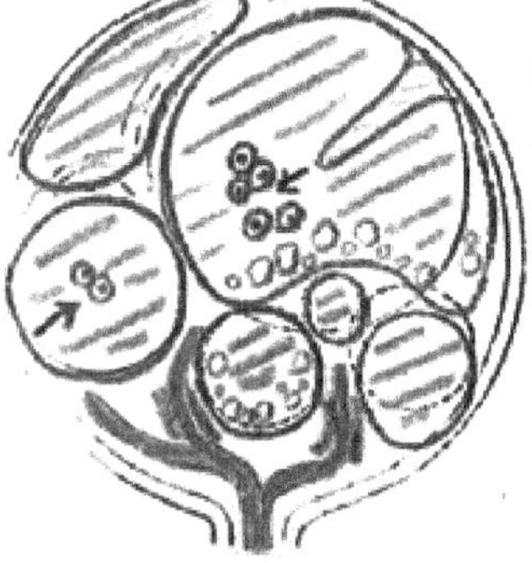

225. Struma colloides diffusa levis.

Slight hyperaemia and pillow-like or papillar increase of epithelial cells with some desquamated epithelial

[redacted]

313

[redacted]

cells in follicles.

318

318. Acute disfiguring of thyroid in medium degree. Considerable congestion and degenerative processes of follicular epithelial cells (flattening, cloudy swelling, pycnotic degeneration, and desquamation of epithel cells). Slight increase of more or less basophilic colloidal masses and at some places considerable collapse of follicles (severe fluidification o
siderable collapse of follicles (severe fluidification of colloidal masse) with increase of colloidal masses in perifollicular connective tissues.

320

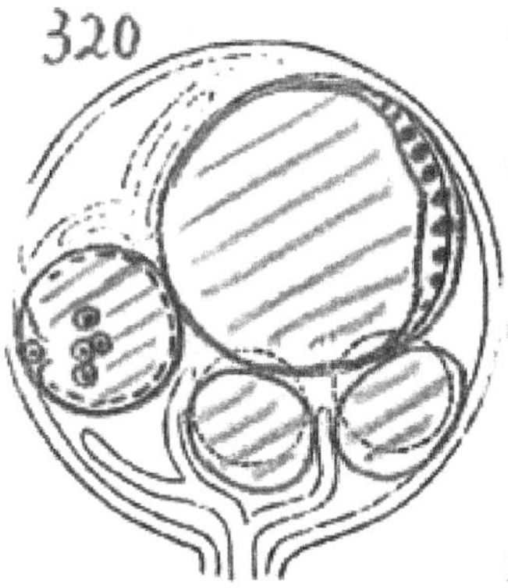

At some places slight hyperplasia of epithelial cells so as to form pillow-like orpapillar arrangements with many microfollicles.

320. Struma collòides non-proliferativa.

Thyreoids in statical state with flattening of epithàl cells. At some places slight desquamation or desolation of epithelial cells and at other places, slight hyperplasia of epithel cells.

328.

Thyreoids instatical state with slight desquamation or desolation of follicular epithelial cells.

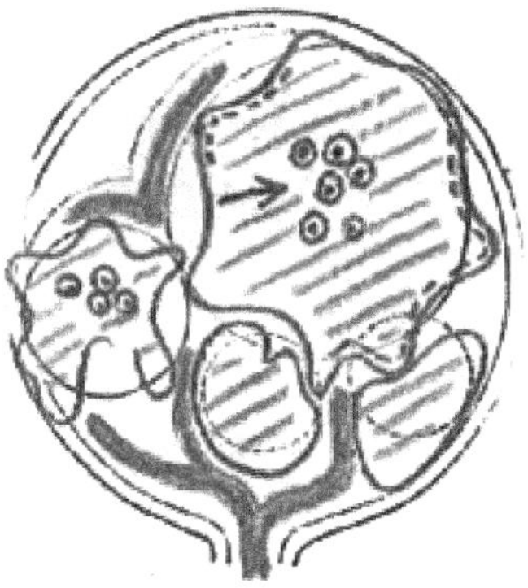

389. Acute disfiguring of thyreoids in medium degree.

Cansiderable congestion and degenerative processes of follicular epithelial cells (flattening, cloudy swelling, pycnosis, desquamation and desolation of epithelial cells).

CONFIDENTIAL 314

[redacted]

393

393.

Acute di[redacted]d in medium degree. Considerable congestion and degenerative processes of follicular epithelial cells (flattening, cloudy swelling, pycnosis, desquamation and some desolation of epithel cells) with increased basophilic colloidal masses and collapse of follicles (fluidified colloidal masses). Without any proliforative changes.

Colloidal masses in lymph-vessel and slight edematous swelling of peri-follicular connective tissues.

396

396. Acute disfiguring of thyreoid in severe degree. Considerable congestion, more or less swelling of blood-vessel walls and slight edematous swelling of perivascular tissues.

Follicles in various forms: some macro-and some microfollicles, with some degenerative processes of follicular epithelial cells (flattening, pycnosis, remarkable desquamation and desolation of epithelial cells). Increase of basophilic colloidal masses and collapse of follicles in severe degree. Colloidal masses in lymph-vessels.

Bacterial masses in follicles without any proliferative changes.

399

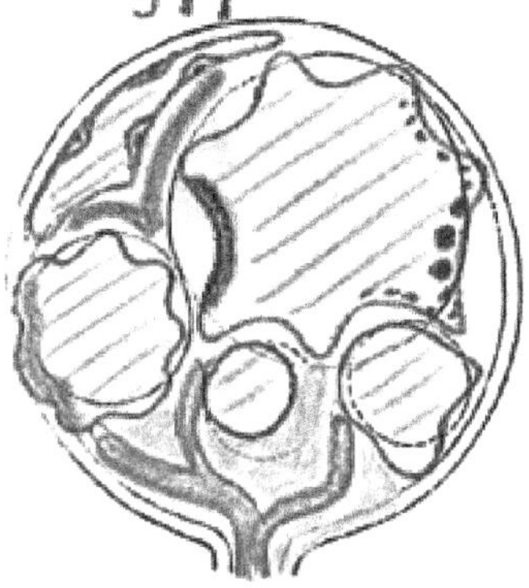

399. Acute disfiguring of thyroids in slight degree. Considerable congestion and slight edema in perivascular tissues. Some degenerative processes of follicular epithelial cells in slight degree and slight

[redacted] 315

[redacted]

increase of colloidal masses in follicles and lymph-vessels.

At some places, with slight hyperplasia of follicular epithelial cells. [redacted]

401

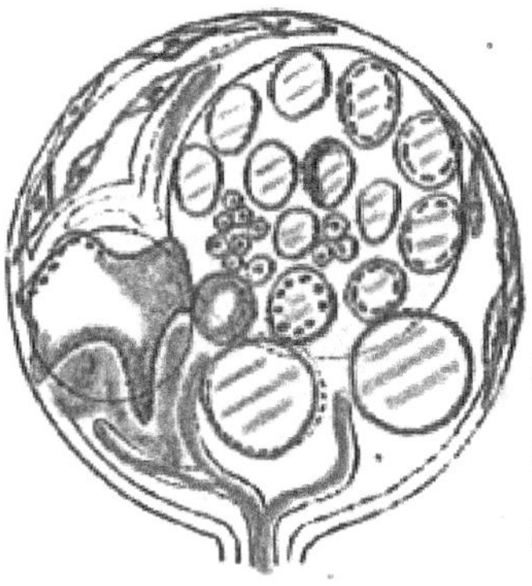

401. Struma parenchymatosaalletis.

With many microfollicles, which are in statical or rather degenerative state and some of them, resulting from considerable follicular collapse.

Slight fibrosis and hyaline degeneration of perifollicular connective tissues.

403

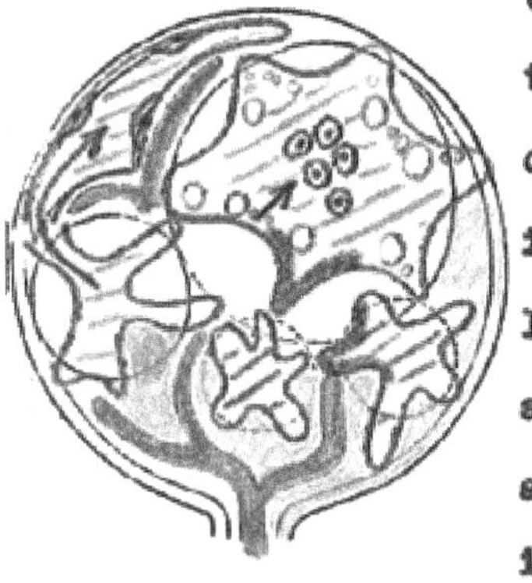

403. Acute disfiguring in severe degree.

Considerable congestion and edematous swelling of interstitial tissues with some degenerative processes of epithelial cells (esp. desquamation and desolation) in high degree.

Increase of more or less basophilic colloidal masses and fluidification of colloidal masses with their accumulations in lymph-vessels. Follicular collapse in severe degree.

405. Thyroids in statical state with slight hyperplasia of follicular epithelial cells.

406

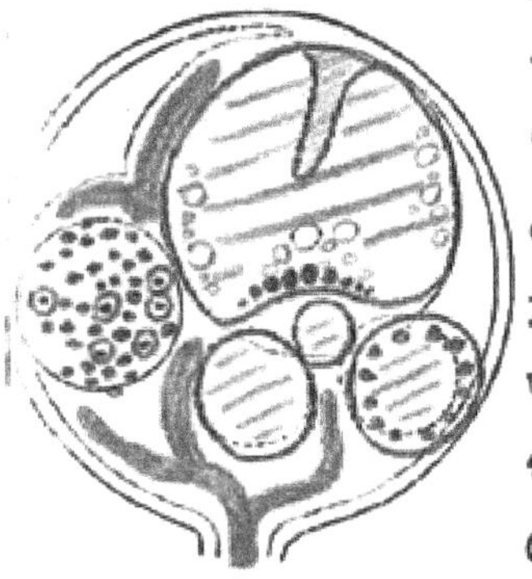

406. Thyroids in activated state in slight degree.

Considerable congestion and hyperplasia of follicular epithelial cells so as to form pillow-like or papillar arrangement and at some places solid cell groups. with some parafollicular cells.

407. Acute disfiguring of thyroid in slight degree.

Considerable congestion and follicular collapse in

[redacted], 316

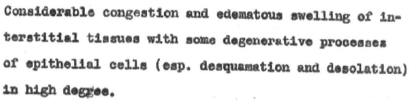

[redacted]

407

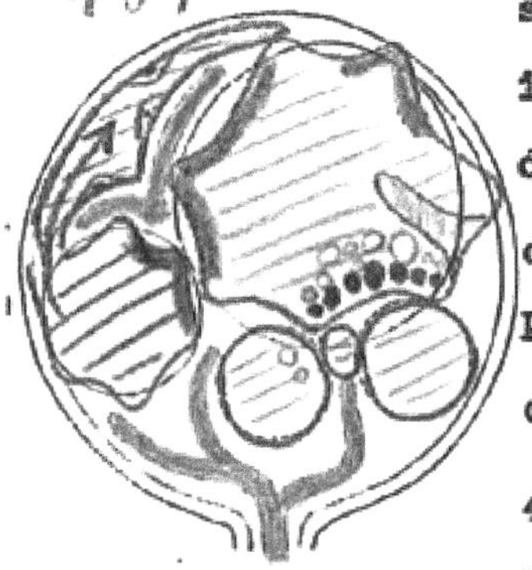

slight degree. Degeneration and desolation of epithelial cells and slight increase of basophilic colloidal masses in follicles and lymphvessels. Follicular collapse with some degenerative processes. At some places slight hyperplasia of follicular epithelial cells to form pillow-like or papaillar arrangements.

410. Acute disfiguring of thyroid in demium degree. Remarkable congestion and perifacular hemorrhages and swelling with remarkable degenerative processes of follicular epithelial cells (cloudy swelling, flattening, desuqamation and desolation of epithel cells) and considerable follicular collapse.
At some places, persistence of lymphonodular tissues with remarkable congestion and some hemorrhages in lymphonoduli.

410

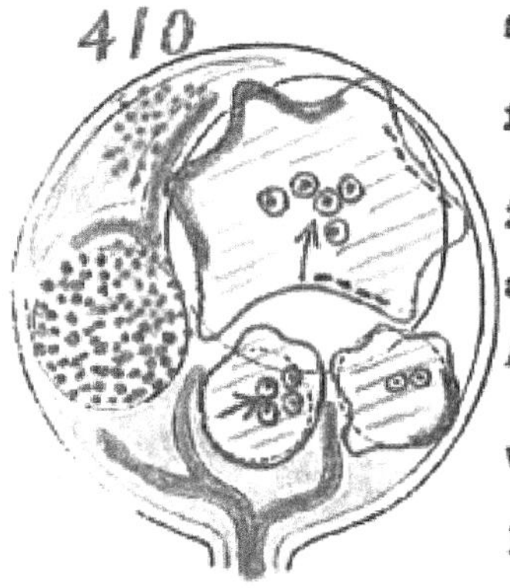

413. Acute disfiguring of thyroid and slight regenerative processes.
Considerable congestion and some perivascular edematous swelling with degenerative processes of follicular epithel cells (flattening, cloudy swelling, pycnosis and desquamation of epithelial cells). Increase of basophilic or fluidified colloid in follicles and lymph-vessels: follicular collapse.
Beside these degenerative changes, slight hyperplasia of epithelial cells to form papillar arrangements.

413

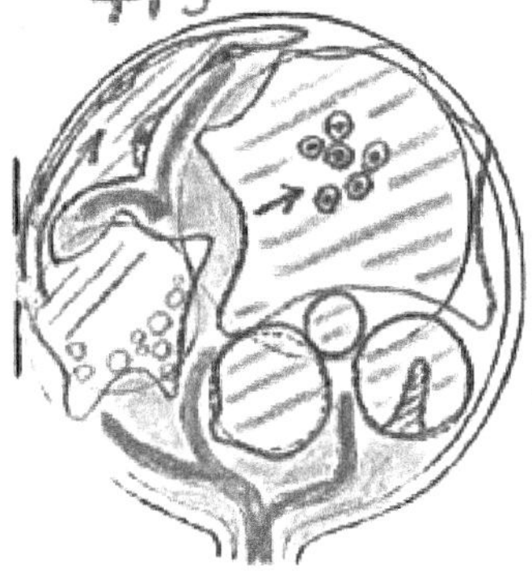

CONFIDENTIAL 317

[redacted]

417

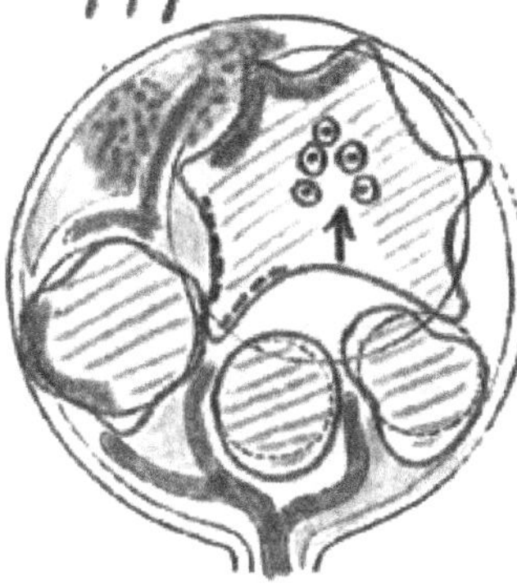

417. Acute disfiguring of thyroid in medium degree. Considerable congestion and slight perivascular hemorrhages and edematous swelling, accompanied with severe degenerative processes of follicular epithelial cells (remarkable degeneration, desquamation and desolation of epithelial cells) and follicular collapse. Without any proliferative changes and increase of colloidal masses.

Some bacterial masses in blood-vessels.

26

26. Acute disfiguring of thyroid.

Congestion and slight fibrosis with some degenerative changes of follicular epithelial cells (desquamation and desolation) to fall into more or less collapse-state of thyroid.

Increase ofcolloidal masses in follicles and lymph-vessels.

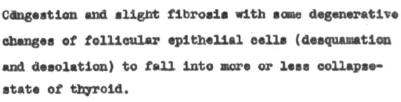

CO[redacted] 318

[redacted]

(B) S U M M A R Y

1) The bird-eye-views of patholigical changes in all cases.

[redacted]

	Changes, due to infection.	Ground-disease.	Note
17	slight activated state	Struma collөides nodosa.	
26	acute disfiguring in slight degree.		
53	staticalsstate (rather degenerative) form	slight fibrosis	some parafolli-cular cells
54	slight activated state.	struma colloides diffusa levis.	some microfolli-cles.
225	slight activated state.	struma colloides diffusa levis.	
318	acute disfiguring in medium degree.		
320	staticalsstate	struma colloides non-proliferativa.	
328	acute disfiguring in demium degree		
393	acute disfiguring in medium degree.		

[redacted]

319

[redacted]

396	acute disfiguring in severe degree.		some bacterial masses in follicles
399	acute disfiguring in slight degree.	[redacted]	
401	statical (rather degenerative) state follicular collapse.	Struma parenchymatosa levis.	
403	acute disfiguring in severe degree.		
405	statical state.		
406	activated state		
407	acute disfiguring in slight degree.		
411	acute desfiguring in medium degree.		persistence of lymphatic apparatus with slight hemorrhages.
413	acute disfiguring in slight degree.		
417	acute disfiguring in demium degree.		some bacterial masses in capillarties.

All microscopically investigated cases in 19 cases.

with acute disfiguring of follicles. in II cases.

in slight degree. in 4 cases.

in medium degree. in 5 cases.

in severe degree. in 2 cases.

with activated state. in 4 cases.

[redacted] 320

[redacted]

with non-activated, statical state. in 4 cases.

with remarkable bacterial accumulations.in follicles. in 8 cases.

Accordingly, the most cases of them fall into acute disfiguring or somewhat activated state of follicles, due to Anthrax-infection. Namely after Anthrax-infection, occured at first some activating of follicles with considerable congestion and some changes of follicular epithelial cells:

Sometimes in slight activated regeneration (slight hyperplasia of epithelial cells) and

sometimes in slight disturbed degeneration (slight degeneration of epthelial cells and furthermore remarkable degeneration or follicular collapse).

These activated state advanced furthermore into the acute disfiguring of follicles with remarkable degeneration of follicular epithelial cells and some signs of follicular collapse.

As remarkable degeneration of epithelial cells:

Flattening, clouding, pycnotic degeneration, desquamation and desolation of epithelial cells and

as signs of functional disturbances (follicular collapse):

increase of basophilic or fluidified colloidal masses in follicles and lymphsinoids.

Accordingly, the developing mechanismus of thyreoidal changes, due to Anthrax-infection are as following:

[redacted] 321

[redacted]

Statical state.
4 cases.

[redacted]

Activated state.
4 cases.

<u>in regenerative form.</u>
2 cases

<u>in degenerative form.</u>
2 cases.

State of
disfiguring.
11 cases.

<u>in follicular collapse.</u>
11 cases.

[redacted] 322

[redacted]

[redacted]

THYROID

			17	26	53	54	225	318	320	328	389	393	396	397
Parenchyma	Follicles	Large Follicles	+++	+	+	++	++	+	+	+	+	+	++	+
		Small Follicles	+	+	+	+	+	+	÷	÷	+	+	+	+
		Cysts	+	−	−	−	−	−	−	−	−	−	÷	−
		Microfollicles	+	÷	+	+	÷	+	÷	÷	÷	÷	+	÷
		Ruin	÷	+	+	÷	(+)	+	(÷)	(++)	+	(+)	++	(+)
	Epithelium	flat	++	+	+	+	+	+	++	+	+	+	+	++
		cuboidal	+	+	+	+	+	+	÷	+	+	+	+	÷
		cylindrical	+	÷	÷	+	+	+	(÷)	(+)	+	+	÷	÷
		Papilla Formation	+	÷	÷	++	+	÷	÷	÷	÷	÷	−	÷
		Pillow Formation	++	(+)	÷	+	++	(++)	(÷)	(+)	++	÷	÷	÷
		Solid Cell Groups	+	÷	÷	÷	÷	∣	÷	÷	÷	+	∣	÷
		Trabecular Arrangement	−	−	÷	−	−	−	−	−	÷	÷	−	÷
		Sack Formation	+	+	÷	+	÷	÷	−	−	÷	÷	+	−
		Desquamation	+	++	÷	÷	++	++	÷	÷	++	++	+	÷
	Changes of Nuclei	Pyknosis etc	+	++	÷	÷	÷	++	÷	+	÷	÷	+	÷
		Increase of Chromatin	÷	+	+	÷	+	+	+	÷	÷	÷	+	÷
		Karyolysis & -rrhexis	÷	÷	÷	÷	÷	+	÷	+	÷	÷	+	−
	Colloid	Quantity	+++↑	+↑	+↑	+++↑	+↑	++↑	++↑	+↑	+↑	++↑	++↑	÷↑
		Vacuoles	++	+	÷	+	÷	+	÷	÷	÷	÷	++	÷
		Fluidification	+	÷	÷	÷	÷	÷	−	÷	÷	÷	+	÷
Stroma		Edema	÷	++	(++)	÷	++	+	+	÷	++	++	++	+
		Hyaline Degeneration	÷	+	÷	+	÷	+	÷	−	÷	÷	÷	−
		Fibrosis	÷	÷	+	÷	÷	+	÷	÷	÷	−	÷	−
		Colloid in Lymph-vessels	(+)	÷	(+)	÷	++	(++)	÷	÷	+	++	++	++
		Hemorrhage	÷	÷	÷	÷	÷	+	−	÷	÷	÷	÷	÷
		Round Cell Infiltration	÷	÷	÷	÷	÷	(+)	÷	÷	÷	÷	÷	÷
	Blood Vessels – Contents	Congestion	+	++	++	+	++	+	÷	÷	++	+	++	÷
		Lymphocytes	÷	÷	÷	÷	÷	÷	÷	÷	÷	÷	+	÷
		Leucocytes	÷	÷	÷	÷	÷	−	−	÷	−	÷	+	÷
		Fibrin	÷	÷	−	−	−	−	÷	−	−	−	−	−
	Blood Vessels	Increase of Endothelium	÷	÷	÷	÷	÷	÷	+	÷	÷	÷	÷	÷
		Degeneration of Endothelium	÷	+	÷	+	+	++	÷	+	+	+	++	÷
		Swelling of Walls	÷	+	+	+	+	÷	÷	+	+	+	+	÷
	Lymphoid Focus	Lymphocytes	∣	∣	∣	∣	∣	∣	∣	∣	∣	∣	∣	∣
		Plasma Cells	∣	∣	∣	∣	∣	∣	∣	∣	∣	∣	∣	∣
		Germinating Center	∣	∣	∣	∣	∣	∣	∣	∣	∣	∣	∣	∣

[redacted] 323

[redacted]

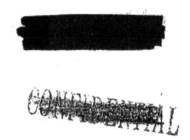

CONFIDENTIAL

THYROID

			399	401	403	405	406	407	409	410	411	414	416	417
Parenchyma	Follicles	Large Follicles	+	÷	+	+	+	+̈	+̈	+	÷	+̈	÷	÷
		Small Follicles	+	++	+	+	+̈	÷	+	++	++	+	++	++
		Cysts	−	−	−	−	−	−	−	(+)	++	−	−	−
		Microfollicles	÷	+	÷	∸	+	∸	∸	∸	÷	∸	+	÷
		Ruin	(+)	++	++	∸	(+)	++	++	++	++	(+̈)	(+̈)	++
	Epithelium	flat	+	+	+	÷	∸	++	+̈	+̈	+++	+	∸	++
		cuboidal	+	÷	+	+	++	+	∸	+	+	+	++	∸
		Cylindrical	÷	−	∸	(÷)	+	−	−	(÷)	−	÷	+	−
		Papilla Formation	÷	÷	∸	∸	++	÷	÷	÷	+	÷	++	−
		Pillow Formation	÷	−	−	∸	+̈	÷	−	−	∸	(+)	++	−
		Solid Cell Groups	÷	++	+	(÷)	+	+	++	++	+	+	+	++
		Trabecular Arrangement	∸	+	÷	−	−	−	−	÷	−	−	−	÷
		Sack Formation	+	÷	∸	(÷)	÷	+	÷	∸	+	÷	+	−
		Desquamation	÷	∸	÷	∸	÷	++	∸	+	+	÷	÷	+
	Changes of Nuclei	Pyknosis etc	∸	+	+	∸	∸	+	+	÷	+̈	÷	∸	+
		Increase of Chromatin	÷	÷	÷	+	++	÷	∸	÷	∸	+	+̈	∸
		Karyolysis & -rrhexis	÷	+	÷	∸	(÷)	+	∸	÷	+	+	+	÷
	Colloid	Quantity	÷↑	+↓	∸↑	−	−	+↑	÷↑	÷↓	++↑	+↑	÷↓	++↓
		Vacuoles	÷	++	+̈	+	÷	÷	÷	÷	++	∸	∸	+̈
		Fluidification	÷	+	÷	(++)	÷	÷	+	÷	++	−	−	÷
Stroma		Edema	+̈	+̈	++	÷	+	+	++	+	+̈	++	+̈	++
		Hyaline Degeneration	−	+	÷	−	−	÷	∸	∸	−	+	−	∸
		Fibrosis	−	++	∸	∸	∸	÷	∸	÷	÷	∸	−	÷
		Colloid in Lymph-vessels	+	+	++	−	(+)	++	++	+	÷	++	(+)	÷
		Hemorrhage	∸	∸	÷	−	∸	(÷)	÷	+̈	+	(÷)	÷	÷
		Round Cell Infiltration	∸	+	∸	∸	∸	+	∸	+	÷	÷	÷	∸
	Blood Vessels – Contents	Congestion	+̈	+̈	++	÷	++	+̈	++	+++	++	+̈	++	+++
		Lymphocytes	÷	÷	÷	∸	÷	+	∸	÷	÷	+	÷	÷
		Leucocytes	÷	∸	÷	−	∸	∸	∸	∸	−	∸	÷	÷
		Fibrin	−	+	∸	−	−	−	÷	÷	−	−	−	−
	Blood Vessels	Increase of Endothelium	÷	÷	∸	÷	÷	+	∸	+	÷	+	÷	÷
		Degeneration of Endothelium	÷	+	÷	∸	∸	÷	÷	÷	+	÷	÷	÷
		Swelling of Walls	÷	+	++	÷	∸	÷	[illegible]	÷	÷	÷	+	+
	Lymphoid Focus	Lymphocytes	|	|	|	|	|	|	|	|	++	|	|	|
		Plasma Cells	|	|	|	|	|	|	|	|	÷	|	|	|
		Germinating Center	|	|	|	|	|	|	|	|	÷	|	|	|

[redacted] 324

[redacted]

CONFIDENTIAL

M.235 Follicular collapse:
Follicles with degenerated
follicular epitheliums.

× 65

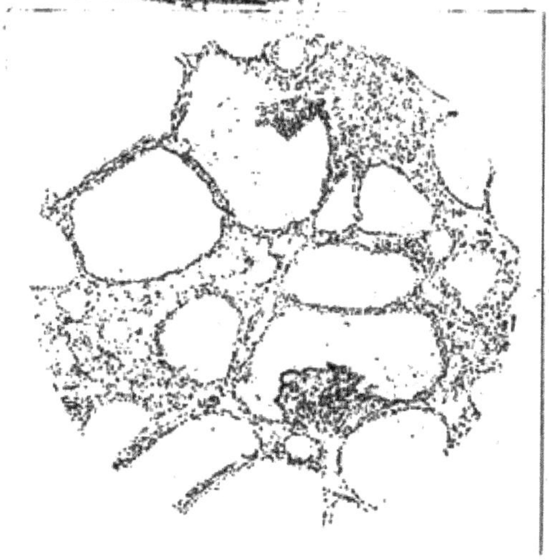

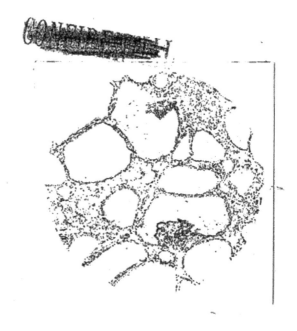

M.401. Follicular collapse ;
In high power.

× 200

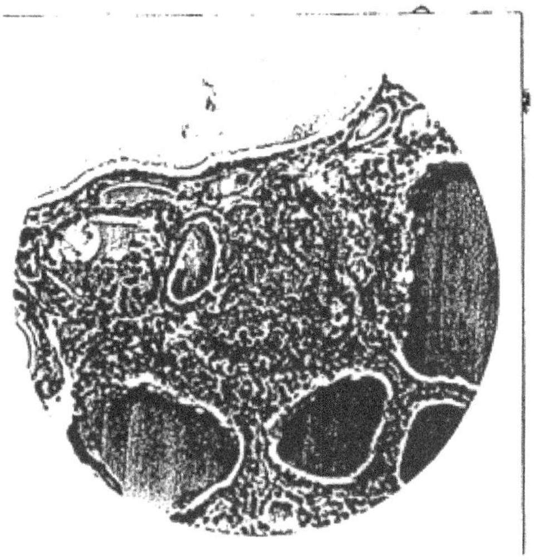

CONFIDENTIAL 325

[redacted]

[redacted]

M.416 Intense follicular collapse, with colloidal masses in lymphsinusoid.

×80

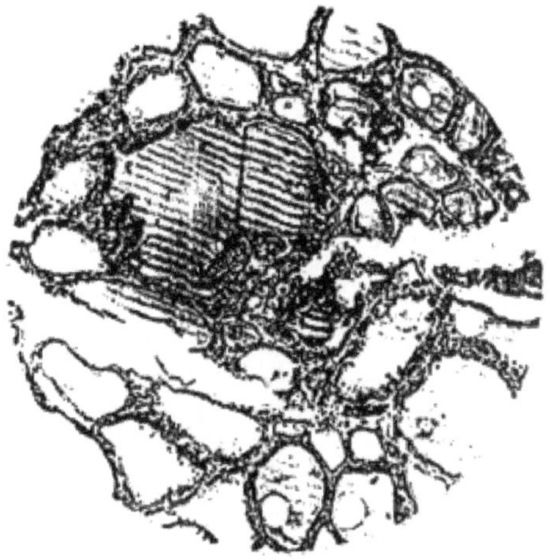

M.346 In activated state , with pillow-like hyperplasia of follicular epitheliums.

×37.5

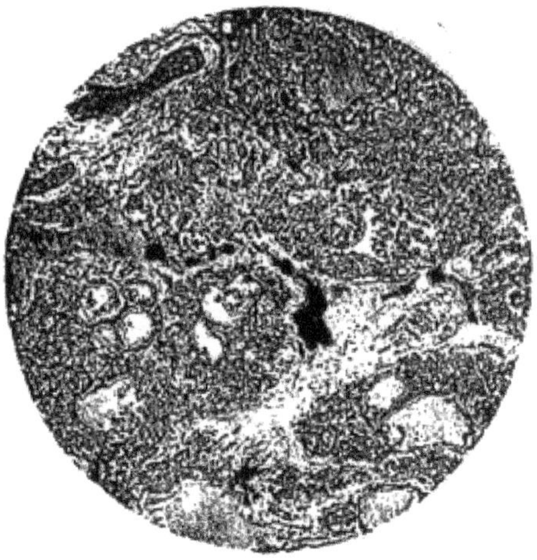

[redacted] 326

[redacted]

CONFIDENTIAL

M.318 Atrophy of lobulus.

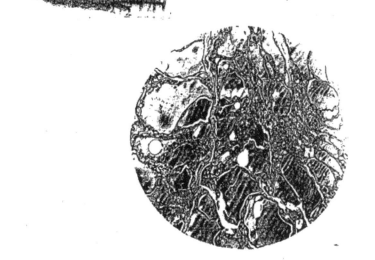

× 31.5

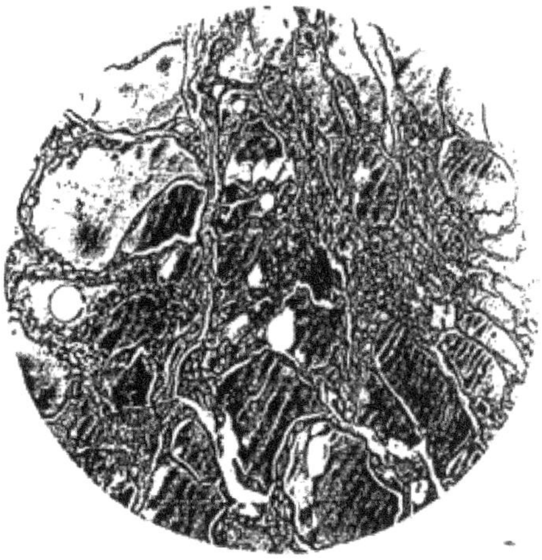

M.4[illegible] Atrophy of lobulus.

× 38

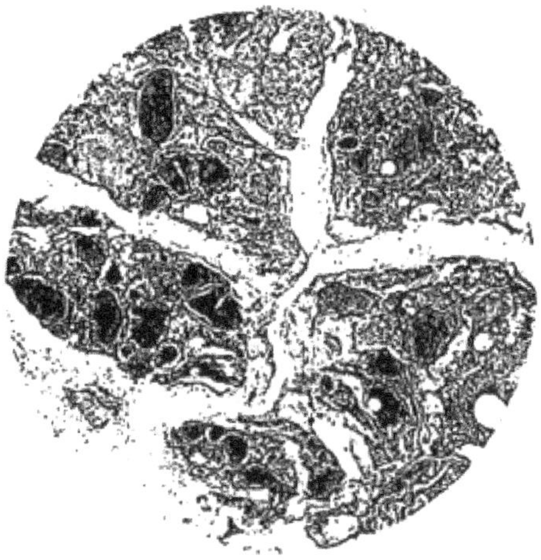

CONFIDENTIAL

327

[redacted]

In activated state with follicular congestion.

x 38.5

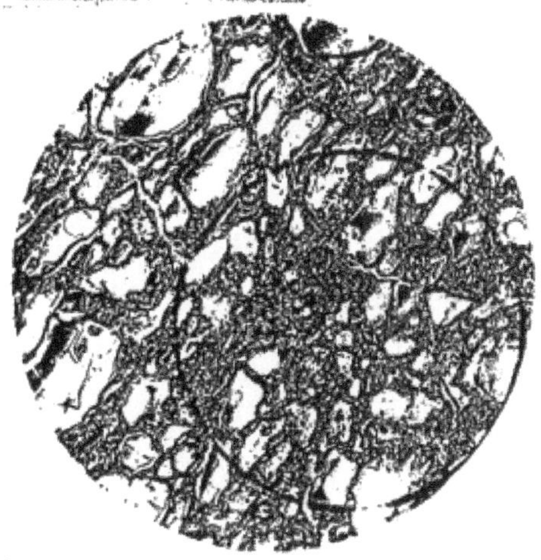

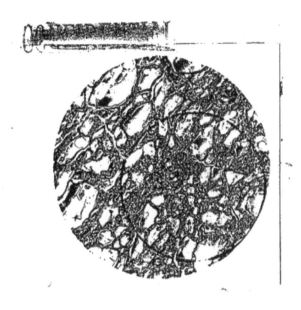

M.496 Follicular congestion in high power.

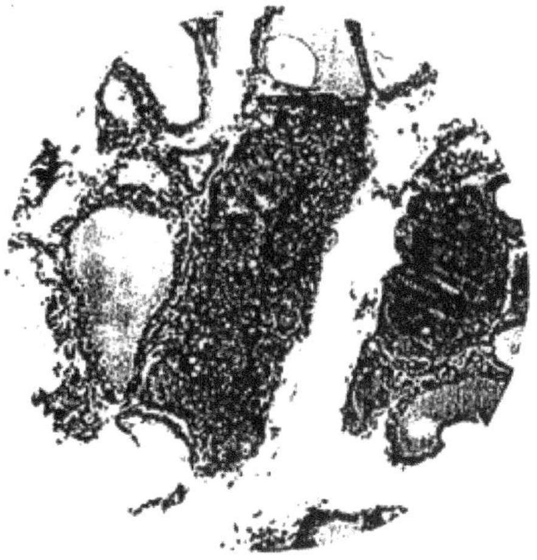

328

[redacted]

CONFIDENTIAL

M.401 Atrophy of lobulus.
x38.5

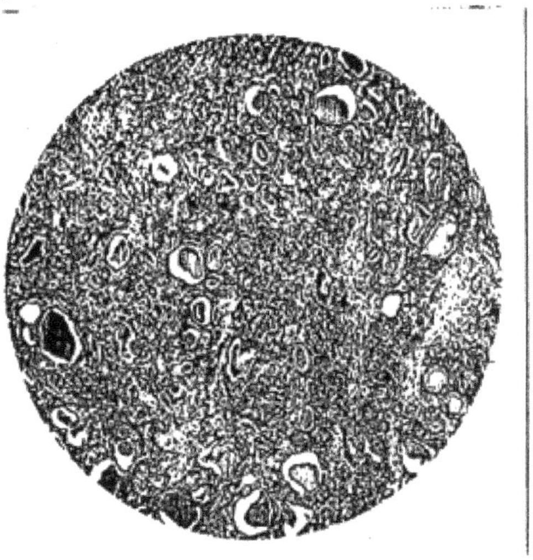

M.410 Lymphoid focus; hyperplasied lymphatic nodulus with some grerminative centres.
x38.5

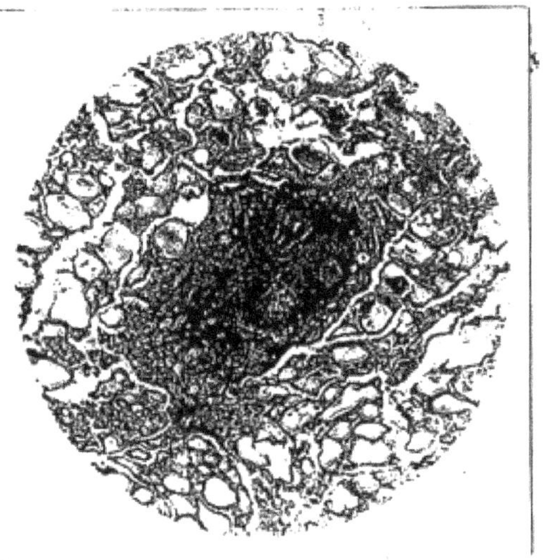

[redacted]

329

[redacted]

[redacted]

Testis

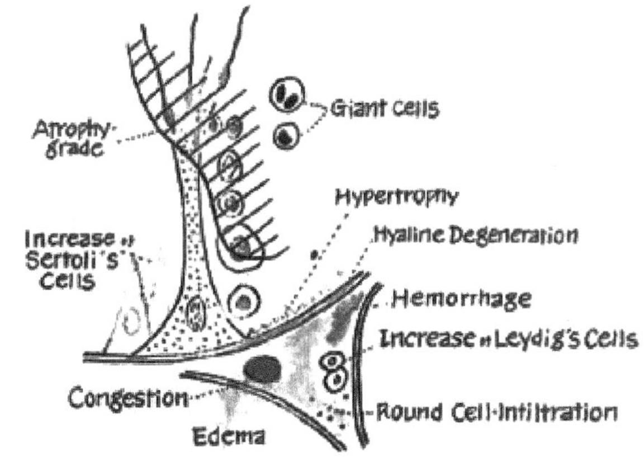

[redacted]

330

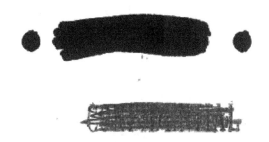

[redacted]

TESTICLE

A) Microscopical [redacted]

a) Parenchyma.

	Reduction of Tubulus	Atrophia testis	Hypertrophia or Hyaline degeneration of T.propria.	Giant cell formation	Hyperplasia of Sertoli's cells
17	I.	III.	+	−	N
54	I.	III.	++	÷	↓
225	I.	III.	÷	÷	↓
318	I.	III.	+	÷	↓

b) Stroma.

	Congestion	Hemorrhages	Roundcell infiltration	Swelling or Roughness	Increase of Leydig's cells
17	+	+	−	+	÷
54	÷	÷	÷	÷	↓
225	+++	÷	÷	+++	N
318	+	−	÷	+	↓

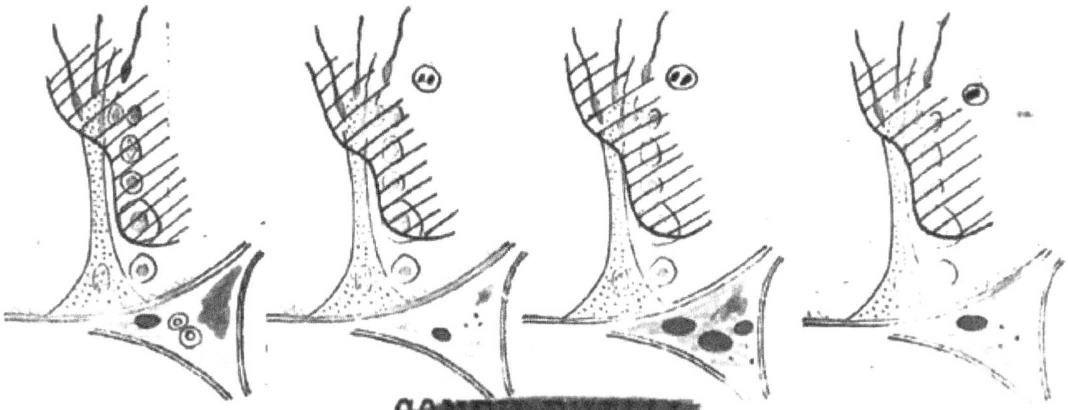

[redacted] 331

• [redacted] •

a) Parenchyma.

	Reduction of Tubulus	Atrophia testis	[redacted]		
			Hypertrophia or Hyaline degeneration of T.propria.	Giant cell formation	Hyperplasia of Sertoli's cells
320	~I.	II.	÷	—	÷
325	I.	II.	÷	—	+
328	—.	I.	±	—	↓
388	I.	I.	±	—	N

b) Stroma.

	Congestion	Hemorrhages	Round cell infiltration	Swelling or Roughness	Increase of Leydig's cells
320	+	±	±	+	÷
325	+	±	±	+	÷
328	++	±	±	++	÷
388	++	±	±	++	÷

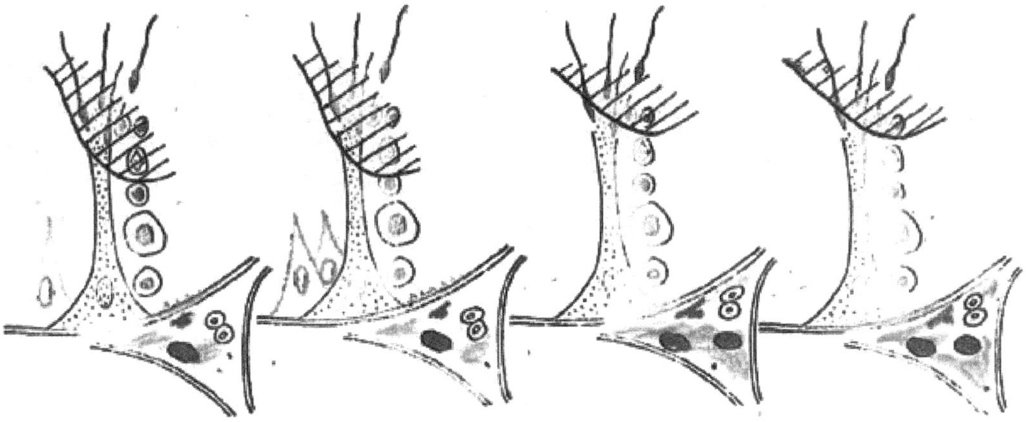

[redacted]

332

• [redacted] •

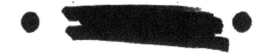

a) Parenchyma. [redacted]

Reduction of Tubulus	Atrophia testis	Hypertrophia or Hyaline-degeneration of T. propria.	Giant cell formation.	Hyperplasia of Srtoli's cells
389 I.	II.	∸	∸	÷
393 II.	III.	∸	—	↓
396 I.	III.	÷	—	÷
397 I.	II.	—	∸	+

b) Stroma.

	Congestion	Hemorrhages	Round cell infiltration	Swelling or Roughness	Increase of Leydig's cells
389	++	∸	∸	++	↓
393	+++	∸	÷	+++	÷
396	+	÷	÷	+	÷
397	++	÷	∸	++	÷

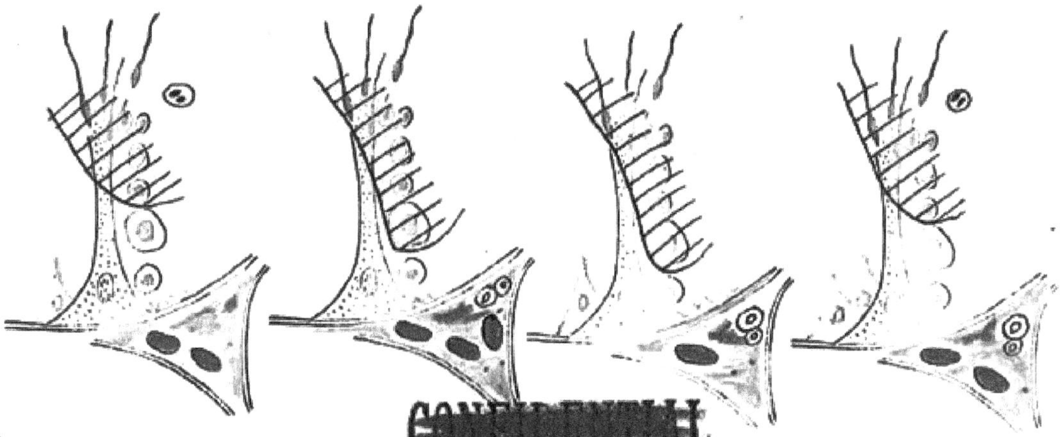

[redacted]

333

[redacted]

(a) Parenchyma. [redacted]

Redaction of Tubulus	Atrophia testis	Hypertrophia or Hyaline degeneration of T.propria.	Formation of Giant cells	Hyperplasia of Sertoli's cells
399 ~ I.	II.	∸	+	N
4o1 I.	III.	−	+	N
403 I.	III.	÷	±	++
405 II.	II.	∸	±	÷

b) Stroma.

	Congestion	Hemorrhages	Round cell infiltration	SWelling or Roughness	Increase of Leydig's cells.
399	÷	±	÷	÷	+
401	++	±	÷	++	÷
403	+++	±	±	+++	N
405	+	∸	÷	+	÷

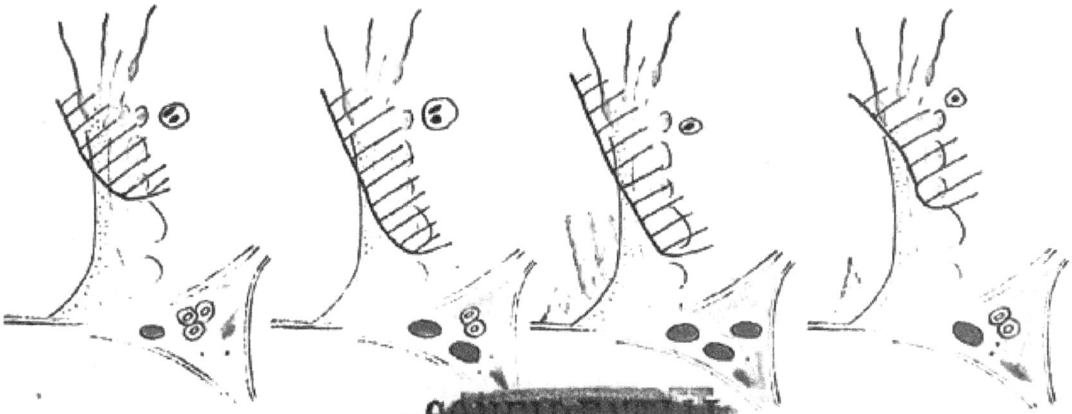

[redacted] 334

[redacted]

a) Parenchyma.

[redacted]

	Rednction of Tubulus	Atrophia testis	Hypertrophia or Hyaline degeneration of T.propria.	Giant cell formation.	Hyperplasia of Seroli's cells
406	II.	III.	−	−	↓
407	I.	III.	÷	∸	N
409	~I.	II.	∸	−	↓
410	I.	II.	÷	÷	↓

b) Stroma.

	Congestion	Hemorrhages	Round cell infiltration	Swelling or Roughness	Increase of Leydig's cells.
406	++	+	∸	++	÷
407	++	∸	∸	++	↓
409	+	∸	∸	+	+
410	+++	∸	∸	+++	N

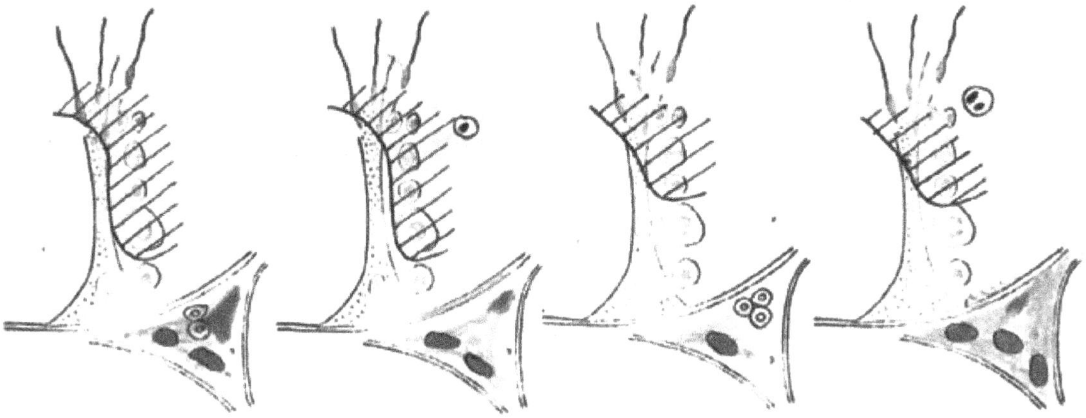

[redacted] 335

[redacted]

a) Parenchyma.

	Reduction of Tubulus	Atrophia testis	Hypertrophia or Hyaline degeneration of T.propria.	Formationn of Giant cells	Hyperplasia of Sertoli's cells
			[redacted]		
411	I.	II.	÷	—	↓
413	I.	II.	∸	÷	N
414	~I.	II.	—	+	N
416	—	II.	—	—	↓

b) Stroma.

	Congestion	Hemorrhages	Round cell infiltration	Swelling or roughness	Increase of Leydig's cells
411	+	∸	∸	+	+
413	+	—	∸	+	↓
414	+	—	∸	+	+
416	÷	—	∸	÷	÷

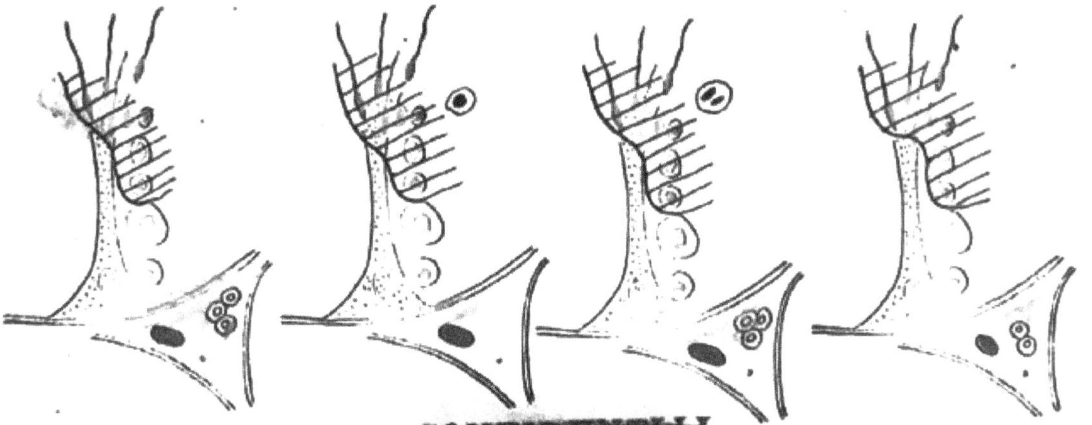

[redacted] 336

[redacted]

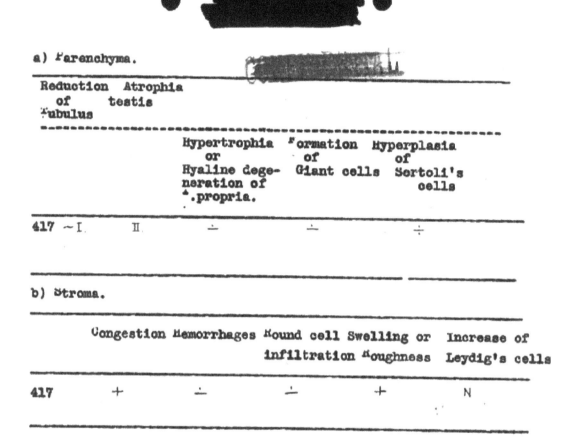

a) Parenchyma. [redacted]

	Reduction of Tubulus	Atrophia testis	Hypertrophia or Hyaline degeneration of T.propria.	Formation of Giant cells	Hyperplasia of Sertoli's cells
417	~I	II	±	±	±

b) Stroma.

	Congestion	Hemorrhages	Round cell infiltration	Swelling or Roughness	Increase of Leydig's cells
417	+	±	±	+	N

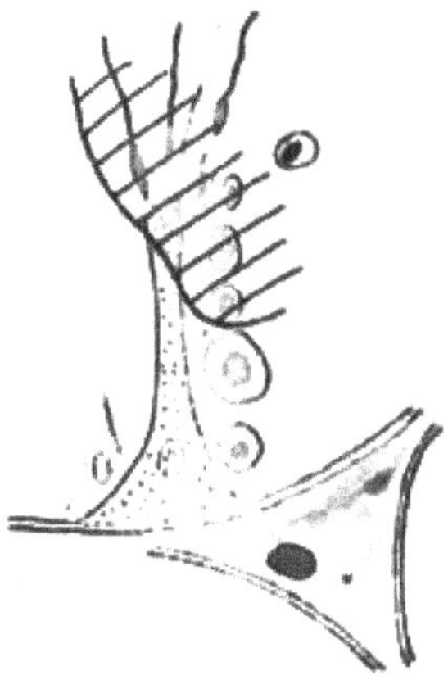

[redacted] 337

[redacted]

B) S U M M A R Y [redacted]

(I)

Our classification of "disturbance of spermatopoietic process".

a) On the "Atrophia testis".

Atrophia testis 1.	Pyknotic spermatozoa. Relative increase of prespermatids and spermatids.
Atrophia testis 11.	Degeneration of prespermatids and spermatids with somewhat considerable excoriation of somewhat giant cell-formation (as signs of degeneration).
Atrophia testis 111.	Remarkable degeneration of prespermatids and spermatids.
Atrophia testis 1V.	Remarkable degeneration or sometimes complete diminishment of spermatocytes. Degeneration and sometimes irregular cell-arrangment o spermatogonien.
Atrophia testis V.	Complete diminishment of spermatic cells. Remarkable swelling and hyaline degeneration of T.propria of tubuli seminiferi.

b) On the reduction o tubuli seminiferi.

Reduction 1.	Diameter of tubulus seminiferus is reduced to 3/4 of normal.(slight atrophia).
Reduction 11.	Reduced to 2/4.(medium atrophia).
Reduction 111.	Reduced to 1/4. (severe atrophia).

[redacted] 338

[redacted]

(2)

Generally infection causes some disturbances of spermato-poietic process: [redacted]

Atrophia testis	1.	2 cases.
"	11.	13 cases.
"	111.	10 cases.

Reduction of tubuli seminiferi

	1.	20 cases.
"	11.	3 cases.

Sometimes accompanied with giant cell-formation of spermatids and prespermatids, as degenerative signs.

14 cases.

Generally infection causes some congestion.

Congestion	in slight degree.	14 cases.
	in medium degree.	7 cases.
	in severe degree.	4 cases.

Sometimes hemorrhages and edema in interstitial tissues.

Hemorrhages	in slight degree.	18 cases.
	in mediun degree.	2 cases.
Edema	in medium degree,	18 cases,
	in severe degree.	4 cases.

Accompanied with sometimes some round cell-infiltration.

in slight degree. 24 cases.

Leydig's cells. Sometimes increase.

in slight degree	12 cases.
in medium degree.	4 cases.

Sometimes decrease.

in slight degree. 5 cases.

in normal state [redacted] cases.

339

[redacted]

CONFIDENTIAL

TESTIS

			17	54	225	318	320	325	328	388	389	393	396	397	399
Tubuli Seminiferi	Grade of Reduction		+	+	+	+	÷	+	∸	+	+	++	+	+	÷
	T.propria	Thickening	÷	+	∸	+	÷	÷	∸	−	∸	∸	÷	−	∸
		Fibrous Degeneration	+	+	÷	÷	+	÷	∸	÷	÷	÷	+	∸	÷
		Hyaline Degeneration	+	++	∸	÷	÷	÷	−	∸	−	−	÷	−	−
	Sertoli's Cells	Quantity	N	↓÷	↓÷	↓÷	↓÷	↑+	↓÷	N	↑÷	↓+	↑÷	↑+	N
		Degeneration	∸	∸	÷	∸	÷	∸	+	−	÷	+	∸	∸	−
	Spermatogonien	Quantity	↓÷	N	↓÷	↓÷	N	↓÷	N	N	N	↓÷	N	N	N
		Degeneration	∸	−	∸	∸	∸	−	−	−	−	∸	−	−	−
	Spermatocytes	Quantity	↓÷	↓÷	↓÷	↓÷	↓÷	N	↓÷	N	↑÷	↓÷	N	N	↓÷
		Degeneration	÷	÷	−	+	∸	÷	∸	÷	+	÷	÷	∸	÷
	Prespermatids	Quantity	↓+	↓÷	↓÷	↓+	↓÷	N	↑÷	N	↓÷	N	↓+	↓÷	↓÷
		Degeneration	+	+	+	÷	∸	∸	−	−	+	+	+	÷	+
	Spermatids	Quantity	↓++	↓+	↓++	↓÷	↓+	N	↑÷	↓÷	↓÷	↓+++	↓+++	↓+	↓÷
		Degeneration	++	+	++	+	+	∸	÷	+	÷	+++	+++	+	÷
	Spermatozoa	Quantity	↓+++	↓+	↓+++	↓++	↓++	↓++	N	↓÷	↓++	↓+++	↓+++	↓+	↓+
		Degeneration	+++	++	+++	++	+	+	÷	÷	+	+++	+++	+	+
	Giant Cells		−	÷	÷	∸	−	−	−	−	∸	−	−	∸	+
Stroma	Congestion		+	÷	+++	+	+	+	++	++	++	+++	+	++	÷
	Edema		+	÷	+++	+	+	+	++	++	++	[illegible]	+	++	÷
	Swelling of Connective Tissue		+	−	∸	∸	+	+	−	÷	∸	+	÷	∸	−
	Hemorrhage		+	∸	÷	−	∸	∸	∸	∸	∸	÷	÷	÷	∸
	Round Cell Infiltration		−	∸	∸	∸	∸	∸	∸	∸	∸	÷	÷	∸	÷
	Increase of Connective Tissue		÷	−	−	−	÷	÷	−	+	∸	÷	+	∸	+
	Vessel wall	Degeneration of Endothelium	∸	÷	+	÷	÷	÷	÷	÷	÷	÷	÷	−	÷
		Hyaline Degeneration	∸	+++	−	−	−	+	−	−	÷	−	−	+	∸
		Swelling	÷	÷	+	∸	÷	÷	÷	∸	÷	÷	−	∸	∸
	Leydig's Cells	Quantity	↑÷	↓÷	N	↓÷	↑÷	↑÷	↑÷	↑÷	↓÷	↑÷	↑÷	↑÷	↑+
		Yellow Granules	÷	∸	−	−	+	−	−	−	−	−	−	−	+
T.albuginea T.vasculosa	Congestion		+	÷	│	÷	+	÷	++	++	│	++	+	++	+
	Hemorrhage		÷	−	│	−	−	−	−	−	│	−	−	−	−
	Round Cell Infiltration		−	÷	│	÷	∸	∸	−	∸	│	−	∸	÷	÷
	Degeneration of Vessel Endothelium		−	−	│	÷	∸	∸	∸	÷	│	∸	−	÷	÷
	Increase of Connective Tissue		−	−	│	−	−	−	−	−	│	−	−	−	−
Grade of Atrophy			III	III	III	III	II	II	I	I	II	III	III	II	II

CONFIDENTIAL 340

[redacted]

[redacted]

TESTIS

			401	403	405	406	407	409	410	411	413	414	416	417
Tubuli Seminiferi	Grade of Reduction		+	+	++	++	+	÷	+	+	+	÷	∸	÷
	T. Propria	Thickening	−	÷	−	−	−	∸	÷	÷	−	−	−	∸
		Fibrous Degeneration	∸	÷	∸	∸	+	∸	÷	÷	+	÷	∸	÷
		Hyaline Degeneration	−	−	−	−	÷	−	∸	÷	∸	−	−	∸
	Sertoli's Cells	Quantity	N	↑++	↑÷	↓+	N	↓÷	↓÷	↓÷	N	N	↓÷	↑÷
		Degeneration	−	∸	∸	÷	−	∸	÷	∸	∸	∸	÷	÷
	Spermatogonien	Quantity	N	↓÷	↓÷	↓÷	N	↓÷	↓÷	↓÷	N	↓÷	↓÷	N
		Degeneration	−	−	−	−	−	−	−	−	−	−	−	−
	Spermatocytes	Quantity	↓÷	↓÷	↓÷	↓÷	↓÷	↓÷	N	↓÷	↓÷	↓÷	↓÷	↓÷
		Degeneration	∸	∸	∸	−	∸	÷	+	+	−	−	+	∸
	Prespermatids	Quantity	↓+	↓+	↓+	↓+	↑÷	↓+	↓÷	↓+	↓÷	↑÷	↓+	N
		Degeneration	+	++	+	++	÷	÷	÷	÷	+	−	+	∸
	Spermatids	Quantity	↓++	↓+	↓+	↓++	↓÷	↓+	↓+	↓+	↑÷	↓÷	↓+	↓÷
		Degeneration	+++	+	++	+++	÷	+	+	+	∸	÷	∸	÷
	Spermatozoa	Quantity	↓++	↓++	↓+	↓++	↓++	↓++	↓+	↓+	↓÷	↓÷	↓+	↓+
		Degeneration	+++	+++	++	+	++	+++	+	+	+	+	+	+
	Giant Cells		+	∸	∸	−	∸	−	÷	−	÷	+	−	∸
Stroma	Congestion		++	+++	+	++	++	+	+++	+	+	+	÷	+
	Edema		++	+++	+	++	++	+	+++	+	+	+	÷	+
	Swelling of Connective Tissue		÷	∸	÷	÷	−	−	−	∸	∸	+	+	∸
	Hemorrhage		∸	∸	∸	+	∸	−	∸	∸	−	−	−	∸
	Round Cell Infiltration		÷	∸	÷	∸	∸	∸	∸	∸	∸	∸	÷	∸
	Increase of Connective Tissue		÷	÷	+	+	−	−	−	−	∸	+	∸	∸
	Vessel Walls	Degeneration of Endothelium	+	÷	÷	∸	∸	∸	−	+	∸	∸	÷	÷
		Hyaline Degeneration	++	++	−	÷	∸	−	+++	−	+	−	+	÷
		Swelling	+	÷	÷	∸	∸	∸	+	∸	∸	∸	∸	÷
	Leydig's Cells	Quantity	↑÷	N	↑÷	↑÷	↓÷	↑+	N	↑+	↓÷	↑+	↑÷	N
		Yellow Granules	∸	∸	−	∸	∸	++	∸	+	−	∸	÷	÷
T. albuginea / T. vasculosa	Congestion		+	+	÷	÷	++	++	+++	I	+	+	÷	+
	Hemorrhage		−	−	−	−	∸	−	−	I	−	−	−	−
	Round Cell Infiltration		÷	∸	∸	∸	∸	∸	∸	I	∸	−	∸	−
	Degeneration of Vessel Endothelium		∸	÷	∸	∸	∸	÷	÷	I	−	∸	÷	∸
	Increase of Connective Tissue		−	−	∸	−	−	−	−	I	−	−	−	−
Grade of Atrophy			III	III	II	III	III	II	II	II	II	II	II	II

N = normal

[redacted] 341

[redacted]

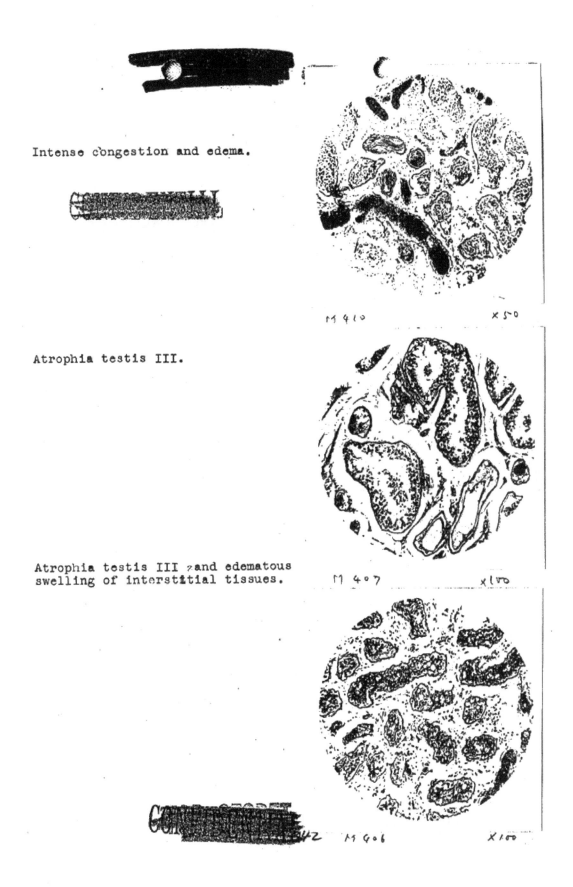

Intense congestion and edema.

[redacted]

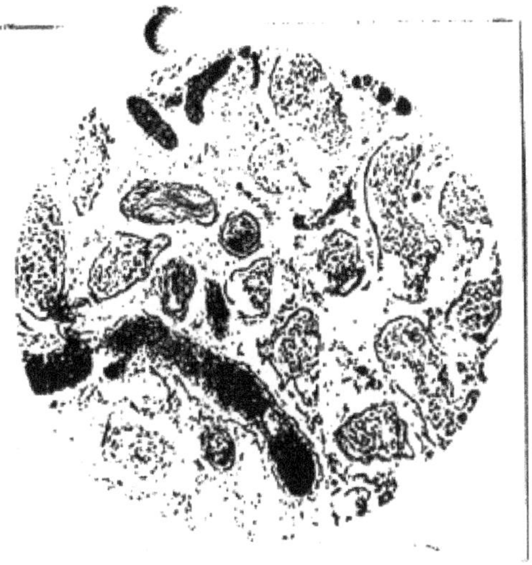

M 410　x 50

Atrophia testis III.

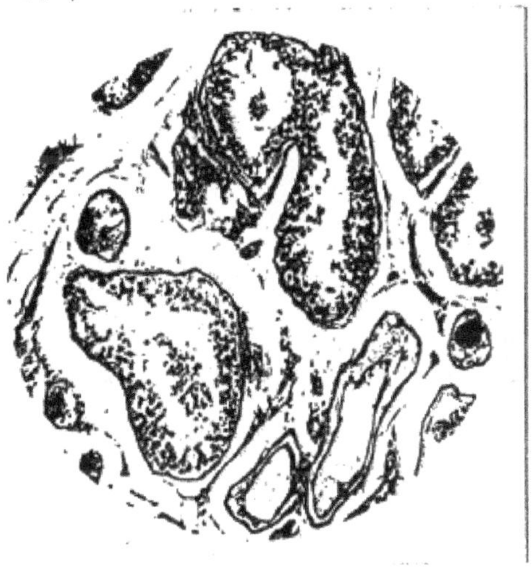

Atrophia testis III and edematous swelling of interstitial tissues.

M 407　x 100

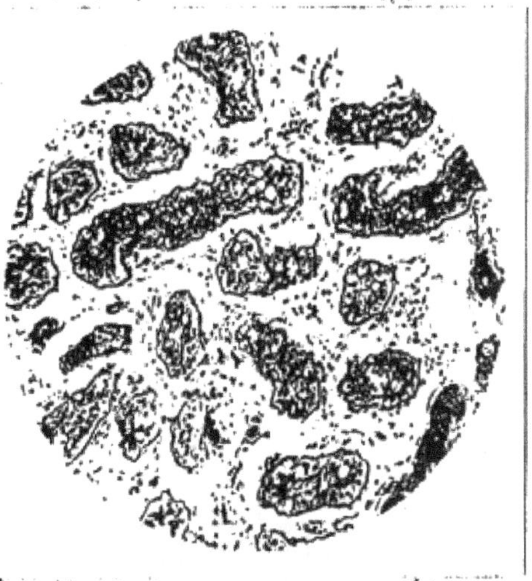

[redacted]

M 406　x 100

[redacted]

[redacted]

Atrophia testis III, accompanied with diminish of spermatozoic cells.

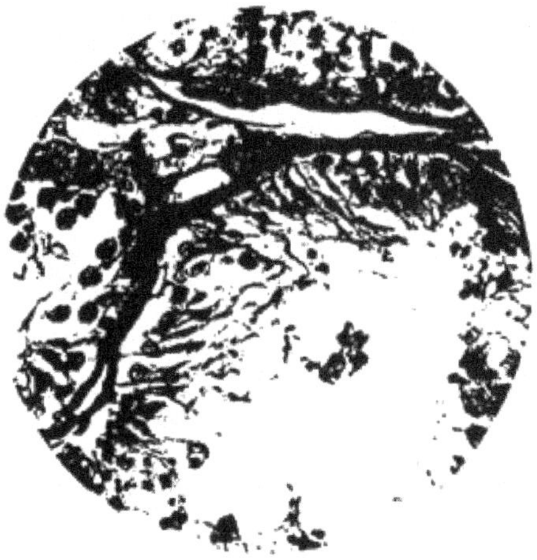

M 403 x210

Atrophia testis III, accompanied with giant cells formation of spermatogonic cells.

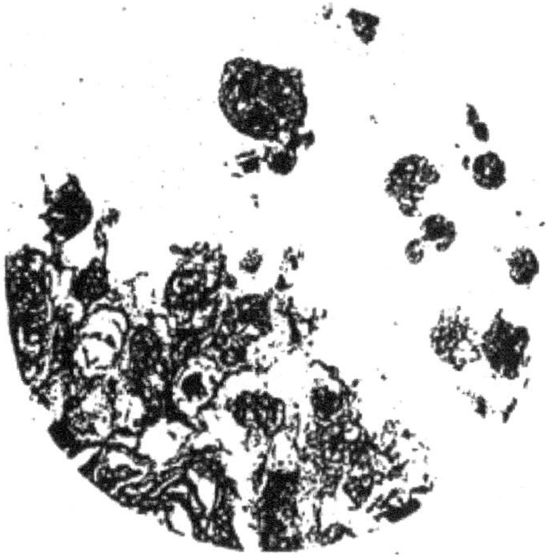

M 399 x520

[redacted] 343

[redacted]

[redacted]

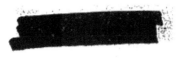

Pituitary body

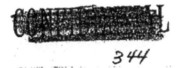

[redacted]

344

[redacted]

PITUITARY-BODY. [redacted]

(A) Microscop. Investigati[redacted]

225.

Partial hemorrhages in capsules. Severe congestion in anterior and posterior lobe (with some leucocytes in capillaries) and edema. Slight parenchymatous degeneration.

318.

Slight partial hemorrhages, severe congestion and subendothelial edema in anterior lobe. Slight parenchymatous degeneration.

401.

More or less atrophic and degenerative glandular cells with slight dissociation of cellular arrangements. Some bacterial masses in capillaries. Slight congestion and flat, non-active endothelial cells.

404.

In posterior lobe, some capillories include leucocytes.

~~404~~.

More or less atrophic and degenerative glandular cells with slight dissociation of cellular arrangements. Non active endothelial cells.

405.

Almost normal with slight proliferative tendency of basal membrane. Wandering of basophilic glandular cells in posterior lobe.

409.

Slight congestion and slight parenchymatous degeneration. No remarkable changes else.

410.

More or less considerable congestion and edema. More or less atrophic

[redacted] 945

[redacted]

[redacted]

and degenerative glandular cells. Slight perivascular round-cell -accumulation in intermediate lobe.

4II.

Intense congestion, edema and partial hemorrhages in anterior lobe. More or less atrophic and degenerative glandular cells. (esp. at hemorrhagic parts).

[redacted] 346

[redacted]

(B) S U M M A R Y. [redacted]

A.) Anterior lobe.

I) Always with somewhat capillar congestion.

Congestion in slight degree.	2 cases.
in medium degree.	1 cases.
in severe degree.	3 cases.
~~in severe degree.~~	~~cases.~~
Congestion with some leucocytes, as capillar contents.	1 cases.
Congestion with some bacterial masses, as cap-contents.	1 cases.
Congestion, accompanied with perivascular hemorrhages.	3 cases.

2) After that, occured some signs of so-called serous inflammatiom.

S-I, With considerable subendothelial edematous swelling. 1 cases.

S-I, accompanied with some dissociation of cellular arrangements. 2 cases.

S-I, accompanied with some degenerative changes of capillar endothlial cells (swelling, clouding and desquamation). 1 cases.

We classified these changes according to the concept "serous inflammation", which we prefered.

Pituitaritis serosa	I degree.	4 cases.
	II degree.	1 cases.
	III degree.	1 cases.

3) Then, it shows some degenerative changes of parenchymatous cells (esp. basophilic cells), esp. at perivascular portions.

Cloudy swelling in slight degree. 2 cases.

[redacted] 347

[redacted]

CONFIDENTIAL

Cloudy swelling in considerable degree. 3 cases.

Cloudy swelling with vacuolar degenerations. 1 cases.

B.) Posterior lobe.

Sometimes, with considerable congestion and following changes.

Considerable congestion. 1 cases.

Considerable with slight perivascular hemorrhages. 1 cases.

Considerable with slight hyperplasia of neuroglia cells. 0 cases.

Accordingly, the significant main pathological changes are slight Pituitaritis serosa (congestion, serous exudation and some parenchymatous degenerations).

CONFIDENTIAL 348

([redacted]

[redacted]

PITUITARY BODY

			225	318	401	404	405	409	410	411
Capsule		Congestion	+	+	−	−	−	∸	ǀ	∸
		Edema	+	++	+	++	−	+	ǀ	+
		Hemorrhage	++	++	∸	−	−	−	ǀ	−
		Infiltration of Round Cells	−	∸	−	∸	−	∸	ǀ	∸
Adenohypophysis		Congestion	+++	+++	+	∸	+	∸	+	++
		Edema	++	∸	÷	+	++	++	+	+++
		Hemorrhage	−	−	∸	−	−	∸	−	++
		Infiltration of Round Cells	−	∸	−	−	−	−	−	−
	Chromophobe C.	Parenchymatous Degeneration	∸	−	∸	∸	−	−	∸	∸
		Atrophia	−	−	∸	∸	−	−	∸	∸
		Pyknosis	−	−	−	−	−	−	−	−
		Karyorrhexis	−	−	−	−	−	−	−	−
		Karyolysis	∸	−	−	−	−	−	−	−
	Eosinophile C.	Parenchymatous Degeneration	+	+	+	+	∸	+	+	+
		Atrophia	−	−	∸	∸	−	−	∸	∸
		Pyknosis	∸	∸	∸	∸	∸	∸	∸	∸
		Karyorrhexis	∸	−	∸	−	−	−	∸	∸
		Karyolysis	∸	∸	∸	∸	∸	∸	∸	∸
	Basophile C.	Parenchymatous Degeneration	+	∸	+	+	+	+	÷	+
		Atrophia	−	−	∸	∸	−	−	∸	∸
		Pyknosis	∸	−	∸	−	−	−	∸	∸
		Karyorrhexis	−	−	−	−	−	−	−	−
		Karyolysis	∸	∸	∸	∸	∸	∸	∸	∸
		Necrosis	−	+	+	−	−	−	−	−
Neurohypophysis		Congestion	+	ǀ	ǀ	−	∸	+	∸	∸
		Edema	+	ǀ	ǀ	+	+	+	+	+
		Hemorrhage	+	ǀ	ǀ	−	∸	+	−	+
		Infiltration of Round Cells	−	+	+	−	−	−	−	−
Pars Intermedia		Hemorrhage	−	−	−	−	−	−	−	−
		Infiltration of Round Cells	−	−	−	−	+	−	−	−
		Color of Colloid	R.	R.	R.	V.	V.	R.	R.	R.
		Vacuole in Colloid	+	+	+	+	+	+	+	+
		Desquamation of Cyst wall cells	+	+	−	+	−	+	+	−

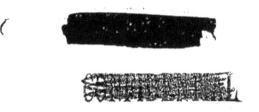

V.······ violet
R.······ red

[redacted] 349

[redacted]

CONFIDENTIAL

Hemorrhages in adeno-pituitary body.

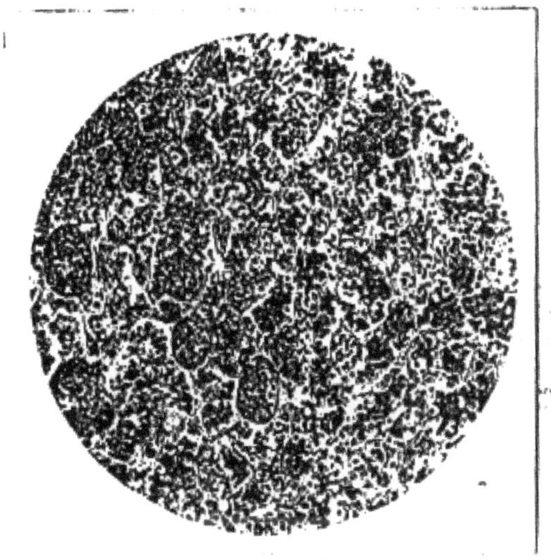

M-225 x130

Hemorrhages in pituitary body (anterior lobe)

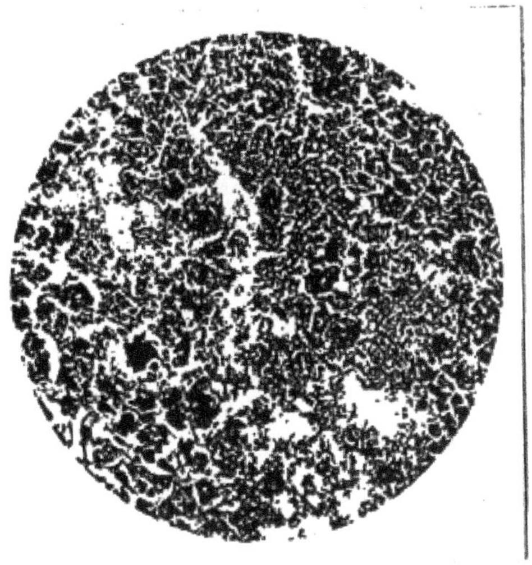

M-411 x130

CONFIDENTIAL 350

[redacted]

CONFIDENTIAL

Bacterial masses in capillaries and perivascular parenchymatous degeneration.

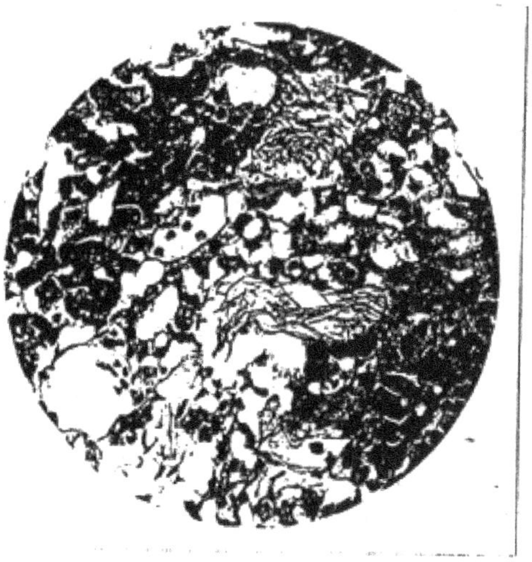

M-401 x320

Leucocytes in capillaries and perivascular edema, in anterior lobe.

CONFIDENTIAL

M-404 x320

351

[redacted]

[redacted]

Edematous swolling of subepithelial layers of acinus.
Degeneration of basophilic cells

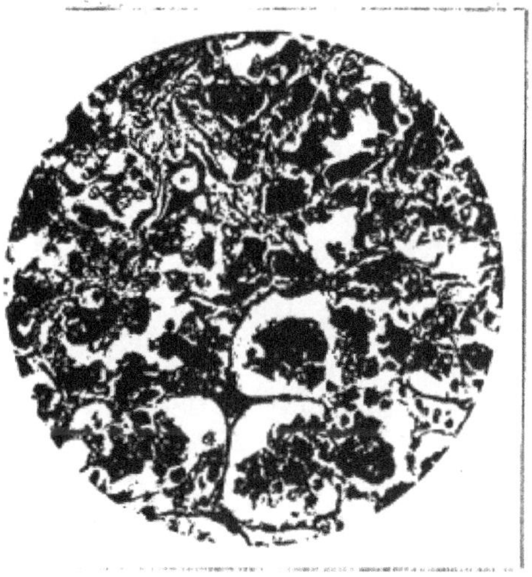

M. 411　　x320

[redacted] 352

[redacted]

[redacted]

Skin

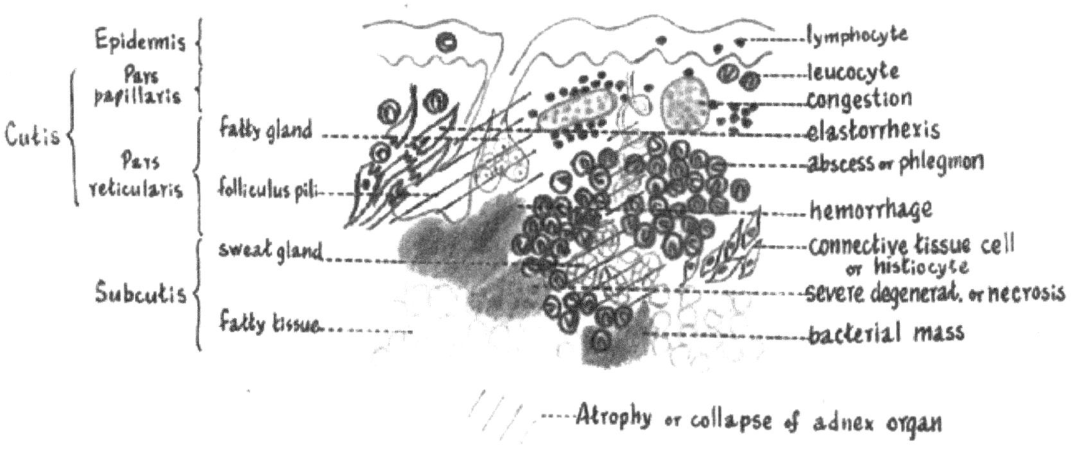

[redacted]L 353

[redacted]

SKIN

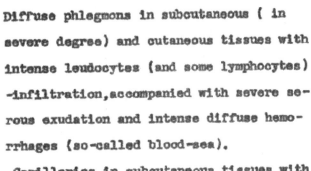

A) Microscopical Investigation.

54. Phlegmona diffusa.

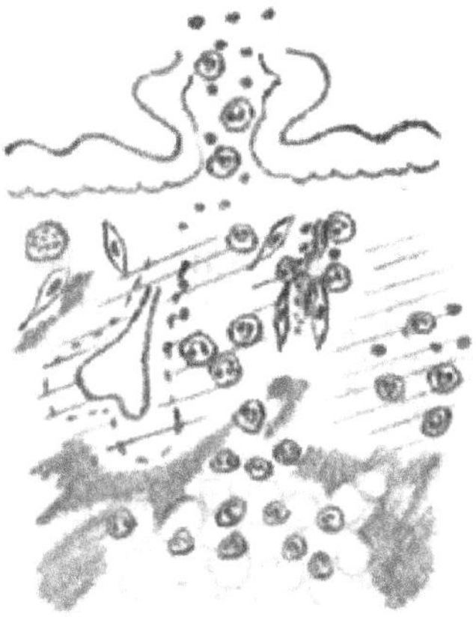

Diffuse phlegmons in subcutaneous (in severe degree) and cutaneous tissues with intense leudocytes (and some lymphocytes) -infiltration,accompanied with severe serous exudation and intense diffuse hemorrhages (so-called blood-sea).

Capillaries in subcutaneous tissues with plentiful leucocytes,necrotic ruin of capillary-walls,intense perivascular edema and hemorrhages,intense leucocytes-emigration(hematogenous-metastatic characters), invading phlegmoneously all over the neighbouring tissues.

Accompanied with atrophic epidermis and atrophy or collapse of adnex-organs.

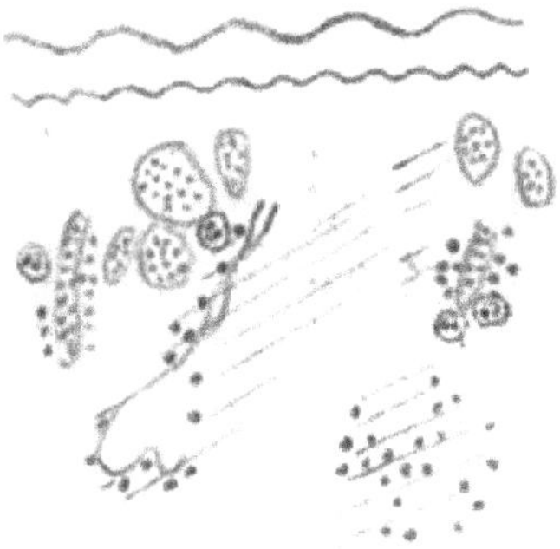

388.

Remarkable congestion of capillaries at Str.subpapillare with some anthrax-bacillus

Accompanied with somewhat necrotic ruins of capillary-walls,perivascular edema in a high degree and some localised hemorrhages.

Some pericapillar lymphocytes (and leucocytes)accumulation and slight collapse of adnex-organs.

CONFIDENTIAL 354

[redacted]

CONFIDENTIAL

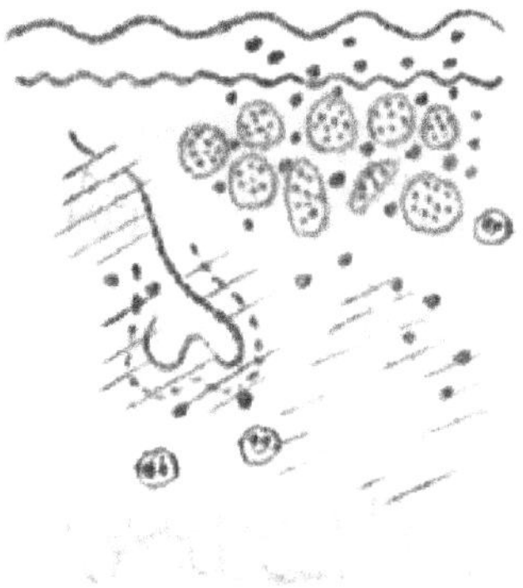

409.

Intense congestion of capillaries and localised hemorrhages at Str.subpapillare and Str.papillare,accompanied with some-what diffuse perivascular cellular infilt-ration.(leucocytes,some of them being eosinophilic,lymphocytes and some histio-cytes).Slight fibrosis of adnex-organs.

In epidermis,slight swelling and atrophia of pickle cells and some parakeratosis above the cutis.

B) S U M M A R Y

Considerable congestion (especially at Str.subpapillare).

Emigration of leucocytes and lymphocytes.

Atrophy of adnex-organs.

In No:54 is diffuded phlegmon with severe hemorrhages and fragmentation of degenerated epidermis.Hematogenous-metastatic charqcter is considered from point of necrotic ruins of vessels and perivascular serous and cellul ar infiltration.

CONFIDENTIAL

356

[redacted]

[redacted]

M-358 Hypermia at Str. papillare.

×69

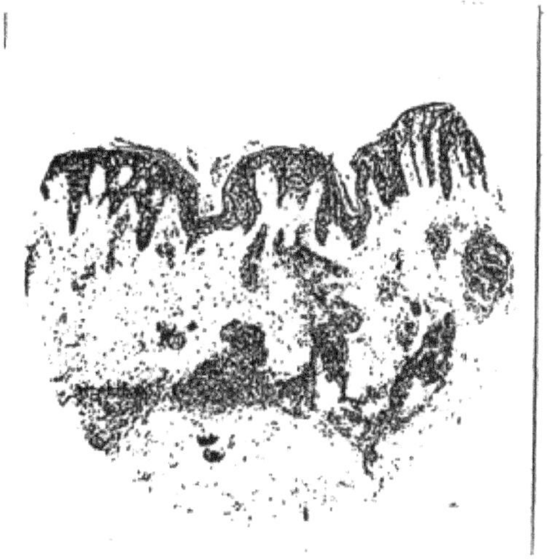

M-56 Hemorrhages and some leucocytes dissemination in subcutaneous tissues.

×80.

[redacted] 356

[redacted]

CONFIDENTIAL

Lymphnode

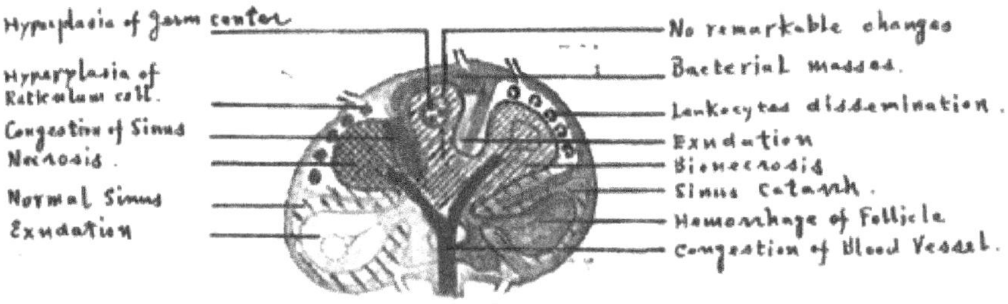

CONFIDENTIAL 357

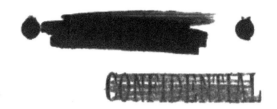

[redacted]

LYMPR-NODULUS.

(A) Microscop. Investigation.

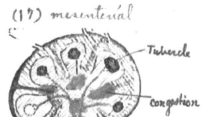

(17) mesenterial

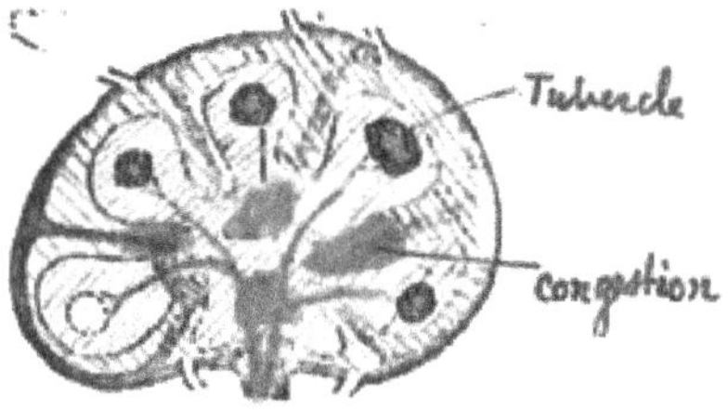

I7. Mesenterial:

Lymphadenitis tuberculosa obsoleta with considerable congestion in medullary sinus, edematous swelling of capillary walls and slight reduction of follicular lymphocytes.

27. Mesenterial:

Extraordinary intense pericapsular hemorrhagic and leucocytic changes and also extremly severe hemorrhagic and necrotic changes in follicular tissues with intense diffuse leucocytees - emigration, various decayed cellular fragments and diffuse intense hemorrhages in follicular tissues.

(27) mesenterial

severe hemorrhagic necrotic change
numerous leucocytes

27. Mesenterial:

dime-large. Severest pericapsular hemorrhages and leucocytes - emigration and remarkable hemorrhagic exudative changes in peripheral sinuses. Intense diffuse hemorrhages, necrotic swelling of reticular tissues with remarkable leucocytes- emigration in medullary sinusos and remarkable

(27) mesenterial

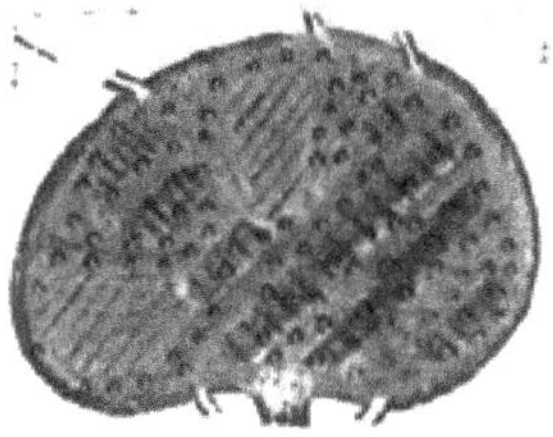

[redacted] 368

[redacted]

(27) peribronchial [redacted]

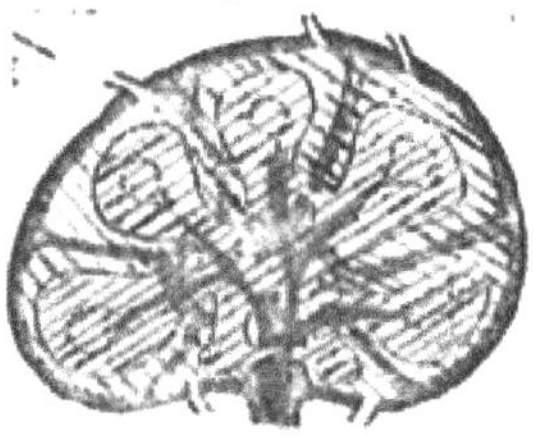

hemorr ghic-exudative processes in some germinative centres.

In yet remained other follicular tissues with remarkable reduction of follicular lymphocytes, and considerable leucocytes-emigrations.

Lymphadenitis haemorrhagico-necroticans in severe degree.

(225) mesenterial

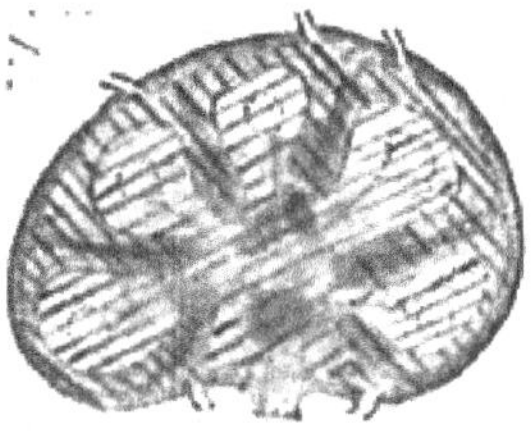

27. Peribronchial:

Anthracosis and considerable congestion (a little leucocytes as capillary contents) and very slight reduction of follicular lymphocytes.

225. Mesenterial:

Slight pericapsular hemorrhages with slight leucocytes- accumulations, and slight catarrh of peripheral sinuses.

Slight swelling of pulpe-meshes and slight congestion and slight hyperplasia of reticulum-cells in medullary sinuses.

(325) mesenterial

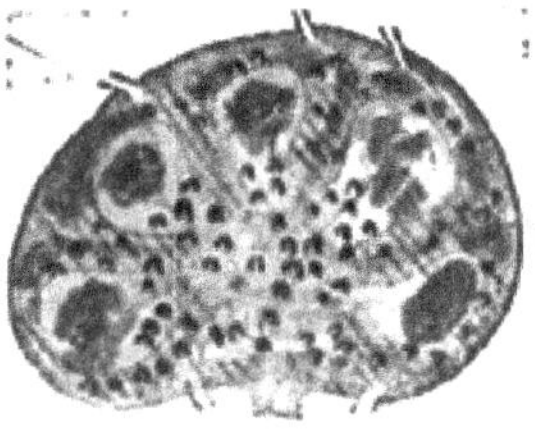

325. Mesenterial:

Sugar-corn large.

Slight pericapsular congestion and hemorrhages and remarkable catarrh of

[redacted] 359

[redacted]

(318) [redacted]

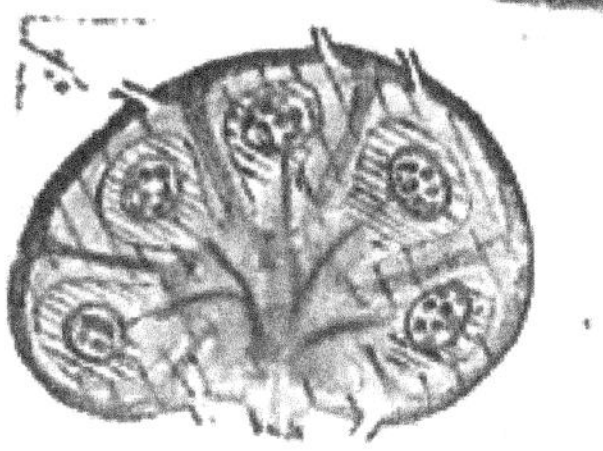

peripheral sinuses.
In medullary sinus; severe congestion, necrotic ruins of blood-vessel-walls and multiple hemorrhages, accompanied with necrotic swelling of medullary tissues.
In pulps-meshes: extremly severe hemorrhages, edematous swelling of reticulum-fibres and remarkable diminution of follicular lymphocytes.
Lymphadenitis haemorrhagico-necroticans gravis.

(318) peribronchial

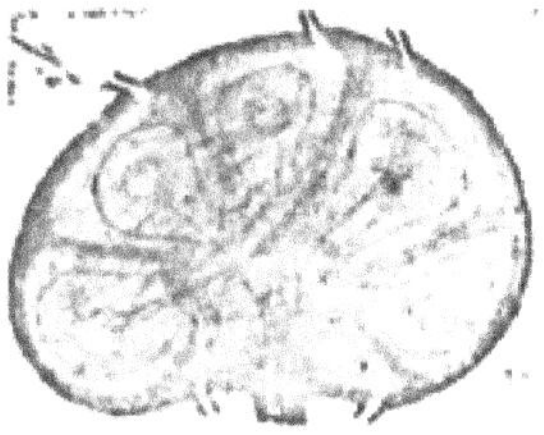

318. Peribronchial:
Organ-corn large. Lymphadenitis caseosa tuberculosa and Anthracosis.
Slight catarrh of peripheral sinus and considerable hyperplasia of germinative centers with some increased histiocytes, accompanied with slight congestion, slight perivascular edema and slight hyperplasia of reticulum-cells (some of them in erythrophagocytosis) in medullary tissues.
320. Peribronchial:
Slight catarrh of peripheral sinuses (slight hyperplasia of histiocytes)

[redacted] 360

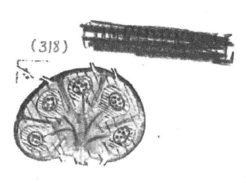

[redacted]

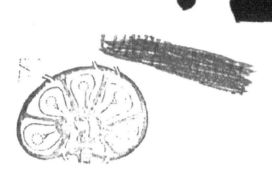

peripheral sinuses (considerable hyperplasia and cloudy swelling of histiocytes, remarkable swelling of reticulum-fibres, plenty of leucocytes and some bacterial masses in peripheral sinuses).

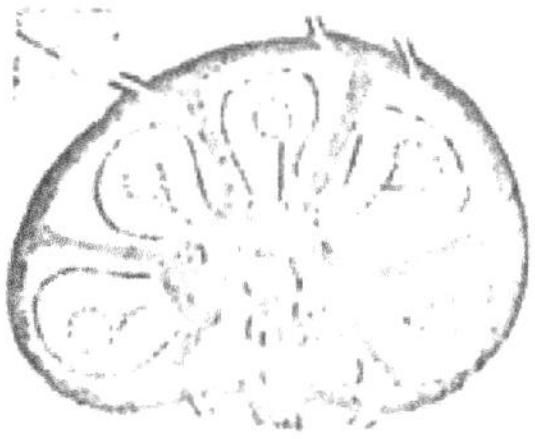

In follicular tissues, at some places miliary bionecrotic changes with some decayed masses of histiocytic and some bacterial accumulation and at other pulpa-meshes, considerable swelling with some leucocytes and slight reduction of follicular lymphocytes.
Germinative centres in considerable hyperplasia with some increased histiocytic cells and some of them fall into cellular fragments and some of them, into submilliary caseous masses.
Bacterial accumulation in surrounding tissues of germinative centers.
Initial stage of acute lymphadenitis, due to [illegible]-infection.

(318) mesenterial

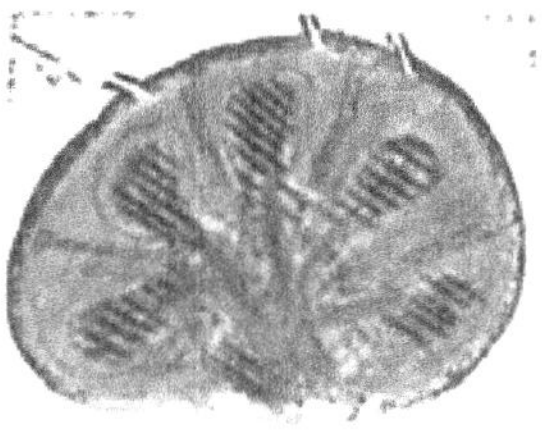

318. Mesenterial:
Severe pericapsular congestion and severe diffuse haemorrhages and severe bleeding with some leucocytes in

[redacted] 361

[redacted]

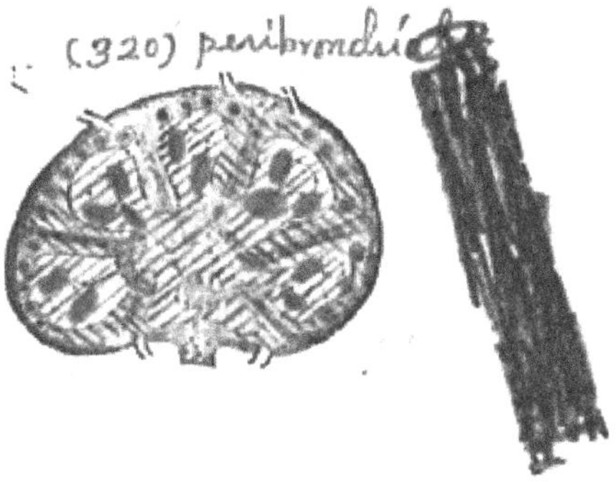

and considerable congestion in follicular tissues, (accompanied with slight
hyperplasia of reticulum-cells in medullary tissues and slight swelling of
pulpa-meshes with considerable reduction of lymphocytes in pulpa-meshes.
Lymphadenitis catarrhalis and haemorrhagica levis.

325. Mesenterial:

Sugar-corn large. Slight catarrh of
peripheral sinuses and considerable
hyperplasia of reticulum-cells in
pulpa-meshes and medullary tissues.
Considerable swelling of pulpa-meshes
and with some leucocytes-emigrations
and considerable diminution of follicular lymphocytes.

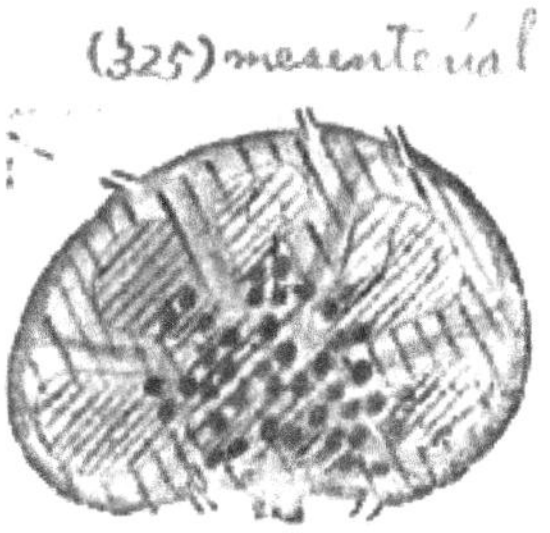

380. Mesenterial:

large.

almost normal, very slight catarrh of
peripheral sinuses, slight hyperplasia of reticulum-cells in medullary
tissues with slight congestion. No
considerable reduction of follicular
lymphocytes.

382. Mesenterial:

[redacted] 362

[redacted]

(380) mesenterial

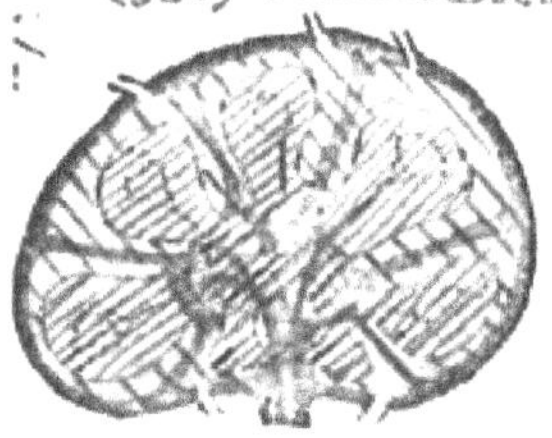

Sugar-corn large[redacted]
Slight pericapsular leucocytes- emigrations and slight hemorrhages and considerable hemorrhagic necrotic changes in peripheral sinuses (considerable hemorrhages, more or less remarkable leucocytes- and bacterial accumulations). Considerable congestion, (plenty bacterial masses in capillaries), necrotic ruins of vessel-walls, severe necrotic swelling and considerable hemorrhages in medullary tissues and multiple submiliary hemorrhagic-necrotic portions in follicular tissues, accompanied with bacterial accumulations, severe edematous swelling and remarkable diminution of follicular lymphocytes in pulpa-meshes.

(388) mesenterial

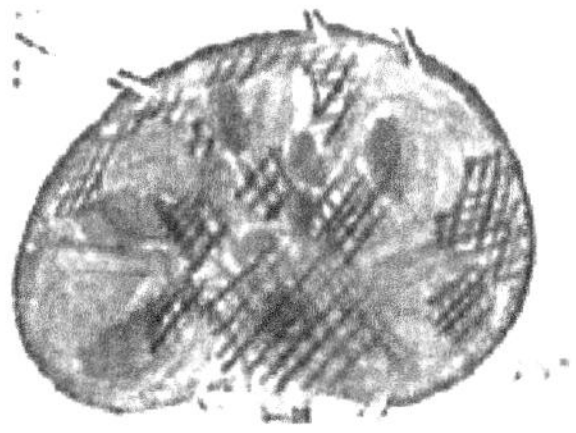

Lymphadenitis haemorrhagico-necroticans.

(388) Peribronchial.

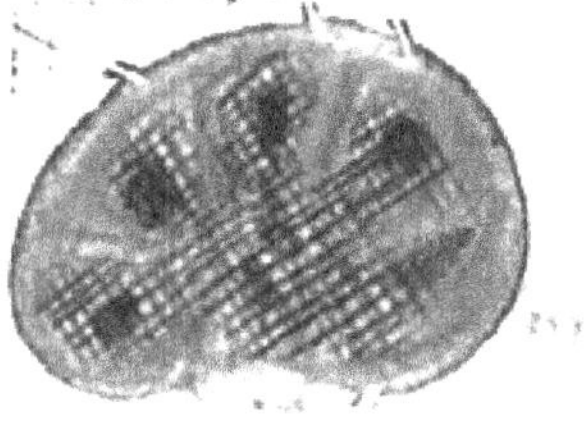

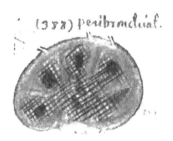

388. Peribronchial:
Sugar-corn large.
The same hemorrhagic-necrotic changes.
388. Submaxillaris:
The same, hemorrhagic-necrotic changes.
388. Axillaris. Some lymphnodus in large.
Extraordinary intens pericapsular hemorr-[redacted]tous swelling and leucocytes-

[redacted] 363

[redacted]

[redacted] severe hemorrhagic-necrotic changes in peripheral sinuses (plenty leucocytes and some bacterial accumulations).

(388) submaxillar

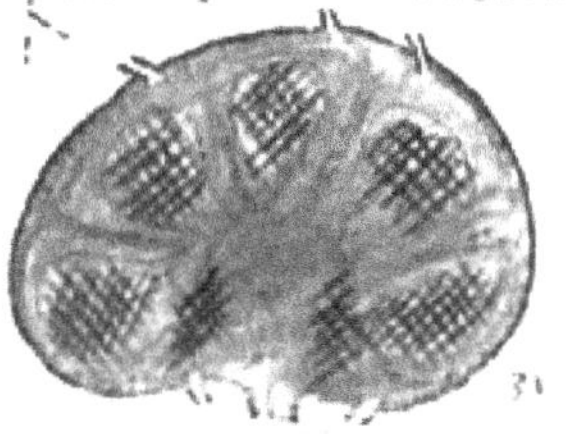

Severe congestion, necrotic ruins of capillary walls, severe perivascular edema and diffuse severe hemorrhages with some leucocytes-emigrations in follicular tissues and multiple hemorrhagic necrotic changes in pulpe-meshes, accompanied with severe swelling, severe leucocytes- emigrations, some bacterial accumulations and severe diminutionof follicular lymphocytes.

(388) Axillar

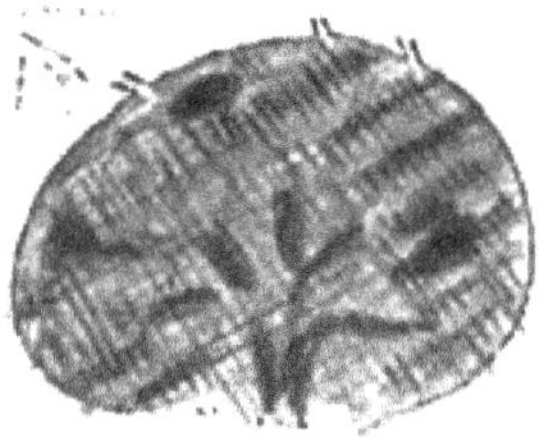

Lymphadenitis haemorrhagico-necroticans.

389. Mesenterial:

Sugar-corn large.

Slight catarrh of peripheral sinuses and slight hyperplasia of reticulum-cells in medullary tissues with considerable congestion.

Slight perivascular edema and slight hemorrhages in medullary tissues and slight swelling of pulpe-meshes (with very slight leucocytes-emigrations).

393. Peribronchial:

[redacted] catarrh in peripheral sinuses

[redacted], 364

[redacted]

(389) mesenterial

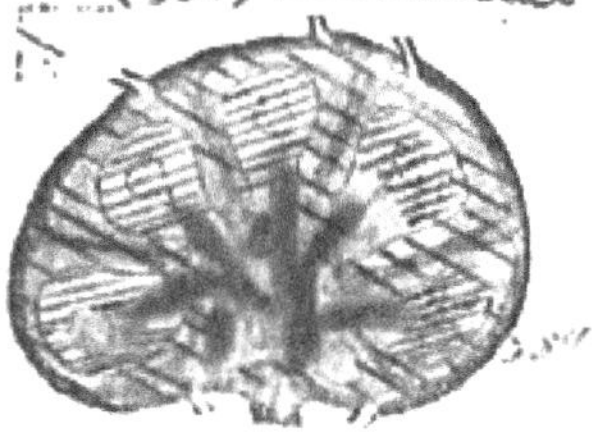

[redacted]kable congestion in medullary tissues, accompanied with slight edematous swelling and slight localised hemorrhages in medullary tissues and considerable swelling with some leucocytes in pulpa-meshes with considerable diminution of follicular lymphocytes.

(393) peribronchial

395. Mesenterial:

Slight catarrh of peripheral & nuses and slight congestion and slight swelling in medullary tissues.

393. Mesenterial:

Lymphadenitis tuberculosa.

Slight cateleuse of peripheral sinuses and multiple caseous parts in follicular tissues with considerable increased histiocytes-cells as perifocal changes (with some giant cells).

No congestion in follicular tissues and slight diminution of follicular lymphocytes.

(395) mesenterial

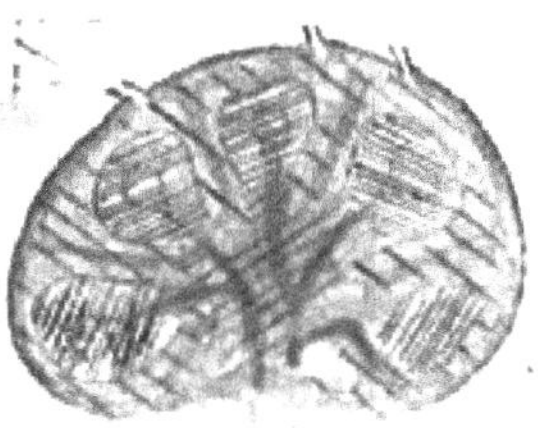

393. Radical mesenterial lymphnodus:

Remarkable pericapsular inflammatory changes (remarkable congestion, considerable hemorrhages with some bacterial accumulations) and severe hemorrhagic-[redacted] changes in peripheral sinuses

365

[redacted]

(393) mesenterial

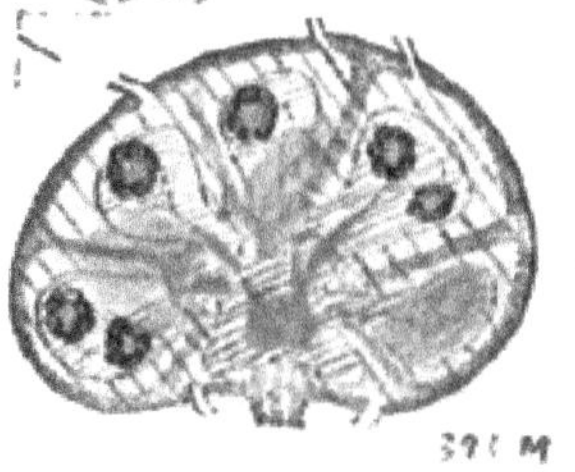

[redacted]

(severe hemorrhages, necrotic swelling of reticulum-fibres and some bacterial masses).

Severe congestion (with some bacterial masses as capillary contents), necrotic ruins of capillary walls, severe necrotic swelling and severe hemorrhagic-exudative changes of medullary tissues.

No significant hyperplasia of reticulum-cells.

(393) Radical mesenterial

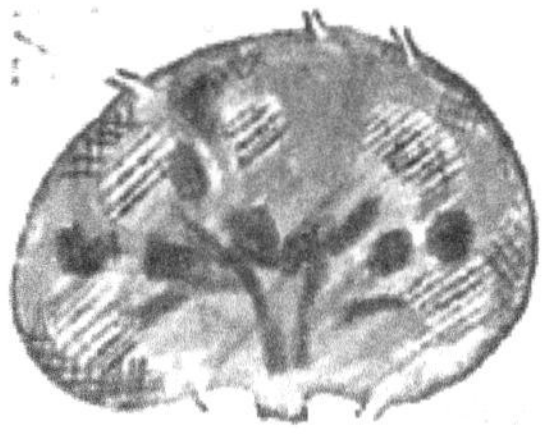

Multiple hemorrhages in pulpa-meshes, accompanied with severe swelling and some bacterial accumulations in pulpa-meshes and remarkable diminutions of follicular lymphocytes.

Lymphadenitis haemorrhagico-necroticans gravis.

395. Peribronchial:

Total hemorrhagic ruins of follicular tissues and severe diffuse pericapsular hemorrhages.

396. Mesenterial:

almost normal, slight hyperplasia of medullary reticulum-cells. No significant congestion.

397. Mesenterial:

[redacted] 366

[redacted]

[redacted]

(395) peribronchial

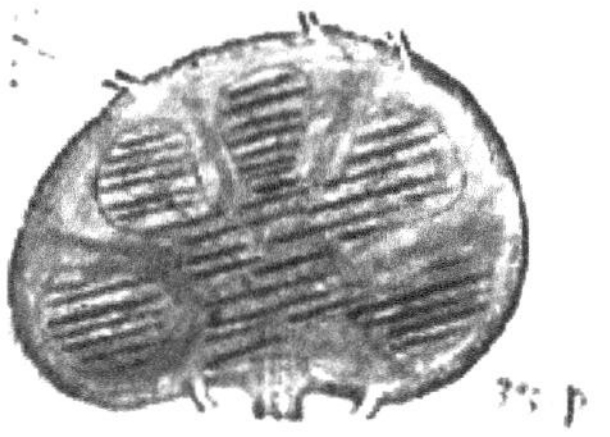

Sugar-corn large.

Slight pericapsular inflammatory changes (slight congestion, slight leucocytes-emigrations and slight edematous swelling) and remarkable hemorrhagic exudative changes in peripheral sinuses (remarkable hemorrhages, remarkable exudation and some decayed cellular masses).

(396) mesenterial

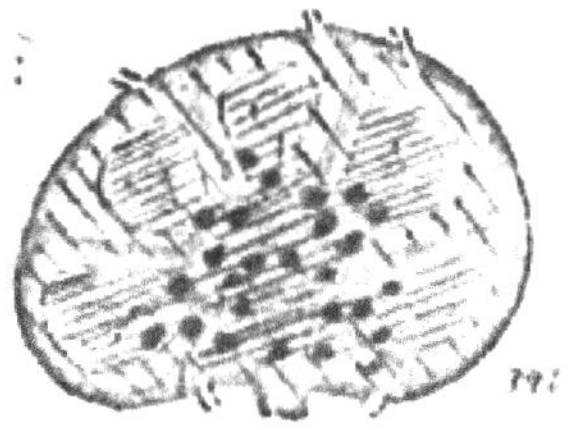

Considerable congestion, necrotic ruins of capillary walls, severe necrotic swelling and severe hemorrhagic-exudative changes in medullary tissues and multiple hemorrhages in pulpa-meshes, accompanied with severe swelling and severe congestion in pulpa-meshes with remarkable diminution of follicular lymphocytes.

397. Peribronchial:

large.

Slight catarrh in peripheral sinuses and remarkable congestion, slight swelling and slight hyperplasia of medullary tissues.

No. significant diminution of follicular lymphocytes.

[illegible]

Slight catarrh in peripheral sinus

[redacted] 367

[redacted]

(397) mesenterial [redacted]

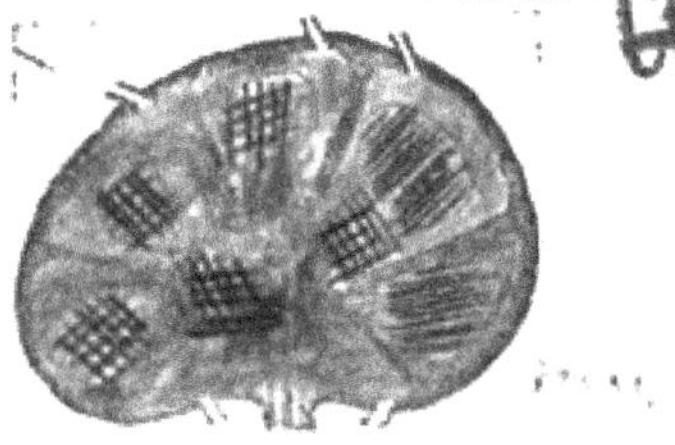

and slight hyperplasia of medullary reticulum-cells. Remarkable congestion, necrotic ruins of capillary walls and severe necrotic swelling of medullary tissues, plenty of leucocytes-emigrations and at some places remarkable hemorrhages in follicular tissues, accompanied with severe swelling and considerable diminution of lymphocytes in pulpa-meshes. Lymphadenitis haemorrhagica.

397. Para-pancreal:

(397) peribronchial

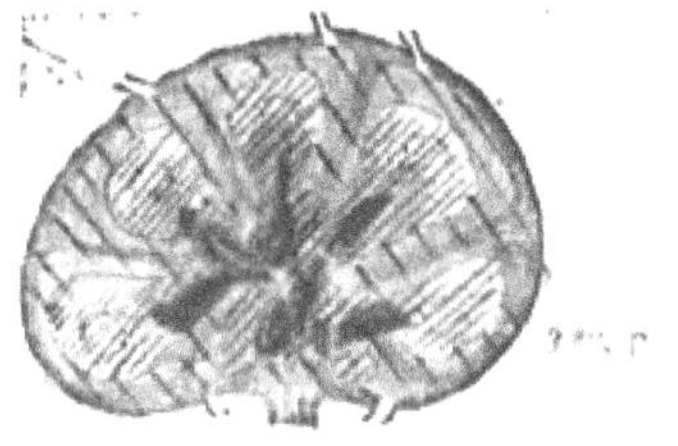

Extremely severe hemorrhagic exudative changes in pericapsular tissues and severest haemorrhagic exudative changes in follicular tissues (severest congestion, necrotic ruins of capillary walls, necrotic swelling, plenty of leucocytes-emigrations, considerable hemorrhages and some bacterial accumulations in medullary tissues and peripheral sinuses). Severest swelling of yet remained pulpa-meshes and remarkable diminution or diminish of follicular lymphocytes.

(397) mesenterial

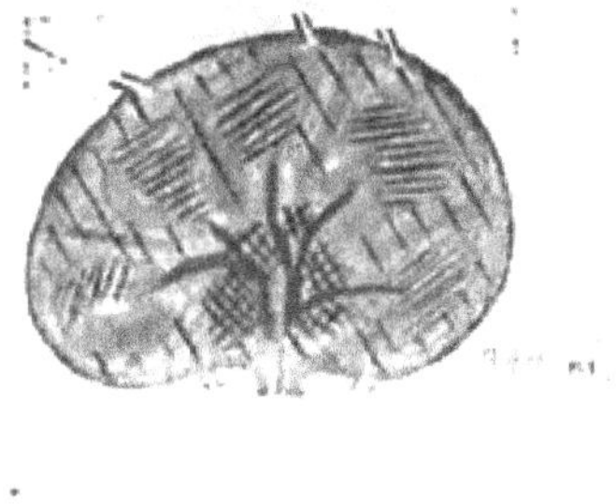

399. Mesenterial:

Almost normal, slight catarrh of peripheral sinuses and slight hyperplasia of

[redacted] 368

[redacted]

CONFIDENTIAL

(397) para-pancreal

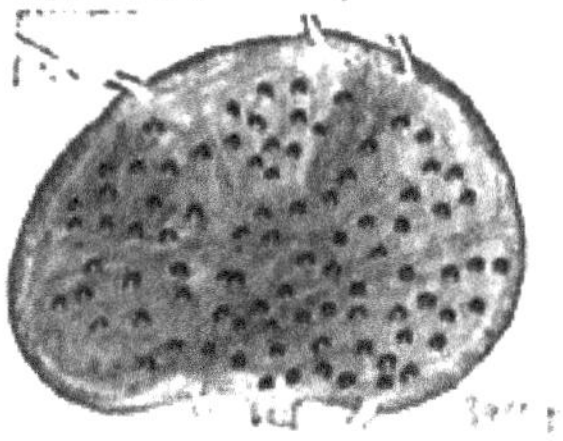

medullary reticulum-cells.

At some places in follicles, slight congestion and slight hemorrhages.

No remarkable changes else.

399. Axillar:

Almost normal.

399. Peribronchial:

Some lymphnodulus in Sugar-corn large.

Extremly severest homorrhagic exudative changes in pericapsular and follicular tissues.

(399) mesenterial

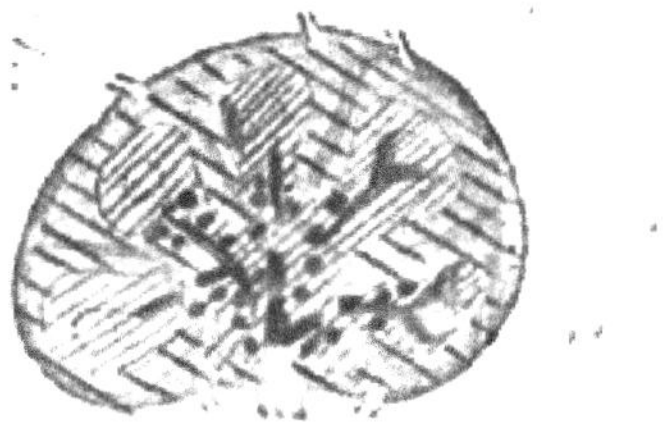

Extremly severest congestion, necrotic ruins of capillary walls, severe necrotic swelling of medullary tissues with remarkable leucocytes- emigrations and severe diffues hemorrhages.

Severest swelling, necrotic swelling of reticulum-fibres (at some places, some submillary necrotic parts) and remarkable diminution of lymphocytes in pulpa-meshes.

Lymphadentis haemorrhagico-necroticans.

400. Peribronchial:

Some lymphnodulr in Sugar-corn large.

Considerable congestion, edematous swelling and some leucocytes-emigration

CONFIDENTIAL 369

[redacted]

(377) axillar [redacted]

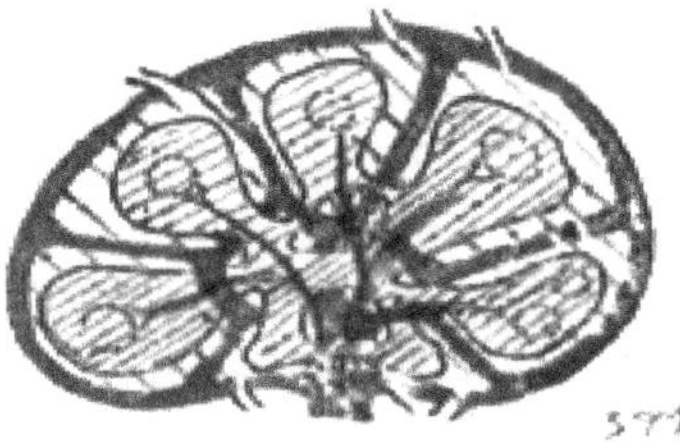

377

(377) peribronchial

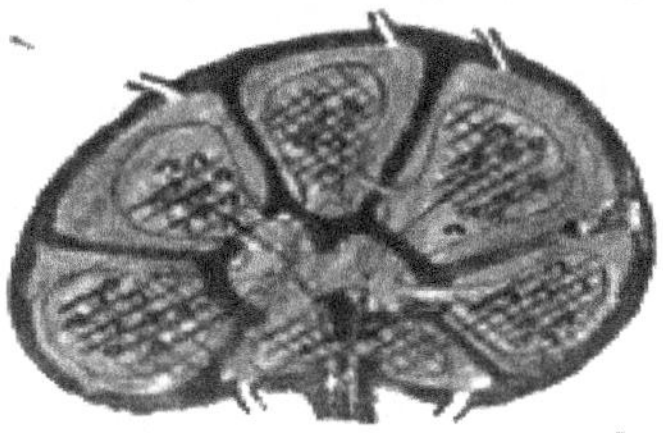

377

[redacted] 370

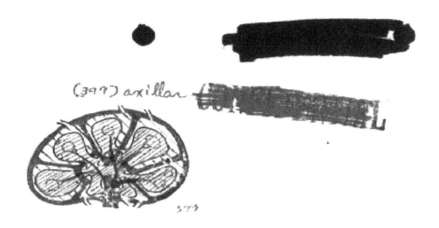

[redacted]

[400] peribronchial

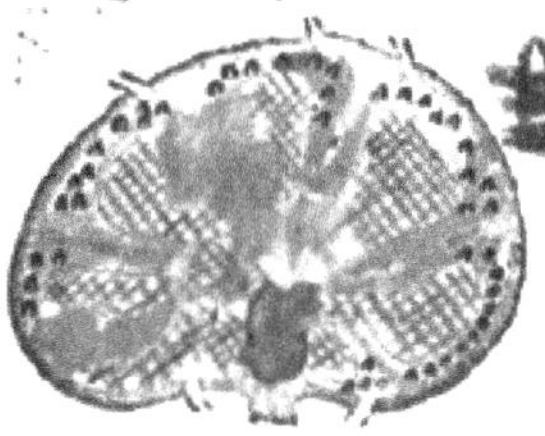

[redacted]ricapsular tissues and remarkable congestion of efferent vessels. Remarkable hemorrhagic- exudative changes in peripheral sinuses (remarkable congestion, severe exudation, plenty of leucocytes and necrtotic ruins of reticulum-fibres or reticulum-cells) and also extremly severe hemorrhagic-necrtotic changes in medullary tissues and pulpa-meshes: remarkable congestion (with some leucocytes as capillary contents), necrotic ruins of capillry walls, severe edematous and hemorrahgic processes in medullary tissues and considerable swelling of pulpa-meshes with remarkable diminution of follicular lymphocytes.

[400] mesenterial

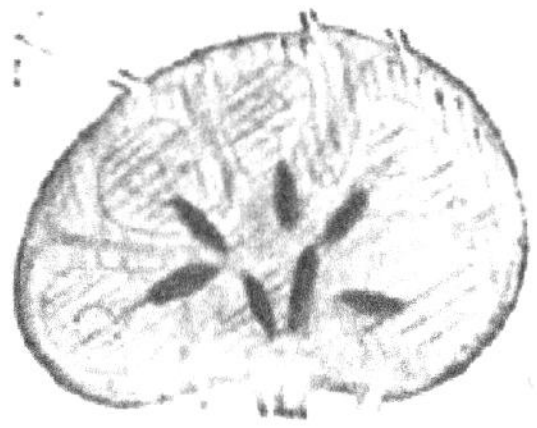

400. Mesenterial:

Very slight pericapsular inflammatory changes and slight catarrh in peripheral sinuses. Considerable congestion and edematous swelling of medullary tissues (with some leucocytes-emigrations) and considerable congestion (at some places, bacterial accumulations) and swelling of pulpa-meshes with considerable diminution of follicular lymphocytes.

[redacted] 371

[redacted]

CONFIDENTIAL

(401) peribronchial

(401) mesenterial

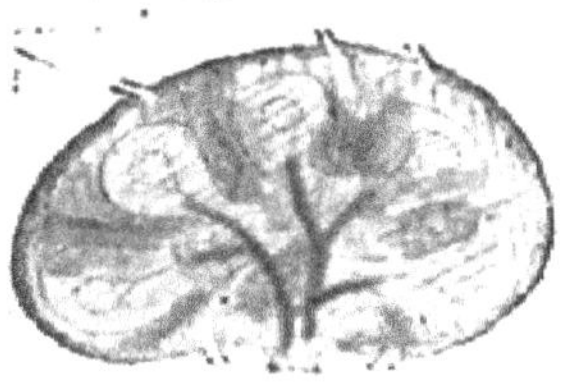

40I. Peribronchial:

Extremly severest hemorrhagic-exudative changes of pericapsular tissues: severe diffuse hemorrhages, some leucocyte -emigrations and necrotic swelling of pericapsular tissues, and also extremly severest hemorrhagic-exudative changes of follicular tissues: severe congestion, severe necrotic swelling of medullary tissues and pulpa-meshes, accompanied with severe diminution or diminish of follicular lymphocytes.

Lymphadenitis hemorrhagico-necroticans.

40I. Mesenterial:

Slight pericapsular inflammatory changes: slight congestion and some leucocytes-emigrations and remarkable hemorrhagic exudative changes of follicular tissues: remarkable congestion, necrotic swelling of capillary walls and more or less considerable diffuse hemorrhages in medullary tissues, Slight swelling of pulpa-mesh with some slightly increased, cloudy swollen histiocytes and slight congestion.

Lymphadenitis haemorrhagica.

40I. Mesenterial:

[redacted] 372

[redacted]

(401) mesenterial

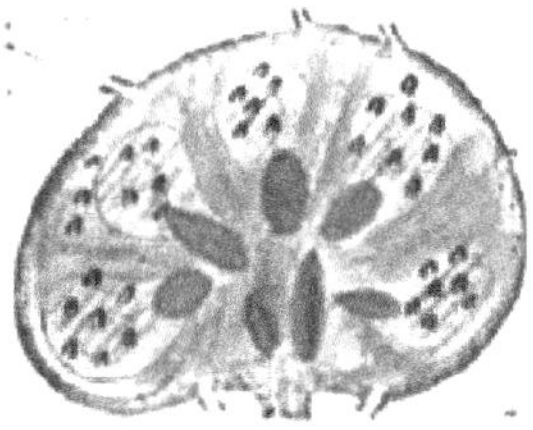

[redacted]

Considerable hemorrhagic-exudative changes in pericapsular tissues and peripheral sinus: considerable congestion, hemorrhages, exudation and some leucocytes-emigrations, and intense hemorrhagic-exudative changes in follicular tissues: severe congestion, necrotic swelling of capillary walls and medullary tissues, diffuse intense haemorrhages and plenty leucocytes-emigrations.

(403) peribronchial

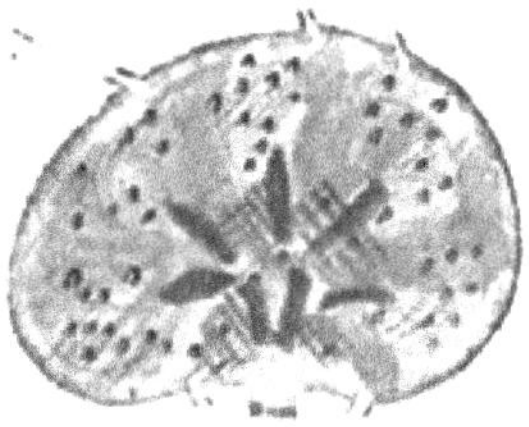

Considerable swelling of pulpa-meshes, with plenty of leucocytes and necrotic swelling of reticulum-fibres in pulpa-meshes, accompanied with remarkable reduction of follicular lymphocytes.

403. Peribronchial:

Remarkable congestion, intense diffuse hemorrhages and plenty of leucocyte-emigrations in pericapsular tissues and peripheral sinues.

Remarkable hemorrhagic-exudative changes in follicular tissues:

Remarkable congestion, necrotic swelling of capillary walls, necrotic swelling of medullary tissues and plenty leucocytes-emigrations and diffuse multiple hemorr-

[redacted] 373

[redacted]

(403) mesenterial

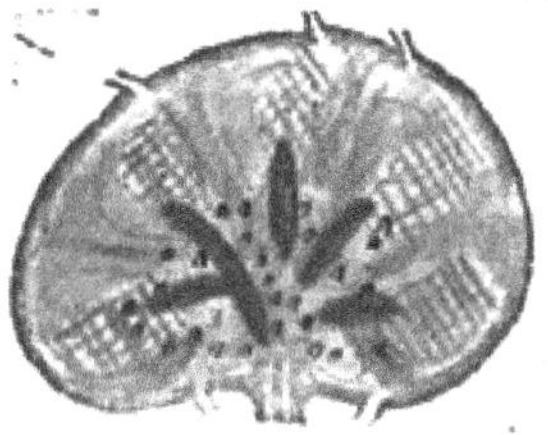

[redacted]hages (at some places, multiple submiliary bionecrotic parts).
Considerable congestion, edematous swelling and some leucocytes-emigration of pulpa-meshes with remarkable reduction of folliculer lymphocytes.

403. Mesenterial:

Extremly severe hemorrhagic exudative changes of pericapsuler tissues and peripheral sinuses and also the same extremly severest hemorrhagic necrotic changes of folliculer tissues: severest congestion and diffuse severe hemorrhages, accompanied with necrotic swelling of medullary tissues and remarkable edematous swelling of pulpa-meshes (with plenty leucocytes-emigration and severe diminution of follicular lymphocytes).

(404) peribronchial

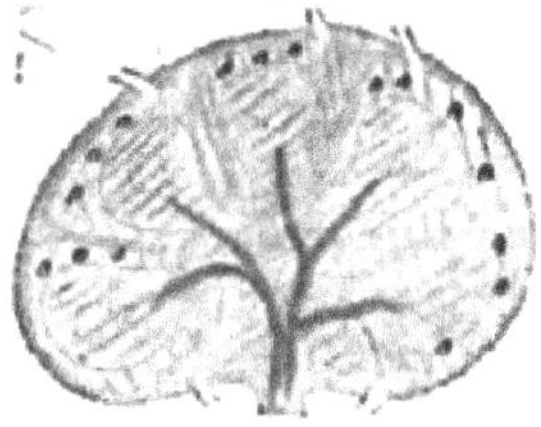

405. Peribronchial:

Slight pericapsular hemorrhagic changes: slight congestion, slight bleeding and some leucocytes-emigration and the some hemorrhagic-exudative changes of peripheral sinuses: slight exudation, some leucocyte-emigration and slight hyperplasia of histiocytes.

[redacted] 374

[redacted]

(405) peribronchial

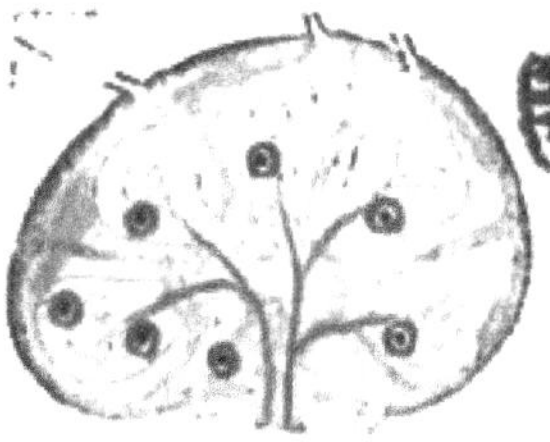

[redacted] Very slight congestion, a few leucocyte-emigrations and slight hyperplasia of swollen histiocytes in medullary tissues, and no considerable reduction of pulpa-meshes.

405. Mesenterial:

Very slight pericapsular inflammatory changes, slight catarrh of peripheral sinuses and slight congestion, slight swelling and slight hyperplasia of medullary tissues.

(405) mesenterial

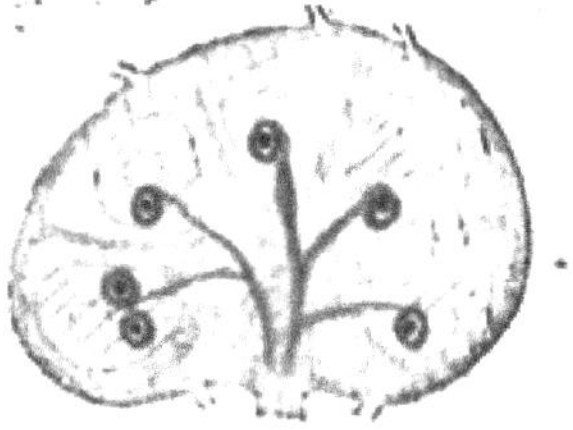

405. Radical mesenterial:

The same changes.

404. Peribronchial:

Extromly severe pericapsular edematous and exudative changes with slight congestion, slight bleeding and some leucocyte-emigrations and slight catarrh of peripheral sinuses (slight exudation, some leucocytes and slight hyperplasia of swollen histiocytes).

(405) Radical-mesenterial

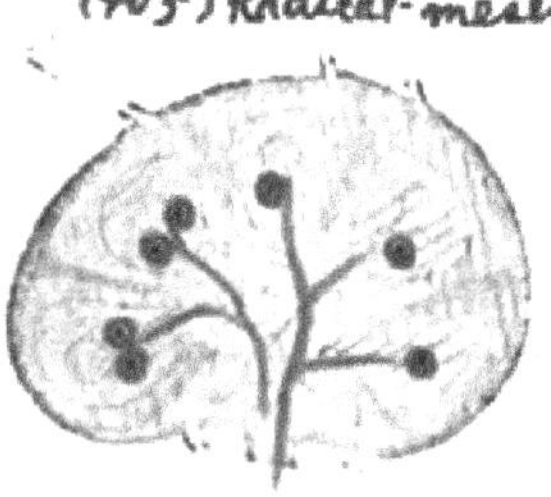

Very slight congestion with a few leucocyter and slight swelling of medullary tissues. Slight swelling and no other significant changes of pulpa-meshes.

407.

CONFIDENTIAL ...ble pericapsular hemorrhagic

375

[redacted]

(407)

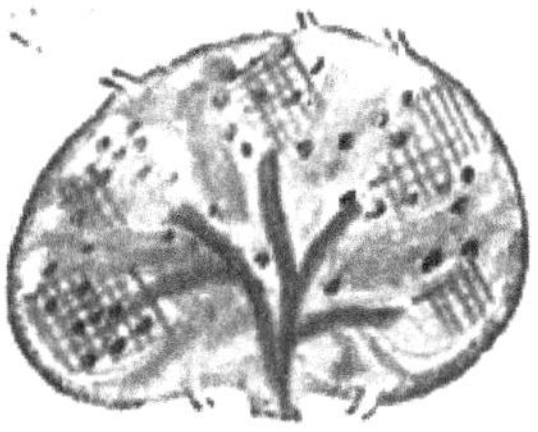

changes with some leucocytes and extremly severe hemorrhagic exudative changes in peripheral sinuses: intense exudation, extremly severe hemorrhages, plenty leucocytes and necrotic swelling or necrotic ruins of reticulum-fibres. In medullary tissues: extremly intense congestion, necrotic ruins of capillary walls, extremly severe necrotic swelling and remarkable diffuse hemorrhages and in pulpa-mesh: remarkable swelling of reticulum-fibres, diffuse intense hemorrhages and exudation, accompanied with remarkable diminution of follicular lymphocytes.

(407) Radical-mesenterial

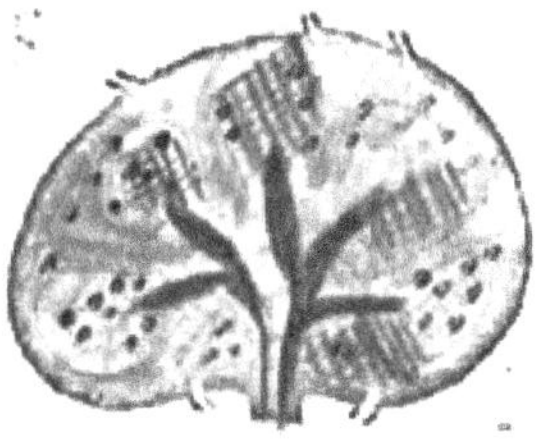

407. Radical mesenterial:
the same changes.

409 γ-heart-sack

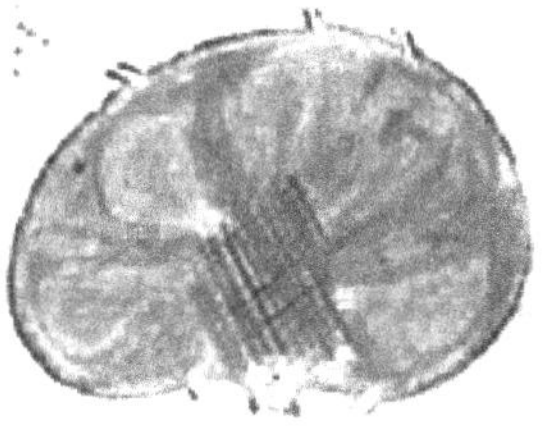

409. Peribronchial:
Extremly severest diffuse hemorrhages with some leucocytes in pericapsular tissues and also extremly intense hemorrhagic changes in follicular tissues, the most intense diffuse hemorrhages all over the follicular tissues with remarkable diminution of all follicular cellular elements: remarkable congestion,

CONFIDENTIAL. 376

[redacted]

(401) axillar [redacted]

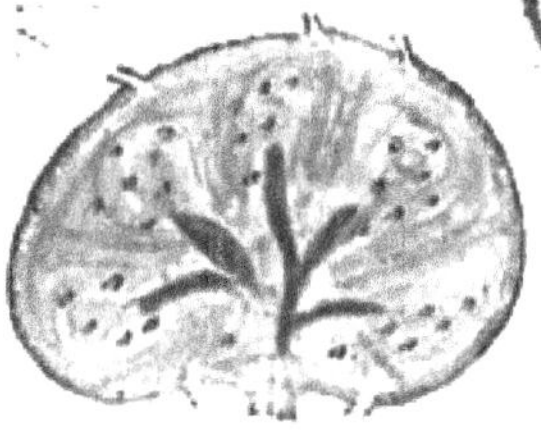

necrotic ruins of capillary walls, diffuse intense hemorrhages and exudation, necrotic swelling or diminish of medullary tissues, remarkable diminuation of pulpa-meshes with remarkable swelling, intense hemorrhage and remarkable reduction of follicular lymphocytes.

409. Axillar:

(4[illegible]) peribronchial

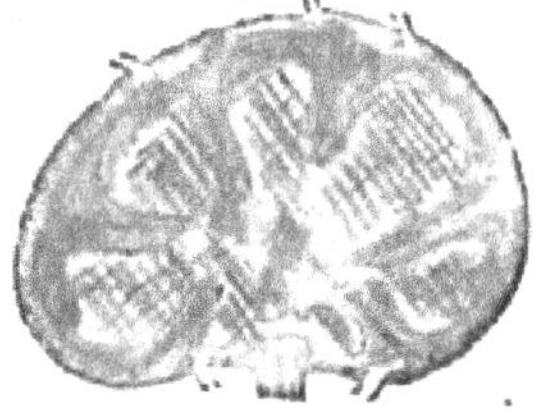

Considerable pericapsular hemorrhages with some leucocytes-emigrations and remarkable hemorrhages with some leucocy-tesemigrations and necrotic swelling of reticulum-fibres in peripheral sinuses. Remarkable congestion, intense edematous swelling and diffuse hemorrhages in medullary tissues and remarkable edematous or bionecrotic swelling of reticulum-fibres, some leucocytes-emigration, considerable hemorrhages and remarkable diminution of lymphocytes in pulpameshes.

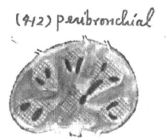

(412) peribronchial

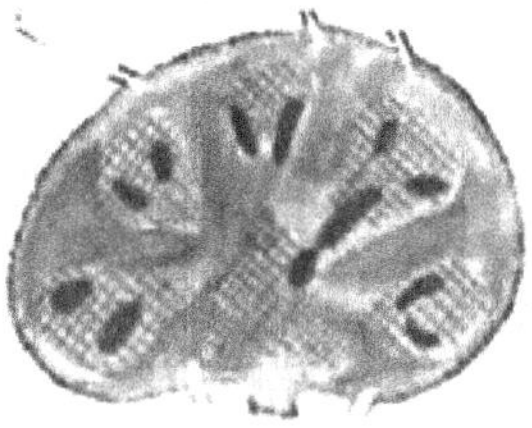

4II. Peribronchial:

Considerable pericapsular inflammation and remarkable hemorrhages in peripheral sinuses.

[redacted]

(4/2) mesenterial

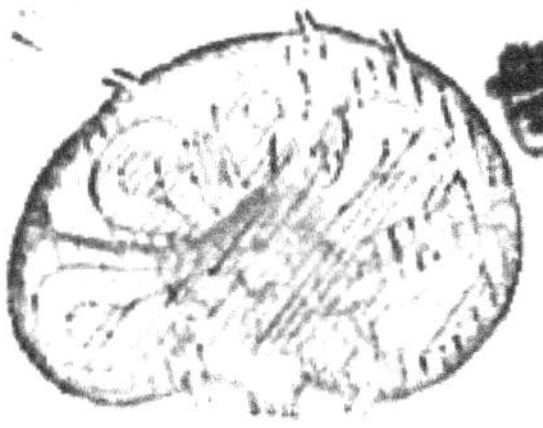

[redacted]

Extremly intense total hemorrhagic-necrotic changes in follicular tissues with remarkable bionecrotic decay or diminution of all follicular cell-components.

Lymphadenitis haemorrhagica gravis.

4I2. Peribronchial:

(4/2) peribronchial

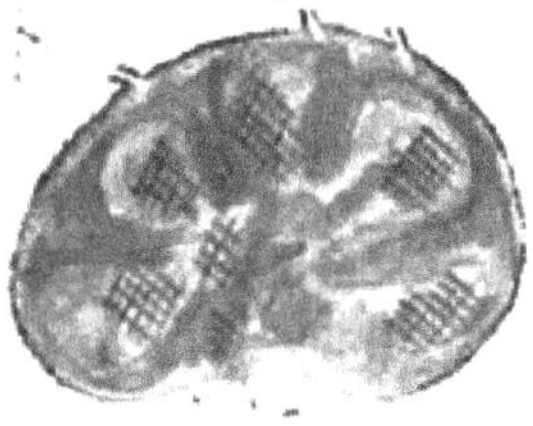

The most intense diffuse hemorrhagic changes (diffuse hemorrhages with some leucocyte-emigrations) in pericapsular tissues and also the same changes (remarkable hemorrhages, considerable exudation, some leucocytes, and necrotic swelling of reticulum-fibres) in peripheral sinuses.

Intense hemorrhagic changes in follicular tissues (severe congestion, bionecrotic swelling and some leucocyte-emigrations in medullary tissues and intense oedematous swelling, severe congestion, localised multiple hemorrhages and intense diminution of lymphocytes in pulpa-meshes).

4I2. Mesenterial:

Almost normal, slight swelling and slight hyperplasia of medullary tissues and slight swelling and slight reduction of pulpa-meshes.

CONFIDENTIAL

378

[redacted]

(412) mesenterial

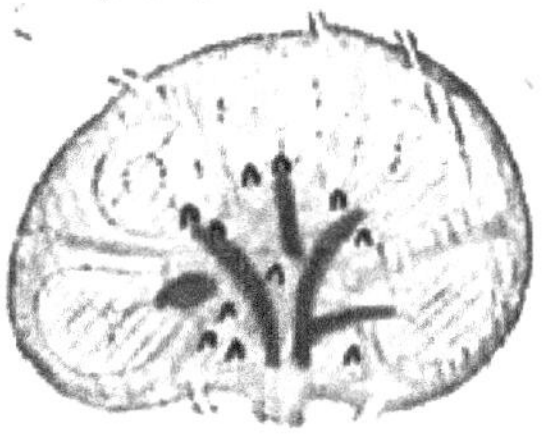

[redacted] No remarkable changes also.

412. Peribronchial:

Extremly intense hemorrhagic changes in pericapsular tissues (intense diffuse hemorrhages and plenty leucocytes-emigrations) and extremly intense diffuse hemorrhagic changes in follicular tissues (the most intense diffuse hemorrhages, necrotic swelling, at some place subuiliary bionecrotic parts and remarkable diminution of ruines follicular cell-elements in medullary tissues and remarkable diminution or diminish of pulpa-meshes).

Lymphadinitis haemorrhagica gravis.

(412) mesenterial

412. Mesenterial:

Slight pericapsular inflammation (with a few leucocytes) and slight catarrh (with some histiocytes) in peripheral sinusos. Considerable congestion and slight edematous swelling of medullary tissues with some leucocytes and slight swelling of pupla-meshos with slight diminution of follicular lymphocytes. No significant congestion in follicular tissues.

412. Mesenterial:

[redacted]379

[redacted]

(417) peribronchial

[redacted] Very slight pericapsular congestion and considerable congestion with very slight swelling in follicular tissues. No remarkable changes else.

417. Peribronchial:

Considerable pericapsular hemorrhages with considerable hemorrhagic-exudative changes in follicular tissues (considerable congestion, swelling slight perivascular hemorrhages, and some leucocytes-emigration in medullary tissues and remarkable hemorrhages, some leucocytes-emigration, edematous swelling of reticulum-fibres and slight hyperplasia of reticulum-cells which fall into bionecrotic cloudy swelling in pulpa-meshes, accompanied with remarkable diminution of follicular lymphocytes.

(417) mesenterial

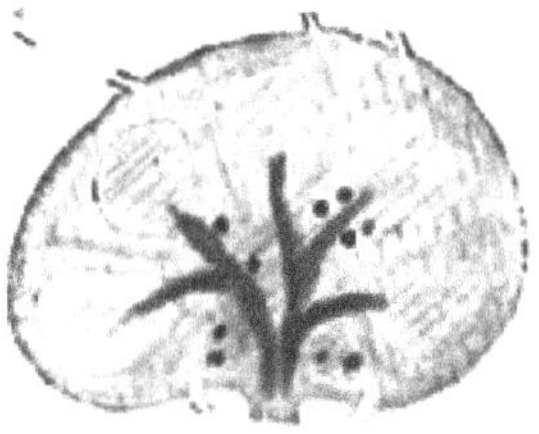

417. Mesenterial:

Almost normal, slight catarrh in peripheral sinuses and considerable congestion with slight hyperplasia of reticulum-cells in medullary tissues. No significant changes else.

(417) axillar

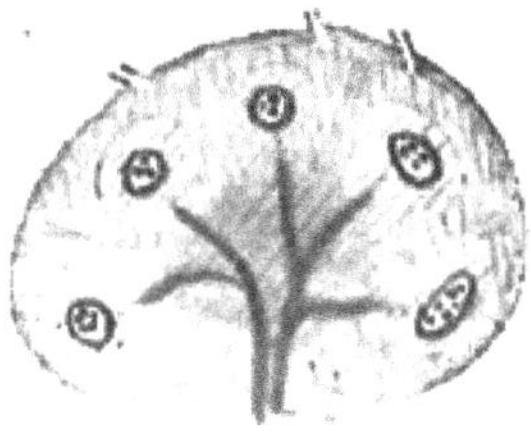

417. Axillar:

Slight catarrh in peripheral sinuses,

[redacted] 380

[redacted]

(417) Radical-mesenterial [redacted]

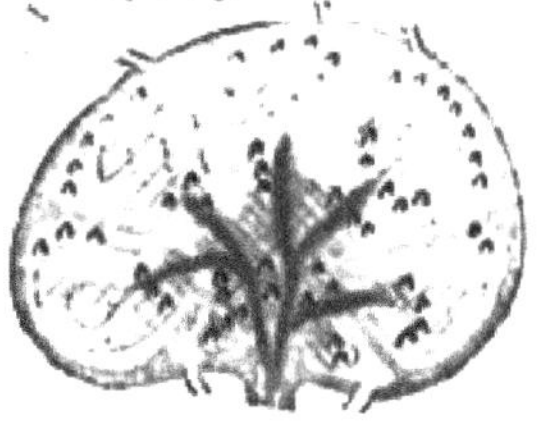

Slight congestion with slight hyperplasia of medullary tissues, slight reduction with slight swelling of pulpa-meshes and slight hyperplasia of germinative centers with some cloudy swollen reticulum-cells.

No remarkable changes else.

(417) peribronchial at bifulcation

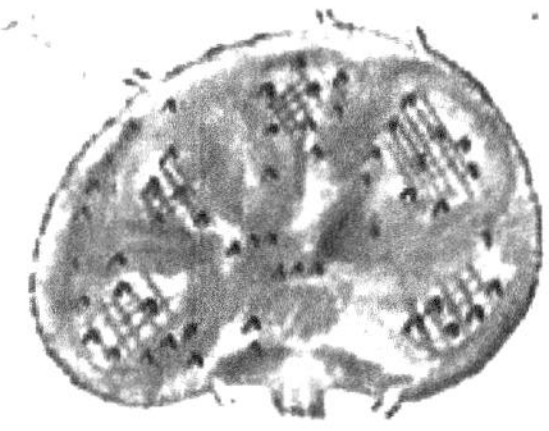

417. Radical mesenterial:

Slight pericapsular inflammation and slight exudation with some leucocytes in peripheral sinuses. Considerable congestion, bionecrotic swelling and plenty leucocytes-emigrations in medullary tissues with considerable reduction of pulpa-meshes (some leucocytes-emigrations, intense swelling of reticulum-fibres and considerable diminution of follicular lymphocytes).

417. Peribronchial:

Lymphnodulus at bifulcation.

Extremely intense hemorrhagic-exudative changes in pericapsular tissues (the most intense diffuse hemorrhages and exudation with leucocytes), in peripheral sinuses (the same changes) and also in follicular tissues (the most intense

CONFIDENTIAL 981

[redacted]

[redacted] congestion, the moste diffuse hemorrhages, plenty leucocytes-emigration, bionecrotic swelling or diminish of cellular components in medullary tissues and the most intense reduction of pulpa-meshes with the most intense exudation, hemorrhages, plenty leucocytes-emigration, necrotic ruins of reticulum-fibres and remarkable diminution of follicular lymphocytes in pulpa-meshes).

Lymphadenitis haemorrhagica gravis.

[redacted] 382

[redacted]

[redacted]

S U M M A R Y.

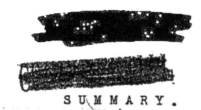

I) The cases of peroral infection.

The bird's-eye-view of pathological changes in all remained microscopical slices.

a) Mesenterial Lymph-nodes.

I7. Lymphadenitis tuberculosa with considerable follicular congestion.

---

27. Lymphadenitis haemorrhagico-necroticans with severe pericapsular inflammation.

---

225. Considerable follicular congestion.
Pericapsular congestion and some hemorrhages, accompanied with some leucocytes as capillary contents.

3I8. Lymphadenitis haemorrhagico-necroticans with severe pericapsular inflammation.

---

325. Lymphadenitis haemorrhagico-necroticans with slight pericapaular inflammation.

---

320. I have only 5 remained microscopical slices of mesenterial lymph-nodes.
3 of them fall into typical hemorrhagic-necrotic inflammation, 2 of them fall into considerable follicular congestion, accompanied with some leucocytes as capillary contents, namely initial stage of acute inflammation.

[redacted] 383

[redacted]

[redacted]

b) Peribronchial lymph-nodes.

27.	Considerable congestion with some leucocytes. Anthracosis.
318.	Lymphadenitis tuberculosa.
320.	Considerable follicular congestion and slight catarrh of sinus.

Only 3 peribronchial lymph-nodes are remained.

2 of them with considerable congestion and some leucocytes, as signs of initial stage of acute inflammation, due to secondary infection.

No remarkable changes else.

II) The cases of pernasal infection;

The bird's-eye-viw of pathological changes in all cases.

	Mesenterial ld.	Peribronchial ld.
388.	Lymphadenitis haemorrhagico-necroticans	Lymphadenitis haemorrhagico-necroticans.
389.	Slight catarrh of sinus. Considerable congestion and some hemorrhages in medullary tissues with some leucocytes.	Lymphadonitis haemorrhagico-necroticans.
393.	Lymphadenitis haemorrhagico-necroticans gravis.	L. haemorrhagica. Slight catarrh of sinus. Medullary congestion and some hemorrhagic places.

[redacted] 384.

[redacted]

390.	Lymphadenitis haemorrhagical [redacted]	Lymphadenitis haemorrhagica gravis.
396.	No remarkable changes.	Lymphadenitis haemorrhagica gravis.
397.	Lymphadenitis haemorrhagico-necroticans gravis.	Lymphadenitis catarrhalis levis.
399.	Lymphadenitis catarrh. levis. Slight congestion and slight hemorrhages.	Lymphadenitis haemorrhagico-levis.
400.	Lymphadenitis and Periadenitis levis. Considerable congestion with some leucocytes in folbicles.	Lymphadenitis haemorrhagico-necroticans.
40I.	Lymphadentis haemorrhagico-purulenta.	Lymphadenitis haemorrhagico-necroticans.
403.	Lymphadenitis haemorhagico-necroticans.	Lymphadenitis haemorrhagico-necroticans.
404.	L. haemorrhagica.	Periadenitis exsudativa gravis. Lymphadenitis catarrh levis (slight congest and some leucocytes)
405.	Lymphadenitis acuta levis. (slight congestion, exudation [redacted]	[redacted]t catarrh and slight con-

[redacted] 385

[redacted]

AND/SOME/LEUCOCYTES/ [redacted]

	And some leucocytes) Slight Pericapsular hemorr-hages.	gestion.
407.	Lymphadenitis haemorrhagico-purulenta. Periadenitis haemorrhagico-purulenta.	Lymphadenits haemorrhagica.
409.	Lymphadenitis haemorrhagica.	Lymphadenitis haemorhagica gravis.
4II.	Lymphadenitis haemorrhagica.	Lymphadenitis haemorhagica gravis.
4I2.	Slight catarrh of sinus. No remarkable changes.	Lymphadenitis haemorrhagica gravis.
4I7.	Lymphadenitis acuta. Slight exudation, congestion some leucocytes. Slight Periadenitis.	Lymphadenitis haemorrhagica.

[redacted] 386

[redacted]

Accordingly the common changes in all cases are as following:

Submaxillar ld. Lymphadenitis haemmrrhagico-necroticans.	Axillar ld. Lymphadenitis haemorrhagico-necroticans.
Mesenterial ld. L. tuberculosa.	
Mesenterial ld. L. haemorrhagica.	
Axillar ld. No remarkable changes.	
Mesenterial ld. L. acuta levis.	
Mediastinal ld. Lymphadenitis haemorrhagica gravis.	Axillar ld. Lymphadenitis haemorrhagico-purulenta.
Peribronchial ld. (at bifulcation). Lymphadenitis haemorrhagica gravis.	Axillar ld. Lymphadenitis catarrhalis levis.

387

[redacted]

[redacted]

2) . Pernasal infection.

a) Peribronchiolar lymph-nodulus.

All investigated I7 cases.

with hemorrhagic (in severe degree).

or hemorrhagic-necrotic changes. I4 cases.

with severe Periadenitis and

considerable follicular congestion. I case.

with slight catarrha and slight

congestion. 2 cases.

Almost all cases fall into intense hemorrhagic or hemorrgagic necrotic changes all over the follicular tissues or severe perifollicular exudation, accompanied with always the most intense hemorrhagic-exudative swelling of mediastinal tissues.

The later, mediastinal tumours (Mediastinitis haemorrhagicp-exsudativa) could be diagnosed easily by X-rays clinically.

2 cases are not attended with severe Lymphadenitis of peribronchial lymph-nodulus : No. 404 and No. 397 case.

In No. 397 case, Anthrax-bacillus broke into alimentary canals after pernasal infection and caused some intestinal disturbances, then severe inflammation (hemorrhagic-necrotic all over the follicular tissues) of mesenterial lymph-nodulus, accompanied with remarkable ascites. The laters was the cause of death.

In. No. 405 cases.

Anthrax-bacillus broke into difectly pulmonal tissues, not accompanied with severe changes of peribronchial lymph-nodulus and caused Endobronchitis and bronchogenous pneumonia: multiple acinous, hemorrhagic-exudativ[redacted]was the cause of death.

388

[redacted]

b) Peri-bronchiolar lymph-nodulus. [redacted]

After capturing peribronchial lymph-nodulus, Anthrax-bacillus intrude furthermore into peribronchiolar lymph-nodulus..

General sketch of these progresses in all investigated cases are as following.

c) Submaxillar or axillar lymph-nodulus.

In some cases (esp. No. 388 and No. 409), submaxillar or axillar lymph-nodulus fall into intense inflammatory changes with hemorrhagicleucocytic infiltration.

[redacted] 389

([redacted] (

d) Mesenterial lymph-nodul[redacted]

All investigated I7 cases.

with severe hemorrhagic or hemorrhagic-necrotic changes. I0 cases.

with some signs of acute inflammation. 4 cases.

Without any remarkable changes. 2 cases.

Most cases of them are attended with severe inflammatory changes of mesenterial lymph-nodes, accompanied with hemorrhagic-exudative swelling of lymph-nodes in heaps, gelatinous swelling of mesenterial fatty tissues and remarkable ascites.

In these cases, Anthrax-bacillus broke into alimentary canal, besides pulmonal tissues and caused some times intense intestinal disturbances so as descriped in chapter ( ), then intense acute inflammatory changes of mesenterial lymph-nodulus.

I0 cases of them are accompanied with acute hemorrhagic inflammation of mesenterial lymphnodulus, but I could found, based on the investigation of survived microscopical slices, which I have recieved during war-time, only 2 cases with severe hemorrhagic fungous swelling of intestinal walls.

In other 8 cases, Anthrax-bacillus should intrude into medenterial lymph-nodulus, not causing severe intestinal symptoms or I may not have obtained the microscopical slices of intesinal di sturbances at inssues.

All all events, Anthrax-baccilus invade into mesenterial lymphnodulus, causing sometimes severe intestinal symptoms or sometimes not.

[redacted] 390

[redacted]

[redacted]

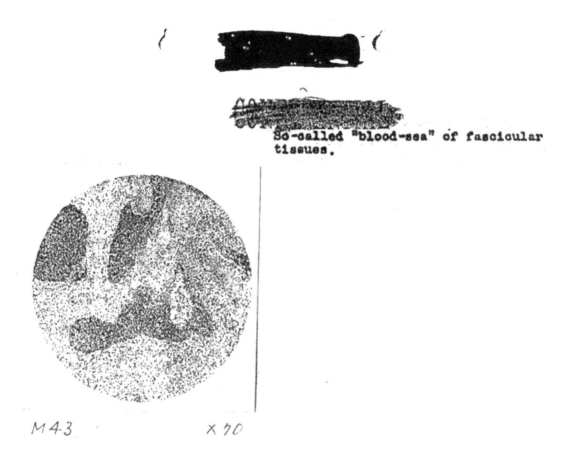

So-called "blood-sea" of fascicular tissues.

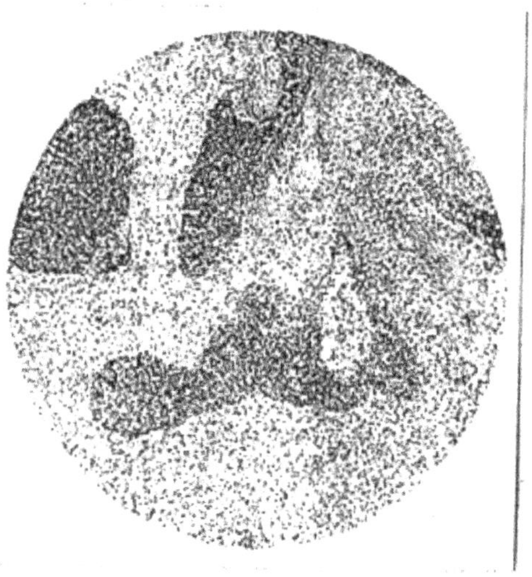

M43 x70

Intense ectasia of sinuses, with some edema.

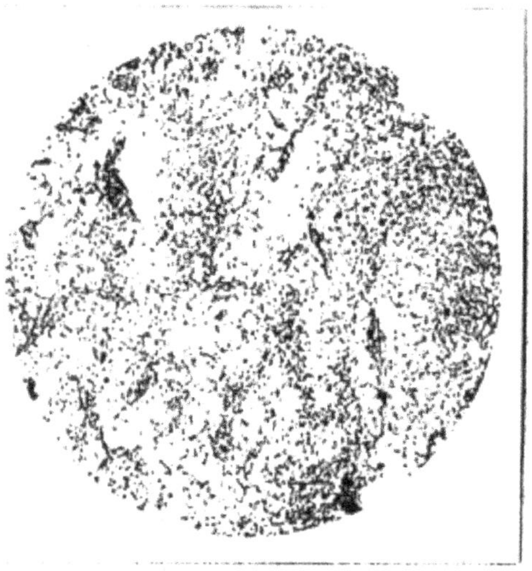

M397 x80

[redacted] 391

([redacted] (

[redacted]

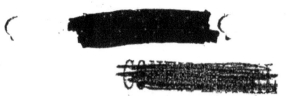

Intese congestion and intense
edematous swelling of follicular
tissues, esp. insubepithelial
tissues.

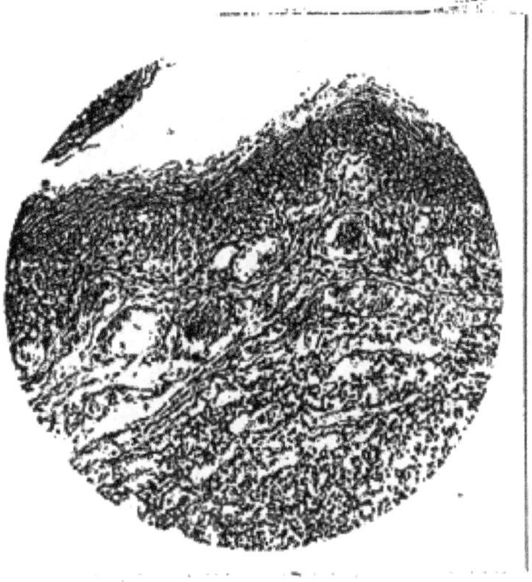

M 412 X100

Remarkble congestion and
edematous swelling of follicular
tissures,

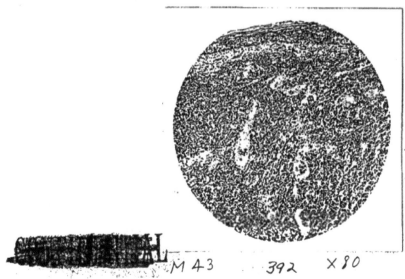

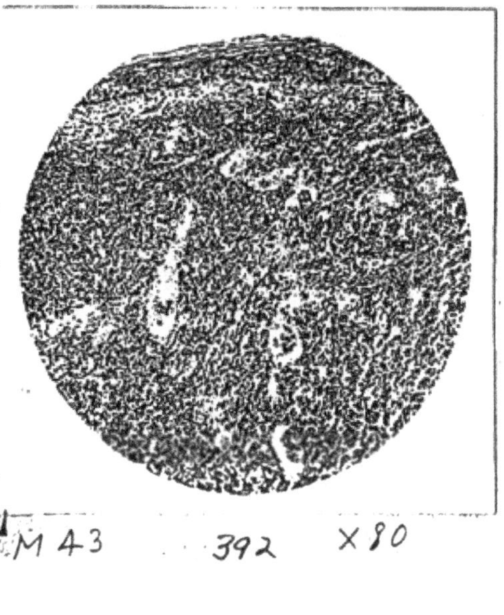

[redacted] M 43 392 X 80

[redacted]

[redacted]

Edematous swelling of follicles,

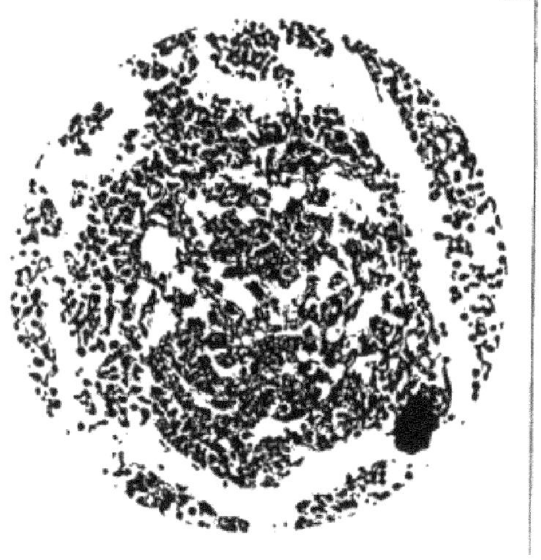

M 393 1. 200

Hyalinous swelling of perifollicular tissues and hyperplasia of retiuuium fibres.

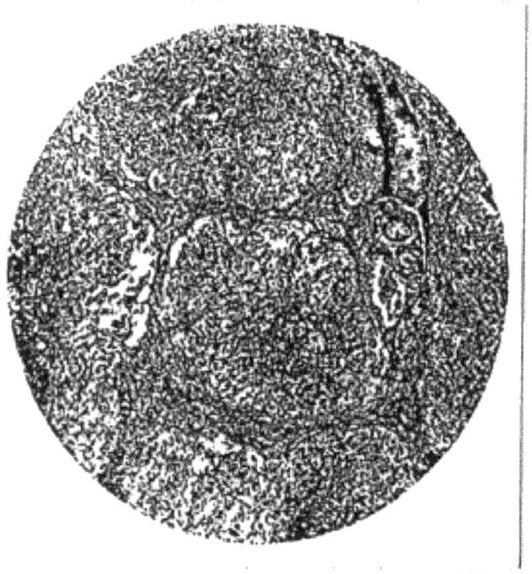

M. 407. 60.

[redacted]43

[redacted]

[redacted]

Intense karyorrhextic changes in fascicular tissues.

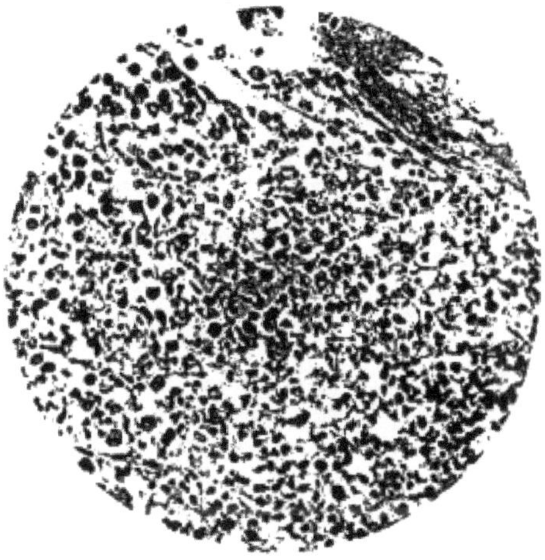

M 318 (b) X240

Intese supprative changes of fascicular tissues.

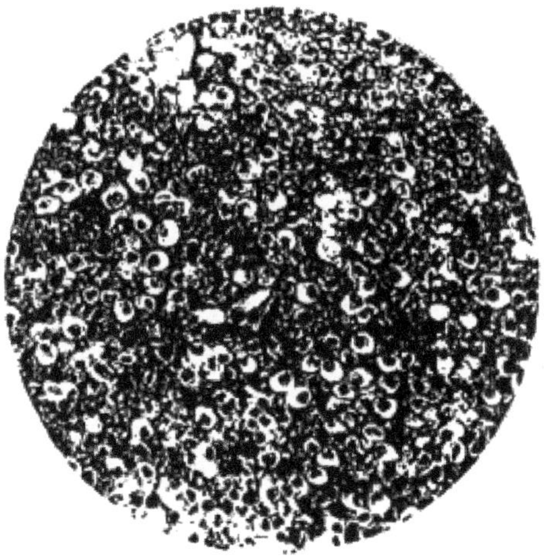

M 403. X330

[redacted] 394

([redacted] (

[redacted]

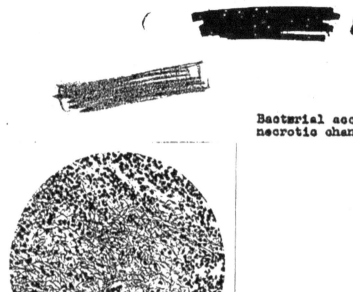

Bacterial accumulation and bio-necrotic changes of fascicular tissues

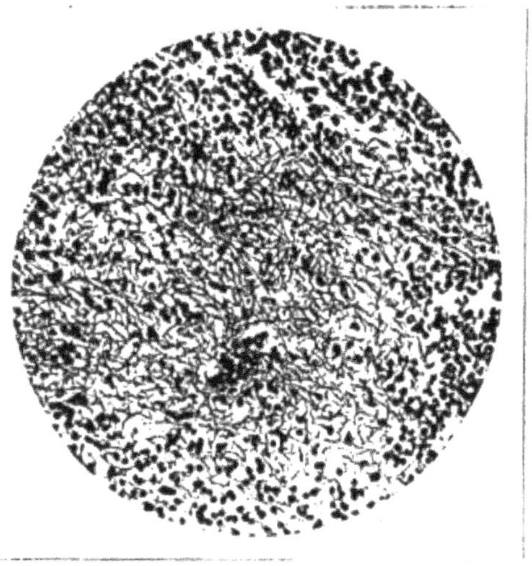

M 385 (b) ×250

Supprative changes of fascucular tissues.

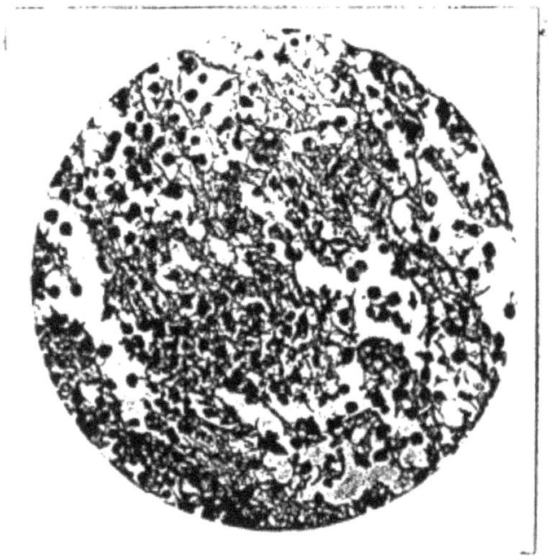

M 393 (a) ×340

CONFIDENTIAL

~~TOP SECRET~~

395

([redacted] (

Bacterial accumulation and diffuse necrosis.

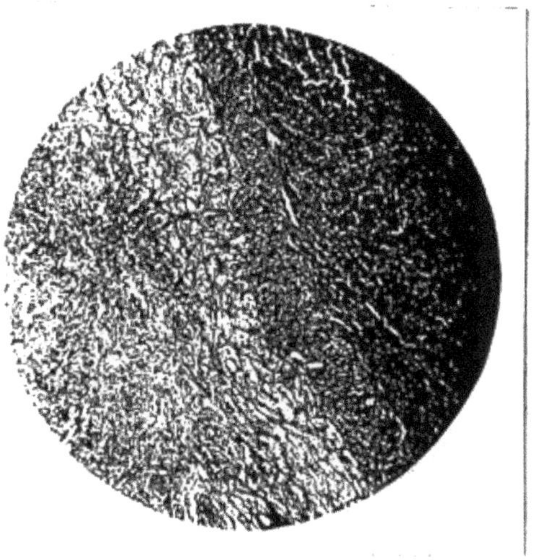

M 318 (c) x 60

Myeloic metaplasia.
Some meylbic cells in sinuses.

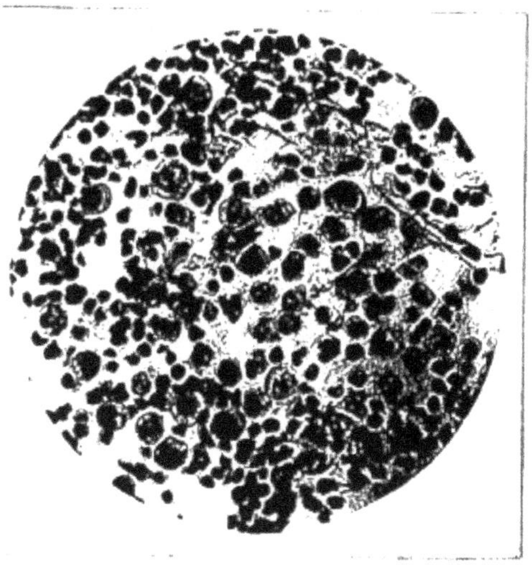

M.413 (a) X 520

~~CONFIDENTIAL~~

396

([redacted]

[redacted]

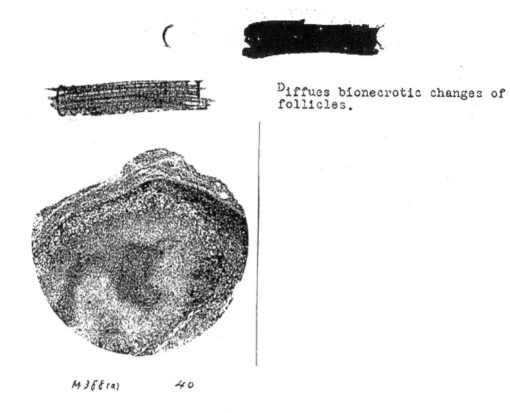

Diffues bionecrotic changes of follicles.

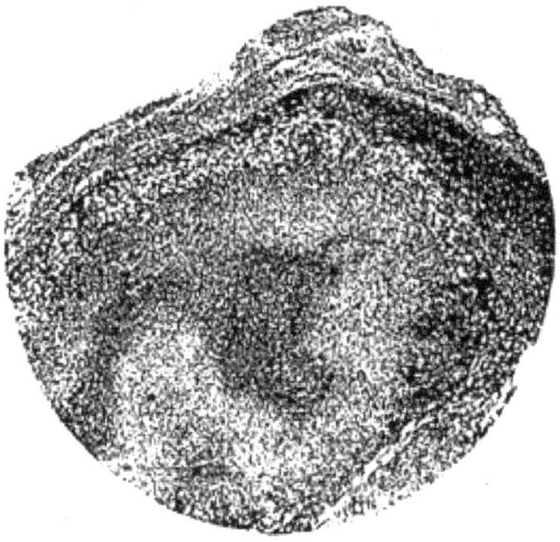

M 368 (a)　　40

Diffuse bionecrotic changes of follicles, in high power.

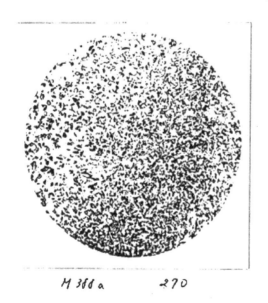

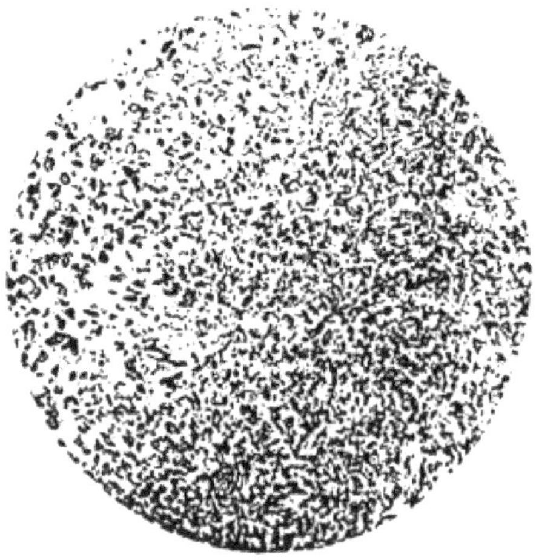

M 368 a　　270

[redacted]L 397

[redacted]

[redacted]

Other Organs

[redacted] 398

[redacted]

BRAIN.

(A) Microscop. Investigation.

CEREBRUM :

225.

Considerable congestion with leucocytic contents. Slight perivascular edema. Slight degeneration of ganglion cells with slight hyperplasia of glia cells.

325.

Slight stasis of meninges.

Slight congestion and slight edema of brain. Slight degeneration of ganglion cells.

411.

Slight stasis of meninges. Considerable congestion and slight perivascular hemorrhages and edematous swelling.

Slight degeneration of ganglion cells with slight hyperplasia of glia cells.

388.

Slight congestion and no remarkable changes else.

417.

Considerable congestion with slight perivascular hemorrhage.

Slight degeneration of ganglion cells.

BRAIN

[redacted] 399

([redacted] (

CEREBELLUM :

225.

Slight edema and congestion with slight perivascular hemorrhage.

Slight degeneration of ganglion cells.

320.

No remarkable changes.

325.

The same changes as above mentioned.

388.

Considerable congestion, slight perivasmular hemorrhages and slight edema of meninges.

Considerable congestion, slight perivascular hemorrhages and slight edematous swelling of brain.

411.

Slight congestion and slight perivascular edema. Slight degeneration of ganglion cells.

[redacted] 400

[redacted]

(B) SUMMARY.

Cerebrum :

·Generaly with very slight, not severe changes.

a) Meninges with slight congestion, sometimes slight perivascular hemorrhages and slight perivascular edema.

b) Brain-masses : slight congestion, slight perivascular edema and sometimes slight perivascular hemorrhages. Slight degeneration of ganglion cells (swelling, atrophia and slight tygrolysis) with more or less degenerative nucleus (pycnosis and Karyolysis in slight degree). Very slight hyperplasia of glia cells.

Cerebellum :

Slighter changes than in brain.

Considerable congestion with sometimes perivascular hemorrhages and perivascular edema. Slight degeneration of ganglion cells.

[redacted] 401

[redacted]

Cr……Cerebrum
M……Mesencephalon
Cl……Cerebellum

BRAIN

			Cr 225	Cr 325	Cr 388	Cr 411	M 411	Cl 320	Cl 388	Cl 411
Meninges	Edema		|	∸	÷	∸	|	÷	÷	÷
	Hemorrhage		|	∸	∸	−	|	−	÷	∸
	Contents of Blood vessels	Erythrocytes	|	+	∸	÷	|	∸	+	#
		Leucocytes	|	−	−	−	|	∸	∸	∸
		Lymphocytes	|	÷	÷	÷	|	−	∸	∸
		Monocytes	|	−	−	−	|	−	∸	∸
	Endothelium	Swelling	|	∸	∸	∸	|	∸	∸	∸
		Desquamation	|	−	÷	∸	|	−	÷	∸
		Hyperplasia	|	−	−	−	|	−	∸	∸
	Infiltration of Leucocytes		|	−	−	−	|	−	∸	∸
	Infiltration of Lymphocytes		|	∸	÷	−	|	−	−	−
	Proliferation of Histiocytes		|	−	÷	−	|	−	−	−
Nerve Cells	Swelling		÷	÷	∸	÷	÷	÷	÷	+
	Atrophia		÷	÷	∸	∸	∸	∸	∸	∸
	Tigrolysis		−	∸	∸	∸	∸	+	÷	+
	Vacuolar Degeneration		−	−	−	−	−	−	−	−
	Changes of Nuclei	Swelling	−	−	−	−	−	−	−	−
		Pyknosis	∸	∸	∸	∸	∸	÷	−	∸
		Karyorrhexis	−	−	−	−	−	∸	∸	∸
		Karyolysis	÷	÷	÷	÷	÷	+	÷	+
	Satellitosis		∸	−	∸	∸	−	∸	−	−
	Neuronophagy		−	−	−	−	−	−	−	−
Glia	Number		↑∸	N.	↑÷	↑∸	N.	↑∸	↑∸	↑∸
	Granular Proliferation of Glia		−	−	−	−	−	−	−	−
	Nodular Proliferation of Glia		−	−	−	−	−	−	−	−
Substance of Brain	Contents of Blood-vessels	Erythrocytes	+	+	∸	+	+	∸	÷	+
		Leucocytes	∸	−	−	−	−	−	∸	−
		Lymphocytes	∸	∸	∸	∸	∸	∸	∸	∸
		Monocytes	∸	−	−	−	−	−	∸	−
	Virchow-Robin Spaces	Erythrocytes	∸	∸	∸	∸	#	∸	+	÷
		Leucocytes	−	−	−	−	−	−	−	−
		Lymphocytes	−	∸	∸	∸	−	−	∸	−
		Adventitial Cells	−	−	−	∸	−	−	−	−
	Edema		∸	÷	÷	÷	÷	÷	÷	÷
	Hemorrhage		−	−	−	−	+	−	÷	∸
	Necrosis		−	−	−	−	−	−	−	−

[redacted]402

[redacted]

AORTA.

17,26, 54,

325, 389, 397, 403, 405, 401,

412, 413, 417.

No remarkable changes.

320, 388, 390, 407, 408, 410.

Slight stasis of periadventitial tissues.

409. Slight stasis of periadventitial tissues and bacterial masses in blood vessels.

393. Slight congestion of vasa vasorum of media.

[redacted] 403

[redacted]

PHARYNX.

(A) Microscop. Investigation.

54.

Slight keratification and desquamation of epitheliums.

Considerable congestion, some edema and some pericapillar round-cell -infiltration in submucous tissues.

225.

Considerable congestion and some round-cell-infiltration at perivascular and periglandular tissues.

Glandulae pharyngese with some desquamative epithelialiums.

318.

Intense congestion and some hemorrhages in submucous tissues.

Slight infiltration of round-cells and some leucocytes in mucous tissues and epithelial layers.

320.

Slight congestion and some edema.

Diffuse round-cell-dissemination (plasma-cells and some lymphocytes) in submucous tissues.

Slight hyperplasia of lymph-nodulus.

[redacted]

404

[redacted] CONFIDENTIAL

MUSCLE.

(A) Microscop. Investigation.

54. Phlegmona diffusa.

Diffuse phlegmons in subcutaneous (in extraordinary intense degree) and cutaneous tissues with intense leucocytes (and some lymphocytes)-infilltration, accompanied with severe serous exudation and intense diffuse hemorrhages (so-called blood-sea) :

Capillaries in subcutaneous tissues with plenty of leucocytes, necrotic ruins of capillar walls, intense perivasculær edema and hemorrhages, intense leucocytes-emigration (hematogenous-metastatic characters), invading phlegmneously all over the neighbouring tissues.

Accompanied with atrophic epidermis and atrophy or collapse of adnex-organs.

388.

Remarkable capillar congestion at Stratum subpapillare with some anthrax-bacillus in some capillaries.

Accompanied with somewaht necrotic ruins of capillar walls, perivascular edema in high degree and some localised hemorrhages.

Some pericapillar lymphocytes (and some leucocytes)-accumulation and slight collapse of adnex-organs.

400.

Interse capillar congestion and localised hemorrhages at Str. subpapillare and Str. papillare, accompanied with somewhat diffuse perivascular cellular infilration. (leucocytes, some of them being eosinophilic, lymphocytes and some histiocytes). Slight fibrosis of adnex-organs.

[redacted] 405 CONFIDENTIAL

[redacted] CONFIDENTIAL

In epidermis, slight swelling and atrophia of pickle cells and some parakeratosis above the cutis.

[redacted] CONFIDENTIAL
406

7.2 The Report of “G”

资料出处： Technical Library, Dugway Proving Grounds, Utah, US.

内容点评： 本资料为日本细菌部队人员向美国提供的人体实验解剖报告“G”报告，即“鼻疽”报告。共21例实验对象，皮肤感染16例，鼻腔感染5例。感染后，4 ~ 45日死亡。为实验对象感染后人体器官病理变化记录报告，按急性、亚急性、亚慢性、慢性顺序排列。

[redacted]

UNCLASSIFIED

The Report of "G"

Reviewed By
Date

Regraded Unclassified by
authority of
by C. V. Hill, on 6 May 60

Regraded Confid, by
authority of
by C. V. Hill, on 6 6 56

CAMP DETRICK CONTROL NO.
SOMC- 1817

~~CONFIDENTIAL~~ UNCLASSIFIED

[redacted]

56-FDTS-20

C[redacted]

[redacted] UNCLASSIFIED

C O N T E N T .

[redacted]

UNCLASSIFIED

56-FDTS-204

[redacted]

UNCLASSIFIED

F O R E W O R D .

I.

I have investigated microscopically 2I cases of glanders-dissease.

These case are divided into 2 groups :

a) Percutaneoué infection and

b) Pernasal infection.

Percutaneous infection.	16 cases.	No. 16. 50. 85. 146. 152. 167. 180. 190. 167.193.205. 207. 221. 222. 225. 254.
Pernasal infection.	5 cases. *	No.176.178.229. 727. 731.

* Some of them, not sure.

I have classified the course of the disease into 4 stages:

I. Acute stage.	0 --------- 14 days.
2. Subacute stage.	14 days ------28 days.
3. Subchronic stage.	28 days ----- 7 weeks.
4. Rather chronic stage.	7 weeks ---- several months.

	Acute stage	Subacute stage	Subchronic stage	Rather chronic stage
Percutaneous infection.	5 cases	7 cases	3	I
Pernasal infection.	3 cases	0	0	2

[redacted] [redacted] UNCLASSIFIED

CAMP DETRICK CONTROL NO. ...ors-204

[redacted]

UNCLASSIFIED [redacted]

(a). Acute stage :

(-) Some cases (8 cases of 21 cases) died in acute stage with some septicemic-toxic symptoms and some adjacent septicemic changes of organs. Not yet accompaneid with remarkable organic changes.

Case.	Days of course.	Toxic-septicemic changes of organs.
224.	4 days.	Traumatic wounds. Congestion in Stomach, Pancreas and Supra-renal glands. Traumatic Wounds. Congestion in Large-Intestine and Pancreas. Interstitial edema of Kidney. Reactive congestion of lung (slight diffuse Alveolitis).

(•) These toxic changes are emphasized in some cases with more intense exudative changes, due to metastasis in various organs.

case	Days of course	Metastatic changes traumatic wounds
3. 180.	12 days.	traumatic wounds. Congestion in stomach. Congestion of lung and pleura, accomapnied with some bacterial dissemination. Miliary glanders-Knots in exudative form, accompanied with someparenchymatous dgeneration in LIVER.
---		Metastatic acute Thyreoiditis :

[redacted]

UNCLASSIFIED

[redacted] 2

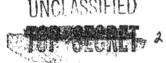

CAMP DETRICK CONTROL NO.
56-FDTS-204

[redacted]

UNCLASSIFIED [redacted]

4. 190.	10 days.	traumatic wounds. Interstitial edema of heart, accompanied with some mesenchymal reactions. Interstitial edema of kidney; accompanied with some round cell accumulation. Slight diffuse Alveolitis of lung, accompanied with slightly hyperplasied alveolar epitheliums. Miliary glanders-Knots in liver, accompanied with some parenchymatous degeneration.
5. 16.	13 days.	traumatic wounds. Some localised hemorrhages and edema of heart. Slight diffuse Alveolitis of lung, accompanied with some bacterial dissemination. Miliary glanders-Knots of liver, accompanied with intense parenchymatous dgeneration. Intense parenchymatous degeneration of pancreas. Metastatic Tonsillitis acuta.
6. 176.	10 days.	Intense congestion of heart, accompanied with some mesenchymal reaction. Intense congestion of large-intestine. Congestion of lung (slight Klveolitis). Hepatitis serosa of liver, accompanied with some hemorrhages in central zone of acinus. Nephrosis, accompanied with considerable interstitial edema and some intense bionecrotic changes of tubular epitheliums.

UNCLASSIFIED

[redacted] [redacted] 3

[redacted]

UNCLASSIFIED [redacted]

---

7. 176. 12 days. Some localised hemorrhages in subendocardial tissues.

Slight Alveolitis and some pulmonal congestion.

Some hemorrhages in pancreas.

Some edema of kidney, accompanied with some pound cell accumulation.

Intense fatty degeneration of liver.

(•). In one case, develop these exudative changes to the most intense.

---

8. 229. 9 days. Intense edema and some mesenchymal reactions of heart.

Exudative-hemorrhagic Bronchitis and Peribronchitis.

Multifocal acinous-lobular pneumonia and Pleuritis sero-fibrinosa.

Intense edema and some round cell accumulation of Kidney.

Intense congestion and some hemorrhages in stomach.

Intense parenchymatous dgeneration of liver.

Moderate parenchymatous degeneration and some round ce-ll accumulation in supra-renal gland.

Parenchymatous degeneration and some subepitheliar edema, in pituitary body.

[redacted] UNCLASSIFIED

[redacted] 4

[redacted]

UNCLASSIFIED

Therfore the main pathelogical changes in acute stage are as following.

UNCLASSIFIED

TOP SECRET 5

[redacted]

UNCLASSIFIED [redacted]

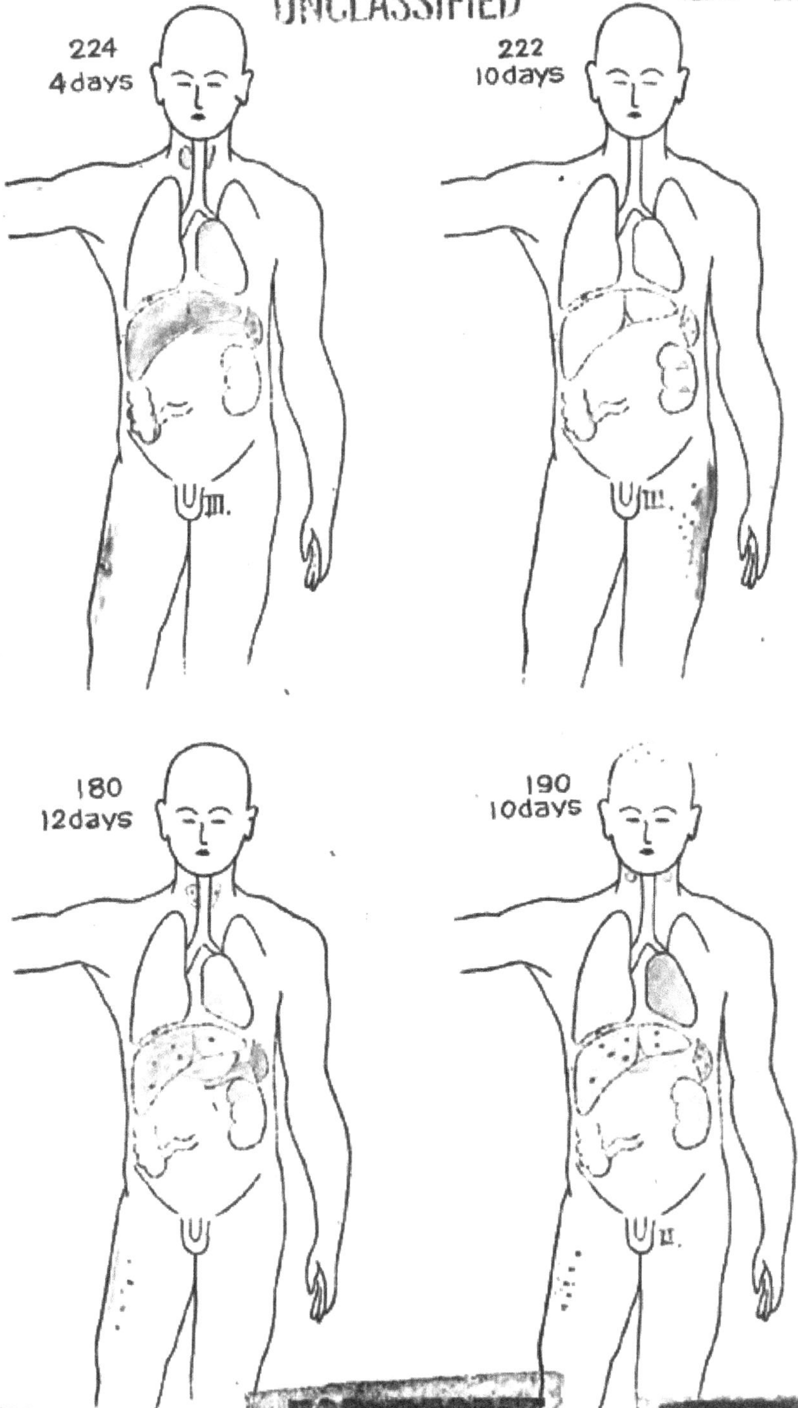

UNCLASSIFIED T[redacted] 6 [redacted]

[redacted]

UNCLASSIFIED [redacted]

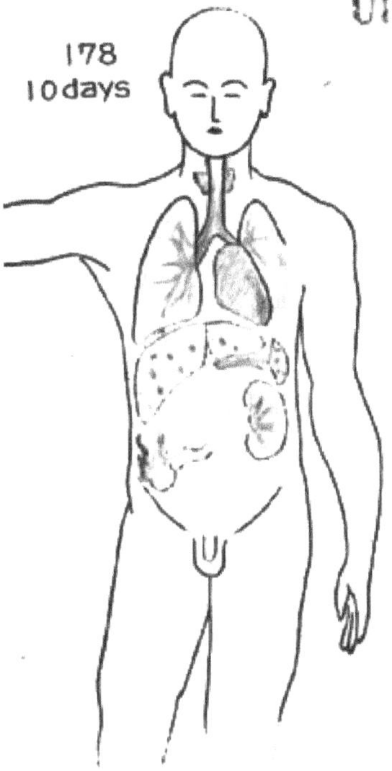

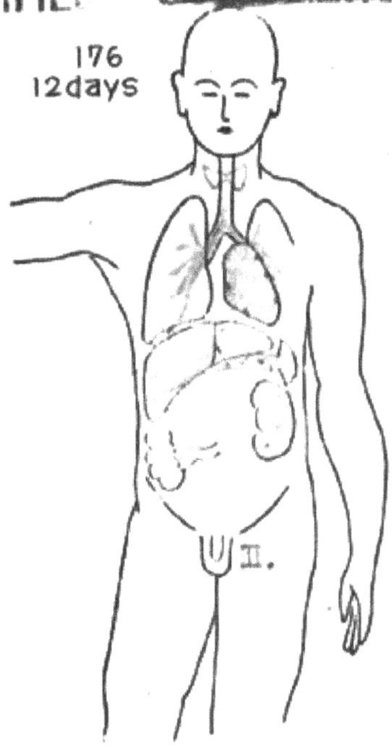

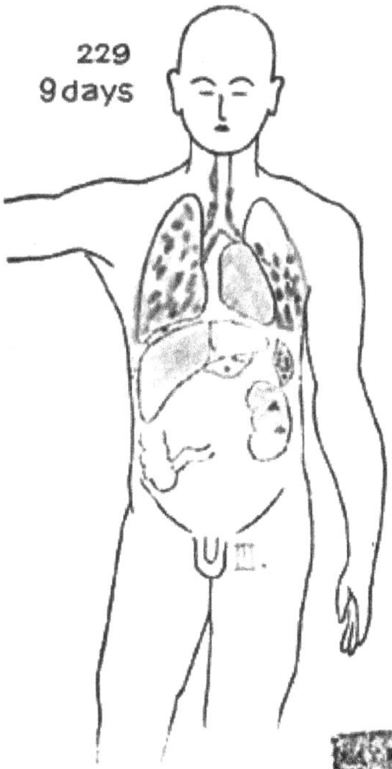

[redacted]

[redacted] 7 UNCLASSIFIED

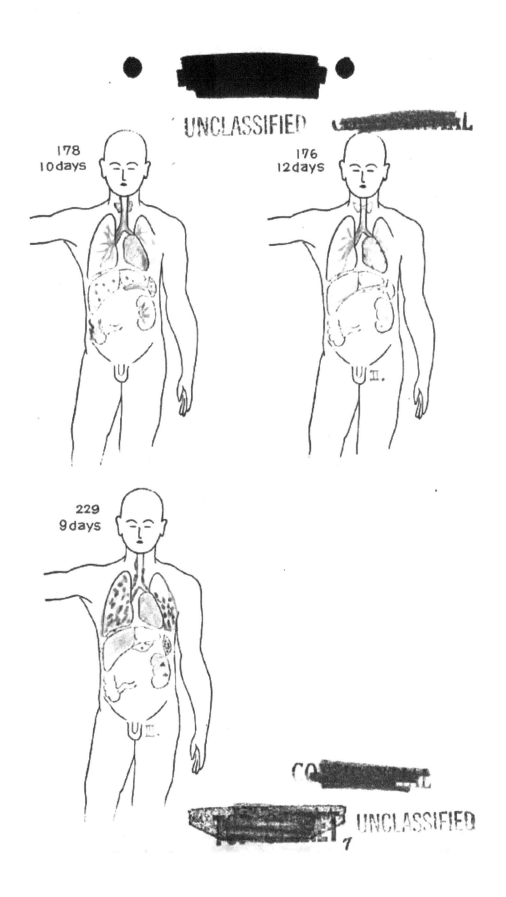

([redacted] (

UNCLASSIFIED [redacted]

(b). Subacute stage:

After labout 2 weeks occured significant and severe symptoms of general metastsis, esp. some pneumonic changes which were frequently accompanied with reactive exudative-hemorrhagic pleuritis.

case	Duys of course.	Changes, due to general metastasis.
I. 167.	15 days.	Lung:Metastatic Endoarteriitis necroticans and multiple acino-lobular pneumonia. Reactive hemorrhagic-fibrinous pleuritis. Liber: Intense fatty degeneration. Some parenchymatous degeneration: Interstitial edema of kidney. Some localised hemorrhages in subepicardial tissues of heart.
2. 50.	16 days.	Lung:Multiple miliary glanders-knots, in intense exudative-hemorrhagic form. Reactive hemorrhagic-fibrinous pleuritis. Other metastatic changes : Metastatic Tonsillitis acuta in the beginning stage. Heart with some mesenchymal reactions.
3. 254.	20 days.	Lung:Multiple acino-lobular,hemorrhagic-leucocytic pneumonia. Subpleural glanders-knots (in exudative form), (Correspond to the primary seat of tuberculous affection). Reactive hemorrhagic pleuritis. Liver ; Multiple millet-corn large glanders-knots (in somewhat proliferative form) and intense fatty degneration. Lymph-node, (Peribronchial) : Lymphadenitis, due to glanders-infection. Small-Intestine : Metastatic glanders-knots in subserous tissues.

UNCLASSIFIED [redacted] 8 [redacted]

([redacted] (

UNCLASSIFIED C[redacted]AL

Some other parenchymatous degeneration:
Heart with intense interstitial edema.
Kidney with intense interstitial edema.
Supra-renal glands with some hemorrhages.
Pancreas with our so-called serous apoplexy of islands (intense exudation in islands).

4\. 85. 21 days.

Lung: Multiple miliary glanders-knots in intense exudative form.

Liver: Intense fatty degeneration and multiple miliary glanders-knots.

Some other parenchymatous degeneration.
Heart with some rheumatoid-knots (in exudative form), due to glanders-infection.
Nephrosis I or III at some places.

5\.207. 18 days.

Lung: Metastatic Endoaretiitis necroticans.
Multiple glanders-knots with slight perifocal reactions.
Multiple acino-lobular pneumonia.
Multiple subpleural glanders-knots.

Liver: Some parenchymatous degeneration and some hemorrhages in the central zone of acinus.

Some other parenchymatous degeneration :
Kidney with slight nephrosis and some interstitial edema.
Heart with some interstitial edema.
Thyreoid in follicular collapse.

6\. 221. 24 days.

Lung: Multiple acino-lobular pneumonia with severe exudative-hemorrhagic perifocal reactions.
Reactive exudative-fibrinous pleuritis.

Liver: Multiple miliary glanders-knots and some parenchymatous degeneration.

Some other parenchymatous degneration+
Heart with intense interstitial edema.etc.

7\.193. 25 days.

Lung: Metastatic Endoarteriitis necroticans.
Multiple submiliary glanders-knots.
Bacterial disemination.

Liver : Multiple submiliriay glanders-knots (in

UNCLASSIFIED [redacted] ? C[redacted]AL

[redacted]

UNCLASSIFIED [redacted]

rather proliferative form).

Some other parenchymatous degeneration :
Heart with some mesenchymal reactions.
Glomerulo-nephrosis with some our so-called.
polar edema.
Thyreoids in follicular collapse.

********* ********* *********

In this subacute stage, occured some intense exudative changes, especially in lung and liver, on the ground of general metastasis. The later two and Nound, infected with glanders. (accomapnied with metastatic muscular abscesses) caused serious clinical syptoms-which cause the death.

METASTASIS in LUNG : in all 7 cases.

a) Necrotic decay of blood vessel wall, due to metastatic Thromboendoa-eteriitis necroticans and Pneumonic changes of perivascular pulmonal tissues.

b) Invasion to alveolar capillaries.

Miliary glanders-Knots formation.
(mainly exudative form in this stage).

Multifocal (exudative-hemorrhagic) acino-lobular pneumonia.

UNCLASSIFIED [redacted]

[redacted] 10

([redacted] (

[redacted]

Accomapnied with exudative-hemorrhagic pleuritis.

(in 4 cases of 7 cases).

METASTASIS in LIVER :

Multiple miliary glanders-Knots formation.

(in 6 cases of 7 cases).

or caused intense parenchymatous degeneration.

METASTASIS in CUTANEOUS or MUSCULAR TISSUES :

Metastatic pustulosis, accompanied with some erythema, pustules, phlegmons or some muscular abscesses or suppurative Peri ostitis.

Mutiple pustulosis head and face. I case.

Abscess in knee-joint. 1 case.

Continual propagation of muscular abscesses, from traumatic wounds. 5 case.

METASTASIS in OTHER PARENCHYMATOUS ORGANS.

Metatasis in small-intestine.

Typical glanders-knots formation in subserous tissues. 1 case.

[redacted] // [redacted]

[redacted]

CONFIDENTIAL

Sometimes accompanied with severe parenchymatous degeneration.

Serous apoplexy of islands. I case.

Glomerulo-nephrosis with intense polar edema. I case.

TOP SECRET CONFIDENTIAL

12

([redacted] (

Sketchy record of general metastasis in subacute stage.

[redacted]

[redacted]

TOP SECRET 13

[redacted]

[redacted]

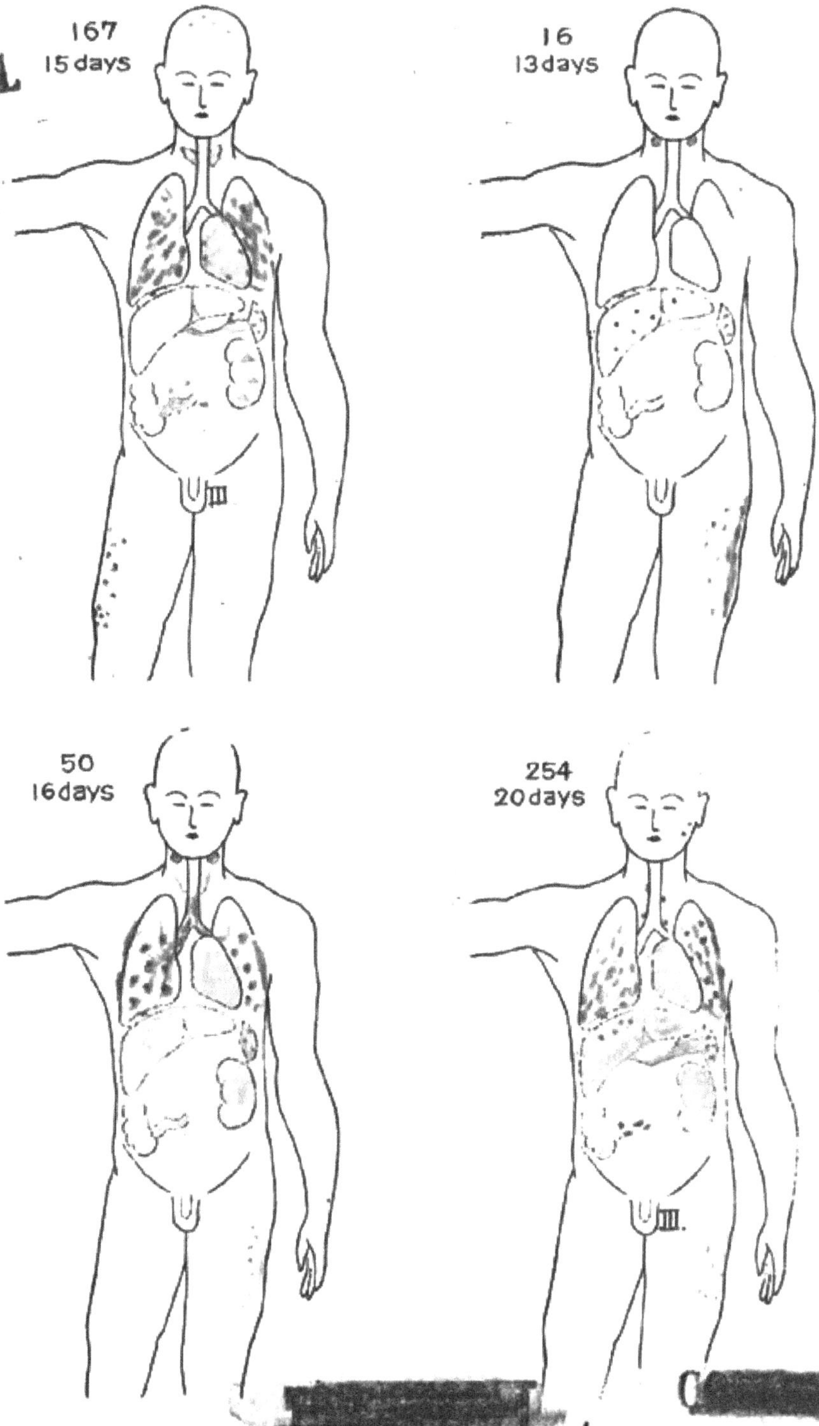

[redacted] 14 [redacted]

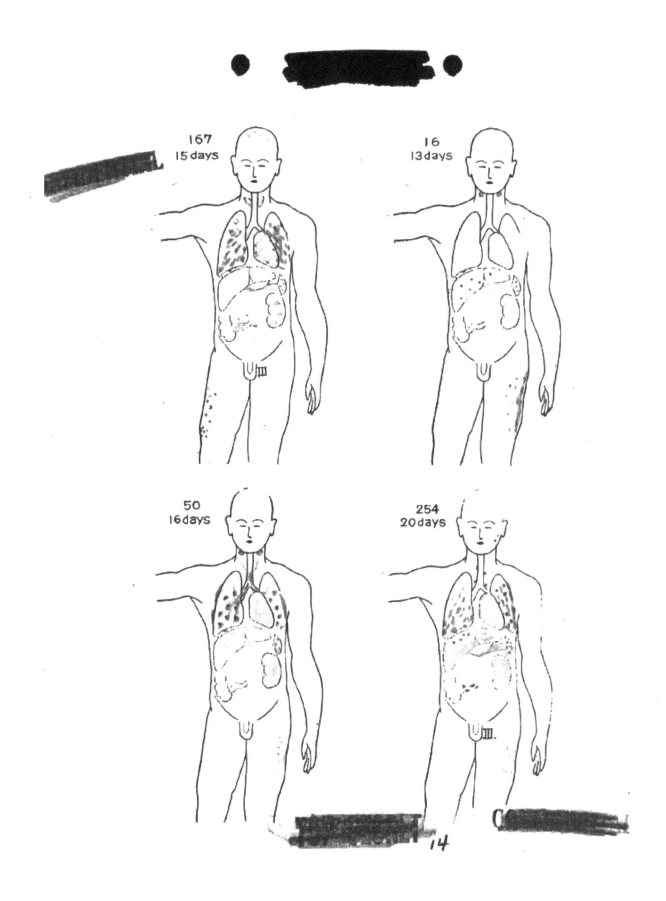

[redacted]

[redacted]

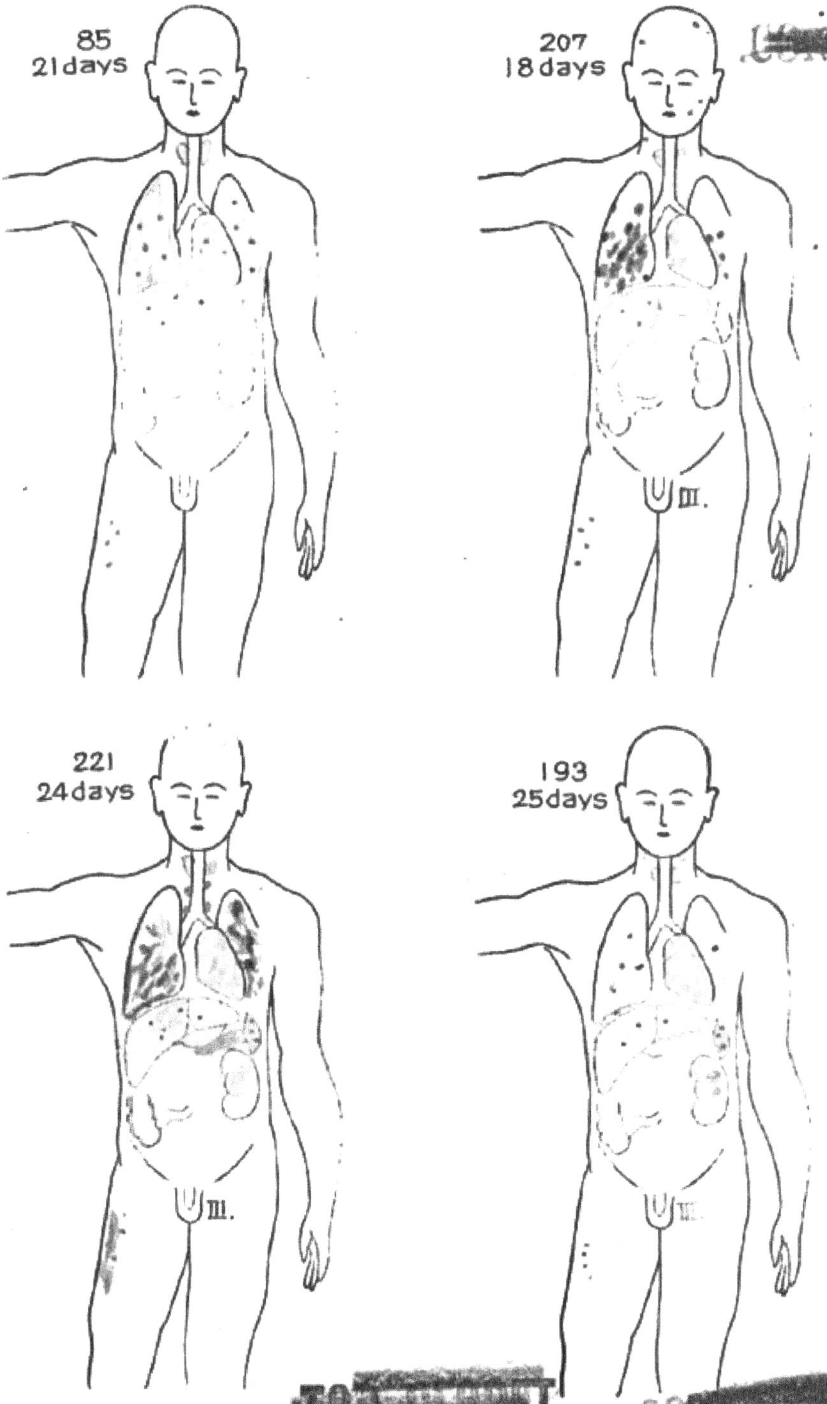

[redacted] 15 [redacted]

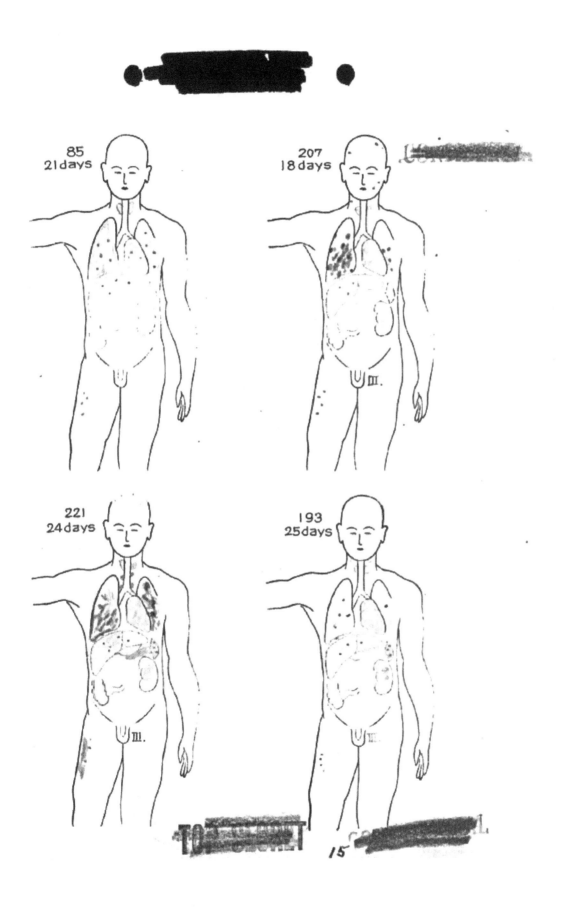

([redacted])

(c). Subchronic stage : 4---7 weeks. 3 cases. CONFIDENTIAL

The main pathlogical changes in this stage are also intense exudative changes :

I. Secondary pneumonia : meatstatic Endoarteriitis necroticans and following hemorrhgic-leucocytic pneumonia. Sometimes accompanied with reactive pleuritis (exudative-fibrinous) pleuritis.

2. Hepatitis serosa and multiple glanders-knots in rather exudative forms.

3. Infected wounds, muscular absecesses and metastatic pustulosis.

4. Some exudative changes of some other parenchymatous organs. Sometimes accompanied with some mesenchymal reaction, due to rather chronic course.

Case.	Days of course.	Main pathlogical changes
I. 205.	37 days.	Lung: metastatic Endoarteriitis necroticans Multiple supermiliary glanders-knots, with intense perifocal reactions. Liver: Multiple submiliary glanders-knots. Other parenchymatous organs : Glomeulo-nephrosis with intense interstitial edema and some round cell accumulation. Pancreas with lymphocytes-accumulation. Supra-renal glands with some lymphocytes accumulation. Mascular abscess and metastatic pustulosis.
2. 146.	39 days.	Lung: Lobular pneumonia in hemorrhagic-leucocytic form. Some bacterial dissemination. Reactive sero-fibrinous pleuritis. Liver: Hepatitis serosa , with intense fatty degeneration.

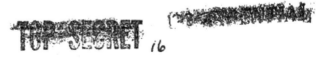

TOP SECRET 16 CONFIDENTIAL

([redacted] (

Some other parenchymatous organs :
Glomerulo-nephrosis with multiple round cell accumulation.
Pancreas with some parenhymatous degeneration and slight hemorrhages.
Intestine with some submucous congestion.
Meninges with congestion and slight hemorrhages.
Supra renal glands with some round cell accumulation and pamenshymatous degeneration.
Multiple pustulosis.

---

3. 152. 46 days. Lung: Moderate diffuse Alveolitis.

Liver: Hepatitis serosa , with intense fatty degeneration and some hemorrhages in central zone of acinuses.

Other parench ymatious organs.
Heart with some localised hemorrhages in subepicardial tissues.
Kidney (Glomeulo-nephrosis) with intense interstitial edema.
Meninges with slight hemorrhages.

No remarkable changes else.

Muscular tissues with abscess and traumatic wounds.

I case with continual propagation of nuscular abscesses and metastatic pustulosis in face.

I case with multiple pustulosis (in face, head, knee-joint, some cutaneous tissues and some periostal tissues, esp. at uper upper arm.).

I case with intense multiple, continual metastatic muscular abscesses and diffuse abscesses.

TOP SECRET 17

[redacted]

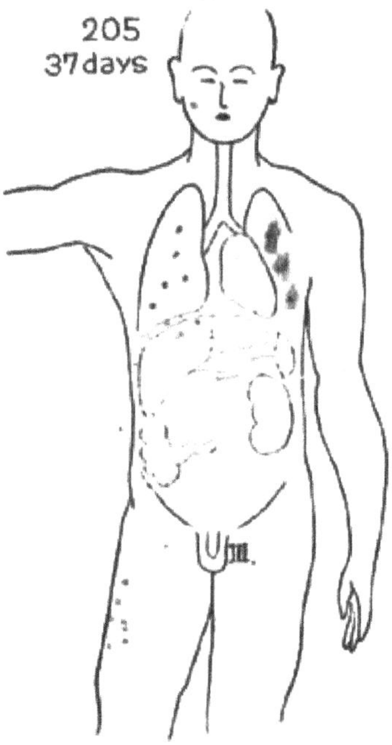

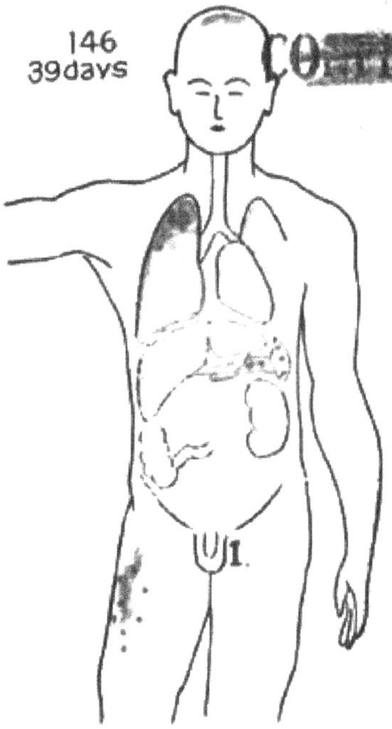

CONFIDENTIAL

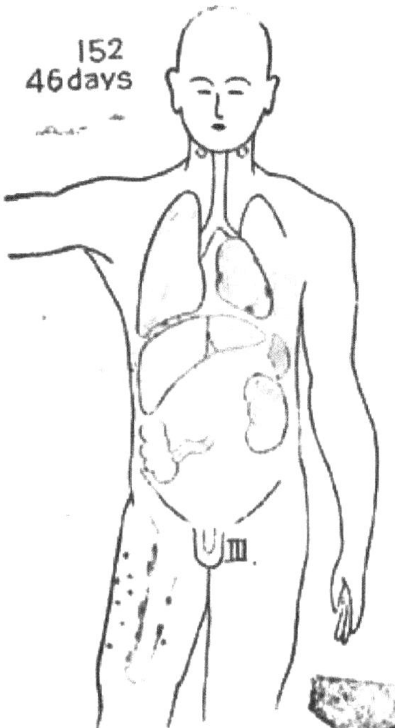

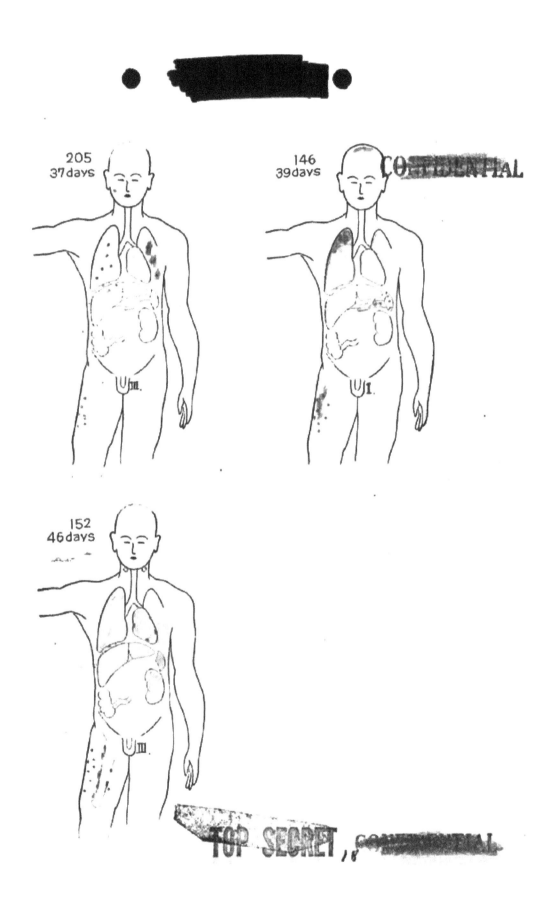

TOP SECRET

([redacted] (

[redacted]

(d). Rather chronic stage :

In this stage I have recognized many metastatic changes, due to general metastasis : in lung, lung, liver, intestines, lymph-nodes, kidney muscles and thyreoid and etc.

Case.	Days of course.	Main pathological changes.
I. 256.	45 days.	Lung: Metastatic Endoarteriitis necroticans. Multiple miliray glanders - Knots. Multifocal hemorrhagic-leucocytic, acinolobular pneumonia. Remarkable papillar increase of alveolar or bronchiolar epitheliums at the intercalary portion of lung. Liver: Hepatitis serosac with some hemorrhages in the central zone of acinuses. Other parenchymatous organs : Glomerulo-nephrosis with some polar edema and some proliferative changes at ^ -areas. Supra-renal glands with slight some hemorrhages. Pituitary body with slight hemorrhages in posterior lobe. Lymphadenitis caseosa, due to perhaps glanders-infection. Muscular absesses.
2. 727.	105 days.	Lung: Metastatic Endoarteriitis necroticans. Lobular pneumonia in intense hemorrhagic -exudative form. At some places with caverns formation. Liver; Hepatitis serósa , with multiple miliary glanders-knots. Some other parenchymatous organs : Small intestine with reactive hyperplasia of

TOP SECRET 19 [redacted]

[redacted]

CONFIDENTIAL

lymphatic nodulus(containing some giant cells, due to chronic course).
Kidney with moderate Glomerulo-nephrosis with some polar edema and interstitial edema.
Supra-renal glands with some hemorrhages and some round cell accumulations.
Thyreoids in follicular collapse.

No remarkable changes at cutaneous tissues, any where.

3.731. ca.3 months.

Lung : Acino-lobûlar pneumonia with intense perifocal reactions.

Liver: Hepatitis serosa with multiple miliary millet-corn large knots and remarkably increased Kupfer's cells.

Some other organs:
Heart with intense interstitial edema and some slight hemorrhages in subepicardial tissues.
Kidney with considerable Glomeulo-nephrosis, accompnaied with some polar edema and some remarkable round cell accumulation at peri-glomerular portions (glanders-knots).
Thyreoditix subacuta with some metastatic glanders-knots.
Supra-renal glands with intense degneration and some hemorrhages.
~~cutaneous tissues.~~
No remarkable changes at cutameous tissues.

In this stage, I have recognized many metastatic changes, due to general metastasis : in lung, liver, intestine. lymph-nod, spleen, kidney, muscles, or thyreoid.

These organic changes are classidfied into 2 types : a) exudative form and b) rather proliferative form.

[redacted] 20 CONFIDENTIAL

([redacted] (

a). Exudative form: [redacted]

The exudative changes, the main pathological reactions in subacute or subchronic stage, develops in this stage to the most intense.

For examples :

.) I have investigated multiple acino-lobular pneumonia with intense hemorrhagic exudative perifocal reactions in I case and furthermonr some cavern formation in I case. The perifocal tissues of these caverns are intensely exudative.

.) I have investigated in some other parenhymatous organs also intense exudative changes : slight hemorrhages and some exudation.

b) Rather proliferative form.

On the other hand, these exudative changes are accompanied in some cases with some proliferative reactions.

For examples :

.) I have recognised remarkable (papillar) hyperplasia of alveolar or bronchiolar epitheliums, especially at the intercalary portions of lung, due to rather chronic course.

[redacted]

TOP SECRET 21

[redacted]

[redacted]

•). In liver : also, hyperplasied some histiocytic cells (Kupfer's cells), as significant proliferative reactions.

Multiple miliary glanders-knots.	Exudative form. ↓ Rather proliferative form, accompanied with hyperplasia of Kupfer's cells.

[redacted]

TOP SECRET 22

([redacted] (

CONFIDENTIAL

•) In some other parenchymatous organs : these exudative changes are accompanied with some mesenchymal reactions.

Consequently , both (rexudative and proliferative) changes in every organs in every organs arē as following.

In shrt short, both exudative and proliferative changes in every organs are as following :

	Acute course.	Rather chronic course.
	Exudative changes.	Rather proliferative changes.
Heart.	Interstitial edema. Slight hemorrhages (in subendocardial tissues). Miliary glanders-knots(in subendocardial tissues).	Some meaenchymal reaction. Rheumatoid-knots formation. fresh exudative ----- (obsolete form).
Lung.	Metastatic Endoarteriitis. Miliary glanders knots in exudative form.	Miliary glanders knots in proliferative form.
	Multiple acinous or acino-lobular pneumonia with intense exudative perifocal reactions.	Some organising process. Papillar increase of alveolar epitheliums, as proliferative reaction.
	Reactive (exudative-fibrinous) Pleuritis.	
Liver.	Exudation In Disse's spaces. (Hepatitis serosa). Hemorrhages in central zone.	
	Miliary glanders-knots in exudative form.	Miliary glanders-knot in proliferative form. Accompanied with remarkable hyperplasia of Kupfer's cells.

TOP SECRET 23 CONFIDENTIAL

([redacted] (

[redacted]

Kidney.	Glomepulo-nephrosis. with somcalled polar edema. Some mesenchymal reaction Miliary glanders-knots formation.	Slight proliferative reactions at popar portions (so-called Δ-areas).
Intestine.	Submucous congestion. Miliary glanders-knots in exudative form.	Hyperplasia of reticulum cells. accompanied with some giant cells formation.
Supra-renal-gland.	Epinephritis serosa (with some edema). Hemorrhages. Some round cell accumulation.	-
Pancreas.	Degeneration. Perivascular edema and hemorrhages. Serous apoplexy of islands.	Some round cells accumulation.
Pituitary body.	Pituitaritis serosa. Slight hemorrhages in posterior lobe.	-
Meninges.	Some congestion and some slight hemorrhages.	
Muscles.	Abscess.	Hyperplasia of myoblasts, histiocytes and fbroblasts.
Spleen.	Angio-folliculitis haemorrhagico-exudativa. Fasciculitis hemorrhagico-exaudativa.	Hyperplasia of reticulo-endotheliar system.

[redacted] 24 [redacted]

[redacted]

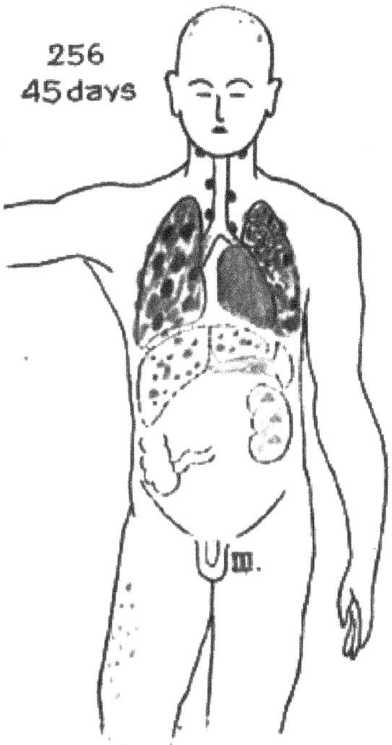

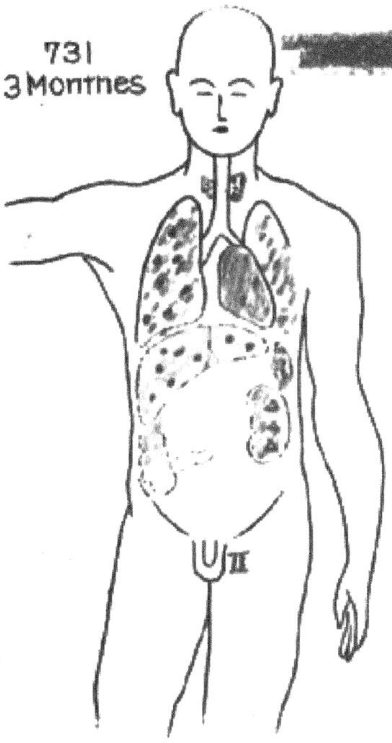

[redacted]

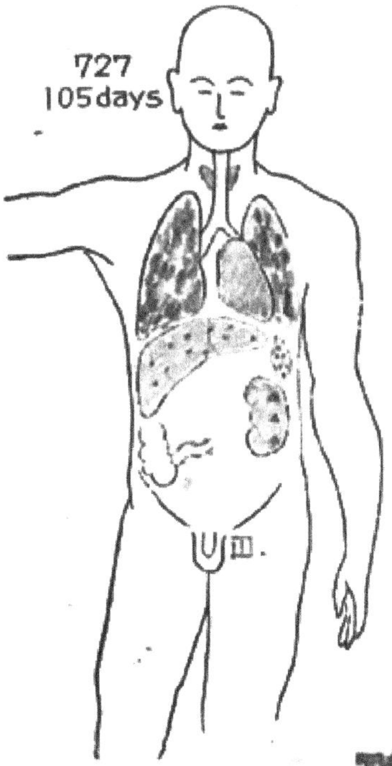

TOP SECRET 25 [redacted]

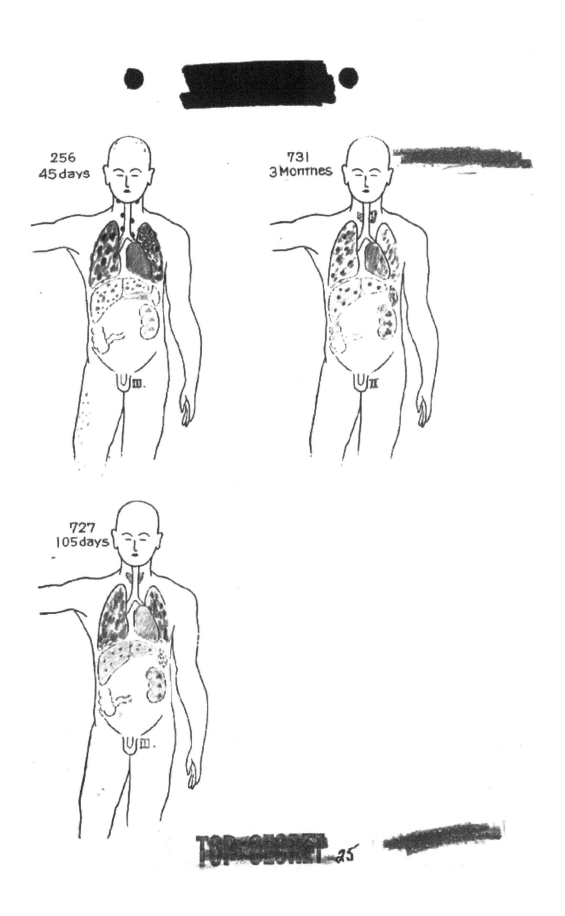

p.25 [redacted]

16.

---

ca. 25 years old.

Days of course. 13 days.

Infect.-mode. Per-cutanous infection.

Skin. Diffuse intense exudative-hemorrhagic-leucocytic infiltration in subcutaneous tissues.

Muscle. Multiple suall abscesses.

Heart. Degeneration myocardii calised hemorrhages in subepicardial tissues.

Aorta. No remarkable chnges.

Ronsil. Tonsillitis acuta.

Reactive hyperplasia of germinative entres with some locali-sed necrosis.

Intense congestion and some leucocytes-dissemination in submucous tissues.

Pharynx. No remarkable changes, macroscopically.

Bronchus. Bronchiolitis catarrhalis lavis.

Lung.

I. sup. Stasis et edema pulmonum.

Slight diffuse Alveolitis with some bacterial dissemination.

TOP SECRET 26

([redacted] (

[redacted]

I. inf.	Stasis et edema pulmonum.	Slight diffuse Alveolitis.
r. sup.	Stasis et edema pulmonum.	Slight diffuse Alveolitis.

Liver.	Hepatitis serosa (II). with multiple miliary necrosis.
Stomach.	No remarkable changes.
Small-Intestine.	Atrophic glandular cells.
Large- Intest.	Almost normal.

Kidney.	Slight Glomerulo-nephrosis. Nephrosis I., with some interstitial edema.

Spleen.	Angio-Folliculitis haemorrhagico-exsudativa. Slpeno-Fasciculitis exsudativa.
Lymph-node.	
Mesenterial.	No remarkable changes.
Peri-bronchial.	Medullary congestion.

Panceas.	Parenchymatous degeneration with hyaline-droplets formation in some acinuses. Vacuolar degeneration of island-cells.
Supra-renal.	Considerable atrophia and degeneration of parenchymatous cells. Considerable edema and slight round-cell -accumulation in cortical tissues.
Thyreoid.	In statical state with slight congestion.
Pituitary body.	missed.
Testicle.	missed.

Brain.	-

TOP SECRET 27 [redacted]

([redacted] (

50. [redacted]

Ca. 30 years old.

Days of course. 16 days.

Infect.-mode. Per-cutaneous infection.

Skin. Phlegmonous cell infiltration in subcutaneous tissues.

Muscle Multiple swall abscesses.

Heart. Degeneration myocardii. Slight mesenchymal reaction with some histiocytes, some Myocytes and some Monocytes.

Aorta. No remarkable changes.

Tonsil. Tonsillitis acuta (partialis).
Remarkable congestion in follicular tissues.
Some localised necrosis (with plenty of bacterial masses, plenty of leucocytes) in germinative centres.

Pharynx. Slight congestion.

Bronchus. Bronchitis catarrhalis with some hemorrhagic masses.

Lung.(r.and l) Severe diffuse Alveolitis.
Multiple miliary glanders-knots with severe hemorrhagic perifocal reactions.
Pleuritis hemorrhagico-fibrinosa auplex.

TOP SECRET . 38 [redacted]

([redacted] (

Liver.	Hepatitis serosa
Stomach.	Considerable congestion in mucous tissues.
Small-Intest.	Enteritis catarrhalis.
Large-Intest.	No remarkable changes.

	Slight Glomerulo-nephrosis.
Kidney.	Nephrosis I (at some places III), with some interstitial edema.

Spleen.	Angio-Folliculitis haemorrhagico-exsudativa.
	Spleno-Fasciculitis exsudativa.
Lymph-nods. peribronchial,	Considerable follicular congestion
Pancreas.	-.
Supra-renal.	-.
Thyreoid.	In slight activated state with slight congestion, slight edema and slight degeneration of parenchym. cells.
Pituitary body.	-
Testicles.	-

Brain.

TOP SECRET 29

([redacted] (

85. CONFIDENTIAL

ca 25 years old.

Days of course.	21 days.
Infect.-mode.	Per-cutaneous infoction.
Skin.	Remarkable diffuse congestion and perivascular vound cell-accumulation in subcutaneous tissues.
Muscle.	Some small abscesses.
Heart.	Degeneratio myocardii. Some rhoumatoids-knots, (due to glanders-infection.)
Aorta.	No remarkable changes.
Tonsil.	No remarkable changes, macroscopically.
Pharynx.	"
Bronchus.	"
Lung.(right and left)	Severe diffuse Alveolitis. Multiple miliary glanders-Rnots with intense exudative perifocal reactions.
Liver.	Hepatitis sweosa I-I^I, with intense fatty degeneration at some places and multiple miliary knots (lymphocytic).
Stomach.	No remarkable changes.
Small-Intestine.	Almost normal.
Large-Intestine	Slight catarrh.

TOP SECRET 30 CONFIDENTIAL

[redacted]

Kidney. Slight Glomerulo-nephrosis(glomeruli in degenerative form).
Nephrosis I (II or III at some places).
Interstitial edema and some calcinated masses in tubular spaces.

Spleen. Angio-Folliculitis exsudativa.
Spleno-Fasciculitis exsudativa.

Lymph-node.
Mesenterial. No remarkable changes.
Peribronchial. Lymphadenitis caseosa tuberculosa.

Pancreas. -
Supra-renal. -
Thyreoid. In slight activated state with slight degeneration of follicular epitheliums.
Pituitary body. -
Testicles. -

Brain. -

TOP SECRET 31

[redacted]

146. [redacted]

ca. 35 years old.

Days of course	39 dayes.
Infect.-mode.	Per-cutaneous infection.
Skin.	Multiple pea-large abscesses with hemorrhages.
Muscle.	Multiple millet-corn large or miliary abscesses, (leucocytic-hemorrhagic).
Heart.	Degeneratio myocardi.
Aorta.	No remarkable changes.
Tonsil.	No remarkable changes (macroscopically).
Bronchus.	Bronchiolitis catarrhalis gravis.
Pharynx.	No remarkable changes, macroscopically.
Lung.	
(I, sup).	Stasis et edema pulmonum. Considerable diffuse Alveolitis.
(I. inf).	Stasis et edema pulmonum. Considerable diffuse Alveolitis, with some bacterial dissemination.
(r, apex).	Lobular pneumonia. Catarrhalic-exudative, sometimes hemorrhagicloucocytic.
(r, median).	Pleuritis sero-fibrinosa with some pleural congestion. Stasis et edema pulmonum. Slight diffuse Alveolitis.
(r,inf).	Stasis et edema pulmonum.

[redacted] 32 [redacted]

([redacted] (

CONFIDENTIAL

Liver.	Hepatitis serosa, with intense fatty degeneration at some places.
Stomach.	Gastritis catarrhalis hypertrophicans.
Small-Intest.	Almost normal with slight congestion in submucous tissues.
Large-Intest.	Considerable edema in mucous tissues and considerable congestion in submuclus tissues.
Kidney.	Slight Glomerulo-nephrosis (glomeruli in degenerative form). Nephrosis I (II or III at some places), with multiple round-cell-infiltration and intense edema.

Spleen.	Angio-Folliculitis haemorrhagico-exsudative. Spleno-Fasciculitis exsudativa.
Lymph-nods.	
Peribronchial.	Considerable follicular congestion.

Pancreas.	Considerable congestion and slight hemorrhages. Parenchymatous degeneration and some hyaline degeneration of islan-cells.
Supra-renal.	Some parenchymatous degeneration with some perivascular round-cell-accumulation. Hyaline masses in medullary tissues.
Thyreoid.	-
Pituitary body.	-
Testicles	Atrophia testis ...

CONFIDENTIAL

TOP SECRET

33

[redacted]

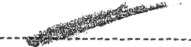

Brain.	Considerable congestion, slight diffuse hemorrhages and some round-cell-infiltration in meningeal tissues. Considerable congestion and some edema of brain.

[redacted]

34

([redacted] (

152. [redacted]

---

ca. 40 years old. ♂

Days of course. 46 days.

Infect.-mode. Per-cutaneous.

Skin.	Multiple pea-large abscesses in Str. reticularis.
Muscle.	Multiple small abscesses. (with periostitis purulenta)
Heart.	Degeneratio myocardii. Some localised hemorrhages in subepicardial tissues. Some Myocytes.
Aorta.	No remarkable changes.
Tonsil.	Reactive hypertrophia with some reactive hyperplasia of germinative centres.
Pharynx.	No remarkable changes, macrossopically.
Bronchus.	No remarkable changes.
Lung.	Edema et stasis pulmonum.
(right and left)	Considerable diffuse Alveolitis.
Liver.	Hepatitis serosa I-II. with intense fatty degeneration at some places and some hemorrhages in central zone of acinuses. [redacted]
Stomach.	Almost normal with some atrophic glandular cells.

[redacted] 35

([redacted] (

[redacted]

Small-Intestine.	Enteritis catarrhalis levis.
Large-intestine.	Almost normal with slight hyperplasia of lymphatic follicles.

Kidney.	Slight or considerable Glomerulo-nephrosis (glomeruli in degenerative form). Nephrosis I (at some places II[I]), with intense interstitial edema.

Spleen.	Angio-Folliculitis exsudativa. Spleno-Fasciculitis exsudativa.
Lymph-node.	No remarkable changes, macroscopically.

Pancreas.	-
Supra-renal.	Atrophia and some parenchymatous degeneration.
Thyreoid.	-
Pituitary body.	Considerable congestion and considerable degeneration of parenchymatous cells (esp. basophilic cells).
Testicle.	Atrophia testis II.

Brain.	Meningeal congestion and slight hemorrhages. Considerable congestion in brain.

[redacted]

[redacted] 36

([redacted] (

167. [redacted]

ca 40 years old. ♂

Days of course. 15 days.

Infect-mode. Per-cutaneous infection.

Skin. Multiple pea-large abscesses in Str. subpapillaris.

Muscle. Multiple small abscesses.
(with joint abscesses).

Heart. Degeneratio myocardii levis. Some localised hemorrhages in subepidar~~k~~dial tssues. Some myocytes.

Aorta. No remarkable changes.

Tonsil. No remarkable changes (macroscopically).

Bronchus. Bronchitis catarrhalis levis.

Lung. (l,inf) Slight diffuse Alveolitis.

Pleuritis haemorrhagico-fibrinosa.

(r). Hemorrhagic-pneumonia (acino-lobular),organised slightly with remarkable hyperplasied alveolar epitheliums.

(l. sup). Endoarteriitis et Endoarteriolitis necroticans with multiple acino-lobular pneumonia.

Pleuritis fibrosa and pleural congestion.

[redacted]

TOP SECRET 37

[redacted]

Liver.	Hepatitis serosa II. with some intense fatty degeneration.
Stomach.	Gastritis catarrhalis hyprtrophicans. some considerable congestion.
Small-Intestine	Enteritis catarrhalis.
Hargo-Intestine.	Almost normal.

Kidney.	Considerable Glomerulo-nephrosis (some glomeruli in degenerative form) with considerable polar edema. Nephrosis I, with intese interstitial edema and some round cell accumulation.

Spleen.	Angio-Folliculitis exsudativa; Spleno-Fasciculitis haemorrhagico-exsudativa.
Lymph-node. (mesenterial)	Slight catarrh.

Pancreas:	Parenchymatous degeneration and some hyaline degeneration or hyaline-droplets formation in some acinuses.
Supra-renal.	Considerable congestion and some hemorrhages in cortical tissues and intense round cell accumulation.
Thyreoid.	Struma colloides proliferans.
Pituitary body.	Slight congestion and considerable edema. Considerable degeneration of parenchymatous cells (esp. basophilic cells).
Teticle.	Atrophia testis III.

[redacted] 38

([redacted]. (

[redacted]

Brain. Considerable congestion, some hemorrhages and slight perivascular round cell infiltration in meninges. Considerable congestion of brain.

[redacted]

[redacted] 39

([redacted] (

176.

[redacted]

---

ca 38 years old.

Days of course.	12 days.
Infect.-mode.	Per-nasal infection ?
Skin.	No remarkable changes.
Muscle.	No remarkable changes.
Heart.	Parenchymatous degeneration. Some localised hemorrhages in epicardial tissues and some myocytes.
Aorta-	No remarkable changes.
Tonsil.	No remarkable changes (macroscopically).
Pharynx.	No remarkable changes (macroscopically).
Bronchns.	Bronchitis catarrhalis.
Lung. (r,l).	Slight pulmonal congestion (Slight diffuse Alveolitis).
Liver.	Hepatisis sarosa I. with intense fatty degeneration.
Stomach.	Intense congestion and some eosinophilic leucocytes in capillaries.
Small-Intestine.	Almost normal.
Large-Intestine.	Almost normal.

[redacted]

[redacted]- 40

[redacted]

[redacted]

Kidney.	Considerable Glomerulo-nephrosis (some glomeruli in degenerative form).
	Nephrosis I, with intense edema and some round cell accumulation.
Prostata.	Some round cell infilatation with some corpora amylaceac.

Spleen.	Missed.
Lymph-node.	No remarkabe changes (macroscopically).
Pancreas.	Considerable congestion and some hamorrhages .
	Hyaline-degeneration or some hyaline droplets formation in some acinuses.
	Intense congestion and some parenchyamatous degeneration of island-cells.
Supra-renal.	Slight parenchymatous degeneration and some hypertrophic cell-groups in cortical titssues.
Thyreoid.	In slight activated state with slight congestion slight hyperplasia of follicular epitheliums.
Pituitary body.	-
Testicle.	Atrophia testis III.

Brain.	-

[redacted]

[redacted] 41

([redacted] (

L78. [redacted]

Days of course. 10 days.

Infect.-mode. Per-nasal infection?

Skin. No remarkable changes, according to autopsy-records.

Muscle. No remarkable changes, according to autopsy-records.

Heart. Degeneratio myocardii., with intense congestion and some histiocytes around capillaries.

Aorta. No remarkable changes (macroscopically).

Tonsil. No remarkable changes (macroscopically).

Pharynx. Intense edema in submucous tissues and hyalinisation of T.muscularis (intense edema).

Bronchus. Bronchitis catarrhalis.

Lung. Slight pulmoanl congesti on. (slight daffuse Alveolitis).

Liver. Hepatisis serosa I-II, with some hemorrhages in central zone.

Stomach. No remarkable changes (macroscopically).

Small-Intestine. No remarkable changes (macroscopically).

Large-Intestine. Remarkable atrophia of glandular cells with considerable congestion in submucous tissues.

Kidney. Slight Glomerulo-nephrosis (some glomeruli in degenerative form) and Nephrosis I (some [redacted]

[redacted] 42

([redacted] (

with vacuolar degeneration). [redacted]
Considerable interstitial edema with some localised bionecrotic places.

Spleen.	Angio-Folliculitis haemorrhagico exsudativa. Spleno-Fasciculitis haemorrhagico exsudativa.
Lymph-node.	No remarkable changes.

Pancreas.	Congestion and considerable parenchymatous degeneration. Atrophic island-cells.
Supra-renal.	Some parenchymatous degeneration with some hemorrhages in Z. glomerulosa.
Thyreoid.	Follicular collapse.
Pituitary body.	-
Testicle.	-

Brain.	Considerable congestion and some round cell accumulation in meninges. Considerable congestion of brain.

[redacted]

[redacted] 43

[redacted]

[redacted]

I80.

ca 28 years old.

Days of course.	12 days.
Infest.-mode.	Per-cutaneous.
Skin.	Phlegmons in cutaneous or subcutaneous tissues.
Muscle.	Multiple milliary or millet-corn large abscesses (hemorrhagic-loucocytic).
Heart.	Slight parenchymatous degeneration, venous congestion and some Myocytes.
Aorta.	No remarkable changes (macroscopically).
Tonsil.	No remarkable changes (macroscopically).
Pharynx.	Slight round cell accumulation.
Bronchus.	No significant changes.
Lung.	Considerable pulmonal congestion and edema.
(r, and l.).	Bacterial accumulation at some places and plerural congestion.
Liver.	Hepatisis serosa II-III. with miliary multiple necrosis (lymphocytes-accumulation).
Stomach.	Slight congestion and considerable catarrh.
Small-Intest.	Almost normal.
Large-Intest.	Almost normal (macroscopically).

[redacted]

[redacted] 44

([redacted] (

[redacted]

Kidney. Slight Glomerulo-nephrosis (some glomeruli in degenerative form) and Nephrosis I.

Spleen. Angio-Folliculits exsndativa.
Spleno-Fasciculitis exsndativa.

Lynph-node. No remarkable changes (macroscopically).

Pancreas. Considerable congestion and edma.
Some parenchymatous degeneration.

Supra-renal. Atrophia and some degeneration of cortical cells.
Considerable edema and some round cell accumulation.

Thyreoid. Subacute Thyreoiditis with some congestion, hemorrhages, some round cell accumulation and some parenchymatous degeneration.

Pituitary body. Considerable congestion and edema.
Slight cloudy degeneration of parenchym. cells (esp. basophilic cells).

Testicle.. -

Brains -

[redacted]

[redacted] 45

([redacted] (

L90 CONFIDENTIAL

ca. 30 years old.

Days of course.	IO days.
Infect.-mode.	Per-cutaneous infection.

Skin.	Multiple perivascular leucocytes-accumulation in subcutaneous tissues and some small abscesses formation.
Muscle.	Multiple small abscesses.

Hoart.	Intense parenchymatous degeneration and intense atrophia. Intense edema and some histicocytes-accumulation.
Aorta.	No remarkable changes (macroscopicaly).

Tonsil.	Almost normal with slight superficial ulcers.
Pharynx.	Edema and some round celi accumulation.
Bronchus.	No significant changes. Intensne congestion.
Lung.	Slight diffuse Alveolitis, with slight hyperplasia of alveolar eptheliums.

Liver.	Hepatitis serosa II. with multiple submiliary lymphocytic accumulation in acinuses.
Stomach.	Considerable catarrh and slight hyperplasia of lymphatic nodulus.
Small-Intest.	Enteritis catarrhalis levis.

46

([redacted] (

Large-Intest.	Almost normal. [redacted]

Kidney.	Slight Glomerulo-nephrosis (some glomeurli in degenerative form) and Nephrosis I, with some interstitial edema and some round cell acumulation.
Seminal vesicles.	No remarkable changes

Spleen.	Angio-folliculitis haemorrhagico-exsudativa. Spleno-Fascilulitis. exsudativa.
Lymph-node.	No remarkable changes macroscopically.

Pancreas.	Venous congestion, considerable atrophia and degeneration.
Supra-renal.	Parenchymatous degeneration, with some hemorrhages in Z. reticularis. Hyaline-droplets formation in medullary tissues.
Thyreoid.	In statsicla state.
Pituitary body.	-
Testicle.	Atrophia testis II.

Brain.	Considerable congestion, slight nemorrhages and some porivascular round cell accumulation in meninges.

[redacted]

[redacted] 47

[redacted]

[redacted]

193.

---

ca. 35 years old.

Days of course. 25 days.

Infect.-mode. Per-cutaneoud infection.

Skin. Considerable diffuse congestion and perivascular lymphocytes-accumulation in subcutaneons tissues.

Muscle. Some swall abscesses.

Hoart. Intense atrophia and degeneration of parenchym.cells. Plenty of Myocytes.

Aorta. No remarkable changes (macroscopically).

Tonsil. Tonsilitis simplex. Reactive hyperplasia of lymphatic follicles.

Pharynx. Some round cell infiltration in submucous tissues.

Bronchus. No significnt changes.

Lung. (r). Endoarteriitis and Endoarteriolis necroticans.
Sumiliary glanders-knots in catchment areas.
Intense pulmonal edema and pleural congestion.

(l). Considerable diffuse Alveolitis.
Edema et stasis pulmonum and some bacterial dissemination.
Considerable pøleural congestion.

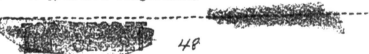

[redacted]

[redacted] 48

([redacted] (

[redacted]

Liver.	Hepatitis serosa (I). with multiple submiliary necrosis , (In proliferative form).
Stomach.,	Slight catarrh.
Small-Intest.	Almost normal.
Large-Intest.	Almost normal, macroscopically.

Kidney.	Considerable Glomerulo-nephrosis (some glomeruli in degenerative form) with some polar edema. Nephrosis I, (some places III), with intense interstitial edema.
Spleen.	Angio-Folliculitis haemorrhagico exsudativa Spleno-Fasciculitis. haemorrhagico-exsudativa.
Lymph-node.	No remarkable changes.

Pancreas.	-
Supra-renal.	-
Thyreoid.	Follicular collapse.
Pituitary body.	-
Testicle.	Atrophia testis III.

Brain.	-

[redacted]

TOP SECRET 49

[redacted]

205. [redacted]

Ca. 23 Years old ♂.

Days of course.	37 days.
Infect,-mode.	Per-cutaneous infection.

Skin.	Multiple pea-large absccsses in subcutaneous tissues.
Muscle.	Multiple millet-cornlarge or miliary abscesses.

Heart.	Degeneratio myocardii levis and some Myocytes.
Aorta.	No remarkable changes, macroscopically.

Ionsil.	No remarkable changes, masroscopically.
Pharynx.	No remarkable changes, macroscopically.
Bronchus.	No significant changes.
Lung. (r).	Endoarteriolitis necroticans.
	Multiple supermiliary glanders-knots (without remarkable perifocal changes).
	Slight pleural congestion.
(l).	Endoarteriolitis necroticans.
	Multiple supermiliary glanders-knots with intense hemorrhagic perifocal reactions.
	Stasis et edema pulm.

Liver	Hepatitis serosa I. with multiple submiliary lymphocytic acculumation. [redacted]

TOP SECRET 50

[redacted]

CONFIDENTIAL

Small-Intestine.	Enteritis catarrhalis levis.
Large-Intestine.	Slight catarrh.

Kidney:	Considerable Glomeulo-nephrosis (glomeruli in considerable congestion).
	Nephrosis I, with considerable interstitial edema and considerable round cell infiltration.

Spleen.	Missed.
Lymph-node.	No remarkable changes.

Pancreas.	Considerable congestion and some edema. Some lymphocytes accumulation at perivascular portions.
	Considerable parenchymatous degeneration.
Supra-renal.	Intense parenchyatous degneration with some round cell accumulation in cortical tissues.
	Some Places with hypertrophic cell groups.
	Some round cell acumulatuion in medullary tissues.
Thyreoid.	
Pituitary body.	
Testicle.	Atrophia testis III.

Brain.	

[redacted] 51 CONFIDENTIAL

([redacted] (

207. [redacted]

---

ca 30 years old. ♂

Days of course	18 days.
Infect.-mode.	Per-cutaneous infection.

Skin.	Considerable diffuse congestion and perivascular lymphocytes-accumulation in subcutaneous tissues.
Muscles.	Some small abscesses.

Heart.	Degeneratio myocardii and intense interstitial edema.
Aorta.	No remarkable changes, macroscopically.

Tonsil.	No remarkable changes, macroscopically.
Pharynx.	No remarkable changes, macroscopically.
Bronchus.	No significant changes.
Lung. (r).	Endoarteriolitis necrosticans. Subpleural glanders-knots and multiple glanders-knots, with slight hemorrhagic perifocal reactions. Some acino-lobular pneumonia.
(l).	Subpleural supermiliary glanders-knots, with slight perifocal hyperemia. No remarkable changes in other general pulmonal tissues.

[redacted] [redacted]

52

([redacted] (

[redacted]

Liver.	Hepatitis serosa II. with some hemorrhages in central zone of acinuses.
Stomach.	No remarkable changes, macroscopically.
Small-Intestine.	Almost normal with slight congestion.
Large-Intestine.	Almost normal.
Kidney.	Slight Glomerulo-nephrosis (some glomeruli in degenerative form). Nephrosis I with considerable interstitial edema.
Spleen.	Missed.
Lymph.-node.	No remarkable changes.
Pancreas.	-
Supra-remal.	-
Thyreoid.	Follicular collapse.
Pituitary body.	-
Testicle.	Atrophia testis III.
Brian.	No significant changes.

[redacted]

[redacted] 53

([redacted] (

221. [redacted]

Yound man.

Days of course.	24 days.
Infect.-mode.	Per-cutaneous infection.
Skin.	Multiple intense perivascular leucocytes-emigration. Intense diffuse homorrhages in subcutsneous tissues.
Muscle.	Some small abscesses.
Heart.	Degenratio et atrophia myocardii levis. intense interstitial edema.
Aorta.	No remarkable changes.
Tonsil.	No remarkable changes.
Pharynx.	No remarkable changes.
Bronchus.	Broncho-Bronchiolitis catarrhalis levis.
Lung. (r).	Pleuro-pnoumonia. Lobular pneumonia et Pleuritis ero-fibrinosa.
(l).	Acinouas or acino-lobular pneumonia, with severe exudative-hemorrhagic perifocal reactions.
(l).	Acinous or acino-lobular pneumonia with multiple glanders-knots.

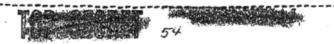

[redacted] 54 [redacted]

([redacted] (

Liver.m	Hepatitis serosa I. with multiple miliary necrosis (lymphocytic histiocytic). Some lymphocytes-accumulation in Glissons capsules.
Stomach.	Slight catarrh and slight congestion, slight hyperplasia of lymphatic nodulus.
Small-Intestine.	Enteritis catarrhalis with reactive hyperplaasia of germinative centres of lymphatic nodulus.
Large-Intestine.	Atrophic mucous tissues. Intense congestion in submucous tissues.
Kidney.	Slight Glomerulo-nephrosis (some glomeruli in degenerative form). Nephrosis I.

Spleen.	Angio-Folliculitis haemorrhagico-exsudativa. m Spleno-Fascilcuits haemorrhagico-exsudativa.
Lymph. node. (Peribronchial).	Slight catarrh. Pericapsular slight hemorrhages. Catarrh and considerable congestion (with some eoninophilic leucocytes in capillaries) in follicular tissues.

Pancreas.	Congestion. Degeneration and atrophia of parenchymatous cells. Intense congestion and intense peripolar edema of island.
Supra-renal.	Considerable congestion and some round cell accumulation.

TOP SECRET CONFIDENTIAL

([redacted] (

[redacted]

	Considerable parenchymatous degeneration.
Thyreoid.	Subacute disfiguring of thyreoids. Some places with disfiguring. Some places with hyperfunction, due to Basedow's disese.
Pituitary body.	Considerable congestion with some leucocytes in capillaies. Slight parenchymatous degeneration.
Testicle.	Atrophia testis III.
Brain.	Some cogestion, slight round cell accumulation and slight hemorrhages in meninges.
Urinary bladder.	No remarkable changes.

[redacted]

[redacted] 56

([redacted] (

222. [redacted]

ca. 25 years old. 1

Days of course.	10 days.
Infect-mode.	Per-cutaneous infection.
Skin.	Diffuse intense sweous-exudative-hemorrhagic -leucocytic infiltration in subcutaneous tiss-nes.
Muscle.	Multiple small abscesses.
Heart.	Degeneratio myocardii.
Aorta.	No remarkable changes, macroscopically.
Tonsil.	No remarkable changes, macroscopically.
Pharynx.	No remarkable changes, macroscopically.
Bronchus.	No significant changes.
Lung.(r and l).	Stasis pulmonum levis.
Liver.	Hepatitis serosa I - II .
Stomach.	Almost normal, macroscopically.
Small-Intestine	Almost normal, macroscopically.
Large-inbestine	Atoohic glandular cells. Remarkable congestion in submucous tissues.

[redacted] [redacted]

57

([redacted] (

[redacted]

Kidney. Considerable Glomeulo-nephrosis (some glomeruli in acute exudation and congestion), with some polar changes. Nephrosis I with consdierable interstitial edema.

Spleen. Angio-folliculitis haemorrhagico-exsudativa-
Spleno-Fascilulitis haemorrhagico-exsudativa.

lymph-node. No remarkable changes, macroscopically.

Pancreas. C/loudy swelling or vacuolar degeneration.
Considerable congestion and slight hemorrhages.

Aupra-renal. Considerable edema in cortical tissues.
Some round cell infiltration in medullary tissuey.
Some hypertorphic cells-groups.

Thyreoid. -

Pituitary body. Considerable congestion and slight edema in subendotheliar layers of acinuses.
Slight degeneration of parenchymatous cells.
Slight congestion and some hemorrhages in posterior lobe.

Testicle. Atrophia testis III.

Spermatic cord. Considerable congestion, slight hemorrhages and slight round cell infiltration.

Brain. -

[redacted] [redacted]

58

[redacted]

224.

	33 years old.
Days of conrse.	4 days.
Infect.-mode.	Per-cutaneous infection.
Skin.	Small spotted wound.Diffuse intense serous-exsudative-hemorrhagic-leucocytic infiltrotion in subcutaneous tissues.
Muscle.	Phlegmonous infiltration of wandering cells.
Heart.	Atrophia et degeneratio myocardii. Intense edema.
Aorta.	No remarkable changes.
Tonsil.	No remarkable changes,macroscopically.
Pharynx.	No remarkable changes, macroscopically.
Bronchus.......	No significant changes.
Lung.	Stasis et edema pulmonum levis.
(r, l)	Slight diffuse Alveolitis.
Liver.	Hepatitis serosa III-IV.
Stomach.	Considerable congestion in muocus tissues.
Small-Intest.	No remarkable changes, macroscopically,
Large-Intest.	Remarkable atrophia of glandular cells.

[redacted] 59

[redacted]

[redacted]AL

Kidney.	Considerable Glomerulo-nephrosis 6 some glomeruli in degenerative form).
	Nephrosis I.
Spleen	Angio-Bolliculitis haemorrhagico-exsudativa.
	Spleno-Fascilcuitis. haemorrhagico-exsudativa.
Lymph-node.	No remarkable changes. macroscopically.
Pancreas.	Considerable degeneration and atrophia of parenchyma-tous cells. Considerable congestion.
	Considerable congestion and atrophia of island-cells.
Supra-renal.	Atrophia, degeneration and dissociation of parenchym-atous cells.
	Slight hemorrhages, intense edema and some round cell accumulation in cortical tissues.
Thyreoid.	In slight activated state (
	Slight congestion, edema and slight degeneration of follicular epitheliums.
Pituitary body.	Considerable congestion and some edema in subendo theliar layers of acinuses.
	Cloudy swelling of parenchymatous cells (esp. basophi-lic cells).
Testicle.	Atrophia testis III.
Brain.	

CONFIDENTIAL

TOP SECRET

60

([redacted] (

229. [redacted]

ca 32. years old.

Days of course. 9 days.

Infect.-mode. Per-cutaneous infection.

Skin. No remarkable changes.

Muscle. No remarkable changes.

Heart. Atrobia and degeneratio myocardii, with intense edema. Some Myocytes.

Aorta. No remarkable changes.

Tonsil. No remarkable changes, macroscopically.

Pharynx. No remarkable changes, macrpscopically.

Bronchus. Exudative-hemorrhagic inflammation of bronchus and peri-bronchial tissues.

Lung.(r). Multiple acinous or acino-lobular pneumonia, with seves exudative perifocal changes.

(l,inf). Multiple acino-lobular pneumonia with glanders-knots.

Pleuritis sero-fibrinosa.

(l,sup). Stasis et edema pulmonum.

Subpleural congestion.

Liver. Hepatitis serosa I.

Stomach. Considerable congestion with slight hemorrhages in

[redacted] [redacted]

61

([redacted] (

	mucous tissues.
Small-Intestine.	Almost normal.
Large-Intestine.	Almost normal.

CONFIDENTIAL

Kidney.	Considerable Glomerulo-nephrosis with some polar changs. Nephrosis I (or II ar some places), with considerable interstitial edema.
Spleen.	Angio-Folliculitis haemorrhagico-exsudativa. et necroticans . Spleno-Fasciculitis haemorrhagico-exsudativa et necroticans.
Lymph-node.	Missed. (Not described in autopsy-records).

Pancreas.	-
Supr-renal.	Parenchymatous dgeneration. Some round cell accumulation and submiliary lymphocytic accumulation at some places.
Thyreoid.	-
Pituitary. body.	Intense congestion and subendothelial edema. Considerable parenchymatous degeneration.
Testicle.	Atrophia testis III.

Brain.	No remarkable changes.

CONFIDENTIAL

TOP SECRET

62

([redacted] (

254. [redacted]

ca. 27 years old.

Days of course. 20 days.

Infect.-mode. Per-cutaneous infection.

Skin.	Multiple millet-corn large abscess or phlegmonous cell infiltration.
Muscle.	Multiple poppy seed-large abscess.

Heart.	Degeneratio et atorophia myocardii.
	Intense interstitial edema and slight Myocytes.
Aorta.	No remarkable changes, macroscopically.

Tonsil.	No remarkable changes, macroscopically.
Pharynx.	No remarkable changes, macroscopically.
Bronchus.	No significant changes.
Lung. (r,sup.).	Multiple miliary glanders-knots with slight proliferat. perifocal changes.
(1).	Acino-lobular hemorrhagic-leucocytic pneumonia with intense exudative-hemorrhagic perifocal reactions and multiple supermiliary glanders-knots.
	Pleurtistis haemorrhagica.
	Remarkable perivascular round cell accumulation.
(r, inf.).	Acino-lobular pneumonia.
	Subpleural glanders-knots. [redacted]

[redacted] 63

[redacted]

Liver. Hepatitis serosa with some [redacted] degnerat. at some places and millet-corn large glanders-Knots in proliferative form.

Stomach. Gastirtis catarrhalis hypertrophicans.

Small-Intestine. Atrophic glandular cells.
Some submiliary glanders-knots (with epitheloid cells, in proliferative form) in subserous tissues.

Large-Intestine. Colitis catarrhalis levis.

Spleen. Angio-folliculitis haemorrhagico-exsudativa.
Spleno-fasciculitis exsudativa.

Lymph-node.Multiple submiliary caseous places in germinative (Peribronchial) centres, (due to glanders-infection?).
Slight catarrh of sinus.

Kidney. Considerable Glomerulo-nephrosis (glomeruli in exudative form), with eonsiderable polar edema.
Nephrosis I, with considerable interstitial edema and some round cell infiltration.

Pancreas. Congestion. Atrophia and degeneration of parenchymatous cells.
Serous apoplexie of islands.

Supra-renal.
Atrophia and some parenchymatous degeneration of cortical tissues (esp. in Z. glomeruloca).
Considerable eedma [redacted]rhages. [redacted]

[redacted] 64

([redacted] (

Thyreoid. -

[redacted]

Pituitary body. -

Testicle. Atrophia III.

Brain. No remarkable changes.

[redacted]

[redacted] 105

([redacted] (

856. [redacted]

25 years sld.

Days of course 45 days.

Infect.-mode. Per-cutaneous infection.

Skin. Multiple small abscesses with hemorrhages.

Muscle. Multiple super-miliary or mollet-corn large abscesses. (leucocytio-hemorrhagic).

Heart. Degeneratio myocardii and Cicatrix myocardii.
Some Myocytes.

Aotta. No remarkable changes, macroscopically.

Tonsil. Tonsillitis acuta levis.
Remarkable edematous swelling, some leucocytes-accumulation, some localised necrosis and intense reduction of follicular tussues.
Considerable congestion and slight diffuse hemorrhages in submucous tissues.

Pharynx. No remarkable changes, macroscopically.

Bronchus. Bronchiolitis catarrhalis, with some decayed masses as bronchiolar contents.

Lung.
1). Multiple miliry glanders-knots in hemorrhagic-leucocytic form, with severe exudative peifocal changes.

2). Multiple lobulo-acinous pneumonia.
Pleuritis hemorrhagico-exsudativa.

3). Multiple Endoarteriolitis necroticans.
Multiple acino-lobular pneumonia in hemorrhagic-exudative form. [redacted]

[redacted] 66

[redacted]

[redacted]

4). Endoarteriolitis necroticans.

Acinous hemorrhagic pneumonia.

5). Endoarteriolitis necroticans.
Subpleural acino-lobular pneumonia, with some exudative-hemorrhagic perifocal reactions.
Papillar increase of bronchiolar and alveolar epitheliums at intercalary portion of lung.

6). Papillar increase of alveolar or bronchiolar epitheliums at intercalary portion of lung.

Liver.	Hepatitis serosa II-III. with some hemorrhages in central zone of acinuses and multiple miliary necrosis (leucocytic-lymphocytic).
Stomach.	Slight catarrh.
Small-Intestine.	No remarkable changes, macroscopically.
Large-Intestine.	No remarkable changes, macroscopically.
Kidney.	Considerable Glomerulo-nephrosis (some glomeruli in rather proliferative form), with some polar edema. Considerable hyperplasia of adventitial cells of v. afferens. Nephrosis I.

[redacted]

[redacted] 67

[redacted]

--[redacted]--------

Spleen.	missed.
Lymph-node.	Mesenterial : No remarkable changes, with somen medulary congestion.
	Peribronchial : Lymphadenitis caseosa, due to Glanders -infection.
	Multiple submiliary caseous plalces in germinative centres.
	Considerable congestion and slight hemorrhages in follicular tissues.

Pancreas.	Considerable parenchymatous degeneration.
	Considerable congestion and slight perivascular round cell accumulation.
	Cloudy swelling or hyaline degeneration of island cells.
Supra-renal.	Atrophia and slight parenchymatous degeneration.
	Intense hemorrhages in cortical tissues and some round cell accumulation.
Thyreoid.	In statical state.
Pituitary body.	Intense congestion (with some leucocytes in capillaries), slight increase of capillary endothel-sells, and parenchmatous degeneration.
	Slight congestion and slight hemorrhages in posterior lobe.
Testicle.	Atrophia testis III.

---[redacted]--------

Brain. -

[redacted]

68

([redacted])

727.

25 years old. [redacted]

Days of course. ca. 105 days.

Infest.-mode. Per-cutaneous infection?

Skin. Hyperkeratosis.

Muscles. No remarkable changes.

Heart. Degeneratio mycardii. Some leucocytes in capillaries.

Aorta. No remarkable changes, macroscopically.

Tonsil. No remarkable changes, macroscopically.

Pharynx. No remarkable changes, macroscopically.

Bronchs. Bronchilotis catarrhalis.

Lung. (r). Lobular pneumonia with severe exsudative -hemorrhagic perifocal changes.

(l). Lobulo-acinous pneumonia (hemorrhagic-exudative), with caseoud necrotic focus and cavern-formations at some places.

Liver. Hepatitis serosa II. with multiple miliary necrosis (lymphocytes-accumuoation).

Stomach. Slight catarrh.

Small-Intestine. Reactive hyperplasia of lymphatic nodulus. Germinative centres with some increased histiocytes and some giant cells, due to chronic [redacted]

[redacted] 69

([redacted] (

Large-Intestine.	No remarkable changes, macroscopically.

[redacted]

Spleen.	Angio-Folliculitis haemorrhagico-exsudativa. Spleno-Fasciculitis exsudativa et necroticans.
Lymph-node.	No remarkable changes, macroscopically.
Kidney.	Considerable Glomerulo-nephrosis (glomeruli mainly in exudative form), with considerable polar edema. Nephrosis I (III at some places) with interstitial edema.
Pancreas.	-
Supra-renal.	Intense atrophia and dissociation. Intense edema and intense round cell accumulation in cortical tissues.
Thyreoid.	Subacute disfiguring with slight congestion and hyalinous degeneration of interstitium. Considerable degeneration of follicular epitheliums.
Pituitary-body.	Considerable congestion and subendothelial edema. Parenchymatous degeneration. (slight).
Testicle.	Atrophia testis III.
Brain.	No remarkable changes.

[redacted]

[redacted]

70

([redacted] (

731.

	ca 25 years old. [redacted]
Days of course.	ca 3 months.
Infect-mode.	Per-cutaneous infection?
Skin.	No remarkable changes.
Muscle.	No remarkable changes.
Heart.	Intense degeneration and trophia. Intense interstitial edema, slight hemorrhages in myocardium.
Aorta.	No remarkable changes, macroscopically.
Tonsil.	No remarkable changes, macroscopically.
Pharynx.	No remarkable changes, macroscopically.
Bronchus.	Bronchiolitis catarrhalis.
Lung. (r).	Miliary necrosis with intense hemorrhagic perifaocal changes.
Lung. (l).	Acino-lobular, leucocytic pneumonia with intense perifocal reactions.
Liver.	Hepatitis serosa III - IV, with remarkably increased Kupfer's cells and multiple millet-corn large glanders-knots.
Stomach.	No remarkable changes, amcroscopically.

[redacted] [redacted]

71

([redacted] (

Small-Infestine.	Colitis catarrhalis. [redacted]
Spleen.	Angio-Folliculitis haemorrhagico-exsudativa et necroticans. Spleno-Fasciculitis exsudativa et necroticans.
Lymph-node.	No remarkable changes, macroscopically.
Kidney.	Considerable Glomerulo-nephrosis (glomeruli mainly in rather degenerative form), with some polar changes. Some remarkable round cell accumulation at peri-glomerular tissues. Nephrosis I, with intase interstitial edema.
Pancreas.	-
Suprarenal.	Intense dissociation and atrophia and some degeneration of parenchymatous cells. Some localised hemorrhages.
Thyreoid.	Subacute Thyreoiditis with multiple glanders-knots.
Pituitary body.	Considerabe congestion, slight increase of capillary endothel-cells. Slight degeneration of parenchymatous cells (esp. basophilic cells).
Testicle.	Atrophia testis II.
Brain.	No remarkable changes, macrosscopically. [redacted]

[redacted]

72

[redacted]

[redacted]

Heart

[redacted]

[redacted]

73

[redacted]

H E A R T

(A) Microscopical Investigation.

[redacted]

I6.

Parenchymatous degeneration. Partial hemorrhages in epicardium.

50.

Parenchymatous degeneration. Slight increase of histocytes in interatitium; Appearance of myocytes around blood-vessels. Monocytes-accumulation in some blood-vessels.

85.

Rheumatoid-knots-formation around veins: miliary sized accoumulation of histiocytic cells and adventitial cells, and myolytic decay of some neighbouring muscle fibres.

I52.

Slight parenchymatous degeneration and slight hemorrhages in interstitium.

I67.

Parenchymatous degeneration and medium appearance of myocytes around some blood-vessels. Partial hemorrhages in epicardium.

I76.

Parenchymatous degeneration. Slight edema and slight appearance of myocytes in interstitium.

I78.

Slight parenchymateus degeneration. Intense venous congestion and increase of histiocytes around blood-vessels.

[redacted]

[redacted] 74

C [redacted]

I80. [redacted]

Slight parenchymatous degeneration. Slight appearance of myocytes in endocardium. Venous congestion.

Slight parenchymatous and, at some place, basophilic degeneration. Slight appearance of myocytes in endocardium and venous congestion.

I90.

Remarkable parenchymatous degeneration. Remarkable edema and histiocytes-accumulation in interstitium.

I93.

Parenchymatous degeneration and intense atrophia of myocardium. Remarkable appearance of myocytes in interstitium.

205.

Parenchymatous degeneration and slight appearance of myocytes in interstitium.

207.

Parenchymatous degeneration and atrophia.
Remarkable edema in interstitium.

22I.

Parenchymatous degeneration and atrophia. Remarkable edema in interstitium.

224.

Parenchymatous degeneration and atrophia. Remarkable edema in interstitium.

229.

In subepicardium and myocardium, multiple miliary sized necrotic places, which united each other to form rather diffuse necrosis.

[redacted] 75

[redacted]

Accumulation of lymphocytes and histiocytes at perifocal parts of these miliary necrosis. [redacted]

In the neighbouring tissues, musclar fibres fall into pieces and collapse aroud these places.

254.

Parencymatous degeneration and atrophia. Remarkable edema and slight myocytes-accumulation in interstitium.

256.

Parenchymatous degeneration and some myocytes in interstitium. Some places are rearranged with callously increased connective tissues and hyaline degeneration of blood-vessel-walls.

727.

Parenchymatous degeneration. Accumulation of leucocytes and monocytes in blood vessels of epicardium.

Remarkable accumulation of myocytes in interstitium.

73I.

Atrophia and intense parenchymatous degeneration, due to intense edema. Slightlhemorrhages in myocadium.

[redacted]

[redacted] 76

([redacted] (

(B) S U M M A R Y.

In vestigation on I9 micro-sl[redacted]

a) Endocardium: Generally no remarkable changes, except 2 cases with slight mesenchymal reactions.

b) Myocardium: some intense edema, some slight hemorrhages (in 4 cases), intense venous congestion in 5 cases, a few of polynuclear leucocytes, lymphocytes and monocytes in blood-vessels. Slight edematous swelling of vessel-walls with more or less intense peri-vascular edema and in 1 case rheumatoid-knots-formation: nemely. miliary sized accumulation of histocytes and adventitial cells around the veins and myolytic decays of some neighbouring muscle-fibres.

Intense cloudy swelling (disappearance of striatioh, various degeneration of nuclei, etc.) in 9 cases and basophilic degeneration in I cases.

In subepicardial myocardium of I case exist multiple miliary necrosis (glanders-knots) in a row. Glanders-knots (most and central parts fall into the caseous or structureless necrosis) are surrounded with extremely intense hemorrhagic and exudative perifocal re-actions (severe hemorrhage, severe edema, lymphocytes-infiltration and decay of muscular cells).

These hemorrhagic and exudative changes propagated themselves to the neighbouring tissues with more or less intense reactions.

Some muscular fibres which degenerated glassy or waxy and broked or losed their nuclei, are scattered in these inflammatory places.

[redacted] 77.

[redacted]

[redacted]

HEART

			16	50	85	146	152	167	176	178	180	190	193	205	207	221	224	229	254	256	727	791
Parenchyma of Myocardium	Fragmentation		÷	—	—	+	+++	—	—	+	—	÷	++	—	÷	÷	—	÷	—	—	÷	—
	Lipofuscin		÷	÷	++	+	+	÷	++	+	+	+	+	+	+	+	+	—	÷	—	++	+÷
	Atrophia		(+)	÷	÷	÷	+	÷	÷	(++)	÷	(+)	+++	÷	(++)	(+÷)	++	÷	+	÷	÷	++÷
	Hypertrophia		÷	÷	—	÷	÷	÷	—	÷	—	—	—	—	—	—	—	—	—	÷	÷	—
	Disappearance of Striations		+	+	++	(÷)	÷	+	+	+	+	(+÷)	+	(+)	+	+	+	(++++)	(+)	÷	÷	++
	Cloudy Swelling		++	+÷	+++	+	÷	++	++	+	+	++	+	(+÷)	+÷	+	+	+	+	(+)	+	++
	Vacuolar Degeneration		÷	÷	÷	—	÷	—	—	—	÷	÷	—	—	÷	—	—	—	—	—	—	÷
	Hyaline Degeneration		—	—	÷	—	—	—	—	—	—	—	—	—	—	—	—	(++)	—	—	—	—
	Basophilic Degeneration		—	—	—	—	—	—	—	—	(+)	—	—	—	—	—	—	—	—	—	—	—
	Waxy Necrosis		—	—	—	—	—	—	—	—	—	—	—	—	—	—	—	—	—	—	—	—
	Changes of Nuclei	Pyknosis	÷	÷	+	÷	÷	÷	÷	÷	÷	÷	÷	—	÷	÷	÷	÷	—	÷	÷	÷
		Swelling	÷	÷	÷	+	÷	÷	÷	÷	÷	÷	÷	÷	÷	÷	÷	—	÷	÷	÷	÷
		Karyolysis	+	÷	+÷	÷	÷	÷	+÷	÷	÷	+	÷	÷	÷	÷	÷	÷	÷	÷	÷	+
		Disappearance	÷	÷	+	÷	÷	÷	÷	÷	—	+	÷	÷	÷	÷	÷	(+++)	÷	[illegible]	÷	÷
Interstitium of Myocardium	Edema		÷	÷	÷	÷	÷	÷	+	+	÷	+÷	+	÷	++	++	++	÷	+÷	÷	÷	++÷
	Hemorrhage		÷	÷	÷	÷	(+)	÷	÷	÷	÷	—	÷	—	—	÷	÷	(+++)	÷	÷	—	+
	Contents of Blood Vessels	Erythrocytes	+	+÷	+	+	+÷	+÷	+	++	++	÷	+	+÷	÷	÷	÷	+	÷	+	+	÷
		Leucocytes	÷	—	(÷)	÷	÷	—	÷	—	(÷)	÷	(÷)	—	—	—	—	—	÷	÷	÷	—
		Lymphocytes	÷	÷	÷	÷	÷	÷	(+)	—	÷	÷	÷	÷	—	÷	—	—	÷	(÷)	÷	÷
		Monocytes	÷	+÷	÷	—	÷	÷	(÷)	÷	÷	÷	÷	—	—	—	—	÷	÷	÷	÷	÷
	Infiltration of Leucocytes		—	—	—	—	÷	—	—	—	—	÷	—	—	—	—	—	—	—	—	—	—
	Infiltration of Lymphocytes		÷	—	÷	÷	÷	÷	÷	÷	—	÷	÷	÷	÷	÷	—	(++)	÷	÷	÷	÷
	Proliferation of Histiocytes		÷	(++)	÷	+	÷	÷	÷	(++)	+	(+)	÷	÷	(+)	÷	÷	(+++)	÷	÷	÷	÷
	Proliferation of Myocytes		—	++	—	+÷	÷	+	÷	—	—	—	+÷	÷	—	—	—	—	÷	+	++	—
	Changes of Vessel Walls	Thickening	—	÷	—	÷	—	—	—	—	÷	—	—	—	—	—	—	—	—	÷	—	—
		Edema	÷	—	÷	—	÷	—	÷	—	—	÷	—	—	÷	+	÷	÷	÷	—	÷	+
		Adventitial cells	÷	÷	(+)	++	÷	÷	÷	÷	÷	—	+	—	—	—	÷	—	÷	(+)	+	—
	Perivascular Edema		+÷	+	÷	+÷	÷	(+)	++	+	÷	+	+	÷	++	++	++	+	++	÷	÷	++
Endocardium	Edema		+	÷	|	÷	—	÷	÷	÷	÷	÷	÷	|	|	|	|	|	++	—	+	|
	Infiltration	Erythrocytes	—	—	|	(+)	—	—	—	—	—	—	—	|	|	|	|	|	—	—	—	|
		Leucocytes	—	—	|	—	—	—	—	—	—	—	—	|	|	|	|	|	—	—	—	|
		Lymphocytes	÷	—	|	—	—	—	—	—	÷	÷	—	|	|	|	|	|	÷	—	÷	|
	Proliferation of Mesenchym-cells		—	÷	|	++	—	÷	—	—	(++)	—	—	|	|	|	|	|	÷	÷	÷	|
Epicardium	Edema		+	÷	+	÷	÷	+	++	÷	÷	+	÷	÷	+	+	++	+	++	|	+	+
	Congestion		÷	+	÷	+	÷	+	+	+	+÷	÷	+	+	÷	÷	+	+	÷	|	÷	÷
	Infiltration	Erythrocytes	(+++)	÷	÷	÷	—	(+)	—	—	—	—	—	—	÷	÷	÷	(+++)	÷	|	—	—
		Leucocytes	—	—	—	—	—	—	—	—	—	—	—	—	—	—	—	—	—	|	—	—
		Lymphocytes	÷	÷	—	—	—	—	—	—	—	—	—	—	—	÷	+	(+++)	÷	|	÷	÷
	Proliferation of Histiocytes		÷	+	÷	÷	÷	(+)	÷	÷	+	÷	+	÷	÷	÷	+	(+++)	+	|	(+)	÷

[redacted]

[redacted] 78

[redacted]

Intense edematous swelling
of blood-vessel-wall.

[redacted]

Typical glanders-knot in
subserous tissues.

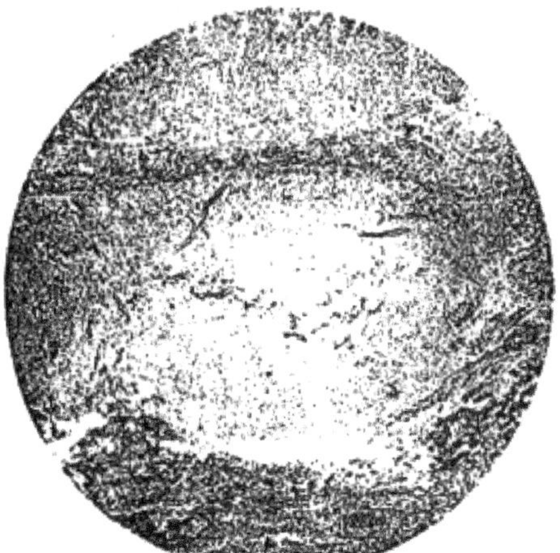

[redacted]

[redacted]

79

[redacted]

Rheumatoid-kont and desolative
decays of the neighbouring parenchymatous
cells.

[redacted]

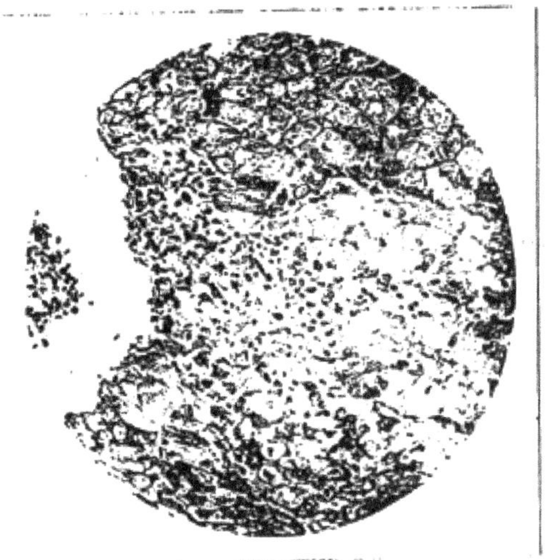

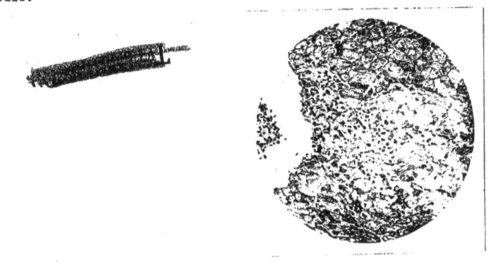

Some round cell infiltration and some
hyperplasia of interstitial connective
tissues.

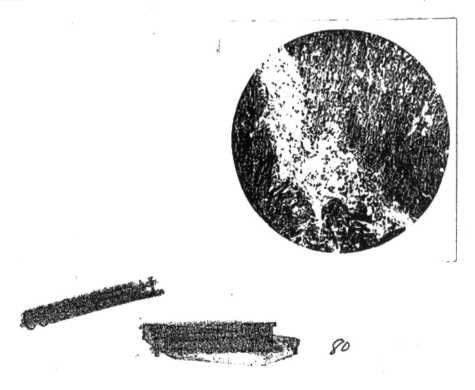

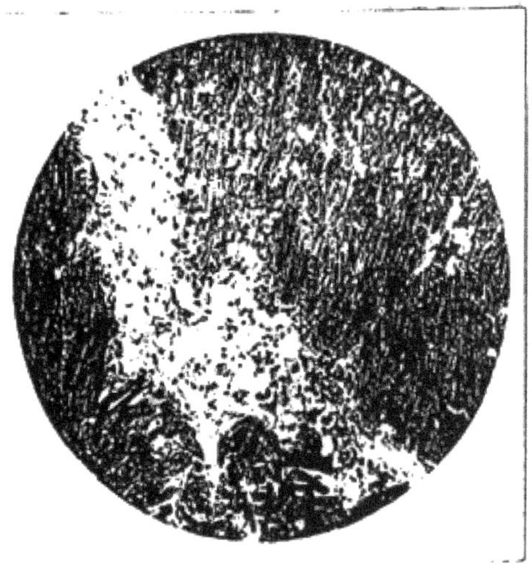

[redacted]

[redacted] 80

• [redacted] •

[redacted] Lung

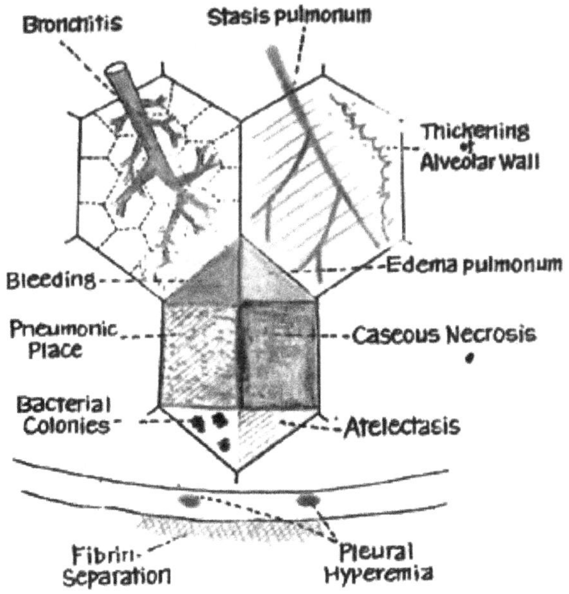

[redacted] [redacted] 81

[redacted]

L U N G

A) MICROSCOPICAL INVESTIGATION

[redacted]

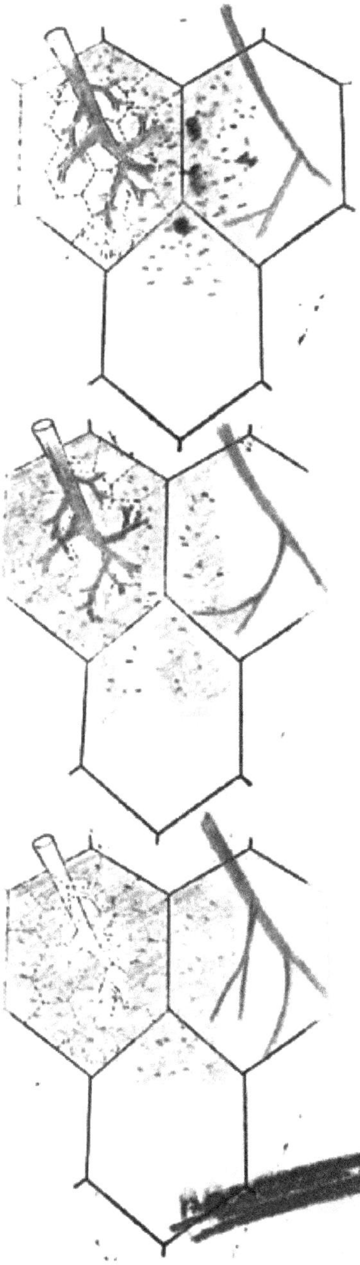

16. (left, superior)

Bronchiolitis catarrhalis and stasis et edema pulmonum.

Considerable congestion and edematous swelling of alveolar walls with inflammatoy edema and slight hemorrhages in alveoli. Some bacterial accumulations in some alveoli.

16. (left inferior)

Bronchiolitis catarrhalis, diffuse Alveolitis and stasis et edema pulm. Considerable congestion, edematous swelling and leucocytes-emigration at alveolar walls with inflammatory edema and leackages of leucocytes in some alveoli. Edematous swelling of interlobular connective tissues.

16 (right)

Stasis et edema pulmonum: considerable congestion and edematous swelling of alveolar walls with inflammatory edema in alveoli.

50.

Multiple miliary glanders-knots, severe pulmonal congestion and pleural hyperaemia and hemorrhages.

Remarkable [redacted]litis: remarkable

[redacted]

82

[redacted]

congestion, edematous swelling, leucocytes-emigrations at alveolar walls and following reactive changes: inflammatory edema and hemorrhages in alveoli.

[redacted]

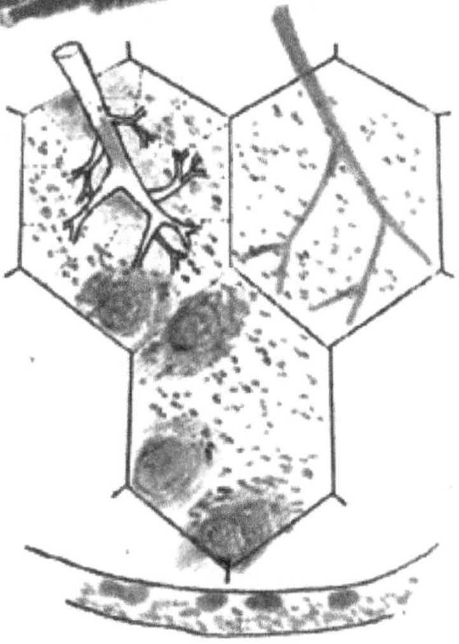

These inflammatory processes develope at some places to multiple Glanders-knots-formation, with numerous leucocytes or their nuclear fragments and residues of decayed capillary walls.

These necrotic changes spread with severe exsudative changes (edema, remarkable congestion and hemorrhages) to neighbouring tissues.

Bronchiolitis catarrahlis with a large quantity of hemorrhagic masses as contents and condiderable peribronchiolar congestion. (Bronchiolitis and Peribronchiolitis).

Severe heperaemia, severe hemorrhages and separation of fibrinous masses in adjacent pleural tissues (Pleuritis haemorrhagico-fibrinosa) and exsudative-hemorrhagic miliary glanders-knots in subpleural tissues.

146. (left superior)

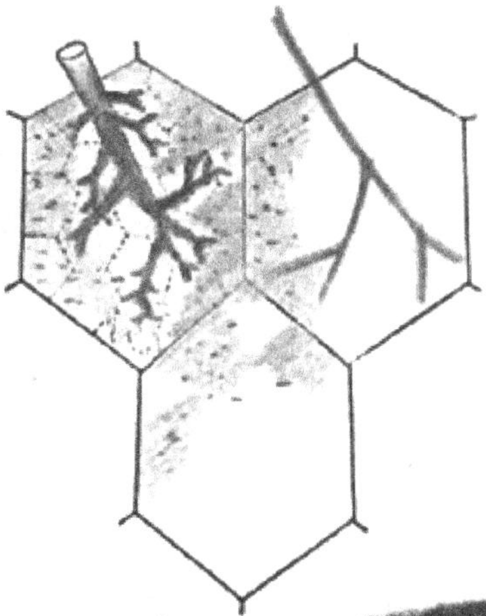

Bronchiolitis catarrhalis in high degree and considerable diffuse Alveolitis: severe edematous swelling and leucocytes-emigration at alveolar walls, accompanied with considerable inflammatory edema in alveoli.

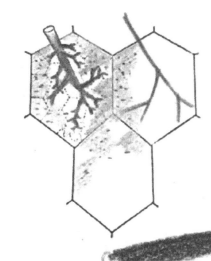

[redacted] [redacted]

83

[redacted]

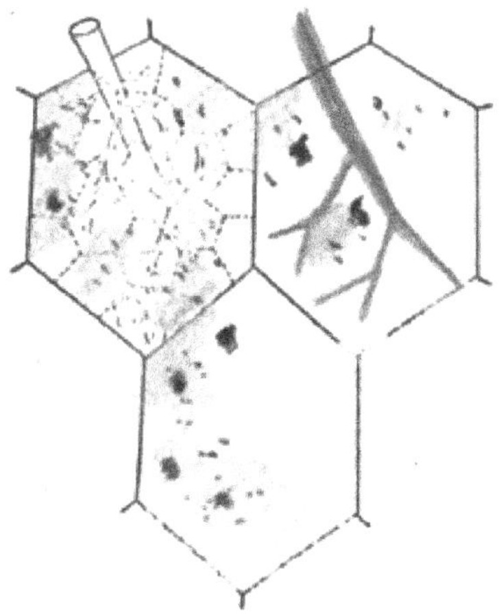

146. (left inferior)

Edematous swelling and congestion of alveolar walls in high degree and slight inf[redacted]tory edema and desquamation of alveolar epithel cells in alveoli. Bacterial accumulations in alveolar walls and alveoli.

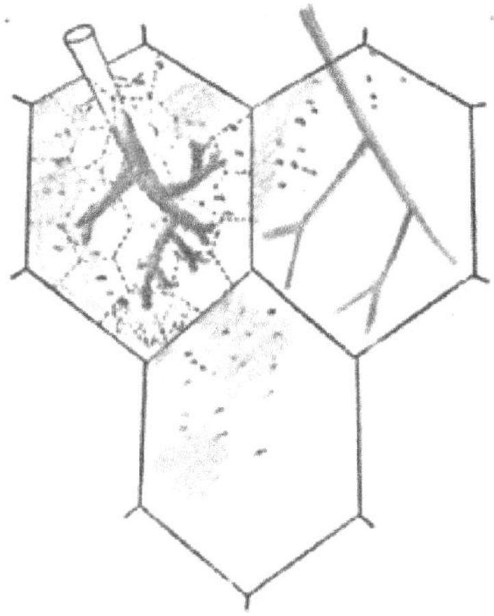

146. (right apex)

Bronchiolitis catarrhalis and slight diffuse Alveolitis: remarkable congestion, remarkable edematous swelling, and slight leucocytes emigration at alveolar walls with inflammatory edema and desquamation of alveolar epithels in alveoli.

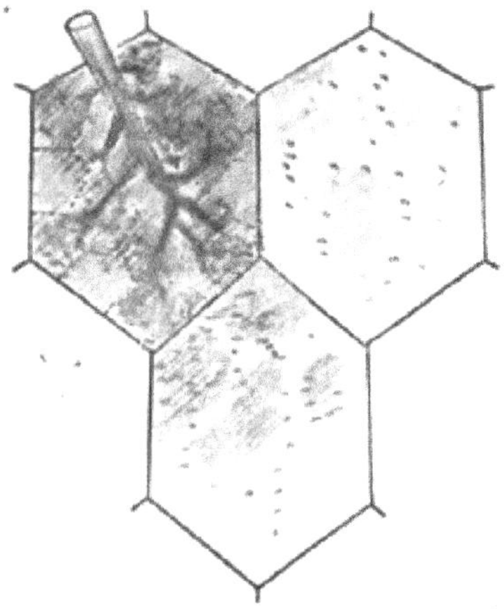

146. (right median)

Bronchiolitis catarrhalis gravis and lobular exsudative pneumonia. Bronchiolitis catarrhalis in high degree with numerous leucocytes, catarrhalic masses, desquamation of bronchial epithel cells and some bacterial colonies as contents.

Remarkable edematous swelling of peribronchial tissues.

Diffuse Alveolitis (remarkabl congestion and desquamation of alveolar epithel cells in alveoli) develope at some peribronchiolar tissues which are attached to damaged bronchiolus,

[redacted] [redacted]

84

[redacted]

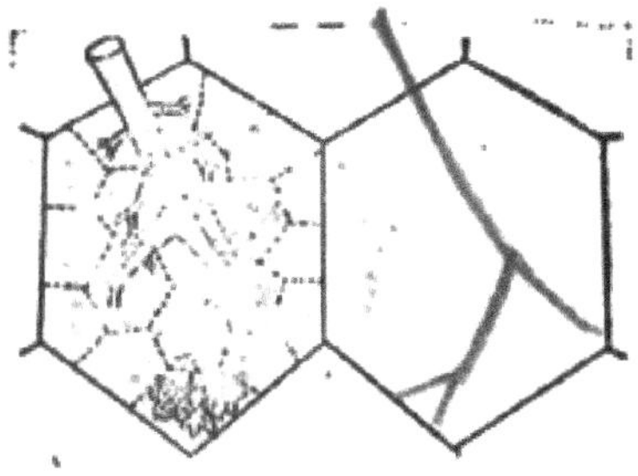

to multiple acinous or acino-lobular pneumonia in leucocytic-exsudative form.

146. (right inferior)

Slight pulmonal congestion. [redacted]

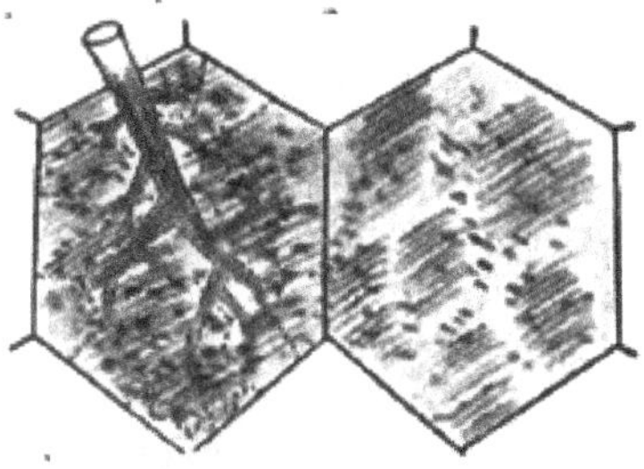

146. (right)

Lobular pneumonia in leucocytic-hemorrhagic form and diffuse inflammatory edema in severe degree.

152.

Edema pulmonum and diffuse Alveolitis.

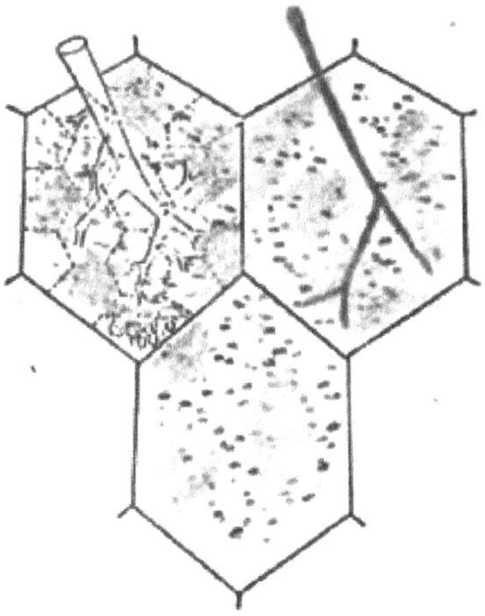

Remarkable edematous swelling, congestion and leucocytes infiltration at alveolar walls, accompanied with slight inflammatory edema and slight hemorrhages in alveoli.

167. (a)

Slight diffuse Alveolitis and Pleuritis haemorrhagico-fibrinosa.

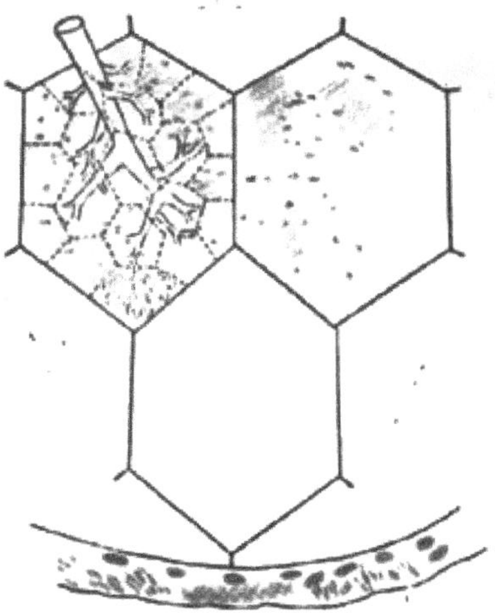

Slight diffuse Alveolitis: slight round cell-infiltration and edematous swelling of alveolar walls with slight desquamation of alveolar epithel cells in alveoli. Atelectatic alveolar spaces.

In pleural tissues: capillary congestion, remarkable hemorrhages at some places and separation of fibrinous masses.

[redacted]

[redacted] 85

[redacted]

167. (b)

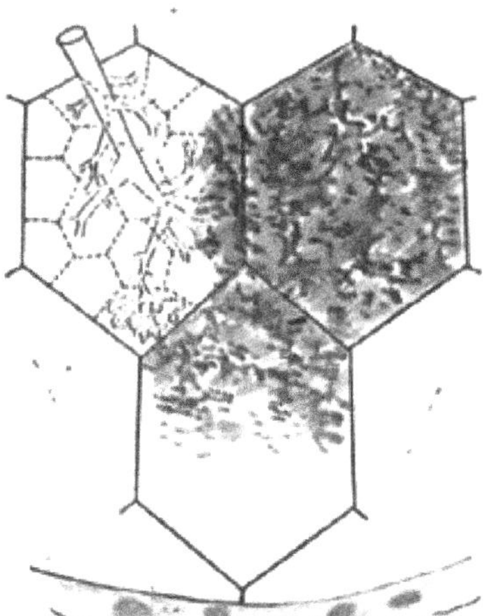

[redacted]

Obsolete lobular hemorrhagic pneumonia in organizing process. In some alveoli of scino-lobular hemorrhagic pneumonia, exist numerous erythrocytes and among them, many proliferated alveolar epitheliums. Some other alveoli of these hemorrhagic places are reamranged almost completely with proliferative cells (alveolar epitheliums, histiocytic cells and fibroplasts). In other general tissues, esp. neighbouring tissues, exist also considerable congestion and considerabl hyperplasia of alveola r epithel cells.

In pleural tissues: considerable congestion and edematous swelling.

167. (c)

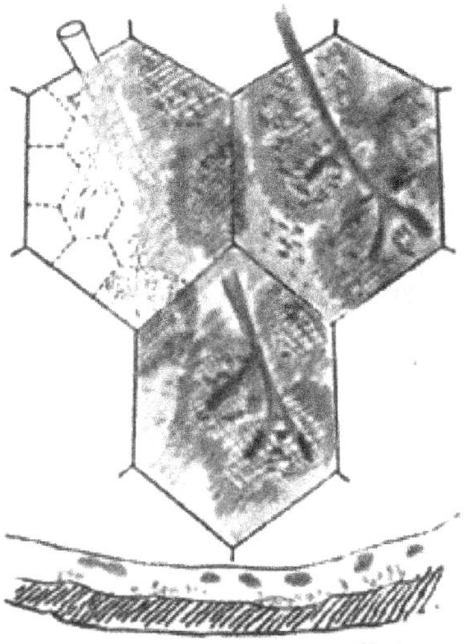

[redacted]

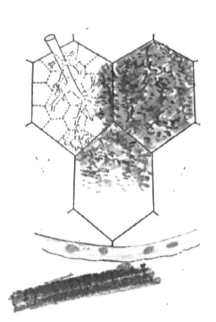

Endoarteriitis and Endoarteriolitis necroticans:

*) In arteries and arterioles, numerous leucocytes and their nuclear decayed fragments, necrotic ruins of arterial walls and perivascular leucocytes-accumulation and edematous swelling in high degree.

*) Multiple lobular pneumonic changes in the catch-areas of the above mentioned damaged blood-vessels.

In the focal parts of pneumonic places exist numerous leucocytes and various decayed masses

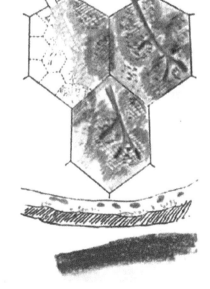

[redacted]

● [redacted]

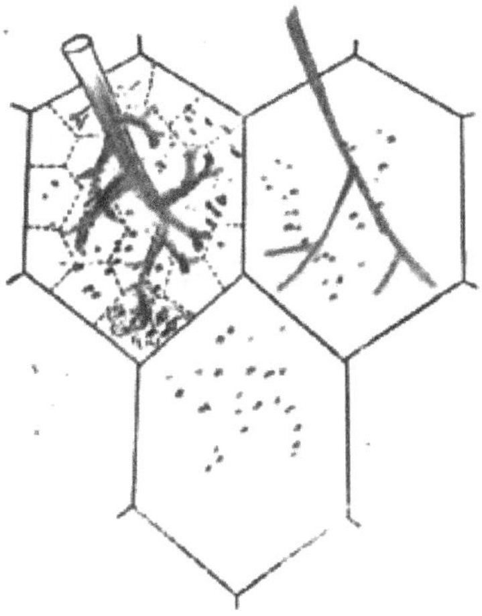

with severe reactive changes (Bleeding, separation of fibrinous masses or inflammatory edema in high degree).

*) and these pneumonic places united each other to form multiple acino-lobular pneumonia.

*) Bronchiolitis catarrhalis with a large quantity of mucous or decayed masses as contents. [redacted]

176.

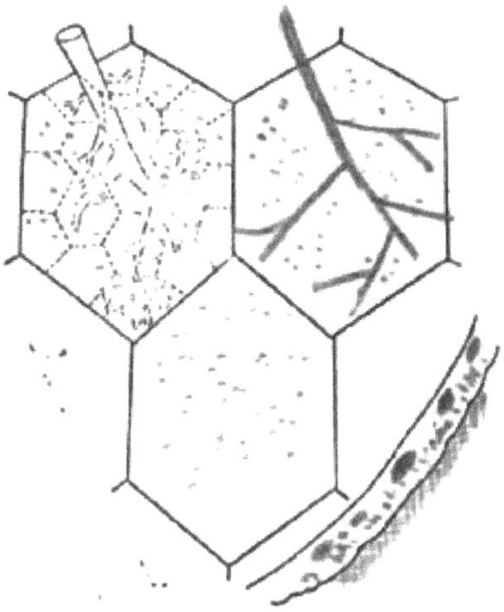

Bronchiolitis catarrhalis with a large quantity of mucous masses, desquamation of epithel cells and erythrocytes as contents.

Slight pulmonal congestion.

~~180.~~ 178.

Considerable congestion and slight diffuse hemorrhages in alveoli.

Remarkable pleural and subpleural congestion and hemorrhages with hemorrhagic-fibrinous masses on the pleural surfaces. (pleuritis haemorrhagico-fibrinosa).

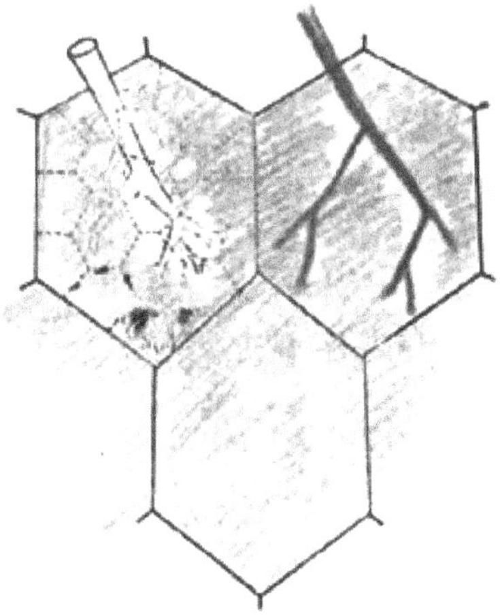

180.

Considerable congestion and edematous swelling of alveolar walls and remarkable inflammatory edema in alveoli. Bacterial accumulation at some alveolar walls.

[redacted]

[redacted] 87

[redacted]

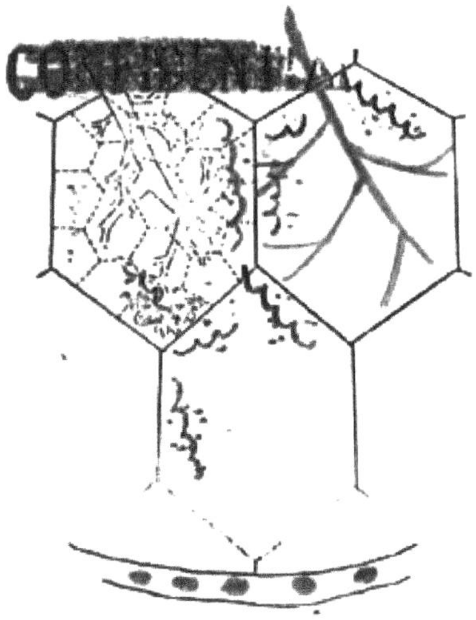

190.

Remarkable congestion, edematous swelling and considerable round cell infiltration at alveolar walls with more or less hyperplasia of alvelar epithel cells.

Pleural and subpleural hyperaemia in high degree.

193.(a)

Endoarteriitis necroticans and multiple supermilary glanders-knots in its following alveoli.

Endoarteriitis necroticans with a large quantity of leucocytes and their fragments as contents and necrotic ruins of walls.

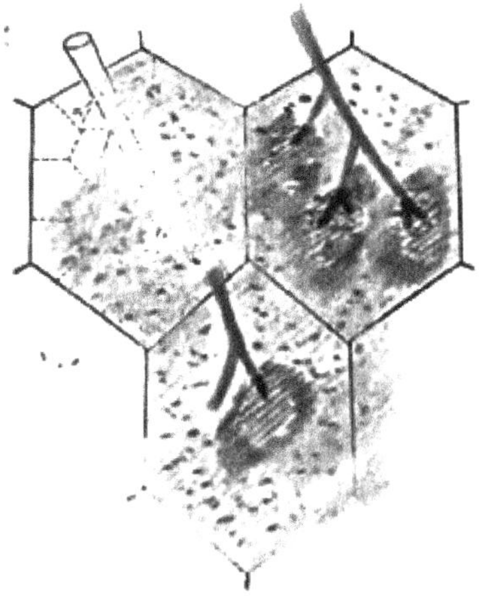

Supermiliary, more or less circumscribed glanders-knots with leucocytes-accumulation in perivascular or catchment-areas of attacked arteries.

These pneumonic knots are more or less localised and bounded sharply with slight hemorrhagic perifocal zone.

In other general lung-tissues: considerable congestion and edematous swelling of alveolar walls and intense inflammatory edem in alveoli.

Severe congestion and edematous swelling of interlobular connective tissues.

193.(b)

Diffuse Alveolitis: considerable congestion,

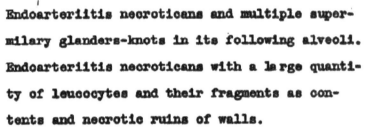

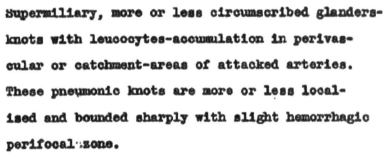

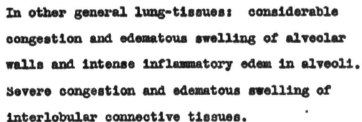

[redacted]

[redacted] 88

[redacted]

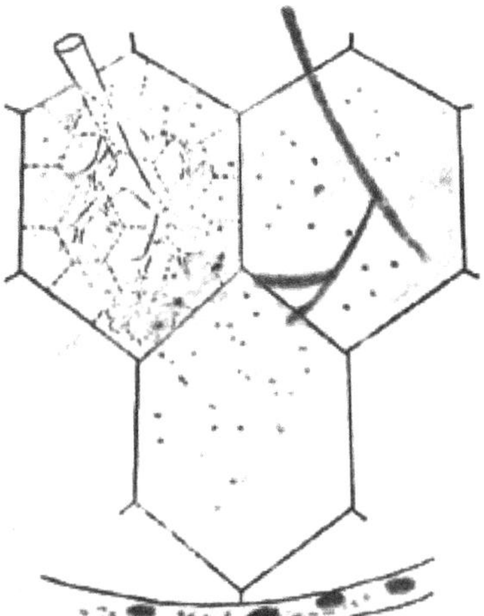

[redacted]

edematous swelling and slight round cell in-filtfation of alveolar walls with slight leackage of leucocytes in alveoli and inflammatory edema.

Bacterial celonies in alveoli and alveolar walls.

Slight hyperaemia and slight hemorrhages in pleural tissues.

205. (a)

Endoarteriitis necroticans and more or less localised miliary glanders-knots.

Endoarteriitis necroticans with a large quantity of leucocytes, necrotic ruins of walls and severe edematous swelling of perivascular tissues.

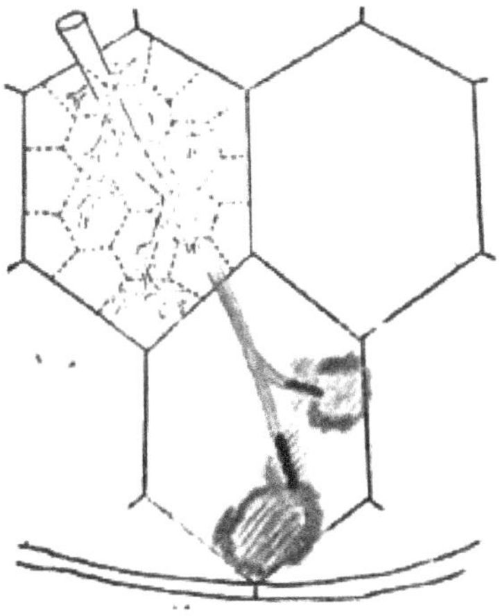

Multiple supermiliary glanders-knots in the attachment-areas of attacked blood-vessels. (hemotogenous glanders-knots).

Supermiliary, măre or less sharply bounded, sphenical knots with numerous leucocytes and their nuclear decayed asses are bounded with slight hemorahgagic perifocal reactive zone more or less sharply to the neighbouring tissues. The neighboring general pulmonal tissues with slight swelling and slight congestion of alveolar walls. No remarkable changes else.

[redacted]

[redacted] 89

[redacted]

205. (b)

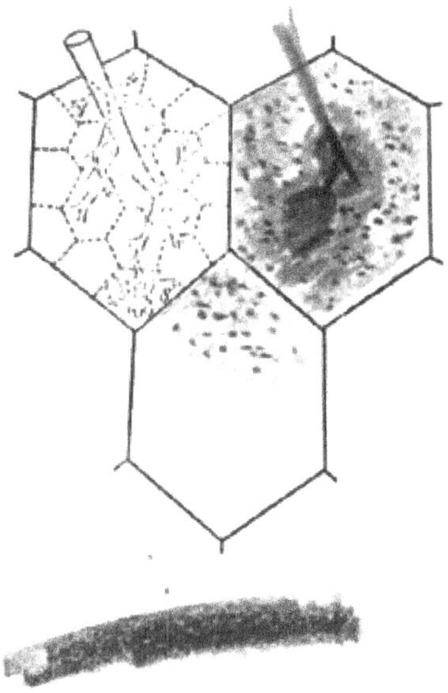

Endoarteriitis necroticans and supermiliary glanders-knots with remarkable reactive changes. Endoarteriolitis necroticans and perivascular reactive changes in high degree. Multiple supermiliary glanders-knots in the catchment-area.

The most parts of glanders-knots are extraordinary leucocytic and nocrotic (nuclear fragments and structureless decayed masses), having remarkable exsudative-hemorohaic perifocal changes (intense hemorhage and inflammatory edema).

The neighbouring general pulmonal tissues fall into also somewhat reactive changes: considerable congestion, edematous swelling, slight round cell emigration in alveolar walls with considerable inflammatory edema and more or less remarkable hemorrhages in alveoli.

207. (a)

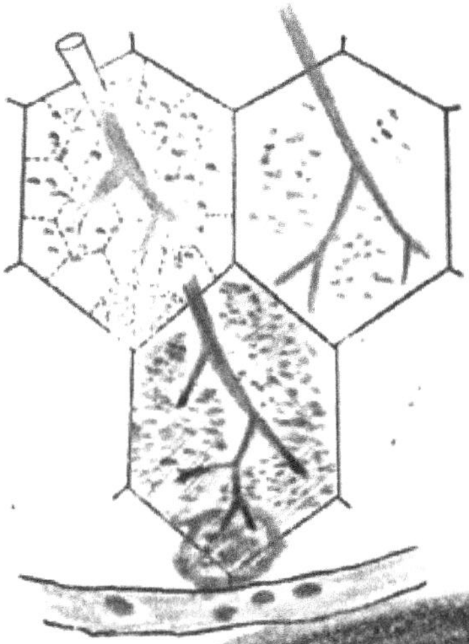

Endoarteriitis nocroticans, subpleural miliary glanders-knots and multiple miliary or acinous pneumonia.

*) Endoarteriitis necroticans and intense perivascular inflammatory reactions.

*) Supermiliary sphenical leucocytes-accumulation in attachment-areas of attacked blood-

[redacted] 90

[redacted]

vessels and subpleural miliary glanders-knots in the same mode.

The most parts of knots are intesively leucocytic and necrotic, and perifocal parts of them slightly hemorrhagic.

[redacted]

These inflammatory processes do not spread so intensely to the neighbouring tissues: considerable clngestion, slight edematous swelling and leucocytes emigration in alveolar walls with slight hyperplasia of alveolar epithel cells.

207. (b, c, d)

Subpleural supermiliary glanders-knots.

In subpleural tissues exist sphenical, more or less sharply bounded supermiliary glanders-knots. The most focal parts of these knots with numerous leucocytes and their nuclear fragments, decayed masses of alveolar epithel cells and slight hemorrhages and perifocal parts with slight hyperaemia. Bounded more or sharply, but without any proliforative processes. Other neighbouring general tissues: slight congestion, slight edematous swelling of alveolar walls and no particular changes else. Intense edematous swelling and hyperaemaia of adjacent pleural tissues.

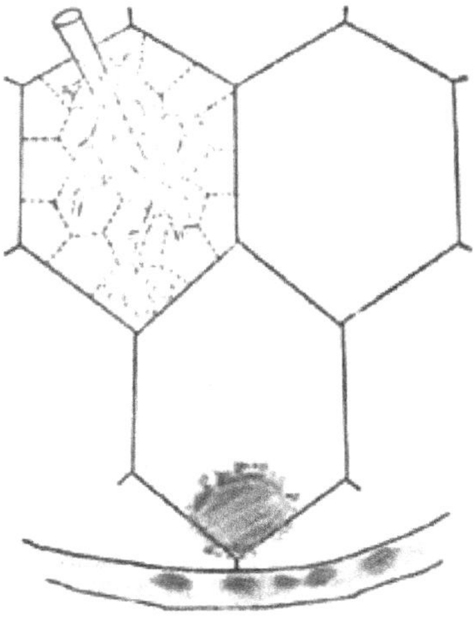

207. (e)

[redacted]

[redacted] 91

[redacted]

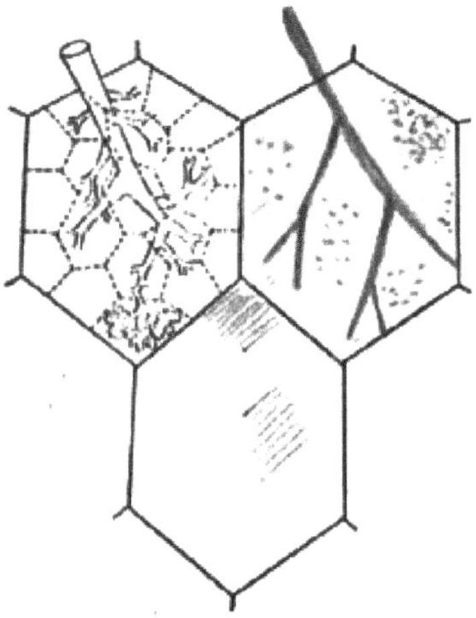

[redacted]

Remarkable congestion and edematous swelling of alveolar walls with slight inflammatory edema and slight haemorrhages in alveoli.

Atelectasis of alveolar spaces.

22f.(a).

Lobular pneumonia with severe perifocal changes and Pleuritis haemorrhagico-fibrinosa. In subpleural tissues exist lobular pneumonic places.

The focal parts with a large quantity of leucocytes and their nuclear fragments, decayed masses of alveolar epithel cells, more or less intense hemorrhagic-exsudative reactions into the neighbouring tissues gradually.

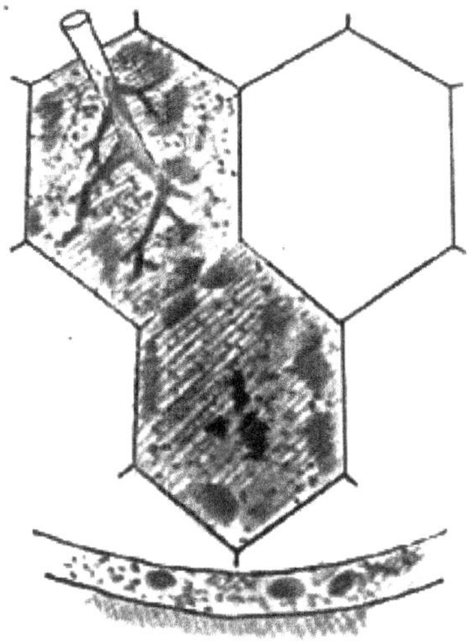

[redacted]

∘) Other general tissues : considerable congestion and edematous or fibrinous swelling of alveolar walls with somewhat remarkable inflammatory edema, slight hemorrhages and leackage of leucocytes in alveoli.

∘) Bronchiolitis catarrhalis of adjacent bronchioli and Pleuritis haemorrhagico-fibrinosa (in pleural tissues, considerable congestion

[redacted] 92

[redacted]

[redacted]

edematous swelling and slight haemorrhage in pleural tissues with the sero-haemorrhagic masses on the pleural surface.

22I (b).

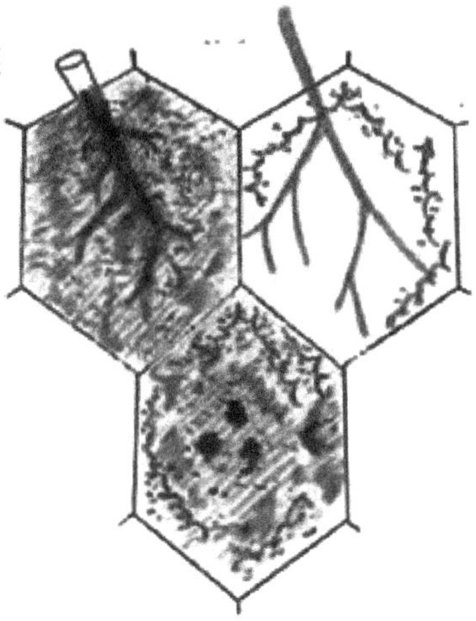

Multiple acinous or acino-lobular pneumonia.

In bronchus and their fragments, serous exsudat, decayed epithel cells and erytrocytes with necrotic ruins of bronchiolar walls and severe inflammatory changes of peribronchiolar tissues:edematous swelling, hyperaemia and leucocytes-infiltrations.

) Multiple acinous pneumonia in the attachments -areas of attacked bronchiolus and these pneumonic places united each other into acino-lobular pneumonia.

In pneumonic areas exist numerous leucocytes and their fragments, decayed masses of alveolar epithel cells and etc, fibrinous separative masses, haemorrhages and numerous bacterial masses.

These inflammatory processes run into the surrounding tissues with severe exsudative-haemorrhagic reactions (congestion, haemorrhages and inflammatory edema). [redacted]

[redacted] 93

[redacted]

[redacted]

Some arteriole in the focal parts show Endo-arteriolits necroticans (embolus-formation with various decayed masses and necrotic ruins of blood-vessel-walls).

) In other general tissues : considerable congestion, edematous swelling, more or less remarkable leucocytes-emigrations of the alveolar walls with exsudative-haemorrhagic changes (inflammatory edema, haemorrhages, leucocytes leackage and desquamation of alveolar epithel cells in alveoli) and slight hyperplasia of alveolar epithel cells.

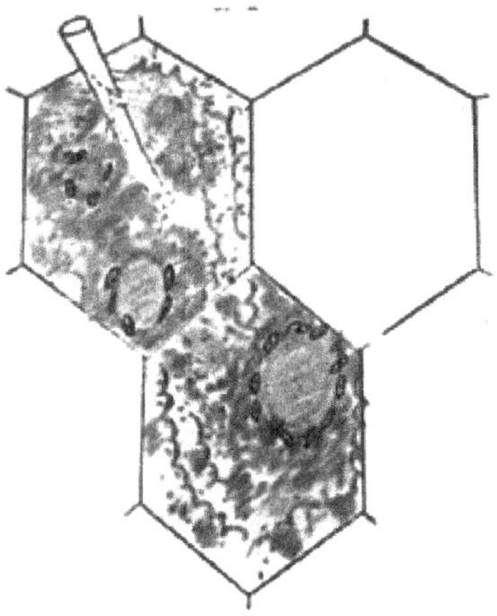

221 (c).

Multiple acinous or acino-lobular pneumonia.

The same changes so as above mentioned, exsudative-necrotic changes of bronchiolus and their following lower pulmonal tissues:

: severe leucocytic and haemorrhagic Endobronchiolitis and peribronchiolitis with multiple acinous or acino-lobular pneumonia.

Acinous pneumonia are formed mainly at my so-called intercalary portions of lung and united each other with more or less remarkable exsudative-haemorrhagic perifocal changes into

[redacted]

[redacted] 94

[redacted]

acino-lobular pneumonia.

[redacted]

In pneumonic areas exist various decayed masses (leucocytes and their fragments, fibrinous masses, haemorrhages or caseous necrtic masses of alveolar epithel cells) and slight hyperplasia of alveolar and bronchial epithel cells with giant cell-formation at some places.

Some arterioles in the focal parts show Endoarteriolitis or Endoarteriolitis obliterans(hyalinous thickning of blood-vessel walls in severe grade, edema and round cell infiltration in media, hyalinous thickening of intima and adventitial tissues).

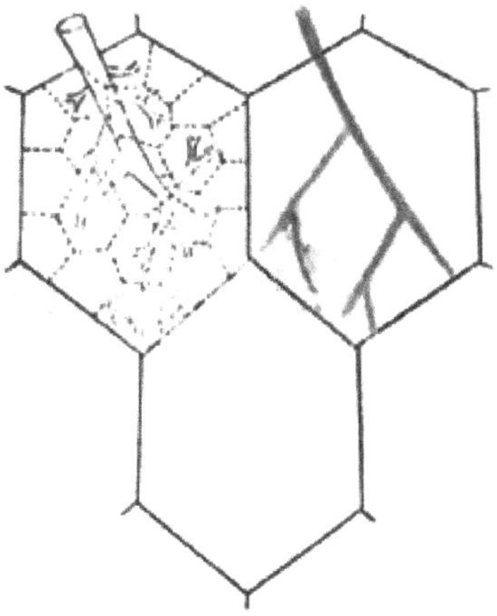

These inflammatory processes run into the neighbouring tissues with somewhat remarkable exsudative reactions (congestion, leucocytes-emigration,edematous swelling of alveolar walls with slight bleeding, inflammatory edema, leucocytes-leackage and desquamation of alveolar epithel cells in alveoli and slight hyperplasia of alveolar epithel cells).

222. Slight congestion and edematous swelling of alveolar walls.

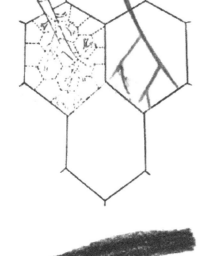

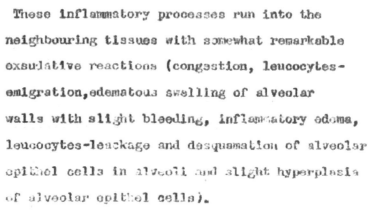

[redacted]

[redacted] 95

[redacted]

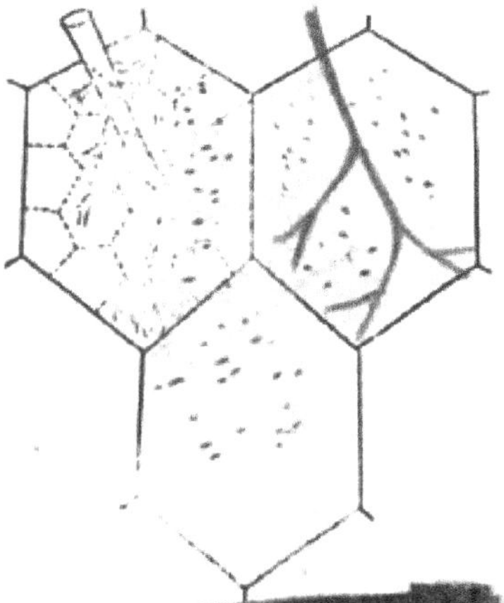

224.

Slight congestion and edematous swelling of alveolar walls with remarkable edema in alveoli.

229. (a)

Multiple lobular or acino-lobular pneumonia.

*) Exsudative-necrotic changes of bronchiolus and peribronchial tissues, in high degree: exsudative necrotic masses in bronchiolus and necrotic ruins of bronchiolar walls with exsudative-necrotic inflammation of peribronchiolar tissues.

[redacted]

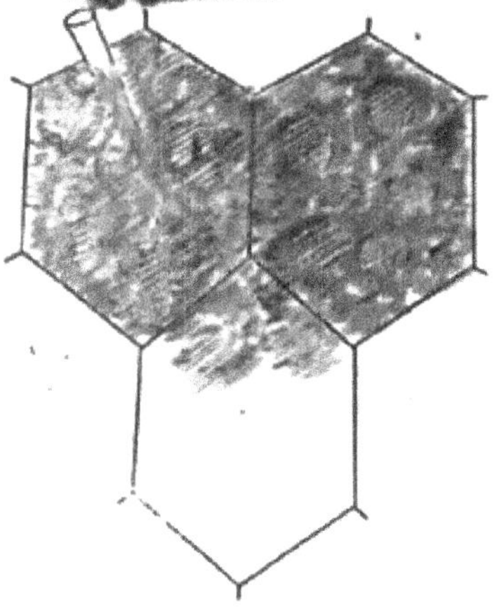

*) Multiple acino-lobular or lobular pneumonic places in the catchment-areas of attacked bronchilolus.

These pneumonic changes with caseous necrotic masses in focal parts run into the neighbouring tissues with severe reactive perifocal reactions (congestion, haemorrhages and fibrinous separation and more or less remarkablo leucocytes-emigrations).

Other general tissues: in inflammatory edema and hemorrhages in high degree.

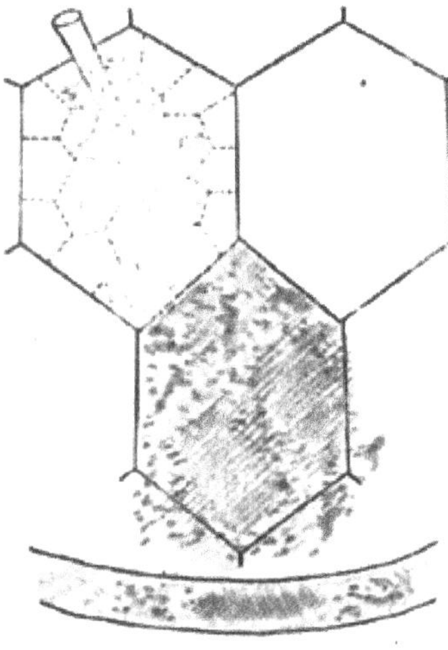

229. (b)

The same glanders-pneumonia (so as above mentioned) with Pleuritis sero-fibrino-hemorrhagica in adjacent pleural tissues.

[redacted]

96

[redacted]

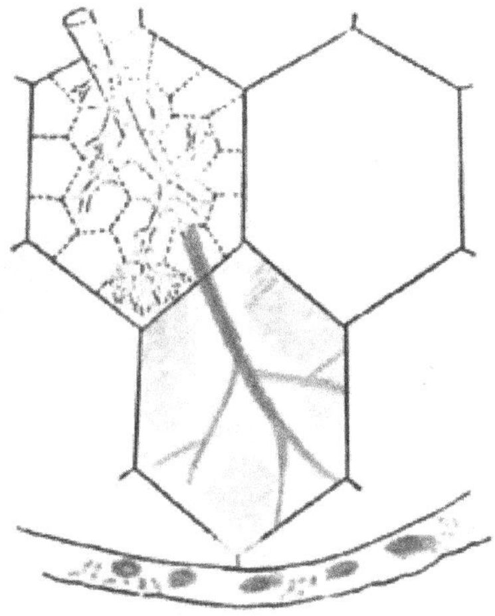

229.(c) [redacted]

Pulmonal congestion, slight pulmonal edema and sunpleural hyperaemia with slight bleeding.

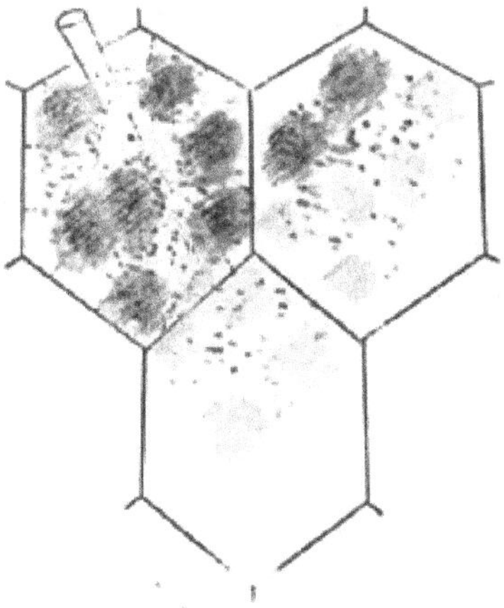

254.(a)

Multiple miliary or supermiliary glanders-knots in more or less proliferative form.

These glanders-nodulus exist mainly at intercalary portions of lung. In the central focus exist numerous decayed fragments of leucocytes and caseous necrotic masses of pulmonal-tissues. In the perifocal parts shows it more or less slight proliferative walls.

Other general tissues are in medium congestion and slight edematous swelling of alveolar walls with slight inflammatory edema and slight hemorrhages in alveoli.

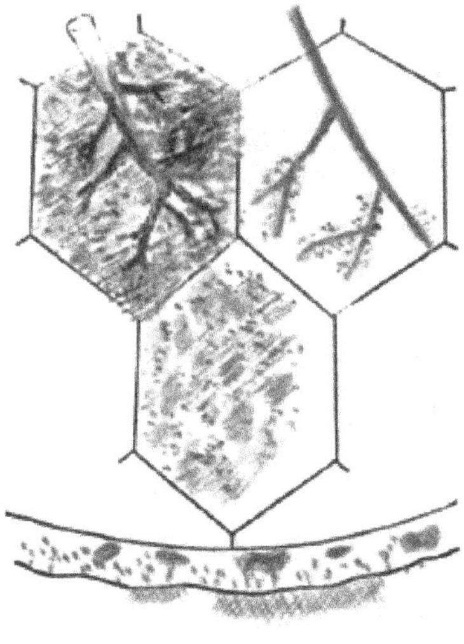

254.(b)

Multiple supermiliar, acinous or acino-lobular pneumonia.

These pneumonic changes occured mainly at the intercalary portions of lung.

In bronchiolus (esp. intercalary portion) and pulmonal tissues of its catchment-area occured pneumonic changes. The most parts (central focus) are caseous necrotic and its perifocal parts, severely leucocytic-hemorrhagic.

These pneumonic changes run into the neighbouring

[redacted] 97 [redacted]

[redacted]

[redacted]

tissues with severe hemorrhagic-exsudative processes gtadually and united each other to form acino-lobular pneumonic changes.

Other general tissues in remarkable congestion, severe edematous swelling and more or less remarkable leucocytes-infiltration of alveolar walls with inflammatory edema and hemorrhages in high degree and round cell infiltration in perivascular (veins and arterioles) tissues.

Pleural tissues in remarkable congestion and hemorrhages with fibrinous hemorrhagic masses on the pleural surface (Pleuritis fibrino-hemorrhagica of adjacent pleura)-

254. (c)

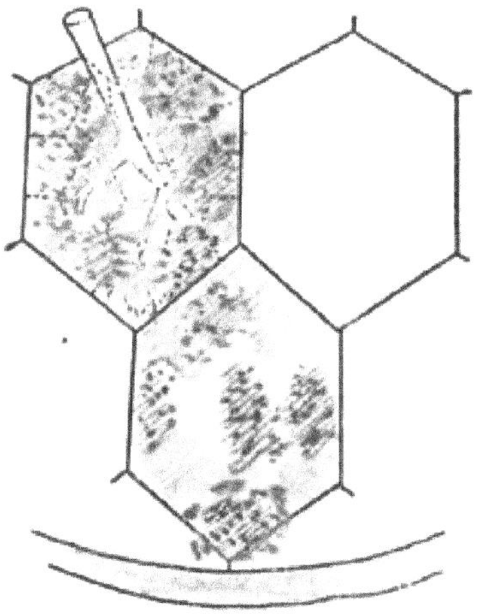

Acino-lobular pneumonia with subpleural miliary glanders-knots.

The same changes as above mentioned.

256. (a)

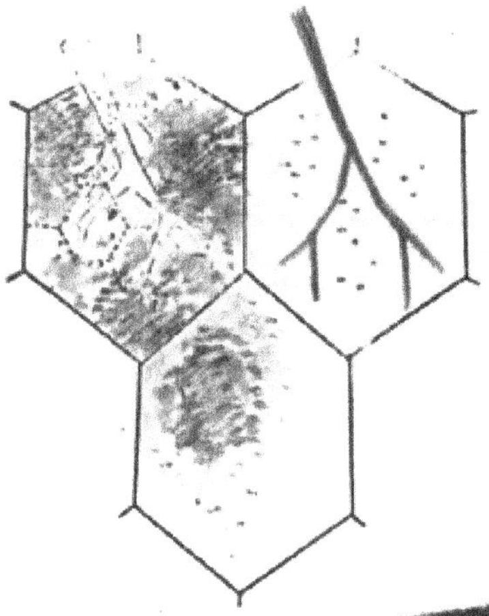

Multiple miliary glanders-knots in leucocytic-hemorrhagic form.

The focal parts with numerous leucocytes and their nucleqr fragments and the perifocal parts with leucocytic-hemorrhagic changes.

These pneumonic reactions run into the neighbouring tissues with severe hemorrhagic-exsudative processes.

[redacted]

[redacted] 95

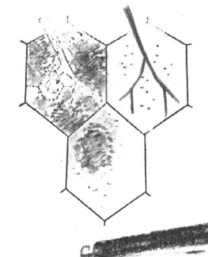

[redacted]

Other general tissues are in considerable congestion, edematous swelling and leucocytic infiltration of alveolar walls with slight hemorrhages and slight leucocytic infiltration in alveoli.

[redacted]

256. (b)

Multiple lobulo-acinous pnemonia and Pleuritis hemorrhagico-exsudativa.

In the focal parts of pneumoniq places exist a large quantity of leucocytes and their fragments and residual masses of ruined arterioles (Endoarteriitids necroticans: Embulus-formation with decayed cellular masses and necrotic ruins of their walls with perivascular leucocytic infiltration in high grade). In adjacent bronchiolus exist numerous and various decayed cell-elements, accompanied with necrotic ruins of bronchiolar walls.

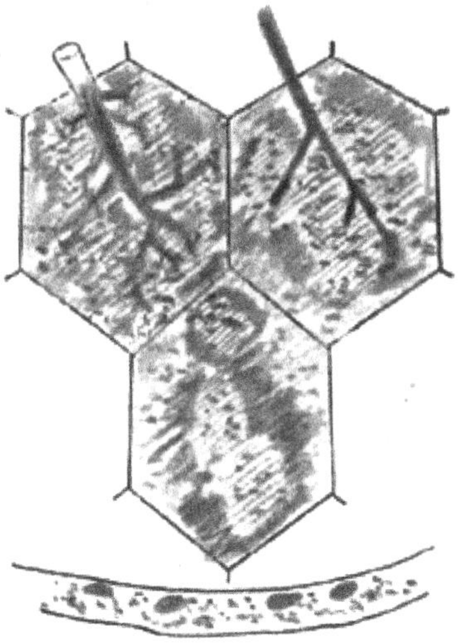

These pneumonic changes united each other to form acino-lobular pneumonia and run into the neighbouring tissues with severe reactive hemorragic-exsudative processes(severe congestion, hemorrhages and leucocytic emigrations).

Other general pulmonaltissues are in severe edema and more or less remarkable hemorrhages in alveoli with medium congestion, edematous swelling and leucocytic infiltration of alveolar walls.

[redacted]

[redacted] 99

[redacted]

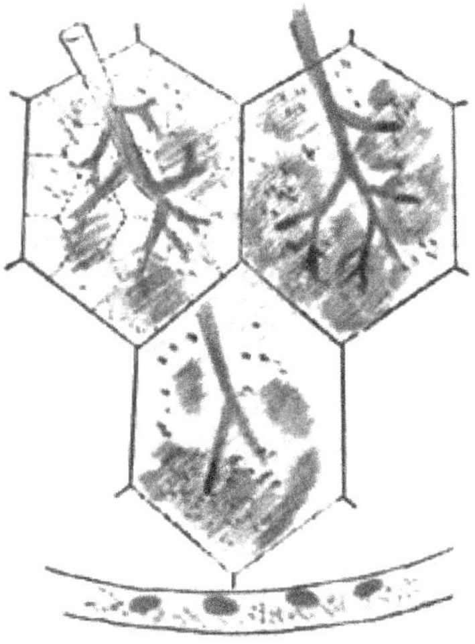

256. (c)

[redacted]

Multiple Endoarteriitis and Endoarteriolitis necroticans and multiple acinous or acino-lobular pneumonia in exsudative-leucocytic-hemorrhagic form. In the catchment pulmonal tissues of attacked blood-vessels break out lobular leucocytic hemorrhagic changes. In the focal parts of the pneumonia exist numerous leucocytes and their fragments, decayed cellular and hemorrhagic masses. These changes run with severe hemorrhagic leucocytic perifocal changes into neighbouring tissues.

Other general pulmonal tissues are in slight congestion and slight edematous swelling of alveolar walls.

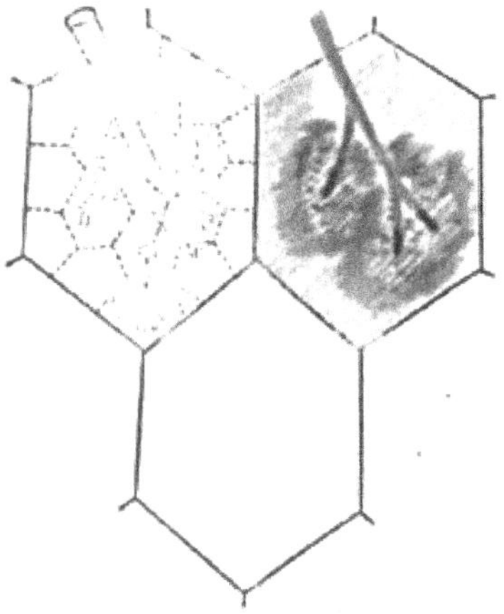

256. (d)

Endoarteriolitis necroticans and lobulo-acinous pneumonia with hemorrhagic perifocal reactions.

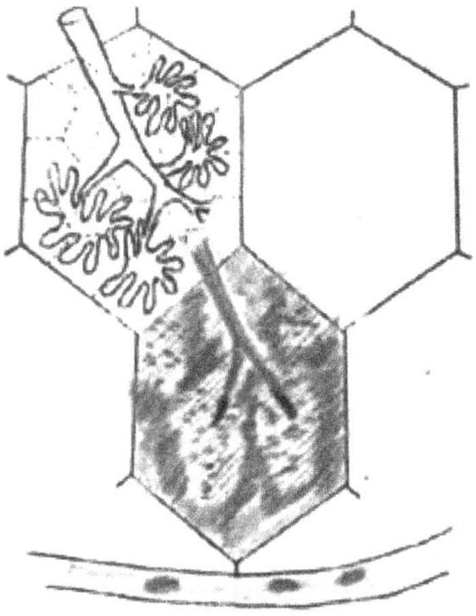

256. (e)

Endoarteriolitis necroticans and subpleural acino-lobular pneumonia.

Multiple acino-lobular pneumonia with the same microscopical changes, as above mentioned.

Attend to the remarkable hyperplasia of bronchiolar or alveolar epithel cells at the intercalary portions of lung to firm papillous increase.

256. (f)

[redacted] Paillous increase of alveolar epitheliums at the

[redacted]

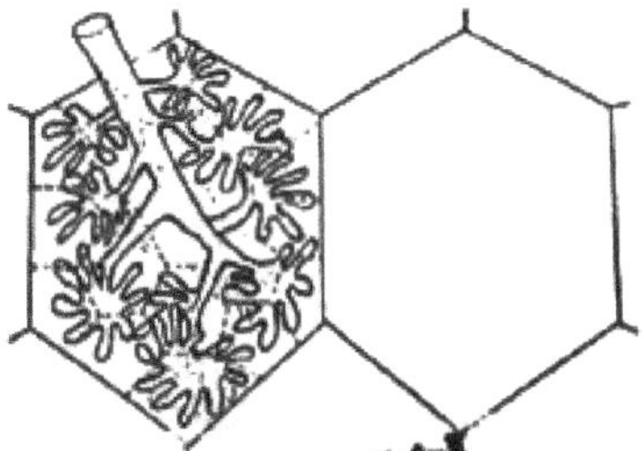

[redacted]

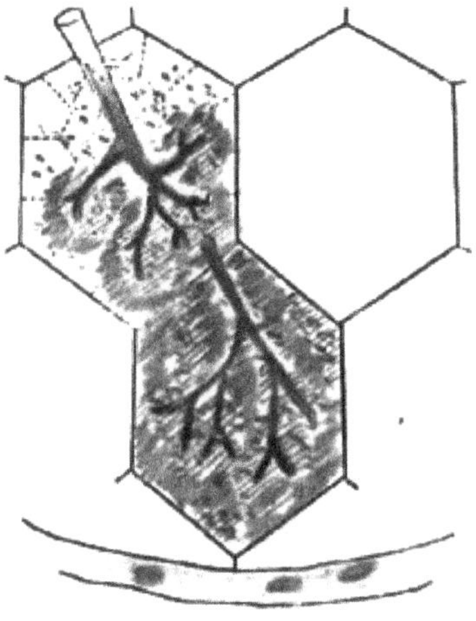

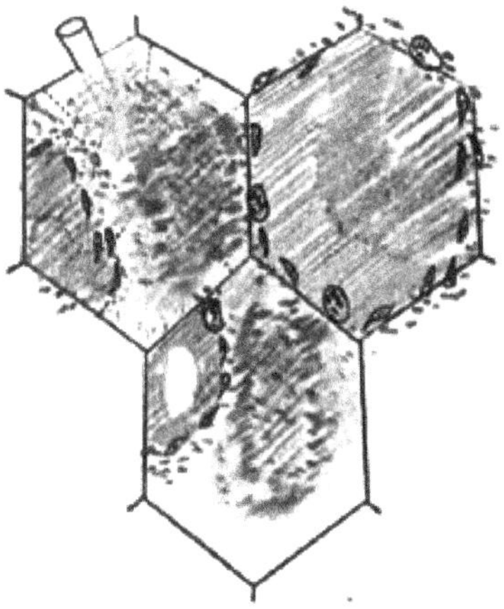

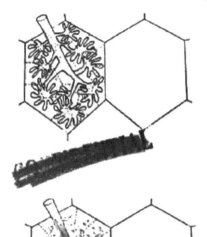

intercalary portions of lung as reactive proliferative changes. No remarkable changes else.

727. (a)

Endoarteriitis and Endoarteriolitis necroticans: Embolus-formation with decayed cellular fragments and necrotic ruins of the blood-vessel walls with severe perivascular leucocytic infiltration.

Diffuse lobular pneumonia in the catchment-area of the attacked blood-vessels. These pneumonic areas are severely hemorrhagic, leucocytic and necrotic and run with severe exsudative changes (hemorrhages, edema and leucocyte-emigration) into the neighbouring tissues.

Adjacent pleural tissues are in considerable congestion and edematous swelling.

727. (b)

Multiple lobulo-acinous pneumonia, which break out in the same processes, as above mentioned. Attend to the cavern-formation in its focal part and caseous ruins of tissues. In its perifocal zone exist slight lymphocytic wall with slight hyperplasia of epitheloid cells and giant cells. These pneumonic changes run with exsudative reactions (congestion, hemorrhages and round cell-infiltration) into the neigh-

[redacted] [redacted] 101

[redacted]

bouring tissues.

[redacted]

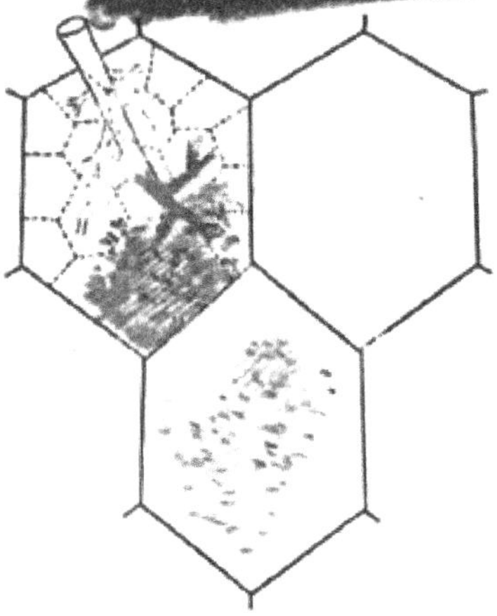

Other general tissues are in congestion and edematous swelling of the alveolar walls with slight edema and slight desquamation of alveolar epithel cells in alveoli and on the other hand slight hyperplasia of alveolar epithel cells.

731. (a)

Miliary glanders-knots (leucocytic focal part and hemorrhagic perifocal part with severe hemorrhagic reactive zones).

Other general tissues, almost normal.

731.

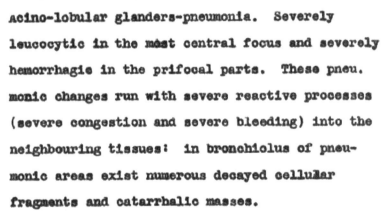

Acino-lobular glanders-pneumonia. Severely leucocytic in the most central focus and severely hemorrhagic in the prifocal parts. These pneu. monic changes run with severe reactive processes (severe congestion and severe bleeding) into the neighbouring tissues: in bronchiolus of pneumonic areas exist numerous decayed cellular fragments and catarrhalic masses.

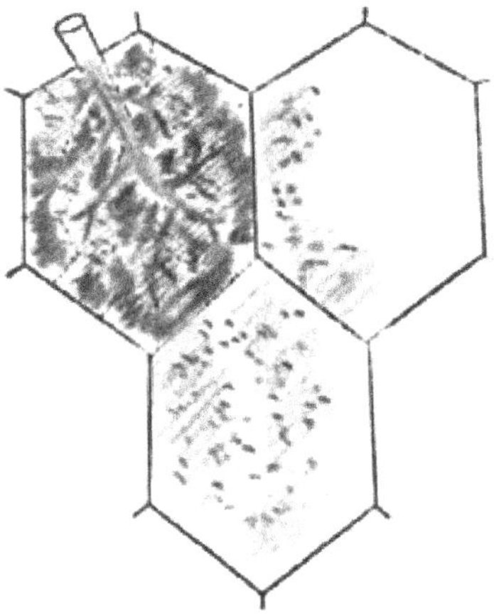

The neighbouring pulmonal tissues are in severe inflammatory edema, more or less leucocytic emigration and bleeding.

[redacted] 102

C [redacted] C

(B) S U M M A R Y

(I)

The birdeye-views of pathological changes in all cases.

16 (l).	Bronchiolitis catarrh.	Stasis et edema pulm. Slight diffuse Alveolitis with some bacterial dissemination.
16 (l,i).	Bronchiolities catarrh.	Stasis et edema pulm. Slight diffuse Alveolitis.
16 (r).	Bronchiolitis catarrh.	Stasis et edema pulm. Slight diffuse Alveolitis.
50.	Bronchiolitis catarrh. (with some haemorrhagic masses) Peribronchiolitis (with remarkable congest.)	Severe diffuse Alveolitis. Multiple milliry glandere-rs-knots with severe haemorrhagic perifocal changes.
146 (l,s).	Bronchiolitis catarh gravis.	Stasis et edema pulm. Considerable diffuse Alveolitis.
146 (l,i).	Bronchiolitis gravis.	Stasis et edema pulm. some desquamative epithels. Consid. diffuse Alveolitis with some bacterial dissemination.
146 (r,ap).	Consid. Bronchiolitis.	Stasis et edema pulm. Slight diffse Alveolitis.
146 (r,m).	Bronchiolitis gravrs.	Lobular pneumonia! catarhalic-exsudative, sometimes. haemorrhagic-leucocytic, sometimes. Stasis pulm.
146 (r,i).	No remarkable changes.	Stasis pulm.

[redacted]

103

([redacted] (

[redacted]

152.	No remarkable changes.	Edema pulm. Consid. diffuse Alveolitis.
167 (a.).	No remarkable changes.	Slight diffuse Alveolitis. Pleuritis haemorrhagico-fibrin.
167 (b.).	Bronchiolitis levis.	Obsolete haemorrhagic pneumonia. (acino-lobular), organised slightly with remarkably hyperplasied alveolar epithels. Pleural congestion.
~~167 (c).~~	~~Bronchiolitis catarrh. (with a large quantity of excreted masses)~~	

[redacted]

[redacted] 104

([redacted] (

167 (C).	Bronchiolitis catarrh. (with a large quantity of excreted masses).	Endoarteritis and Endoarteriàlitis necroticans. Multiple acino-lobular pneumonia. Pleuritis obsolets and pleural congestion. [redacted]
176 ( ).	Bronchiolitis catarrh.	Slight pulmonal cdngestion.
178 ( ).	Bronchiolitis catarrh. in very slight degree.	Severe pulmonal congestion. Pleuritis haemorrhagico-fibrin.
180 ( ).	No significant changes.	Consid. pulmonal congestion and edema. Bacterial accumulation at some Places. Pleural congestion.
190 ( ).	No significant changes.	Slight Alveplitis, accompanied with slight hyperplasia of alveolar epithels. Remark. congestion.
193 (a).	No significant changes.	Endoarteriolitis necroticans. Supermiliary glanders-knots in its catchment-areas. Severe edema pulm. Consid. pleural cOngestion.
193 (b).	No significant changes.	Cònsid. diffuse Alveolitis. Edema et stasis pulm. Some bacterial dissemination. Cdnsid. pleural congestion.
205 (a).	No significant changes.	Endoarteriolitis necroticans. Multiple supermiliary glanders-knots. (without remarkable reactive perifocal zone). Slight pleural congestion.
205 (b).	No significant changes.	Endoarteriolitis necroticans. Multiple supermiliary glanders-knots. (without remarkable hemorrhagic perifocal changes). Stasis et edema pulm in general tissues.

[redacted]

[redacted] 105

([redacted] (

207 (a).	No significant changes.	Endoartariolitis necroticans. Subpleural glanders-knots. Multiple supermiliary glanders-knots, with slight perifocal hemorrhagic reactions.
207 (b).	No consid. changes. [redacted]	Some acino-lobular Pneumonia. Subpleural supermiliary glanders-knots, with slight perifocal hyperaemia. No remarkable changes in other general tissues.
221 (a).	Broncho-Bronchiolitis levis.	Pleuro-pneumonia: Lobular pneumonia. Pleuritis sero-fibrinosa.
221 (b).	Broncho-Bronchilitis gravis.	Acinous or acino-lobular pneumonia. with severe exsudative-hemorrhagic perifocal changes.
221 (c).	Broncho-Bronchiolitis.	Acinous or acino-lobular pneumonia with multiple glanders-knots at intercalary portions of lung.
222 (r,I).	No signicant changes.	Stasis pulm. levis.
224 (r,I).	No significant changes.	Stasis et edema pulm. levis. Slight diffuse Alveolitis.
229 (a).	Exsudative-hemorrhagic changes of bronchus and peribronchial tissues.	Multiple acinous or acino-lobular pneumonia, with severe exsudative perifocal changes.
229 (b).	"	Multiple acino-lobular pneumonia with glanders-knots formations. Pleuritis sero-fibrinosa.
229 (c).	No remarkable changes.	Stasis et edema pulm. Subpleural congestion.
254 (a).	No signicicant changes.	Multiple miliary glanders-knots at intercalary portions of lung, with slight proliferative perifocal changes.

[redacted]

[redacted] 106

C [redacted] C

254 (b).	No significant changes.	Multiple supermiliary glanders-knots and Acino-lobular hemorrhagic-leucocytic pneumonia with severe exsudative perifocal changes. Pleuritis hemorrhagica. Remarkable perivascular round cell accumulations.
[redacted]		
254 (c).	No significant changes.	Acino-lobular pneumonia. Subpleural glanders-knots
256 (a).	No significant changes.	Multiple miliary glanders-knots in hemorrhagic-leucocytic form, with severe exsudative perifocal changes.
256 (b).	"	Multiple lobulo-acinous pneumonia: Pleuritis hemorrhagico-exsudativa.
256 (c).	"Bronchiolitis catarrh with some decayed masses as bronchial contents.	Multiple Endoarteriitis and Arteiolitis necroticans. Multiple acino-lobular pneumonia in hemorrhagico-exsudative form, at intercalary portions of lung. Pleural congestion.
256 (d).	No significant changes.	Endoarteriitiset arteriolitis necroticans and perivascular acinous reactive hemorrhagic pneumonic places.
256 (e).	Bronchiolitis catarrh. with some decayed masses as bronchiolar contents.	Endoareteriitis and Endoarteiolitis necroticans. Subpleural acino-lobular pneumonia, perifocal reactions. Papillous increase of bonchiolar or Alveolar epithels at intercalary portions of lung.
256 (f.).	No significant changes.	Papillous increase of alveolar or bronchiolar epithels at intercalary portions of lung.
727 (a.).	Bronchiolitis catarrhalis with some decayed masses as bronchiolar contents.	Endoarteriitis and Endoarteriolitis necroticans. Lobular pneumonia with severe exsudative-hemorrhagic perifocal changes.
727 (b).	"	Lobulo-acinous, hemorhagic-exsudative pneumonia with caseous necrotic focus and cavern formations at some places.
[redacted]		

[redacted] 107

[redacted]

731 (a).	Bronchiolitis catarrh. with some decayed masses as bronchiolar contents.	Miliary glanders-knots with severe hemorrhagic perifocal reactions.
731 (b)	[redacted]	Acino-lobular leucocytic pneumonia with severe hemorrhagic perifocal reactions.

[redacted]

[redacted] 108

[redacted]

[redacted]

I divide all cases into 2 groups:

a) groups of perbronchial infection and

b) group of metastatic secondary pulmonal infec

A). Perbronchial infection.

Investigation, based on only 4 cases of perbronchial infection (No. 176, 178, 229 and 731). Perbronchial infection with somewhat large quantity of ganders-bacillus, cause after several weeks some pulmonal changes.

(I can not explain "the methods of infection and clinical symptoms" in details, while I have not received these records.)

\- - -   - - -   - - -

a) At first, it causes after some days or some weeks (in 1 case), considerable bronchiolitis catarrhalis.

[redacted] [redacted] 109

([redacted] (

*) Then in 1 case, some considerable reactive changes: pulmonal or pleural congestion.

[redacted]

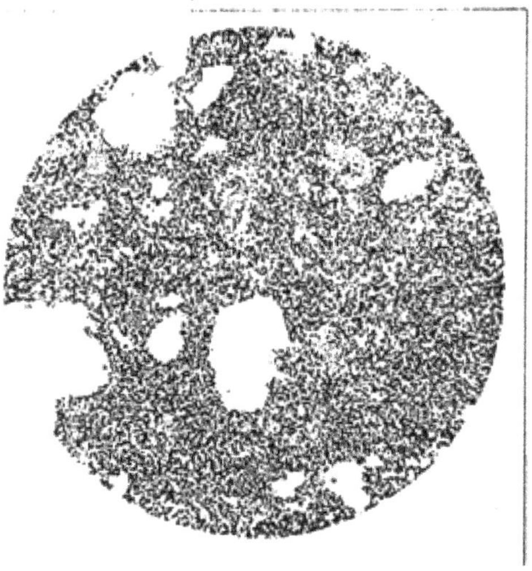

No. 190 (x60)

*) After 2 or 3 weeks (I can not indicate the days of course exactly), it causes some pneumonic changes:

a) In 1 case, multiple peribronchiolar hemorrhagic pneumonia (Broncho-pneumonia in some peribronchiolar acinous parts), and some acino-lobular lenco-cytic pneumonia, due to peribronchiolar proceeding of changes.

[redacted] [redacted] 110

C [redacted] C

No. 207

[redacted]

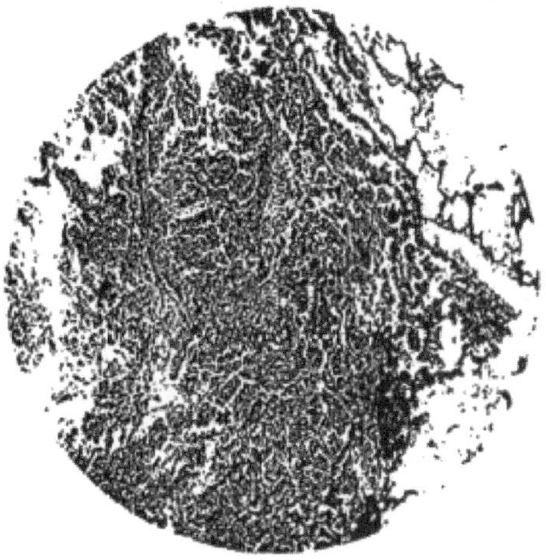

(x30)

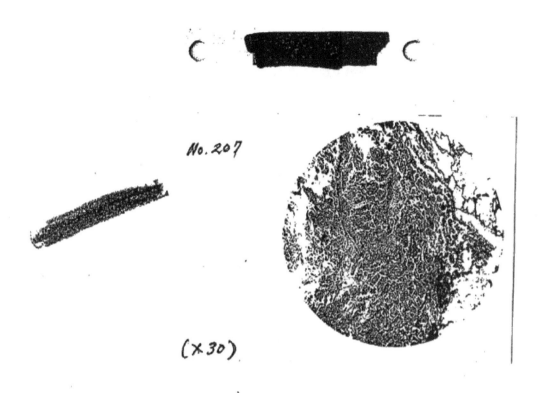

b) In 1 case, multiple acino-lobular pneumonia with some glanders-knots formation and reactive Pleuritis (Intense Bronchiolitis and following acino-lobular pneumonia with some glanders-knots formation and reactive Pleuritis sero-fibrinosa).

[redacted] /11

([redacted] (

[redacted]

No. 254 (b)

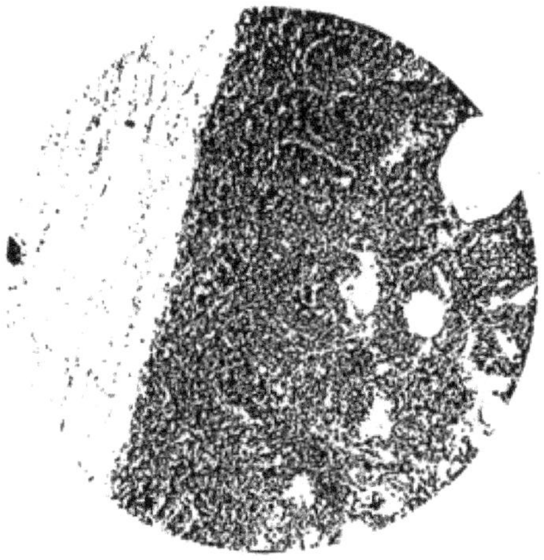

(×60)

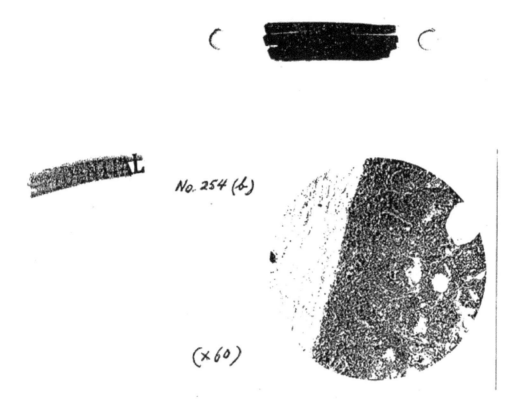

Accordingly the modus of primary lung infection, due to peribronchiolar infection are as following:

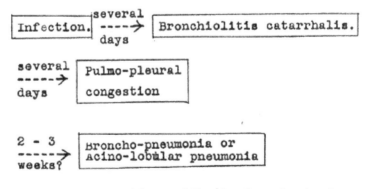

Infection. —several days→ Bronchiolitis catarrhalis.

—several days→ Pulmo-pleural congestion

—2 - 3 weeks?→ Broncho-pneumonia or Acino-lobular pneumonia

*sometimes with glanders-knots formation

[redacted] [redacted] 112

[redacted]

* sometimes with some reactive pleural
  changes.

[redacted] P13

[redacted]

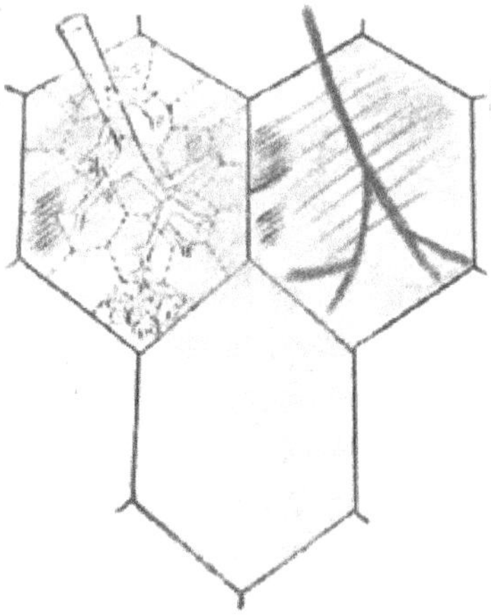

CO[redacted]

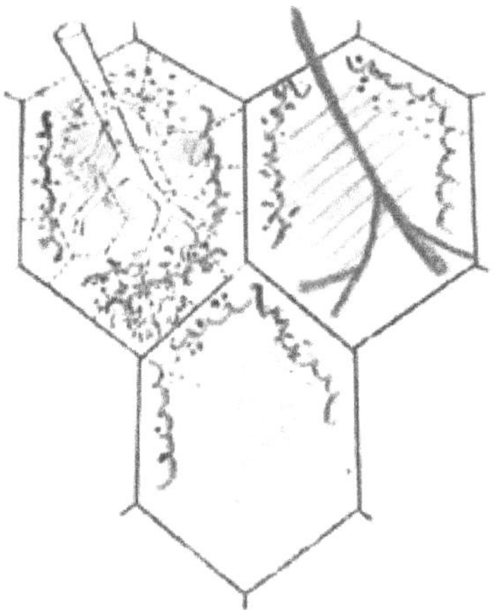

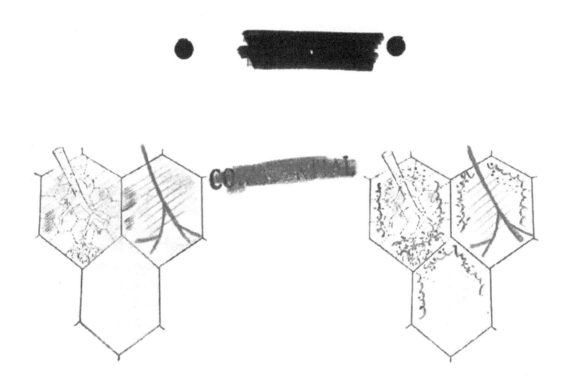

Rather exsudative.

(Edema and bacterial disseminations)

Rather productive.

(Some increased Alveolar epithel cells).

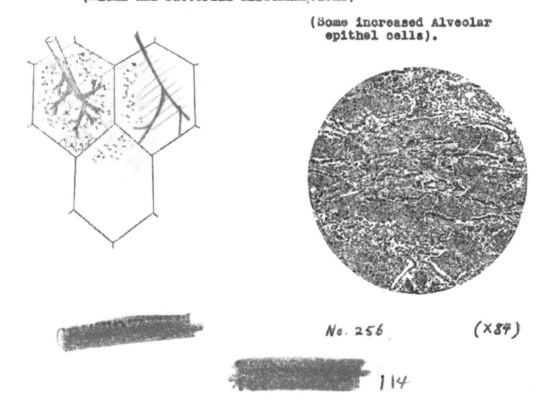

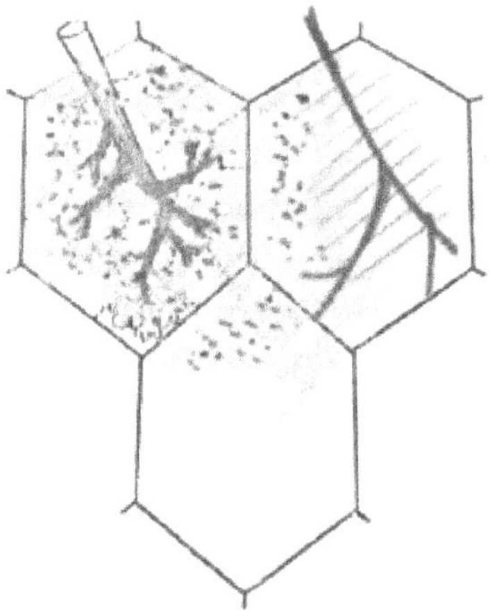

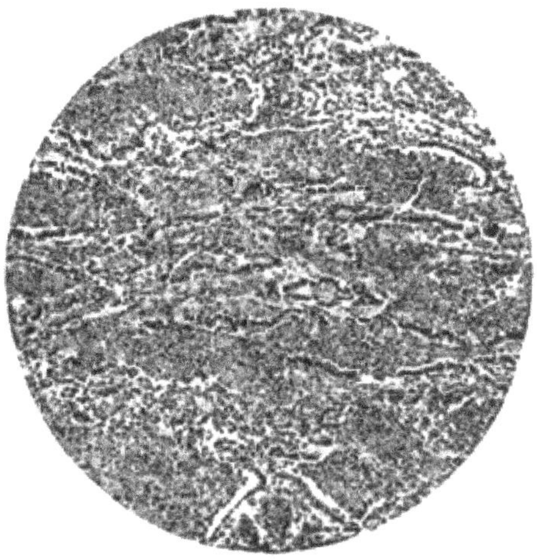

[redacted]

No. 256 (X84)

[redacted] 114

([redacted] (

B) Cecondary Pulmonal infetion. [redacted]

Infected wounds (owing to glanders- infection) cause sometimes metastatic secondary pulmonal infection.

All microscopically investigated 7 cases.

a) Without any remarkable reactive pulmonal changes in 2 cases.

No. 222. Slight pulmonal congestion.

No. 224. Pulmonal congestion and edema.

b) With some diffuse Alveolitis.

(Deucocytes- or lymphocytes- infiltration in alveolar walls, accompanied with considerable pulmonal edema and congestion). Some times with bacterial disseminations. in 5 cases.

No. 180. Considerable pulmonal congestion and edema with some bacterial disseminations.

No. 16. Bronchiolitis catarrhalis and slight diffuse Alveolitis with some bacterial disseminations.

No. 152 Considerable diffuse Alveolitis and pulmonal edema.

No. 167. (a) Slight Alveditis and atelectasis, accompanied with subpleural congestion, slight hemorrhages and fibrinous separation.

No. 190. Round cell infiltration in alveolar walls and some hyperplasia of alveolar epithel cells. (namely in rather chronic course).

[redacted]

[redacted] 115

([redacted] (

[redacted]

B)'. Sometimes occured metastatic severe inflammation of arterioles, due to bacteriaemia;

Endoarteritis or Endoarteriolitis necroticans.

(Necrotic ruins of blood-vessels-walls with extraordinary plenty decayed cellular masses-embolus)

and following inflammations of alveolar walls :

(Diffuse Alveolitis).

No 207. (X20)

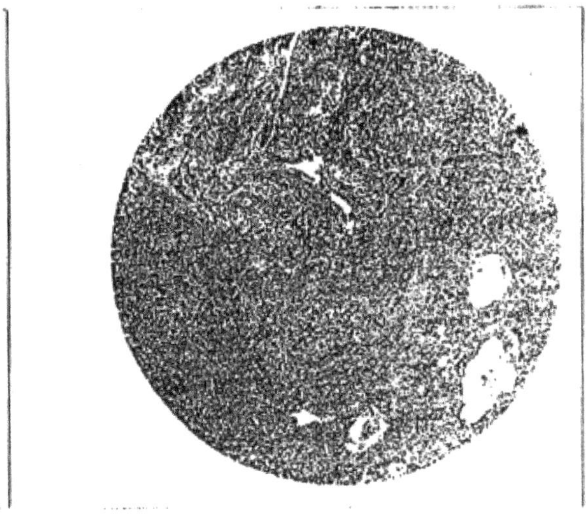

No. 256 (x40)

C). Then diffuse Alveolitis (some times with Endoarteriolits) proceed to

a) Miliary knots formations (without reactive, exsudative-hemorrhagic, acino-lobular, changes.)

b) Multiple acino-lobular pneumonia, and

[redacted]

[redacted] 116

([redacted] (

c) With both changes: miliary knots formation and severe reactive, acino-lobular pneumonia.

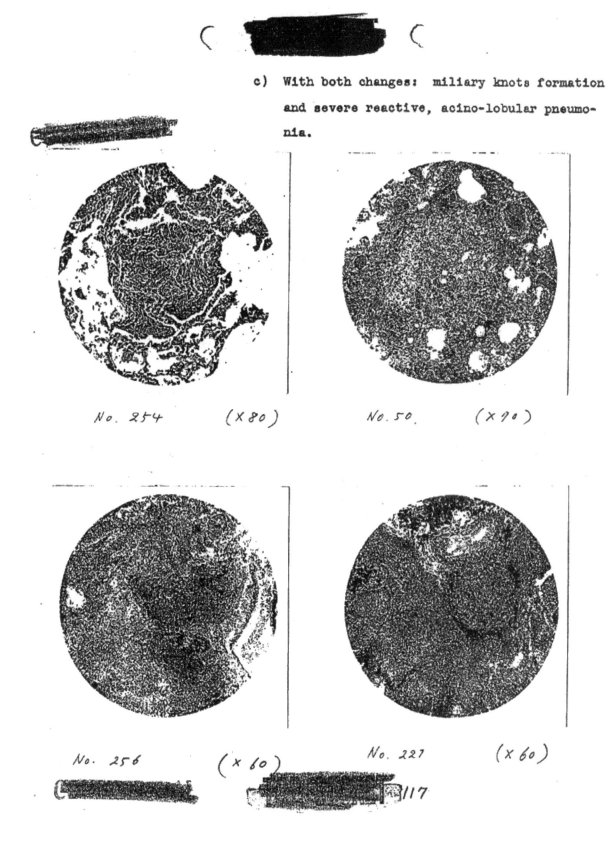

[redacted]

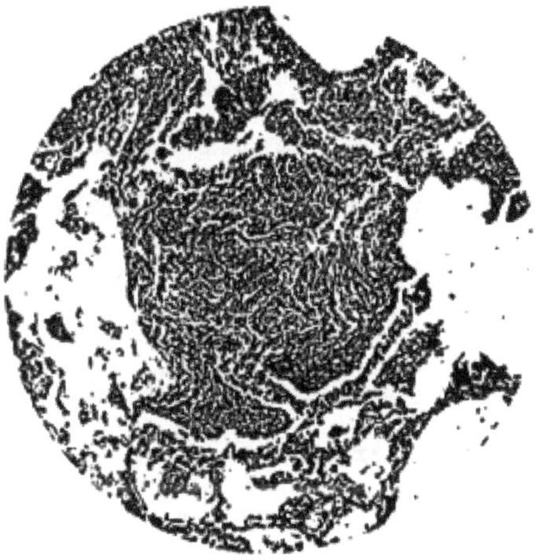

No. 254 (x80)

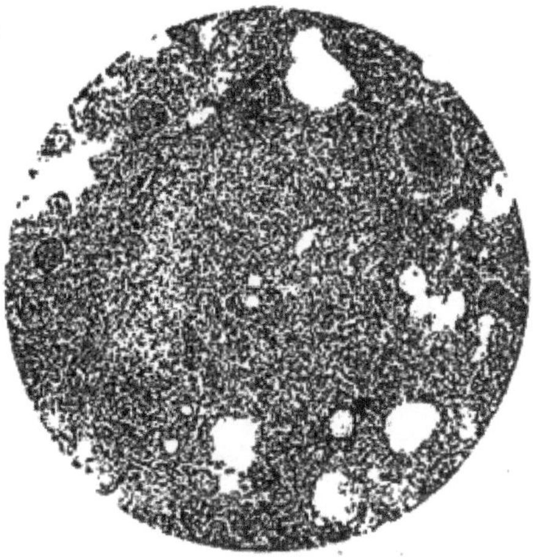

No. 50. (x70)

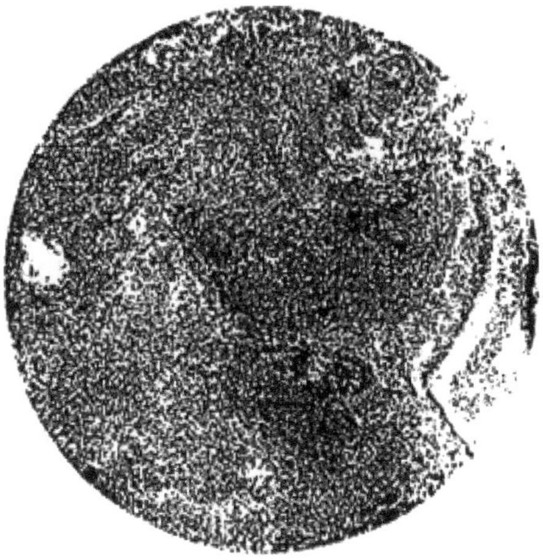

No. 256 (x 60)

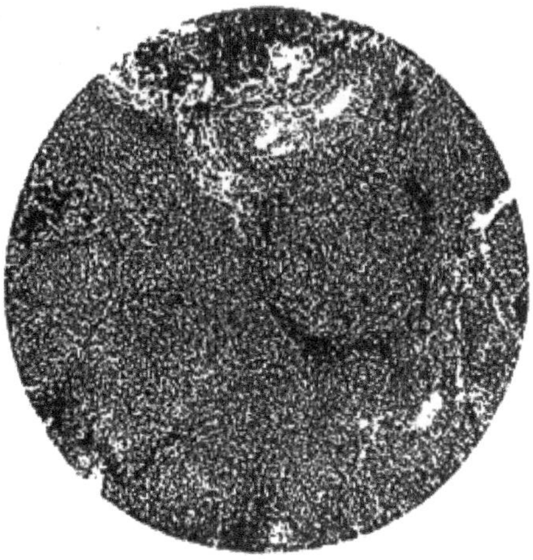

No. 227 (x 60)

[redacted] [redacted]117

[redacted]

a) Miliary knots formation, without reactive pneumonic changes in the neighboring pulmonal tissues, in 4 cases.

[redacted]

No. 254. (a) Glanders-knots in somewhat proliferative for. Multiple Miliar and supermiliar glanders-knots, mainly at the intercalary portions of lung. With slight proliferative perifocal reactions: some hyperplasia of alveolar epitheliums.

No. 205 (a) Glanders-knots formation without remarkable perifocal reactions.

~~No~~ Endoarteriolitis necroticans and multiple supermiliary glanders-knots.

b) Miliary knots are attended sometimes furthermore with (multiple acino-lobular or lobular) pneumonic changes, as reactive exsudative reactions. in 4 cases.

No. 256 (g) Multiple miliary glanders.mnots in hemorrhagic-leucocytic form, with severe exsudative perifocal reactions.

No. 205 (b) Endoarteriolitis necroticans and multiple supermiliary glanders knots with remarkable hemorrhagic

[redacted]

[redacted] 118

([redacted] (

perifocal changesandaslight pleural congestion.

No. 207. (a) Endoarteriolitis necroticans and multiple supermiliary glanders-knots with slight hemorrhagic perifocal reactions, attended with some acino-lobular pneumonic changes.

[redacted]

No. 254. (b) Multiple supermiliary glanders knots and multiple acino-lobular hemorrhagic-leucocytic pneumonia with severe exsudative perifocal changes and following pleuritis hemorrhagica.

c) Diffuse Alveolitis proceed to multiple acino-lobular or lobular pneumonia, sometimes accompanied with miliary glanders-knots (as described in b) and sometimes not. in 4 cases.

1) No. 256. (c) Endoarteriolitis necroticans and multiple acino-lobular pneumonia in hemorrhagic-exsudative form, accompanied with pleuritis hemorrhagicico-exsudative.

No. 256. (b) Multiple lobulo-acinous pneumonia and pleuritis hemorrhagica.

2) No. 221. (a) Lobular pneumonia and reactive perifocal inflammatory edema,

[redacted] [redacted] 119

[redacted]

accompanied with Pleuritis sero-fibrinosa and Bronchiolitis Catarrhalis gravis.

[redacted]

3) No. 146. (h.m.) Lobular pneumonia (sometimes catarrhalic-exsudative, sometimes hemorrhagic-leucocytic) and Bronchiolitis catarrhalis gravis, accompanied with diffuse pulmonal stasis in other pulmonal tissu s.

3) No. 727. (a) Endoarteriolitis necroticans and lobular pneumonia with severe exsudative-hemorrhagic perifocal changes. accompanied with some Bronchiolitis catarrhalis.

d) After several weeks, pneumonic places fall into necrosis or caverns, in 1 case.

No. 727. (b) Lobulo-acinous pneumonia in hemorrhaic-essudative form fall into caseous necrotic masses at focal parts and furthermore caverns-formation.

Accordingly the developing-mode of exsudative-hemorrhagic pulmonal changes are as following:

[redacted] [redacted] 120

([redacted] (

(I). Diffuse Alveolitis.

↓

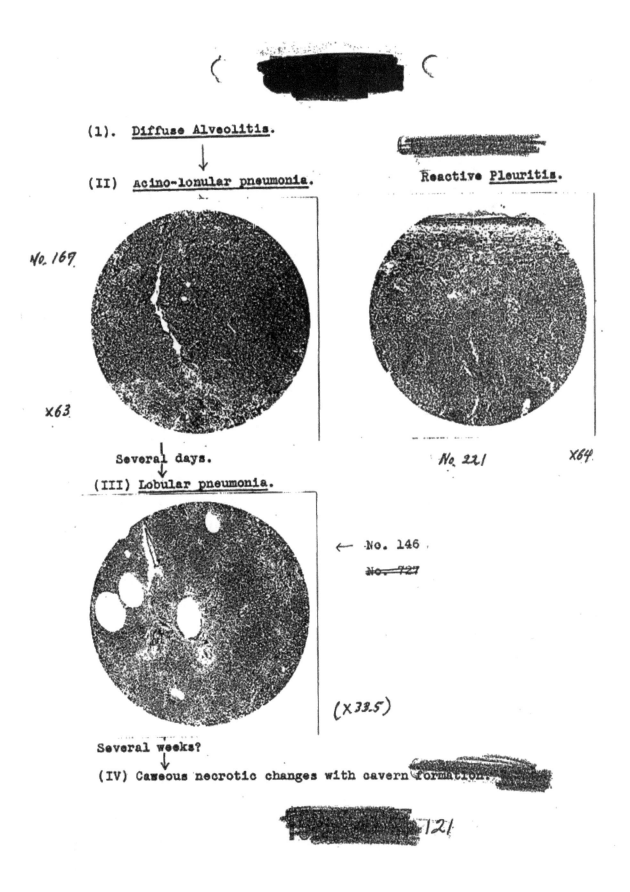

(II) Acino-lonular pneumonia.

No. 167

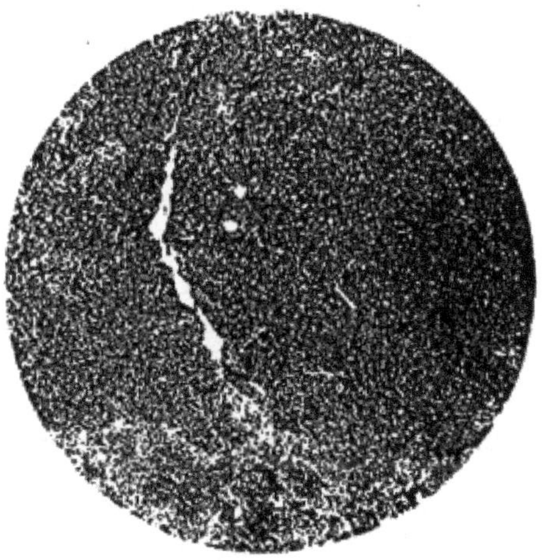

x63

[redacted]

Reactive Pleuritis.

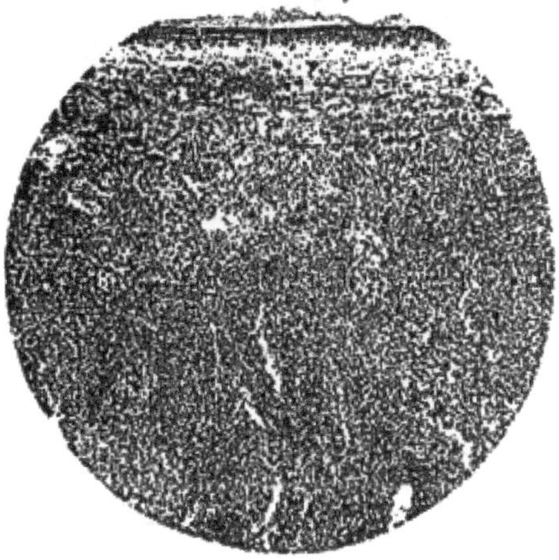

No. 221　　x64

↓ Several days.

(III) Lobular pneumonia.

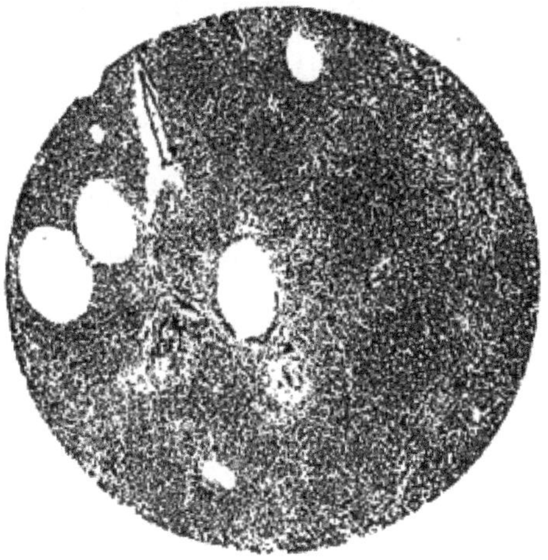

← No. 146

~~No. 727~~

(x33.5)

↓ Several weeks?

(IV) Caseous necrotic changes with cavern [redacted]

[redacted] 121

[redacted]

No. 727

[redacted]

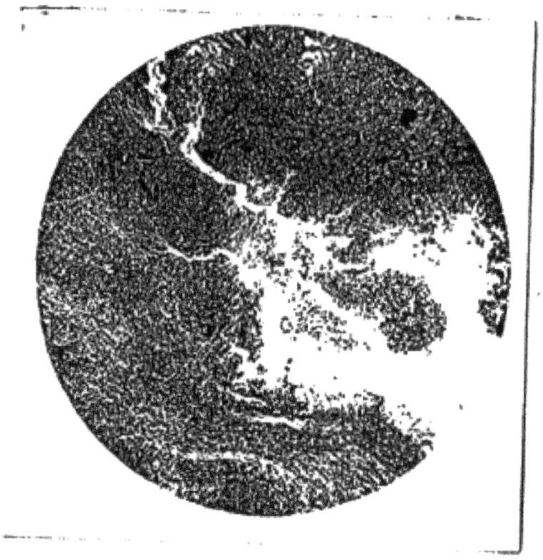

(x64)

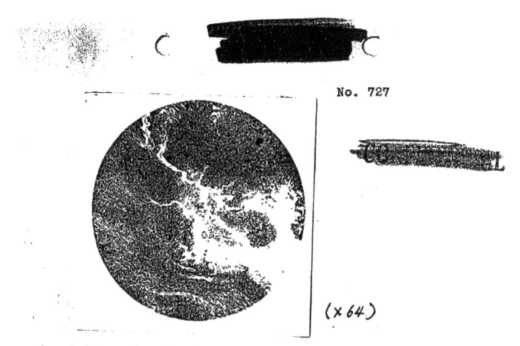

f). On the other hand, exsudative changes are attended gradually with somewhat proliferative reactions, namely slight or remarkable hyperplasia of alveolar epithel cells.

No. 221 (b) Multiple acinous or acino-lobular pneumonia with severe exsudative-hemorrhagic perifocal reactions, accompanied with slight hyperplasia of alveolar epithel cells.

No. 190 Congestion pulmonum in high degree and some round-cell-infiltration in alveolar walls, accompanied with somewhat hyperplasia of alveolar epithel cells. (Alveolitis productive).

No. 167 Obsolete hemorrhagic pneumonia (acinous-lobular), organised with remarkably increased alveolar epithel cells.

No. 254 (a) Multiple miliary or supermiliary glanders-knots with slight proliferative walls (slight increase of

[redacted] 122 [redacted]

C [redacted] C

alveolar epithel cells at perifocal portions).

No. 221 (c) Multiple acious or acino-lobular pneumonia with multiple glanders knots (in rather productive form) at the intercalary portions of lung.

[redacted]

These pneumonic places are in rather productive form: focal necrotic caseous parts and perifocal somewhat productive walls with some hyperplasia of alveolar epithel cells and some giant cell formation.

No. 256 (e) Endoarteriolitis necroticans and subpleural acino-lobular pneumonia with some exsudative-hemorrhagic perifocal reactions, accompanied with papillar increase of bronchiolar or alveolar epithel cells at the intercalary portions of lung.

No. 256 (f) Remarkable hyperplasia of alveolar or bronchiolar epithel cells (papillar increase) at the intercalary portion of lung, without any significant inflammatory signs.

Accordingly the developing mechanismus of productive pulmonal changes by glanders-disease are as followed:

1) Exsudative-hemorrhagic changes.

2) Slight hyperplasia of alveolar epithel cells.

a) In acino-lobular pneumonic parts.

b) In so-called diffuse Alveolitis. (Alveolitis productive)

[redacted]

[redacted] 123

([redacted] (

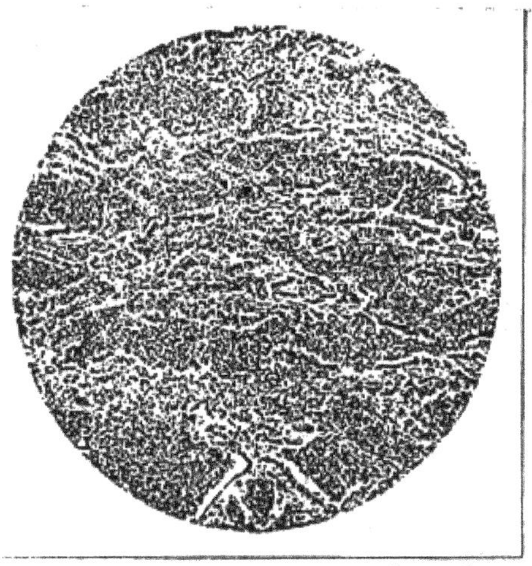

No. 256 (x80)

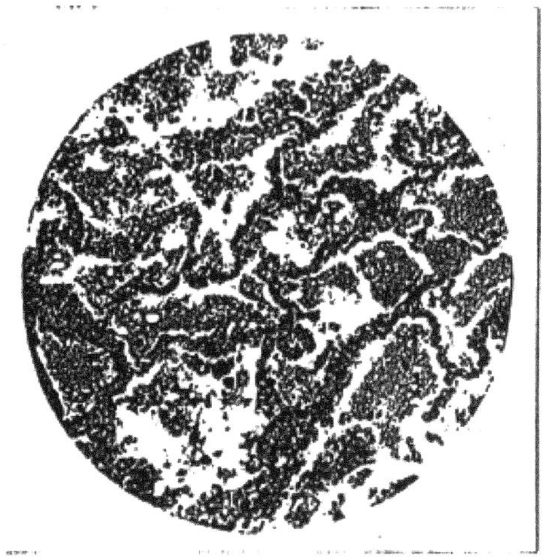

No. 221. (x100).

3) Remarkable hyperplasia of alveolar epithel cell.

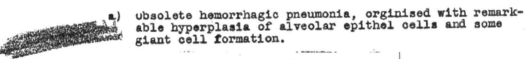

[redacted] a) Obsolete hemorrhagic pneumonia, orginised with remarkable hyperplasia of alveolar epithel cells and some giant cell formation.

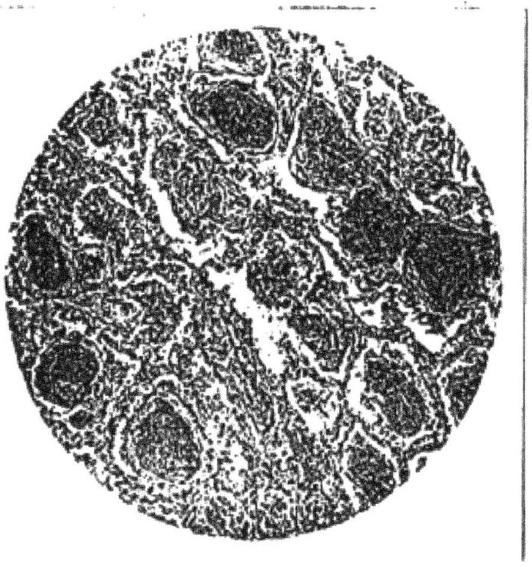

No. 167.

(x80)

b) Rather productive glanders-knots formation. Remarkable hyperplasia of alveolar epithel cells and some giant cell formation.

[redacted] [redacted] 124

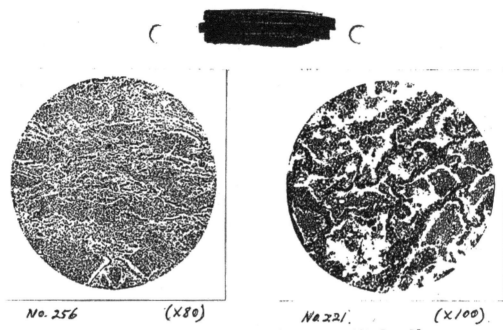

([redacted] (

4) Intense hyperplasia of alveolar epithel cells, especially at the intercalary portion of lung.

[redacted]

Remarkable reactive hyperplasia (papillar increase) of alveolar or bronchiolar epithel cells at the intercalary portions of lung, due to chronic affection of lung.

Generally alveolar epithel cells at the intercalary portions are apt to increase easily.
(Such remarkable papillar increase occurs scarcely in other diseases).

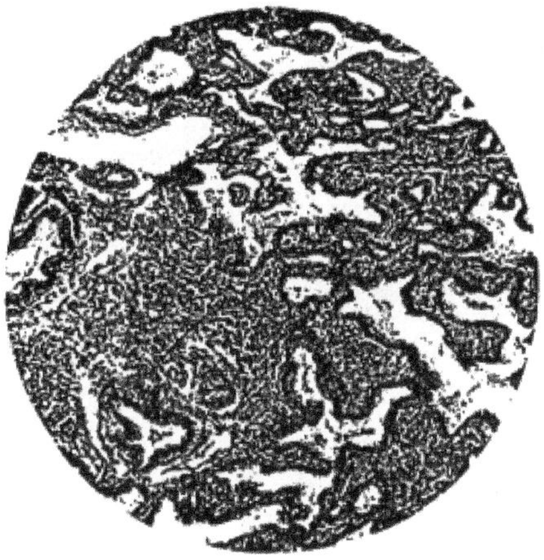

No. 256

(x64)

g) Even in one and the same individual occured some different various pulmonal changes, some places hemorrhagic-exsudativ and some pl ces rather productive: may be, due to the days of each pulmonal changes.

[redacted]

[redacted] 125

[redacted]

1) No. 221 (b) — Acino-lobular pneumonia in exsudative-hemorrhagic form.

No. 221 (e) — Multiple productive glanders-knots formation.

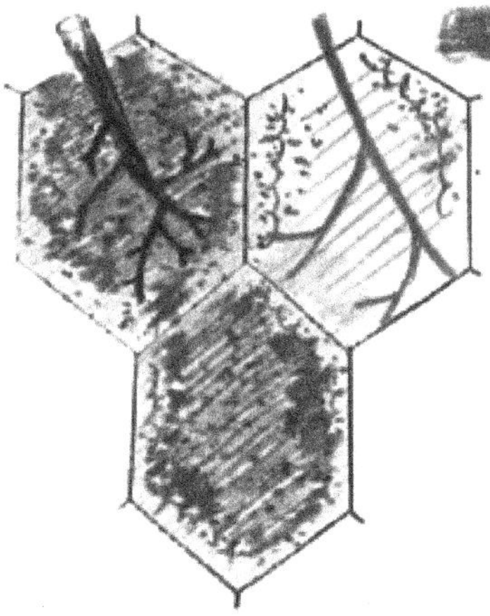

[redacted]

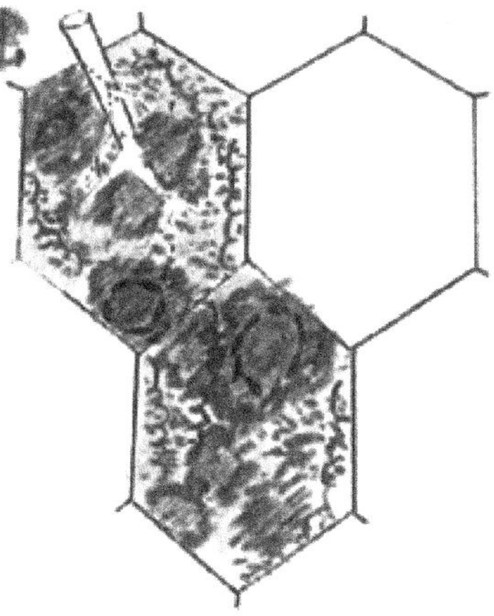

2) No. 256 (b) — Lobulo-acinous pneumonia in exs.-hem. form

No. 256 (e) — Acino-lobular pneumonia with papillar increase of alv. epithel.

No. 256 (f) — Remarkable papillar increase of alv. epith.

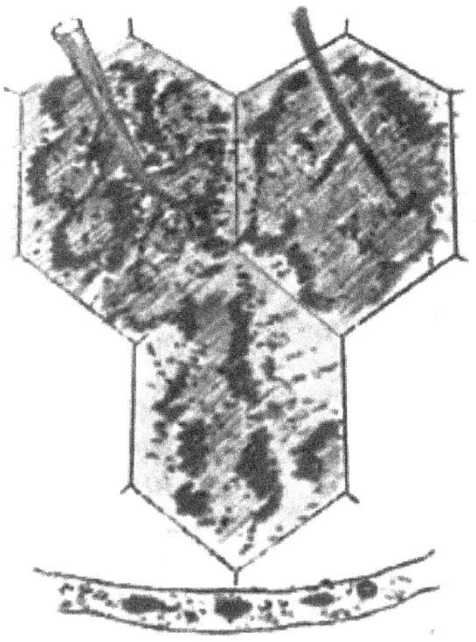

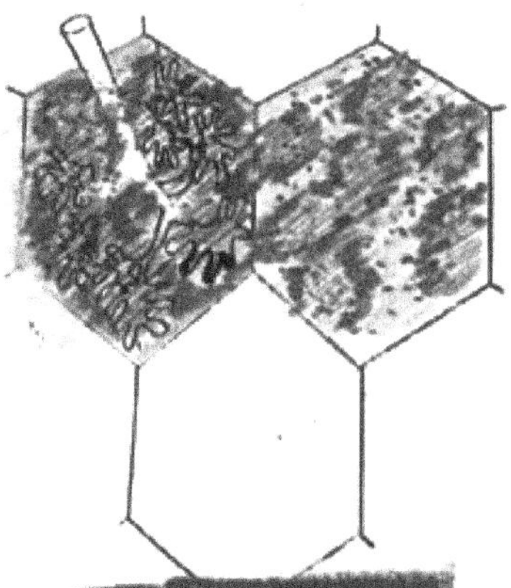

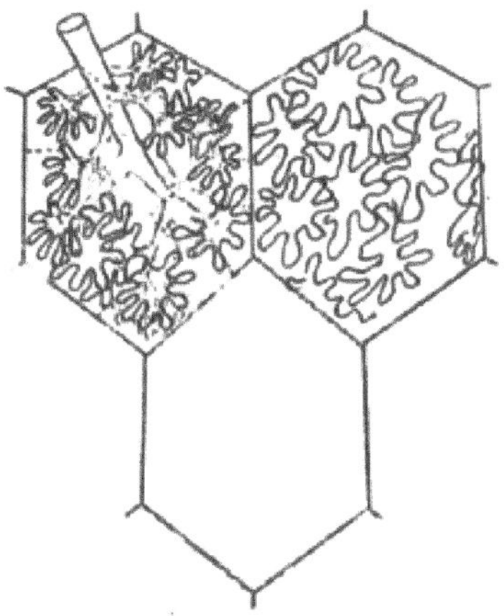

[redacted]

126

[redacted]

3) No. 254 (b)

Multiple miliary glanders-knots, with severe exsudative hemorrhag. perifocal reaction.

[redacted]

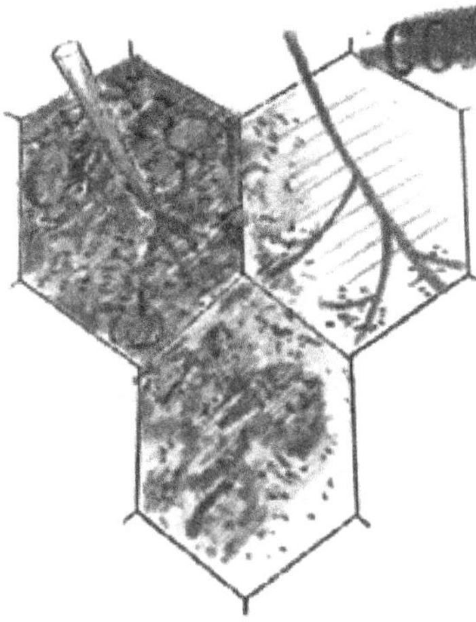

No. 254 (a)

Multiple miliary glanders-knots, without severe perifocal reactions.

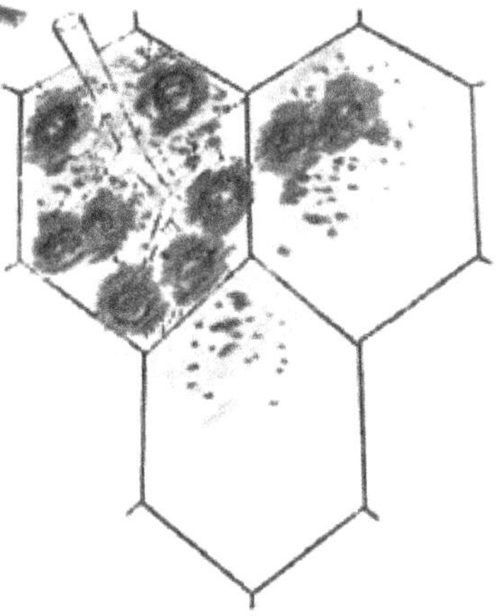

4) No. 167 (c)

Multiple lobular pneumonia in exsud, hemorrhag, form.

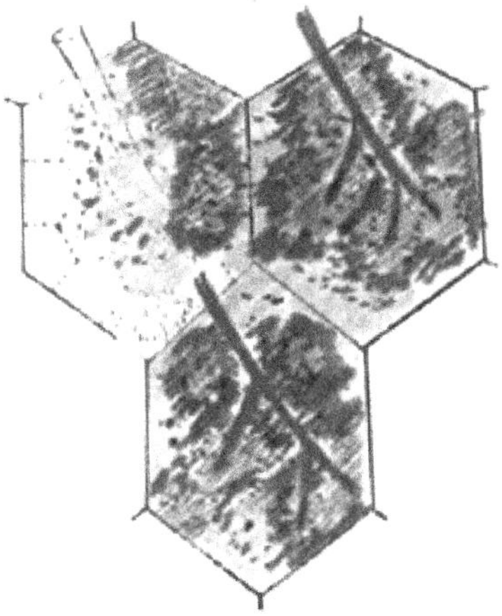

No. 167 (b)

Multiple hemorrhagic pneumonia, organised with some hyperplasia of alveolar epithel cells.

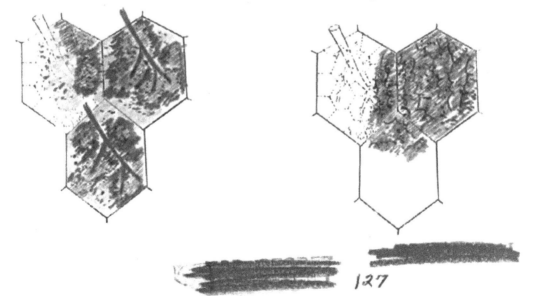

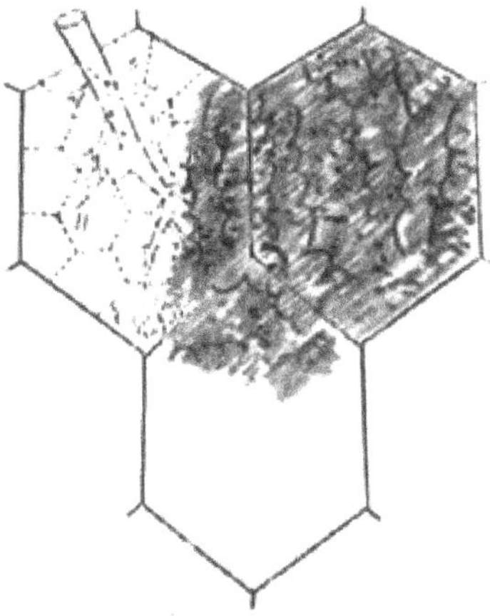

[redacted] 127 [redacted]

([redacted] (

(3)

The classification of general courses of pulmonal changes.

1. Divide all cases into 2 groups:

I) Bronchogenous and 2) haematogenous infection.

[redacted]

I) Course of bronchogenous infection.

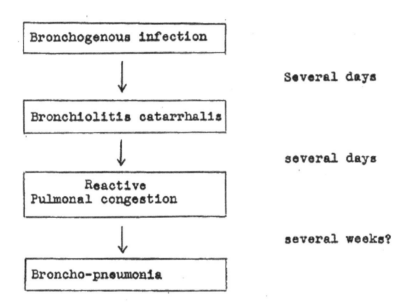

Bronchogenous infection

↓ Several days

Bronchiolitis catarrhalis

↓ several days

Reactive Pulmonal congestion

↓ several weeks?

Broncho-pneumonia

* Sometimes with pleural reaction.

* Sometimes with glanders knots formation ↗ exsudative form. ↘ productive form.

2) Course of hematogenous infection.

I divide all these cases into 2 forms: 1) exsudative form and 2) rather productive form.

[redacted]

[redacted] 128

([redacted] (

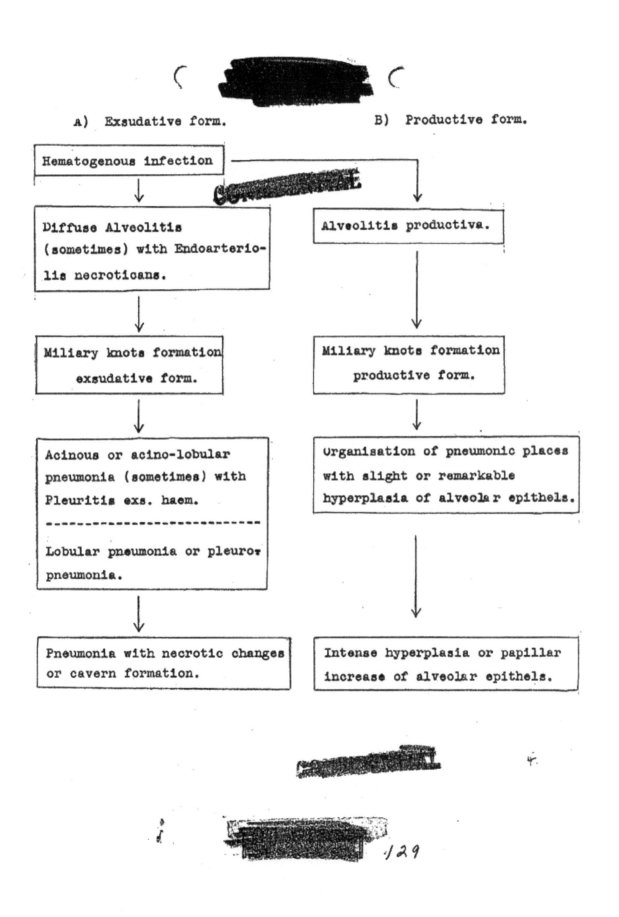

A) Exsudative form.

Hematogenous infection

↓

Diffuse Alveolitis (sometimes) with Endoarteriolis necroticans.

↓

Miliary knots formation exsudative form.

↓

Acinous or acino-lobular pneumonia (sometimes) with Pleuritis exs. haem.

Lobular pneumonia or pleuro-pneumonia.

↓

Pneumonia with necrotic changes or cavern formation.

B) Productive form.

Hematogenous infection

↓

Alveolitis productiva.

↓

Miliary knots formation productive form.

↓

Organisation of pneumonic places with slight or remarkable hyperplasia of alveolar epithels.

↓

Intense hyperplasia or papillar increase of alveolar epithels.

[redacted]

[redacted] 4.

[redacted] 129

([redacted] (

LUNG [redacted]

			16	"	"	50	146	"	"	"	"	"	152	167	"	"	176	178
Alveoli		Emphysema	∸	∸	∸	∸	—	∸	∸	∸	÷	|	∸	∸	÷	—	÷	—
Alveoli		Atelectasis	∸	÷	∸	÷	÷	÷	∸	÷	÷	|	+	++	÷	∸	∸	—
Alveoli		Necrosis or Grander-knots	—	—	—	+	—	—	—	—	—	—	—	—	—	++	—	—
Alveoli	Alveolar Spaces	Edema	++	÷	++	÷	÷	+	+	+	—	+++	++	—	—	(+)	—	∸
Alveoli	Alveolar Spaces	Erythrocytes	∸	(÷)	∸	(+++)	÷	(÷)	÷	÷	—	++	÷	—	(++)	(++)	(∸)	∸
Alveoli	Alveolar Spaces	Leucocytes	—	∸	—	÷	—	—	—	++	—	++	∸	—	—	(+++)	—	—
Alveoli	Alveolar Spaces	Lymphocytes	∸	÷	∸	∸	—	—	—	∸	—	∸	∸	—	÷	(+)	—	—
Alveoli	Alveolar Spaces	Desquamated Epithelial Cells	∸	+	÷	÷	÷	+	∸	++	∸	+++	∸	÷	++	(++)	÷	—
Alveoli	Alveolar Spaces	Heart Desease Cells	—	—	—	—	÷	+	—	÷	∸	∸	—	(∸)	÷	÷	∸	—
Alveoli	Alveolar Spaces	Fibrin	—	÷	—	—	∸	∸	—	÷	—	∸	—	—	÷	(+)	—	—
Alveoli	Alveolar Spaces	Colonies of Bacterium	÷	—	—	—	—	+	—	∸	—	÷	—	—	—	—	—	—
Alveoli	Alveolar Walls	Swelling	÷	+	÷	++	+	÷	+	++	÷	++	+	+	÷	++	÷	—
Alveoli	Alveolar Walls	Hyperplasia of Wall Cells	—	÷	—	÷	÷	—	—	—	—	—	÷	÷	+++	+	÷	∸
Alveoli	Alveolar Walls	Erythrocytes in Capillaries	+	++	+	++	+++	++	++	÷	+	++	+	÷	+	(++)	÷	+++
Alveoli	Alveolar Walls	Leucocytes in Capillaries	∸	÷	∸	+	÷	÷	∸	+	∸	+	÷	÷	—	÷	÷	∸
Alveoli	Alveolar Walls	Lymphocytes in Capillaries	∸	+	∸	÷	÷	∸	∸	—	÷	∸	∸	÷	÷	+	∸	÷
Bronchioli	Contents	Secretion of Mucus	++	++	|	∸	+	÷	+	÷	—	÷	∸	÷	÷	+	++	∸
Bronchioli	Contents	Desquamated Epithelium	++	++	|	∸	+++	++	++	+++	÷	+++	+	÷	∸	÷	+	÷
Bronchioli	Contents	Erythrocytes	∸	—	|	(++)	—	∸	—	—	∸	÷	—	—	(+)	÷	÷	—
Bronchioli	Contents	Leucocytes	∸	∸	|	∸	∸	÷	—	+	—	÷	—	—	÷	—	—	—
Bronchioli	Contents	Lymphocytes	∸	∸	|	—	—	—	—	÷	—	∸	(∸)	—	—	—	—	∸
Bronchioli	Contents	Fibrin	—	÷	|	—	—	(+)	—	—	—	—	—	—	÷	÷	—	—
Bronchioli	Contents	Colonies of Bacterium	÷	÷	|	(÷)	—	÷	—	+	—	÷	—	—	—	—	—	∸
Bronchioli	Peribronchial Tissues	Congestion	÷	+	÷	+++	÷	++	÷	÷	+	++	—	∸	÷	++	÷	++
Bronchioli	Peribronchial Tissues	Edema	+	÷	+	+	÷	+	÷	÷	∸	∸	∸	÷	÷	∸	÷	∸
Bronchioli	Peribronchial Tissues	Hemorrhage	—	—	—	(+)	—	—	—	—	—	—	—	—	—	(+)	—	—
Bronchioli	Peribronchial Tissues	Infiltration Leucocytes	—	—	—	∸	∸	∸	—	÷	—	∸	—	—	—	∸	∸	—
Bronchioli	Peribronchial Tissues	Infiltration Lymphocytes	∸	∸	∸	÷	∸	÷	—	—	÷	∸	—	—	÷	÷	∸	∸
Bronchioli	Peribronchial Tissues	Proliferation of Histiocytic Cells	—	÷	∸	+	÷	÷	—	∸	∸	÷	—	∸	∸	+	÷	+
Blood Vessels	Contents	Erythrocytes	++	++	++	+++	++	+++	++	÷	+	+++	+	÷	+	++	÷	++
Blood Vessels	Contents	Leucocytes	—	÷	(∸)	÷	÷	∸	—	÷	∸	∸	∸	∸	∸	(+++)	∸	∸
Blood Vessels	Contents	Lymphocytes	∸	∸	(∸)	—	—	—	—	÷	—	÷	∸	∸	—	(+)	∸	∸
Blood Vessels	Contents	Monocytes	∸	÷	(∸)	÷	∸	—	—	∸	—	—	∸	—	—	—	—	—
Blood Vessels	Perivascular Tissues	Edema	+	÷	+	÷	÷	÷	+	÷	∸	+	÷	÷	÷	∸	+	—
Blood Vessels	Perivascular Tissues	Hemorrhage	—	—	—	(++)	—	—	—	—	—	—	—	—	—	(+++)	—	—
Blood Vessels	Perivascular Tissues	Infiltration Leucocytes	∸	∸	(∸)	∸	∸	∸	—	—	—	—	—	—	—	(++)	—	—
Blood Vessels	Perivascular Tissues	Infiltration Lymphocytes	÷	—	(∸)	÷	∸	—	—	∸	∸	∸	—	∸	∸	+	∸	—
Blood Vessels	Perivascular Tissues	Proliferation of Histiocytic Cells	∸	∸	∸	∸	∸	∸	∸	∸	—	—	—	∸	+	+	÷	—
Pleura		Covering Masses	|	|	—	∸	+	—	—	—	—	—	|	—	+	—	—	—
Pleura		Thickening	|	|	—	∸	∸	—	—	—	—	—	|	+	÷	+++	—	∸
Pleura		Edema	|	|	÷	÷	+	+	÷	∸	÷	+	|	+	++	+++	+	∸
Pleura		Congestion	|	|	++	+++	+	++	+	—	—	++	|	+	++	++	—	+++
Pleura		Hemorrhage	|	|	—	+	—	—	—	—	—	÷	|	÷	+	++	—	++
Pleura		Infiltration Leucocytes	|	|	—	(+++)	÷	∸	—	—	—	—	|	—	—	—	—	∸
Pleura		Infiltration Lymphocytes	|	|	—	∸	∸	∸	—	—	—	—	|	÷	—	—	—	∸
Pleura		Proliferation of Histiocytic Cells	|	|	∸	∸	÷	÷	∸	—	—	∸	|	÷	(÷)	—	—	—

[redacted] 130

([redacted] (

LUNG [redacted]

			180	190	193	"	205	"	207	"	"	"	"	221	"	"	222	224
Alveoli		Emphysema	−	−	−	−	∸	∸	−	∸	÷	÷	−	−	−	−	∸	÷
Alveoli		Atelectasis	−	÷	−	−	÷	∸	÷	∸	−	−	+	÷	÷	÷	∸	÷
Alveoli		Necrosis or Glander-knots	−	−	+	−	+	+	+	+	+	+	−	+	+	+	−	−
Alveoli	Alveolar Spaces	Edema	++	÷	+++	+++	÷	+++	∸	−	−	−	+	(++)	++	∸	∸	+++
Alveoli	Alveolar Spaces	Erythrocytes	÷	−	+	÷	∸	++	÷	(−)	−	∸	++	÷	÷	++	∸	÷
Alveoli	Alveolar Spaces	Leucocytes	÷	∸	−	++	−	(−)	(+)	(÷)	(+)	∸	÷	+++	+	∸	−	÷
Alveoli	Alveolar Spaces	Lymphocytes	∸	+	∸	∸	−	(÷)	÷	−	−	−	÷	∸	∸	(+)	−	∸
Alveoli	Alveolar Spaces	Desquamated Epithelial Cells	∸	÷	−	÷	∸	÷	+	(÷)	(÷)	∸	÷	++	++	(++)	∸	÷
Alveoli	Alveolar Spaces	Heart Desease Cells	−	−	−	−	−	−	−	−	−	−	−	−	−	−	−	−
Alveoli	Alveolar Spaces	Fibrin	−	−	−	−	−	−	−	−	−	−	−	÷	−	∸	−	∸
Alveoli	Alveolar Spaces	Colonies of Bacterium	+	−	−	++	−	−	−	−	−	−	÷	++	−	−	−	−
Alveoli	Alveolar Walls	Swelling	+	++	÷	++	÷	÷	÷	∸	∸	÷	+	÷	+	÷	÷	+
Alveoli	Alveolar Walls	Hyperplasia of Wall Cells	−	+	−	−	−	−	÷	−	−	∸	−	÷	++	++	−	−
Alveoli	Alveolar Walls	Erythrocytes in Capillaries	+++	++	+	+++	÷	++	+	(+)	÷	+	+++	+	++	÷	+	++
Alveoli	Alveolar Walls	Leucocytes in Capillaries	+	÷	−	÷	∸	∸	∸	∸	∸	÷	∸	+	(+)	∸	−	∸
Alveoli	Alveolar Walls	Lymphocytes in Capillaries	∸	+	∸	−	(÷)	∸	∸	∸	∸	∸	∸	−	∸	÷	−	∸
Bronchioli	Contents	Secretion of Mucus	+	−	(+)	|	(∸)	÷	÷	−	−	|	|	−	|	−	−	÷
Bronchioli	Contents	Desquamated Epithelium	++	÷	∸	|	(∸)	+	÷	(÷)	−	|	|	−	|	−	÷	|
Bronchioli	Contents	Erythrocytes	÷	÷	−	|	−	÷	−	−	−	|	|	∸	÷	+	−	−
Bronchioli	Contents	Leucocytes	÷	−	−	|	−	∸	−	−	−	|	|	+	(+++)	−	−	−
Bronchioli	Contents	Lymphocytes	∸	−	−	|	−	−	−	−	−	|	|	−	∸	−	−	∸
Bronchioli	Contents	Fibrin	−	−	−	|	−	−	−	−	−	|	|	−	(++)	−	−	−
Bronchioli	Contents	Colonies of Bacterium	−	−	−	+	−	−	−	−	−	|	|	−	(++)	−	−	−
Bronchioli	Peribronchial Tissues	Congestion	|	++	++	+++	−	+++	∸	÷	+	|	|	+	÷	++	÷	−
Bronchioli	Peribronchial Tissues	Edema	+++	∸	÷	+++	÷	++	∸	÷	÷	|	|	÷	−	−	∸	÷
Bronchioli	Peribronchial Tissues	Hemorrhage	|	−	∸	÷	−	÷	−	−	−	|	|	−	÷	−	−	−
Bronchioli	Peribronchial Tissues	Infiltration – Leucocytes	|	÷	−	∸	∸	∸	−	−	−	|	|	+	∸	−	−	−
Bronchioli	Peribronchial Tissues	Infiltration – Lymphocytes	|	+	∸	−	∸	÷	(÷)	−	−	|	|	÷	∸	∸	−	∸
Bronchioli	Peribronchial Tissues	Proliferation of Histiocytic Cells	|	+	−	−	−	∸	−	−	−	|	|	÷	−	÷	∸	−
Blood Vessels	Contents	Erythrocytes	+++	++	+++	+++	++	+++	++	++	++	++	+++	++	+	+	++	++
Blood Vessels	Contents	Leucocytes	(++)	∸	−	−	÷	(++++)	(++++)	−	∸	∸	∸	÷	(+++)	∸	∸	∸
Blood Vessels	Contents	Lymphocytes	÷	∸	−	−	−	|	|	−	−	−	−	∸	−	∸	−	−
Blood Vessels	Contents	Monocytes	÷	∸	−	−	−	+	+	−	−	−	−	−	−	−	−	−
Blood Vessels	Perivascular Tissues	Edema	+	−	∸	+++	÷	++	÷	+	+	∸	÷	∸	|	∸	÷	+
Blood Vessels	Perivascular Tissues	Hemorrhage	−	−	−	−	−	÷	−	−	−	−	∸	−	|	−	−	−
Blood Vessels	Perivascular Tissues	Infiltration – Leucocytes	−	÷	−	−	−	(+)	(+++)	−	−	−	−	÷	(+++)	∸	−	−
Blood Vessels	Perivascular Tissues	Infiltration – Lymphocytes	−	(+)	−	−	−	−	−	−	−	−	(÷)	∸	|	(÷)	−	∸
Blood Vessels	Perivascular Tissues	Proliferation of Histiocytic Cells	−	÷	−	−	−	−	−	−	−	−	(∸)	∸	|	∸	−	−
Pleura		Covering Masses	−	−	−	−	−	−	−	−	−	−	−	÷	−	|	|	−
Pleura		Thickening	−	−	−	÷	−	−	∸	−	∸	÷	−	∸	−	|	|	−
Pleura		Edema	∸	−	÷	÷	÷	∸	÷	+	++	÷	÷	+	÷	|	|	÷
Pleura		Congestion	+	+++	+++	+++	+++	++	++	++	+++	+++	++	++	−	|	|	÷
Pleura		Hemorrhage	−	−	∸	∸	÷	÷	÷	∸	∸	÷	∸	÷	−	|	|	(∸)
Pleura		Infiltration – Leucocytes	−	∸	−	−	−	−	−	−	−	−	−	÷	∸	|	|	−
Pleura		Infiltration – Lymphocytes	−	+	−	−	−	−	(÷)	−	−	−	−	+	−	|	|	−
Pleura		Proliferation of Histiocytic Cells	−	÷	−	∸	−	−	∸	−	−	−	−	÷	∸	|	|	−

[redacted]

C [redacted] C

LUNG [redacted]

			229	"	"	254	"	"	256	"	"	"	"	"	727	"	731	"
Alveoli		Emphysema	−	−	−	∸	∸	−	−	∸	∸	−	∸	∸	−	−	+÷	−
		Atelectrasis	−	∸	÷	÷	÷	−	∸	÷	+	−	÷	÷	÷	+	÷	∸
		Necrosis or Glander-Knots	++	++	−	+	+	+	+	++	+	+	+	−	+	++	÷	++
	Alveolar Spaces	Edema	+++	∸	÷	÷	++	+	÷	++	(++)	(+++)	(+)	∸	+	÷	÷	+++
		Erythrocytes	+++	∸	∸	∸	++	∸	∸	(+)	(+++)	(+++)	(++)	(÷)	++	−	÷	+
		Leucocytes	÷	∸	∸	−	+	+÷	∸	÷	+	÷	(+÷)	(+)	(+++)	−	−	÷
		Lymphocytes	+	∸	−	(÷)	÷	∸	−	−	∸	−	−	−	÷	÷	∸	∸
		Desquamated Epithelial Cells	++÷	÷	∸	÷	+	+	(+)	(++)	++	÷	(+÷)	÷	÷	∸	∸	÷
		Heart Desease Cells	÷	∸	∸	∸	÷	∸	∸	÷	+	∸	−	∸	(+)	−	∸	∸
		Fibrin	+÷	−	−	−	−	−	(÷)	−	−	(÷)	−	−	−	−	−	(÷)
		Colonies of Bacterium	−	−	−	∸	−	−	−	−	−	−	−	−	−	−	−	+
	Alveolar Walls	Swelling	++	÷	÷	÷	++	÷	++	÷	++	÷	÷	÷	+	÷	∸	÷
		Hyperplasia of Wall Cells	÷	∸	∸	−	÷	∸	+÷	÷	÷	÷	(++)	÷	(÷)	(÷)	−	−
		Erythrocytes in Capillaries	++	÷	++	÷	++	+	+	+	++	++	+	+	+÷	+	÷	÷
		Leucocytes in Capillaries	÷	∸	∸	−	∸	∸	+	÷	+	÷	÷	∸	∸	−	−	+
		Lymphocytes in Capillaries	÷	∸	÷	(+)	∸	∸	∸	∸	∸	−	−	−	∸	(+)	−	−
Bronchioli	Contents	Secretion of Mucus	−	−	−	∸	−	|	÷	÷	∸	∸	÷	−	|	|	÷	÷
		Desquamated Epithelium	∸	∸	÷	÷	÷	|	÷	÷	+	÷	(+÷)	∸	|	|	(++)	+÷
		Erythrocytes	÷	−	−	∸	+÷	|	÷	÷	(++)	(++)	(++)	−	|	|	−	∸
		Leucocytes	÷	−	−	−	÷	|	−	∸	(+++)	(+)	(+++)	−	|	|	−	(++)
		Lymphocytes	∸	−	−	−	÷	|	−	−	−	÷	−	−	|	|	−	÷
		Fibrin	−	−	−	−	∸	|	÷	−	(÷)	(+)	−	−	|	|	−	−
		Colonies of Bacterium	−	−	−	−	−	|	−	−	−	−	−	−	|	|	−	−
	Peribronchial Tissues	Congestion	+÷	−	+÷	÷	+++	÷	++	+	+	÷	+÷	÷	|	|	÷	(+++)
		Edema	÷	∸	−	÷	÷	∸	÷	÷	+	|	÷	÷	|	|	÷	(+++)
		Hemorrhage	÷	−	−	−	+÷	−	÷	−	(++)	(++)	(+)	−	|	|	−	(÷)
		Infiltration: Leucocytes	∸	−	−	−	÷	÷	÷	∸	∸	÷	∸	∸	|	|	−	(÷)
		Infiltration: Lymphocytes	÷	−	−	+	÷	+	∸	∸	∸	÷	∸	−	|	|	−	−
		Proliferation of Histiocytic Cells	÷	−	−	÷	÷	∸	−	∸	−	∸	(+)	−	|	|	−	−
Blood Vessels	Contents	Erythrocytes	++÷	+÷	++	+	++	++	++	++	++÷	+++	++	++	++	++	÷	+
		Leucocytes	∸	∸	∸	−	−	−	÷	÷	(+++)	(+++)	(+++)	−	∸	−	−	∸
		Lymphocytes	∸	−	−	∸	−	−	−	−	∸	∸	−	−	−	∸	−	(÷)
		Monocytes	−	−	−	−	−	−	−	−	∸	∸	−	−	−	∸	−	−
	Perivascular Tissues	Edema	÷	÷	∸	+	÷	−	÷	÷	÷	+	÷	÷	÷	∸	÷	+
		Hemorrhage	÷	−	−	−	÷	−	−	−	÷	++	−	−	−	−	∸	−
		Infiltration: Leucocytes	∸	∸	−	−	∸	−	−	−	(+++)	(++)	−	−	−	−	−	−
		Infiltration: Lymphocytes	÷	÷	−	(+)	++	∸	−	−	−	−	−	−	−	+	−	−
		Proliferation of Histiocytic Cells	÷	∸	−	(+)	+	∸	−	−	−	−	−	−	−	−	−	−
Pleura		Covering Masses	|	(+)	−	|	−	−	−	+	−	−	−	−	−	−	−	−
		Thickening	|	++	−	|	∸	−	−	(÷)	÷	(÷)	−	−	−	÷	−	−
		Edema	|	(÷)	÷	|	++	÷	∸	÷	÷	÷	+	÷	÷	÷	(÷)	÷
		Congestion	|	(+)	+++	|	+++	÷	++	+++	+++	+++	++	++	+	÷	÷	÷
		Hemorrhage	|	−	−	|	++	−	(+)	+÷	+	+	∸	−	÷	−	−	−
		Infiltration: Leucocytes	|	∸	−	|	−	−	(÷)	(++)	−	−	−	−	−	−	−	−
		Infiltration: Lymphocytes	|	÷	−	|	÷	∸	∸	+	−	−	−	−	−	(÷)	−	−
		Proliferation of Histiocytic Cells	|	(++)	−	|	∸	÷	(+)	÷	−	−	−	−	−	÷	−	−

[redacted]

[redacted] /32

([redacted] (

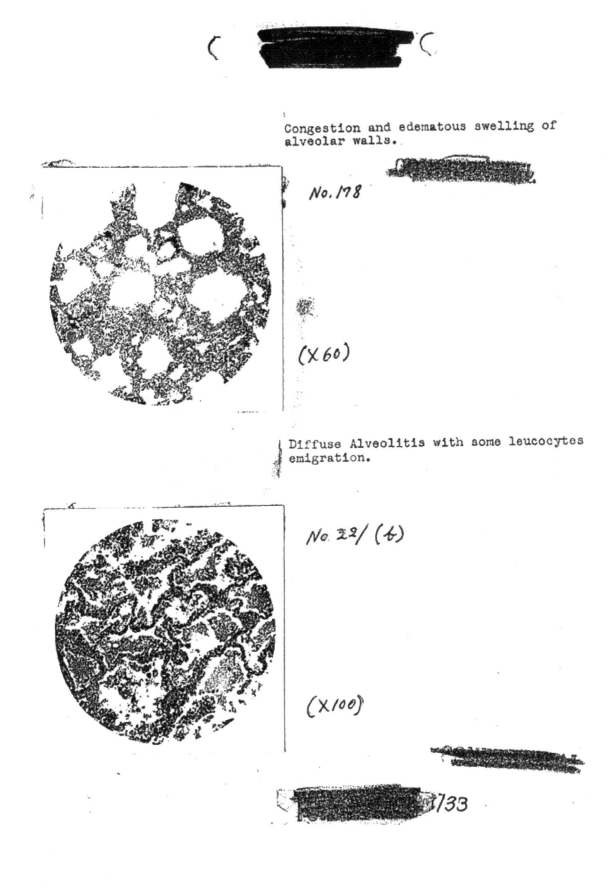

Congestion and edematous swelling of alveolar walls.

[redacted]

No. 178

(X 60)

Diffuse Alveolitis with some leucocytes emigration.

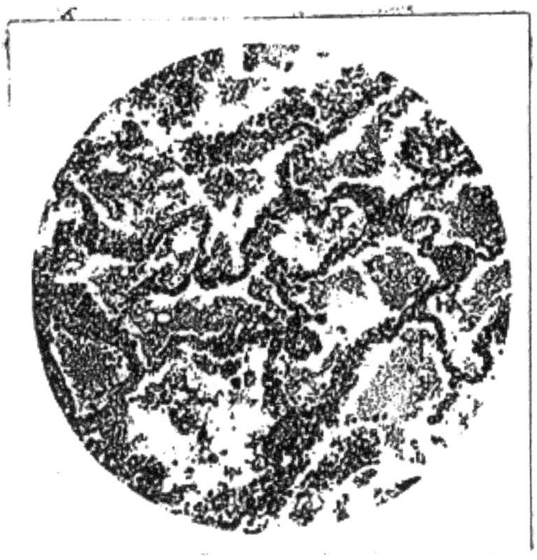

No. 221 (b)

(X100)

[redacted]

[redacted]733

([redacted])

Bronchiolitis and Peribronchiolitis gravis.

[redacted]

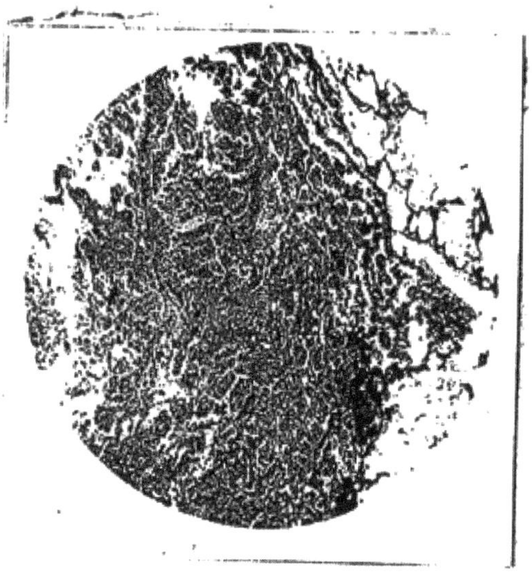

No. 207(c)

(×30)

Bronchitis catarrhalis gravis with massive desquamated epitheliums.

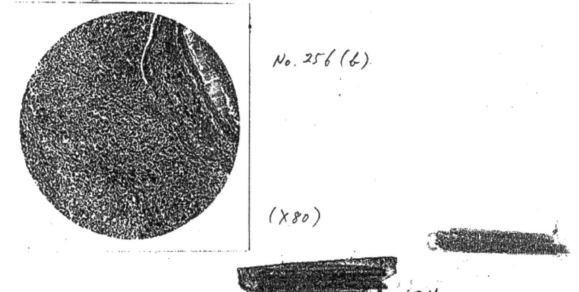

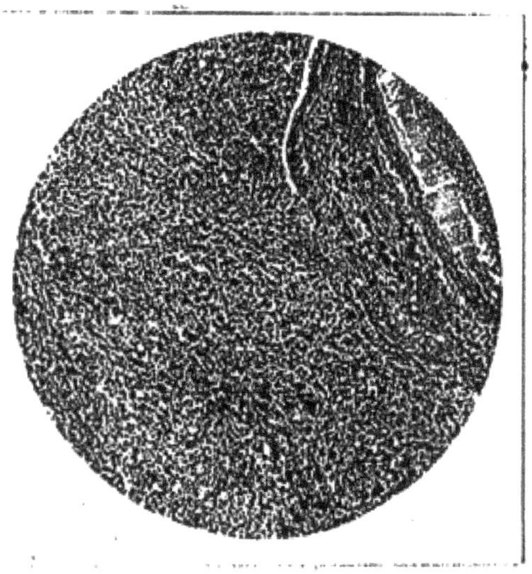

No. 256(b)

(×80)

[redacted]

[redacted] 134

([redacted] (

Endoarteriitis necroticans.

[redacted]

No. 207 (a)

(×20)

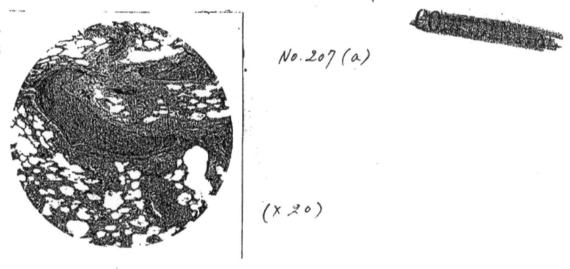

Endoarteriitis necroticans, in high power.

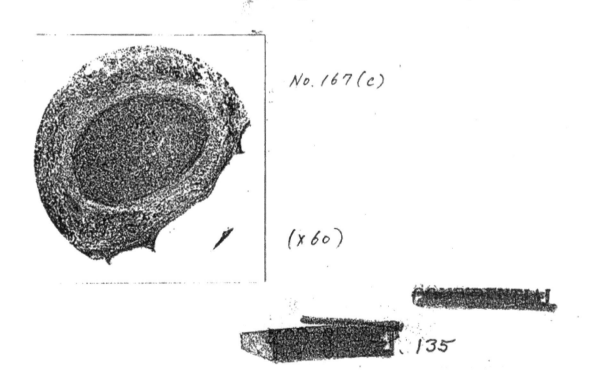

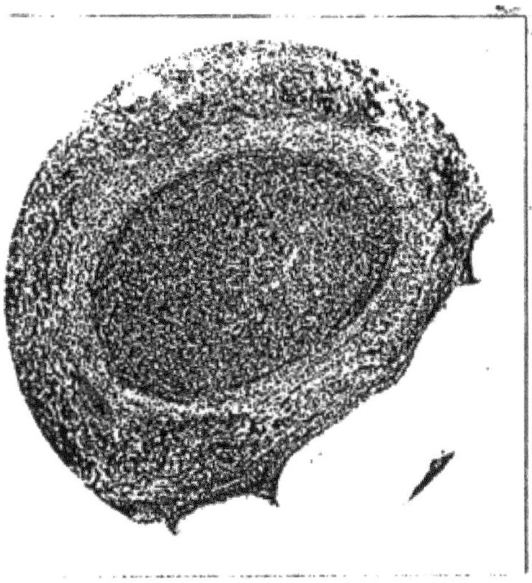

No. 167 (c)

(×60)

[redacted]

[redacted] . 135

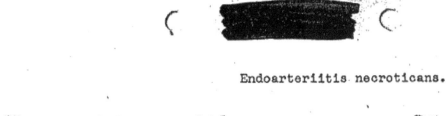

([redacted])

[redacted]

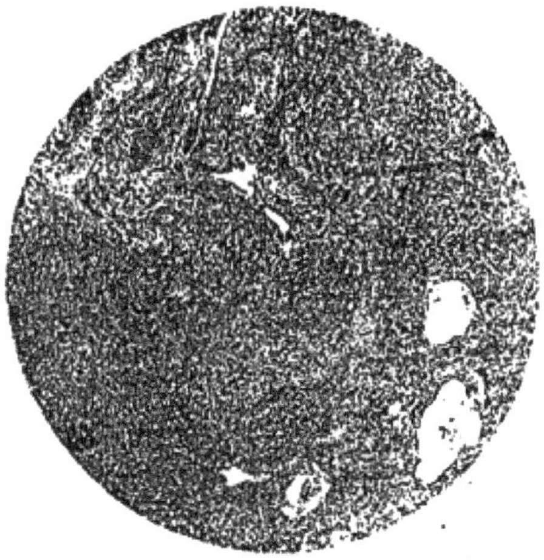

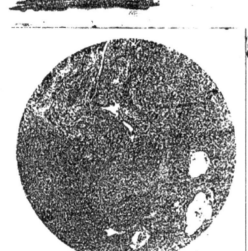

Endoarteriitis necroticans and diffuse hemorrhages in the neighbouring pulmonal tissues.

No. 256 (c)

(x 40)

[redacted]

[redacted] 136

C [redacted] C

[redacted]

Miliary exudative glanders-knot, in high power.

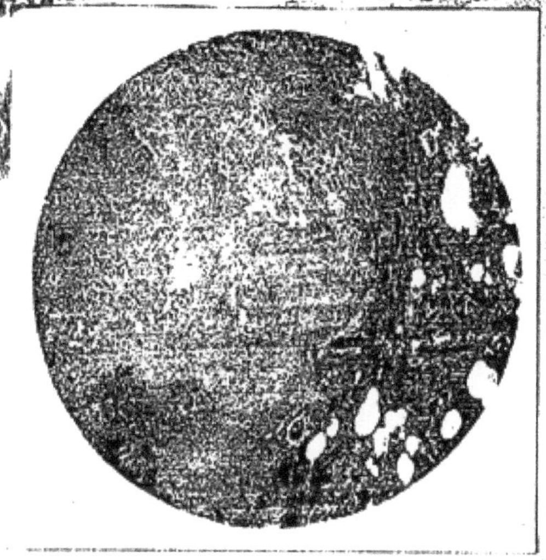

No. 205 (b)

(×20)

Miliary exudative glanders-knot. Leucocytic-exudative peripheral zone of knot, in high power.

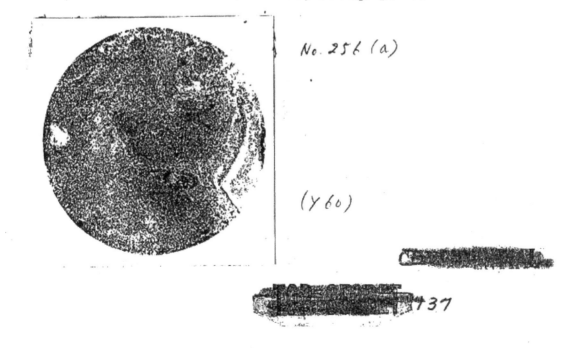

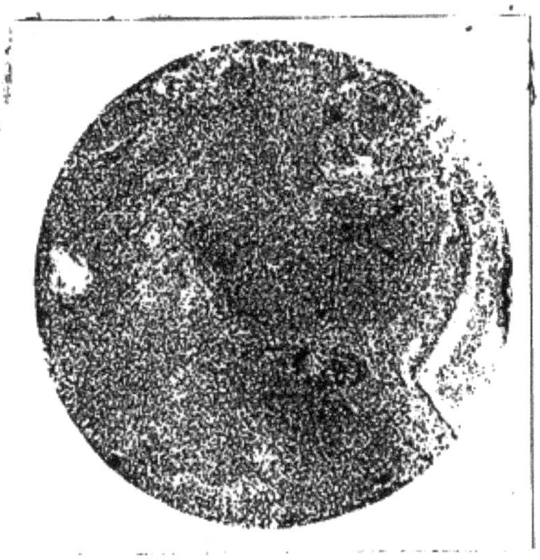

No. 256 (a)

(×60)

[redacted]

[redacted] 137

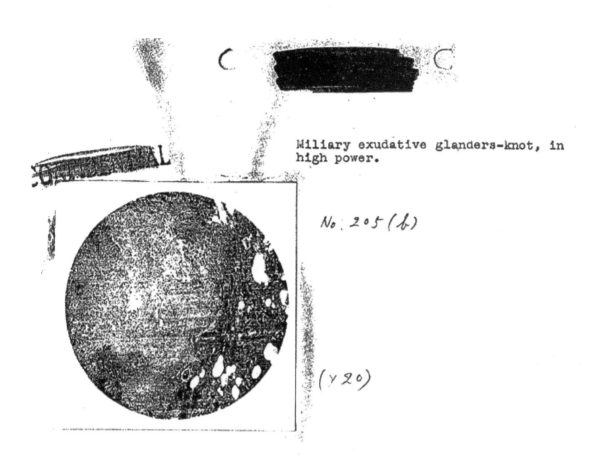

C [redacted] C

[redacted]

Miliary glanders-knot in rather exudative form.

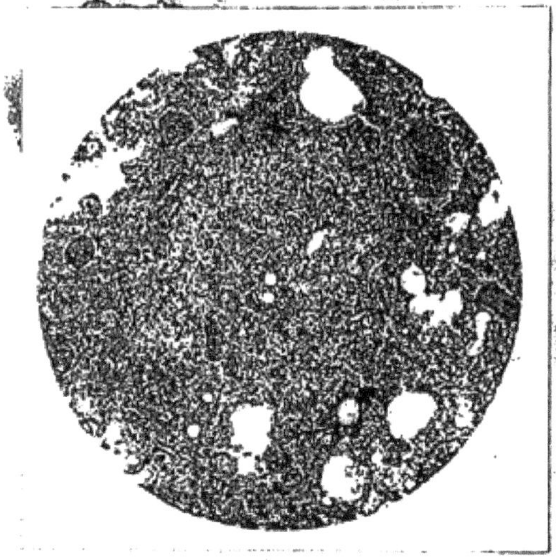

No. 50

(x70)

Miliary glanders-knot in rather exudative form, with intense perifocal reaction.

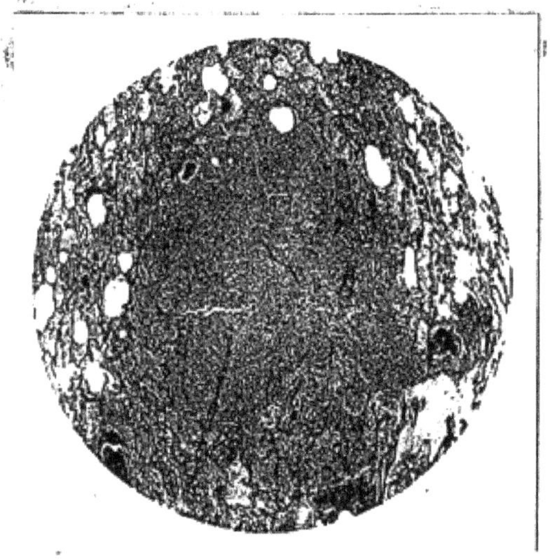

No. 193 (a)

(X20)

[redacted]

[redacted] 138

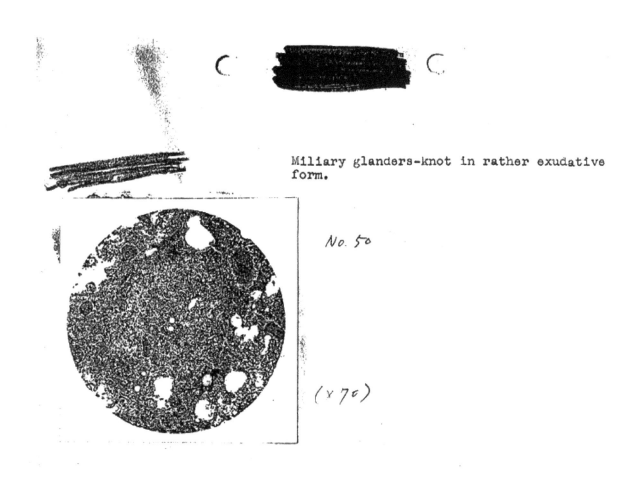

[redacted]

Endoarteriitis necroticans and pneumonic changes in the neighbouring pulmonal tissues.

[redacted]

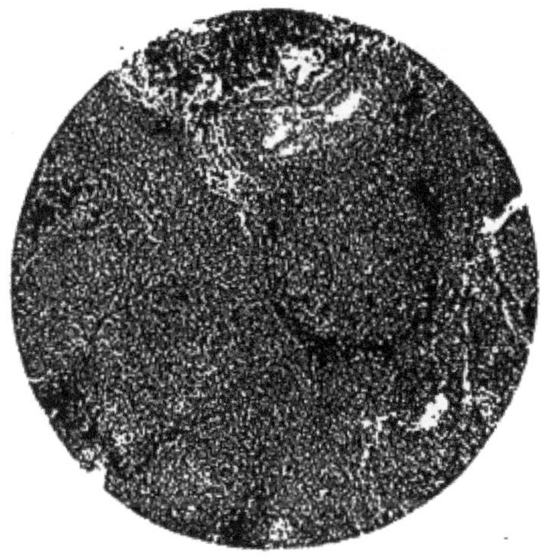

No. 221 (b)

(x60)

Endoarteriolitis obliterans.
Intense thickning of walls of arteriole, accompanied with remarkable round cell accumulation in intima.

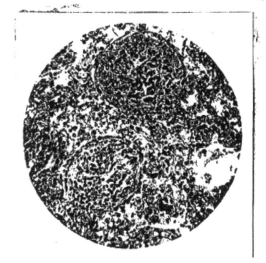

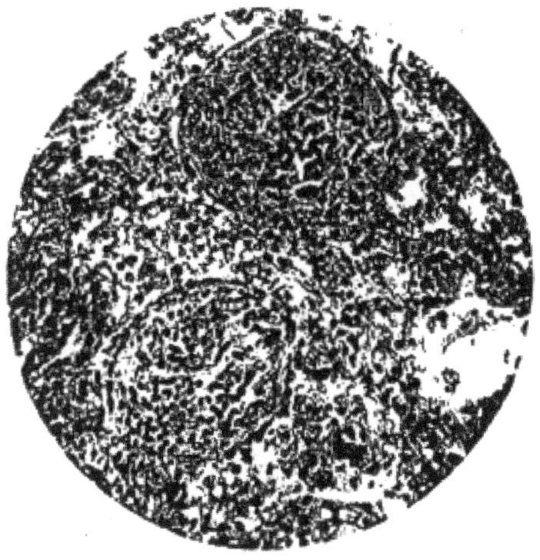

No. 221 (c)

(x180)

[redacted]

[redacted] 139

([redacted] (

Miliary glanders-knot, in rather productive form.
Without any perifocal reaction.

[redacted]

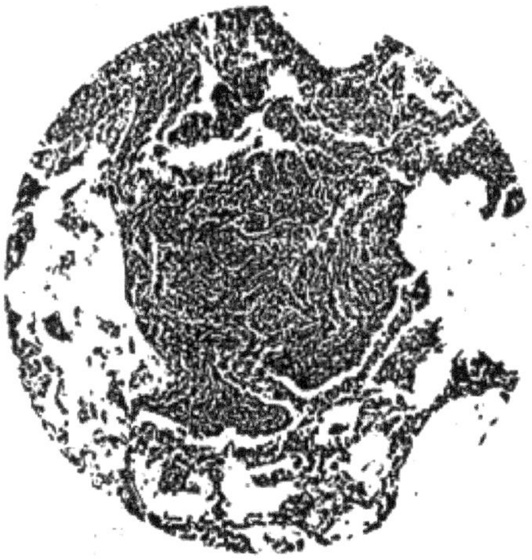

No. 254 (a)

(x 80)

Some miliary glanders-knots with central caseous focus.

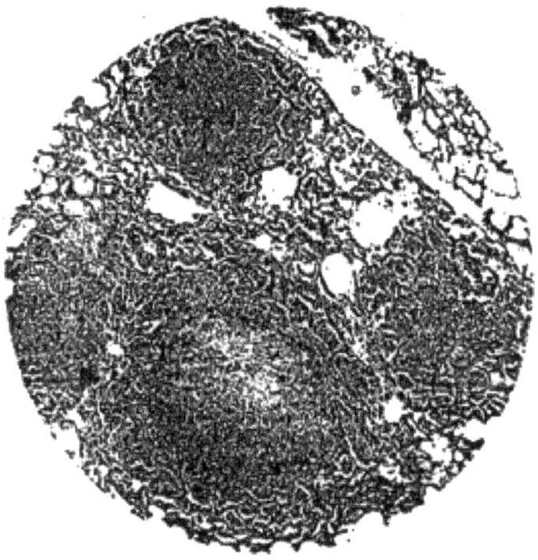

No. 254 (a)

(x 20)

[redacted]

[redacted] 140

([redacted] (

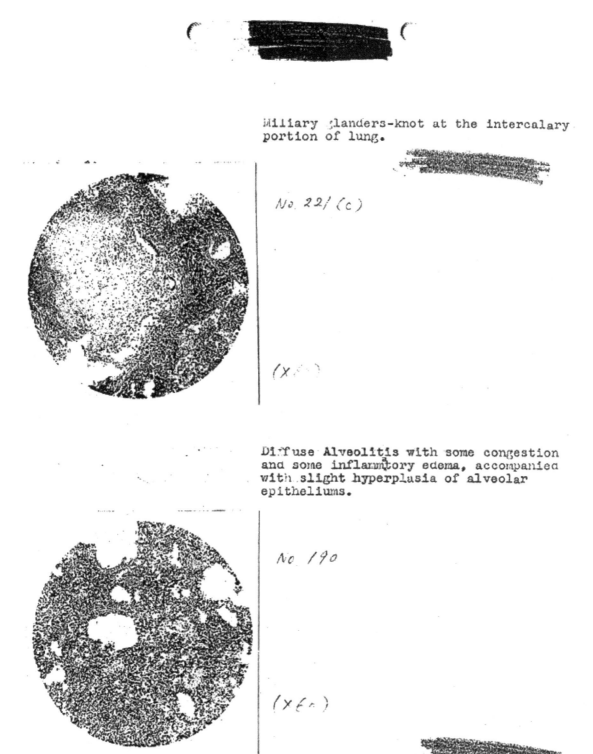

Miliary glanders-knot at the intercalary portion of lung.

[redacted]

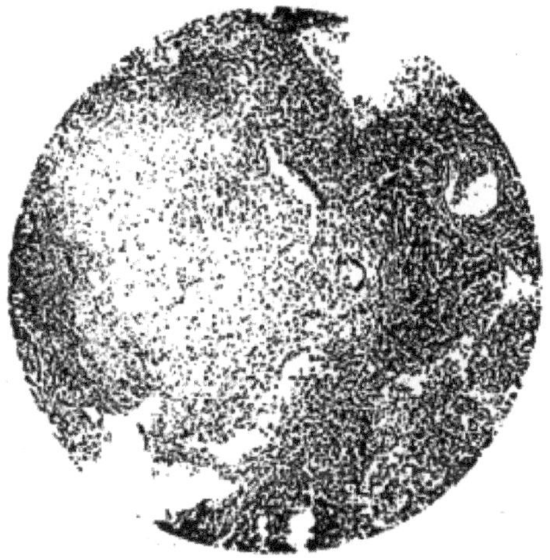

No. 221 (c)

(X[illegible])

Diffuse Alveolitis with some congestion and some inflammatory edema, accompanied with slight hyperplasia of alveolar epitheliums.

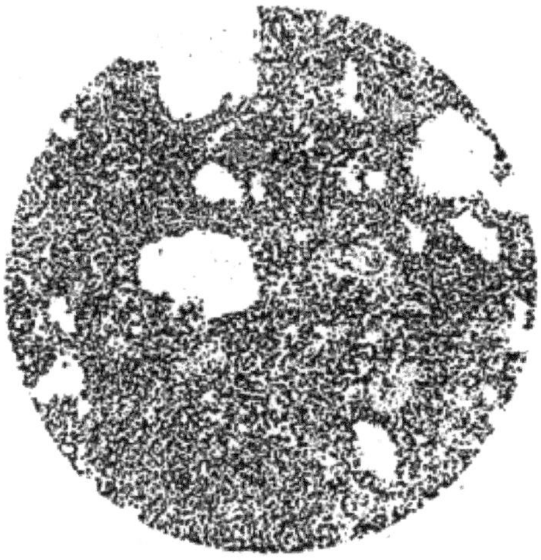

No. 190

(X 60)

[redacted]

[redacted] 141

[redacted]

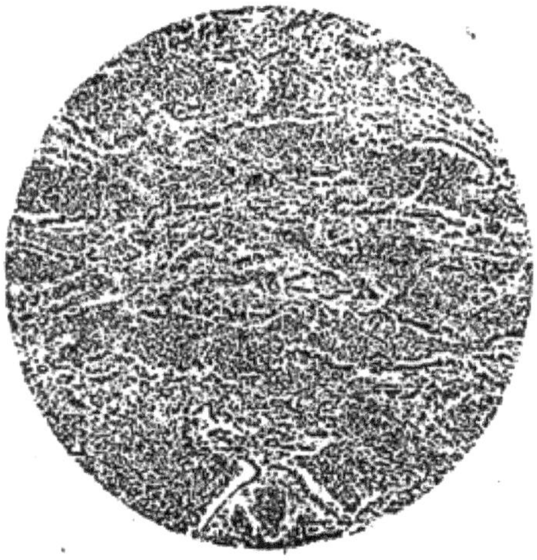

Lobular pneumonia with some increased alveolar and bronchiolar epitheliums.

[redacted]

No. 256 (e)

(x 80)

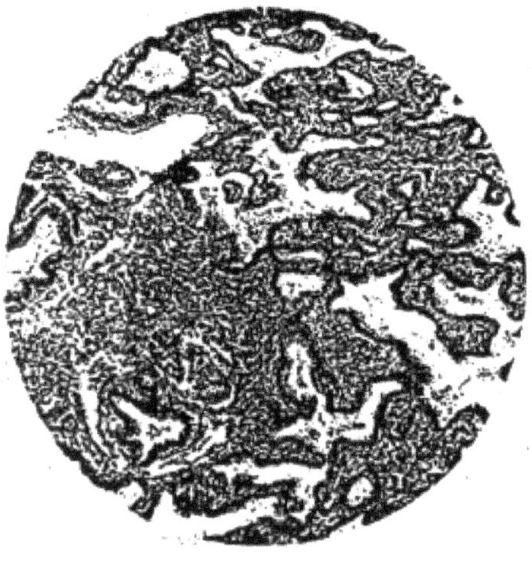

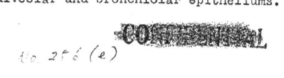

Papillar hyperplasia of alveolar epitheliums in lobular pneumonic places, due to chronic course.

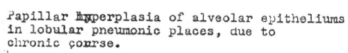

No. 256 (f)

(x 60)

[redacted]

[redacted]

142

([redacted] (

Some proliferative changes, accompanied with slight hyperplasia of alveolar epitheliums.

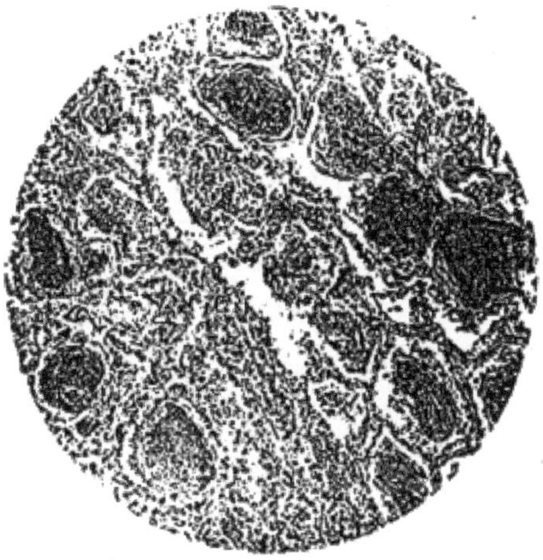

No. 167(4) [redacted]

(×80)

Lobular pneumonia in slight carnification.

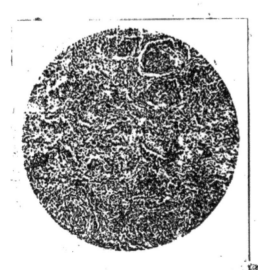

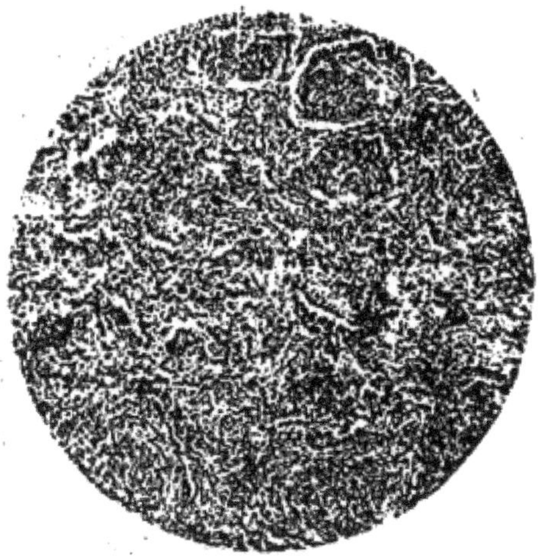

No. 167(4)

[redacted]

143

([redacted] (

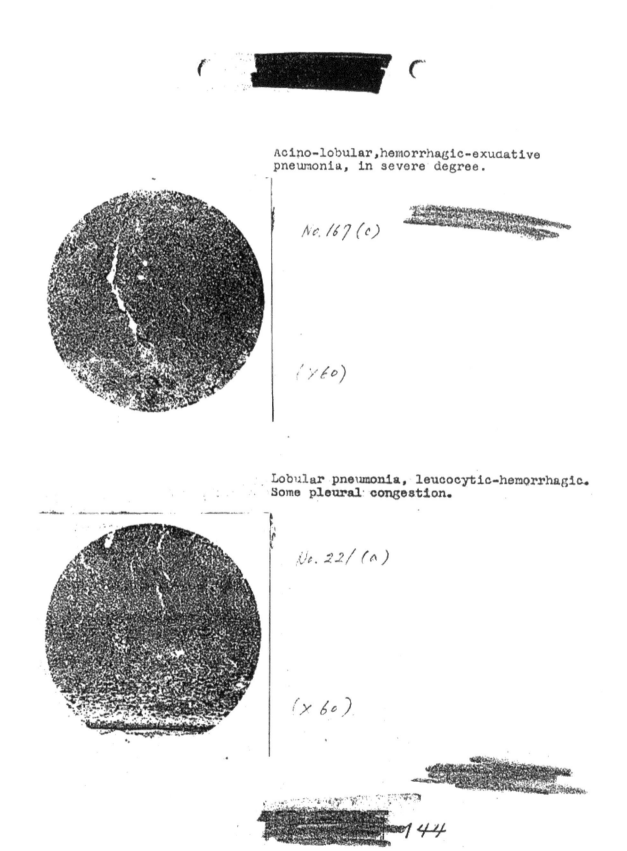

Acino-lobular,hemorrhagic-exudative pneumonia, in severe degree.

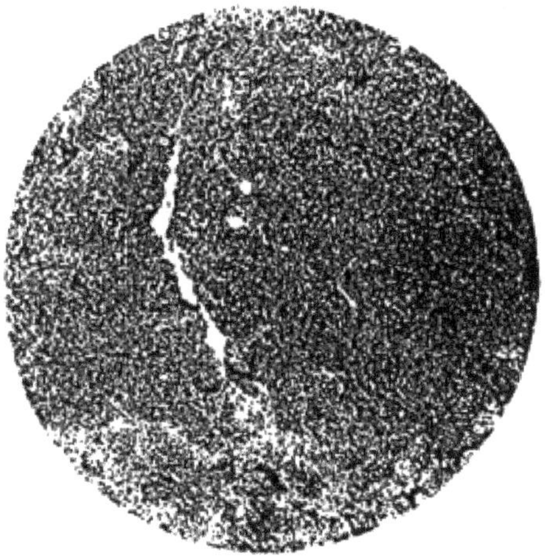

No. 167 (c) [redacted]

(×60)

Lobular pneumonia, leucocytic-hemorrhagic. Some pleural congestion.

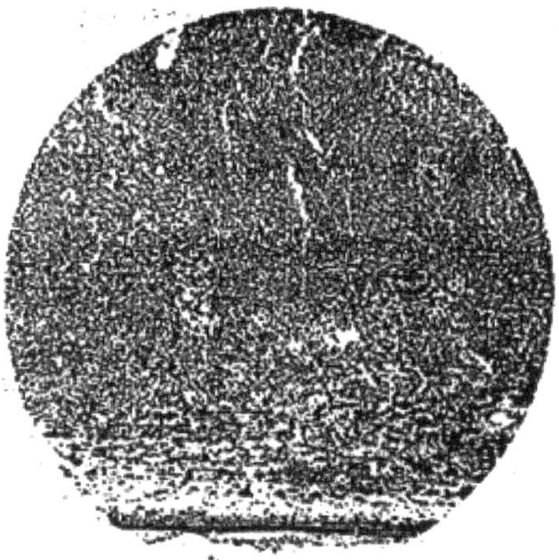

No. 221 (a)

(×60)

[redacted]

[redacted] 144

([redacted] (

Lobular pneumonia, leucocytic-hemorrhagic.
In severe degree.

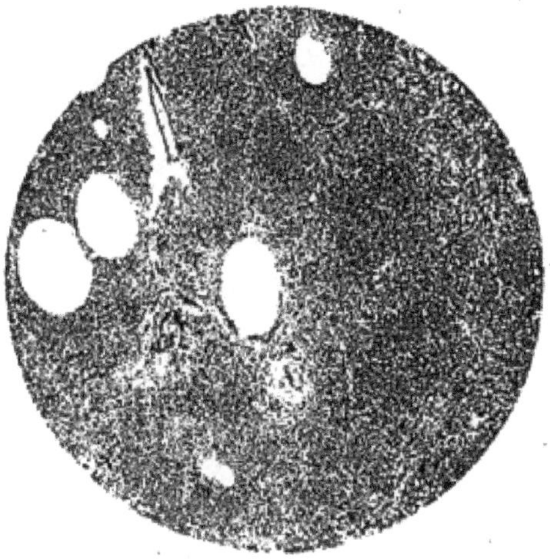

No. 146 [redacted]

(×80)

Lobular pneumonia with cavern formation.
Intense exudative form.

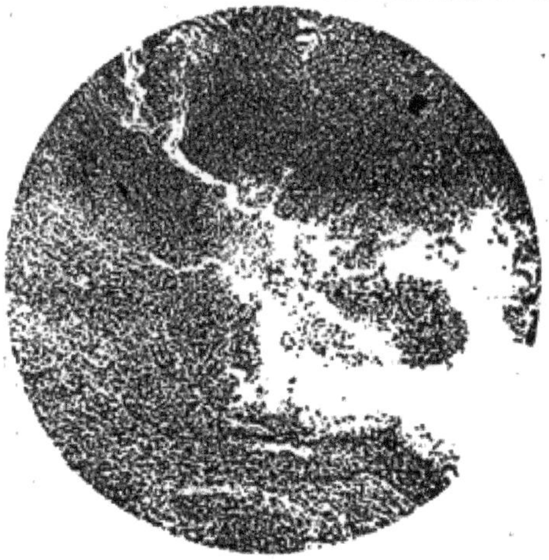

No. 727 (f)

(×60)

[redacted]

[redacted] 145

[redacted]

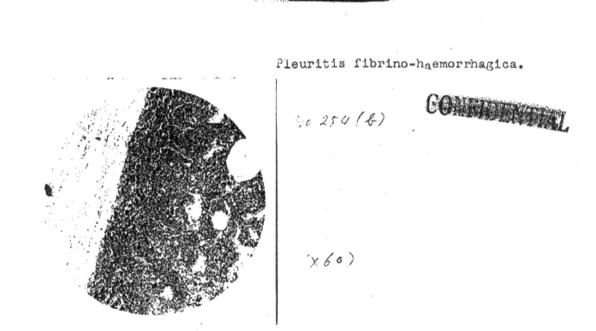

Pleuritis fibrino-haemorrhagica.

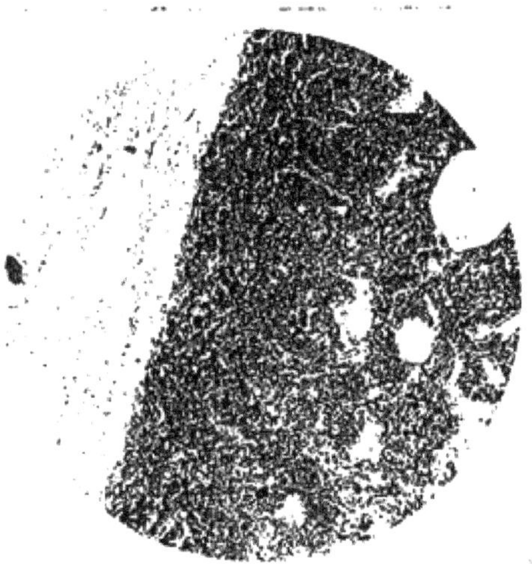

No 254 (b)

CONFIDENTIAL

(x60)

CONFIDENTIAL

[redacted] 146

([redacted] (

CONFIDENTIAL

Tonsil

CONFIDENTIAL

[redacted] 5-47

C [redacted] C

T O N S I L

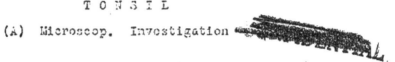

(A) Microscop. Investigation [redacted]

16.

In lacuna, desquamated epitheliums, fibrinous masses and some erythrocytes and edematous swelling of mucous membrane with slight localised necrosis. Slight hyperplasia of follicles and germinative centres with slightly increased and slightly swollen reticulum-fibres and some leucocytes, some lymphocytes and etc.

In submucous tissues: remarkable congestion, edematous swelling of capillary-walls and fibrinous separation, with remarkable leucocytes and lymphocytes infiltrations.

In other general tissues, slight edema, considerable congestion and slight plasma-cells and lymphocytes infiltration.

50.

Remarkable edematous swelling and leucocytes infiltration in mucous layers with some localised necrosis which spreads furthermore to the submucous tissues. In such necrotic parts exist massive bacterial accumulation, fibrinous masses, plenty of leucocytes and some lymphocytes. Remarkable congestion, edematous and at some places hyalinous swelling of capillary walls (desquamation and swelling of capillary endothel-cells), and remarkable edema in mucous tissues.

In lymph-follicles exist edematously swollen reticulum-fibres with some increased makrophagen and epitheloid cells.

In general tissues, edematous swelling and some lymphocytes-infiltration. In crypt, some desquamated epitheliums, fibrinous and bacterial masses.

[redacted] 148 [redacted]

[redacted]

193.

In crypt, desquamated epitheliums, fibrinous and bacterial masses.
Edematous swelling of mucous membrane. Reactive hyperplastic lymph-follicles with some lymphocytes and plasma-cells-emigration in the neighbouring tissues diffusely and slight congestion and edematous swelling of capillary-walls in surrounding connective tissues.
In submucous tissues, at some places remarkable congestion and partial hemorrhages with remarkable plasma-cell-infiltration and fibrinous separation in connective tissues-slits.

152.

desquamated epitheliums in crypts and slight edematous swelling of mucous membranes.
Slight hyperplasia of lymph-follicles and slightly increased reticulum-fibres (lymphfollicles in reticular form Ohno's) with slight edematous swelling of reticulum-fibres and fibrinous separations.
Slight edema in submucous tissues and no remarkable changes else.

190.

Slight swelling and partial localised necrosis of mucous tissues and desquamated epitheliums, fibrinous masses some lymphocytes and erythrocytes leakages in crypts.
No remarkable changes else.

236.

Remarkable edema, atrophia and some localised necrosis in mucous tissues with some leucocytes-infiltrations.
Remarkable reductions of lymph-follicles and germinative centres with some swollen reticulum-fibres and slight hemorrhages.

[redacted] 149

[redacted]

Namely follicles in hyalinous or reticular form Ohno's.
In the neighbouring tissues, considerable congestion, edematous swelling of capillary walls and slight diffuse hemorrhages.
In crypts, some leucocytes, fibrinous masses, hyalinous drops, bacterial colonies and desquamated epitheliums.
Considerable congestion and edematous swelling of submucous tissues.

[redacted]

[redacted]

[redacted] 150

[redacted]

(B) S U M M A R Y [redacted]

Conclusions based on 6 cases, which have some inflammatory changes macroscopically (and except other cases with no remarkable macroscopic changes).

These all 6 cases fall into somewhat bacterial affections, caused by secondary hematogenous metastasis (judging from infection-mode: namely subcutaneous infection).

All investigated cases 6 cases.

.). with remarkable edema and localised ulcers in mucous membrane and some slight inflammation in lymph-follicles and in submucous tissues. 3 cases.

.). with considerable edema in mucous membrane and slight hyperplasia of lymph-follicles with some increased germinative centres, accompanied with slight perifollicular congestion. I cases.

.). with slight hyperplasia of lymph-follicles and slight hyperplasia of germinative centres. I cases.

.). with no remarkable changes. I case.

Other cases have no remarkable changes macroscopically.

Accordingly.

3	cases	in somewhat inflammatory changes.
2	cases	in some reactive hyperplasia of lymph-follicles.
other cases		no remarkable changes.

[redacted] 151 [redacted]

C [redacted] C

On pernasal infection

[redacted]

)

I can't investigate tonsils of pernasal infection-cases microscopically, which have some slight congestion of mucous membrane of pharynx
and tonsila, macroscopically.

)

As if these affection are caused by glanders, can not be determined
definitely, since I have not any micro-slices to investigate.

[redacted]

[redacted] 152

([redacted] (

[redacted]

TONSIL

				16	50	152	190	193	256
Epithelium	Atrophia			−	÷	÷	∸	∸	∸
	Cell edema			÷	+	+	++	+	+
	Desquamation			+	++	+	++	+++	++
	Necrosis			+	++	÷	++	++	++
	Infitration	Leucocytes		÷	÷	∸	∸	÷	+
		Lymphocytes		+	++	+	+	++	+
Lymph nodules	Size			↑	↓	↑	↑	↓	↓
	Blood Vessels	Contents	Erythrocytes	+	+	∸	∸	+	+
			Leucocytes	÷	÷	−	−	÷	+
			Lymphocytes	+	+	÷	÷	++	+
		Endothelium	Swelling	+	++	÷	÷	+	++
			Desquamation	÷	÷	∸	∸	∸	+
			Hyperplasia	+	+	−	−	+	+
	Lymph Vessels	Dilatation		+	+	÷	÷	÷	+
		Lymphocytes		+	+	÷	÷	+	+
		Endothelium	Swelling	+	÷	÷	÷	÷	+
			Desquamation	÷	÷	÷	∸	÷	÷
			Hyperplasia	÷	+	−	−	+	÷
	Edema			÷	++	+	+	+	++
	Leucocytes			+	÷	−	−	÷	÷
	Eosinophile Leucocytes			−	−	−	−	−	−
	Plasma cells			+	++	∸	−	+	−
	Hyalin			÷	+	÷	÷	+	+
	Fibrin			÷	++	÷	+	++	÷
	Flemming's Center	Size		↓	↓	↑	↑	↓	↓
		Leucocytes		−	+	−	−	∸	−
		Contents of Capillaries	Erythrocytes	+	+	−	∸	+	+
			Leucocytes	−	÷	−	−	∸	+
			Lymphocytes	+	+	−	÷	+	+
T. submucosa	Congestion			+	+	÷	∸	+	++
	Edema			÷	+	+	∸	+	++
	Hemorrhage			+	++	÷	÷	+	+
	Fibrin			+	+	÷	÷	++	÷
	Cellular Infiltration			+	+	−	÷	+	+
T. muscularis	Hemorrhage			+	+	∸	∸	+	+
	Necrosis			−	−	−	−	−	−
	Cellular Infiltration			+	+	÷	÷	++	÷

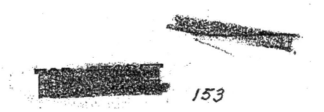

[redacted]

[redacted] 153

([redacted] (

Desquamated masses in lacuna and necrotic changes of epitheliums.

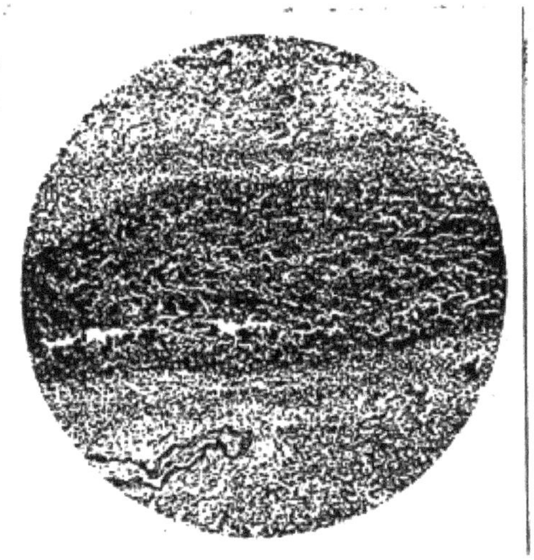

[redacted]

Desquqmated masses in lacuna and necrotic changes of epitheliums.

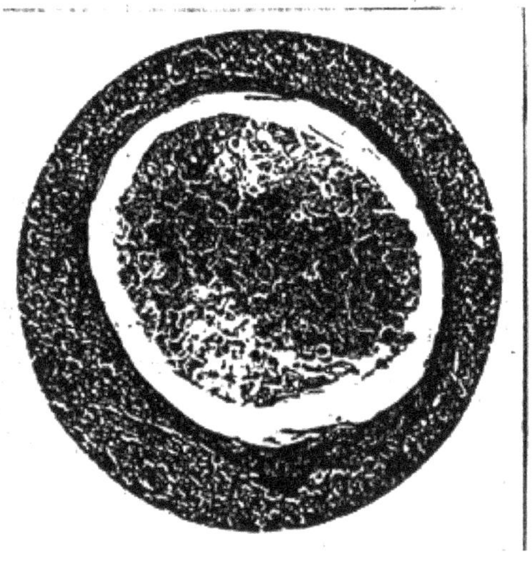

[redacted]

[redacted] 154

[redacted]

Desquamated masses in lacuna.
Exudative-leucocytic.

[redacted]

R. 50

Diffuse hemorrhages in subepitheliar tissues.

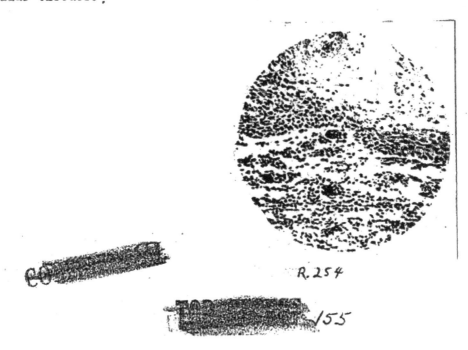

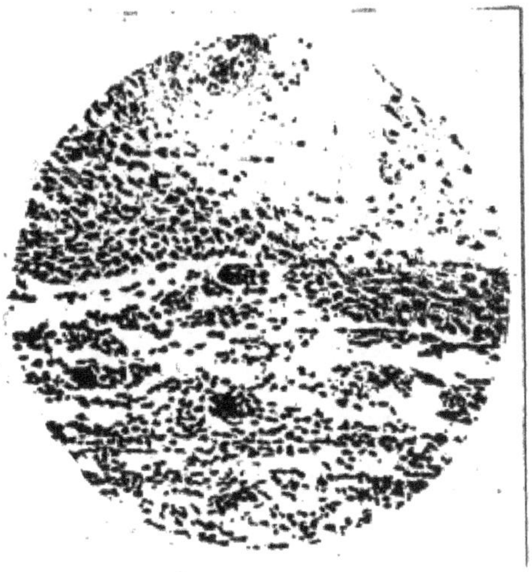

[redacted]

R. 254

[redacted] /155

[redacted]

Reactive hyperplasia of germinative centre.

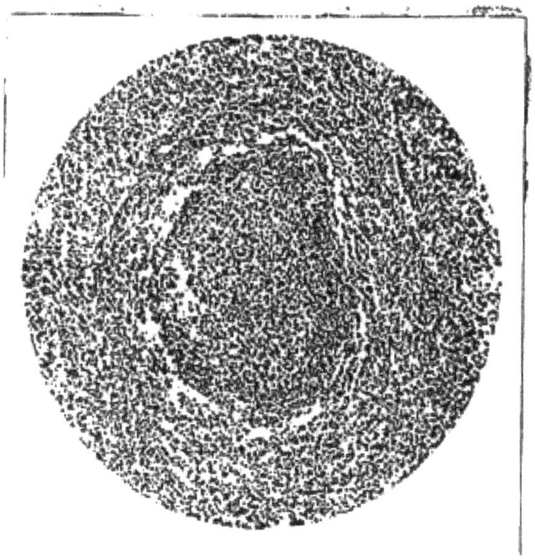

[redacted]

Reactive hyperplasia of germinative centre, in high power.

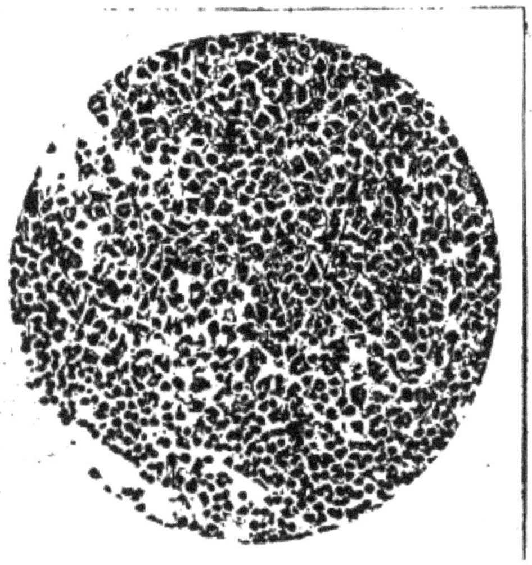

[redacted]

[redacted] 156

• [redacted] •

Liver [redacted]

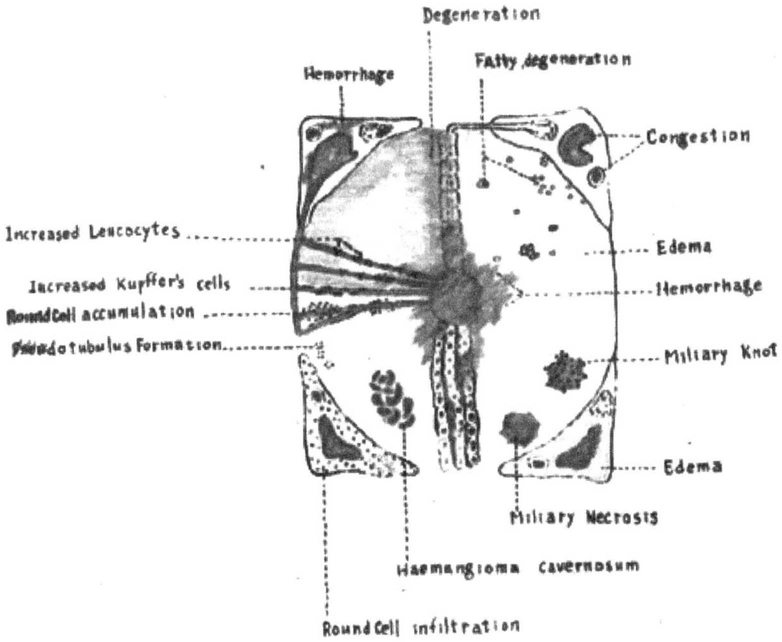

[redacted]

[redacted]

157

• [redacted] •

[redacted]

L I V E R.

(A) Microscop. Investigation.

16.

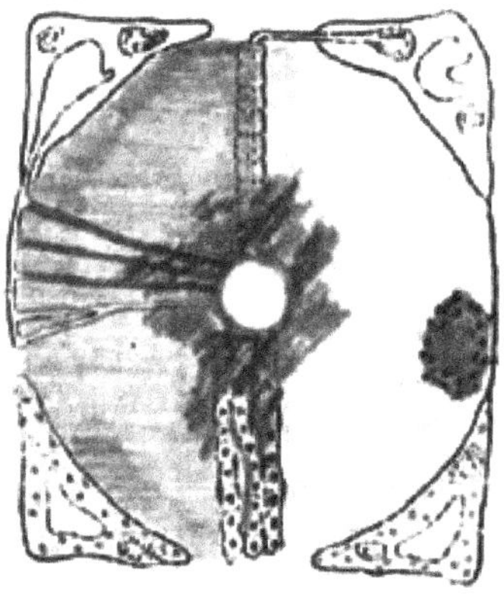

16.

Hepatitis serosa II. Stasis and exudative changes in Disse's spaces, esp. remarkable hemorrhages in central zone of acinus.

More or less considerable parenchymatous degeneration with brown pigments, esp. in central zone of acinus.

Multiple miliary glander-knots with focal necrosis (decayed masses of parenchymal cells) and perifocal lymphocytic cells and more or less considerable histiocytic cells. Bounded more or less sharply.

5o.

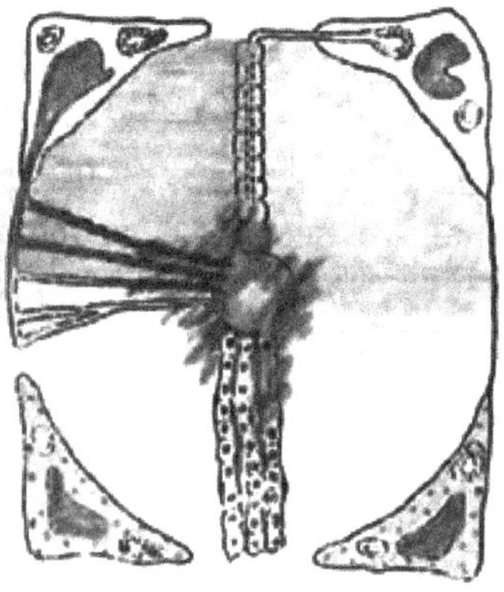

50.

Hepatitis serosa. I. Slight parenchymatous degeneration with considerable congestion in acinus and V.hepatica. Some lymphocytes and slightly increased histiocytic cells as capillary contents.

85. Hepatitis serosa . I-II . Cloudy or fatty degeneration with considerable conges-

[redacted]

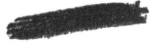

[redacted]

151

[redacted]

85.

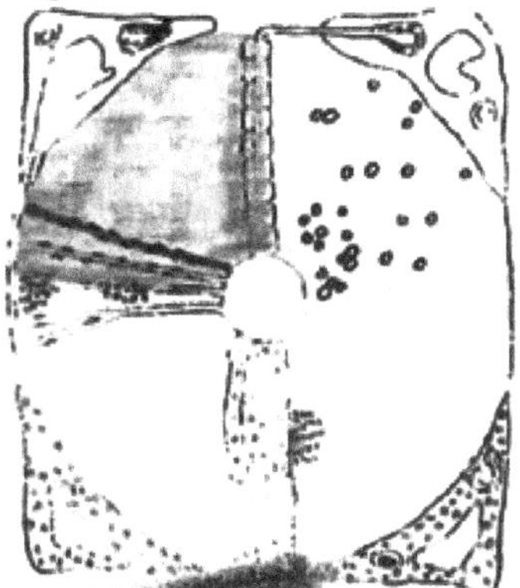

[redacted]

152.

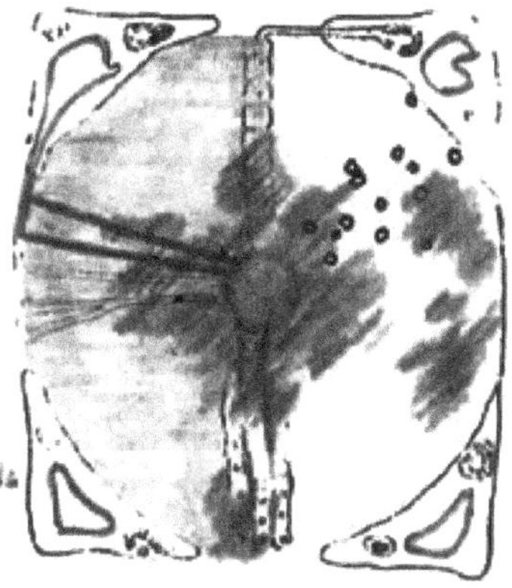

167.

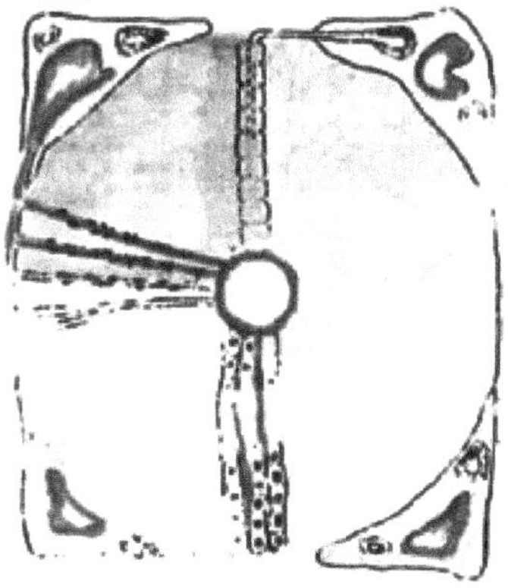

tion. Multiple submiliary lymphocytes accumulations in acinus with slight hemorrhagic perifocal reactions.

146.

Hepatitis serosa . II. Slight parenchymatous degeneration with slight congestion.

152.

Hepatitis serosa I-II. Severe congestion, severe exudative changes in Disses's spaces with remarkable hemorrahges in central zone of acinus. Parenchymatous cells at these hemorrhagic central parts fall into bionocrotic masses (severe congestion, severe hemorrhage, fatty degeneration or furthermore decayed massed of parenchymatous cells etc).

167.

Hepatitis serosa II. Parenchymatous degeneration with slight congestion in acinus . More or less remarkable increase of Kupffer's cells.

176.

Hepatitis serosa . I. Slight congestion, slight degenration, more or less clarified parenchymal cells.

[redacted]

[redacted] 159

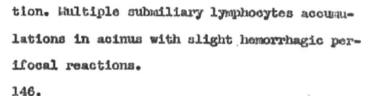

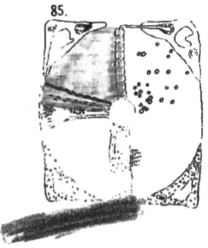

● [redacted] ●

178.

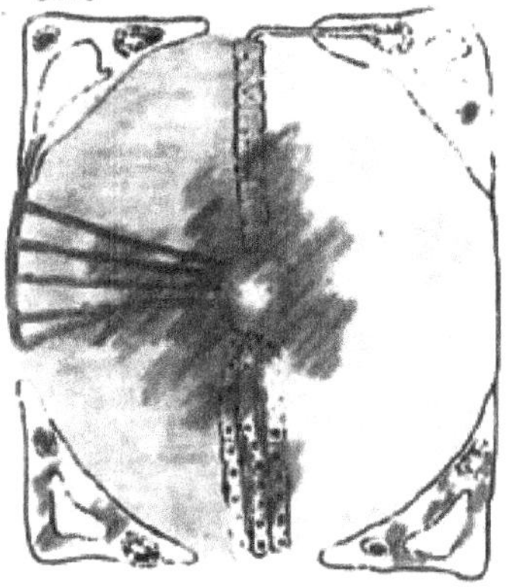

178.

Hepatitis serosa I-II. Extremly remarkable congestion with edematous swelling of capillar -walls, exudative changes in Disse's space and more or less considerable hemorralges in central zone of acinus.
Sometimes slight lymphocytes-accumulations at the walls of central veins (subendothelial lymphocytes-accumulations).
Atrophia and degeneration of parenchymal cells, esp. in central zone of acinus.

[redacted]

180.

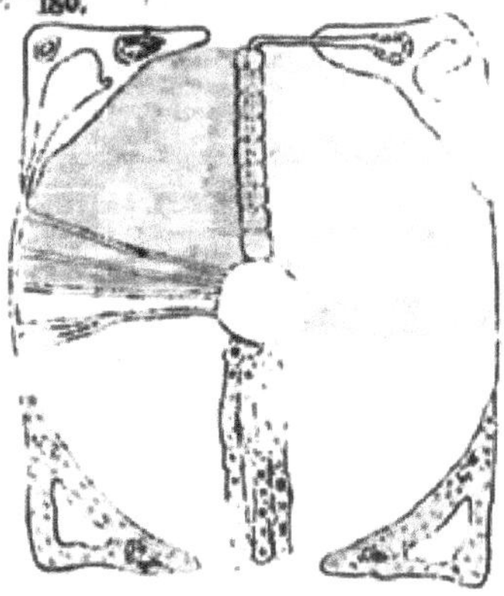

180.

Hepatitis serosa II-III. Slight parenchymatous degeneration with slight congestion slight lymphocytes-infiltration at Glisson's capsule.

190. Hepatitis serosa II.

190.

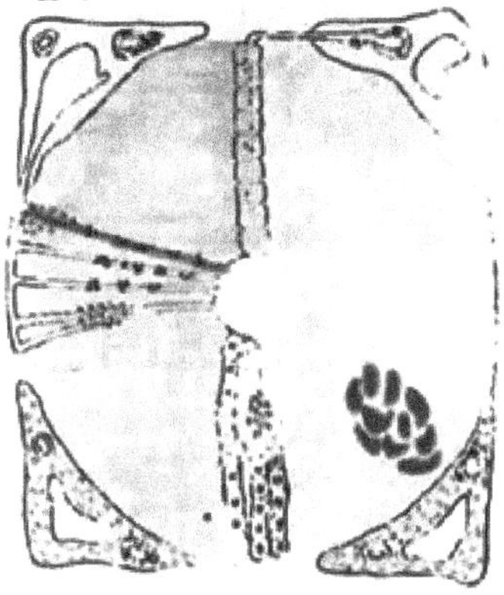

Parenchymatous degeneration in medium degree with increased lymphocytes and leucocytes in capillaries of acinus and multiple submiliary lymphocytes-accumulation in acinus and Glisson's capsule. With Haemoangioma cavernosum hepatis.

[redacted]

160

[redacted]

193.

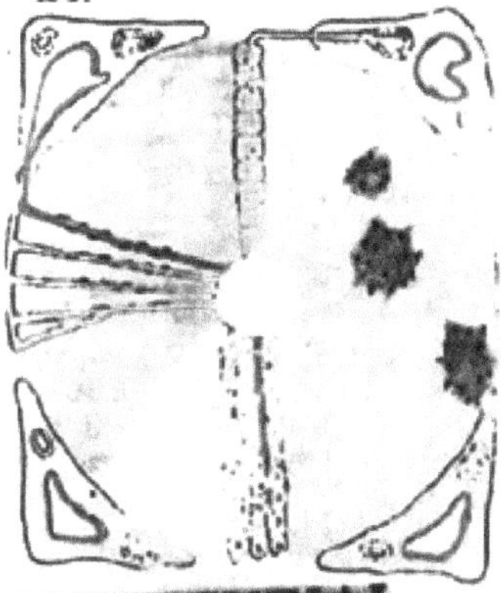

[redacted]

205.

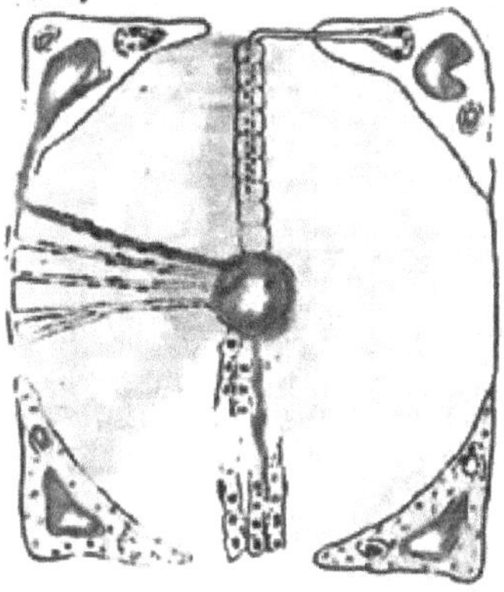

207.

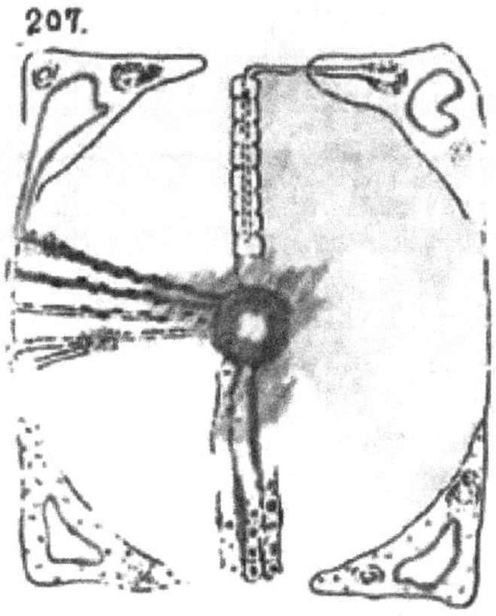

193. Hepatitis serosa I.

Slight parenchymatous degenration with remar-kable hyperplasia of kupfer's cells and multiple submiliary glander-knots in remarkable proliferative form, which are formed mainly by histiocytic cells and a few residues of leucocytes and bounded sharply

205. Hepatitis serosa I.

Slight parenchymatous degeneration. Congestion with increased lymphocytes as capillary contents and multiple lymphocytes-a-ccumulations at some places in acinus.

207. Hepatitis serosa II.

Parenchymatous degeneration in medium degree with remarkable congestion, exudative hemorrhagic changes in Disse's spaces and slight hemorrahge in cntral zone of acinus. Increased lymphocytes and leucocytes as capillary contents a and multiple submiliary lymphocytes-accumulations as glander-knots. At other hands slight increased histiocytic ce lls as proliferative changes.

[redacted]

[redacted] 161

[redacted]

221.

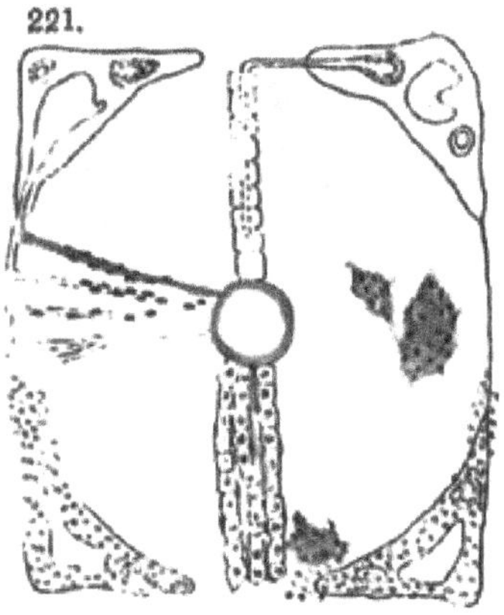

[redacted]

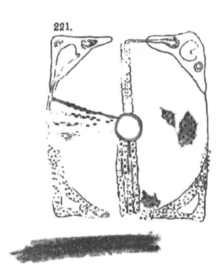

221. Hepatitis serosa I.

Severe parenchymatous degeneration with remarkable congestion and exudative-hemorrhagi changes in Disse's spaces whcih are accompanie with a large quantity of lymphocytes, a few loucocytes and slightly increased histiocytic cells as capillary contents and formation of multiple supermilliary or milliary knots in acinus which are foemed mainly by lymphocytes, necrotic residues of parenchym cells and slightly increased histiocytic cells.

At some perfocal parts of milliary knots, now formation of capillaries and pseudotubulus in slight degree.

The same exsyuative lymphocytic reactions are recognized at the walls of cntral veins (edematous swelling and lymphocytes-accumula-tion in subendotheliar layers of central veins and hopatic veins) or at Glisson's (edematous swelling and lymphocytes-infiltra-tion in Glisson's capsule).

222. Hepatitis serosa I-II.

Remarkable parenchymatous degeneration with severe congestion and remarkable exudative changes in Disse's spaces [redacted]

[redacted] 162

[redacted]

222.

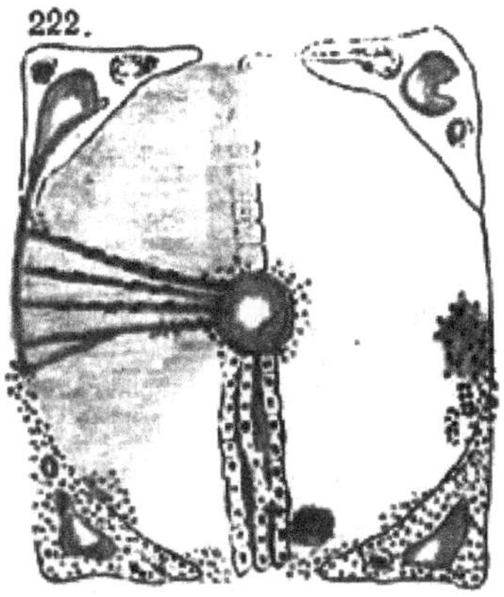

[redacted]

224.

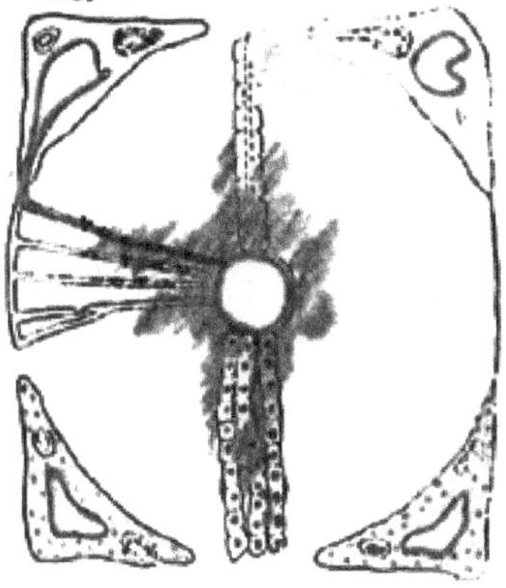

229.

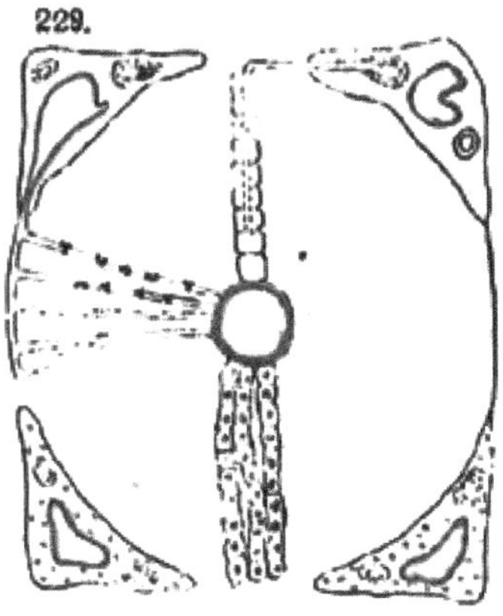

[redacted]

A large quantity of lymphocytes and increased histiocytic cells as capillary contents.
Multiple submiliary knots in acinus which are formed mainly by lymphocytes and slightly increased histiocytic cells.
At some perifocal parts of miliary knots, new formation of pseudotubulus in slight degree.
The same exudative lymphocytic reaction are recognised at the walls of central veins or at Glisson's capsule.

224. Hepatits serosa III-IV.
With postmoltal changes. More or less (fatty) degenration of parenchymal cells with central stasis.

229. Hepatitis serosa I.
Slight parenchymatous degeneration with considerable congestion and slight exudative changes in Disse's spaces.
And remarkable leucocytes as capillary content.

254. Hepatitis serosa III.
Attention to multiple millet-corn large or supermiliary Glander-knots in acinus !
Glander-knots with central caaseous focus are bouned with the proliferative walls of remarkable increased epitheloid cells

[redacted] 163

[redacted]

254

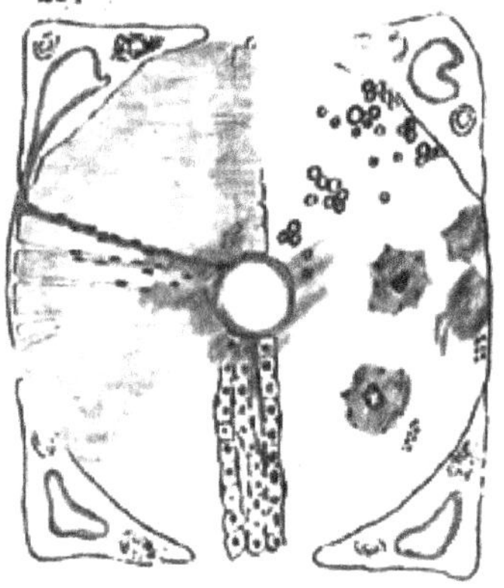

(at some places giant cells), and a few lymphocytes and with new formation of capillaries or pseudetubulus at their perifocal parts. In other general liver-tissues: considerable increase of lymphocytesa and Kupffer's cells and slight parenchymatous degenerations. [redacted]

256. Hepatitis serosa II-III.

Considerable degenerative atrophia of parenchymal cells, esp. in central zone, caused by severe congestion, exudative changes in Disse' spaces and more or less remarkable hemorrhages As capillary contents, it shows some lymphocytes and leucocytes. These exudative, leucocytic and lymphocytic cell reactions growed at some places (esp. at intercalary-portion of acinus and subendothelial layers of central veins) to submiliary cell-accumulation (lymphocytes and leucocytes) with exudative changes.

256.

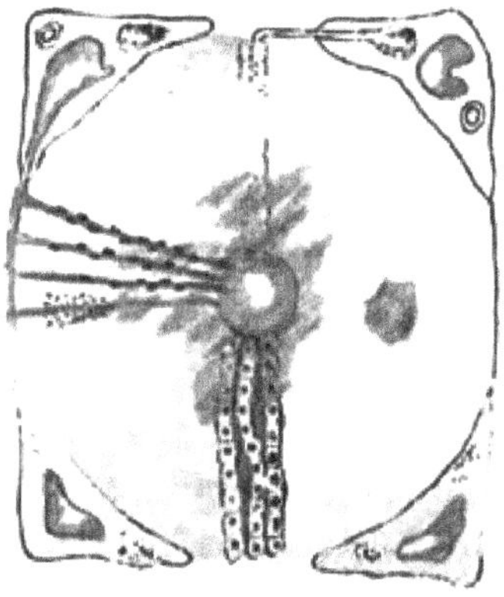

727. Hepatitis serosa II.

Considerable parenchymatous degeneration, esp. in central zone of acinus which are caused by remarkable congestion and more or less increased lymphocytes and leucocytes as

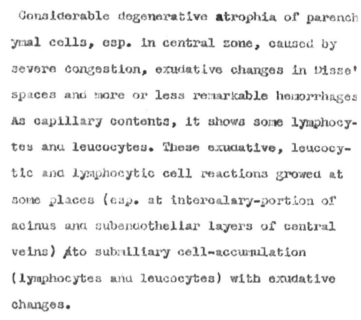

[redacted] [redacted]

[redacted]

727.

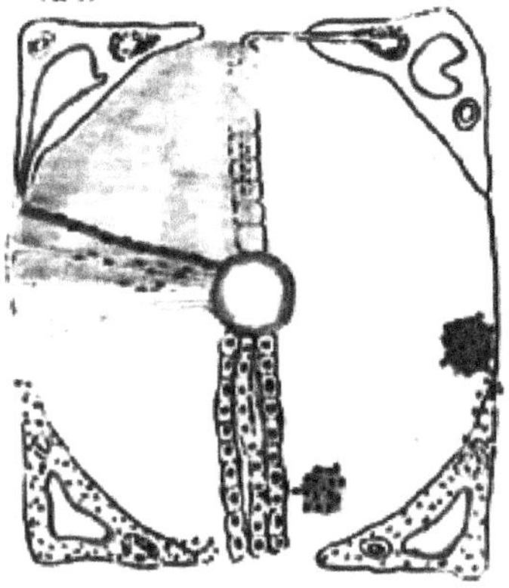

[redacted]

731.

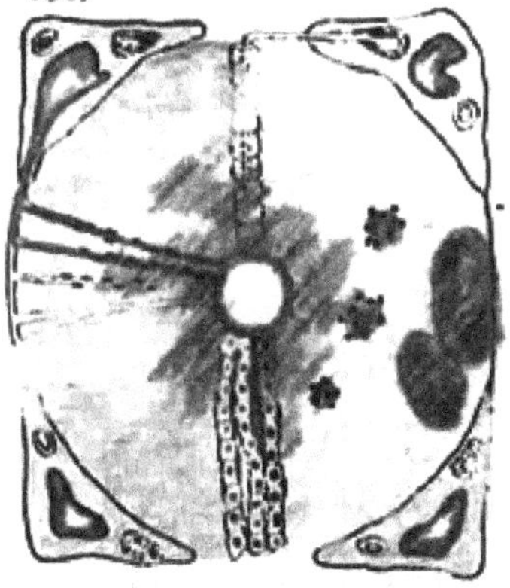

capillary contents) and edematous swelling of capillary-walls and serous exudation.

And multiple miliary knots with many histiocytic cells in acinus.

731. Hepatitis serosa III-IV.

Multiple millet-corn large, supermiliary or miliary glander-knots in acinus.

The most parts of millet-corn large knots fall into caseous structurelose masses and bounded with thin walls slightly increased epitheloid cells and lymphocytes, with more or less exudative changes (edematous swelling, congestion and slight bleeding).

Miliary knots are formed with more or less increased histiocytic cells, lymphocytes and a few residues of parenchymal cells.

In other general liver-tissues : remarkable hyperplasia of Kupffer's cells with slight congestion (and a few lymphocytes as capillary contents).

[redacted]

[redacted] 165

([redacted] (

(B) S U M M A R Y

The bird's-eye view of pathological changes of liver tissues in all cases as follows : [redacted]

1) According to these results, I classified parenchymatous disturbances of liver-tissues as follows :

Hepatitis serosa	I	6 cases.
"	I-II	4 cases.
"	II	6 cases.
"	II-III	2 cases.
"	III	I case.
"	III-IV	2 cases.
"	IV	0 case.

With hemorrhages 15 cases.

with milisry glanders-knots 7 cases.

Gnerally mor or less considerable congestion:

in rather anemic stage 4 cases of them.

with congestion in slight degree 2 cases.

in medium degree 9 cases.

in severe degree 3 cases.

in remarkable degree 6 cases.

And more or less remarkable exudative changes in Disse's spaces,

in slight degree 2 cases.

in medium dgree 4. cases.

in remarkable degree 13 cases.

in severe degree 2 cases.

In preparation to these exudative-hemorrhagic processes, more or less considerable parenchymatous degeneration and diddociation of cell- arraggments. [redacted]

Generally with cloudy swelli [redacted] m in severe degree.

166

[redacted]

L case with remarkable fatty degeneration, o case of them in severe degree.

Frequently emigration of some lymphocytes, or leucocytes in capillary nets in acinus and furthermore formation of miliary knots, acused by accumulation of these wandering cells ,esp- in peripheral zone of acinus.

2) [redacted]

.) No remarkable changes in 5 cases of them:

No.224.229.176.180.

With Hepatitis seroaa 11. 6 cases.

No.16.146. 167. 190.207.727.

With slightly increased histiocytic cells.

No,167. 205.

With Hepatitis serosa. III. 1 case.

No.254.

With Hepatitis serosa IV. 0 case.

With subendotheliar round cell accumulation of central veins.

No.178. 222.

With hemorrhages and miliary-knots.

In initial stage No.35. 190.

In exudative stage No.256.222.731.

With miliary knots and (Hepatitis sersa II).

In rather productive stage No.193.221.

..) Increase of wandering cells in capillary-nits develop to pericapillar cell-accumulation and furthermore miliary knots,as pericapillar cell-accumulations:

[redacted]

[redacted] 167

([redacted] (

a) Subendotheliar lymphocytes-accumulation at central veins-$w_a$lls as its initial stage.

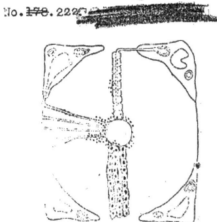

No.~~178~~.222[redacted]　　No.~~222~~ 178.

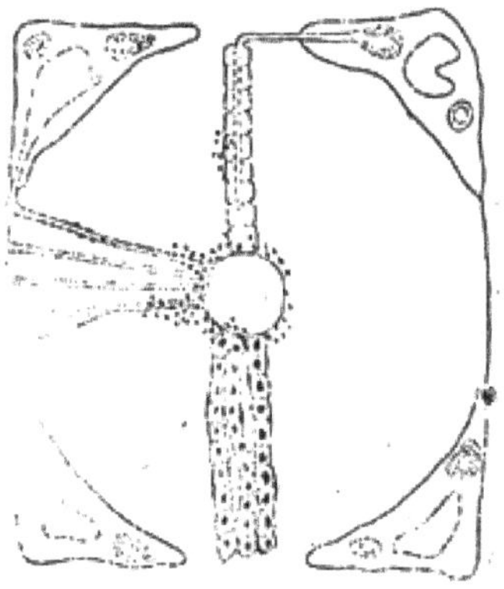

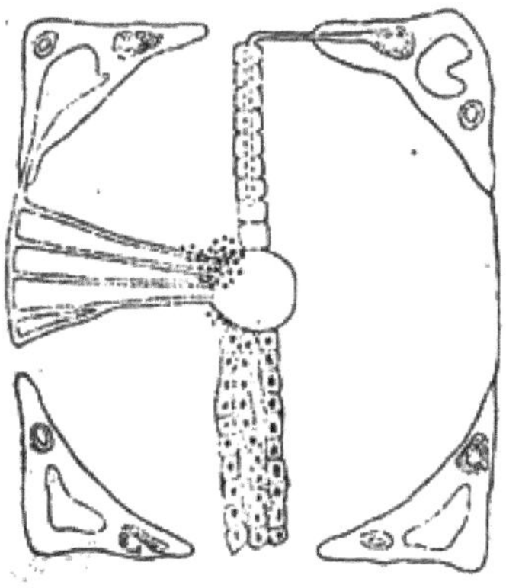

b) Multiple submiliary lymphocytes-accumulation, esp. in peripheral zone of acinus.

No.190.

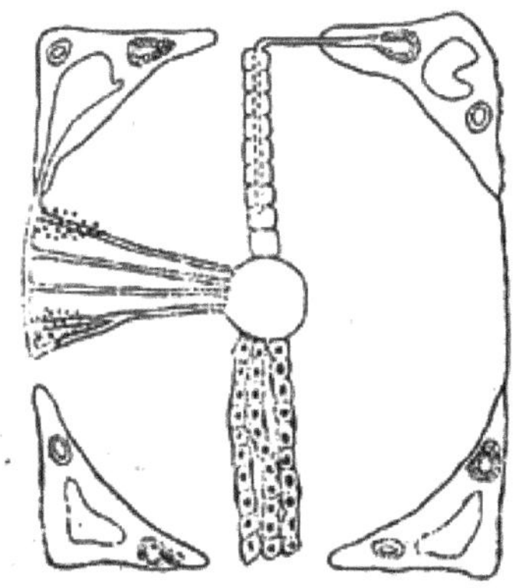

[redacted]

[redacted] 168

([redacted] (

And then these changes grow with exudative reaction to necrosis:

c) Multiple miliary knots(lymphocytes and leucocytes accumulation) with perifocal exudative changes(exudation and hemorrhages) etc.) at intercalary portions of acinus or subendotheliar layers of central veins etc. [redacted]

No.256.

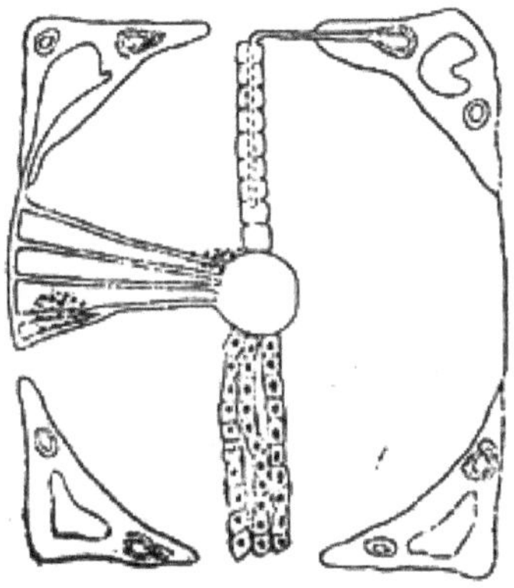

d) And multiple muluary knots with focal caseous necrosis(decayed masses of parenchym cell etc) and perifocal reactive(exudative-hemorrhagic-lymphocytic) reactions.

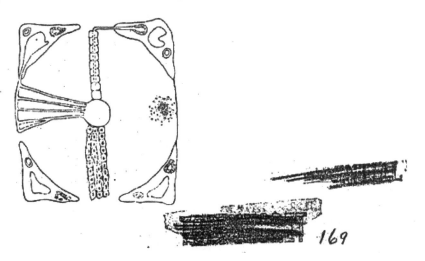

No.16.

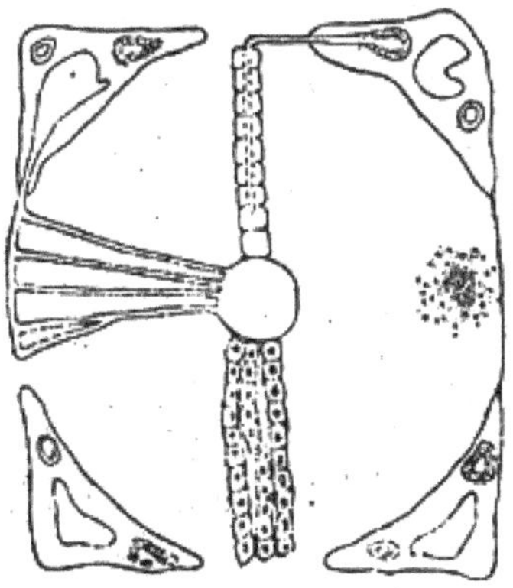

[redacted]

[redacted] 169

([redacted]

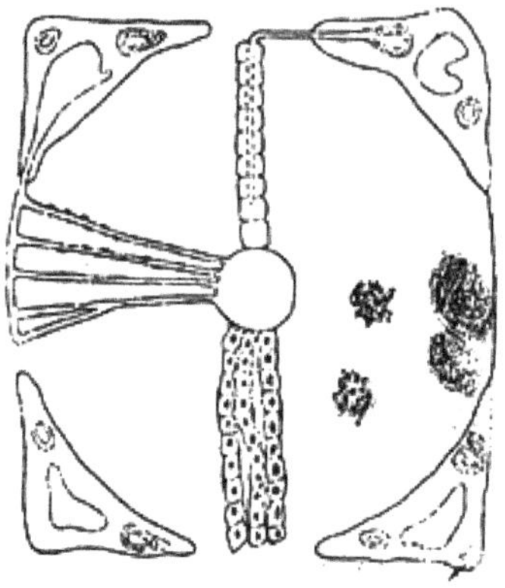

[redacted]

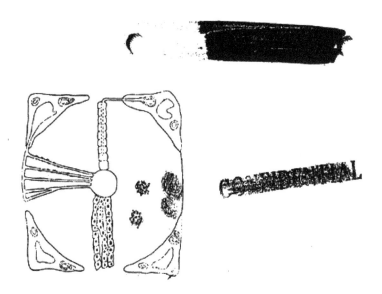

This case(No.731.) died in course of more than 6 months with rather large(millet-corn sized) multiple necrosis in liver.These necrosis are bounded in the lapse of time,-with slightly and gradually increased histiocytic cells and accompanied with slightly increased Kupffer's cells in other general tissues.

Contrary to this case, died No.222. after shorter course(several months in extremly exudative stage(with slighter proliferative cell-reactions).

...) Miliaryg glander-knots are classified into 2 types, a) exudative amd b) prolįferative forms, I say.

All abobe mentioned cases are exudative or tather exudative.
Contraly to these, some cases are rather proliferative with silightly increased histiocytic cells. For example:No.193. with subniliary knots in remarkable proliferative form, which are formed mainly histiocytid cells and a few residuew of leucocytes add bounded more or less sharply.

[redacted]

Glissons's capsule: generally with edematous swelling, 3 cases of them in severe degree and 9 cases of [redacted]

([redacted] (

In the lapse of time, slightly increase histiocytic cells as proliferative reactions.

For example,No.222, Multiple [redacted]iliary knots, which are formed by lymphocytes or necrotic residues of parenchymal cells. Besides them, as proliferative, more or less reparative reactions at some perifocal parts of miliary knots, slightly increased histiocytid cells and new formation of capillaries or pseudotubuls.

No222.

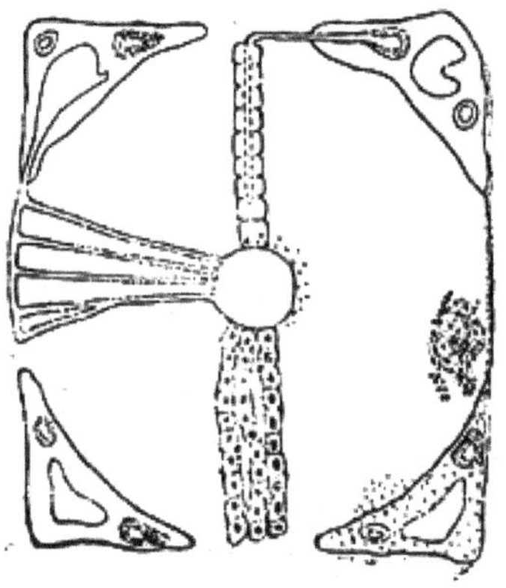

Or multiple millot-corn large and supermiliaru knots. The most parts of knots falled into caseous structure-lose masses and bounded with thin walls of slightly increased epitjeloid cells(occaisionally giant cells) , lymphocytes and more or less exudative perifocal changes.

Other general liver-tissues are soemwhat proliferative with remarkably increased kupffer's cells and slight congsetions.

No.731.

[redacted]

170

([redacted] (

LIVER [redacted]

			16	50	85	146	152	167	176	178	180	190	193	205	207	221	222	224	229	254	256	727	731
Cell Cord	Irregular Arrangement		++	÷	+	+	++	+	÷	÷	÷	÷	÷	+	++	+	++	|	÷	++	(+++)	÷	+++
	Dissociation		++	−	−	(+)	+	+	−	(+)	÷	÷	(÷)	÷	÷	÷	÷	|	÷	+	÷	÷	+++
Liver Cells	Clouding		(++)	+	+	++	++	+	+	++	+	++	++	++	÷	÷	++	|	÷	++	++	+	++
	Atrophia		(+++)	÷	÷	(+)	(++)	(++)	÷	(++)	÷	÷	÷	(+)	(++)	++	(+++)	|	(÷)	++	(+++)	+	+++
	Hypertrophia		÷	+	÷	÷	÷	÷	−	÷	−	−	÷	÷	−	−	+	−	−	−	−	−	−
	Fatty Degeneration	Central	÷	÷	+	÷	÷	−	÷	−	−	−	−	−	÷	÷	−	÷	−	÷	−	−	−
		intermediary	−	÷	÷	÷	÷	−	÷	−	−	−	−	−	÷	−	−	÷	÷	÷	−	−	−
		Peripheral	−	÷	÷	÷	÷	−	÷	−	−	−	÷	÷	−	−	−	÷	−	(+)	−	−	−
	Brown Pigment		++	−	÷	÷	÷	+	(++)	÷	÷	÷	−	+	÷	÷	++	+	+	÷	−	++	(++)
Blood Vessels	V. centralis	Dilatation	÷	+	−	÷	÷	÷	÷	÷	÷	÷	÷	+	−	÷	+	÷	+	−	+	÷	−
		Congestion	+	++	÷	÷	++	+	÷	++	÷	÷	÷	++	++	+	++	+	+	+	++	+	+
	Contents	Dilatation	+	+	+	+	++	++	÷	+++	÷	+	++	++	(++)	++	+++	÷	(+)	++	+++	+	++
		Congestion	(++)	++	+	(+)	++	++	÷	(+++)	|	+	+	+	++	+	+++	+	÷	+	++	+	++
		Leucocytes	÷	÷	÷	÷	÷	+	(+)	÷	|	++	−	÷	÷	÷	÷	+	+	−	÷	−	−
		Lymphocytes	÷	÷	+	÷	+	÷	+	+	|	(+)	÷	+	+	+	+++	÷	÷	÷	÷	÷	+
		Monocytes	÷	+	÷	÷	÷	+	−	÷	|	÷	÷	÷	÷	÷	÷	÷	÷	÷	÷	÷	÷
	Edema		++	+	+	++	++	++	÷	++	+	++	++	++	++	++	++	+	÷	++	+++	++	++
	Hemorrhage		(++)	+	÷	+	(+++)	÷	−	(+++)	|	÷	÷	÷	÷	÷	÷	++	−	+	++	÷	++
	Kupffer's Cells	Proliferation	÷	+	+	−	÷	++	−	÷	÷	÷	++	++	++	+	++	÷	÷	+	+	+	+
		Swelling	÷	+	++	÷	+	++	÷	÷	÷	÷	÷	++	÷	++	+	+	+	÷	÷	÷	÷
		Hemosiderin	÷	−	(+++)	−	(+)	−	−	−	−	−	−	−	−	÷	++	−	−	−	−	−	−
	Bacterium		−	−	−	−	−	−	−	−	−	−	−	−	−	−	−	−	−	−	−	÷	−
	Congestion of V. hepatica		÷	+++	÷	÷	+	÷	+	÷	÷	÷	÷	++	+	÷	++	÷	+	÷	++	(÷)	+
Glisson's Capsule	Production of Connective Tissue		−	−	−	−	−	−	−	−	−	−	−	÷	−	÷	÷	−	−	÷	−	÷	−
	Pseudobiliary Tract		−	−	−	−	−	−	−	−	−	−	−	−	−	−	−	−	−	−	−	−	−
	Edema		+	+	+	++	÷	+	÷	÷	+	+	+	+	÷	÷	÷	+	÷	÷	++	+	++
	Hemorrhage		−	÷	÷	−	−	−	−	+	−	−	−	−	−	(÷)	−	÷	−	÷	−	−	−
	Round Cell Infiltration		+	+	++	+	÷	÷	÷	÷	++	(+++)	÷	+	+	++	+++	+	+	÷	÷	++	÷
	Leucocyte Infiltration		−	−	−	−	−	−	−	−	−	−	−	−	−	−	−	−	−	−	−	−	−
	Congestion of A. hepatica		÷	÷	÷	÷	÷	÷	÷	(+++)	|	÷	÷	+	+	÷	+	÷	÷	÷	+	÷	+
	Congestion of V. pforte		÷	+++	÷	÷	+	+	+	÷	+	+	+	++	+	÷	++	+	+	+	++	+	++
Miliary Necrosis	Necrosis		+	|	|	|	|	|	|	|	|	|	÷	|	|	÷	+	|	|	++	÷	÷	+
	Lymphocytes		÷	|	|	|	|	|	|	|	|	|	÷	|	|	+	+++	|	|	+	÷	÷	÷
	Leucocytes		−	|	|	|	|	|	|	|	|	|	÷	|	|	−	−	|	|	−	÷	÷	−
	Histiocytic Cells		÷	|	|	|	|	|	|	|	|	|	+	|	|	÷	÷	|	|	+	÷	++	÷
	Erythrocytes		−	|	|	|	|	|	|	|	|	|	−	|	|	−	−	|	|	−	−	−	−

[redacted]

[redacted] 171

([redacted])

Intense congestion and some
hemorrhages in the central zone
of acinus.

[redacted]

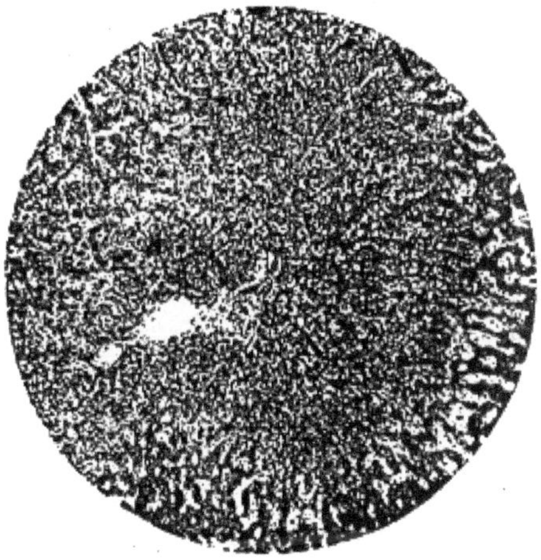

152 x90

Intese congestion and some
round cell accumulation around
the central vein.

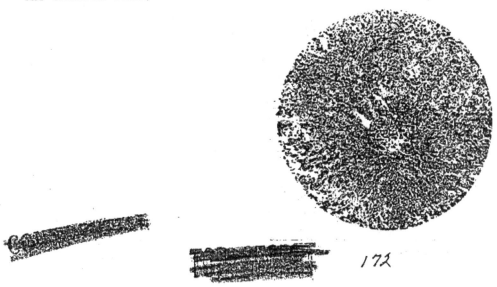

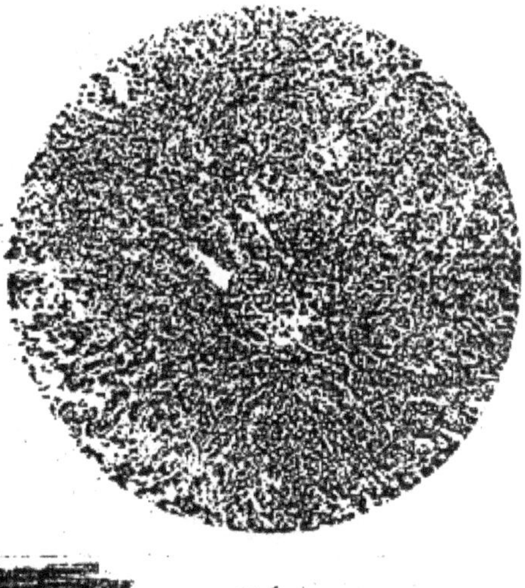

[redacted] [redacted] 172

[redacted]

Remarkable round cell accumulation in the peripheral zone of acinus (mainly at the intercalary portion), accompanied with some parenchymatous degeneration.

[redacted]

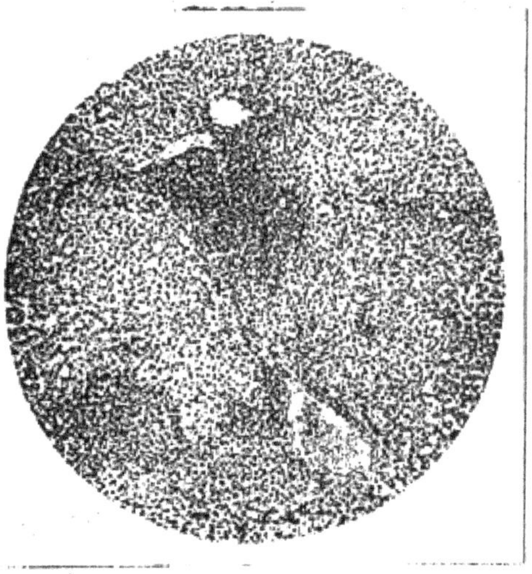

222 X60

Intense congestion and hemorrhates, in high power.

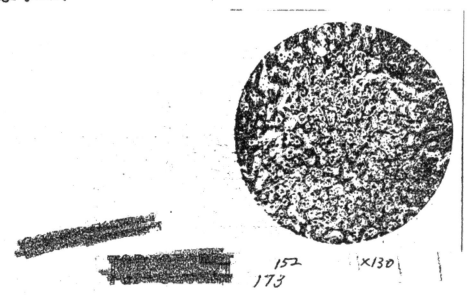

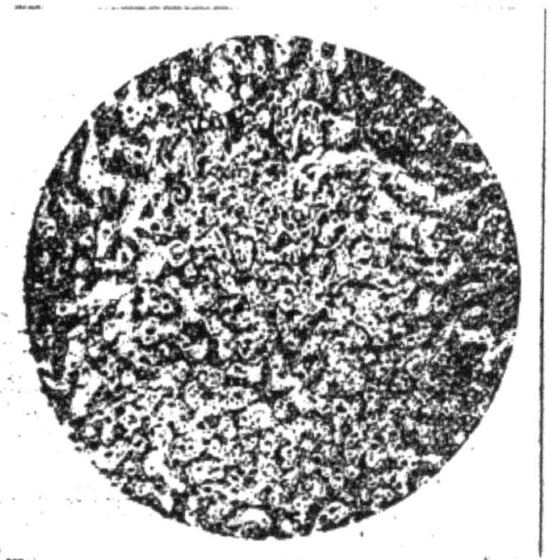

[redacted]

152 X130

173

[redacted]

Remarkable round cell accumulation,
esp. around the central vein.
In high power.

[redacted]

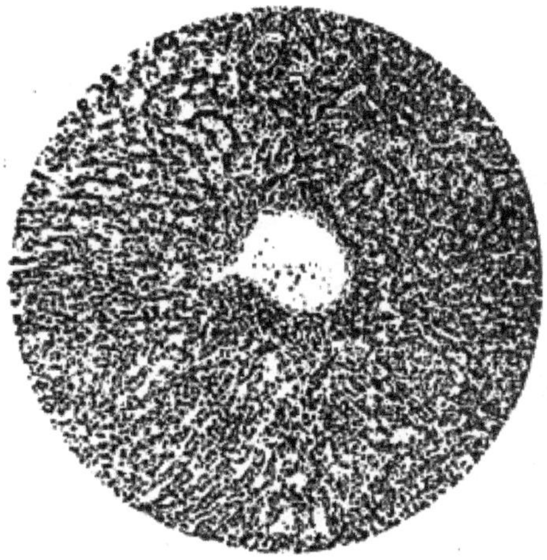

222　　X80

Remarkable round cell adcumulation,
esp. at the peripheral zone of acinus.

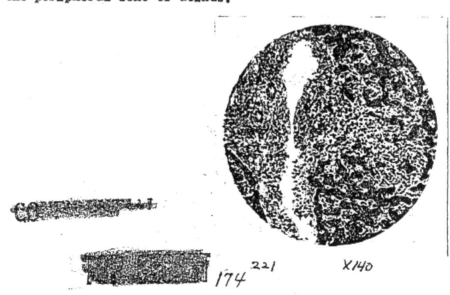

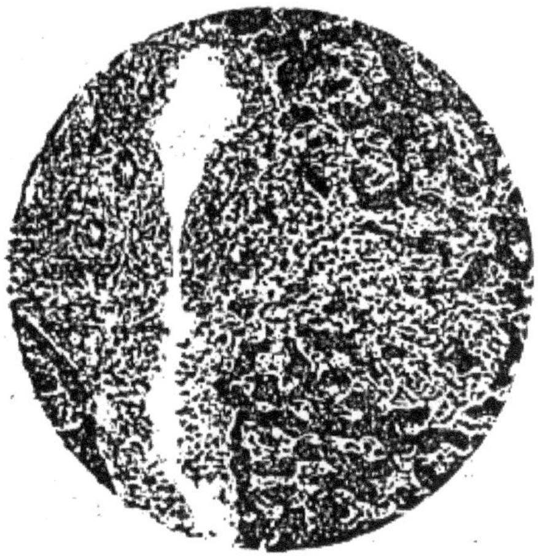

[redacted]

[redacted] 174　221　　X140

([redacted] (

Some round cell accumulation,
initial stage of glanders-knot formation.

[redacted]

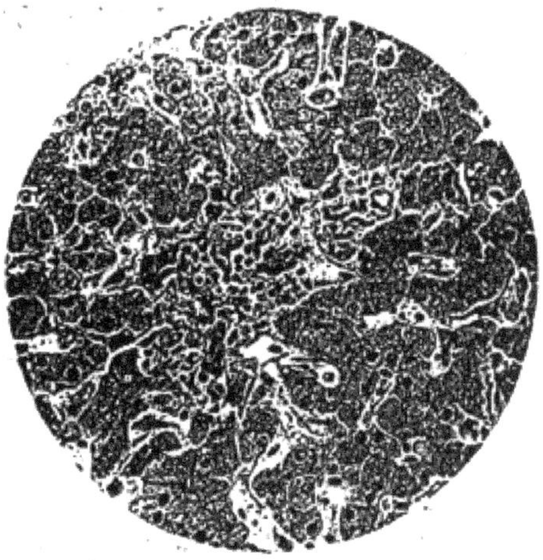

207 x260

Some miliary glanders-knots, in
rather proloferative form.

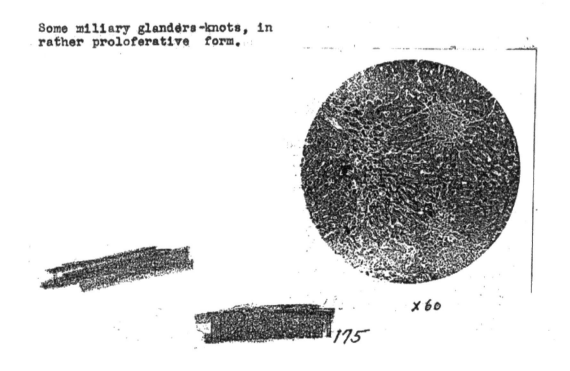

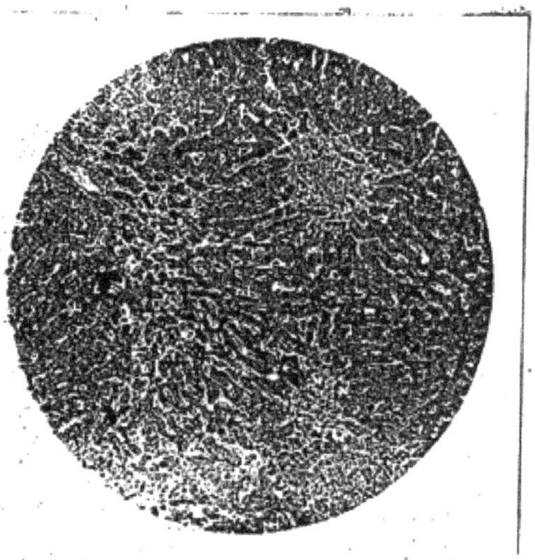

[redacted]

x60

[redacted] 175

[redacted]

Miliary glanders-knot,in
rather productive form.
In high power.

[redacted]

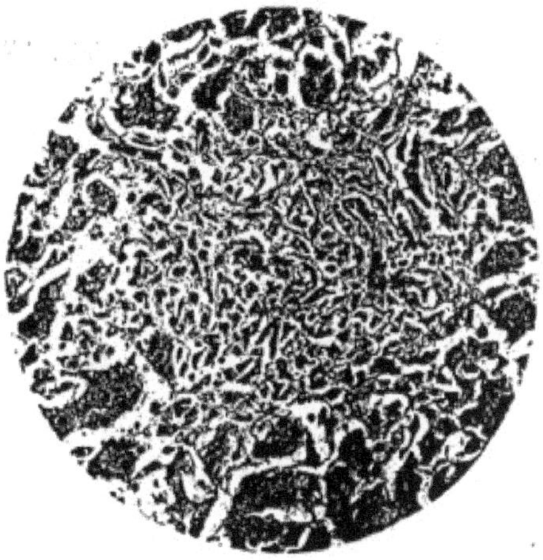

731 X240

Miliary glanders-knot, in
rather productive form.
In high power.

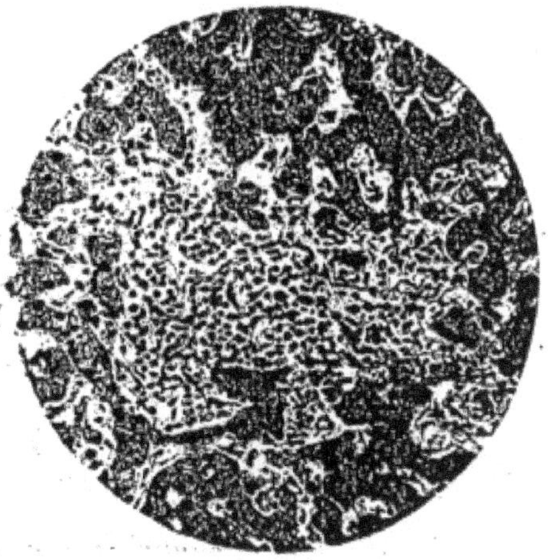

[redacted]

x190

[redacted] 176

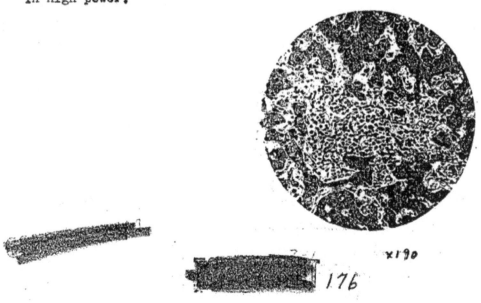

C [redacted] C

Glanders-knot in productive form,
with giant cell formation.

[redacted]

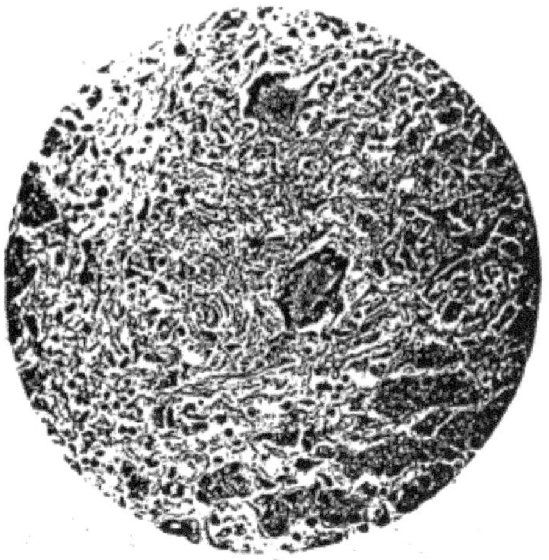

254 x210

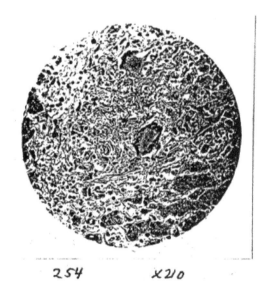

Millet-corn large glanders-knot,
in rather exudative form.

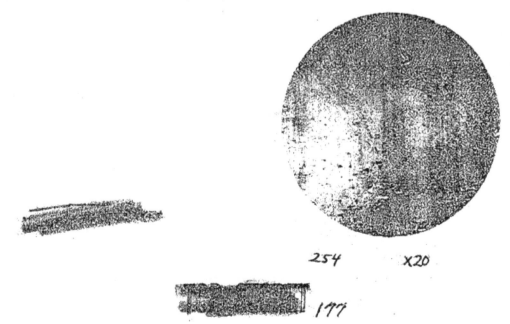

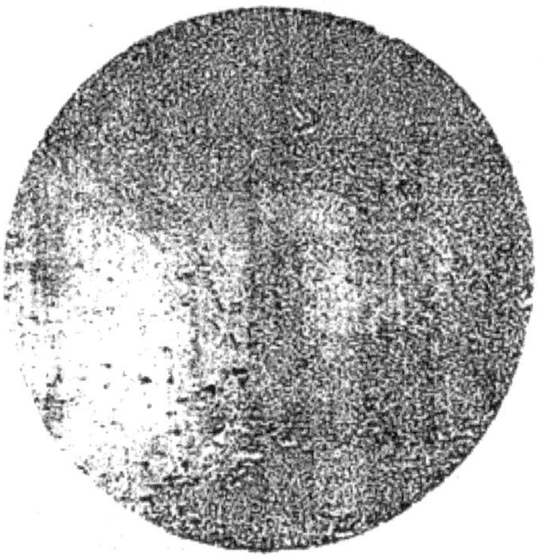

[redacted]

254 x20

[redacted] 177

([redacted] (

Miliary glanders-knot, in
exudative form.

[redacted]

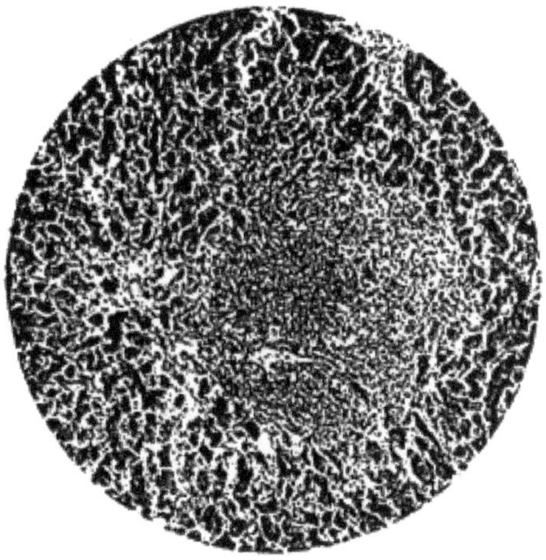

16 X100

Miliary glanders-knot,in
rather exudative form.

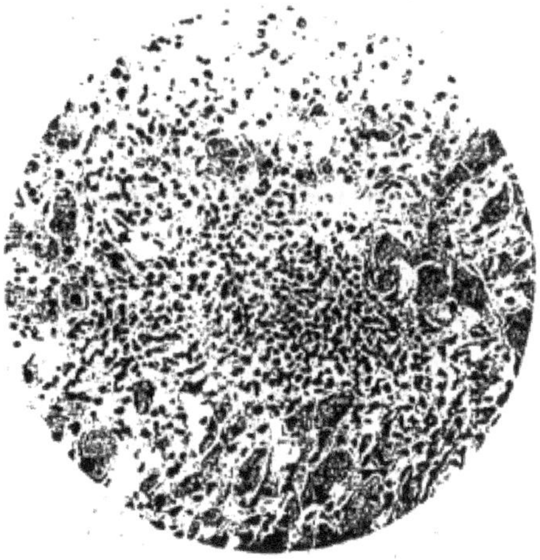

727 X240

[redacted]

[redacted] 178

([redacted] (

Glanders-knot with pseudo-tubulus formation.

[redacted]

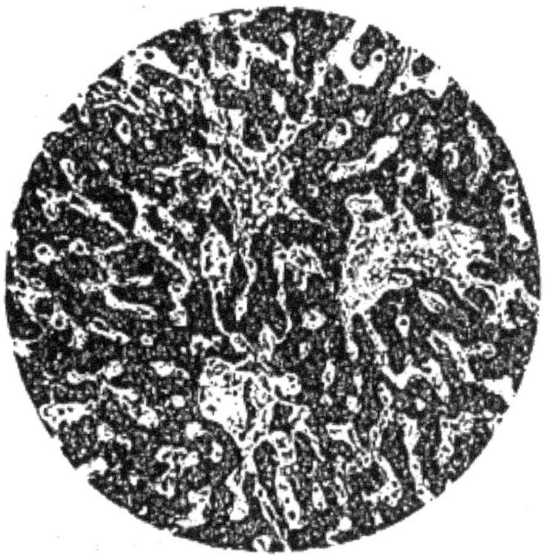

221 X150

Glanders-knots in rather exudative form.
At the margin-portion of knot.

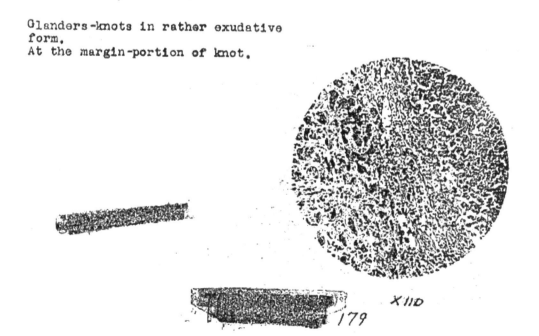

[redacted]

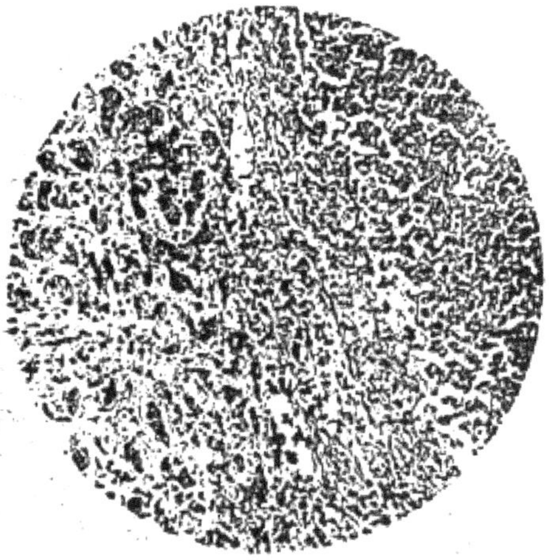

[redacted] 179 X110

[redacted]

Submiliary glanders-knot with
some pseudo_tubulus formation.

[redacted]

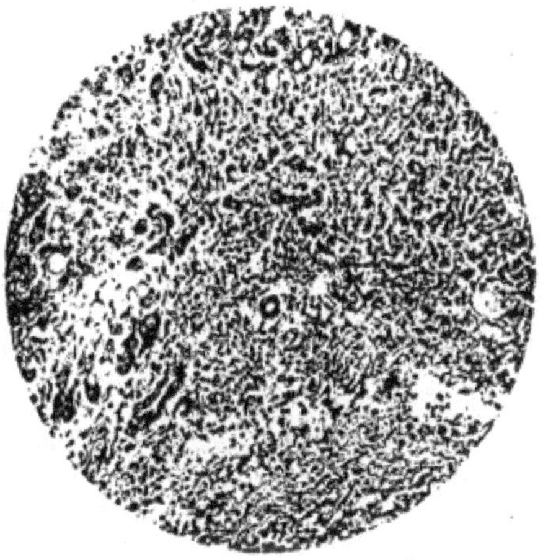

254 X150

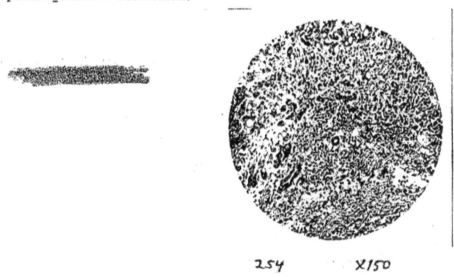

Glanders-knot with pseudo-tubulus
formation.
In high power.

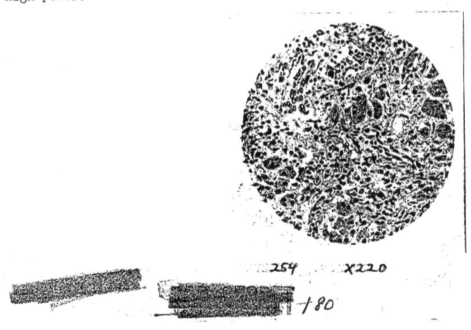

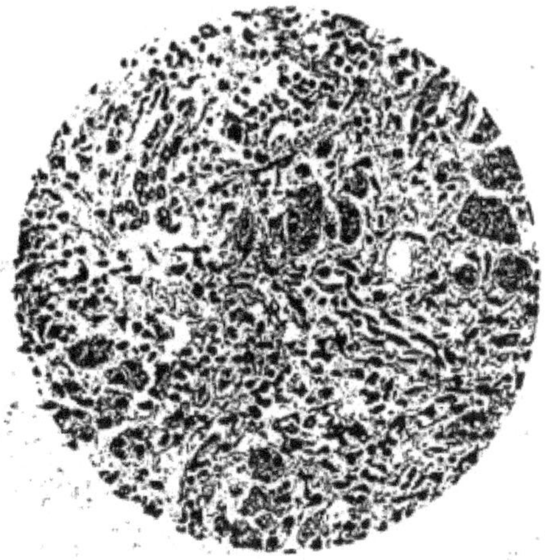

254 X220

[redacted] [redacted] -180

[redacted]

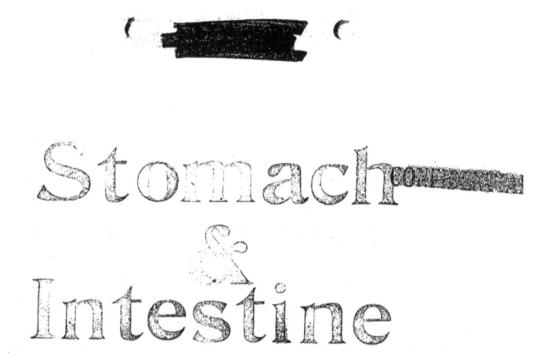

Stomach [redacted]
&
Intestine

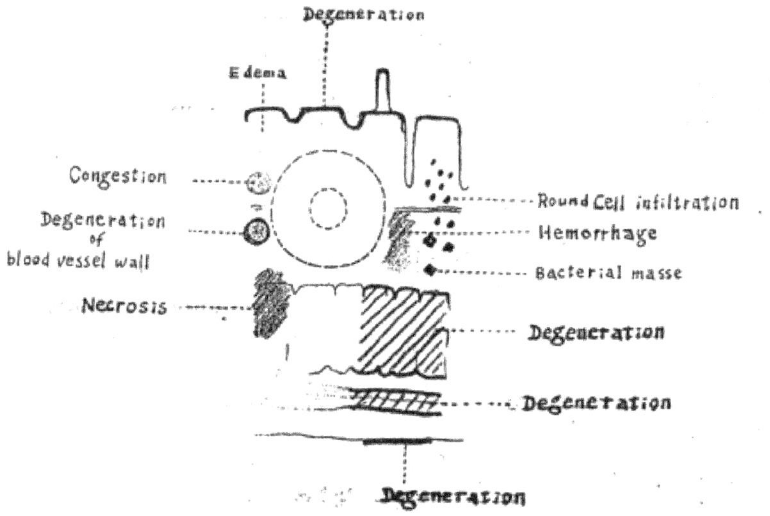

[redacted]

[redacted] 181

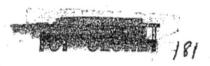

[redacted]

S T O M A C H

(A) Microscopical Investigation.

I6. [redacted]

Almost normal,more or less atrophic glandular cells.

85.

Considerable congestion in T. submucosa and T. propria.

I46.

Gastritis catarrhalis hypertrophicans. Considerable congestion in T. sumbucosa and T. propria.

I52.

Almost normal,more or less atrophic glandular cells.

I67.

Gastritis catarrhalis hypertrophicans. Considerable congestion in T. propria.

I78.

Slight congestion, and slight leucocytes (some of them, eosinophilic leucocytes)- infiltration in mucous layers with slight congestion in T. submucosa.

Remarkable congestion in T. muscularis and subscrous layers with more or less remarkable perivascular leucocytes and round-cell-infiltrations.

I80.

More or less atrophic glandular cells and slight congestion in T. propria.

[redacted]

I90.

More or less considerable catarrh and slight hyperplasia of lympha-

[redacted] 192

[redacted]

tic nodulus.

193.

Slight catarrh and no remarkable changes else. [redacted]

205.

Slight catarrh and slight congestion in mucous layers. No remarkable changes else.

221.

Slight catarrh, slight congestion in mucous layers and slight hyperplasia of lymphatic nodulus.

224.

Considerable congestion of mucous layers and submucous layers with slight edematous swelling.

229.

Considerable congestion in mucous layers, especially at their upper layers with slight hemorrhage.

254.

Gastritis catarrhalis hypertrophicans and no remarkable changes else.

256.

Slight hypersecretion with slight congestion in mucous layers and slight congestion in T. submucosa.

727.

More or less considerable hypersecretion and no remarkable changes else.

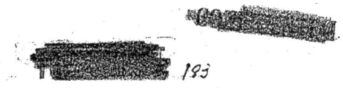

[redacted]

[redacted] 183

([redacted] (

(B) SUMMARY.

I can't point out any significant changes in all cases, exept No. I76 case with considerable or remarkable congestion and some perivascular leucocytes-or lymphocytes-infiltrations.

Other cases without any significant changes; [redacted]

Atrophic glandular cells	3 cases.
Slight catarrh.	4 cases.
Chronic catarrh, due to the other factors.	cases.
Slight or considerable congestion in T. propria	4 cases.
and T. submucosa.	4 cases.

[redacted]

[redacted] 194

[redacted]

R.176

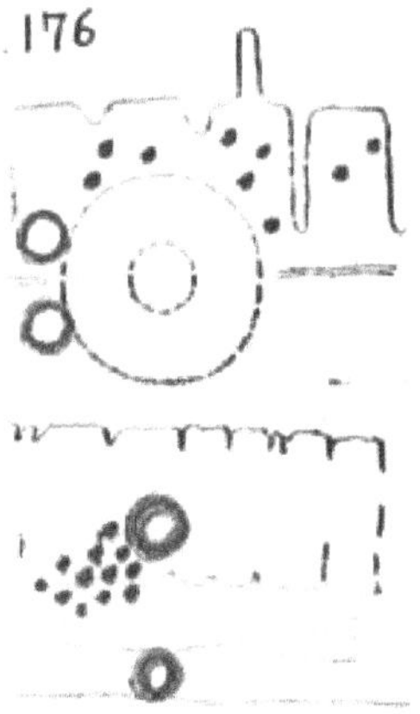

[redacted]

[redacted]

[redacted] 185

[redacted]

STOMACH

[redacted]

			16	85	146	152	167	176	180	190	193	205	221	224	229	254	256	727
T. mucosa		Thickness	|+	N	↑+	↓÷	↑+	N	↓÷	N	N	N	N	N	N	↑+	N	N
		Mucus	−	−	∔	−	∔	−	−	÷	÷	÷	−	−	−	÷	∸	+
		Atrophia of Glands	+	−	−	−	−	−	÷	−	−	−	−	−	−	−	−	−
	T. propria	Edema	÷	∸	÷	÷	∸	÷	÷	∸	∸	∸	÷	÷	÷	−	÷	∸
		Congestion	−	+	∔	÷	∔	+	+	÷	÷	+	+	⧺	∔	∔	+	−
		Hemorrhage	−	−	−	−	−	−	−	−	−	−	−	−	÷	−	−	−
		Leucocytes	−	−	−	−	−	+	−	−	−	−	−	−	−	−	−	−
		Plasma Cells	−	−	−	−	−	∸	−	−	−	−	÷	−	−	−	−	−
Lymph-Nodules		Size	|	−	−	−	−	−	−	↑+	−	|	↑+	|	−	−	|	−
		Indistinction of Limit	|	∸	∸	+	∸	+	+	+	⧺	|	∸	|	∸	∸	|	+
		Edema	|	÷	−	÷	∸	−	−	÷	÷	|	−	|	∸	−	|	∸
		Congestion	|	+	+	−	−	∸	−	−	÷	|	+	|	−	∔	|	−
		Leucocytes	|	−	−	−	−	−	−	−	−	|	−	|	−	−	|	−
		Eosinophil Leucocytes	|	−	−	−	−	∸	−	−	−	|	−	|	−	−	|	∸
		Plasma Cells	|	−	−	−	−	−	−	−	−	|	−	|	−	−	|	−
		Appearance of Germinating Center	|	−	−	−	−	−	−	+	−	|	+	|	−	−	|	−
T. submucosa		Edema	÷	∸	÷	÷	∸	−	÷	∸	∸	∸	−	+	∸	∸	∸	∸
		Congestion	−	∔	∔	−	⧺	+	∸	÷	÷	∸	÷	∔	÷	∔	+	−
		Hemorrhage	−	−	−	−	−	−	−	−	−	−	−	−	−	−	−	−
	Endothelium of Bloodvessels	Hyperplasia	−	−	−	−	−	−	−	∸	−	−	−	−	−	∸	−	−
		Desquamation	−	−	−	−	−	−	−	−	−	−	−	−	∸	∸	−	−
	Lymph-Vessels	Dilatation	−	−	−	÷	−	−	−	−	−	−	−	÷	−	−	−	−
		Lymphocytes	−	−	−	÷	−	−	−	−	−	−	−	−	−	−	−	−
	Infiltration	Leucocytes	−	−	−	−	−	÷	−	−	−	−	−	−	−	−	−	−
		Eosinophil Leucocytes	−	−	−	−	−	÷	−	−	−	−	−	−	−	−	−	−
		Lymphocytes	−	−	−	−	−	−	−	∸	−	−	÷	−	−	−	−	−
		Plasma Cells	−	−	−	−	−	−	−	−	−	−	−	−	−	−	−	−
		Histiocytes	−	−	−	−	−	−	−	÷	−	−	−	−	∸	∸	−	−
T. muscularis		Atrophia	−	−	−	−	−	−	−	−	−	−	−	−	−	−	−	−
		Edema	∸	÷	÷	÷	∸	÷	÷	÷	∸	∸	÷	−	∸	−	∸	∸
		Congestion	÷	+	∔	−	+	∔	+	÷	−	÷	÷	÷	÷	+	÷	÷
		Cellular Infiltration	−	−	−	−	−	+	−	÷	−	−	−	−	−	−	−	∸
T. subserosa		Edema	÷	∸	−	÷	∸	÷	∸	−	−	−	∸	∸	−	÷	∸	÷
		Cellular Infiltration	−	−	∸	−	−	+	−	÷	−	−	−	−	−	−	−	−

N = normal

[redacted]

[redacted] 786

[redacted]

Consìderable congestion in mucous membrane.

[redacted]

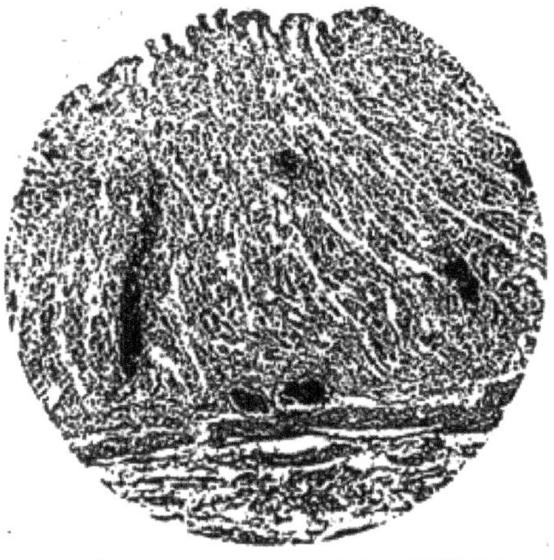

R 224 X70

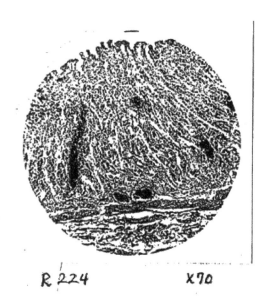

Considerable congestion and some hemorrhages in mucous membrane.

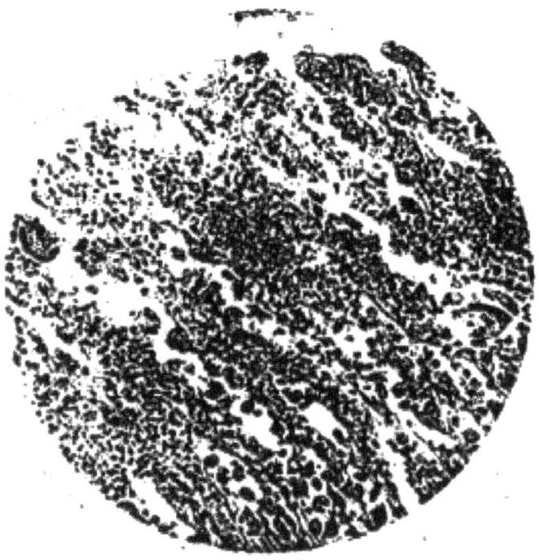

[redacted]

R 229 X130

[redacted] 187

([redacted] (

SMALL INTESTINE

(A) Microscopical Investigation.

I6. [redacted]

Duodenal parts with more or less atrophic glandular cells.

50.

Enteritis catarrhalis with considerable hypersecretion and some desquamated epithelial cells. Slight congestion in mucous membrane.

85.

Almost normal and slight hypersecretion.

I46.

Slight edematous swelling and more or less atrophic glandular cells of mucous membrane. Slight hyperplasia of lymphatic nodulus and slight congestion in T. submucosa.

I52.

Enteritis catarrhalis levis with some desquamated epithelial cells. Slight congestion in mucous membranes.

I67.

Enteritis catarrhalis levis with considerable congestion and slight edematous swelling of mucous membrane. Congenital hyperplasia of lymphatic nodulus and considerable congestion in T. submucosa.

I75.

Almost normal. Slight cogention in mucous and submucous layers.

I80.

Post mortal changes with more or less atrophic glandular cells.

[redacted]

[redacted] 188

([redacted] (

I90.

Enteritis catarrhalis levis with some desquamatied epithelial cells.

[redacted]

205.

Enteritis catarrhalis levis with slight congestion in mucous and submucous layers.

207.

Slight edematous swelling of mucous membrane with more or less atrophic glandular cells and slight congestion in submucous layers.

22I.

Enteritis catarrhalis levis with some separated masses of desquamated epithelial cells and catarrhalic masses. Reactive hyperplasia of germinative centeres of lymphatic nodulus.

More or less slight congestion in submucous layers.

224.

Remarkable congestion in mucous and submucous layers with slight edematous swellung of mucous membrane.

229.

Attention to remarkable changes in submucous layers! Some ruined blood vessels with numerous decayed masses of leucocytes and their nuclear fragments as capillary contents and ruins of capillary-walls. Remarkable congestion and edematous swelling with more or less remarkable perivascular diffuse round-cell-infiltrations. These inflammatory processes propagate themselves to mucous membrane,

[redacted]

[redacted] 189

([redacted] (

which fall into edematous swelling with considerable congestion and at some places structure-less decayed masses. [redacted]

254.

More or less atrophic glandular cells and slight congestion in submucous layers. Some submilliary glanders-knot with epitheloid cells in T. serosa.

727.

Slight edematous swelling of mucous membranes with reactive hyper-plasia of lymphatic nodulus. In germinative centers of lymphatic nodulus exist some increased epitheloid cells with some giant-cells (perhaps due to glander-infection). Without ulcer-formation.

[redacted]

[redacted] 190

([redacted] (

(B) S U M M A R Y.

Investion of 16 micro-slices.

[redacted]

We could assume, based on 4 cases (No. 224, 229, 254 and 727 case), general sketchs of hematogenous infection of glanders in small intestine: namely,

a) in acute stage,

At first, reactive remarkable congestion with some edematous swelling in submucous and mucous tissues (No. 224 or No. 224 with typical miliary glanders-knots-formation with some perifocal changes in subserous tissues).

B) Then diffuse inflammatory propagation came into questions: namely in (No. 229): in focus (in submucous tissues), remarkable congestion and necrotic ruins of capillary-walls with more or less remarkable diffuse inflammatory propagation in the neighbouring mucous tissues with some ruining processes.

C) in chronic stage:

We can't find chronic cases with diffuse inflammatory reactions or remarkable abscess-formation.

In 727 case, acute severe inflammatory signs disappeared already and occured only slight chronic changes in germinative centres of lymphatic nodulus with slight hyperplasia of some reticulum cells and some giant cells formation.

[redacted]

[redacted] 191

([redacted] (

As not so significant complication-signs:

with Enteritis catarrhalis in slight degree.	6	cases.
with slight congestion in mucous tissues.	8	cases.
[redacted] and submucous tissues.	7	cases.
with slight atrophic glandular cells.	5	cases.
with no considerable changes else.	1	cases.

[redacted] 192 [redacted]

• [redacted] •

R229

[redacted]

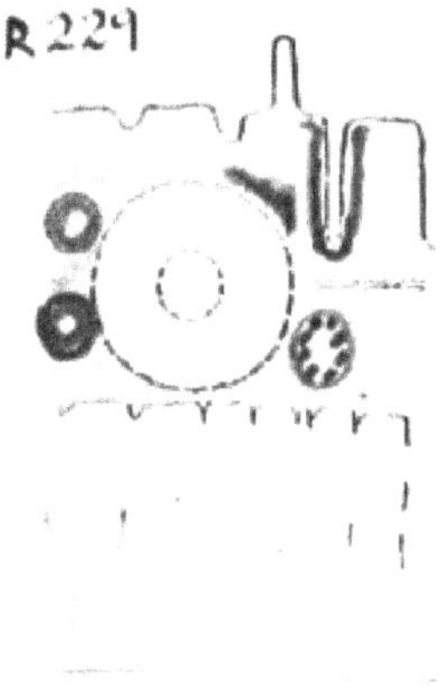

R727

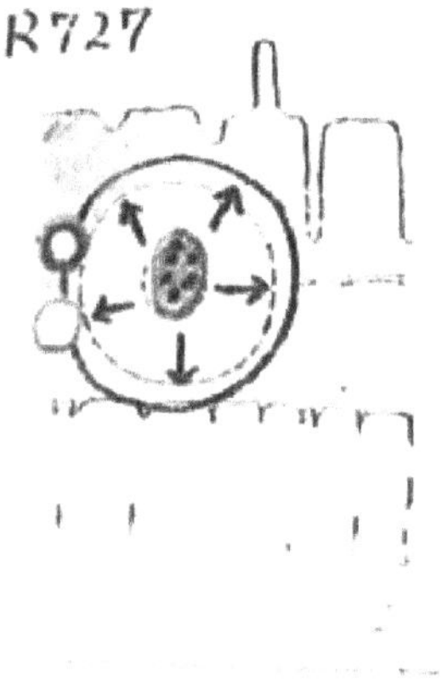

R.254

[redacted]

143

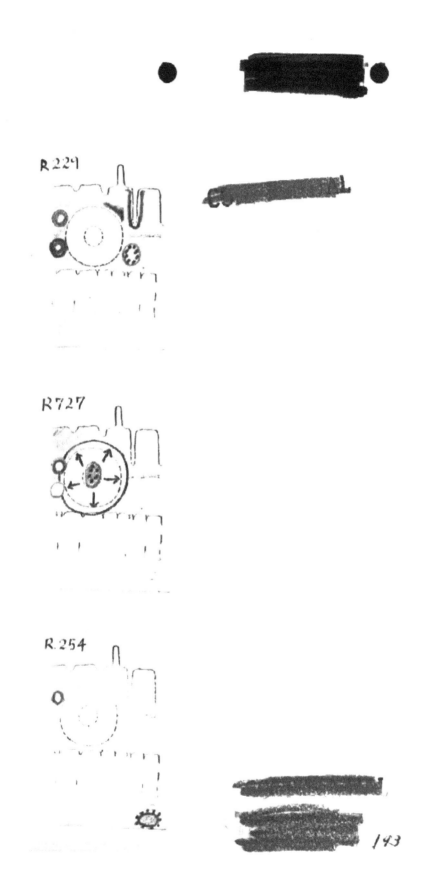

([redacted] (

SMALL INTESTINE [redacted]

			16	50	85	146	152	167	176	180	190	193	205	207	221	224	229	254	727
T. mucosa		Thickness	+++	−	−	+++	−	−	−	|	−	+++	±	|±	−	±	−	|±	−
		Mucus	−	+	±	−	+	±	−	|	±	−	+	−	±	−	−	−	−
		Atrophia of Glands	+	−	−	±	−	±	−	+	−	±	−	±	−	−	−	±	−
	T. propria	Edema	±	±	±	+	±	+	±	|	±	±	−	+	−	+	++	±	+
		Congestion	−	+	±	−	−	++	+	|	−	±	+	±	+	++	++	±	+
		Hemorrhage	±	−	−	−	−	−	−	|	−	−	−	−	−	−	−	−	−
		Leucocytes	±	−	−	−	−	−	−	|	−	−	−	−	−	−	−	−	−
		Plasma Cells	±	−	−	−	−	−	−	|	−	−	−	±	±	−	−	−	−
Lymph-Nodules		Size	|	−	−	+++	−	+++	−	|	|	|	−	−	+++	|	−	−	+++
		Indistinction of Limit	|	±	++	±	++	±	++	|	|	|	+	+	±	|	++	+	+
		Edema	|	±	±	±	±	−	−	|	|	|	−	±	−	|	±	−	+
		Congestion	|	−	−	−	−	+	+	|	|	|	+	±	+	|	±	±	+
		Leucocytes	|	−	−	−	−	−	−	|	|	|	−	−	−	|	−	−	−
		Eosinophil Leucocytes	|	−	−	−	−	−	−	|	|	|	−	−	−	|	−	−	−
		Plasma Cells	|	−	−	−	−	−	−	|	|	|	−	−	−	|	−	−	−
		Appearance of Germinating Center	|	−	−	−	−	−	−	|	|	|	−	−	+	|	−	−	−
T. submucosa		Edema	±	−	±	±	±	−	±	±	±	±	±	−	±	±	++	±	±
		Congestion	−	+	±	+	+	++	+	±	±	±	+	+	+	++	++	+	−
		Hemorrhage	−	−	−	−	−	−	−	−	−	−	−	−	−	−	−	−	−
	Endothelium of Blood Vessels	Hyperplasia	−	−	−	−	−	−	−	−	−	−	−	−	−	−	−	−	−
		Desquamation	−	−	−	−	−	−	−	−	−	±	−	±	−	−	−	±	−
	Lymph-Vessels	Dilatation	−	−	−	−	−	±	−	−	−	−	−	±	+	−	−	−	±
		Lymphocytes	−	−	−	−	−	±	−	−	−	−	−	±	±	−	−	−	±
		Leucocytes	−	−	−	−	−	−	−	−	−	−	−	−	−	−	±	−	−
		Eosinophil Leucocytes	−	−	−	−	−	−	−	−	−	−	−	−	−	−	−	−	−
		Lymphocytes	−	−	−	−	−	−	−	−	−	±	−	±	−	−	+	−	−
		Plasma Cells	−	−	−	−	−	−	−	−	−	−	−	±	−	−	−	−	−
		Histiocytes	−	−	−	−	−	−	−	−	−	−	−	±	−	−	±	−	−
T. muscularis		Atrophia	−	−	−	−	−	−	−	−	−	−	−	−	−	−	−	−	−
		Edema	±	−	±	±	±	±	±	±	−	±	−	−	−	±	±	−	±
		Congestion	−	−	±	−	−	±	±	−	−	−	±	±	±	+	±	±	−
		Cellular Infiltration	±	−	−	−	−	−	±	−	−	±	−	±	−	−	−	−	−
T. subserosa		Edema	−	−	±	−	−	−	±	±	±	±	−	−	±	−	±	±	−
		Cellular Infiltration	±	−	−	−	±	−	−	−	−	−	−	−	−	−	−	+	±

[redacted]

[redacted] 194

([redacted] (

Intense congestion and some edematous swelling of mucous membrane. [redacted]

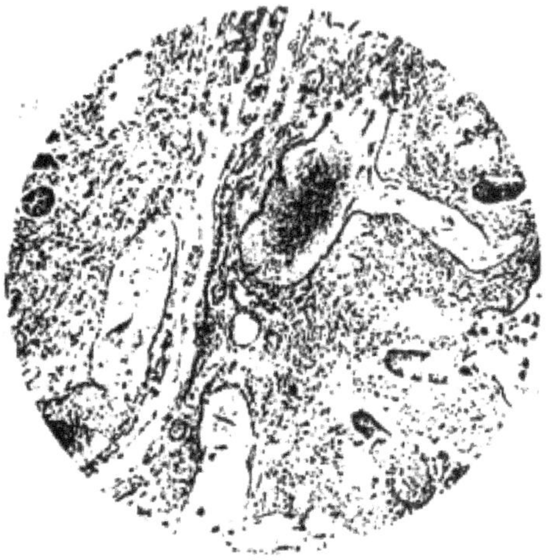

D.D. R.152 100

[redacted]

[redacted] 195

([redacted] (

Ruined blood-vessel and some leucocytes dissemination, in high power.

[redacted]

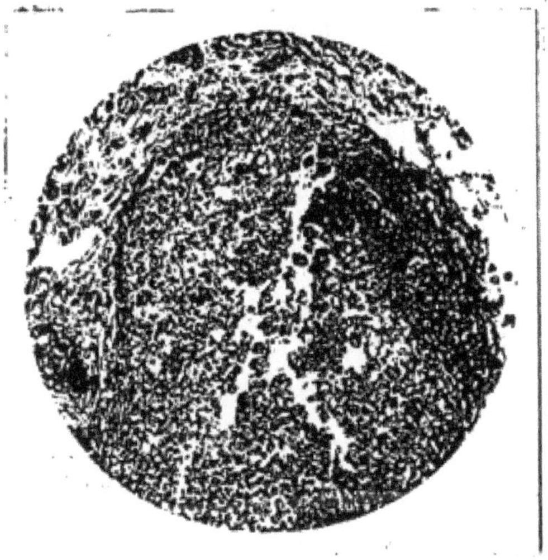

DD R 229 x170

Typical glanders-knot in T.subserosa.

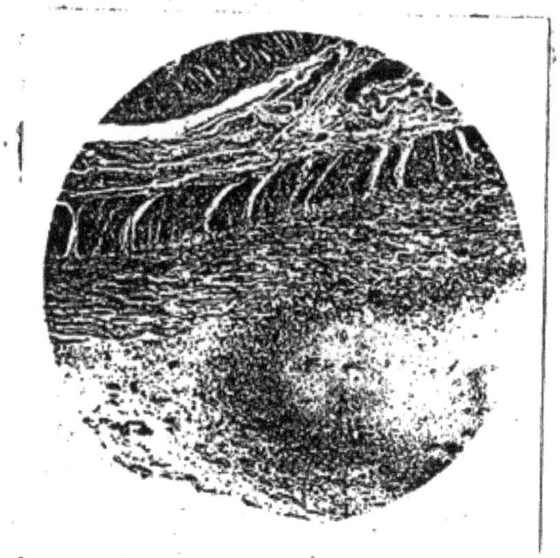

DD R 256 x40

[redacted]

[redacted] 196

[redacted]

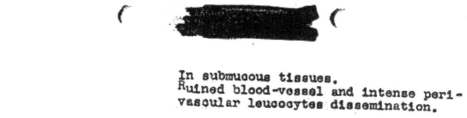

In submucous tissues.
Ruined blood-vessel and intense perivascular leucocytes dissemination.

[redacted]

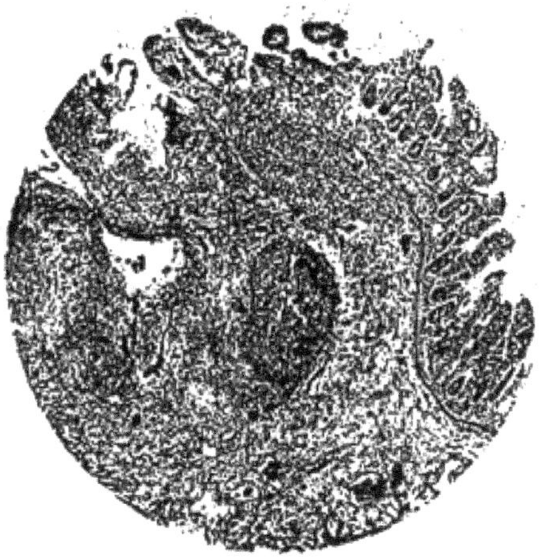

229 X40

Round cell accumulation at perivascular
portion.

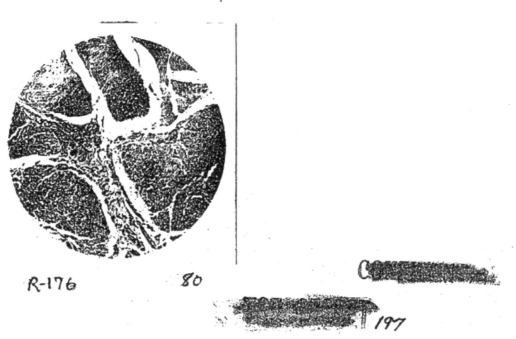

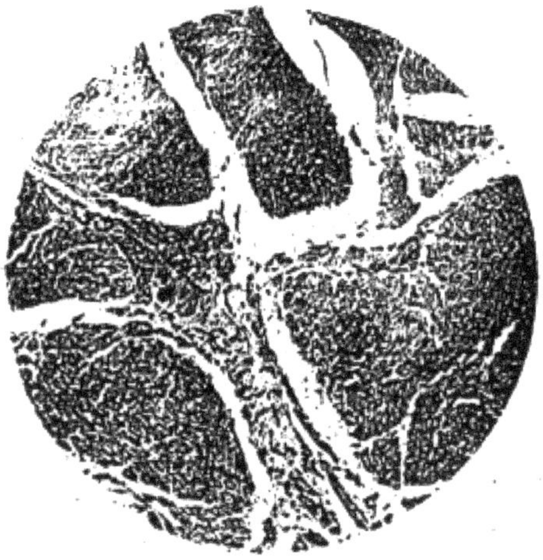

R-176 80

[redacted]

[redacted] 197

([redacted] (

Reactive hyperplasia of germinative centre, with giant cell formation.

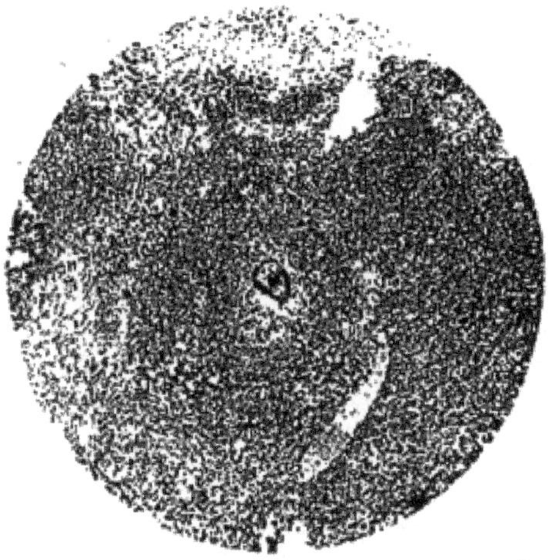

[redacted]

DD R727 x60

Reactive hyperplasia of germinative centre, with giant cell formation, in high power.

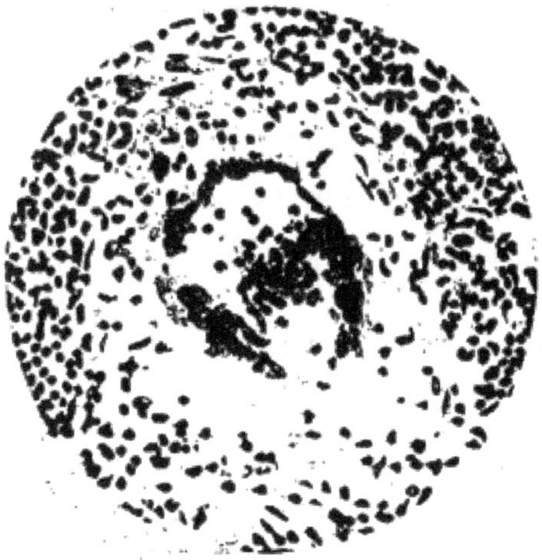

DD R.727 x370

[redacted]

[redacted] /198

([redacted] (

LARGE INTESTINE

(A) Microscopical Investigation.

50. [redacted]

Almost normal. Slight desquamated cells.

85.

Slight catarrh and slight congestion in mucous and submucous layers. No remarkable changes else.

I46.

Edematous swelling of mucous layers with more or less atrophic glandular cells and considerable congestion in submucous layers.

I67.

Almost normal and slight edematous swelling of mucous layers.

I52.

Almost normal and slight hyperplasia of lymphatic nodulus.

I76.

Colitis catarrhalis chronica with a large quantity of separated masses (desquamated epithelial cells and catarrhalic masses) and slight eosinophilic leucocytes infiltrations in mucous layers. Slight congestion in muocus and submusous layers and remarkable hyperplasia of lymphatic nodulus with more or less considerable reactive hyperplasia of germinative centers.

I78.

Remarkable atrophia of muocus layers and considerable congestion in submucous layers. [redacted]

I90.

Almost normal and no remarkable changes else.

[redacted] 199

([redacted] (

205.

Slight catarrh and no remarkable changes else.

[redacted]

207.

Slight atrophic mucous layers and no considerable changes else.

222.

More or less atrophic mucous layers and remarkable congestion of muocus and submucous layers with slight edematous swelling.

224.

Remarkable atrophic mucous layers with slight edematous swelling.

224.

Remarkable atrophic mucous layers with slight congestion in T. submucosa.

229.

Slight catarrh with considerable congestion in T. submucosa.

No remarkable changes else.

254.

Colities catarrhalis levis and no remarkable changes else.

731.

Colitis catarrhalis with slight edematous swelling of mucous layers and slight degeneration of Auerbach's plexus.

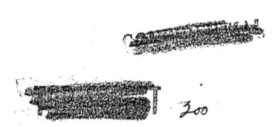

[redacted]

[redacted] 300

([redacted] (

(B) S U M M A R Y.

I can't point out any significant changes: almost all cases have rather atrophic glandular cells and no remarkable changes else. Sometimes with slight or considerable congestion and sometimes with slight or considerable and chronic (due to the other factors) catarrh.

[redacted]

[redacted] 201

([redacted] (

LARGE INTESTINE

[redacted]			50	85	146	152	167	176	178	190	193	205	207	222	224	229	254	731
T. mucosa		Thickness	—	—	++	—	—	—	+++	—	—	—	++	÷	+++	—	—	—
		Mucus	—	÷	—	—	—	+	—	÷	—	÷	—	—	—	÷	÷	+
		Atrophia of Glands	—	—	+	—	—	—	+	—	—	—	+	—	+	—	—	—
	T. propria	Edema	÷	÷	+	÷	+	÷	÷	—	÷	÷	÷	÷	÷	÷	÷	+
		Congestion	—	+	÷	—	—	+	—	÷	—	÷	÷	++	+	÷	÷	÷
		Hemorrhage	—	—	—	—	—	—	—	—	—	—	—	—	—	—	—	—
		Leucocytes	—	—	—	—	—	—	—	—	—	—	—	—	—	—	—	—
		Plasma Cells	—	—	—	—	—	—	—	—	÷	—	÷	—	—	÷	—	—
Lymph-Nodules		Size	—	—	—	++	∣	+++	∣	—	—	—	—	∣	∣	∣	—	—
		Indistinction of Limit	++	++	÷	++	∣	—	∣	++	++	++	+	∣	∣	∣	+	++
		Edema	÷	÷	—	÷	∣	—	∣	—	÷	—	—	∣	∣	∣	—	÷
		Congestion	÷	+	—	—	∣	+	∣	÷	—	+	÷	∣	∣	∣	—	—
		Leucocytes	—	—	—	—	∣	—	∣	—	—	—	—	∣	∣	∣	—	—
		Eosinophil Leucocytes	—	—	—	—	∣	—	∣	—	—	—	—	∣	∣	∣	—	—
		Plasma Cells	—	—	—	—	∣	—	∣	—	—	—	—	∣	∣	∣	—	—
		Appearance of Germinating Center	—	—	—	—	∣	+	∣	—	—	—	—	∣	∣	∣	—	—
T. submucosa		Edema	÷	÷	÷	÷	÷	÷	÷	÷	÷	÷	—	+	÷	÷	÷	—
		Congestion	—	+	++	—	—	+	++	÷	÷	÷	÷	+	+	+	÷	÷
		Hemorrhage	—	—	—	—	—	—	—	—	—	—	—	—	—	—	—	—
	Endothelium of Blood Vessels	Hyperplasia	—	—	—	—	—	—	—	—	—	—	—	—	—	—	÷	—
		Desquamation	÷	—	÷	—	—	—	÷	—	—	—	÷	—	—	—	÷	—
	Lymph-vessels	Dilatation	÷	—	—	÷	—	+	—	—	—	÷	—	—	—	—	—	—
		Lymphocytes	—	—	—	÷	—	+	—	—	—	÷	—	—	—	—	—	—
		Leucocytes	—	—	—	—	—	—	—	—	—	—	—	—	—	—	—	—
		Eosinophil Leucocytes	—	—	—	—	—	—	—	—	—	—	—	—	—	—	—	—
		Lymphocytes	—	—	—	—	—	—	—	—	—	—	—	—	—	—	—	—
		Plasma Cells	—	—	—	—	—	—	—	—	—	—	—	—	—	—	—	—
		Histiocytes	—	—	—	—	—	—	—	—	÷	—	—	—	—	—	÷	—
T. muscularis		Atrophia	—	—	—	—	—	—	—	—	—	—	—	—	—	—	—	—
		Edema	÷	÷	÷	÷	—	÷	÷	÷	—	—	÷	÷	÷	÷	÷	÷
		Congestion	—	÷	+	—	—	÷	—	÷	÷	—	÷	÷	÷	÷	÷	÷
		Cellular Infiltration	—	—	—	—	—	—	—	—	÷	—	—	—	—	—	÷	—
T. subserosa		Edema	÷	÷	÷	÷	÷	—	÷	÷	—	—	÷	÷	÷	÷	÷	—
		Cellular Infiltration	—	—	—	—	—	÷	—	—	—	—	—	—	—	—	—	—

[redacted]

[redacted] 202

[redacted]

Reactive hyperplasia of germinative center.

[redacted]

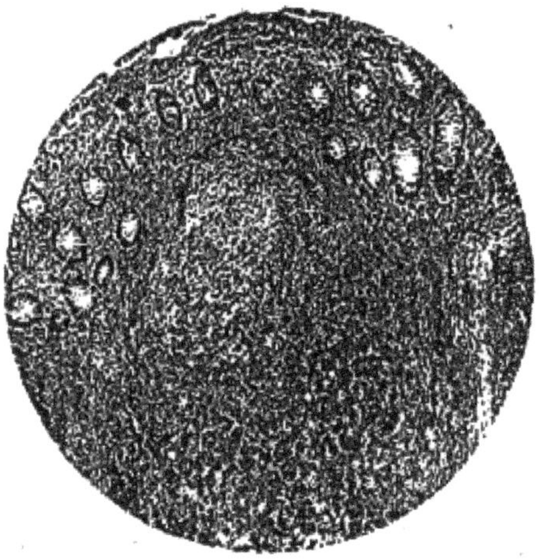

~~221~~ 176   x60

[redacted]

[redacted] 203

• [redacted] •

[redacted]

Spleen

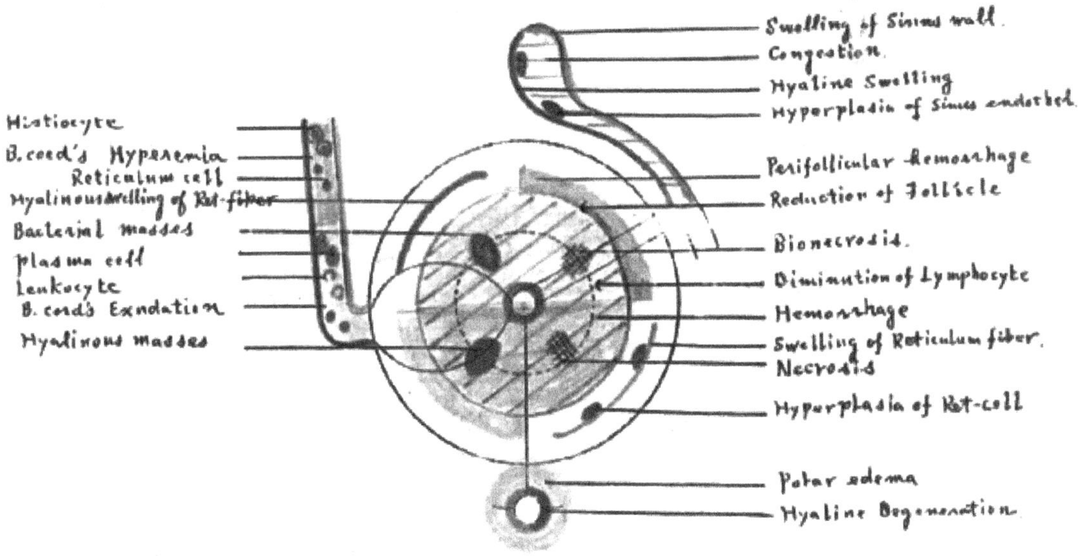
Swelling of Sinus wall.
Congestion.
Hyaline Swelling
Hyperplasia of Sinus endothel.
Histiocyte
B. cord's Hyperemia
Reticulum cell
Hyalinousswelling of Ret-fiber
Bacterial masses
plasma cell
Leukocyte
B. cord's Exudation
Hyalinous masses
Perifollicular hemorrhage
Reduction of Follicle
Bionecrosis.
Diminution of Lymphocyte
Hemorrhage
Swelling of Reticulum fiber.
Necrosis
Hyperplasia of Ret-cell
Polar edema
Hyaline Degeneration

[redacted]

204

[redacted]

SPLEEN

(A) MICROSCOPICAL INVESTIGATION

16.

[redacted]

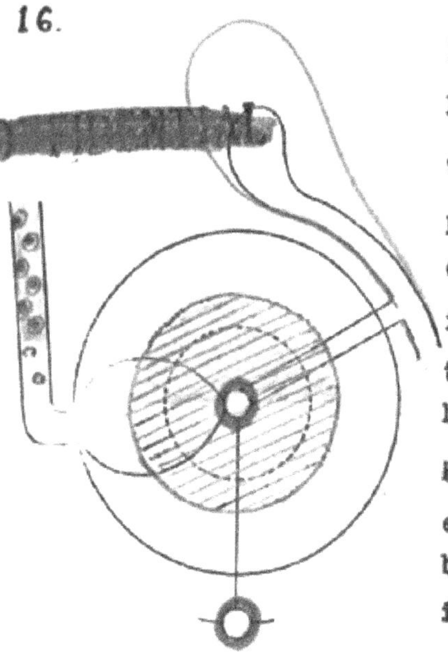

16.

Follicles: Considerable diminution of follicles with hyalinous swelling of walls of central and penicilliary arteries and perivascular edema which caused edematous swelling, multiple hemorrhages in follicular tissues and considerable diminution of follicular lymphocytes. No significant hyperplasia of histiocytic cells. Pulpa-meshes: Remarkable congestion in sinuses and considerable exudative changes (serous exudation, slight bleeding or so-called blood-sea, edematous swelling of reticulum-fibres and diminution or diminish of lymphocytes.), with slight proliferative tendency (slight proliferation of reticulum cells and endothelial cells of sinus-walls.).

50

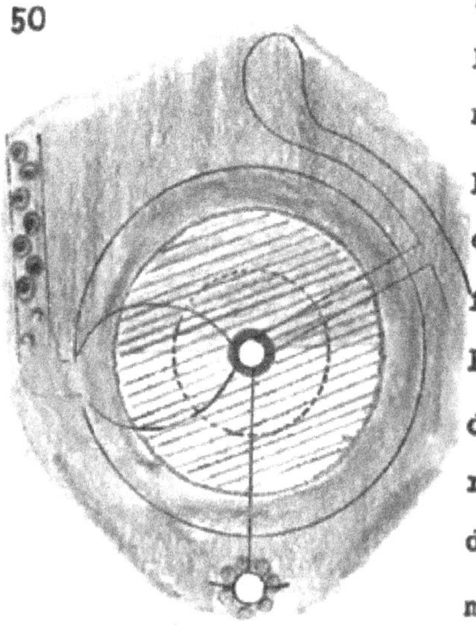

50.

Follicles: Slight reduction of follicles with moderate hyalinous degeneration of central and penicilliary arteries and slight diminution of follicular lymphocytes. Considerable perifollicular congestion and bleeding.

Pulpa-meshes: Severe stasis of venous sinus and diffuse blood-sea with edematous swelling of reticulum-fibres and sinus-walls. Remarkable diminution or diminish of lymphocytes in pulpa-meshes. [redacted]

[redacted]

[redacted]

Beside these exudative changes, slight hyperplasia of reticulum cells or histiocytic cells.

85

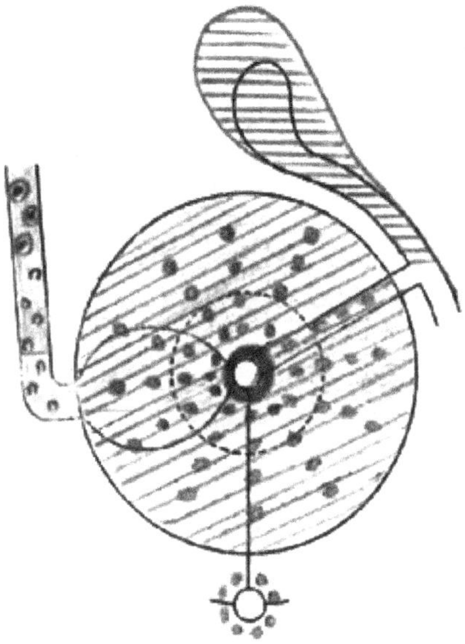

[redacted]

85.

Follicles: Slight diminution of follicles with considerable hyalinous swelling of walls of centra and penicilliary arteries and slight hyperplasia of histiocytic cells in follicular tissues. Considerable perifollicular cängestion and bleeding.

Pulpa-meshes: Severe stasis of venous sinuses and hemosiderosis. Considerable hyperplasia of reticulum cells or histiocytic cells, esp. at perifollicular and peri-penicilliar portions (our sà-called slight "proliferative reactions at polar parts").

146

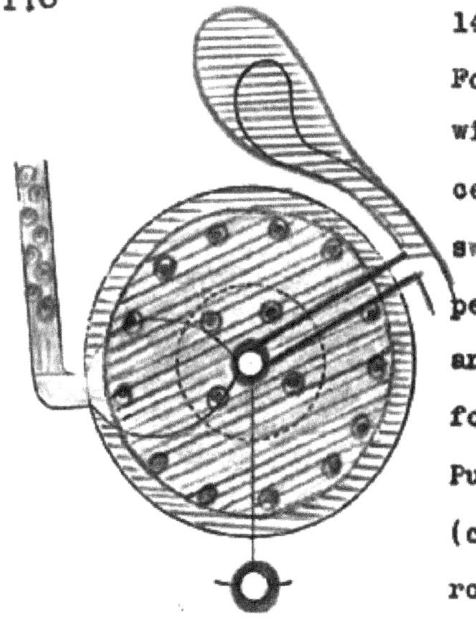

[redacted]

146.

Follicles: Cänsiderable reduction of follicles with considerable hyalinous swelling of walls of central and penicilliary arteries and edematous swelling of follicular tissues. Considerable peri-follicular edema (our so-called polar edema) and slight hyperplasia of histiocytic cells in follicular tissues.

Pulpa-meshes: Considerable exudative processes (considerable cängestion in sinuses, hemosiderosis, leakage of erythrocytes and edematous swelling of reticulum-fibres) and on the other hand slight hyperplasia of reticulum cells,

[redacted] 206

[redacted]

152

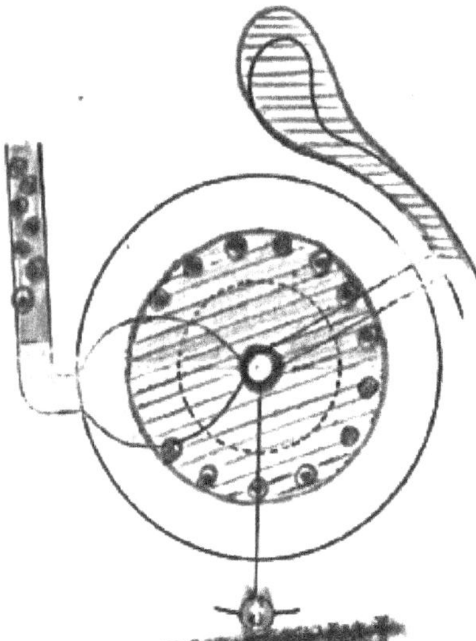

[redacted]

167

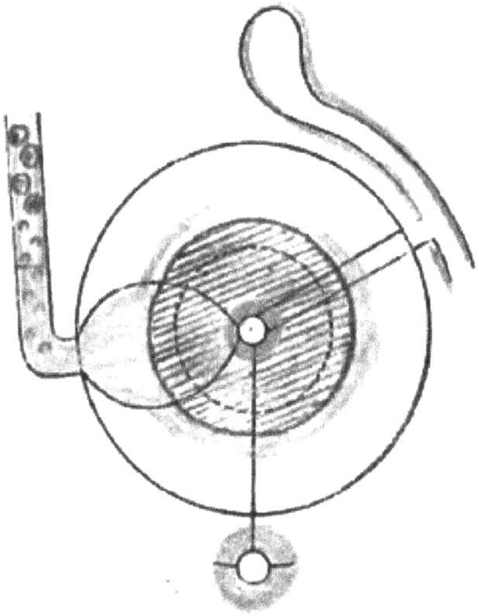

esp. at perifollicular portions.

152.

Follicles in considerable reduction with considerable hyalinous degeneration of central arteries and intra- and perifollicular edema. Slight hyperplasia of histiocytic cells in germinative centers.

Pulpa-meshes: Considerable congestion in venous sinuses, leakage of erythrocytes, and slight edematous swelling of reticulum-fibres. On the other hand, slight hyperplasia of histiocytic cells, esp. at perifollicular portions and slight hyperplasia of reticulum-fibres.

167.

Follicles: Considerable reduction of follicles with edematous swelling of walls of central arteries and considerable edematous swelling of intra- and perifollicular tissues.

Diminution or slight diminish of follicular lymphocytes.

Pulpa-meshes: Consederable congestion in sinuses, leakage of erythrocytes (so-called blood-sea) with plenty leucocytes-emigrations and edematous swelling of reticulum-fibres. With typical our so-called polar edema.

178.

Follicles: Considerable reduction of follicles

[redacted]

201

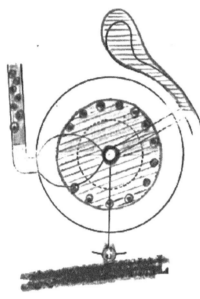

[redacted]

178.

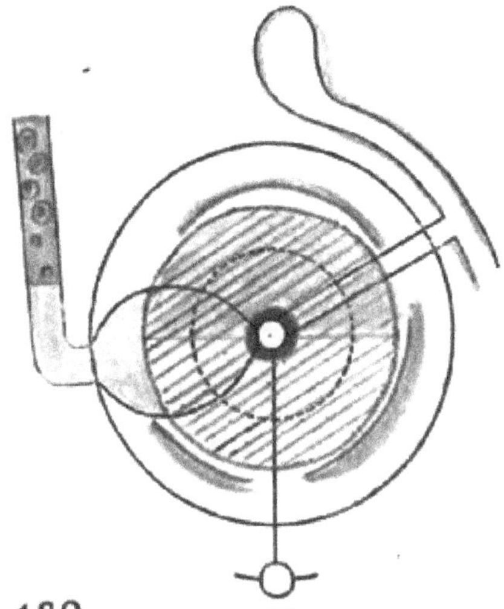

180.

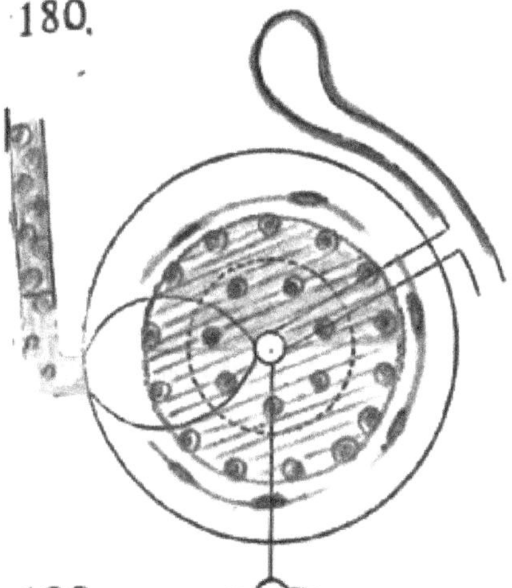

190

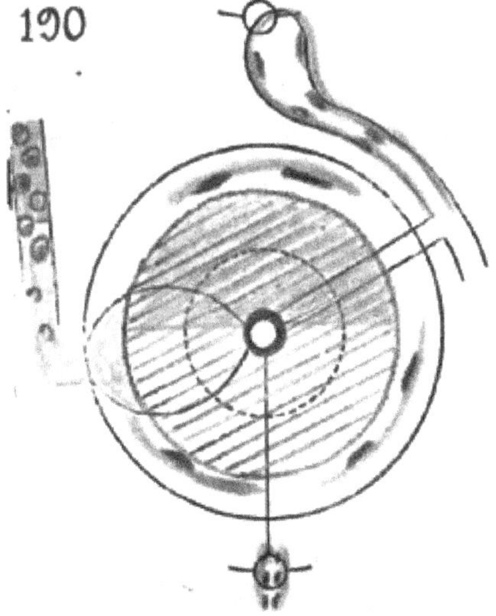

with edematous swelling of walls of central arteries and intra- and peri-follicular edema. Considerable diminution of follicular lympho-cytes. [redacted]

Pulpa-meshes: Slight congestion in sinuses and edematous swelling of reticulum-fibres. Slight hyperplasia of histiocytic cells.

18υ.

Follicles: Considerable reduction of follicles with slight hyalinous swelling of central ar-teries and intra- and peri-follicular edema. Slight diminution of follicular lymphocytes and hyperplasia of histiocytic cells in follicular tissues.

Pulpa-meshes; Considerable congestion in simuses and slight swelling of reticulum-fibres. Moderate hyperplasia of histiocytic cells and endothel cells of simus-walls.

19υ.

Follicles: Considerable reduction of follicles with slight hyalinous swelling of walls of central arteries and slight intra- and peri-follicular edema. Slight hyperplasia of histiocytic cells in follicular tissues.

Pulpa-meshes: Considerable congestion slight leakage of erythrocytes (slight blood-sea) and edematous swelling of reticulum-fibres. Slight hyperplasia of histiocytic cells, esp.

[redacted] 208 [redacted]

[redacted]

193

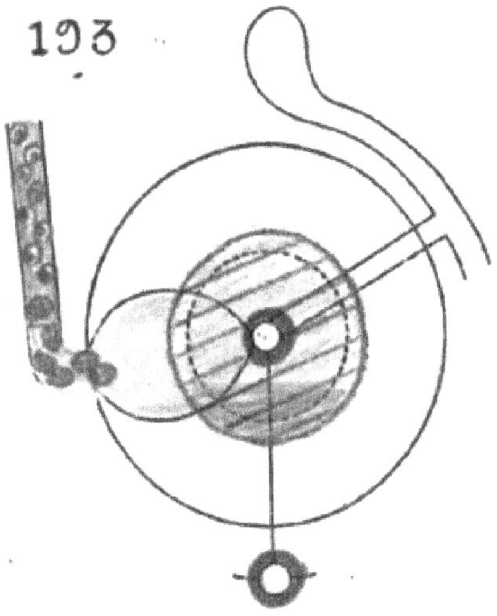

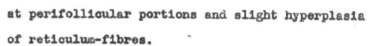

at perifollicular portions and slight hyperplasia of reticulum-fibres.

193. [redacted]

Follicles: Considerable reduction of follicles with hyalinous swelling of walls of central arteries and considerable intra-and perifollicular edema, accompanied with considerable diminution of follicular lymphocytes.

Pulpa-meshes: Considerable congestion, leakage of erythrocytes and edematous swelling of reticulum-fibres. Considerable hyperplasia of histiocytic cells and plasma cells, esp. at perifollicular portions.

221

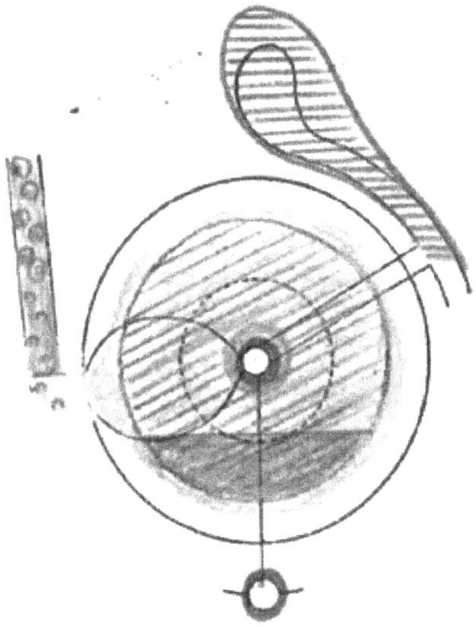

221.

Follicles: Slight reduction of follicles with hyalinous swelling of central and penicillary arteries and considerable intra-and perifollicular edema, accompanied with remarkable diminution of follicular lymphocytes.

Pulpa-meshes: Considerable congestion, leakage of erythrocytes and slight swelling of reticulum-fibres. On the other hand, slight hyper plasia of histiocytic cells (with erythrophagy) and slight hyperplasia of reticulum-fibres.

222.

Follicles: Considerable reduction of follicles with slight hyalinous swelling of central arteries and intra-and peri-follicular edema. Considerable diminution of follicular lymphocytes.

[redacted]

[redacted] 209

[redacted]

222.

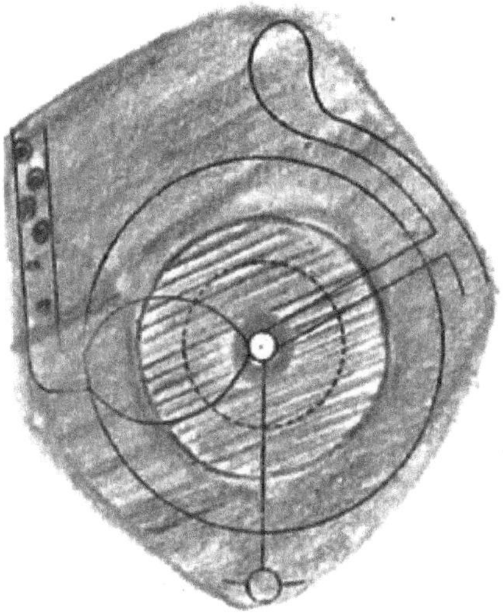

Pulpa-meshes: Considerable congestion in'sinuses, remarkable leakage of erythrocytes (blood-sea) and edematous swelling of reticulum-fibres and sinus-walls.

224. [redacted]

Follicles: Considerable reduction of follicles with hyalinous degeneration of central and penicilliar arteries and severe intra-and perifollicular edema, accompanied with slight hemorrhages and diminution of lymphocytes in follicular tissues.

Perifollicular edema and perifollicular hemorrhages (exudative hemorrhagic changes at our so-called polar portioms).

Pulpa-meshes: Considerable congestion, leakage of erythrocytes (blood-sea) and severe edematous swelling of reticulum-fibres.

224

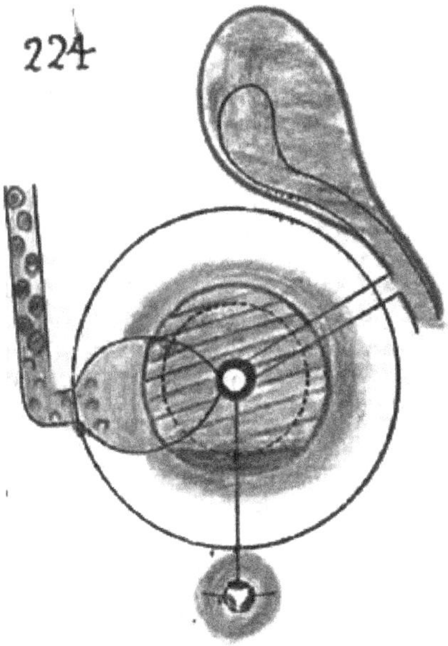

229.

Follicles: Severe reduction of follicles with severe hyalinous degeneration of central arteries and severe exudative hemorrhagic changes in follicular tissues (severe edematous swelling of intra- and perifollicular tissues, considerable hemorrhages andat some places submiliary necrosis etc), accompanied with multiplesubmiliary necrosis at our so-called polar portions (perifollicular portions). These glanders-knots are completely caseous and structureless in focal parts andsurrounded with severehemorrhagic-exud

[redacted]

[redacted] 210

[redacted]

229

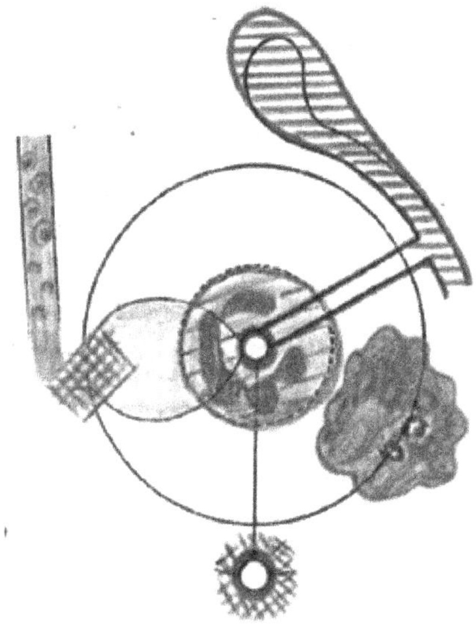

254

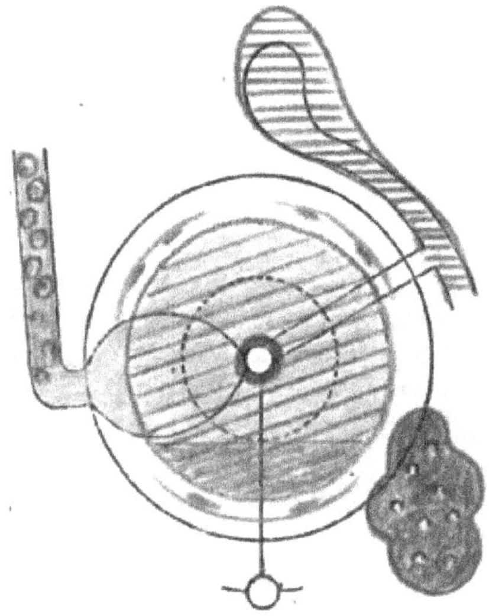

[redacted]

ative perifocal changes, accompanied with slight proliferative reactions (slight increase of histiocytes and some giant-cell-formations).

Pulpa-meshes: Severe congestion in venous sinuses (so-called blood-sea) and severe edematous swelling of reticulum-fibres, accompanied with diminution of lymphocytes in pulpa-meshed in high degree.

[redacted]

With multiple polar miliary necrosis.

254.

Multicple miliary necrosis with slight proliferative processes.

Multiple miliary glanders-knots at polar portions and intrafollicular tissues. These are totally caseous and structureless in focal parts and surrounded more or less sharply with slight proliferative perifocal cellular reactions (slight hyperplasia or reticulum-fibres, reticulum cells and at some places giant-cell-formations).

Follicles: Considerable reduction of follicles with severe edematous swelling of walls of central arteries, severe perivascular edema, edema of intra- and perifollicular tissues, considerable hemorrhages and at some places submiliary glanders knots-formation in follicular tissues.

Pupa-meshes: Considerable congestion in sinuses, remarkable blood-sea and edematous swelling of reticulum-fibres, accompanied with slight hyperplasia of reticulum-fibres and histiocytic cells

[redacted] 211

[redacted]

727

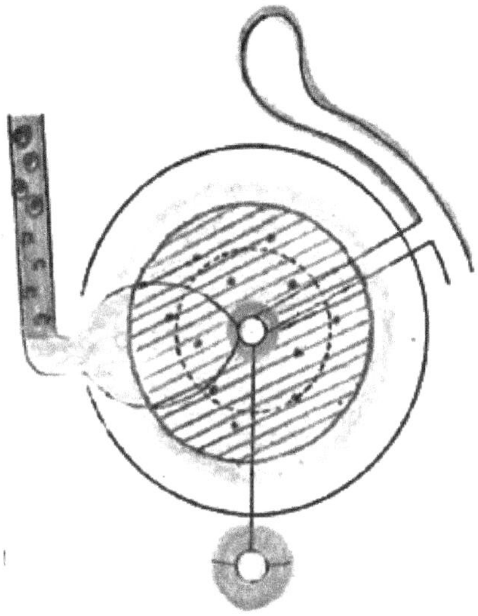

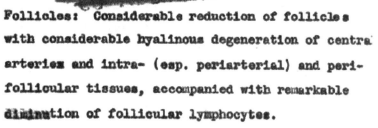

at some localised places.

With multiple miliary glanders-knots in slight proliferative type.

727. [redacted]

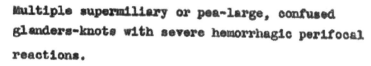

Follicles: Considerable reduction of follicles with considerable hyalinous degeneration of central arteries and intra- (esp. periarterial) and perifollicular tissues, accompanied with remarkable diminution of follicular lymphocytes.

Pulpa-meshes: Considerable congestion and remarkable blood-sea. Considerable edema (esp. our so-called polar edema) and edematous swelling of reticulum-fibres.

731.

Multiple supermiliary or pea-large, confused glanders-knots with severe hemorrhagic perifocal reactions.

720

731

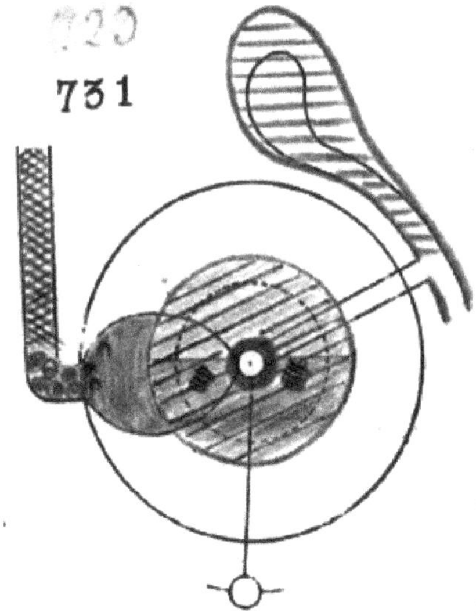

These are severely structureless and necrotic in focal parts and surrounded with severe hemorrhagic perifocal changes.

Follicles: Severe reduction of follicles with severe edematous or hyalinous swelling of central and penicilliary arteries and intra-(esp. periarterial) and perifollicular edema, perivascular multiple hemorrhages, emigration of leucocytes and severe diminution of follicular lymphocytes.

Pulpa-meshes; Considerable congestion and remarkable blood-sea with severe emigration of leuco-

[redacted] [redacted] 812

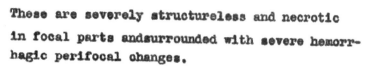

[redacted]

[redacted]

cytes. Severe edematous swelling of reticulum-fibres and on the other hand slight hyperplasia of reticulum-fibres and sinus-walls. Severe diminution of lymphocytes in pulpa-meshes. With multiple polar or intrafollicular super-miliary glanders-knots.

[redacted]

[redacted] 213

([redacted] (

SUMMARY.

(I) [redacted]

I think, the patholigical changes of spleen develope in the following peocesses : namely,

A) NOXIS (bacteria and agens) in Blood.

B) DISTURBANCES OF BLOOD VESSEL SYSTEMS.

At first, at central arteries of follicles and penicilliar arteries.

a) CHANGES OF WALLS.

Hyalinous or edematous swelling of walls.

b) EXSUDATIVE CHANGES OF PERIVASCULAR TISSUES IN FOLLICLES.

Perivascular edema.

Perivascular hemorrahges.

Perivascular wandering cells-accumulations.

Perivascular necroisis. (milliary necrosis, so-called glanders-Knots.)

Then these perivascular localised changes proceed to the following diffuse changes : namely.

C) DISTURBANCES OF FOLLICLES.

c) DIFFUSE EXSUDATIVE CHANGES IN FOLLICLES.

Edematous swelling of tissues.

Haemorrhages.

Wandering cells disseminations. [redacted]

Necrosis. (multiple confused milliary necrosis).

Diminution of follicular lymphocytes. [redacted]

214

C [redacted] C

D) DISTURBANCES OF BILOTH'S CORDS. [redacted]

d) EXSUDATIVE CHANGES IN PULPA+MESHS.

stasis.

Leatkages of erythrocytes (so-called blood-sea).

Hemosiderosis.

Edema, serous exsudation.
Edematous swelling of reticulum-fibres.
Wandering cell disseminations.

Leucocytes-dissemination.

Myelocytes-appearance (myelioc metaplasia).

Diminution of lymphocytes in pulpa-meshs.

Necrosis in pulpa-meshs.

After these exsudative changes, occured slightly rather proliferative changes in follicles and cords.

E) PROLIFERATIVE CHANGES IN FOLLICLES.

Hyperplasia of histiocytes.

Hyperplasia of plasma cells.

Hyperplasia of connective tissues.

F) PROLIFERATIVE CHANGES IN BILLOTH'S CORDS.

Hyperplasia of reticulum-cells and reticulum-fibres.

Hyperplasia of plasma cells.

Etc. (More chronic changes).

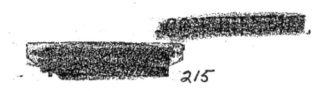

[redacted]

[redacted] 215

([redacted] (

(II). [redacted]

The classification of the pathological findings of spleen, according to the above mentioned developing mechanismus are as followed :

a) Disturbances of central arteries.

Hyalinous swelling of walls in slight degree.	2	cases.
in medial degree.	12	cases.
in severe degree. (necrotic swelling)	3	cases.

b) Disturbances of perivascular tissues or follicular tissues.

. Edema = our so-called ANGIO-FOLLICULITIS EXSUDATIVA.

Angio-folliculitis exsudativa in slight degree.
(Edema in perivascular portions).
Angio-folliculitis exsudativa in medial degree.
Angie-folliculitis exsudativa in severe degree.
(Diffuse edema in follicular tissues).

. Hemorrhages = our so-called ANGIO-FOLLICULITIS HAEMORRHAGICA.

Angio-folliculitis hemorrhagica in slight degree.	6	cases.
Angio-folliculitis hemorrhagica in medial degree.	6	cases.
Angio-folliculitis hemorrhagica in severe degree.	0	cases.

[redacted] 216

([redacted] (

. Leucocytes-emigration = our so-called ANGIO-FOLLICULITIS SUPPRATIVA
[redacted]

Angio-folliculitis with leucocytes-emigration in slight degree. 7 cases.

Angio-folliculitis with leucocytes-emigration im medial degree. 1 cases.

Angio-folliculitis with leucocytes-emigration in severe degree. 0 cases.

. Necrosis-formation = our so-called ANGIO-FOLLICULITIS CUM NECROSIS MILLIARIS.

Multiple milliary necrosis in rather exsudative form. 1 cases.

Multiple milliary necrosis in rather proliferative form. 2 cases.

Diminution of follicular lymphocytes or reduction of follicles are caused by these exsudative changes in follicles.

c) Disturbanses of cords.

. Edema (serous exsudation and edematous swelling of reticulumfibres) = our so-called (SPLENO)-FASCICULITIS EXSUDATIVA.

Fasciculitis exsudativa in slight degree	0	cases.
in medial degree	3	cases.
in severe degree	14	cases.

[redacted]

. Hemorrhage (stasis or so-called blood-sea) = our so-called
[redacted] 217

([redacted]

(SPLENO)-FASCICULITIS HAEMORRHAGICA. [redacted]

Fasciculitis hemorrhagica	in slight degree.	1	cases.
	in medial degree.	4	cases.
	in severe degree.	2	cases.

. Leucocytes-dissemination or myeloic metaplasia = our so-called (SPLENO) FASCICULITIS EXSUDATIVA with leucocytes-dissemination.

Fasciculitis exsudativa with leucocytes disseminations			
	in slight degree.	8	cases.
	in medial degree.	3	cases.
	in severe degree.	5	cases.
Fasciculitis exsudativa with myeloic metaplasia.		2	cases.

Diminution of lymphocytes in cords are complications of these fascicular changes.

(d) Proliferative changes.

In follicles — ANGIO-FOLLICULITIS PROLIFERATIVA.

In cords — (SPLENO)-FASCICULITIS PROLIFERATIVA.

Besides these above mentioned exsudative changes, it shows in this disease, slight, not so significant proliferative changes.

[redacted] [redacted] 218

[redacted]

Folliculo-splenitis exsudativa with slight proliferative tendency :

with some histiocytic cell in follicles. 8 cases.

with some increased reticulum cells or-fibres. 2 cases.

with some plasma cells reactions, esp. at perifollicular portions (our so-called " polar plasma cells reactions")
0 cases.

[redacted]

e) On our so-called polar changes of spleen.

Our so-called polar portions (perifolicular tissues and peri-penicilliar tissues) corespond to so-called "intercalary portions of spleen", so I say. Generally the intercalary portions are the favorite-seats of various cellular changes : inflammatory, degenerative and regenerative changes.

Angio-folliculitis with remarkable polar edema. 10 cases.

" with remarkable polar hemorrhages. 2 cases.

" with some polar milliary necrosis. 2 cases.

" with considerable plasma cells reactions.
0 cases.

[redacted]

[redacted] 219

[redacted]

(III) [redacted]

I profer " SPLENON ", as functional-anatonical unit of sleen.

The general sketch of splenon is as following.

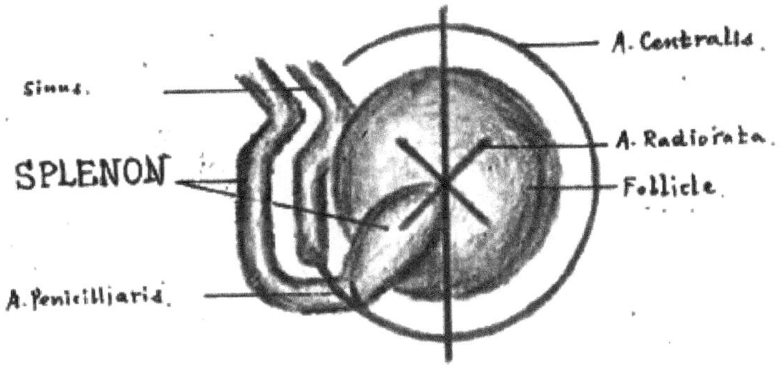

I point out as splenon, a) the attachment-areas of A. radiolata (branch of A.centralis) in follicles and b) Billoth's cords , attached to these follicular sections.

These structures of splenon are completely analogenous to the NEPHRON , functional-anatomical unit of kidney.

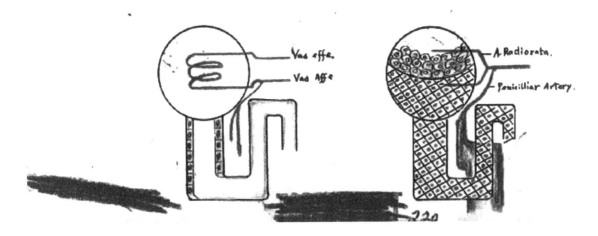

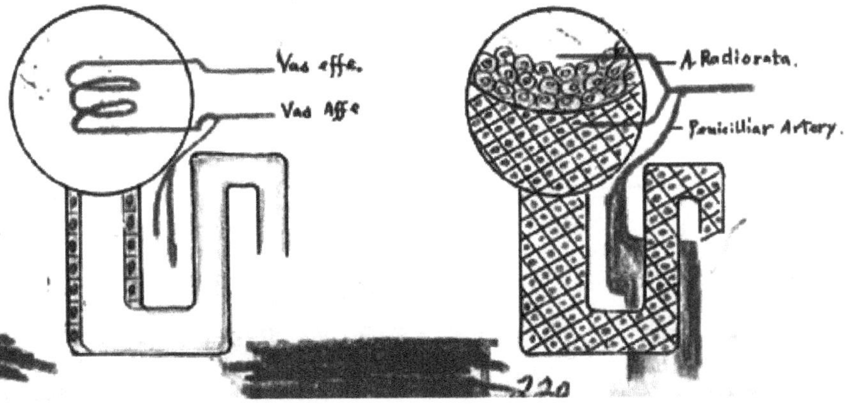

[redacted]

([redacted] (

Based on these facts,

[redacted]

	NEPHRON	SPLENON
Afferent arterie.	Vasa afferens.	A. radiolata. A. penicilliaris.
Filtration-part	Glomerulus.	Germinative centres.
Transport-part.	Tubulus.	Billot's cords.
	Glomerulitis	Angio-folliculitis °
	Tubulitis (Nephrose).	Fasciculitis (Splenose) °
	Glomerulo-nephrose.	Folliculò-fasciculitis. (Folliculo-Splenese)
	Polar-complex. ●●	Polar-complex.
	Nephro-cirrhosis. [redacted]	Spleno-cirrhosis (Banti's disease).

[redacted] 221

([redacted] (

o) I classified the changes of spleen, according to such my concept, Angio-folliculitis and Fasciculitis. [redacted]

oo) Explaining of "polar-complex", concerned in our stand-point on" inflammation"-concept, should be described later in the chapter of kidney.

[redacted]

[redacted] 222

([redacted] (

(IV).

The bird's-eye views of all splenal changes are as following.

[redacted]

223

[redacted]

Thr bird's eye view of all investigated cases , [redacted]

16.	Angio-folliculitis hemorrhagico-exudativa.	Hemorrhagic changes in slight degree. Exudative changes in medium degree.
	Fasciculitis exudativa.	Exudative changes in medium degrre. with some leucocytes dissmination. with some bionecrotic chages.
50.	Angio-folliculitis haemorrhagico-exsudativa.	Hemorrhagic changes in slight degree. Exudative changes in medium degree. with polar edema in slight degree. with polar hemorrhages in slight degree.
	Fasciculitis haemorrhagico-exsudativa.	Hemorrhagic changes in severe degree. Exudative changes in severe degree. with some leucocytes dissemination.
85.	Angio-folliculitis exsudativa.	Exudative changes in severe degree. with some leucocytes dissemination. with polar edema in severe degree. with polar hemorrhages in medium degree.
	Fasciculitis haem exsudativa.	Exudative changes in severe degree. with intense leucocytes dissemination.
146.	Angio-folliculitis haemorrhagico-exsudativa.	Hemorrhagic changes in slight degree. Exddative changes in severe degree. with polar edema in severe degree. with slight proliferative tendency.
	Fasciculitis exsudativa.	Exudative changes in sevrre degree. with some leucocytes dissemination.
152.	Angio-folliculitis exsudativa.	Exudative changes in severe degree. with polar edema in severe degree. with slight proliferative tendency.

[redacted] [redacted] 224

([redacted] (

Fasciculitis exsudativa. [redacted]	Exudative changes in severe degree. with some leucocytes dissemination. with some myeloic metaplasia. with slight proliferative tendency.

---

157. Angio-folliculitis	Exudative changes in severe degree. with some leucocytes dissemination. with polareedema in severe degree. with slight proliferative tendency.
Fasciculitis	Hemorrhagic changes in medium degree. Exudative changes in severe degree. with intense leucocytes dissemination. with slight proliferative tendency.

---

178. Angio-folliculitis	Hemorrahigic changes in medium degree. Exudative changes in severe degree.
Fasciculitis haemorrhagico-exsudativa.	Hemorrhagic changes in slight degree. Exudative changes in severe degree. with some leucocytes dissemination.

---

180. Angio-folliculitis exsudative.	Exudative changes in severe degree. with slight proliferative tendency.
Fasciculitis exudative.	Exudative changes in medium degree. with some leucocytes dissemination. with slight proferative tendency.

---

190. Angio-folliculitis haemorrhagico-axsudativa.	Hemorrhagic changes in slight degree. Exudative changes in severe degree. with polar edema in medium degree. with slight proliferative tendency.
Fasciculitis exudative.	Exudative chages in severe degree. with some leucocytes dissemination. with slight proliferative tendency.

[redacted] [redacted] 225

([redacted] (

---

193. Angio-folliculitis haemorrhagico-exsudativa.. — Hemorrhagic changes in medium degree. Exudative changes in segere degree. with slight proliferative tendency.

[redacted]

Fasciculitis haemorrhagico-exsudativa. — Hemorrhagic changes in medium degree. Exudative chages in severe degree. with slight proliferative tendency.

---

221. Angio-folliculitis haemorrhagico-exsudativa. — Hemorrhagic changes in medium degree. Exudative changes in severe degree. with some leucocytes dissemination. with some polar edema.

Fasciculitis haemorrhagico-exsudativa. — Hemorrhagic changes in medium degree. Exudative changes in severe degree. with intense leucocytes dissemination. with slight proliferative tendency.

---

222. Angio-folliculitis haemorrhagico-exsudativa. — Hemorrhagic changes in slight degree. Exudative changes in severe degree. with slight leucocytes dissemination.

Fasciculitis haemorrhagico-exsudativa. — Hemorrhagic changes in severe degree. Exudative changes in severe degree. with leucocytes dissemination in medium degree. with slight proliferative tendency.

---

224. Angio-folliculitis haemorrhagico-exsudativa. — Hemorrhagic changes in medium degree. Exudative changes in severe degree. with slight leucocytes dissamination. with intense polar edema.

Fasciculitis exsudativa. — Exudative changes in severe degree. with intense leucocytes dissamination. with some myeloic metaplasia.

[redacted] [redacted]

226

([redacted] (

229. Angio-folliculitis haemorrhagico-exsudativa. et necroticans.
Hemorrhagic changes in medium degree.
Exudative changes in severe degree.
Nedrotic changes in medium degree.
(miliary necrosis)
with some leucocytes dissemination.
with polar miliary necrosis.

[redacted]

Fasciculitis haemorrhagio-exsudativa.
Hemorrhagic changes in medium degree.
Exudative vhanges in severe degree.
with intense leucocytes dissemination.
with slight proliferative tendency.

---

229. Angio-folliculitis necroticans.
Necrotic ruins of angio-follicular tissues.

Fasciculitis necroticans.
Necrotic changes all over the fascicular tissues.

---

254. Angio-folliculitis haemorrhagico-exsudativa.
Hemorrhagic changes in medium degree.
Exudative changes in severe degree.
with polar miliary necrosis.
with some polar edema.
with some leucocytes dissemination.

Fasciculitis
Exudative changes in severe degree.
with multiple miliary necrosis,
in rather proliferative form.
with some leucocytes dissemination.

---

727. Angio-folliculitis haemorrhagico-exsudativa.
Hemorrhagic changer in slight degree.
Exudative changes in severe degree.
with polar edema.
with leucocytes dissemination in medium degree.

Fasciculitis exsudativa.
Exudative changes in severe degree.
with intense leucocytes dissemination.

[redacted] [redacted] 227

([redacted] (

---

731. Angio-folliculitis haemorrhagico-exsudativa et necroticans.	Hemorrhagic changes in medium degree. Exudative changes in medium degree. Necrotic changes at some places.
Fasciculitis [redacted]	Exudative changes in medium degree. with diffuse necrosis. with some leucocytes dissemination.

[redacted]

[redacted] 228

([redacted]

[redacted]

Accordingly.

I)

Angio-folliculitis exsudativa	17	cases.
in slight degree.	0	cases.
in medial degree.	3	cases.
in severe degree.	14	cases.
with leucocytes-emigrations.	8	cases.
with milliary necrosis.	3	cases.
with hemorrhage, Angio-folliculitis hemorrhagico-exsudativa.	14	cases.
in slight degree.	6	cases.
in medial degree.	6	cases.
in severe degree.	0	cases.

Angio-folliculitis with remarkable polar changes.	14	cases.
with remarkable polar edema.	10	cases.
with remarkable polar hemorrhages.	2	cases.
with some polar milliary necrosis.	2	cases.
with considerable polar plasma cells reaction	0	cases.

Angio-folliculitis with slight proliferative tendency.	6	cases.

[redacted] [redacted] 229

([redacted] (

2) [redacted]

Fasciculitis

exsudativa. 17 cases.

in slight degree. 0 cases.

in medial degree. 3 cases.

in severe degree. 14 cases.

with so-called "blood-sea", Fasciculitis hemorrhagica. 7 cases.

in slight degree. 1 cases.

in medial degree. 4 cases.

in severe degree. 2 cases.

with leucocytes-dissemination 16 cases.

in slight degree. 8 cases.

in medial degree. 3 cases.

in severe degree. 5 cases.

with myeloic metaplasia. 2 cases.

with multiple milliary necrosis 4 cases.

in rather exsudative form. 1 cases.

in rather proliferative form. 3 cases.

with slight proliferative tendency 8 cases.

[redacted] [redacted] 230

([redacted]

3) Classification of splenal changes according to "Folliculo-Fasciculitis"-concept, analogenous to" Glomerulo-nephrosis" in kidney.

[redacted]

Folliculo-Fasciculitis exsudativa 17 cases.

in slight degree. 0 cases.

in medial degree. 3 cases.

in severe degree. 14 cases.

with hemorrhages. Folliculo-fasciculitis hemorrhagico-exsudativa.

12 cases.

in slight degree. 4 cases.

in medial degree. 6 cases.

in severe degree. 2 cases.

leucocytes-disseminations. Folliculo-fasciculitis Suppprativa.

16 cases.

in slight degree. 8 cases.

in medial degree. 3 cases.

in severe degree. 5 cases.

with myeloic metaplsia. 2 cases.

with multiple milliary necrosis.

5 cases.

in rather exsudative form. 2 cases.

in rather proliferative form. 3 cases.

with slight proliferative tendency.

[redacted] [redacted] 231

([redacted])

ooo ooo ooo [redacted]

Consequently, the main pathological findings are considerable exsudative (at sometimes, hemorrhagico-exsudative) changes, accompanied at some times with glanders-knots formations (in rather exsudative form).

[redacted]

[redacted] 232

[redacted]

SPLEEN

			16	50	85	146	152	167	178	180	190	193	221	222	224	229	254	727	731
Capsule	Thickness		↑±	↑−	N	↓±	↑±	↓±	↓(+±)	↑±	N	↓(+++)	N	|	↓+±	↓+±	N	N	↓±
Capsule	Curve		±	±	±	±	±	±	±	+	+	±	+	|	±	±	±	−	±
Trabeculae	Thickness		↑±	N	N	N	↑±	↓±	↓(++±)	↑±	↓(++±)	↓(+++)	N	↓++	↓+±	↓+	N	↓±	↓±
Trabeculae	Blood Vessels	Congestion	±	++	+	++	+	±	+	±	++	(+±)	+	+	(++)	±	(+±)	(+±)	±
Trabeculae	Blood Vessels	Swelling of Walls	+	+	+±	±	±	+	±	+	±	+	(+±)	+	(++)	±	(+±)	+	+
Trabeculae	Blood Vessels	Loosening of Walls	±	±	+	±	±	+	±	+	±	+	(++)	+	+±	+±	+	±	++
Trabeculae	Blood Vessels	Hyaline Degeneration	+	(++)	+±	±	±	±	±	±	+	(+±)	(+)	+	±	++	±	±	+
Reticulum	Hyperplasia		±	±	±	+±	+±	−	±	±	±	±	±	−	±	±	(+)	−	±
Reticulum	Swelling		++	++	++	+±	+	++	++	+±	+±	++±	±	++	+	+±	++	++	±
Reticulum	Hyaline Degeneration		+	+	±	++	±	−	+±	+	+±	+	+	±	±	+±	±	±	±
Reticulum	Hyperplasia of Reticular Cells	in Follicles	±	±	++	±	±	±	±	±	±	−	±	±	±	±	±	±	±
Reticulum	Hyperplasia of Reticular Cells	perifollicular	+	+	+±	±	±	+	±	±	±	−	±	+	±	±	±	±	±
Reticulum	Hyperplasia of Reticular Cells	peritrabecular	+	±	+±	±	±	+	±	±	±	−	±	±	±	±	±	±	±
Follicles	Size		↓+±	↓+±	N	↓(+±)	↓(++)	↓(++±)	↓++	↓++	↓(++)	↓+++	↓+±	↓+±	↓(+++)	↓+±	↓++	↓(+±)	↓(+++)
Follicles	Number		↓++±	↓++	N	↓+	↓+	↓+	↓++±	↓++	↓++	↓+++	↓++	↓+	↓++±	↓+±	↓++	↓+	↓++±
Follicles	Decrease of Lymphocytes		++	+	+	+±	(++)	±	+	+	+±	+++	+	+	++	+	+±	+	++
Follicles	Edema	in Follicles	+	+	+±	++	±	++	+	+	+	++	+±	++	++	+±	+±	++	±
Follicles	Edema	perifollicular	+±	+±	++	++	+	++	+	+	+	++	+±	++	++	++	++	+++	+
Follicles	Hemorrhage	in Follicles	±	±	±	±	±	±	+	±	±	+	+	±	++	+	±	±	+
Follicles	Hemorrhage	perifollicular	+	++	+±	+±	±	±	+	±	±	+	+	±	+++	++	+	+	+±
Follicles	Histiocytes	in Follicles	±	±	−	±	±	±	±	+	+	+++	±	±	±	±	(+)	±	±
Follicles	Histiocytes	perifollicular	+±	±	±	+±	+±	±	+	++	+±	+++	+±	±	+±	±	±	±	±
Follicles	Central Artery	Congestion	±	+	±	±	(+)	±	+	−	±	+	±	+	±	+±	(+)	±	±
Follicles	Central Artery, Endothelium	Swelling	(+±)	+±	+	+	+	+	(+±)	±	+	+±	+	+±	+	+	(+±)	±	+
Follicles	Central Artery, Endothelium	Hyperplasia	+	+	+	−	±	+	+	−	±	±	−	±	−	−	−	−	−
Follicles	Central Artery, Endothelium	Desquamation	±	±	±	(+)	±	+	±	−	+	±	±	±	+	±	(+±)	±	+
Follicles	Central Artery, Walls	Swelling	+	+±	++	+	±	++	+	±	+	++	+	+±	+	+	+±	+	+
Follicles	Central Artery, Walls	Loosening	(++)	+	+	±	±	+	+	±	+	+	+	+	+	+	+±	+	+±
Follicles	Central Artery, Walls	Hyaline Degeneration	+	+	++	+	+	±	+	±	+±	++	+	+	+	+	+	±	+
Follicles	Exist of Germinating Center		−	−	−	−	−	−	−	−	−	−	−	−	−	−	−	−	−
Follicles	Necrosis	central	−	−	−	−	−	−	−	−	−	−	−	−	−	−	−	−	+
Follicles	Necrosis	peripheral	−	−	−	−	−	−	−	−	−	−	−	−	−	+	+	−	+
Cavernous Sinuses	Width		+	+	+±	(++)	+	+	+	±	+	(+±)	+±	(++)	++	(++)	(+±)	+	(++)
Cavernous Sinuses	Cavernous Sinuses		±	±	+	±	+	±	±	−	±	±	±	±	+±	±	±	±	+
Cavernous Sinuses	Congestion		±	+++	+±	++	++	+±	+	±	+	++	+	++	(+++)	(++)	++	++	(+±)
Cavernous Sinuses	Cellular Inclusion	Leucocytes	±	±	+	±	±	+±	−	±	±	−	±	±	++	±	±	±	±
Cavernous Sinuses	Cellular Inclusion	Lymphocytes	+	+	±	+	+	±	+	+	+	+	±	+	+	±	±	+	±
Cavernous Sinuses	Cellular Inclusion	Histiocytic Cells	+	±	±	+	+	+	+	+	±	+	+	±	+±	±	±	±	+
Cavernous Sinuses	Endothelium	Swelling	(+±)	+±	++	+	±	++	+	±	(+±)	(+)	+	+	+	+±	(++)	+	±
Cavernous Sinuses	Endothelium	Resolution	±	±	+	+	±	+	(+±)	±	+	+	(+±)	(+±)	+±	+±	−	+	±
Cavernous Sinuses	Endothelium	Phagocytosis	±	+±	±	+	+±	±	+	±	(+)	++	++	+	+	+	+	+	+
Billoth's Cord	Edema		+	++	++	++	+	++	+	±	(+±)	++	+	++	+++	++	++	++	+
Billoth's Cord	Hemorrhage		+	++	+±	++	(+±)	+	+	+	±	+±	±	++	+++	++	++	++	+
Billoth's Cord	Necrosis		±	−	−	−	−	−	−	−	−	−	−	−	−	±	−	−	+++
Billoth's Cord	Lymphocytes		+	+	+	+	(+±)	+±	(+±)	(+±)	+	+	+	+	+	+	±	+±	+±
Billoth's Cord	Leucocytes		±	±	+±	±	±	++	±	±	±	−	+±	±	++	(+)	(±)	+	±
Billoth's Cord	Plasma Cells		−	−	−	±	±	±	±	±	−	++	±	±	−	±	−	−	−
Billoth's Cord	Splenocytes		+±	+±	±	++	+±	+	+	++	+±	+++	+±	+	++	+	+±	+	+±
Billoth's Cord	Reticular Cells		±	+	+±	±	±	+	±	±	±	−	±	±	±	(+)	±	±	±
Hemosiderosis			±	±	±	±	++	±	++	±	+	+	++	±	+	±	±	+	+

[redacted] 233

([redacted] (

Our so-called polar edema:
intense edematous swelling of penicillar artery walls and intense edematous swelling around penicillar arteries.

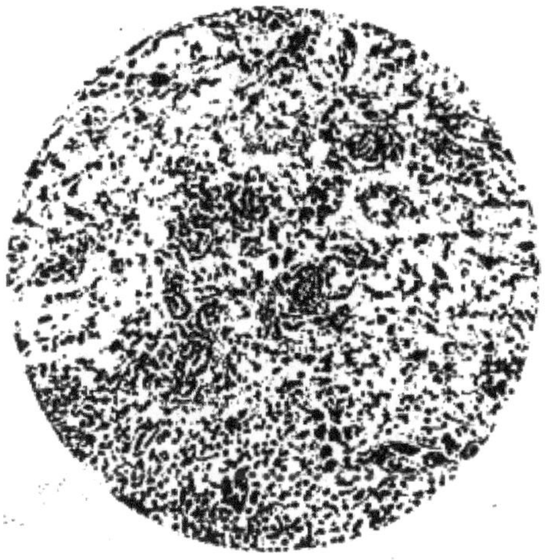

[redacted]

R.152 X170

Edematous swelling of penicillar artery walls.
Polar edema, in high power.

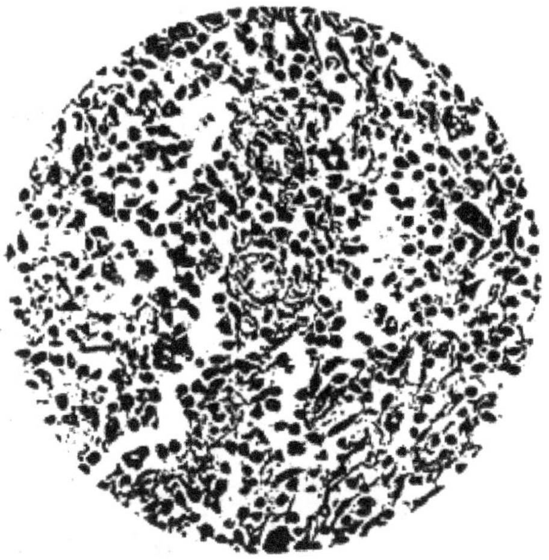

[redacted]

R 193 X320

[redacted] 234

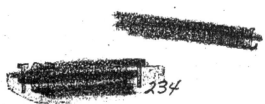

([redacted] (

Hyperplasia of adventitia cells, of A.radiolata (bronch of A.centralis in germinative center) and some reticulum cells.

[redacted]

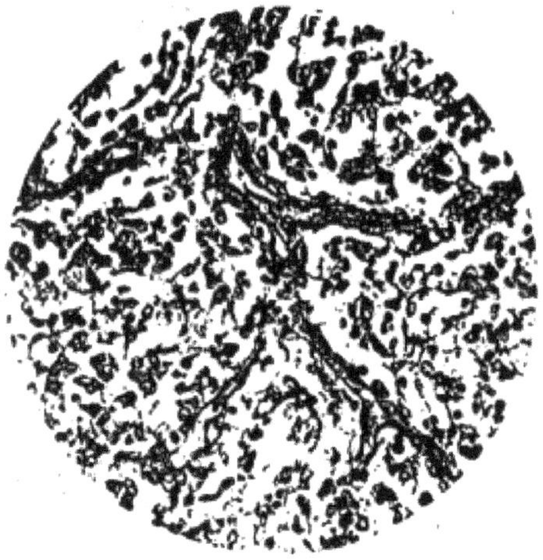

R 16 x310

Hyperplasia of adventitia cells of A.radiolsta and some reticulum cells.

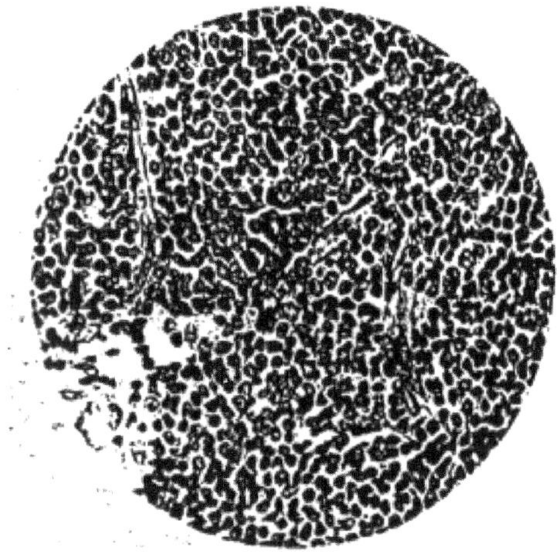

[redacted]

R 85(a) x360

[redacted] 235

([redacted] (

Reactive hyperplasia of germinative centre, in high power.
Remarkable hyperplasia of reticulum cells, in epitheloid cell form.

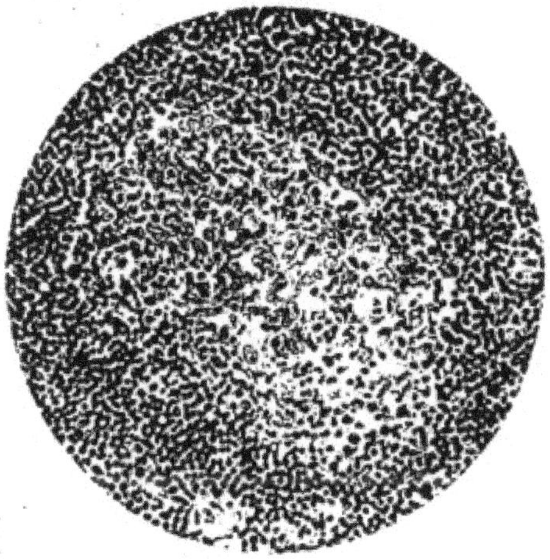

[redacted]

R#50　　　　　X 230

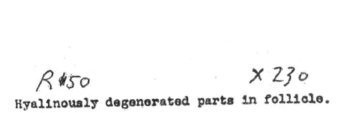

Hyalinously degenerated parts in follicle.

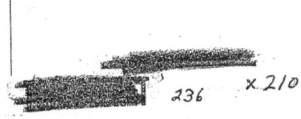

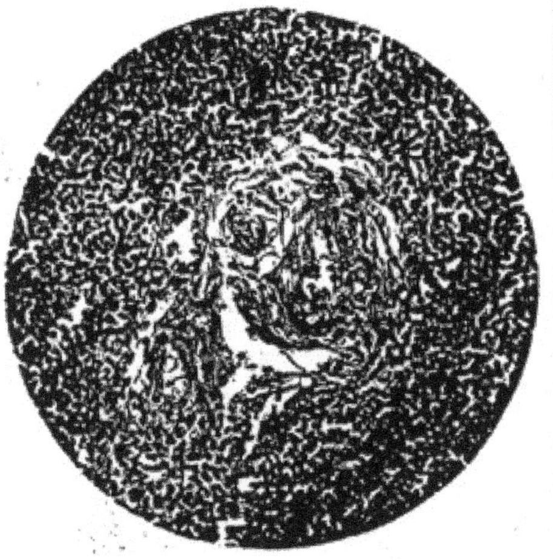

[redacted] 236　　x 210

([redacted] (

Edematous swelling of central artery walls.

[redacted]

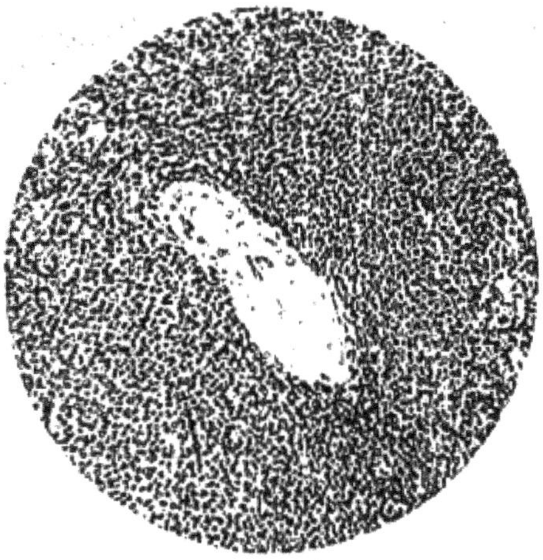

R 85 (a) x 160

Hyalinous degeneration of central artery wall.

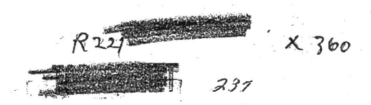

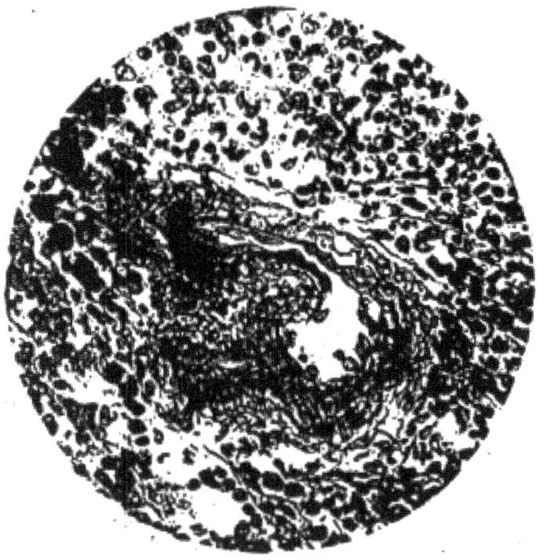

[redacted] R22[redacted] x 360

[redacted] 237

([redacted] (

Glanders-knot in fillicular tissues.
Caseous central focus and the margin
portion of knot with sone giant cells.

[redacted]

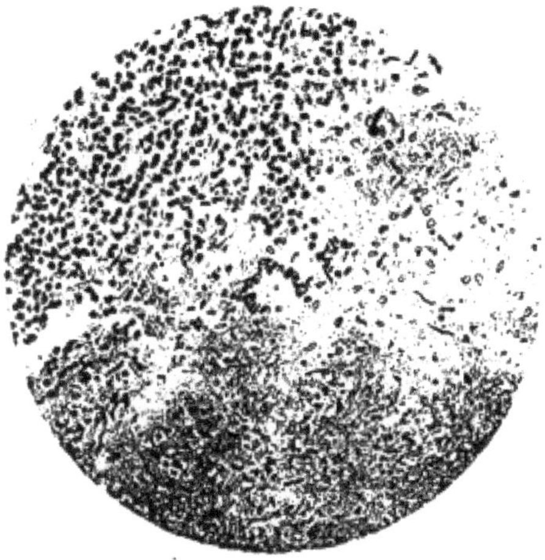

R 229 (a)　　　X 210

Diffuse intense necrosis of follicul,r
tissues.

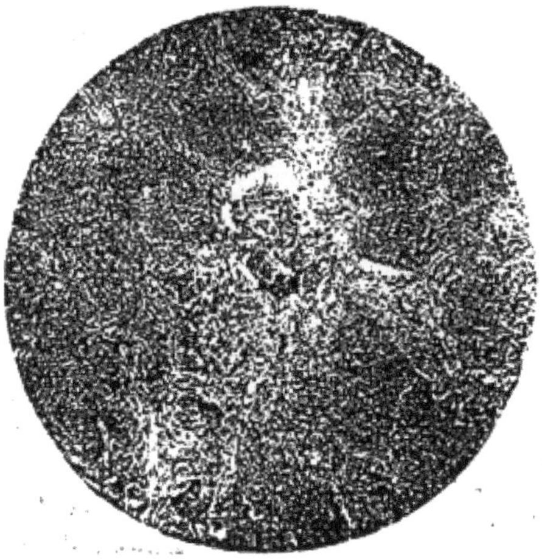

[redacted]

[redacted] 238　　　X 70

([redacted] (

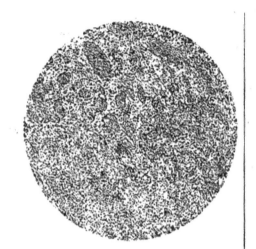

Fasciculitis exsudativa with intense edema in fascicular cords and intense stasis in sinuses.

[redacted]

R 50 x 90

Sinus-ectasia with intense stasis. In high power.

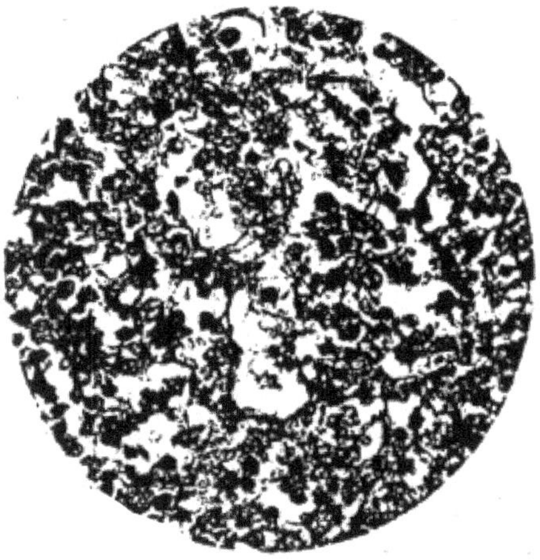

[redacted]

19.16 x 400

TOP SECRET 239

([redacted]

Considerable hyperplasia of wall cells
of penicillar artery.
Considerable proliferative reaction
at polar portion.

[redacted]

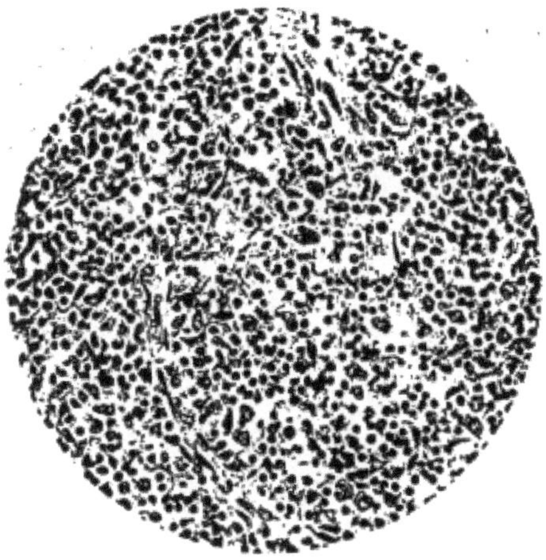

R 180 X 260

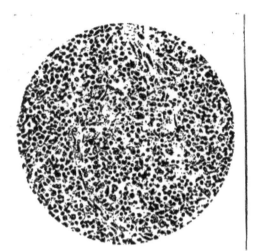

Hyalinous degeneration of penicillar
artery wall-.

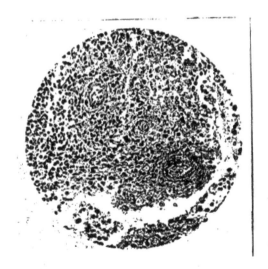

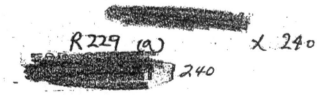

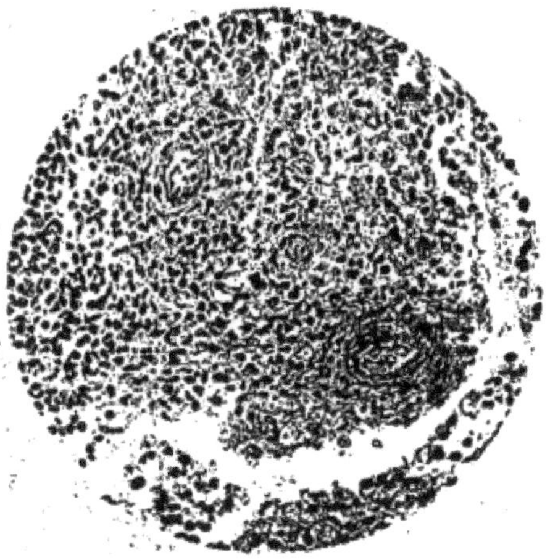

[redacted]

R229 (a) X 240

[redacted] 240

[redacted]

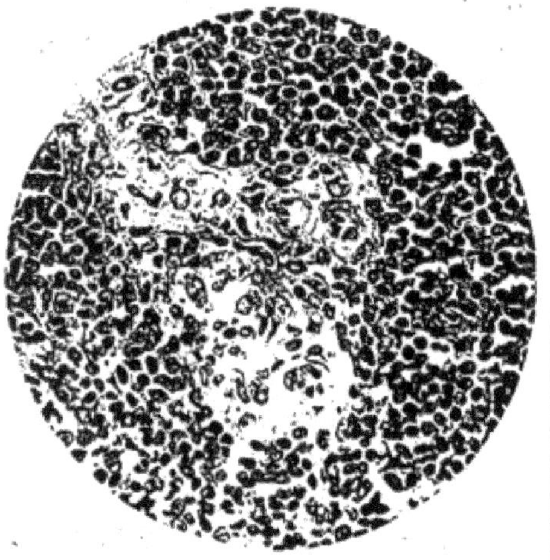

Proliferative reaction around A.radiolata
Some increased reticulum cells and
some increased adventitia cells.

[redacted]

R 85 (b) X380

Hyalinously degenerated follicles.

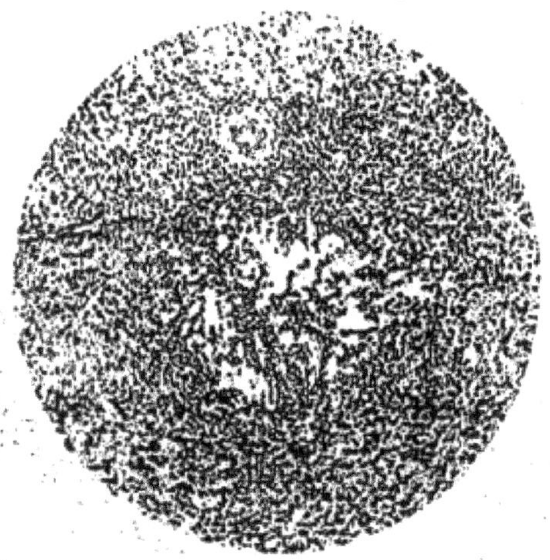

[redacted]

R 229(c) X100

[redacted] 241

([redacted] (

Proliferative reaction at polar portion.
Some increased reticulum cells.

[redacted]

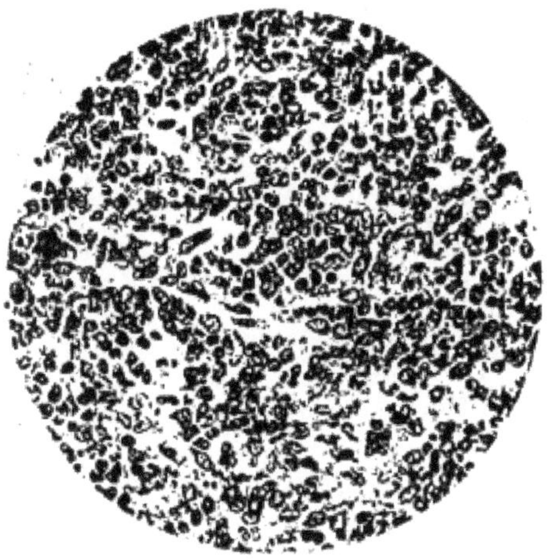

R 85(b)　　X 390

Proliferative reaction at polar portion
with some increased reticulum cells.

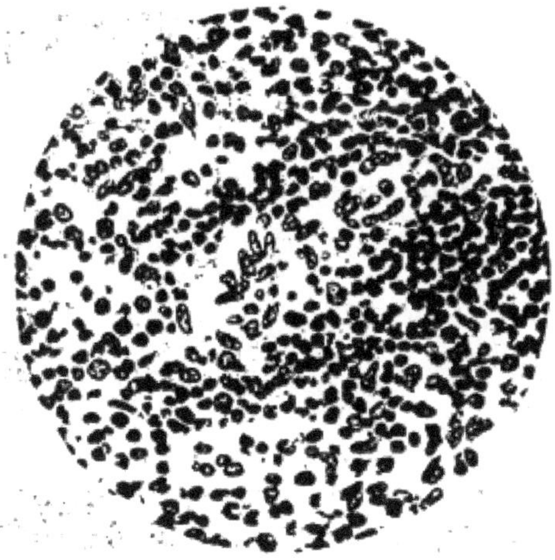

[redacted]

[redacted] 242　　X 380

• [redacted] •

[redacted]

Kidney

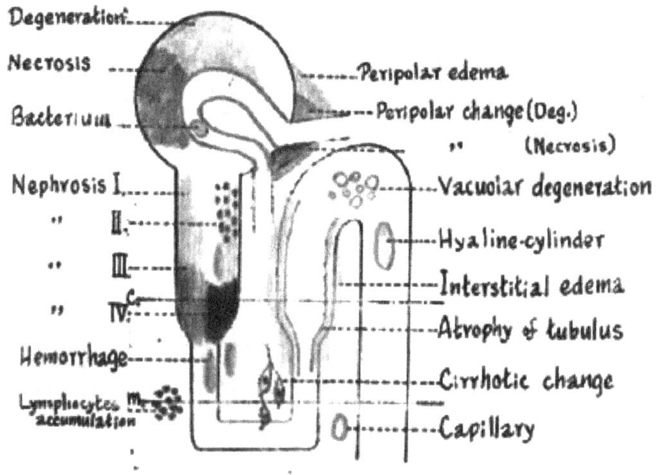

[redacted]

[redacted] 243

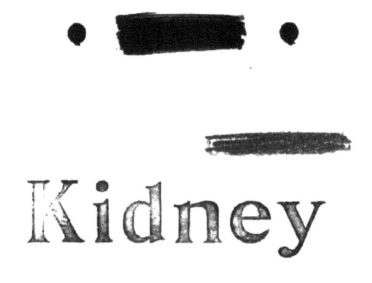

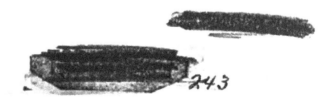

[redacted]

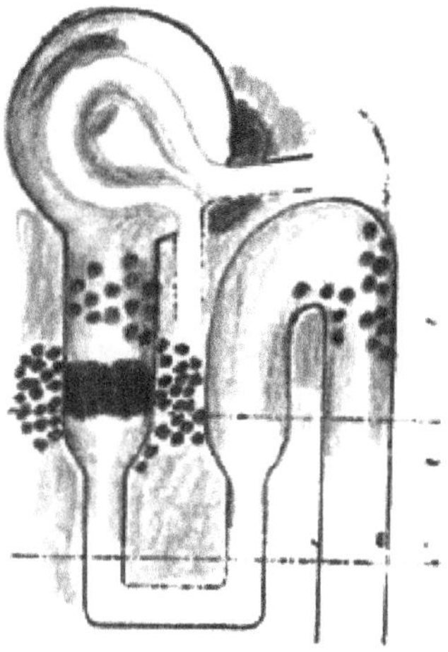

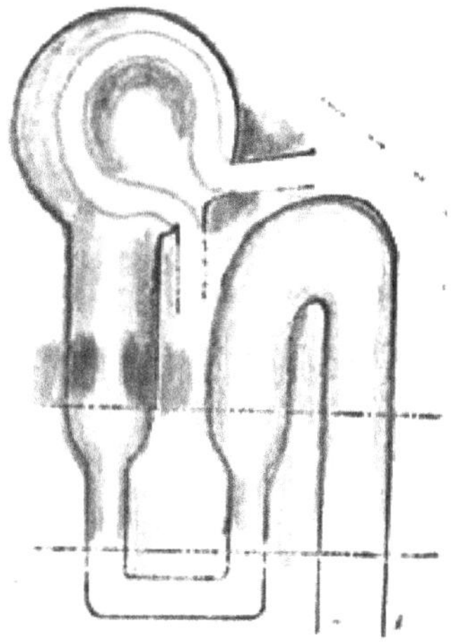

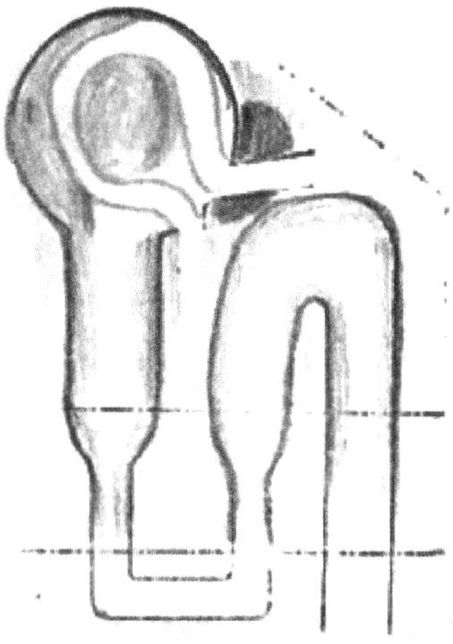

K I D N E Y .

[redacted]icroscop. Investigation.

I46.

Slight Glomerulo-nephrosis (mainly in degenerative form) with slight our so-called peripolar changes and Nephrosis in Ist stage; some places in II stage with some erythrocytes-leakages and some places in IV th stage with remarkable interstitial edema and considerable multiple round-cells-accumulation.

I52.

Slight or at some places considerable Glomerulo--nephrosis (glomeruli mainly in degenerative form) with considerable our so-called peripolar changes.

Nephrosis in I. stage and at some places in III. stage with considerable interstitial edema.

I57.

Considerable Glomerulo-nephrosis (glomeruli in rather degenerative form) with considerable our so-called peripolar changes.

Nephrosis in I. stage with considerable interstitial edema. [redacted]

[redacted] 244

[redacted]

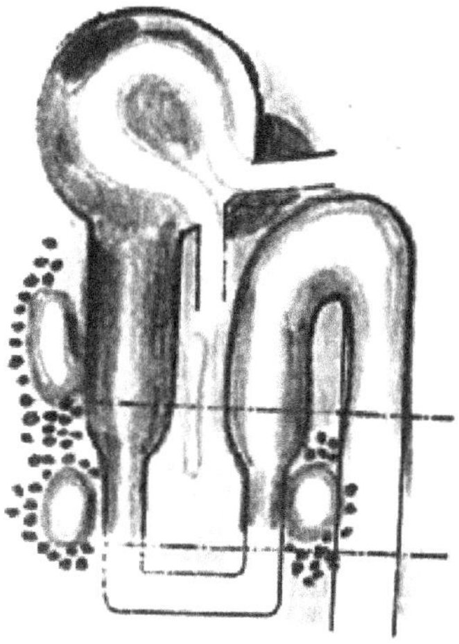

I76. [redacted]

Considerable Glomerulo-nephrosis (glomeruli in rather degenerative form) with considerable our so-called peripolar changes and Nephrosis in M stage with considerable interstitial edema, accompanied with fibrinous swelling of blood-vessel-walls and considerable perivascular round-cells accumulations.

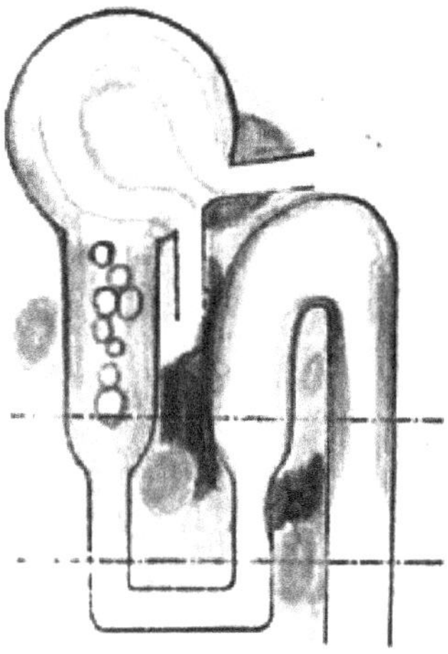

I78.

Slight Glomerulo-nephrosis (glomerular loops in rather degenerative form) with slight our so-called peripolar changes.

Nephrosis in I. stage (at some places partial vacuolar changes of tubular epithel iums) and considerable interstitial edema, accompanied with remarkable edema at some places and localised bio-necrotic swelling of connective tissues at some places.

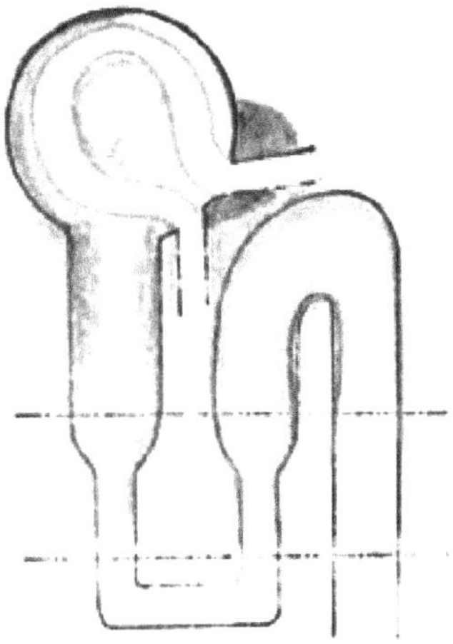

I80.

Slight Glomerulo-nephrosis (glomeruli in rather degenerative form) with slight our so-called peripolar changes.

Nephrosis in I. stage with consdierable intersti al edema.

[redacted]

[redacted] 245

[redacted]

190
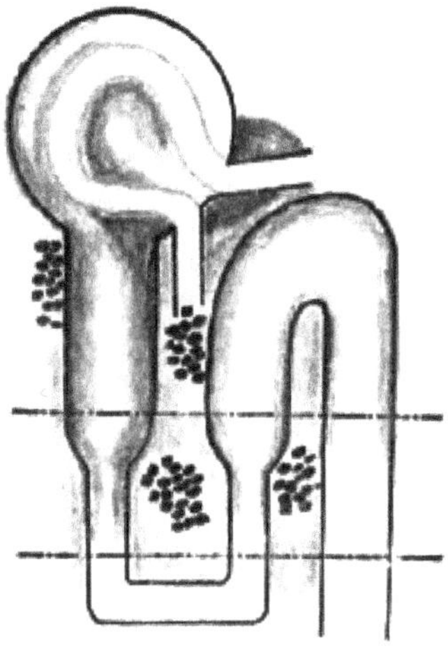

I90.

Slight Glomerulo-nephrosis (mainly in degenerative form) and slight our so-called peripolar [redacted]
changes.

Nephrosis in I. stage and considerable interstitial edema, accompanied with considerable mulpiple round-cell-accumulations.

193
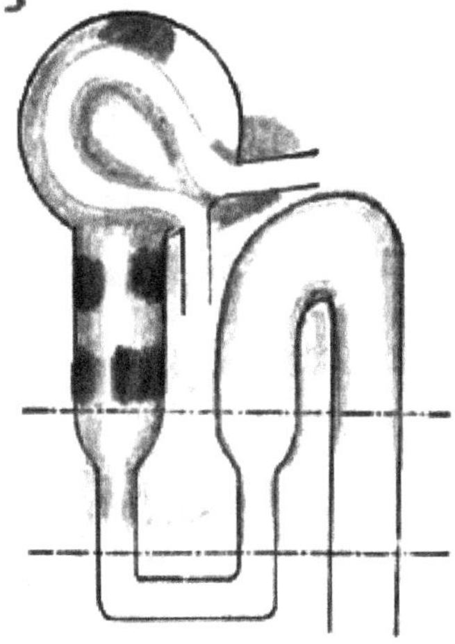

I93.

Considerable Glomerulo-nephrosis (glomeruli mainly in degenerative form) with considerable our so-called peripolar changes and Nephrosis in I. stage or at some places in III. stage with remarkable interstitial edema.

205
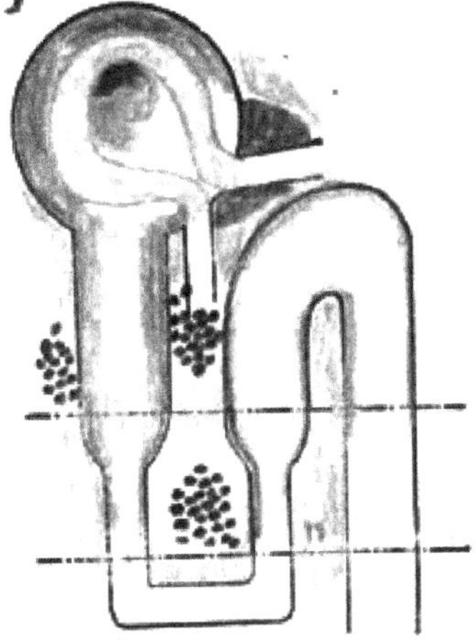

205.

Considerable Glomerulo-nephrosis with considerable congestion (glomeruli in hyperaemic form) with slight peripolar changes and Nephrosis in I. stage with considerable interstitial edema and considerable round-cell-accumulations.

207.

Slight Glomerulo-nephrosis (mainly in degenerative form) with slight our so-called peripolar changes and Nephrosis in I.stage with considerable interstitial [redacted]

[redacted]

246

[redacted]

222

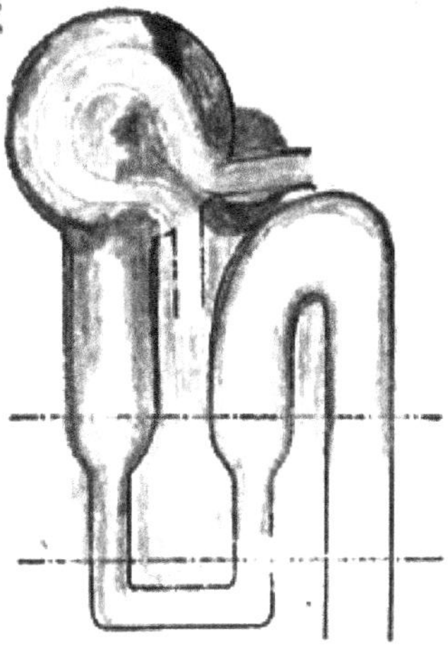

229

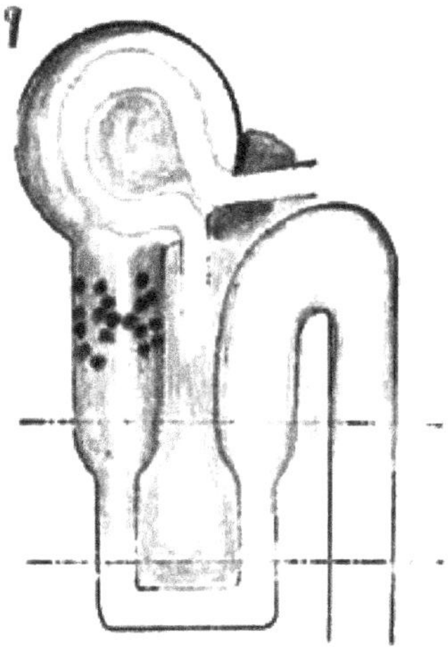

254

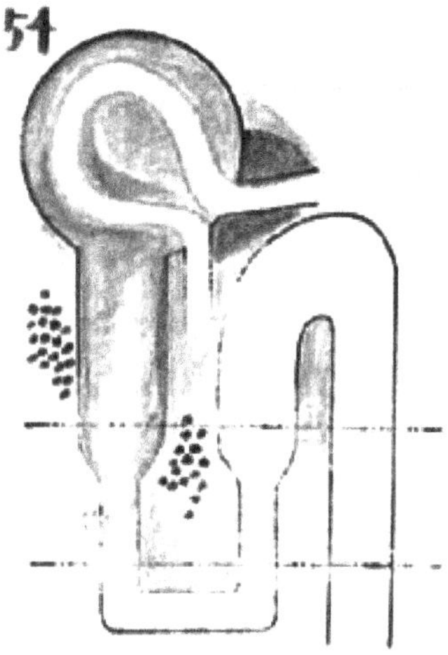

221. missed [redacted]

222.

Considerable Glomerulo-nephrosis (some glommerul in acute hyperaemic form and some in rather exudative form) with considerable peripolar changes (remarkable hyperaemia of vasa afferens). Nephrosis in I st. stage with considerable interstitial edema.

224.

Considerable Glomerulo-nephrosis (mainly in degenerative form) with slight peripolar changes and Nephrosis in I. stage with considerable interstitial edema.

229.

Considerable Glomerulo-nephrosis (mainly in acute form) with some our so-called peripolar changes and Nephrosis in I. stage or at some places in II. stage with considerable interstitis edema.

254.

Considerable Glomerulo-nephrosis (some glomeruli in exudative form, some in rather degenerative form) with considerable our so-called peripolar changes. [redacted]

[redacted] 247

[redacted]

256

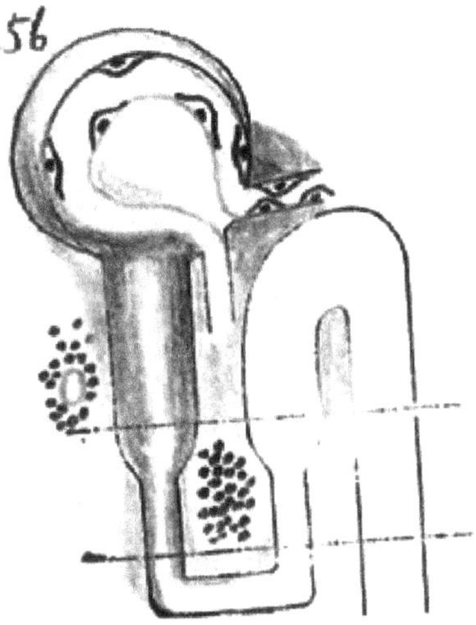

Nephrosis in I. stage with considerable interstitial edema and some round-cell-accumulations. [redacted]

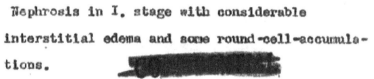

256.

Considerable Glomerulo-nephrosis (some glomeruli in proliferative form) with considerable peripolar changnes (considerable our so-called peripolar edema and considerable proliferation of adventitial cells of Wasa afferens).

727

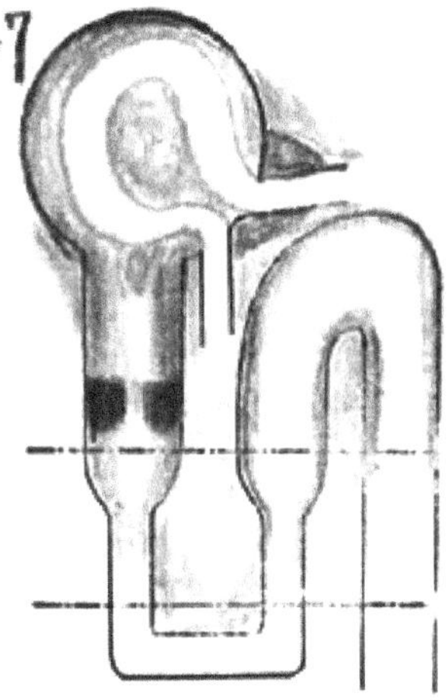

Nephrosis in I. stage with considerable interstitial edema and considerable round-cell-accumulations (perivascular round-cell-accumulations).

727.

Considerable Glomerulo-nephrosis (mainly in exsudative form) with considerable our so-called peripolar changes.

731

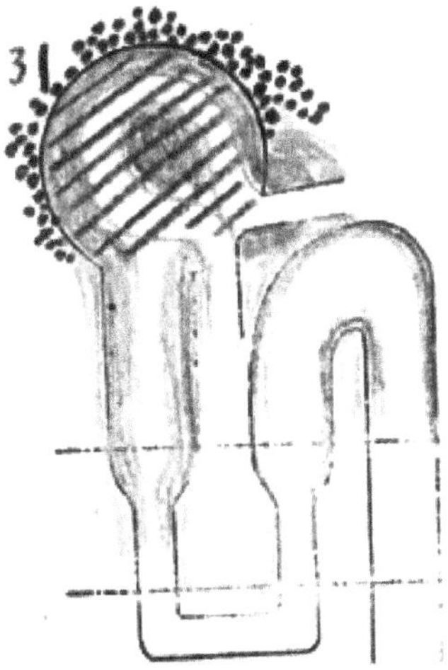

Nephrosis in I. stage or at some places in III rd stage with considerable interstitial edema.

73I.

Considerable Glomerulo-nephrosis (mainly in rather degenerative form) with slight or considerable our so-called peripolar changes.

(esp. some remarkable round-cell-accumulations at peri-glomerular portions and these glomeruli

[redacted]

248

([redacted] (

[redacted] falled into hyaline cirrhosis).

Nephrosis in I. stage with considerable inter-

stitial edema.

[redacted]

[redacted] 249

([redacted] (

S U M M A R Y

A) Tubular changes :

Generally occured some cloudy swelling of tubular epitheliums, with some various cylinders in tubular spaces. [redacted]

Nephrosis	I.degree	18 cases(all investigated cases).
Nephrosis	II. degree	2 cases of them.
Nephrosis	III.degree.	
	with partialbionecrotic swelling.	5 cases of them.
	with partial necrotic changes.	I case of them.

---

tubular contents.	Protein-masses.	Hyaline cylinders.	Calcinated masses
very small quantity	1	1	1
small quantity	8	1	
medium quantity	4	11	4
large quantity	5	7	1

B) Glomerular changes.

Generally occured some glomerular changes : glomerulo-nephrosis Randerath's v with some edematous swelling of capillary walls of glomerular loops, swelling and slight increase of capillary wall-cells and some serous exsudation in Bowmann's spaces. [redacted]

[redacted] 250

([redacted] (

Glomerulo-nephrosis.		
in very slight degree.	0 cases.	[redacted]
in slight degree.	10 cases.	
in medium degree.	6 cases.	
in severe degree.	2 cases.	
Peripolar changes :		
in slight very degree.	1 case.	
in slight degree.	11 cases.	
in medium degree.	3 cases.	
in more or less intense degree.	3 cases.	

C). Interstitium.

Some cases with slight perivascular edema or some hemorrhages. Some cases are accompanied with some round cell accumulation and I case (No. 176) with remarkable round cell accumulation (Glanders-knots).

[redacted]

[redacted] 251

([redacted] (

On polar changes :

Our so-called polar portions of kidney fall within like periglomerular areas at afferent portions of blood-vessels, bounded with 2 blood-vessels (V.afferens and defferens) and intercalary portion of tubulus and equipped with special cellular arragnements with neuro-myo-angio-epitheilar segments, which belong to so-called diffuse endocrinic system. [redacted]

These areas are very chemoreceptoric, and able to regulate blood-quantity in glomeruli and furthermore favorite-seats of various inflammatory changes.

Noxae, advenced hemotogenously to kidney, cause inflammatory changes firstly at afferent portions, due to their chemoreceptoric properties, then at glomeruli and sometimes at V. defferens.

Thus occured inflammatory changes angio-vasrulally at perivascular portions in △-areas.

These noxae are filtrated at glomerular loops, then excreted in tubulus with nephrosis and some of themabsorbed again mainly at intercalary portions of tubulus, accompanied with considerable degeneration of tubular epitheliar cells and some peritubular inflammatory changes in neighbouring △-areas.

Thus occured inflammatory changes epitheliogenously at peritubular portions in △-areas.

△-areas are very sensitive to inflammatory changes, which occured in 2 manners, a) angiovasculallu at perivascular portions with mesenchymal reactions and b) epitheliogenously at peritubular portions with epitheliogenous reactions and accompanied with varoius complicated changes, due to chemoreceptoric and regenerative properties of these

[redacted] 252 [redacted]

([redacted] (

intercalary portions.

In -areas, inflammatory changes apt to be occured and if occured, in 2 manners, not only with mesenchymal reactions, but also with epitheliogenous reactions . [redacted]

Such special cellular arrangements with mesenchymal and epithelial segments which belong to diffuse endocrinic system, are expected to exist in each organs(for example, discovery of "lung-island" by us) and inflammatory changes of these portions are named by us "polar changes" of each organs.

[redacted]

[redacted] 253

([redacted] (

[redacted]

KIDNEY

			85	146	152	167	176	178	180	190	193	205	207	222	224	229	254	256	727	731
Glomeruli	Glomerular Loop	Dilatation	+	+	±	+	+	+	+	+	+	+	+	+	+	±	+	+	+	+
	Capillary-walls	Swelling	±	+	+	+	+	+	+	+	++	+	±	+	+	±	+	+	+	+
		Deposition of Hyaline or Albuminoid Substance	±	+	+	±	+	±	±	±	+	±	±	+	-	+	+	+	+	±
	Changes of Nuclei	Increase of Nuclei	±	±	±	+	+	-	-	±	±	±	-	+	-	±	±	+	±	±
		Swelling	+	±	+	+	+	+	+	±	+	+	±	+	±	±	±	++	+	+
		Pyknosis	+	+	±	-	-	+	+	+	±	-	+	±	+	+	±	-	±	-
	Contents of Capillaries	Erythrocytes	+	+	++	++	+	++	+	++	+	+++	+	+++	+	+	+	++	+	-
		Round Cells	-	-	-	-	-	-	-	-	-	-	-	-	-	-	-	-	±	-
	Bowman's Lumen	Dilatation	↑-	↓-	↓-	↓±	↑-	↓-	↓-	↓-	↓-	↓-	↑±	↓-	↑±	↓-	↓-	↑-	↑-	↑-
		Hyaline or Albuminoid Casts	±	-	±	-	-	-	±	-	+	±	-	±	-	-	±	-	-	-
		Penetrative Fluid	-	-	±	-	-	-	-	±	+	±	±	±	±	-	-	-	-	±
	Epithelium of Bowman's Capsule	Cloudy Swelling	±	±	±	±	-	±	±	+	+	±	-	±	±	-	-	±	-	±
		Proliferation	-	-	±	-	-	-	-	-	-	-	-	±	-	-	-	-	-	-
	Bowman's Capsules	Swelling	±	±	+	±	±	±	±	±	±	±	-	±	-	±	-	±	±	±
		Hyaline Degeneration	-	(+)	±	-	-	-	-	-	±	-	-	-	-	-	-	-	-	-
	Vasa afferentia	Congestion	-	+	+	+	±	±	±	+	++	++	+	+	+	+	+	+	+	±
	Endomedial Cells	Swelling	-	-	-	±	±	-	-	-	±	-	-	±	±	-	-	-	±	-
		Proliferation	-	-	-	-	-	-	-	-	-	-	-	-	-	-	-	+	+	-
		Desquamation	-	-	-	-	-	-	-	-	-	-	-	-	-	-	-	-	-	-
	Media	Swelling	+	+	-	±	+	±	±	±	+	-	-	(+)	±	±	±	+	+	±
		Hyaline Degeneration	±	+	±	-	+	±	-	-	±	-	-	-	-	-	±	+	+	±
		Tendency to Necrosis	±	±	-	-	±	-	-	-	±	-	-	-	-	±	-	±	±	-
	Adventitial Cells	Swelling	+	-	-	-	±	-	-	±	-	-	-	±	±	-	±	+	±	±
		Proliferation	-	-	-	+	+	-	-	-	+	-	-	+	-	-	-	+	±	-
	Adjoining Portion	Peripolar Edema	+	+	+	±	(++)	±	±	±	+	+	+	+	+	±	+	+	+	+
		Appearance of "Polkissen"	-	±	±	+	±	-	±	±	-	-	-	+	-	±	+	+	-	-
		Macula densa	-	-	±	+	-	-	-	±	±	-	-	±	-	-	+	+	-	-
Parenchyma	Tubules Epithelium	Cloudy Swelling	+	+	++	+	+	+	+	++	++	+	+	+	+	++	+	++	+	+
		Hyaline Droplet Degeneration	(+)	(+)	-	-	-	-	-	-	-	-	-	-	-	(+)	-	-	-	-
		Vacuolar Degeneration	+	+	±	-	±	(++)	+	±	-	±	++	-	+	+	+	±	-	++
		Fatty Degeneration	±	±	-	-	-	(+)	+	-	-	-	++	-	+	+	-	-	-	+
		Necrosis	±	±	(+)	-	-	-	-	-	±	-	-	-	-	±	-	-	±	-
		Degenerations of Nuclei	+	±	±	±	±	±	±	±	±	±	+	±	-	±	-	±	±	+
	Tubules Contents	Cloudy or Massive Albuminoide Substance	++	±	±	+	±	-	-	±	±	±	±	++	±	+	++	+	±	+
		Fibrinous Substance	-	-	-	-	-	-	-	-	-	-	-	+	-	-	-	-	-	-
		Hyaline or Colloid Cylinder	++	(+)	(++)	(+)	(++)	(+)	-	+	(+)	(±)	-	(+)	+	±	+	(+)	(+)	+
		Various Calcium Casts	(+++)	(+)	-	-	-	-	(+)	(+)	-	-	-	-	-	(+)	-	-	-	-
		Erythrocytes	-	-	(+)	-	-	-	-	-	-	-	-	-	-	-	-	-	-	-
Interstitium	Congestion	Cortex	±	+++	++	++	+	+	+	+++	(++)	++	+	+	+	±	+	++	±	+
		Medulla	(+)	++	+	++	(+)	+	+	+++	+	++	++	+	+	++	+	+	+	±
	Edema	Cortex	+	+	+	+	+	+	±	(+)	++	+	+	+	+	+	++	+	+	++
		Medulla	(+)	++	+	+	(+)	++	+	+	++	+	++	+	+	+	+	+	+	++
	Hemorrhage	Cortex	-	-	(+)	-	-	-	-	-	-	-	-	-	-	-	-	-	-	-
		Medulla	-	-	-	-	-	-	-	-	-	-	-	-	-	-	-	-	-	-
	Round Cell Infiltration	Cortex	+	+	±	-	+++	-	-	+	±	+	-	-	(±)	-	(+)	(+)	±	+
		Medulla	-	-	-	-	-	-	-	-	-	-	-	-	-	-	-	-	-	-
	Vessel Walls	Hyaline Degeneration	-	±	±	±	+	-	-	±	±	-	-	-	-	-	±	-	+	±
		Tendency to Necrosis	-	±	-	-	±	-	-	-	±	-	-	-	-	±	-	(+)	±	-
		Proliferation of Adventitial Cells	-	-	-	+	++	-	-	±	±	-	-	±	-	±	-	(+)	±	-
	Colonies of Bacterium		-	-	-	-	-	-	-	-	-	-	-	-	-	-	-	-	-	-

[redacted]

[redacted] 254

([redacted] (

Intense edema in Δ areas.
Our so-called polar edema.

[redacted]

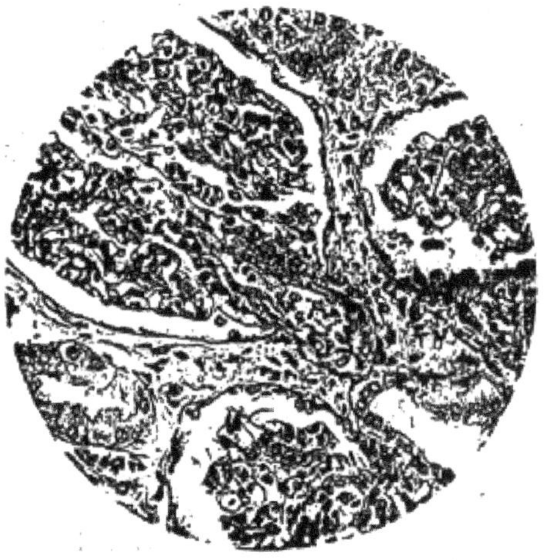

-256 X230

Miliary glanders-knot, at peri-
glomerular portion.

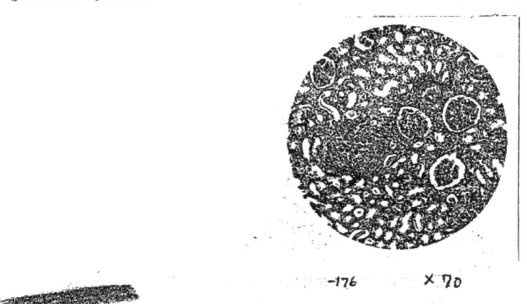

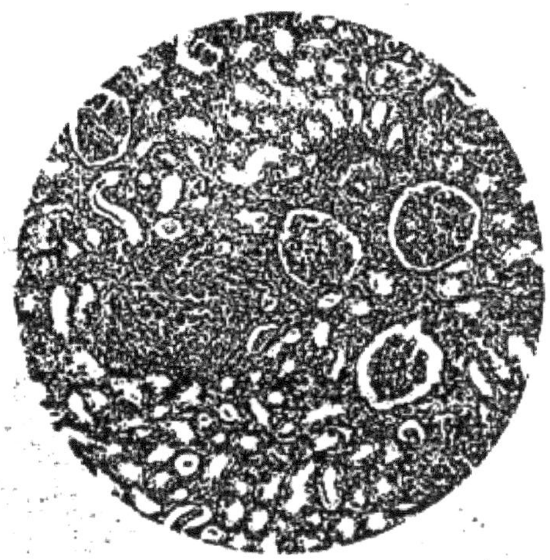

-176 X 70

[redacted]

[redacted] 255

([redacted] (

Round cell accumulation ar perivascular portion.

[redacted]

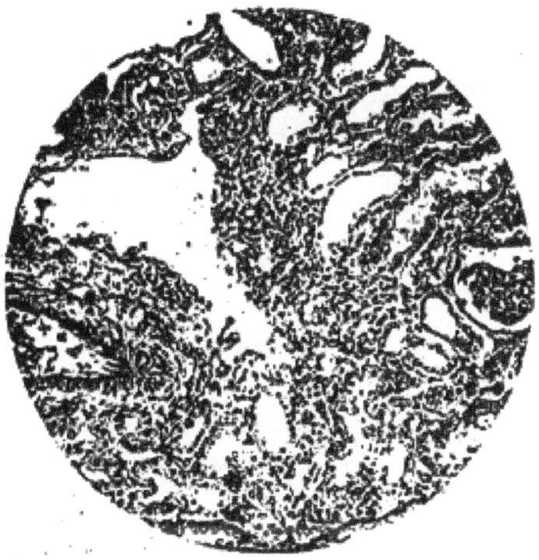

R 256 X120

Calcificated masses in cortical tissues.

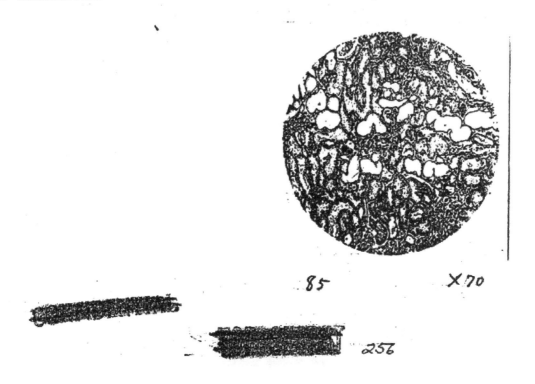

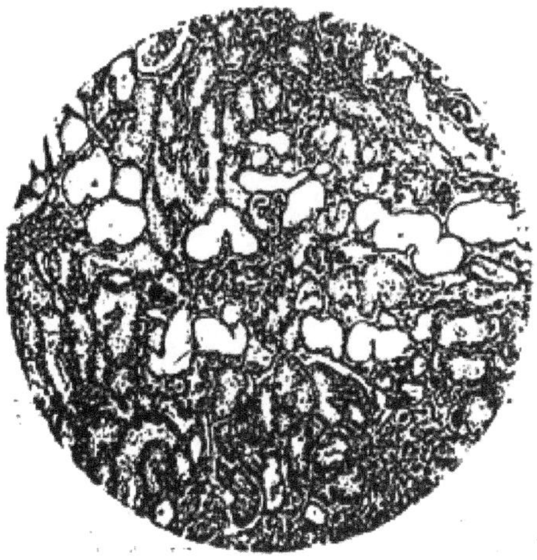

85 X70

[redacted]

[redacted] 256

([redacted] (

Miliary glanders-knot, in high power.

[redacted]

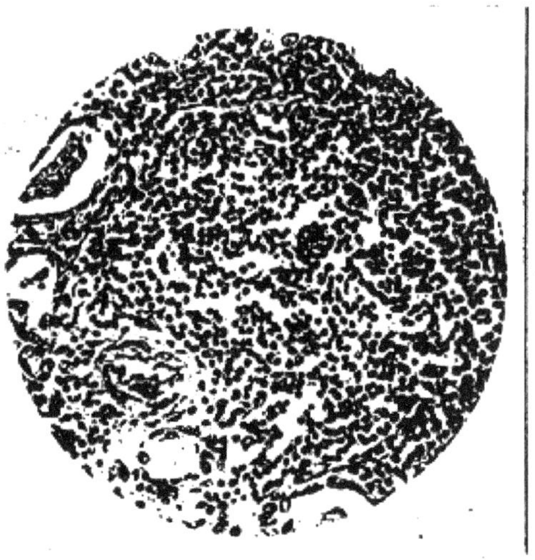

176 X240

“ound cell accumulation at peri-glomerular portion.

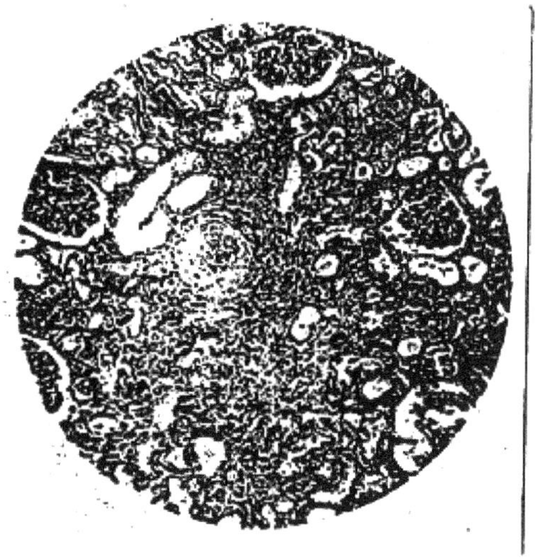

731 X70

[redacted] [redacted] 257

• [redacted] •

[redacted]

Pancreas

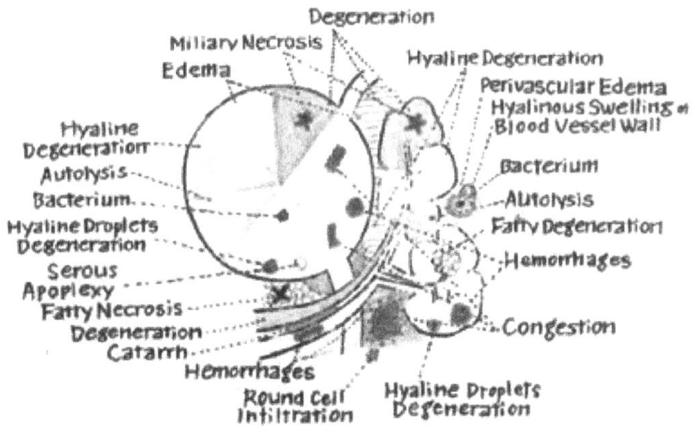

[redacted] [redacted] 258

[redacted]

[redacted]

( ) P A N C R E A S

(A) Microscopical Investigations.

86.

Hyaline degeneration of blood-vessel-walls and slight increase of connective tissues, which are in more or less hyalinous degeneration.
Slight degeneration of parenchymatous cells with hyaline-droplets at some places. Considerable vacuolar degeneration of island-cells.
Considerable catarrh of efferent ducts.

I46.

Slight increase of connective tissues, which are slightly hyalinously degenerative.
Considerable venous congestion and slight hemorrhages in connective tissues. Slight degeneration of parenchymatous cells.
Considerable hydropic and hyalinous degeneration of island-cells with hyaline-droplets at some places.

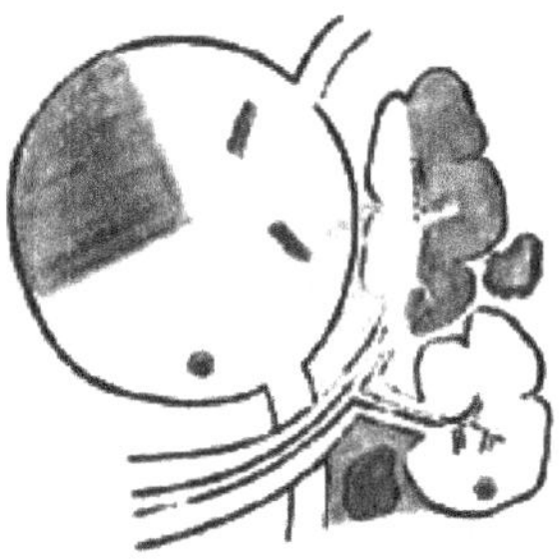

[redacted] [redacted] 257

[redacted]

[redacted]

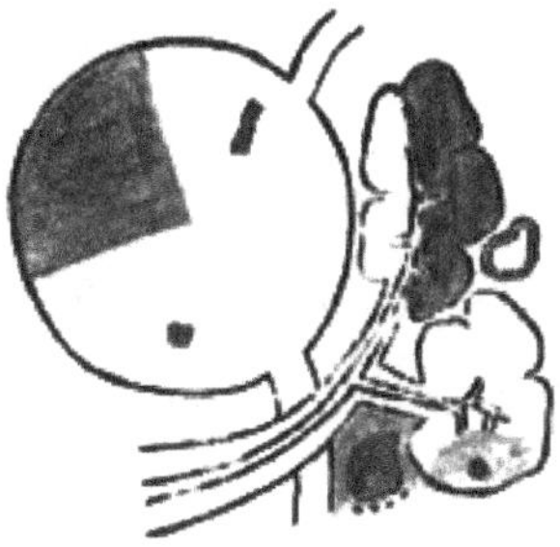

167.

Condiderable venous congestion and considerable cloudy swelling of parenchymatous cells. Some of them in edematous or furthermore hyaline degeneration with hyaline-droplets at some places. Slight swelling and degeneration of island-cells.

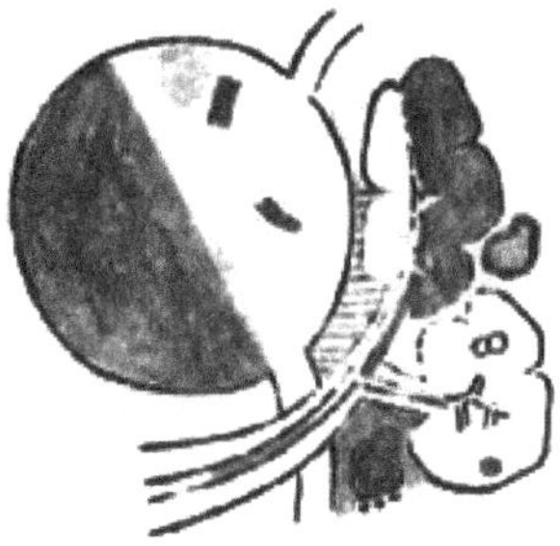

176.

Considerable venous congestion, edematous swelling of blood-vessel-walls (some of them, hyalinous) and slight hemorrhages in connective tissues.

Considerable degeneration of parenchymatous cells with some hyaline-droplets at some places.

Remarkable stasis of island-capillaries and hyalinous swelling of their walls. Atrophia and degeneration (partially hyalinously) of island-cells and catarrh of efferent ducts.

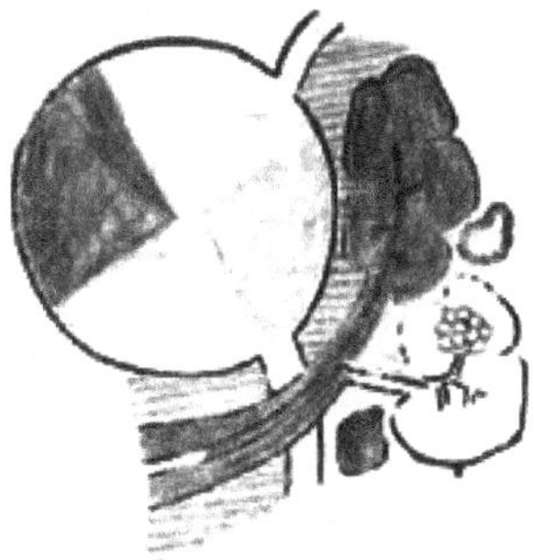

178.

Considerable venous congestion and edematous swelling of connective tissues. Considerable cloudy

[redacted] [redacted] 260

• [redacted] •

swelling of parenchym. cells and
catarrh of efferent ducts.

[redacted]

Island-cells, atrophic.

I80.

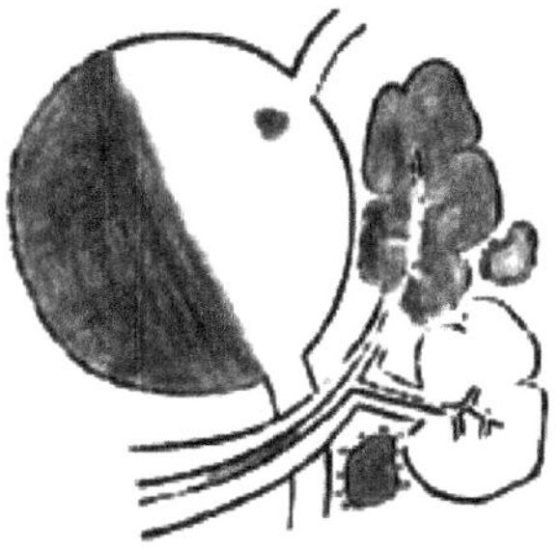

Considerable venous congestion and
edematous swelling of bloodvessel-
walls and perivascular tissues.
Parenchymatous cells in cloudy
swelling and island-cells also in
considerable cloudy swelling and
atrophia or partial hemorrhages in
islands.

I90.

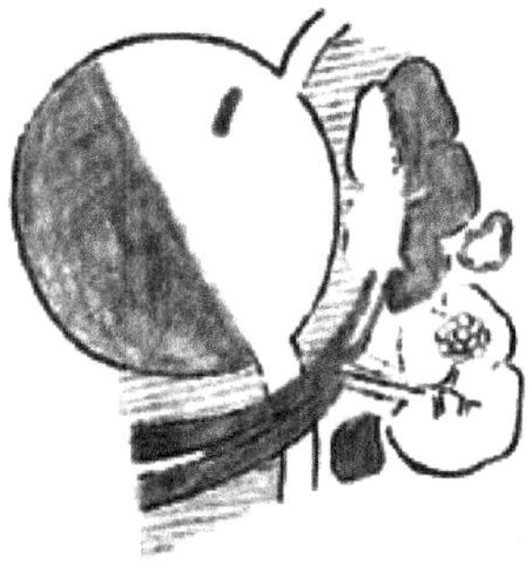

Consid. venous congestion and edematous swelling of connective tissues.
Condiderable atrophia and cloudy swelling of parenchymatous cells and
atrophia or cloudy swelling of island-
cells.
Catarrh and polypous hyperplasia of
efferent ducts.

205.

Considerable venous congestion and
edematous swelling of connective
tissues with perivascular accumulation
of lymphocytes at some places.

[redacted]

[redacted] 261

[redacted]

[redacted]

Cloudy swelling of parenchymatous cells, esp. in severe degree at pericapillar portions. Edematous swelling and slight degeneration of island-cells.

221.

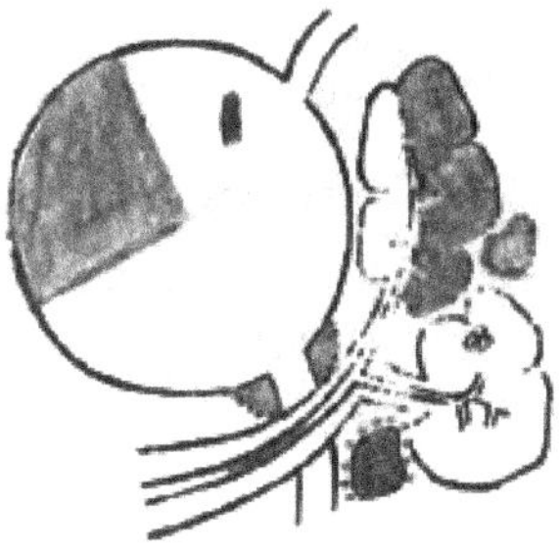

Considerable venous or capillary congestion, edematous swelling of blood-vessel-walls and perivascular tissues.

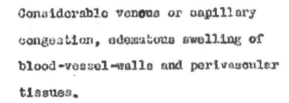

Considerable atrophia and cloudy swelling of parenchym. cells.

Remarkable stasis of island-capillaries and edematous or bionecrotic swelling at their afferent portions (our so-called "polar edema").

Slight edematous swelling of island-cells.

222.

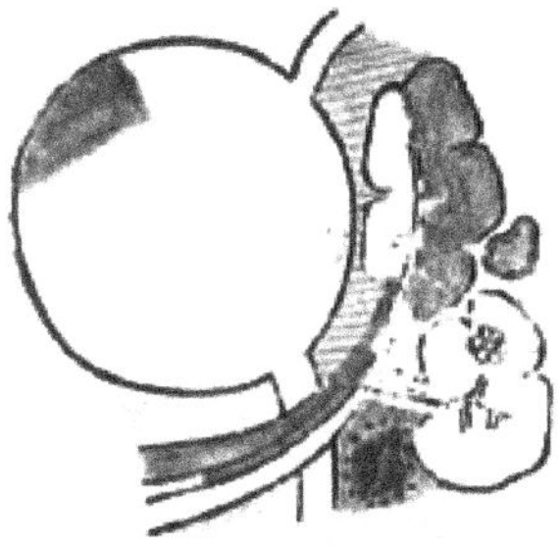

Considerable venous congestion, edematous swelling and slight hemorrhages in connective tissues.

Considerable cloudy and vacuolar degeneration of parenchymatous cells and slight degeneration of island-cells.

[redacted] [redacted] 262

[redacted]

[redacted]

224.

Considerable venous stasis, edematous swelling of connective tissues and dissociation of cell-arrangements. Remarkable atrophia and considerable degeneration of parenchymatous cells and island-cells.

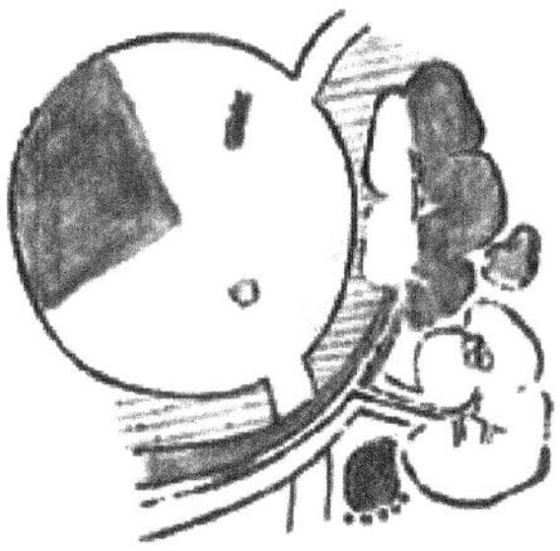

254.

Consid. venous congestion and slight swelling of connective tissues. Atrophia and degeneration of parencymatous cells, esp. at pericapillar portions.

Slight stasis of island-capillaries and remarkable serous exudation in some islands (our so-called "serous apoplexy of islands").

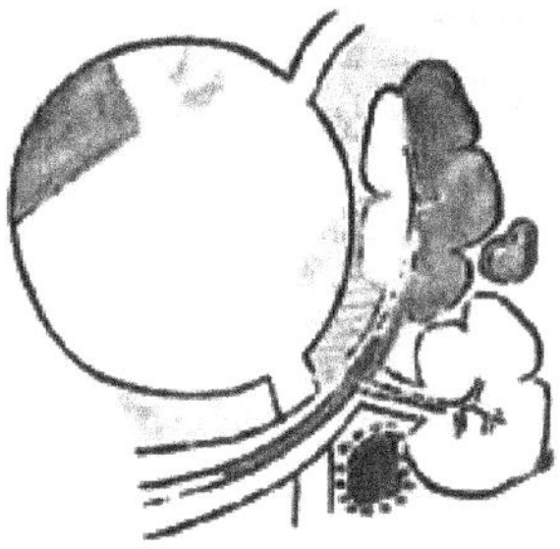

256.

Considerable venous congestion, edematous swelling of connective tissues and slight perivascular round-cell-accumulation at some places. Slight dissociation of cell-arrangements.

Considerable degeneration of parenchymatous cells, esp. at pericapillar

[redacted]

263

([redacted] (

[redacted]

portions.
Cloudy swelling and furthermore at some places hyalinous degeneration of island-cells.

[redacted]

[redacted] 264

([redacted] (

[redacted]

(B) S U M M A R Y

SUMMARY, bases on Investigation on I3 Micro-Slices.

A). Acinus.

I) In the most I3 cases, with somewhat congestion of inter- and intraa-acinous capillaries.

Congestion in slight degree.
2 cases.

Congestion in medium degree.
5 cases.

Congestion in severe degree.
6 cases.

Congestion with hyalinous swelling or degeneration of capillary walls.
3 cases.

Congestion, accompanied with considerable perivascular edema.
2 cases.

Congestion, accompanied with slight perivascular hemorrhages.
3 cases.

Congestion, accompanied with slight perivascular lymphocytes-accumulations.
10 cases.

[redacted]

265

([redacted] (

[redacted]

Accordingly, the main pathological processes are following:
Congestion ___ Edematous swelling of capillary walls ___
Sometimes, pericapillary edema, hemorrhages and slight round-cell-accumulations.

2) After that, occured some degenerative changes of parenchymatous cells, esp- at pericapillar portions.

with rather atrophic glandular cells.
2 cases.

with cloudy or edematous swelling of parenchymatous cells.
18 cases.

in slight degree.	10 cases.
in considerable degree.	3 cases.
with hyalinous degene	0 cases.
(with hyaline-droplets)	4 cases.

Accordingly, it shows generally some slight parencprymatous degenerations and sometimes, some remarkable changes with hyalinous degeneration or hyaline-droplets formations in acinus.

[redacted]

266

([redacted] (

B). Islands.

[redacted]

I) Sometimes with considerable congestion of island-capillaries.

Congestion in considerable degree.

I cases.

Congestion in remarkable degree, accompanied with edematous swelling of capillary walls.

I case.

Congestion, accompaied with remarkable our so-called "polar edema" (remarkable capillary congestion with edema or bionecrotic swelling of pericapillarg tissues at afferent portions).

I case.

Congestion with our so-called "serous apoplexy of islands". (serous exsudation in islands).

I case.

Congestion with our so-called "(hemorrhagic) apoplexy of islands". (hemorrhages in islands).

I case.

[redacted]

2) Sometimes, some degenerative changes of island-cells.

[redacted] 267

([redacted] (

[redacted]

With rather atrophic cells.

7 cases.

With cloudy swelling.

13 cases.

With slight vacuolar degeneration.

2 cases.

[redacted]

[redacted] 268

[redacted]

[redacted]

PANCREAS

			85	146	167	176	178	180	190	205	221	222	224	254	256
Acinus		Size	↓÷	↓÷	↓÷	↓÷	↓÷	↓+	↓÷	↓÷	↓+	↓+	↓++	↓+	↓+
		Dissociation	−	−	−	−	−	−	−	−	−	−	−	−	−
		Necrosis	−	−	−	−	−	−	−	−	−	−	−	−	−
Parenchyma	Parenchymatous Cells	Clouding	+	+	+	+	++	++	+	++	+	+	+	+	+
		Swelling	+	+	+	+	+	++	+	++	+	+	+	+	+
		Zymogen Granules	÷	−	÷	+̇	−	÷	+	++	+	−	−	÷	+̇
		Honeycombed Degeneration	−	÷	÷	+	++	÷	+	÷	+̇	++	+̇	−	+̇
	Changes of Nuclei	Swelling	−	−	−	−	−	−	−	−	−	−	−	−	−
		Pyknosis	+	+	++	−	++	++	+̇	++	++	÷	+	+	++
		Karyolysis	−	−	÷	−	+	÷	+	÷	÷	+	÷	÷	+
		Hyperplasia of Centroacinar Cells	−	−	−	−	−	−	−	−	−	−	−	−	−
		Dsq. of Epithelcells of Efferent Ducts	−	−	−	−	++	+	+	÷	÷	+	÷	÷	+
Interstitium		Edema	÷	÷	÷	+	++	+	++	+	+	++	++	+	÷
	Contents of Capillaries	Erythrocytes	++	++	+̇	++	+	++	+̇	++	++	++	+̇	++	++
		Leucocytes	÷	÷	÷	÷	÷	÷	÷	÷	+	÷	+	−	+
		Lymphocytes	÷	−	÷	÷	−	÷	÷	÷	+	÷	+	−	÷
		Hemorrhage	−	−	−	−	−	−	−	−	−	−	−	−	−
	Infiltration	Leucocytes	−	−	−	−	−	−	−	−	−	÷	−	−	−
		Lymphocytes	−	−	−	−	−	−	−	−	−	÷	−	−	÷
	Proliferation	Plasma cells	÷	−	−	−	−	−	−	÷	−	−	−	−	−
		Histiocytes	+̇	−	÷	÷	−	÷	−	+̇	÷	÷	÷	÷	+
		Capillarywall-Cells	−	−	−	−	−	−	−	−	−	−	−	−	−
Langerhans's Island		Number	↓÷	↓÷	↓÷	↓÷	↓++	↓÷	↓÷	↓÷	↓+̇	↓+	↓+̇	↓÷	↓+
		Atrophia	−	÷	÷	++	++	++	++	+	++	+	++	++	−
		Necrosis	−	−	−	−	−	−	−	−	+	−	−	−	−
	Parenchymatous Cells	Size	↓+̇	↓+̇	↓÷	↓+̇	↓++	↓+	↓++	↓÷	↓+	↓+	↓+̇	↓+	↓+̇
		Clouding	+	+	+	++	+	++	++	+	+	÷	+	+	÷
		Swelling	+	+	−	+	+	++	++	−	−	−	−	−	−
		Honeycombed Degeneration	÷	−	−	+	+	÷	++	+̇	+	÷	++	÷	÷
	Changes of Nuclei	Swelling	−	−	−	−	−	−	−	−	−	−	−	−	−
		Pyknosis	(++)	÷	÷	÷	++	+̇	++	÷	+̇	+	+	−	÷
		Karyolysis	−	−	−	÷	÷	÷	−	−	−	−	÷	−	−
		Congestion of Capillaries	++	+	÷	+	−	−	÷	÷	÷	−	−	÷	−
		Hemorrhage	−	−	−	−	−	÷	−	−	−	−	−	−	−
		Hyperplasia of Capillary-wall-Cells	+	+	÷	+̇	÷	+	+̇	÷	÷	−	−	−	−

[redacted] 269

([redacted] (

Parenchymatous degeneration of pancrea~~s~~ s.

[redacted]

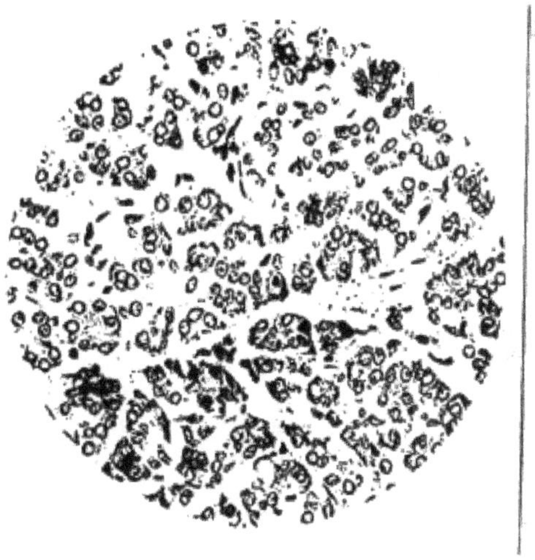

R254 X310

[redacted]

[redacted] 270

([redacted] (

Hyalnie droplets degeneration
of parenchymatous cells.

[redacted]

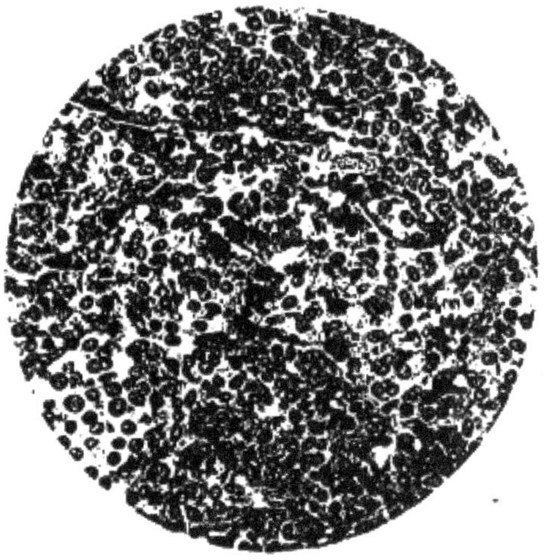

R167 x370

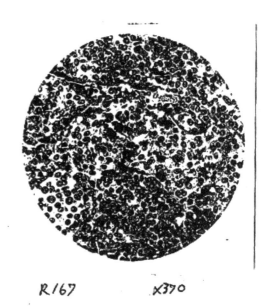

Vacuolar degeneration of
Parenchymatous cells.

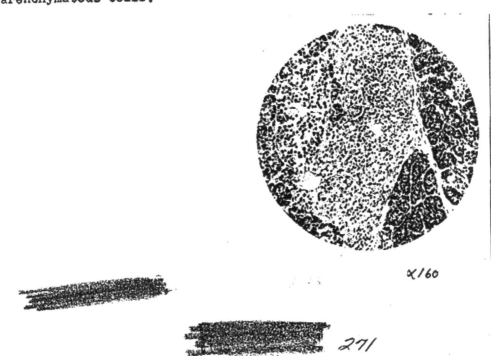

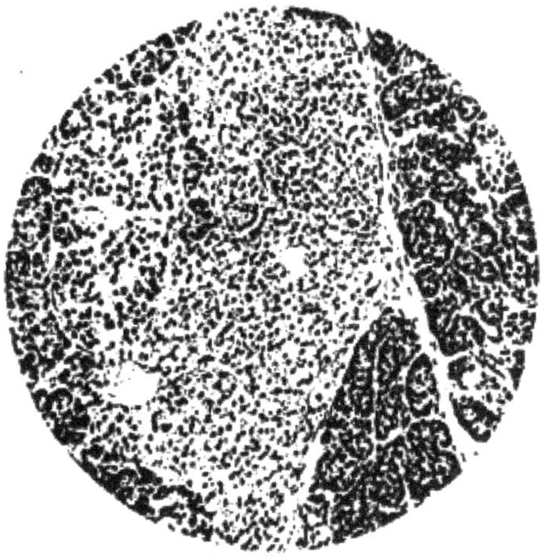

x160

[redacted]

[redacted] 271

([redacted] (

Intense parenchymatous degeneration,especially at pericapillary portion.

[redacted]

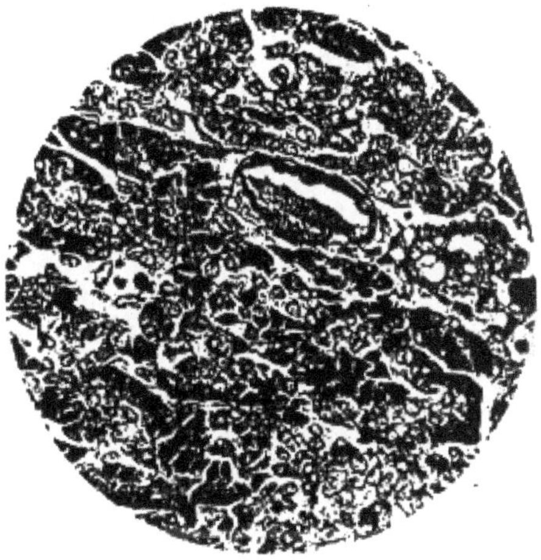

R 205 x330

Intense parenchymatous degeneration, especially at pericapillary portion..

[redacted]

R 222 x270

[redacted] 272

([redacted] (

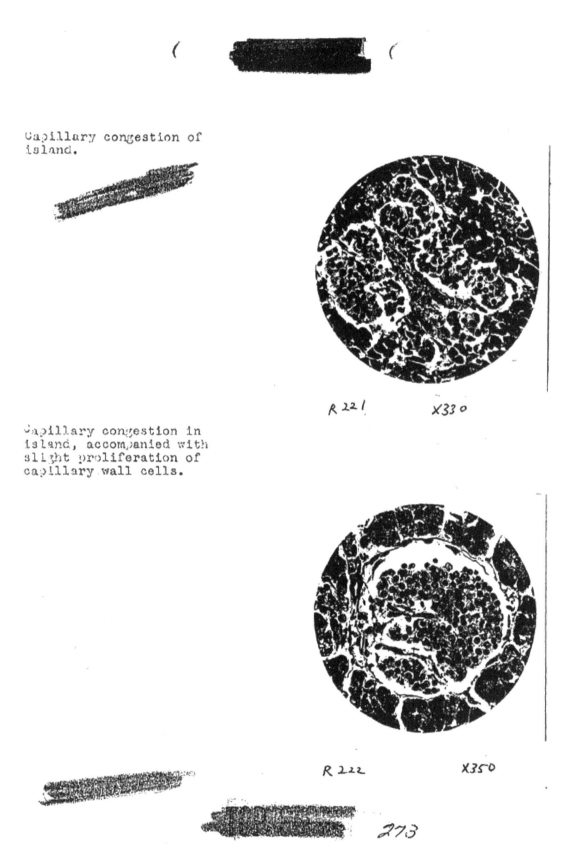

Capillary congestion of island.

[redacted]

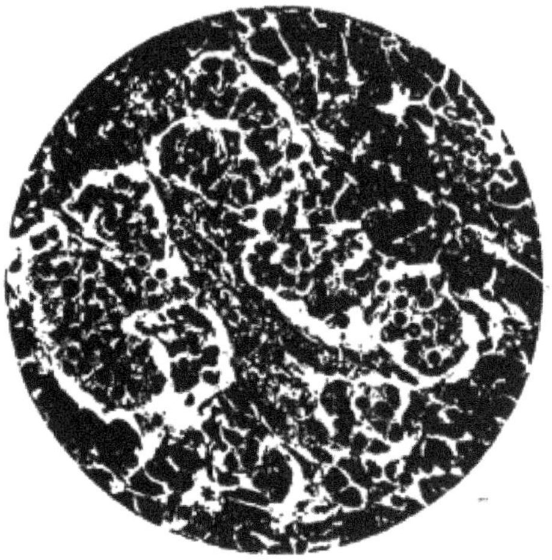

R 221 X330

Capillary congestion in island, accompanied with slight proliferation of capillary wall cells.

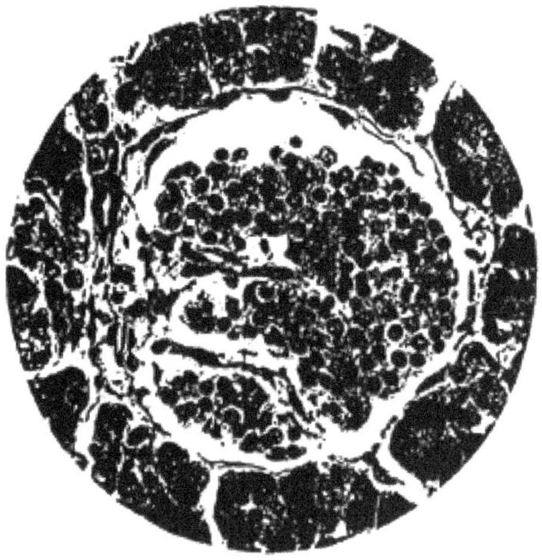

R 222 X350

[redacted]

[redacted] 273

([redacted] (

Edematous swelling of island, accompanied some parenchymatous degeneration.

[redacted]

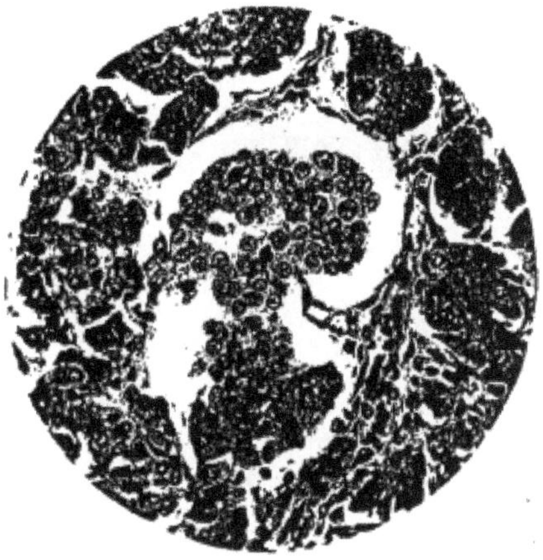

R 221 x330

Intense edematous swelling of island.
Accompanied with vacuolar degeneration of parenchymatous cell.

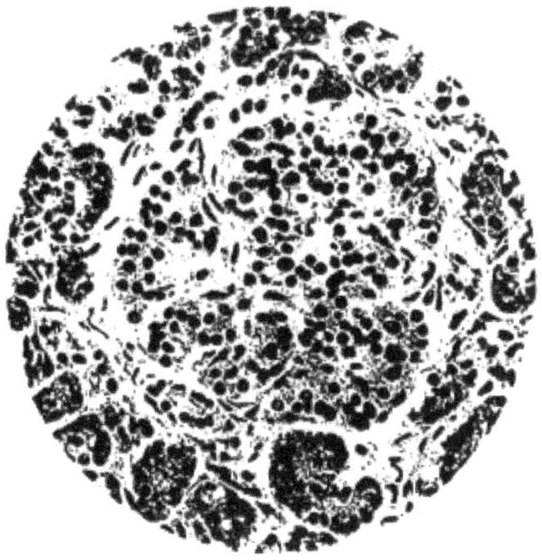

[redacted] R166 x160

[redacted] 274

[redacted]

Edema at polar portions of island.

[redacted]

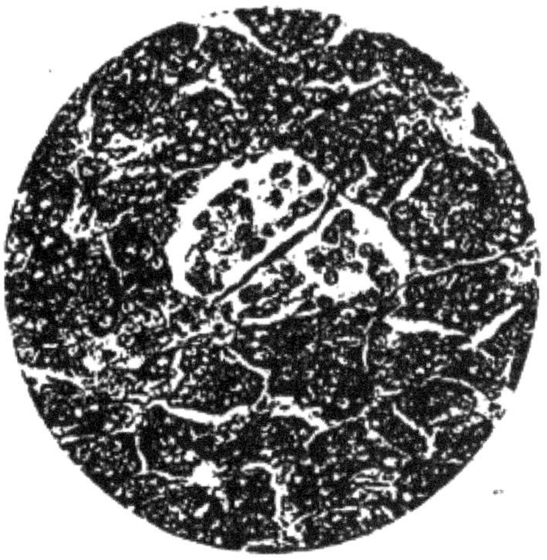

R 85 x330

Round cell accumulation at polar portion of island.

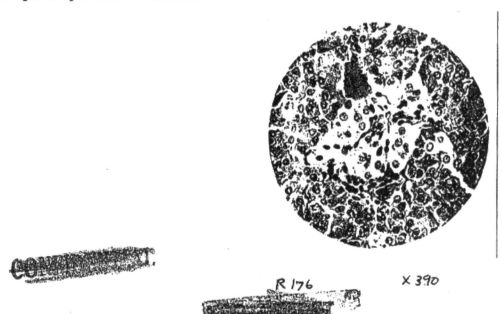

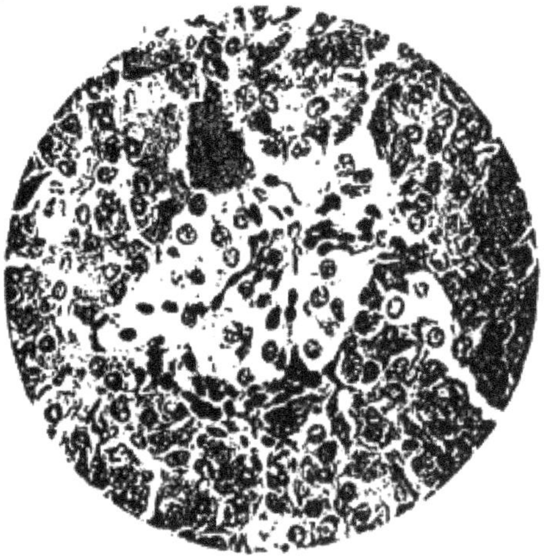

[redacted]

R 176 x 390

[redacted]

275

([redacted] (

Perivascular round cell
infilltration.

[redacted]

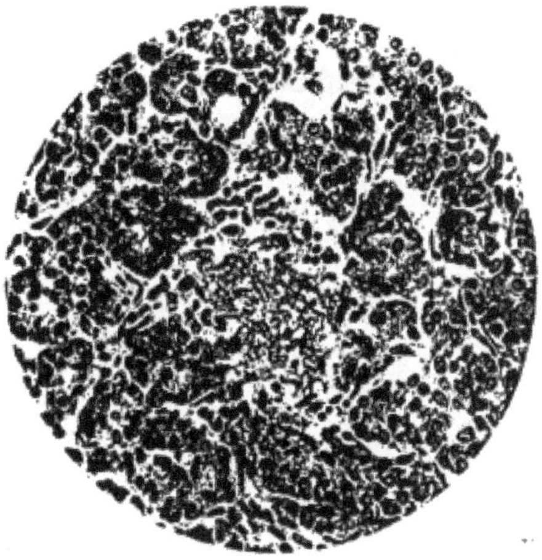

R166 x160

Perivascular round cell
infiltration in high power.

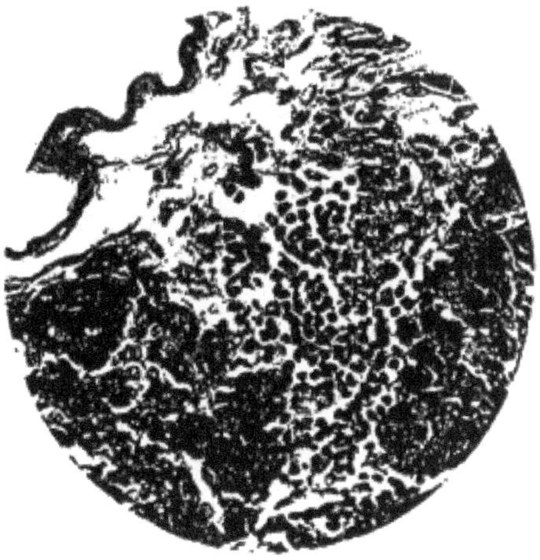

R205 x330

[redacted]

[redacted] 276

([redacted] (

Hemorrhage in islands.
(so-called apoplexy of island).

[redacted]

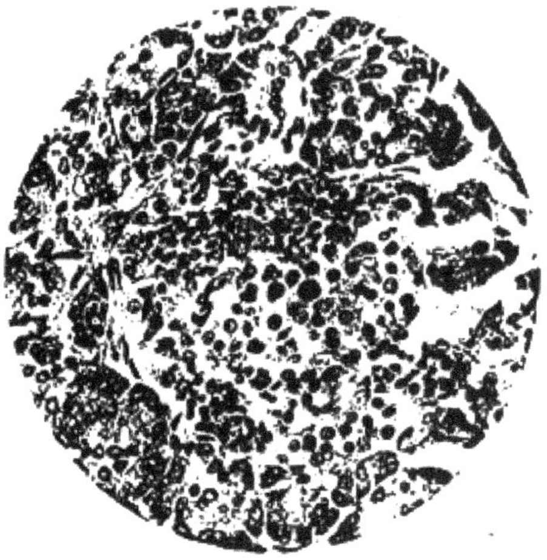

R.180 x330

Exudation in island.
(so-called serous apoplexy
of island).

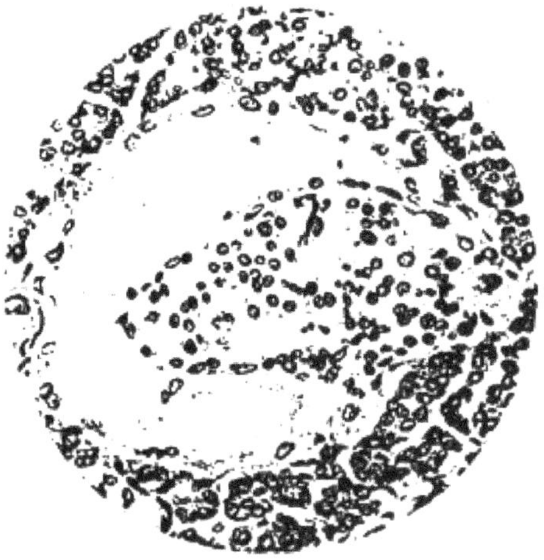

R256 x310

[redacted]

[redacted] 277

• [redacted] •

Suprarenal

[redacted]

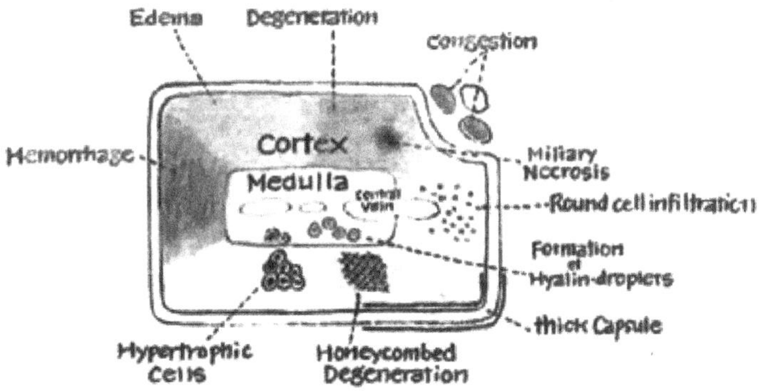

[redacted] [redacted] 278

[redacted]

SUPRA-RENAL GLAND.

(A) Microscoopic[redacted]tigation.

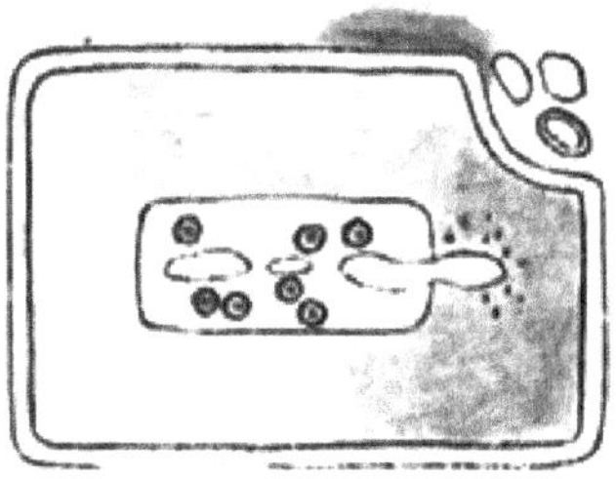

I6.

Considerable atrophia and degeneration of ~~degeneration~~ of parenchymatous cells. Formation of acious lumina in cords of cells of Z. fasciculata. Considerable odema. Perivascular small round-cell-accumulation in Z. reticularis.

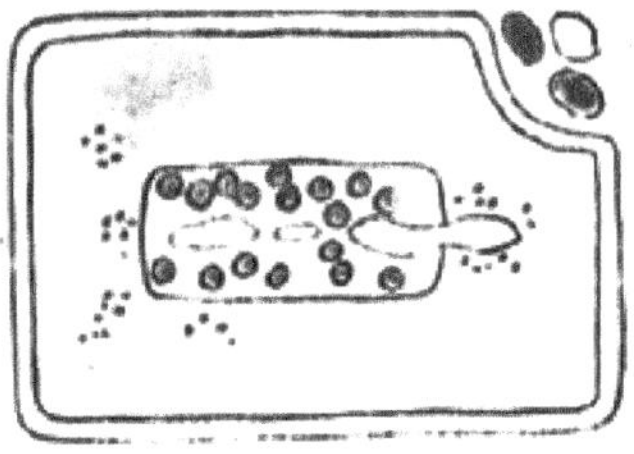

I46.

Perivascular small round-cell-accumulation in Z. reticularis. Some medullar cells with large nuclei (initial stage of medullar hypertrophy). Remarkable formation of hyalin-droplets in medullar cells.

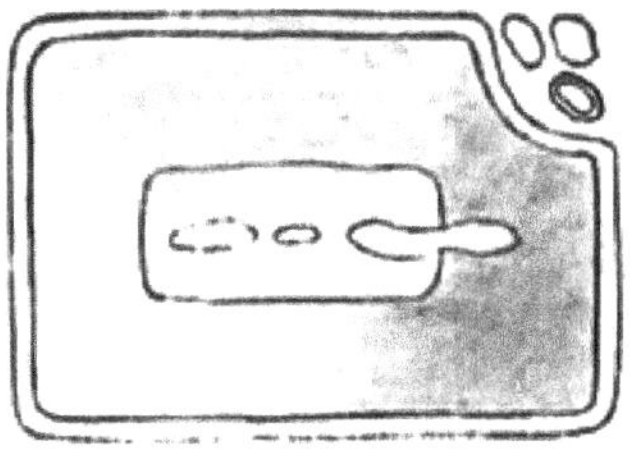

I52.

Considerable atrophia, degenertion and dissociation of parencymatous cells. Some medullar cells with large nuclei.

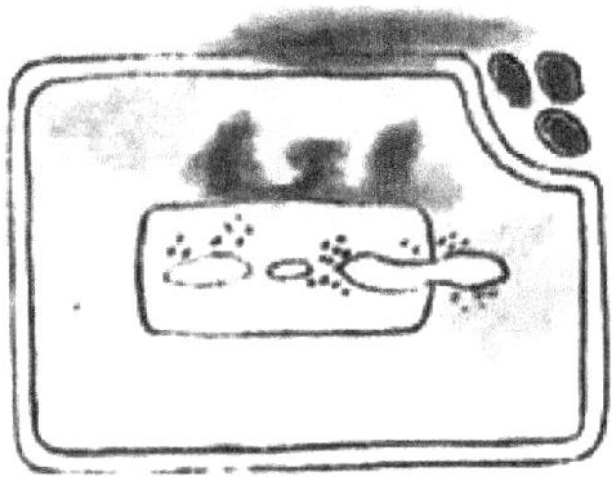

I67.

Considera-ble congestion and hemorrhage in Z. fasciculata and Z. reticularis. Remarkable accumulation of round cells (contained many plasma cells) around subcapsular blood-vessels, central veins and in medulla.

[redacted] [redacted] 279

[redacted]

I76.

Increase of fatty contents in cortex (deposits of fats even in Z. glomerulosa). Some districts of cortex with hypertrophic cell-groups. Accumulation of small round cells in Z. reticularis ~~Also in medulla.~~ and in medulla. [redacted]

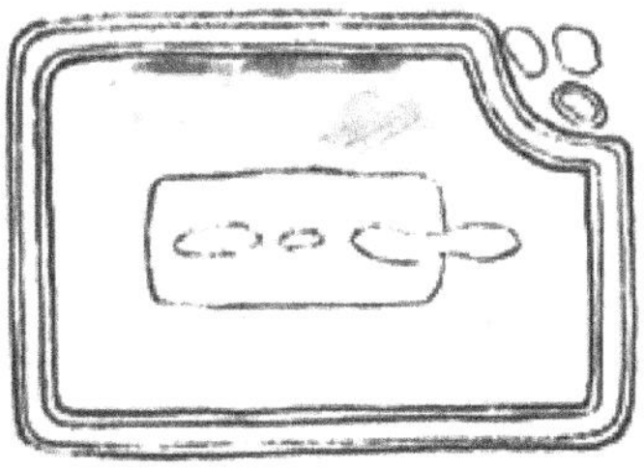

I78.

With very thick capsule. Homorrhages in Z. glomerulosa. Considerable hyperplasy of capillay-wall-cells.

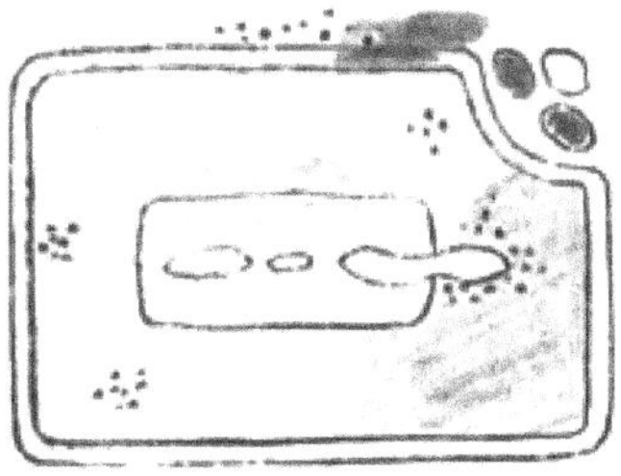

I80.

Dissociation and atrophia of parenchymatous cells. Considerable edema, Perivascular small round cells accumulation in cortex. Considerable hyperplasia of capillary-wall-cells.

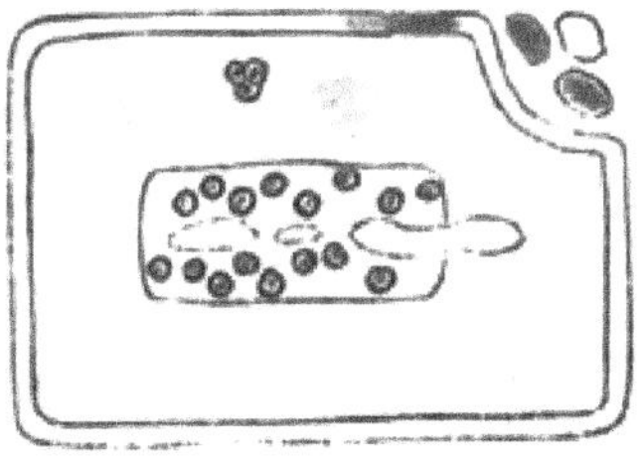

I90.

Homorrhages in Z. reticularis. Some medullar cells with large nucleis. Remarkable formation of hyalin-droplets in medullar cells.

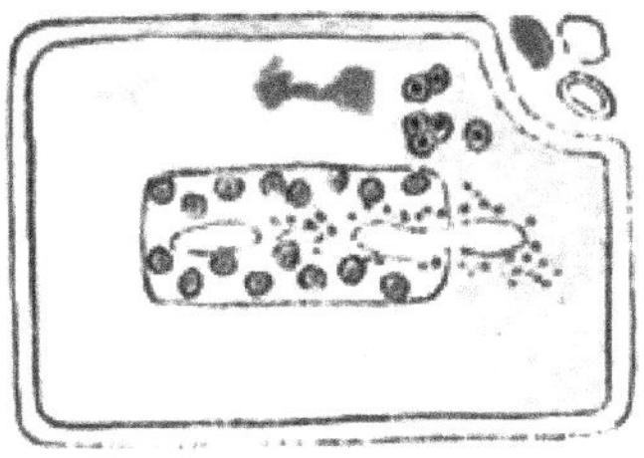

205.

Some hypertrophic cell-groups in cortex. Perivascular round cell accumulation (lymphocytes and plasma cells) in cortex and also in medulla. Parenchymatous degeneration with remarkable pycnosis and ~~furthermore Z. fasciculata and Z. reticularis.~~ honeycombed degenerated cells. Considerable congestion and hemorrhages chiefly in Z. fasciculata. Remarkable formation of hyalin-droplets in medullar cells.

[redacted]

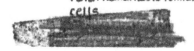

280

● [redacted]

221.

Considerable edema. Perivascular small round-cell-infiltration in Z. fasciculata and Z. reticularis.

[redacted]

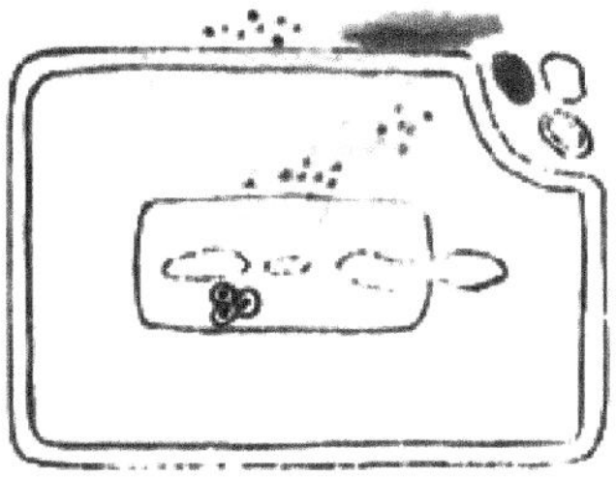

222.

Considerable edema. Perivascular round cell (lymphocytes and plasma cells) accumulation in Z. fasciculata and Z. reticularis. Appearance of some hypertrophic medullar cells.

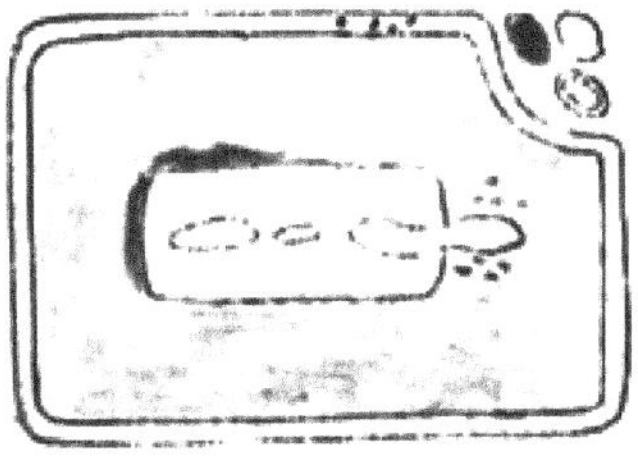

224.

Considerable atrophia, degeneration and dissociation of parenchymatous cells. Slight hemorrhages in Z. reticularis. Perivascular small round-cell-accumulation in cortex. Severe edema.

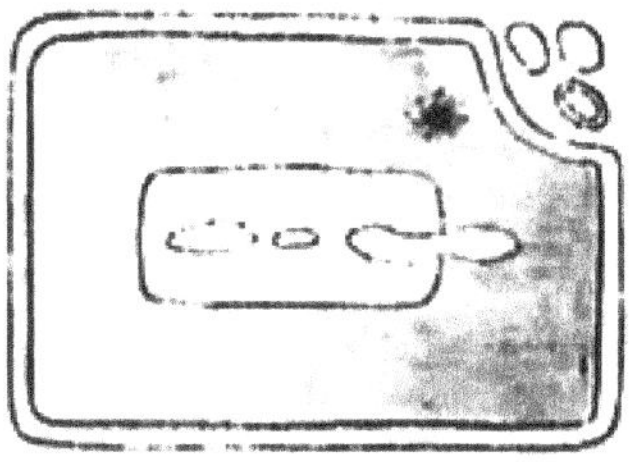

229.

Perivascular small-round-cell-accumulation in Z. fasciculata to form miliary knots. In these places cortical cells fall into severe degeneration or decayed masses. Considerable hyperplasia of capillary wall-cells.

254.

Atrophia of Z. glomerulosa. Localised hemorrhages in Z. reticularis and Z. fasciculata. Considerable edema.

[redacted] [redacted] 281

[redacted]

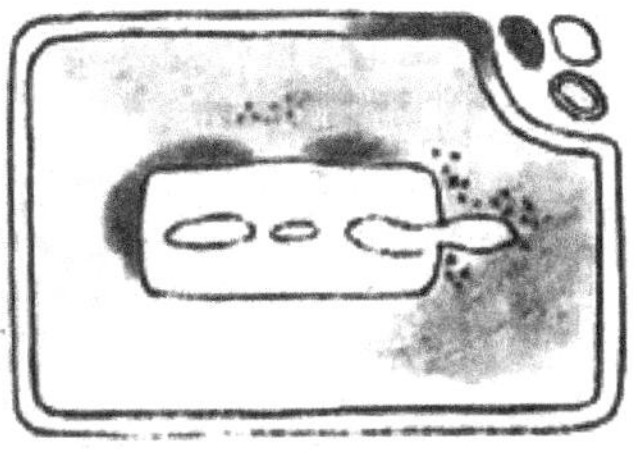

256.

Considerable atrophia of parenchymatous cells. Z. reticularis with more or less remarkable hemorrhages. Considerable edema. Perivascular small-round-cell-accumulation in Z. reticularis. Some hyperplasia of capillary-wall-cells.

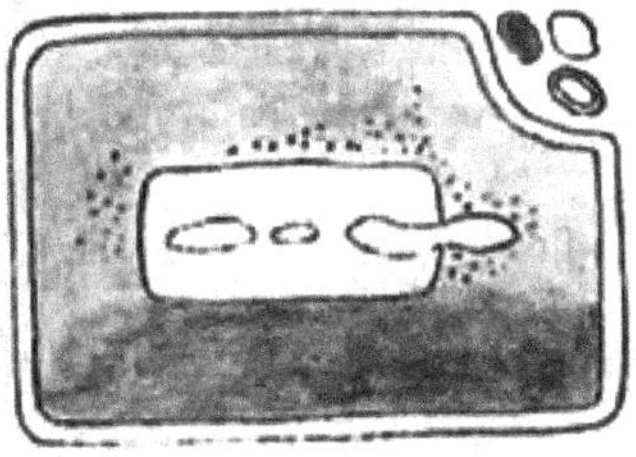

727. [redacted]

Severe dissociation and atrophia of parenchymatous cells. Severe edema. Remarkable perivascular small-round-cellaccumulation at some places in Z. reticularis and around central veins in cortex.

731.

Severe dissociation and atrophia of parenchymatous cells. Severe edema. Some localised hemorrhages in Z. reticularis. Some perivascular small-round-cell-infiltration in Z. fasciculata.

[redacted]

[redacted] 282

([redacted] (

(B) SUMMARY.

a) Pericapsular tissues: slight small-round-cell-infiltration in all cases and considerable hemorrhages in 7 cases.

[redacted]

b) Capsular tissues: Generally slight edematous swelling and more or less considerable hemorrhages in 5 cases.

c) Cortex: In all cases (except only I case with slight increase of fatty contents in cortex) it shows more or less remarkable decrease of fatty contents (splitting of fatty substances and degenerative changes to form dark or homogenous protoplasma).
Severe atrophia in 7 cases and dissociation of cell-arrangements in 5 cases.
Cortex with hypertrophic cell-groups, besides general atrophia in 7 cases.
Generally without vacuolar degeneration, but in 1 case with cellgroups in honeycombed degeneration.
In all cases with severe edematous swelling and in several cases with more or less considerable congestion in Z. reticularis and subcapsular tissues. In all cases (except I)

[redacted]

[redacted] 283

([redacted] (

with a few leucocytes and lymphocytes in capillaries and in 1 case with plenty of them.

[redacted]

In 5 cases with slight hyperplasia of capillary wall-cells (endothel cells or adventitial cells). Small-round-cell-infiltration in I2 cases, 3 of them in high degree and 2 of them with plasma cells. We classify parenchymatous disturbances, according to concept "serous inflammation", as following:

Epinephritis serosa	I.	in	IO	cases
	II.	in	6	cases

d) Medullar tissues: In all cases with edematous swelling and in 4 cases hyaline-droplets-formation. In all cases with more or less slight vacuolar degeneration. Small-round-cell-infiltration (generally with plasma cells) in 7 cases.

[redacted]

[redacted] 284

([redacted] (

[redacted]

SUPRARENAL

			16	146	152	167	176	178	180	190	205	221	222	224	229	254	256	727	731
Serous Inflammation			I	I	II	I	—	I	II	I	I	I	I	II	I	I	II	II	II
Pericapsular Tissue	Congestion		+	+:	−	++:	÷	÷	++	++	+	÷	+	+	÷	++	+	+	÷
	Hemorrhage		+	÷	÷	++:	+++	−	+	÷	÷	++	+	÷	÷	+	÷	÷	÷
	Infiltration of Leucocytes		÷	−	−	−	−	−	−	−	−	÷	−	−	−	−	−	−	−
	Infiltration of Lymphocytes		÷	÷	÷	÷	÷	÷	++	÷	÷	÷	+	÷	÷	÷	(÷)	÷	÷
	Proliferation of Histiocytic Cells		÷	+	÷	+:	÷	÷	÷	÷	+	÷	÷	÷	+	+	÷	÷	+
Capsule	Edema		+:	÷	++	+	++	÷	+	÷	(++)	+	++	÷	+	+	÷	++	+++
	Hemorrhage		÷	÷	÷	+	+	−	(+++)	+	÷	÷	÷	−	−	÷	+	−	÷
	Cellular Infiltration		÷	−	÷	÷	÷	−	÷	÷	÷	−	÷	(+)	÷	÷	−	÷	÷
Parenchyma of Cortex	Decrease of Fat		+:	++	+	+:	−	++	++	++	++	+	+	+:	++	++	++	++	++
	Cortical Cells	Dissociation	÷	−	(++)	÷	−	−	(++)	(÷)	+	÷	÷	++:	÷	÷	+	+++	+++
		Atrophia	+:	÷	(++)	÷	÷	÷	(+:)	÷	+	+	−	++	+	+	++	+++	+++
		Hypertrophia	÷	÷	−	−	+:	−	÷	÷	+	−	÷	−	−	−	−	−	−
		Splitting of Lipoid-drops	++	+++	++	++:	÷	+++	+++	+++	+++	+:	+	++	+++	+++	+++	+++	+++
		Vacuolar Degenerat. (Dietrich)	−	−	−	−	−	−	−	−	−	−	−	−	−	−	−	−	−
		Honeycombed Degener. (Dietrich)	−	−	−	−	−	−	−	÷	(+)	−	−	−	−	−	−	−	−
		Formation of Lumina	+	−	÷	÷	−	÷	−	−	−	−	÷	÷	÷	÷	÷	÷	÷
		Brown Pigment	÷	+:	++	÷	++	÷	+	++	+	+	+	+	÷	÷	+	+	+
		Changes of Nuclei: Pyknosis	+	−	÷	+	÷	÷	÷	÷	++	÷	÷	÷	÷	÷	÷	÷	+
		Changes of Nuclei: Karyolysis	+:	÷	++	÷	+	÷	÷	÷	+	÷	÷	+	+	+	+	++	+
		Changes of Nuclei: Dissapperance	+	÷	++	÷	+	÷	÷	(÷)	+	÷	÷	+:	+:	÷	÷	++	++
Interstitium of Cortex	Congestion of Subcapsular Blood v's		++	++	+	÷	+:	++	÷	++	+	+	++	+	÷	+	++	+	+
	Edema		++	÷	++:	+	÷	+	++	(+)	(+)	++	++	(+++)	+:	++	++	+++	+++
	Contents of Capillaries	Erythrocytes	(+:)	++	+	+++	+	(+)	ǀ	++	+++	+:	++	++	÷	(+)	++	÷	÷
		Leucocytes	÷	−	÷	÷	÷	÷	ǀ	÷	÷	−	−	−	−	÷	+:	−	÷
		Lymphocytes	÷	÷	−	÷	÷	÷	ǀ	÷	÷	÷	÷	÷	÷	÷	÷	+	÷
		Large Mononuclears	−	−	−	÷	−	÷	ǀ	−	÷	÷	÷	−	÷	÷	÷	÷	÷
	Hemorrhage		÷	÷	÷	+++	÷	+	ǀ	+	+	÷	÷	+	÷	+	+	−	+
	Circumscribed Round cell-Infiltration		÷	+	÷	+:	+:	−	++	÷	++	+	+:	+:	÷	−	++	+++	÷
	Hyperplasia of Vessel Wall Cells		−	÷	−	÷	÷	+	+	÷	+	÷	÷	÷	+	÷	+:	÷	(÷)
Medulla	Parenchyma	Hyalindrops	++	+++	÷	÷	−	ǀ	(+)	+++	+++	÷	−	ǀ	−	+	÷	ǀ	+
		Vacuolar Degenerat.	++	+	(+)	++	+	ǀ	÷	÷	++:	÷	+	ǀ	÷	+	+	ǀ	+
	Edema		+	÷	++	+	++	ǀ	++:	÷	÷	+	++	ǀ	+	++	++	ǀ	−
	Congestion		÷	+	÷	÷	+	ǀ	(+)	+	÷	÷	÷	ǀ	−	+	+	ǀ	÷
	Hemorrhage		÷	÷	÷	−	÷	ǀ	(÷)	÷	÷	÷	÷	ǀ	−	÷	÷	ǀ	÷
	Circumscribed Round cell-Infiltration		÷	÷	÷	++	++	ǀ	+	+	+:	−	÷	ǀ	÷	÷	++	ǀ	+

[redacted]

[redacted] 285

[redacted]

Epinephritis serosa III, in low power.

[redacted]

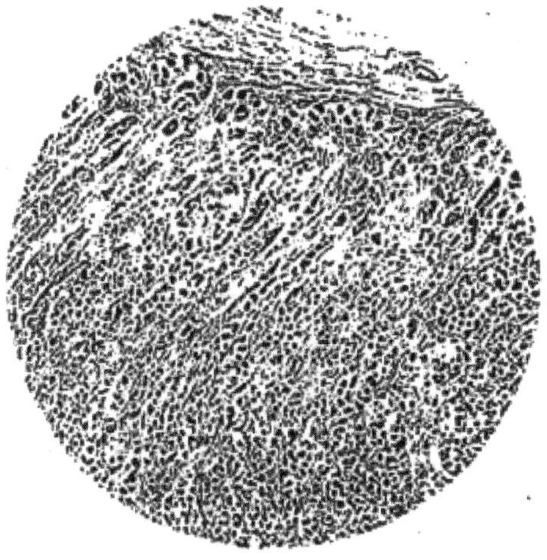

Epinephritis serosa, with remarkable congestion and edematous swelling of cortical tissues.

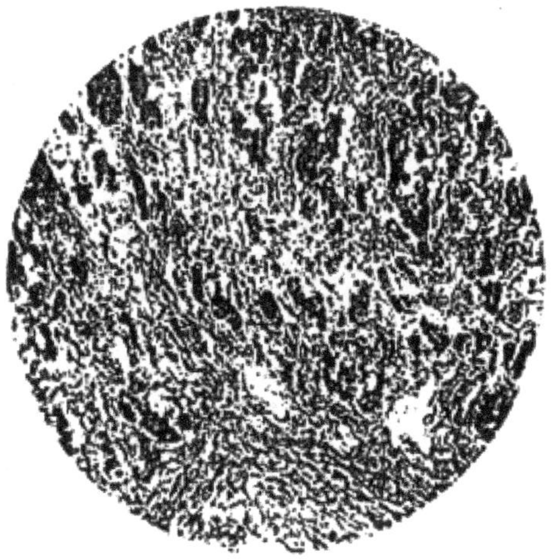

[redacted]

286

[redacted]

Honeycombed degeneration of cortical tissues.

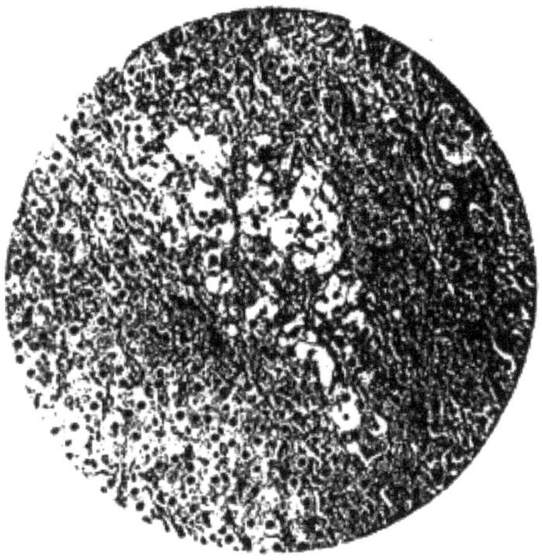

[redacted]

Miliary necrosis in cortical tissues.

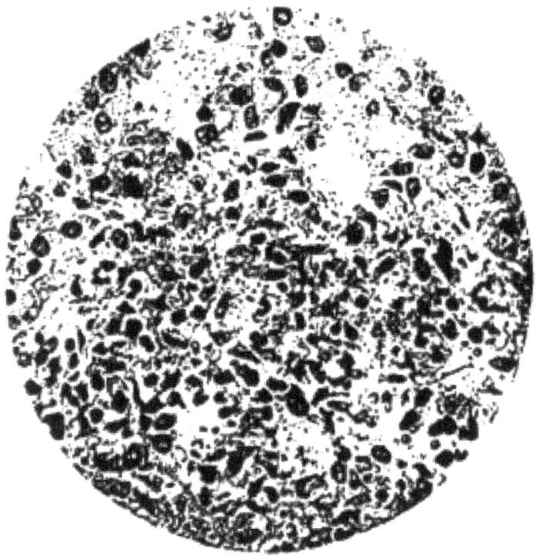

[redacted]

[redacted] 287

[redacted]

Small round cell accumulation around the central vein.

[redacted]

Round cell accumulation in medullary tissues.

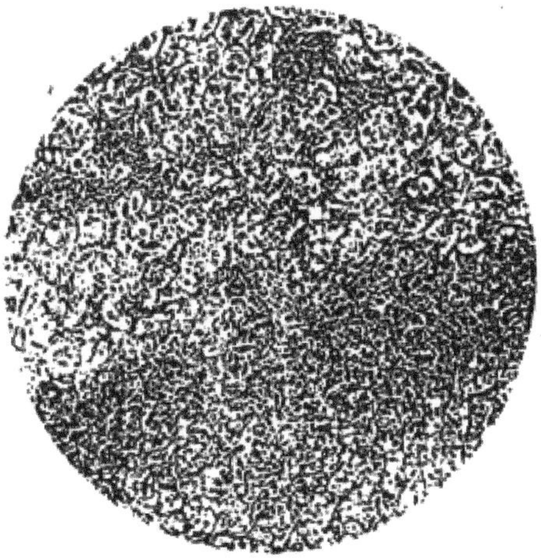

[redacted]

[redacted] 288

([redacted] (

Hyaline droplets degeneration of medullary cells.

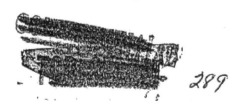

[redacted]

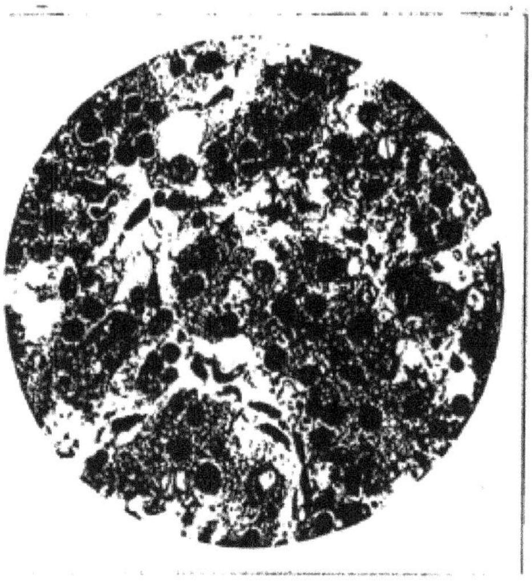

[redacted]

289

[redacted]

[redacted]

Thyroid

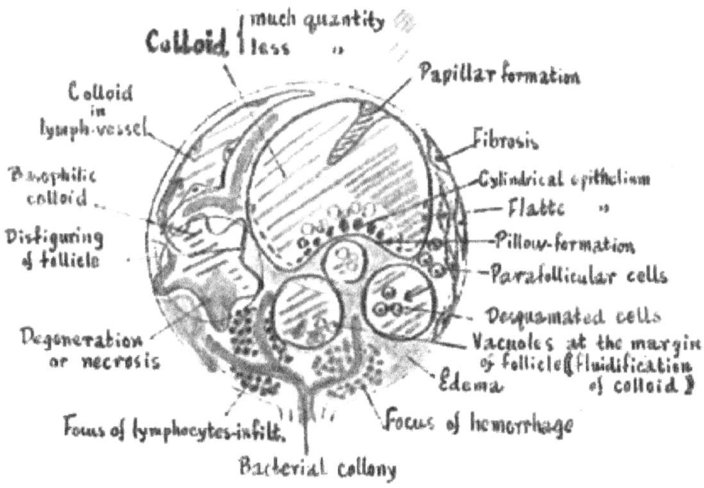

[redacted]

291

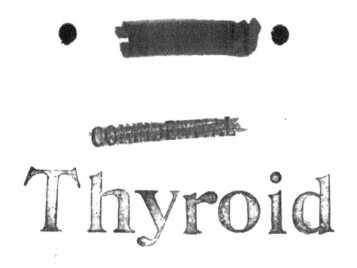

[redacted]

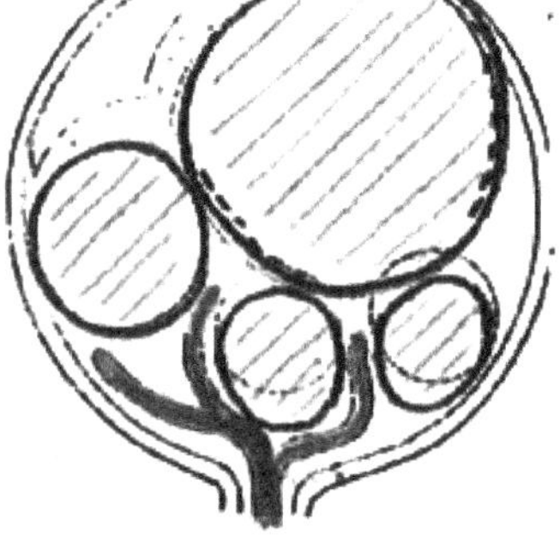

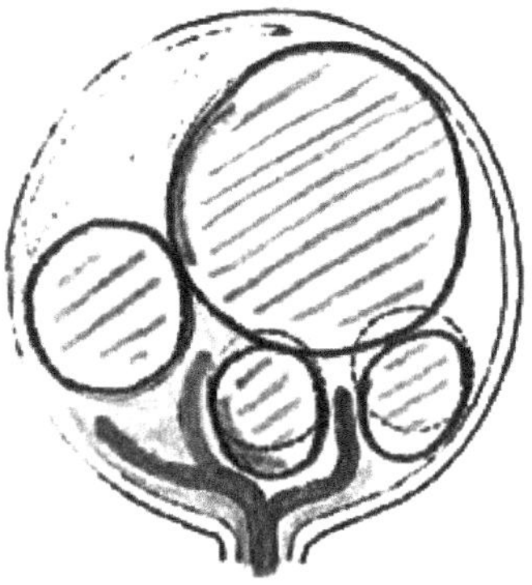

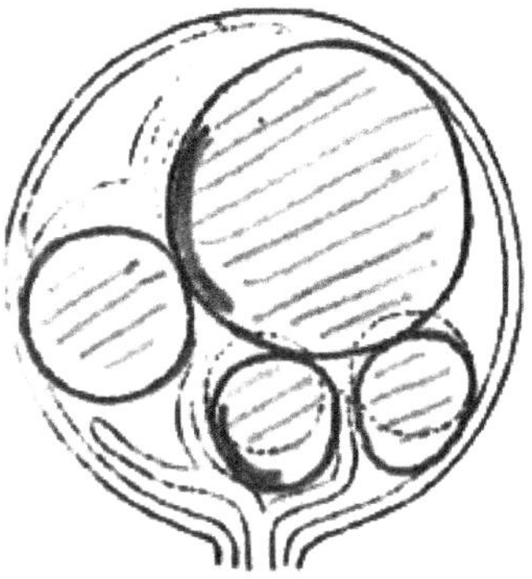

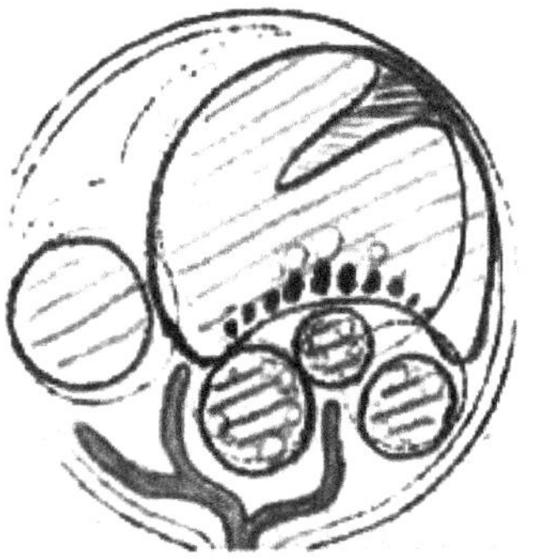

THYROID.

(A) Microscopical Investigation.

I6.

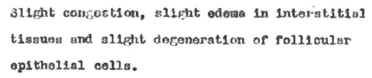

Slight congestion and follicles in statical state.

50.

Slight congestion, slight edema in interstitial tissues and slight degeneration of follicular epithelial cells.

At some places with pillow-like or papillar increase of epithelial cells and many microfollicles-formation in the attachment-area.

85.

Slight degenerative changes of follicular epithelial cells (degeneration and desquamation).

I67.

Struma colloides proliferativa.

Slight congestion and some macrofollicles with papillar or pillow-like increase of epithelial cells and many microfollicles-formation in the area attached to these proliferative follicles.

A large quantity of colloidal masses in follicles.

[redacted]

[redacted] 291

[redacted]

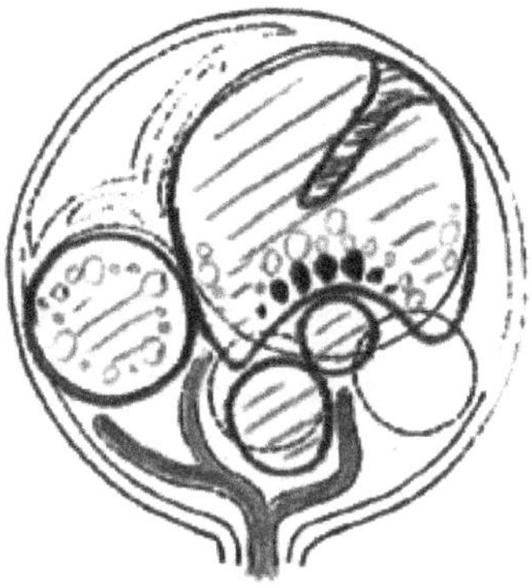

I79.

Slight congestion without any degenerative changes. [redacted]

Slight hyperplasia of follicular epitheial cells to form pillow-like or papillar arrangement. Vacuole-formation in colloidal masses at the margin of follicles (increase of resorption).

I78.

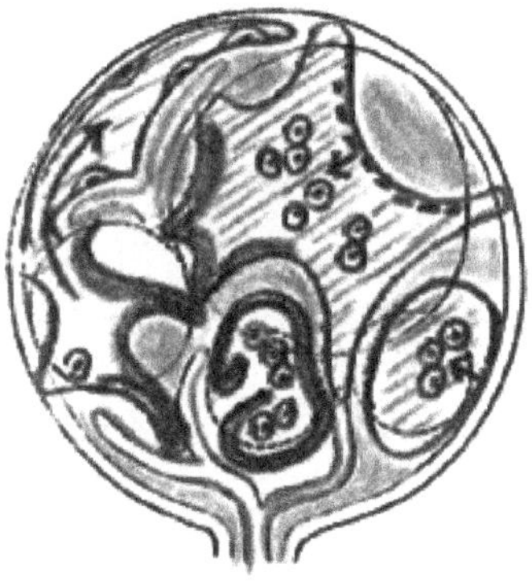

Collapse of follicles.

Rather anaemic edematous swelling of interstitium and remarkable degenerative changes of epithelial cells (flattening, cloudy swolling, pycnosis, desquamation and desolation), without any proliferative tendency: namely follicles in collapse.

Increase of colloidal masses in follicles and also in lymph-vessels.

I80.

Chronic thyreoiditis.

Considerable congestion, edematous swelling and hyaline degeneration of interstitial tissues with some round cell infiltrations.

[redacted]

292

● [redacted]

[redacted]

So many micro-follicles all over the thyroidal tissues with remarkable degeneration of epithelial cells (flattening, cloudy swelling, pyconsis, desquamation and desolation of epithelial cells, especially desquamation and desolation in high degree).

In follicles: a large quantity of desquamative epithelial cells and remarkable decrease of colloidal masses and at some places, basophilic masses.

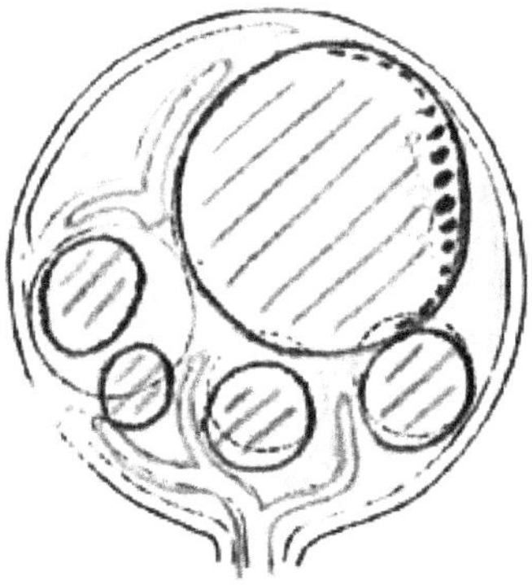

At some places, localised slight hemorrhages in follicles.

I90.

Slight swelling of interstitial tissues and follicles in statical state (with slight hyperplasia) and many micro-follicles.

No remarkable degenerative changes.

I93.

Thyreoid in collapse.

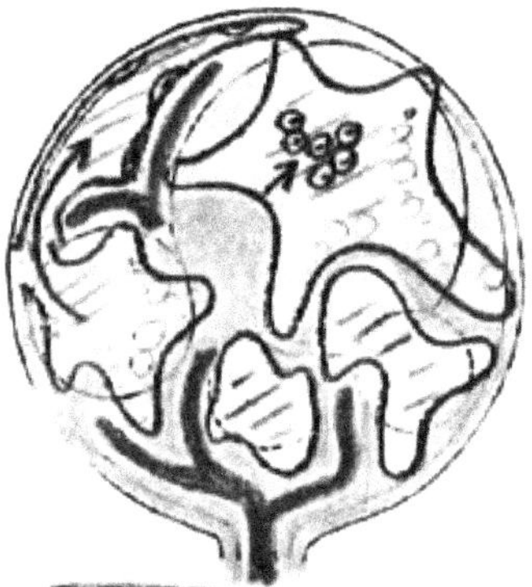

Considerable congestion and edematous swelling of interstitial tissues with follicles in collapse-state with remarkable degenerative changes (flattening, cloudy swelling, desquamation and desolation in a high degree). In follicles, increase of more or less basophilic or fluidified colloidal masses.

[redacted]

[redacted] 293

● [redacted]

Also in lymph-vessels, some colloidal accumu-

[redacted] lations.

207.

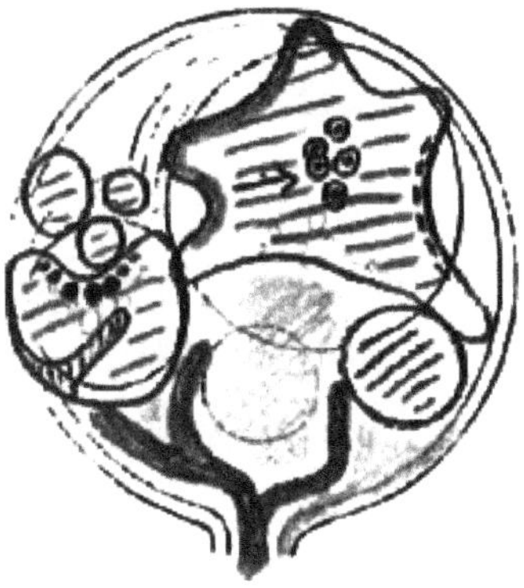

Follicular collapse with some slight regenerative processes.

Considerable congestion and edematous swelling of interstitial tissues with follicles in subacute shove with some degenerative changes at some places and some regenerative changes at the other places.

As degenerative changes: flattening, cloudy swelling, pycnosis, desquamation and desolation of follicular epithelial cells. And increase of more or less basophilic or fluidified colloidal masses in follicles: namely follicular collapse.

As regenerative changes, slight hyperplasia of epithelial cells to form pillow-like or papillar arrangements.

221.

(a). Subacute disfiguring in Graves's thyreoid. Slight fibrosis, slight edematous swelling of interstitial tissues and some significant changes of precapiller arterioles (Increase of endothelial cells, swelling of intima, edematous

[redacted]

294

[redacted]

swelling of adventitial tissues, thickning of media and leaf-knots formation at bifulcating portions of arterioles).

[redacted]

Parenchymatous follicles are in the hyperfunctional state with many micro- and macrofollicles or in the knotty hyperplasia.

Macrofollicles with papillary increased epithelial cells and microfollicles with papillarily, or trabecularily increased epithelial cells and with somany parafollicular cells.

Beside these hyperfunctional changes exist some degenerative processes of epithelial cells (flattening, pycnosis, desquamation, and desolation of epithelial cells).

221.

(b). Considerable congestion and some macrofollicles with papillarily or pillow-likely increased epithelial cells and so many micro-follicles in the attachment areas of these proliferative follicles.

Considerable degenerative changes of these follicular epithelial cells (flattening, pycnosis, desquamation and desolation of epitheial cells) and slight increase of colloidal masses in follicles and lymphvessels.

[redacted]

[redacted] 295

[redacted]

At some places, some follicles with somewhat regenerative changes (papillar arrangements of epithelial cells).

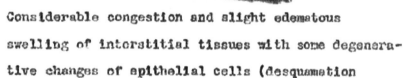

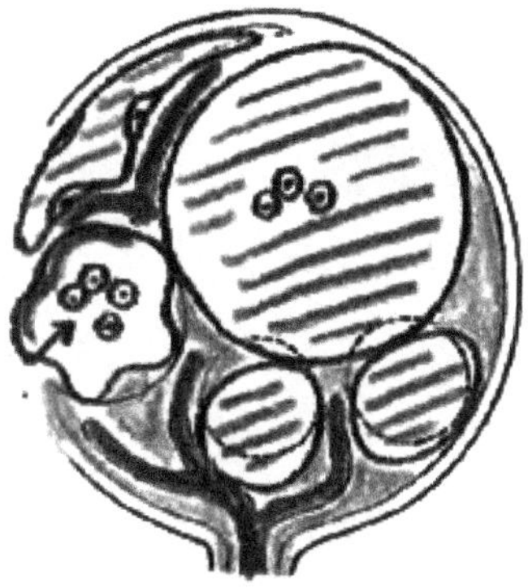

224. [redacted]

Considerable congestion and slight edematous swelling of interstitial tissues with some degenerative changes of epithelial cells (desquamation and desolation).

Considerable increase of colloidal masses in follicles (decrease of resorption) and in lymph-vessels.

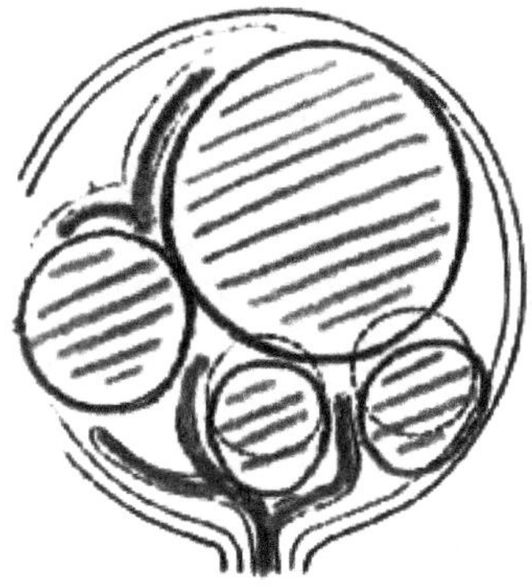

256.

Slight congestion and no remarkable changes else. With some macro- and many microfollicles.

727.

Subacute disfiguring of thyreoid.

Slight congestion, edematous swelling and hyaline degeneration of interstitial tissues.

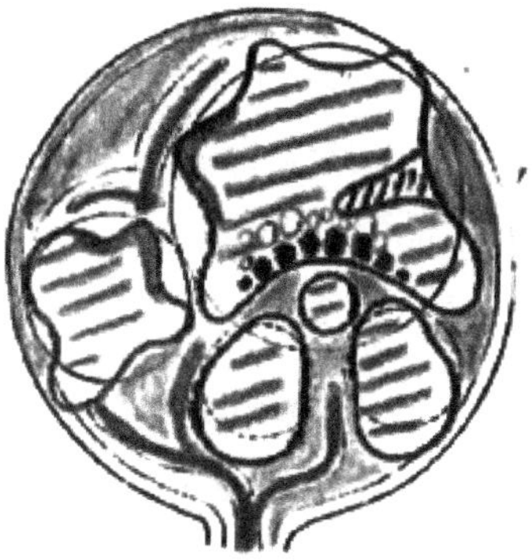

Follicular epithelial cells are at some places more or less degenerative and at the other places, somewhat regenerative.

As degenerative changes: cloudy swelling, pyconosis, desquamation and desolation of epithelial cells and as regenerative changes; papillar or pillow-like increase of epithel cells.

[redacted] 296

[redacted]

771.

These thyreoid are in confusion with so many micro- macro or cytic follicles and various reactive changes. [redacted]

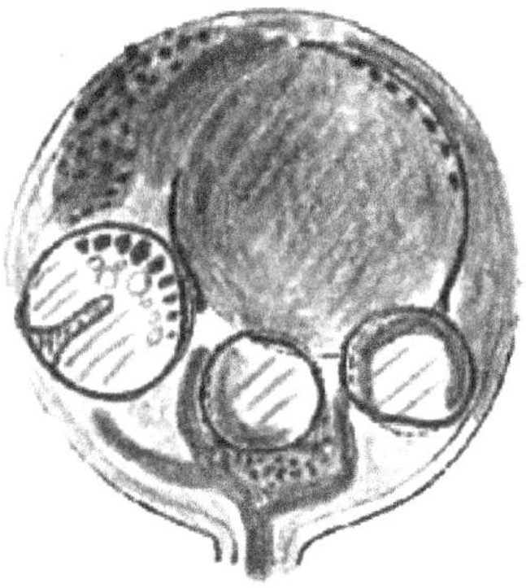

Micro- and macro- follicles with remarkable degenerative changes:

a) considerable congestion, edematous swelling, more or less remarkable hemorrhages and diffuse lymphocytes-infiltration of interstitial tissues and b) remarkable degenerative changes of epithelial cells (flattening, pycnosis, desquamation and desolation of epithelial cells) with slight proliferative tendency (papillar arrangements of epithelial cells).

At some portions exist multiple caseous structureless, miliary places, due to glanders-infection with severe exsudative perifocal changes.

In the focal parts, totally caseous and structureless and in perifocal parts, remarkable hemorrhages and considerable increase of phagoepithelial cells (erythrocytes- and decayed masses- phagocytosis).

In the neighbouring tissues, slight hyperplasia of follicular epithelial cells to form new follicles. [redacted]

[redacted] 297

([redacted] (

(B) SUMMARY.

I) The birdeye-views of pathological changes in all cases.

[redacted]

I6.	Statical state.	
50.	Slight activated state, degenerative form.	Slight congestion and edema Slight degeneration
85.	Slight activated state. degenerative form.	Slight degeneration
I67.	Struma colloides proliferativa.	
I76.	Slight activated state. regenerative form.	Slight congestion Slight hyperplasia of epithelial cells.
I78.	Follicular collapse.	
I80.	Chronic Thyreoiditis.	Considerable congestion Some round cell-accumulation Some hemorrhages. Some degeneration of epithelial cells.
I90.	Statical state.	
I93.	Follicular collapse.	
207.	Follicular collapse.	
22I.	Subacute disfiguring of Graves's thyroid.	Hyperfunctional findings, as Graves's disease. Disfiguring-findings, due to Glanders-infection.
224.	Slight activated state. degenerative form.	Slight congestion, edema. Slight degeneration of epithelial cells.

[redacted] 298

([redacted] (

256.	Statical state.	
727.	Subacute disfiguring. [redacted]	Slight congestion. Hyaline degeneration of interstitial tissues. Considerable degeneration.
73I.	Subacute Thyreoiditis with multiple glanders-knots.	

[redacted]

[redacted] 299

([redacted] (

Therefore, the frequency of pathological changes:

I)	Statical state.	3	cases.
	Struma colloides proliferativa.	I	case.
2)	Slight activated state.		
	in regenerative form.	I	case.
	in degenerative form.	3	cases.
3)	Follicular collapse.	3	cases.
4)	State of acute disfiguring.	0	case.
	State of subacute disfiguring.	2	cases.
5)	Slight thyreoiditis.	I	case.
	Subacute Thyreoiditis.		
	with multiple glanders-knots.	I	case.
6)	All microscopically investigated	I5	cases.

Because of chronic processes of glanders-disease, sometimes thyreoids are not so activated or sometimes slightly activated. Instead of acute severe disfiguring, occured sometimes subacute or rather chronic disfiguring, which advanced occaisionally furthermore to chronic inflammation of thyroids and one of them had multiple glanders-knots, as a rare occurance.
In multiple abscesses played follicular epithelial cells as so-called "phago-epithelium" the main role, so as mentioned in the section of microscopical investigations.

[redacted] [redacted] 300

([redacted] (

2) The developing mechanism of pathological, changes due to glanders-infection are as following:

[redacted]

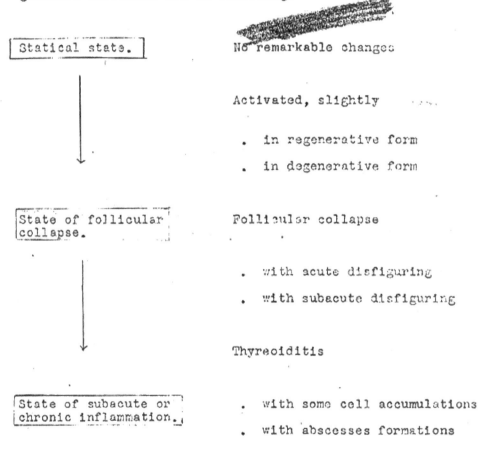

Statical state.	No remarkable changes
↓	Activated, slightly
	. in regenerative form
	. in degenerative form
State of follicular collapse.	Follicular collapse
	. with acute disfiguring
	. with subacute disfiguring
↓	Thyreoiditis
State of subacute or chronic inflammation.	. with some cell accumulations
	. with abscesses formations

x) cf. Chapter of "Thyreoids of Anthra-disease".

[redacted]

[redacted] 301

([redacted]

CO[redacted]L

THYROID

			16	50	85	167	176	178	180	190	193	207	221	224	229	256	727	731
Parenchyma	Follicles	Large Follicles	+	+	+	++	++	+	—	+	+	+	+	++	+	+	+	++
		Small Follicles	÷	+	+	+	+	+	++	++	+	+	++	÷	÷	++	++	++
		Cysts	—	—	—	—	—	—	—	—	—	—	—	—	—	÷	—	+++
		Microfollicles	—	+	÷	(+)	÷	÷	++	+	—	÷	++	—	—	÷	+	+
		Ruin	÷	—	++	—	—	++	++	÷	++	++	(++)	—	÷	÷	+	+++
	Epithelium	flat	++	+	+	+	+	++	++	+	++	+	++	++	+	+	+	+
		cuboidal	+	+	÷	+	+	÷	÷	+	÷	+	++	÷	+	(+)	+	++
		Cylindrical	÷	÷	(+)	(++)	(+)	—	÷	÷	—	÷	÷	—	÷	(+)	+	(+++)
		Papilla Formation	—	+	+	+	+	÷	—	+	—	÷	(+)	(+)	÷	+	+	++
		Pillow Formation	—	++	÷	(++)	(+)	÷	—	÷	—	÷	(+)	(++)	(+)	(+)	+	++
		Solid Cell Groups	—	+	(+)	|	+	|	++	|	—	+	(+)	÷	|	+	++	++
		Trabecular Arrangement	—	—	—	—	—	—	÷	—	—	—	÷	—	—	—	—	(+)
		Sack Formation	+	+	+	÷	÷	÷	÷	++	÷	÷	(+)	—	—	+	+	+
		Desquamation	—	—	—	—	—	—	—	—	—	—	—	—	—	—	—	—
	Changes of Nuclei	Pyknosis etc.	+	+	++	(+)	÷	+	++	÷	++	+	(++)	++	+	+	+	++
		Increase of Chromatin	÷	+	+	(++)	+	÷	÷	+	÷	+	+	|	+	+	+	+
		Karyolysis & -rrhexis	+	÷	+	+	÷	÷	++	÷	÷	++	(++)	÷	+	+	+	++
	Colloid	Quantity	++	—	÷	++	+	++	÷	+	+	++	+	++	++	÷	+	+
		Vacuoles	+	÷	—	÷	(÷)	+	÷	—	÷	÷	+	÷	÷	+	+	÷
		Fluidification	÷	÷	—	—	—	÷	÷	—	÷	+	÷	—	—	|	÷	÷
Stroma		Edema	+	÷	+	+	÷	++	++	÷	++	++	++	÷	+	—	++	++
		Hyaline Degeneration	—	÷	÷	—	÷	—	÷	—	÷	÷	—	÷	÷	÷	—	(+)
		Fibrosis	—	÷	÷	÷	—	—	+	÷	(+)	÷	+	—	÷	+	÷	++
		Colloid in Lymph-vessels	(++)	(÷)	+	(+)	(++)	+++	++	(÷)	++	++	(+)	+	÷	(+)	+	(++)
		Hemorrhage	÷	÷	÷	(÷)	÷	÷	++	—	(+)	+	÷	—	÷	—	+	(+++)
		Round Cell Infiltration	—	++	÷	—	—	|	+	÷	++	|	—	|	(+)	+	+	+
	Blood Vessels: Contents	Congestion	++	+	÷	++	+	÷	++	÷	+	+	+	+	+	+	+	+
		Lymphocytes	÷	÷	÷	÷	÷	÷	+	÷	+	÷	÷	÷	÷	÷	÷	÷
		Leucocytes	+	÷	÷	÷	÷	÷	÷	—	—	÷	÷	—	—	—	++	÷
		Fibrin	—	—	—	—	—	—	+	—	—	—	—	—	—	—	÷	(+)
	Blood Vessels	Increase of Endothelium	(÷)	÷	+	+	÷	÷	÷	—	+	÷	++	—	+	÷	÷	÷
		Degeneration of Endothelium	++	÷	++	÷	÷	+	++	÷	++	+	÷	++	+	÷	+	+
		Swelling of Walls	(+)	÷	÷	+	÷	÷	+	÷	++	÷	++	÷	+	÷	+	+++
	Lymphoid Focus	Lymphocytes	|	|	|	|	|	|	|	|	|	|	|	|	|	+	|	|
		Plasma Cells	|	|	|	|	|	|	|	|	|	|	|	|	|	—	|	|
		Germinating Center	|	|	|	|	|	|	|	|	|	|	|	|	|	—	|	|

[redacted]

[redacted] 302

[redacted]

R-256 Atrophy of lobulus.
x40

[redacted]

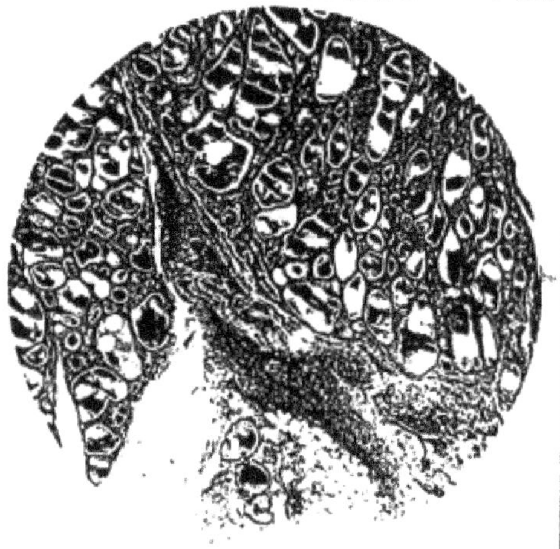

R-180 Intense atrophy of lobulus.
x60

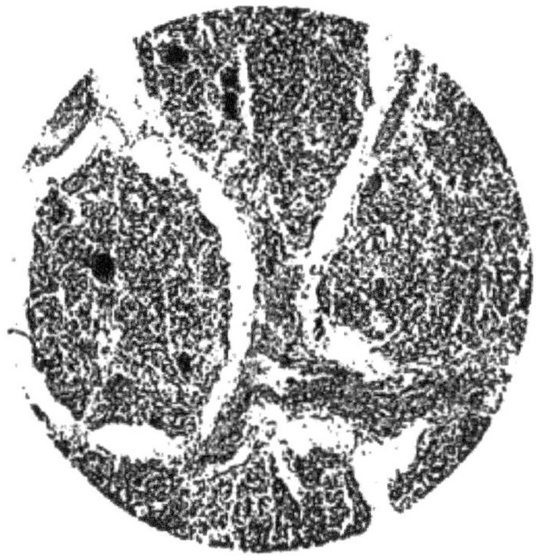

[redacted]

[redacted] 303

([redacted] (

R224 Intense atrophy or ruins of follicles.

x 21.8

[redacted]

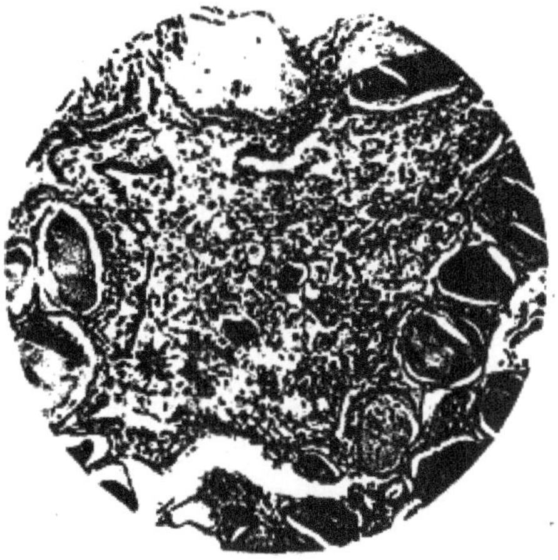

R-85 Activation of follicular epitheliums, as so-called phago-epitheliums.

X140

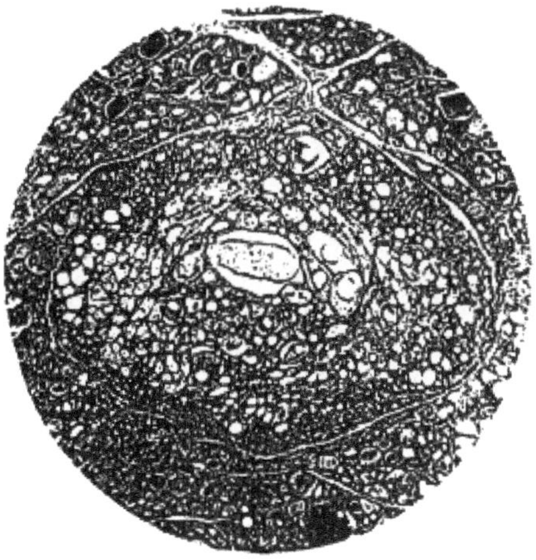

[redacted]

[redacted] 304

([redacted] (

R-178 Follicular collapse, with intense edema and some colloidal masses in ~~lymphsinuspid~~. lymphsinusoid.

x90

[redacted]

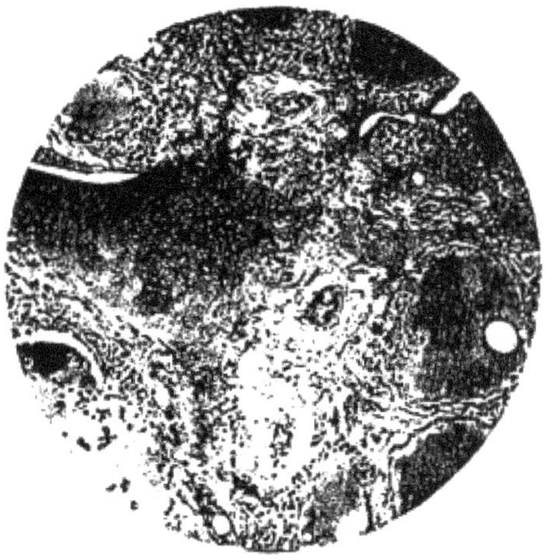

R-190 Follicular collapse , with desquamation of follicular epitheliums.

x130

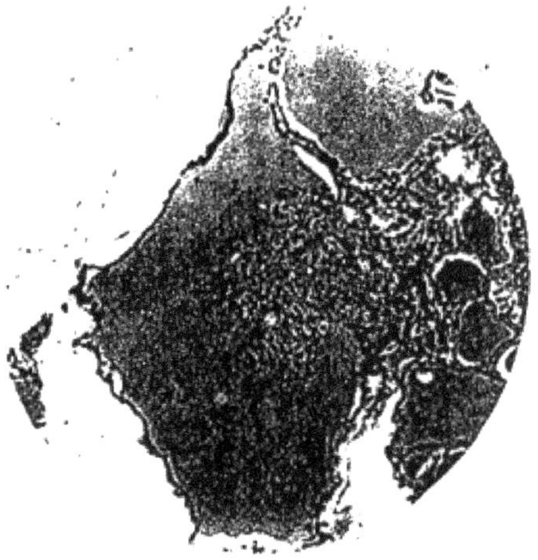

[redacted] [redacted] 305

[redacted]

R-167 Active follicles.
x80

[redacted]

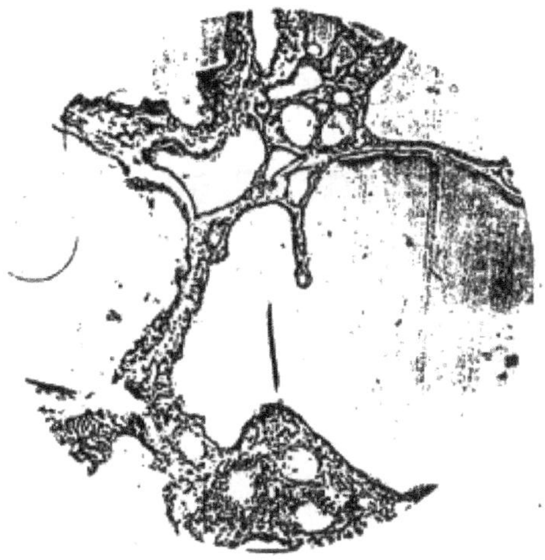

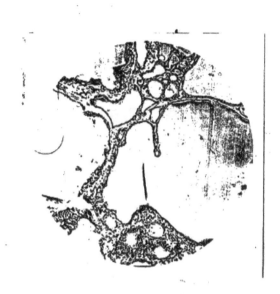

R-176 Active follicles: with some pillow-like hyperplasia of follicular epitheliums to form micro-follicles.

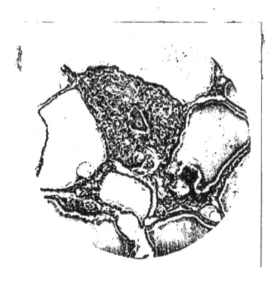

x120

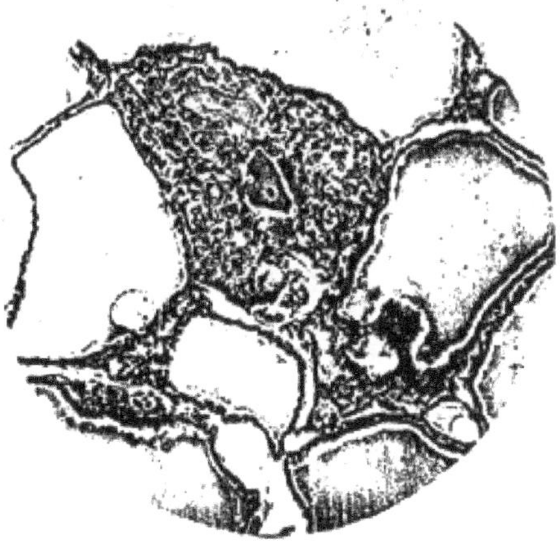

[redacted]

[redacted] 306

([redacted] (

R-731 Thyreoiditis acuta, with multiple glanders-knots.

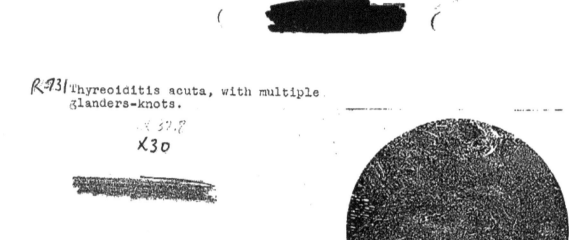

37.8

X30

[redacted]

[redacted]

[redacted] 307

[redacted]

[redacted]

Testis

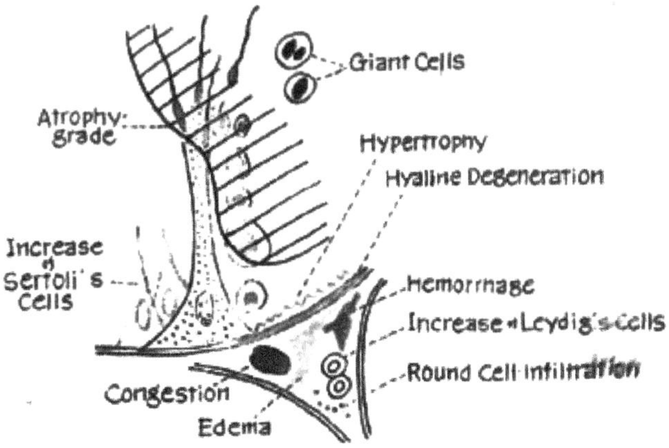

[redacted]

[redacted]

[redacted]

TESTICLE

A) Microscopical Investigation

a) Parenchyma

[redacted]

	Reduction of Tubulus	Atrophia testis	Hypertrophia or Hyaline degeneration of T.propria	Formation of Giant cells	Hyperplasia of Sertoli's cells
146	I.	I.	−	+	N
152	~I.	II.	−	÷	N
167	II.	III.	∸	∸	÷
176	I.	III.	÷	−	÷

b) Stroma

	Congestion	Hemorrhages	Round cell infiltration	Swelling or Roughness	Increase of Leydig's cells
146	∸	−	−	+	N
152	−	−	−	−	÷
167	∸	+	÷	+	÷
176	∸	−	÷	++	N

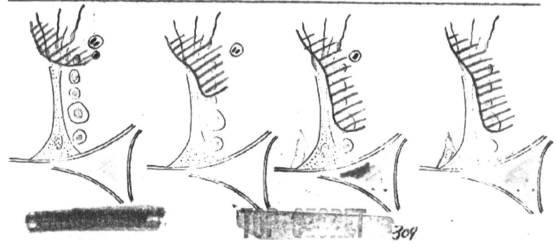

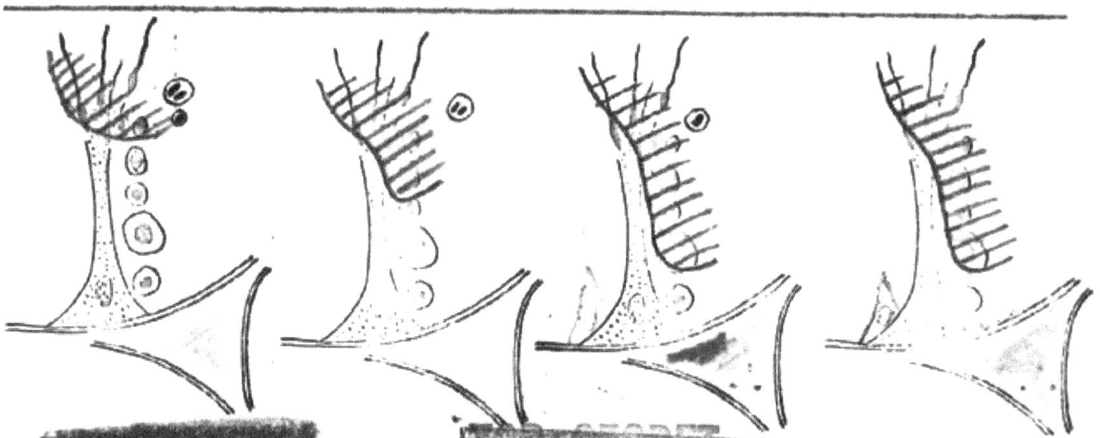

[redacted] TOP SECRET 309

[redacted]

a) Parenchyma.

	Reduction of Tubulus	Atrophia testis	[redacted]		
			Hypertrophia or Hyaline degeneration of T.propria.	Formation of Giant cells	Hyperplasia of Sertoli's cells
190	I.	II.	÷	÷	÷
193	II.	III.	+	—	÷
205	II.	III.	+	—	+
207	~I.	III.	+	÷	÷

b) Stroma.

	Congestion	Hemorrhages	Round cell infiltration	Swelling or Roughness	Increase of Leydig's cells.
190	÷	—	—	—	N
193	÷	—	÷	+	÷
205	÷	÷	÷	÷	+
207	÷	—	÷	÷	÷

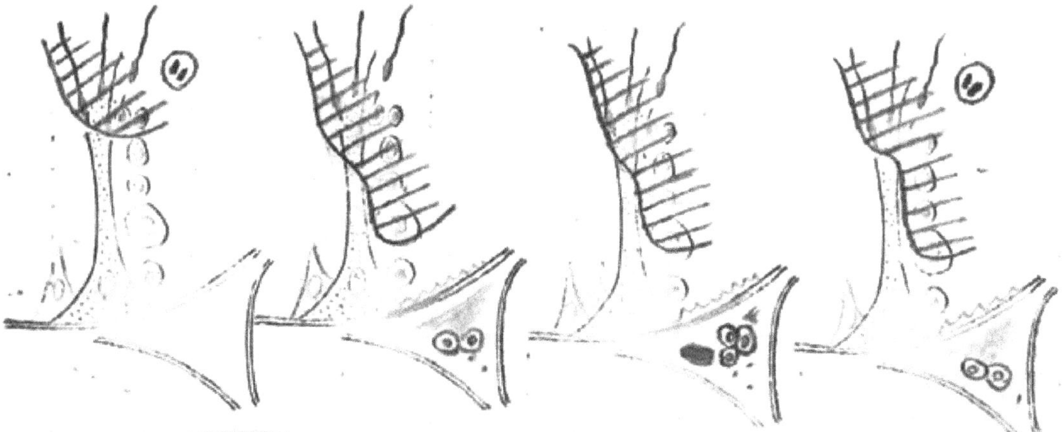

[redacted] [redacted] 310

[redacted]

a) Parenchyma

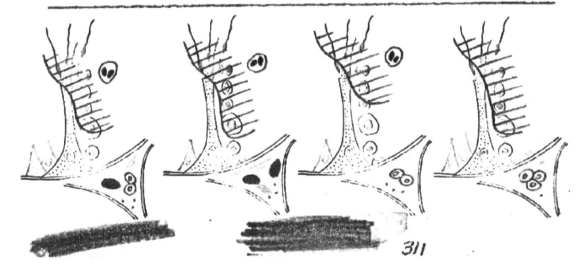

	Reduction of Tubulus	Atrophia testis	[redacted]		
			Hypertrophia or Hyaline degeneration of T.propria	Formation of Giant cells	Hyperplasia of Sertoli's cells
221	I.	III	÷	÷	+
222	I.	III.	÷	÷	÷
224	I.	II.	÷	÷	÷
229	II.	III	+	−	+

b) Stroma

	Congestion	Hemorrhages	Round cell infiltration	Swelling or Roughness	Increase of Leydig's cell s.
221	+	−	÷	÷	÷
222	++	−	÷	+	N
224	∸	−	÷	∸	÷
229	∸	−	∸	∸	+

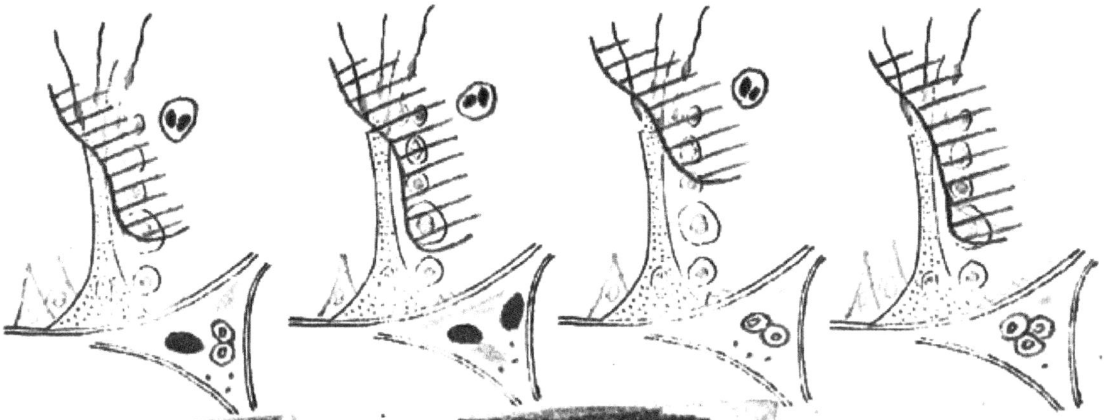

[redacted] [redacted] 311

[redacted]

a) Parenchyma

	Reduction of tubulus	Atrophia testis	[redacted]		
			Hpertrophia or Hyaline degeneration of T.propria	Formation of Giant cells	Hyperplasia of Sertoli's cells
254	II.	III.	+	−	++
256	−.	II.	−	÷	N
727	~I.	II.	÷	∸	+
731	I.	II.	÷	∸	N

b) Stroma.

	Congestion	Hemorrhages	Round cell infiltration	Swelling or Roughness	Increase of Leydig's cells
254	∸	∸	÷	∸	N
256	÷	−	∸	∸	÷
727	+	−	÷	−	+
731	+	÷	+	∸	÷

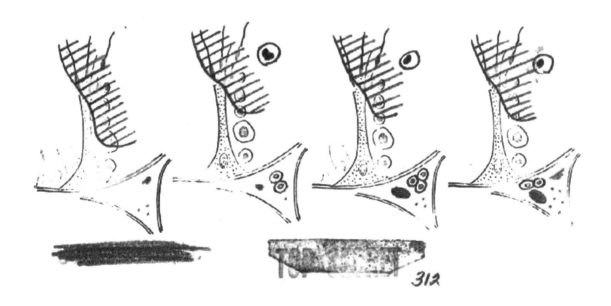

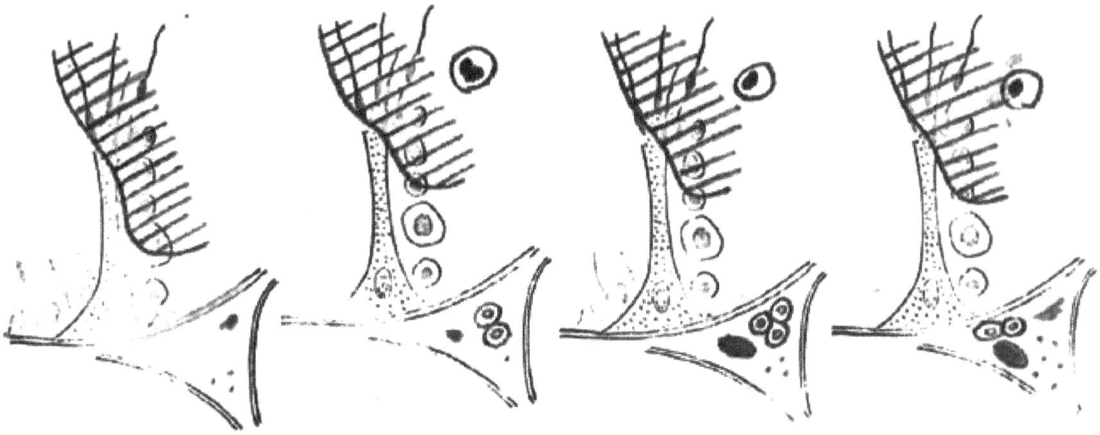

[redacted] [redacted] 312

([redacted] (

(B) S U M M A R Y

(1)

Our classification of "disturbance of spermatopoietic process".

a) On the "Atrophia testis". [redacted]

Atrophia testis 1. Pyknotic spermatozoa.
Relative increase of prespermstids and spermatids.

Atrophia testis 11. Degeneration of prespermatids and spermatids with somewhat considerable excoriation or sometimes giant cell-formation(as signs of degeneration).

Atrophia testis 111. Remarkable degeneration of prespermatids and spermatids.

Atrophia testis 1V. Remarkable degeneration or sometimes complete diminishment of spermatocytes.
Degeneration and sometimes irregular cell-arrangment of spermatogonien.

Atrophia testis V. Complete diminishment of spermatic cells.
Remarkable swelling and hyaline degeneration of T.propria of tubuli seminiferi.

b) On the reduction of tubuli semifliferi.

Reduction 1. Diameter of tubulus seminiferus is reduced to 3/4 of normal.(slight atrophia).

Reduction 11. Reduced to 1/2.(medium atrophia).

Reduction 111. Reduced to 1/4.(severe atrophia).

[redacted]

[redacted]

313

([redacted] (

(2)

Generally infection causes some disturbances of spermato-poietic process: [redacted]

Atrophia testis 1. 1 case.

" 11. 6 cases.

" 111. 9 cases.

Reduction of tubuli seminiferi

1. 10 cases.

" 11. 5 cases.

Sometimes accompanied with giant cell-formation of spermatids and prespermatids, as degenerative signs.

11 cases.

Generally infection causes some congestion.

Congestion. in slight degree. 3 cases,

Sometimes hemorrhages and edema in interstitial tissues.

Hemorrhages in slight degree. 3 cases.

Edema in slight degree.10 cases.

" in medium degree 5 cases.

Accompanied with sometimes some round cell-infiltration.

in slight degree. 12 cases.

in medium degree. 1 case.

Leydig's cells. Sometimes increase.

in slight degree. 8 cases.

in medium degree. 3 cases.

in mormal state. 5 cases.

[redacted]

[redacted] 314

([redacted] (

[redacted]

TESTIS

			146	152	167	176	190	193	205	207	221	222	224	229	254	256	727	731
Tubuli seminiferi	Grade of Reduction		+	÷	++	+	+	++	++	÷	+	+	+	++	++	−	÷	+
	T.propria	Thickening	−	−	∸	÷	∸	+	+	+	÷	÷	÷	+	+	−	÷	÷
		Fibrous Degeneration	÷	÷	÷	÷	∸	÷	∸	÷	÷	÷	÷	∸	−	−	−	−
		Hyaline Degeneration	−	−	∸	−	−	÷	÷	−	−	−	−	−	+	−	−	−
	Sertoli's Cells	Quantity	N	N	↑÷	↑÷	↑÷	↑÷	↑+	↑÷	↑+	↑÷	↑÷	↑+	↑++	N	↑÷	N
		Degeneration	−	∸	∸	−	−	−	−	−	−	−	−	−	−	−	−	−
	Spermarogonien	Quantity	N	N	N	N	N	N	N	N	N	N	N	N	N	N	N	N
		Degeneration	−	∸	−	−	−	∸	∸	∸	∸	−	−	−	−	−	−	−
	Spermatocyres	Quantity	N	N	N	N	N	↓+	↓+	N	↓÷	N	N	↓++	↓++	N	↓÷	N
		Degeneration	−	÷	+	+	∸	+	+	÷	÷	∸	∸	−	−	−	−	−
	Prespermatids	Quantity	N	↓÷	↓+	↓++	↓+	↓++	↓++	N	↓+	↓+	↓+	↓+++	↓+++	↓+	↓+	↓÷
		Degeneration	÷	+	++	++	++	++	++	+	+	+	++	+++	+++	+	++	++
	Spermatids	Quantity	N	↓÷	↓++	↓++	↓+	↓++	↓+++	N	↓+	↓++	↓+	↓+++	↓+++	↓+	↓+	↓÷
		Degeneration	÷	+	++	+++	++	++	+++	+	+	++	++	+++	+++	+	++	++
	Spermatozoa	Quantity	↓+	↓+	↓++	↓+++	↓+++	↓+++	↓+++	↓+	↓+	↓+++	↓+	↓+++	↓+++	↓++	↓+++	↓+
		Degeneration	+	+	++	+++	+++	+++	+++	+	++	+++	++	+++	+++	+++	+++	++
	Giant Cells		+	÷	∸	−	÷	−	−	÷	÷	÷	÷	−	−	÷	∸	∸
Stroma	Congestion		∸	−	∸	∸	∸	∸	÷	∸	+	++	∸	∸	∸	÷	+	+
	Edema		+	−	+	++	−	+	∸	÷	÷	+	∸	∸	∸	∸	−	∸
	Swelling of Connective Tissue		∸	−	÷	++	−	+	÷	÷	÷	+	∸	∸	∸	∸	−	÷
	Hemorrhage		−	−	+	−	−	−	∸	−	−	−	−	−	∸	−	−	÷
	Round Cell Infiltration		−	−	÷	÷	−	∸	÷	∸	÷	÷	÷	∸	÷	∸	÷	+
	Increase of Connective Tissue		−	−	−	−	∸	∸	÷	∸	∸	∸	∸	÷	÷	−	+	÷
	Vessel Walls	Degeneration of Endothelium	∸	÷	∸	−	−	÷	∸	÷	÷	∸	∸	−	−	−	∸	−
		Hyaline Degeneration	−	−	−	−	+	÷	÷	−	÷	÷	∸	−	−	+	−	÷
		Swelling	∸	∸	÷	÷	−	∸	−	÷	÷	∸	÷	∸	−	−	−	−
	Leydig's Cells	Quantity	N	↑÷	↑÷	N	N	↑÷	↑+	↑÷	↑÷	N	↑÷	↑+	N	↑÷	↑+	↑÷
		Yellow Granules	∸	+	+	∸	÷	∸	+	∸	÷	∸	∸	∸	∸	÷	+	÷
T. albuginea T. vasculosa	Congestion		+	−	|	|	∸	|	+	÷	÷	+	|	|	∸	÷	÷	+
	Hemorrhage		∸	−	|	|	−	|	÷	∸	−	+	|	|	−	∸	−	÷
	Round Cell Infiltration		∸	−	|	|	−	|	÷	+	∸	+	|	|	∸	∸	∸	+
	Degeneration of Vessel Endothelium		−	−	|	|	∸	|	−	+	∸	+	|	|	∸	−	∸	∸
	Increase of Connective Tissue		−	−	|	|	−	|	−	∸	−	÷	|	|	−	−	−	−
Grade of Atrophy			I	II	III	III	II	III	III	II	III	III	II	III	III	II	II	II

↓+++ = Disapperance

[redacted] [redacted] 315

([redacted] (

Hemorrhages in interstitial tissues.

[redacted]

R 167 X 210

Edematous swelling of interstitial
tissues and atrophy of testicular tissues.

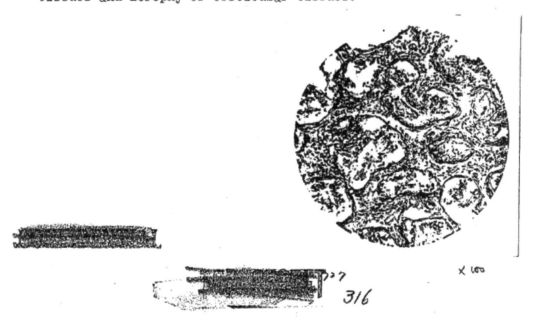

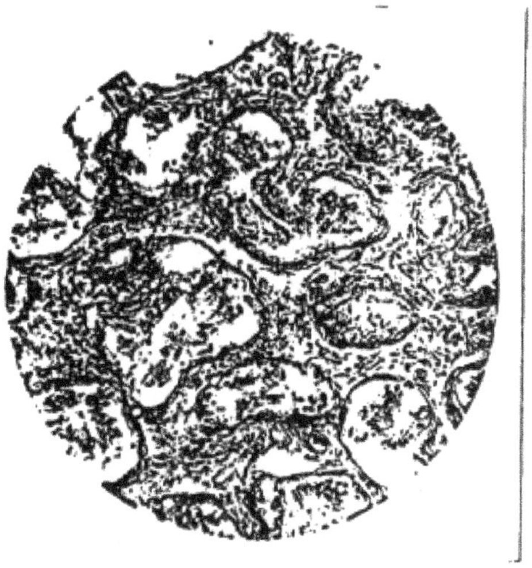

[redacted]

X 100

[redacted] 7

316

([redacted] (

Atrophia testis III.

[redacted]

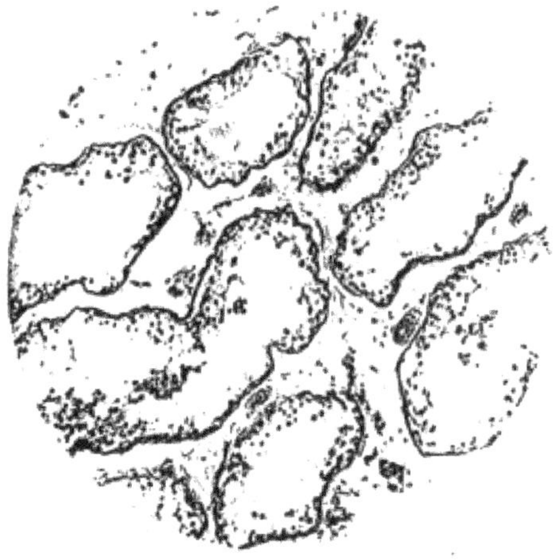

R176 X100

Atrophia testis III.

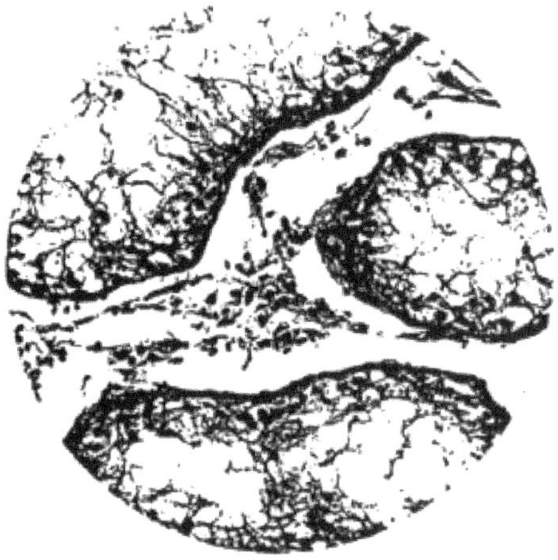

R205 X210

[redacted] [redacted] 317

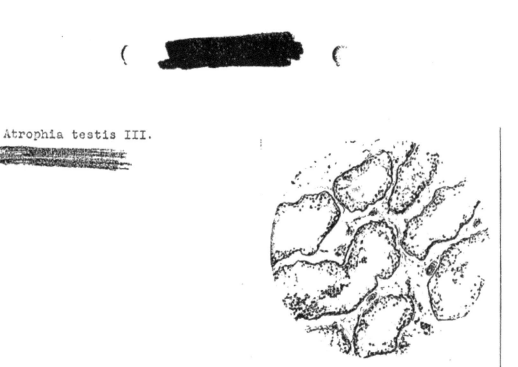

([redacted] (

[redacted]

Pituitary body

[redacted]

[redacted] 318

([redacted] (

P I T U I T A R Y - B O D Y.

(A) Microscop. Investigation.

I52. [redacted]

Moderate capillary congestion and edematous swelling of capillary -walls with slight swelling of pericapillar tissues. Slight hyperplasia, swelling and desquamation of endothelial cells.

Considerable degeneration of basophilic parenchymatous cells.

I67.

Slight capillary-congestion and middling severe perivascular edematous swelling. Slight hyperplasia of endothelial cells.

Moderate cloudy swelling and vacuolar degeneration of basophilic and other parenchymatous cells.

Slight edematous swelling of posterior lobe.

I80.

Moderate capillary congestion and slight perivascular edema.

Slight cloudy swelling of basophilic cells and slight edematous swelling of posterior lobe.

22I.

Capillary congestion with some leucocytes (esp. eosinophilic leucocytes) as capillary contents. Slight hyperplasia, swelling and desquamation of endothelial cells.

Slight parenchymatous degeneration and slight edematous swelling of posterior lobe.

[redacted]

[redacted] 319

([redacted] (

[redacted]

222.

Moderate capillary congestion, swelling of capillary-walls and edema of subendothelial layers. Slight degeneration of parenchymatous cells and dissociation of cell-arrangements.

Slight congestion and slight perivascular hemorrhages of posterior lobe.

224.

Moderate congestion of capillary and edema of subendothelial layers. Cloudy swelling of parenchymatous cells (esp.basophilic cells), and dissociation of cellular-arrangements with edematous swelling of basal membrane.

Slight hyperplasia and desquamation of capillary endothelial cells.

229.

Severe capillary congestion and swelling of capillary-walls. Dissociation of cellular-arrangements and considerable parenchymatous degeneration.

256.

Severe capillary congestion with some leucocytes as capillary contents. Slight hyperplasia and swelling of capillary endothelial cells.

Leakage of erythrocytes in lumina of acinus.

Almost intact parenchymatous cells.

Slight congestion and slight hemorrhages of posterior lobe.

727.

Moderate capillary congestion, edematous swelling of subendothelial layers and perivascular edema. Slight dissociation of cell-arrangements and degeneration of parenchymatous cells esp.at perivascular portions.

[redacted] [redacted] 320

([redacted] (

[redacted]

Swelling of basal membrane.

Slight hyperplasia of neuroglia-cells at posterior lobe.

731.

Moderate capillary congestion and edematous swelling of capillary-walls with slight hyperplasia of endothelial cells.

Dissociation of cell-arrangements and slight degeneration of parenchymatous cells, esp. vacuolar degeneration of basophilic cells. Edematous swelling of basal membrane.

[redacted]

[redacted] 321

([redacted] (

(B) S U M M A R Y

[redacted]

A). Anterior lobe.

I) Generally with some capillary congestion.

Congestion in slight degree. 2 cases.

" in medium degree. 6 cases.

" in severe degree. 2 cases.

Congestion with some leucocytes as capillary contents.

2 cases.

Congestion with some bacterial masses as capillary-contents.

0 cases.

Congestion, accompanied with perivascular hemorrhages.

0 cases.

2) After that, occured some signs of so-called serous inflammatoins, with considerable subendotheiliar edematous swelling.

Serous inflammation, accompanied with some dissociation of cellular arrangements. 4 cases.

Serous inflammation, accompanied with some degenerative changes of capillary endothelial cells (swelling, clouding and desquamation). 2 cases.

I classified these changes, according to the concept "Pituitaritis serosa".

Pituitaritis serosa I. degree. 2 cases.

II. degree. 4 cases.

III. degree. 1 cases.

[redacted] [redacted] 322

([redacted] (

[redacted]

3) Then it shows some degenerative changes of parenchymatous cells, esp. at perivascular portions.

Cloudy swelling in slight degree. 4 cases.

" in medium degree. 4 cases.

" in severe degree. 1 cases.

Cloudy swelling with considerable vacuolar degeneration. 2 cases.

B). Posterior lobe.

Sometimes, with considerable congestion and following changes.

Considerable congestion. 2 cases.

" ,with perivascular hemorrhages. 2 cases.

" ,with slight hyperplasia of neuroglia cells. 1 cases.

Accordingly, the significant main pathological changes are considerable Pituitaritis serosa (congestion,serous exudation and some parenchymatous degeneration).

[redacted]

[redacted] 323

([redacted] (

[redacted]

PITUITARY BODY

			152	167	180	221	222	224	229	256	727	731
Capsule		Congestion	|	|	+	+	+	∸	+	+	∸	+
		Edema	|	|	+	+	+	÷	+	+	+	+
		Hemorrhage	|	|	∸	∸	+	−	+	+	−	∸
		Infiltration of Round Cells	|	|	−	−	−	−	−	+	∸	+
Adenohypophysis		Congestion	+	+	+++	+	+++	++	+++	++++	++	++
		Edema	++	++	+	÷	+	++	+	+	+++	++
		Hemorrhage	−	−	+	−	−	−	−	−	−	−
		Infiltration of Round Cells	−	−	−	−	−	−	−	−	−	−
	Chromophobe C	Parenchymatous Degeneration	∸	∸	−	∸	÷	+	−	−	+	∸
		Atrophia	−	∸	−	−	−	−	−	−	∸	−
		Pyknosis	−	−	−	−	−	−	−	−	∸	∸
		Karyorrhexis	−	∸	∸	−	−	−	−	−	−	∸
		Karyolysis	−	−	−	∸	∸	+	−	−	∸	−
	Eosinophile C	Parenchymatous Degeneration	÷	+	∸	+	+	++	−	−	+	+
		Atrophia	−	−	−	−	−	−	−	−	+	+
		Pyknosis	∸	−	−	+	−	+	−	−	÷	+
		Karyorrhexis	−	−	−	−	−	+	−	−	−	−
		Karyolysis	−	÷	∸	−	+	+	−	−	−	−
	Basophile C	Parenchymatous Degeneration	++	+	+	÷	+	++	∸	∸	+	+
		Atrophia	−	−	−	−	−	−	−	−	∸	+
		Pyknosis	−	−	−	∸	−	+	∸	∸	−	−
		Karyorrhexis	−	−	−	−	−	−	−	−	−	−
		Karyolysis	+	+	+	∸	+	+	−	∸	÷	+
		Necrosis	−	−	−	−	−	−	−	−	−	−
Neurohypophysis		Congestion	++	+	++	+	+	÷	+	+	÷	∸
		Edema	+	++	−	++	+	+	∸	−	∸	∸
		Hemorrhage	−	−	−	−	+	−	−	+	−	+
		Infiltration of Round Cells	−	−	−	+	∸	−	−	∸	∸	÷
Pars intermedia		Hemorrhage	+	−	−	−	−	−	−	−	−	|
		Infiltration of Round Cells	−	−	−	−	−	−	−	−	−	|
		Color of Colloid	V.	R.	V.	R.	R.	R.	R.	R.	R.	|
		Vacuole in Colloid	−	+	+	+	+	+	+	+	+	|
		Desquamation of Cyst wall cells	+	−	÷	+	++	+	+	+	+	|

V. …… violet
R. …… red

[redacted] 324

[redacted]

Edematous swelling of subepitheliar layers and some degeneration of parenchymatous cells.

[redacted]

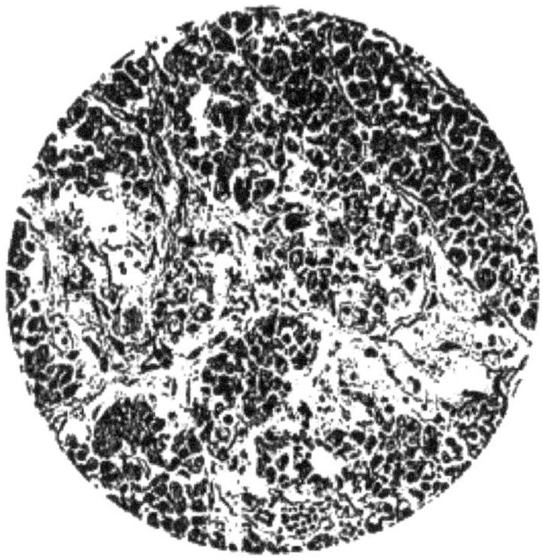

222　　　X 270

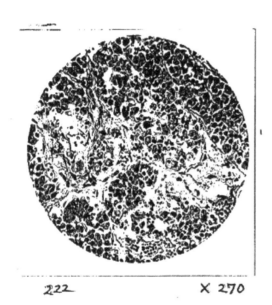

Congestion and slight hemorrhages, accompanied with some increased glia cells, in posterior lobe.

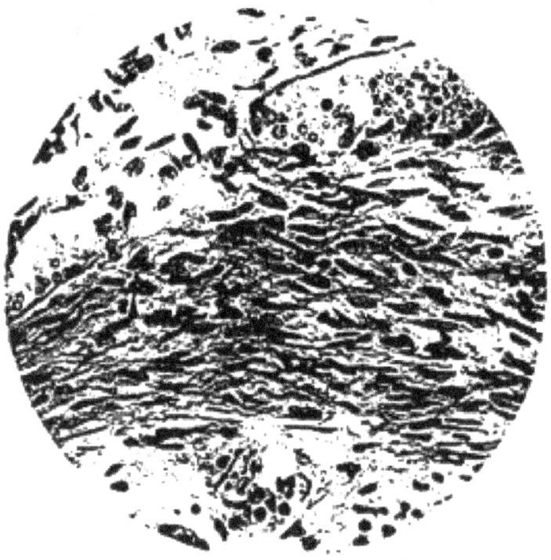

727　　　x 210

[redacted]

325

([redacted] (

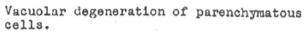

Vacuolar degeneration of parenchymatous cells.

[redacted]

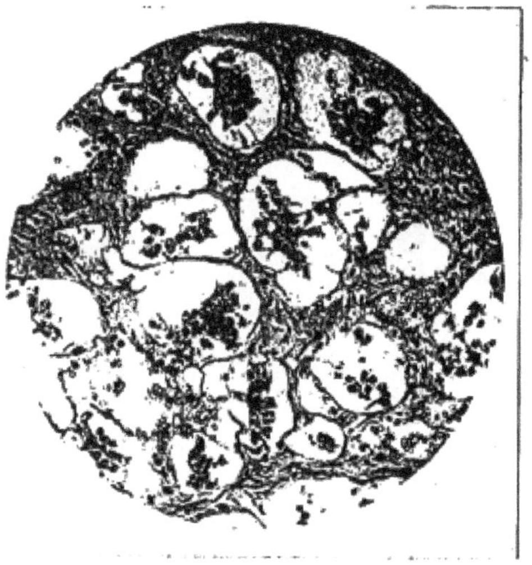

224 x220

Pycnotic changes of basophilic cells.

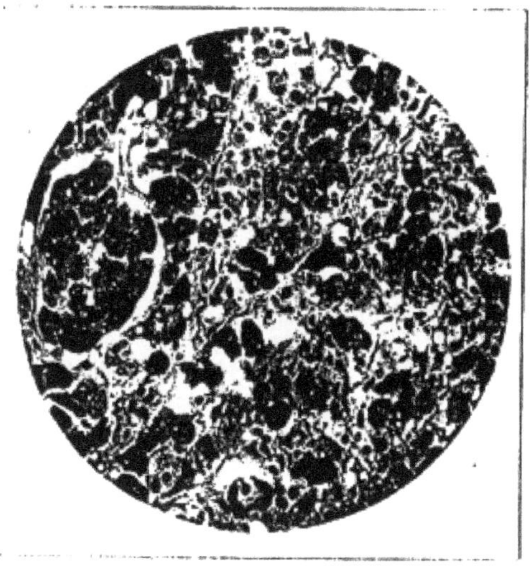

152 X270

[redacted]

326

[redacted]

Skin

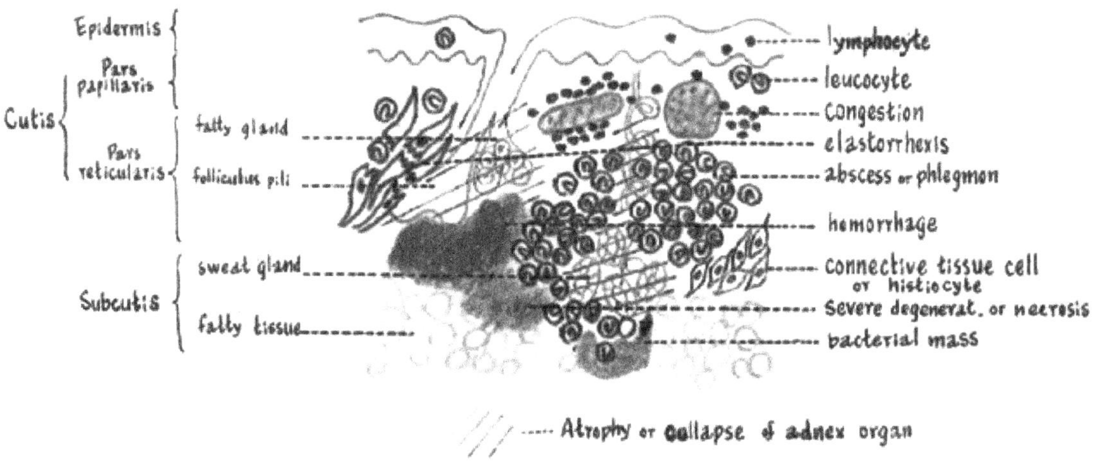

[redacted]

[redacted]

327

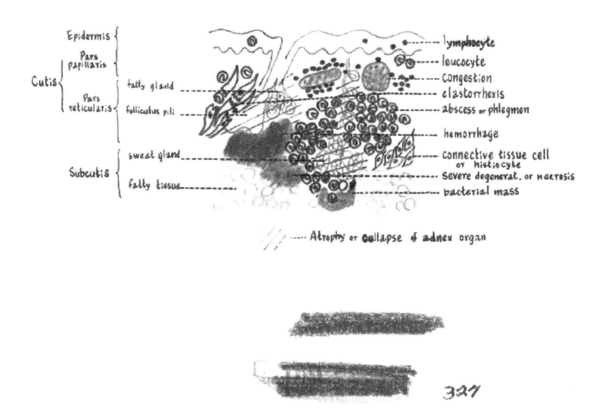

[redacted]

S K I N

(A) Microscopical Investigation.

152

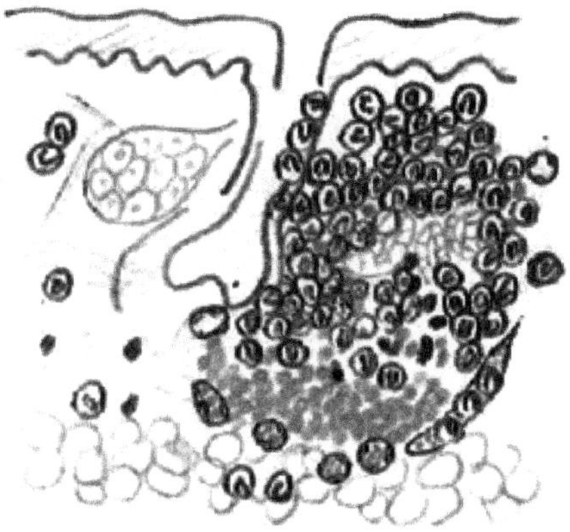

152. [redacted]

Multiple pea-large abscesses in Str. reticulare: with plenty leucocytes, some erythrocytes and their fragments, and some ruined masses of connective tissues and sweat gland cells, accompanied with severe perifocal hemorrhagic reactions.

In the neighbouring tissues, exist some congested blood-vessels, basophilic stained degenerative connective tissues and sweat glands in collapse.

Edema of epidermis, with pycnotic or karyolytic pickle cells.

167

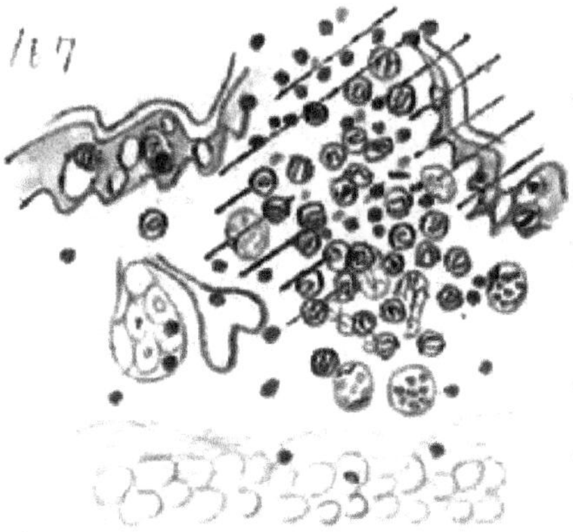

167.

Multiple pea-large abscesses in Str. subpapillare with plenty of leucocytes, some lymphocytes and erythrocytes, and their fragments, accompanie with degenerated or ruined adnex-organs.

Neighbouring tissues with some congested blood-vessels and lymph-vessels.

Considerable edema of adjacent epidermis and with somewhat pycnotic or karyolytic pickle cells.

180

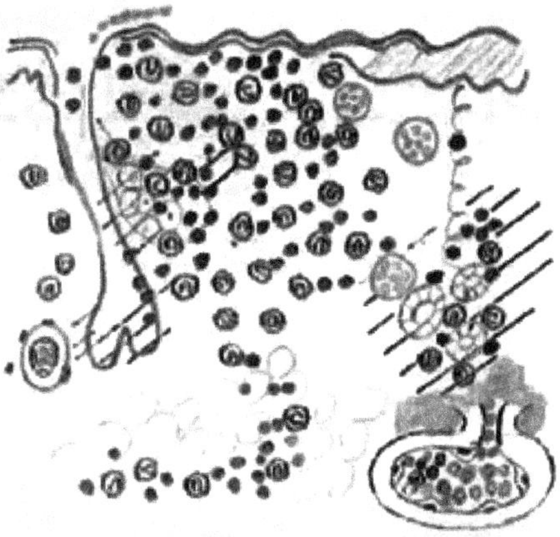

180.

Phl[redacted]r subcutaneous tissues:

[redacted]

328

[redacted]

18[redacted]

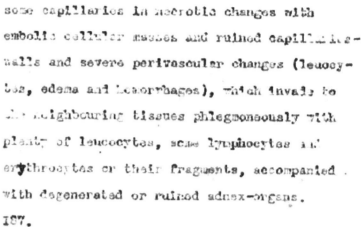

some capillaries in necrotic changes with emboli cellular masses and ruined capillaries-walls and severe perivascular changes (leucocytes, edema and haemorrhages), which invade to the neighbouring tissues phlegmoneously with plenty of leucocytes, some lymphocytes and erythrocytes or their fragments, accompanied with degenerated or ruined adnex-organs.

187.

Considerable capillary congestion in subcutaneous tissues with somewhat edema and slight perivascular lymphocytes-accumulation.

Sweat glands in slight collapse.

190

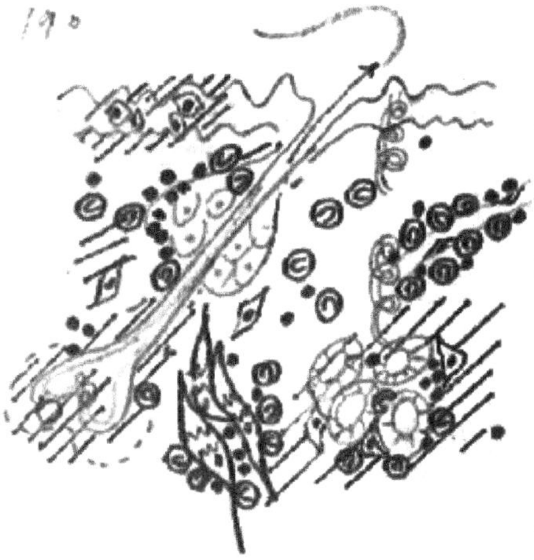

190.

Considerable capillary congestion and some perivascular leucocytes (and some lymphocytes) accumulation in subcutaneous tissues, esp. along folliculi pili, invading into the neighbouring adnex-organs to form some abscesses.

207

Accompanied with edematous swelling of connective tissues and Folliculi pili and some considerable degenerative changes of epidermis (edema and pickle cells in necrosis or karyolysis).

207.

Considerable congestion and some perivascular lymphocytes infiltration, broadly in subcutaneous

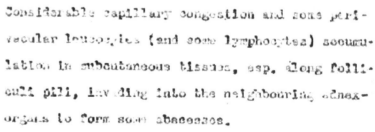

[redacted] [redacted] 329

[redacted]

[redacted]

221

222

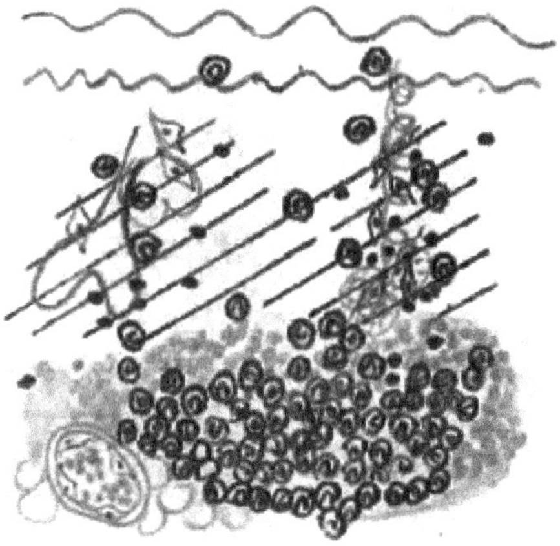

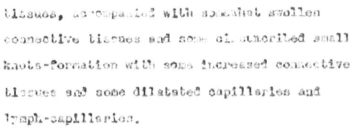

tissues, accompanied with somewhat swollen connective tissues and some circumscribed small knots-formation with some increased connective tissues and some dilatated capillaries and lymph-capillaries.

Edema of epidermis, with some pycnotic or karyolytic cells of Stratum Malpighi.

221.

Multiple remarkable perivascular leucocytes-emigration, necrotic ruing of capillaries walls and following diffuse hemorrhages (with some leucocytes) and severe edema in subcutaneous fatty tissues.

Slight [illegible] and some lymphocytes accumulation in subpapiller tissues along the blood-vessels and afferent ducts of sweat glands.

Atrophy of Folliculi pili.

222.

[illegible] intense leucocytic-hemorrhagic infiltration in subcutaneous fatty tissues:

Some blood-vessels in severe necrotic changes with plenty of leucocytes or their fragments, severe necrotic ruins of walls and the most [illegible] perivascular leucocytic-hemorrhagic [illegible] and [illegible].

These inflammatory [illegible] spread furthermore

[redacted]

[redacted] 330

[redacted]

[redacted]
727

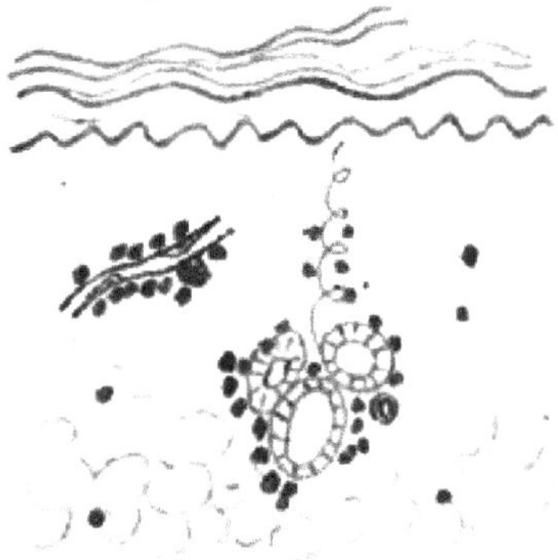

all over the neigh-bouring subcutaneous tissues or cutaneous and epidermal tissues, accompanied with severely degenerated or ruined adnex-organs.

727.

Hyperkeratosis.

Slight edema in cutis and epidermis, very slight lymphocytes infiltration along blood-vessels and sweat glands and no remarkable changes else.

[redacted] [redacted] 3 31

([redacted] (

[redacted] (B) S U M M A R Y

(I)

The bird's-eye view of all investigated cases.

152. Multiple pea-large abscesses in Str. reticulare.Severe perifocal hemorrhagic reactions with congestion, degenerative connective tissue fibres and ruin of sweat gland.

167. Mulitple pea-large abscesse in Str. subpapollare. Congestion of blood- and lymph-vessels and edema.

180. Phlegmons in cutaneous or subcutaneous tissues. Some capillaries in necrotic chagnes with embolic cellular masses and diffuse hemorrhagic infiltration.Ruin of adnex. organs.

187. Considerable capillary congestion and perivascular lymphocytes infiltration. Ruin of sweat glands.

190. Multiple supermiliary abscesses(which involve adnex organs in ruin). Congestion and perivascular leucoxytes accumulations.

207. Congestion and perivascular lymphocytes infiltration broadly in subcutaneous tissues. Some small circumscribed knot-formation with connective tissues cells, surrounded with dilated vessels and lymphocytes-accumulation.

221. Phlegmoneous leucocytes infiltration in cutaneous and subcutaneous tissues with hemorrhages amd severe edema. Ruin of adnex organs.

222. Diffuse intense leucocytic-hemorrhagic infiltration in subcutaneous fatty tissue. Some blood-vessels in severe necrotic changes. Ruin of adnex organs.

[redacted]Slight lymphocytes inf[redacted].Slight hyperkeratosis.

332

([redacted] (

[redacted] (2)

Plegmons or abscesses in 6 cases, Multiple miliary or super-miliary abscesses in 3 cases, with more or less perifocal reactive hemorrhages. Phlegmoneous infiltration extends broadly to subcutaneous fatty tissues in 3 cases.

In these foci, some blood vessels with severe necrotic walls and in many cases, much bacterial-cellular embolic masses in spaces of blood vessels. Much leucocytes-accumulation in center of focus and perivascular leucocytes and lymphocytes infiltration with severe congestion and hemorrhafes in perifocal tissues. Cutaneous tissues and adnex organs, especially folliculi pili and sweat glands fell into degeneration or in ruin in neighbouring parts of focus. Epidermis upon these foci fell also into degeneration, espácially in rete Malpighii.

Slighter degeneration are recognised in other 3 cases: considerable congestion and perivascular serous and round cell infiltration, and ruin of adnex organs. In 1 case of them is knot-formation in Str. subpapillare, -namely, accumulation of connective tissue cells, with perafocal dilated blood- and lymph-vessels and lymphocytes infiltration.

[redacted] [redacted] 333

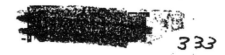

C [redacted] C

R-221 Hemorrhages in subcutaneous tissues.

x59

[redacted]

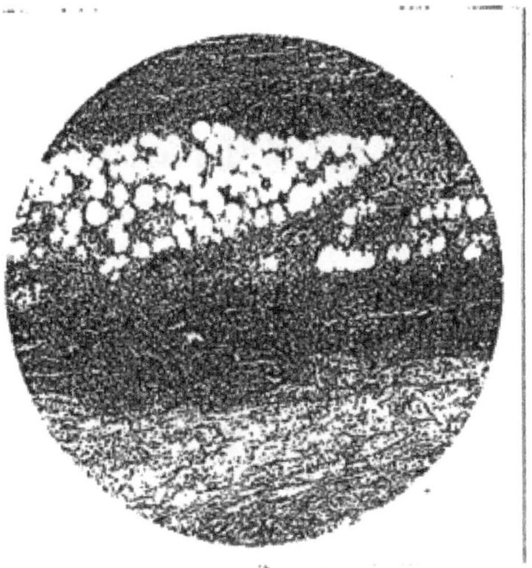

R-180 Perivascular hemorrhages.

x58

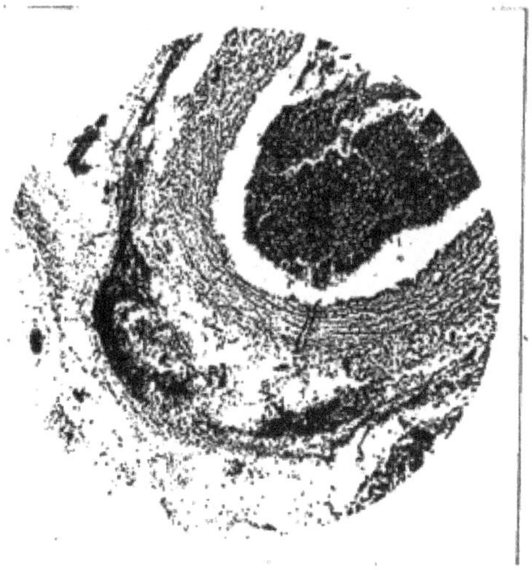

[redacted] [redacted]

334

[redacted]

R-222 Collapse of admex-organs.

x 43.8

[redacted]

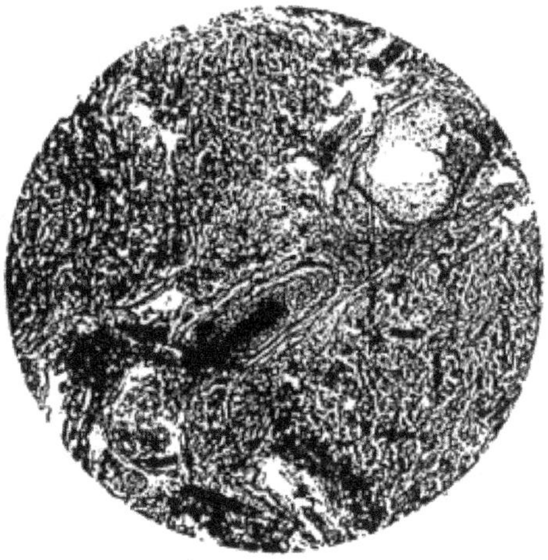

R-207 Accumulation of some histiocytes in Str.papillare.

X130

[redacted] [redacted] 335

([redacted] (

R-167 Abscess in cutis.

x19.5

[redacted]

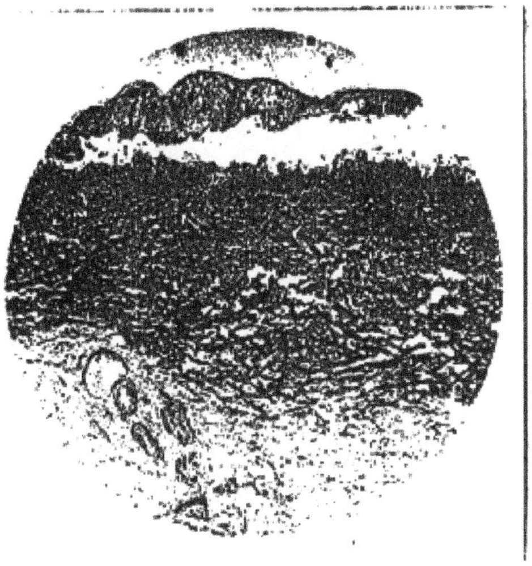

R-152 Absøccss in cutis, in high power.

x66

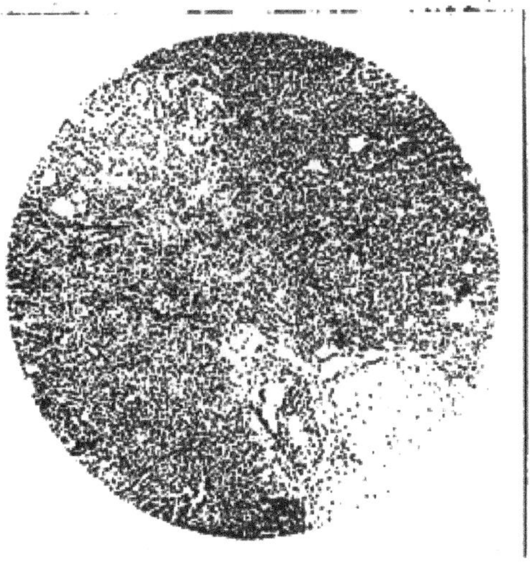

[redacted] [redacted] 336

● [redacted] ●

[redacted]

Lymphnode

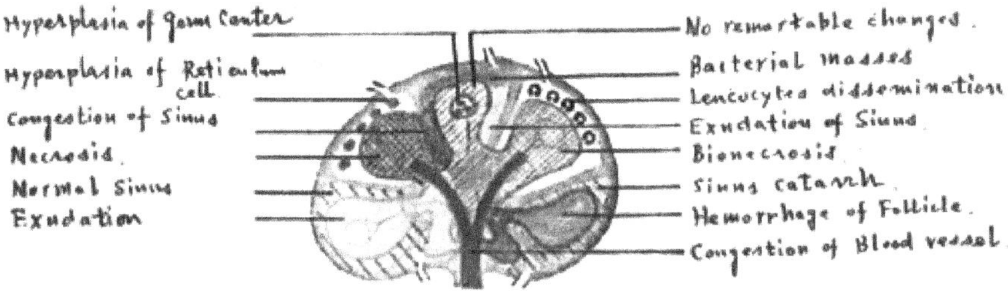

[redacted] [redacted] 337

([redacted] (

[redacted]

LYMPH-NODULUS.

(A) Microscop. Investigation.

I6. Mesenterial : No remarkable changes.

I6. Peribronchial : Considerable congestion in medullary sinuses and slight perivascular edema with very slight hyperplasia of reticulum-cells.

85. Peribronchial lymph-nodulus :
Lymphadenitis tuberculosa obsoleta, with caseous masses in focal parts and considerab/ele histiocytes-walls with some giant cells in perifocal parts.

85. Mesenterial :
Remarkable hyperplasia of reticulum-cells in medullar sinuses, without remarkable congestion.

IC7. Mesenterial.
Almost normal. Slight catarrh of peripheral sinuses and slight hyperplasia of reticulum-cells in medullary sinuses. No remarkable congestion and no considerable reduction of follicular tissues.

207. Peribronchial.
Fibrous capsule. No remarkable changes in peripheral sinus. Slight congestion and slight swelling of pulpa-meshes with some increased reticulum-cells. No considerable reduction of pulpameshes.

[redacted] [redacted] 338

([redacted] (

[redacted]

22I. Mesenterial.

Slight catarrh of peripheral sinuses with considerable congestion (with some leucocytes, especiaaly some eosinophilic cells in capillaries) in follicular tissues.

Considerable congestion and some slight hemorrhages in pericapsular tissues.

254. Mesenterial.

No remarkable changes in capsule and slight catarrh of peripheral sinuses. Multiple submiliary caseous changes in some germinative centres with slight hyperplasia of histiocytes in perifocal parts. In other yet remained follicular tissues, slight hyperplasia of reticulum-cells in pulpa-meshes and slight swelling and slight reduction of lymphocytes in pulpa-meshes.

256. Mesenterial.

No significant changes in capsules and peripheral sinuses. Considerable congestion and slight hyperplasia of reticulum-cells in medullary sinuses. Slight swelling of pericapillar tissues.

256. Peribronchial : Lymphadenitis caseosa.

Multiple supermiliary caseous changes in some germinative centres with considerable proliferative changes (slight hyperplasia of histiocytes). Considerable congestion of medullary sinuses with edematous swelling of capillary-walls and some localised hemorrhages.

Slight swelling and considorable diminution of lymphocytes in other yet remained follicular tissues.

[redacted] [redacted]

[redacted]

[16] mesenterial

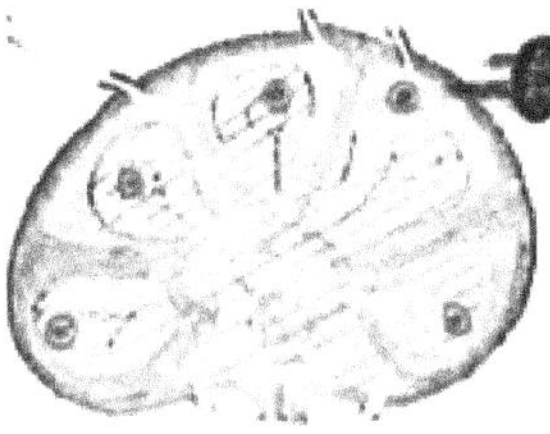

[redacted]

[85] mesenterial

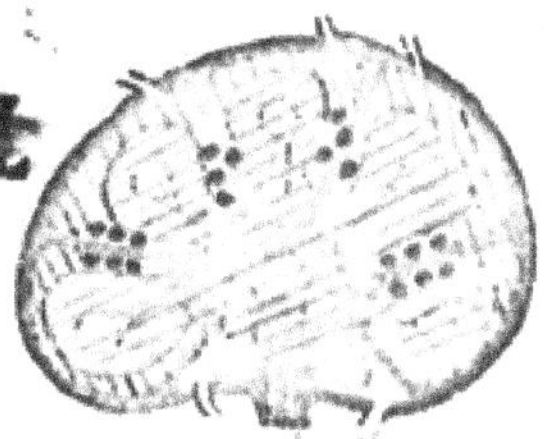

[16] peribronchial

[85] peribronchial

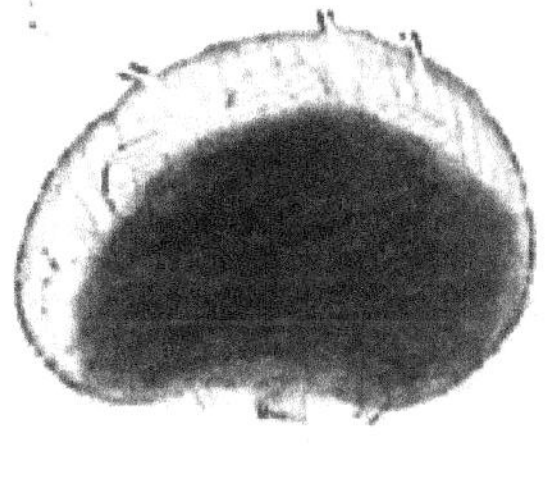

[redacted] [redacted] 340

[redacted]

[146]

[207]

[redacted]

[167]

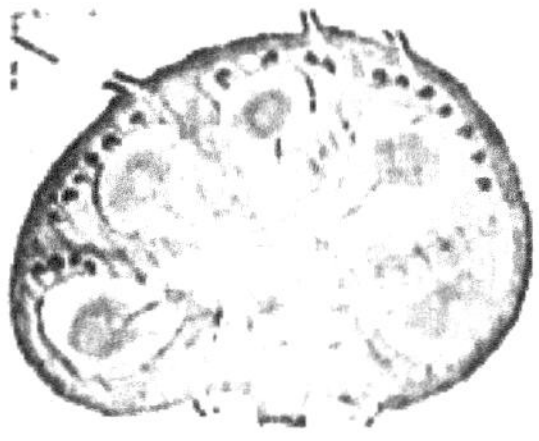

[221](a)

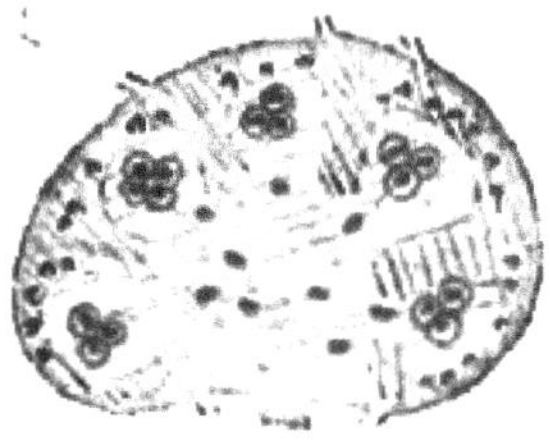

[redacted]

[redacted] 341

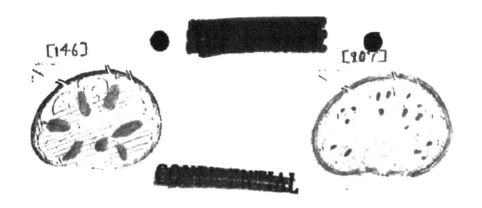

● [redacted] ●

[221] (b)

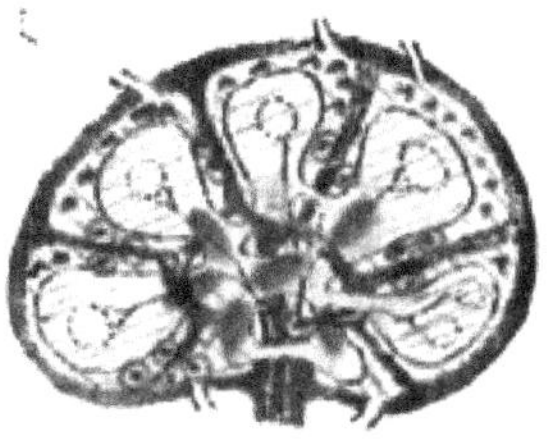

[256]

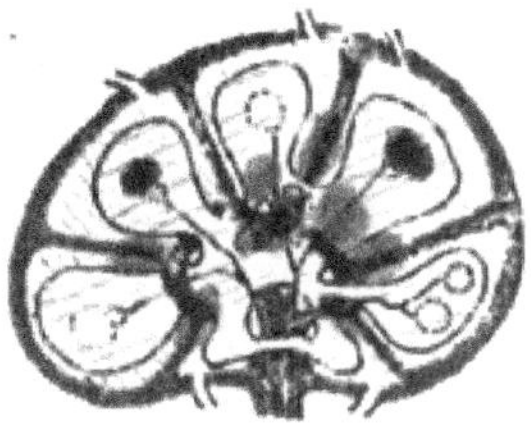

[redacted]

[256]

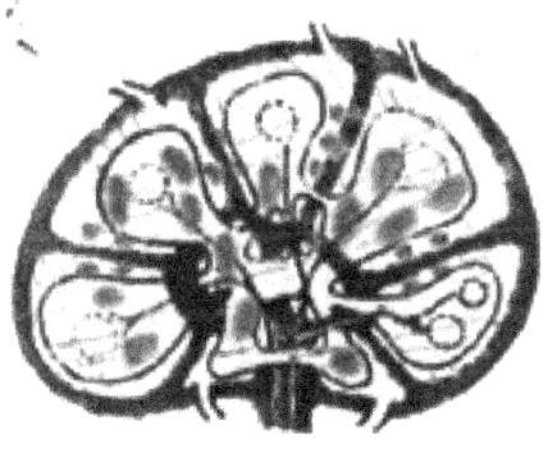

[256] op

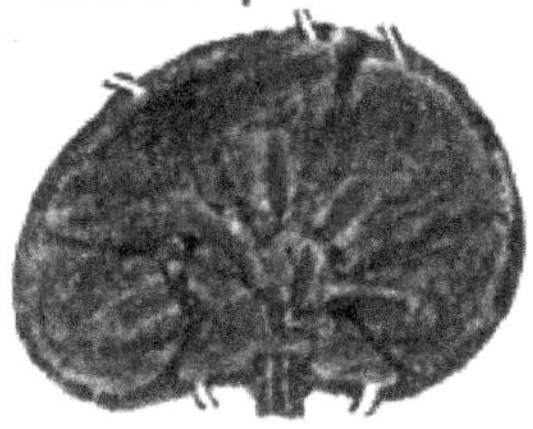

[redacted]　[redacted] 342

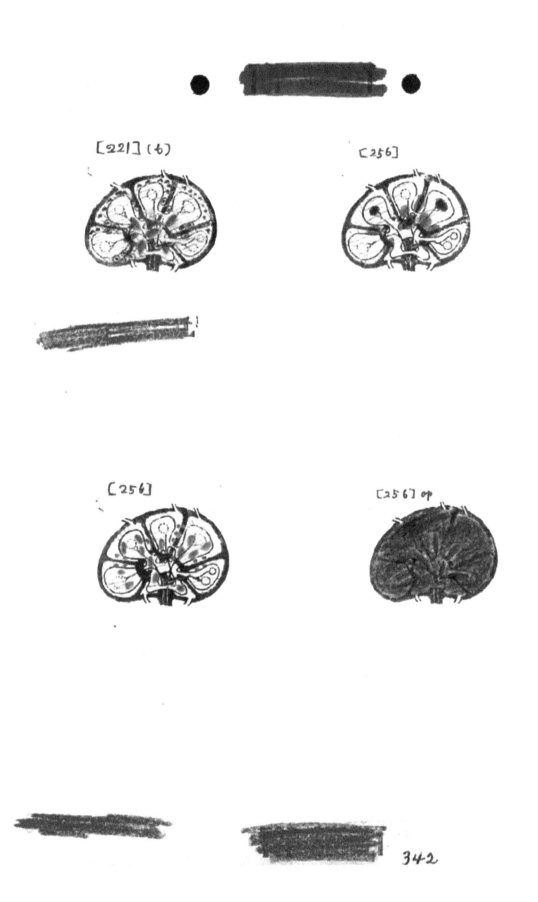

● [redacted] ●

[254] op

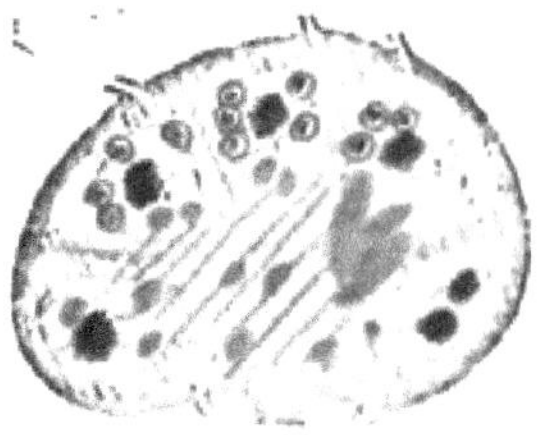

[redacted]

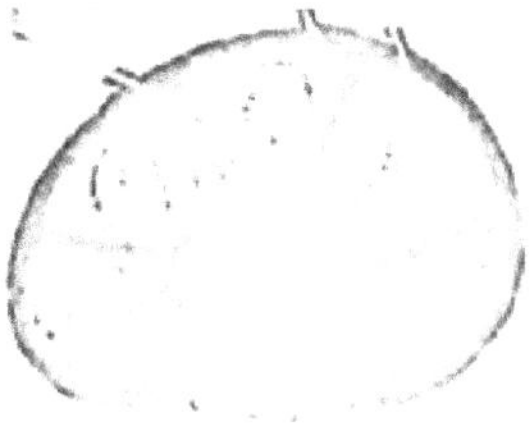

[redacted]

[redacted] 343

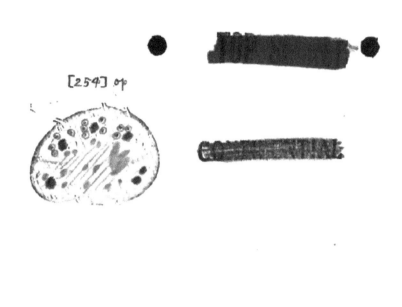

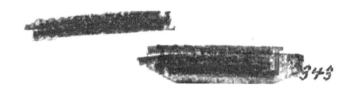

([redacted] (

[redacted]

The bird's-eye-view of the pathological changes in some microscopical slices, which I have recieved.

Other cases are nor accompanied with any signiticant changes macroscopically.

I6. Peribronchial.	Medullary congestion.
	Slight pericapsular edema.
I6. Mesenterial.	No remarkable changes.
85. Peribronchial.	Lymphadenitis tuberculosa obsoleta.
85. Mesenterial.	Slight catarrh, remarkable medullary congestion.
I67. Mesenterial.	Slight catarrh of sinus.
207. Peribronchial.	No remarkable changes.
22I. Mesenterial.	Slight catarrh of sinus.
	Considerable congestion with some leucocytes (esp. eosinophilic cells) as capillary contents.
	Considerable congestion and some slight hemorrhages in pericapsular tissues.
254. Mesenterial.	Slight catarrh of sinus.
	Multiple submiliary caseous changes in germinative centres, due to glanders-infection?
256. Peribronchial.	Lymphadenitis caseosa.
256. Mesenterial.	Considerable medullary congestion.

[redacted] Considerable congestion and some leucocytes:

[redacted] 344

([redacted] (

[redacted]

as signs of initial stage of acute inflammation.

In 2 cases, with some caseous changes in germinative centres :

perhaps due to glanders-infection. (※)

In some other cases, with slight reactive catarrh of sinus :

as not so significant changes.

※). It can't be determined exactly, whatever due to glanders- or tuberculosis-infection.

[redacted]

[redacted] 345

([redacted] (

[redacted]

Follicular congestion, accompanied with some hyperplasia of reticulum cells and histiocytic cells.

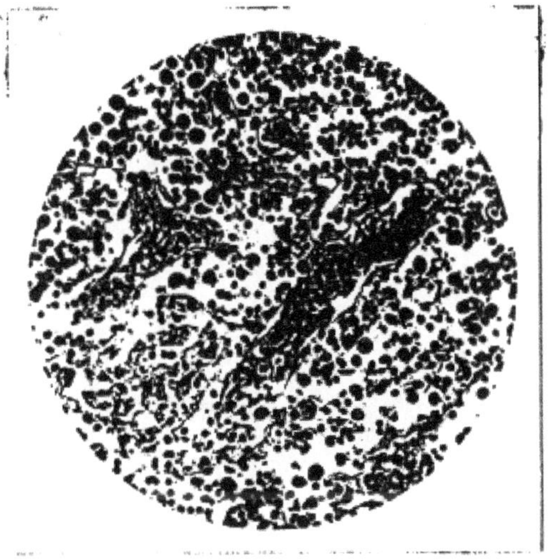

R 207　　　x 270

The same changes, in high power.

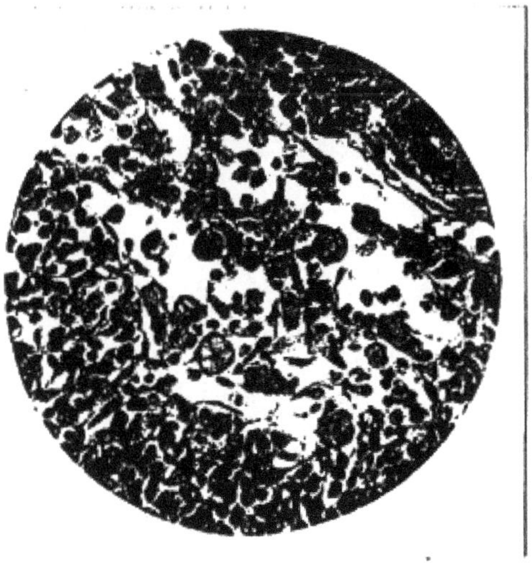

[redacted]　　[redacted] 346　　x310

[redacted]

[redacted]

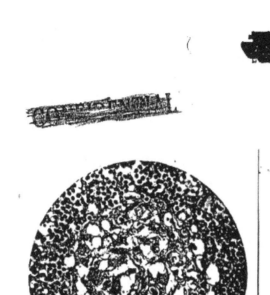

Edematous swelling of reticulum cells and reticulum faser in follicle.

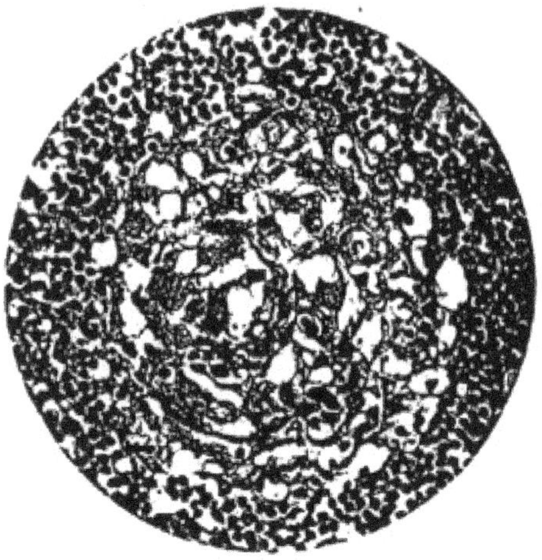

R 167 x310

Hyalinisation of follicular tissues, accompanied with slight hemorrhages.

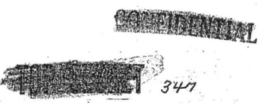

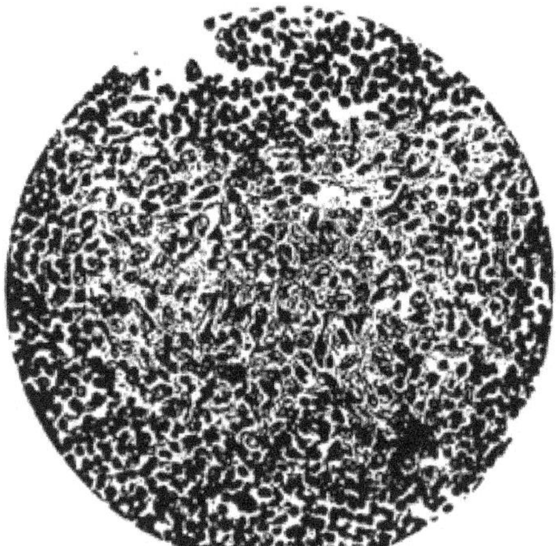

CONFIDENTIAL

[redacted] 347

x 280

([redacted] (

[redacted]

Serous fluids(edematous swelling)
and edematous swelling of reticulum
faser.

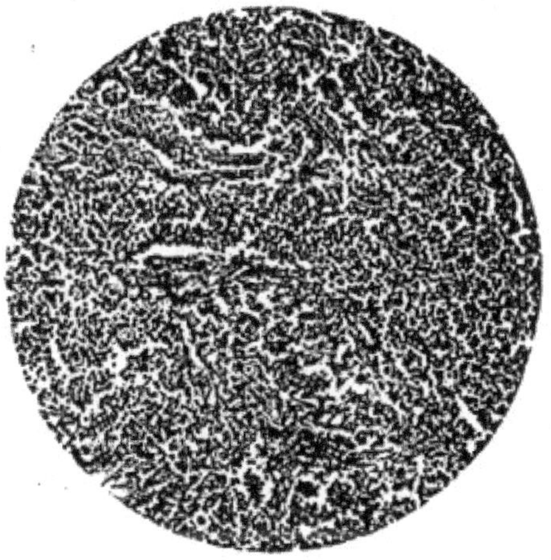

R 207 x150

Germinative centre in reticular form,
accompanied with hyperplasia of
reticulum cells.

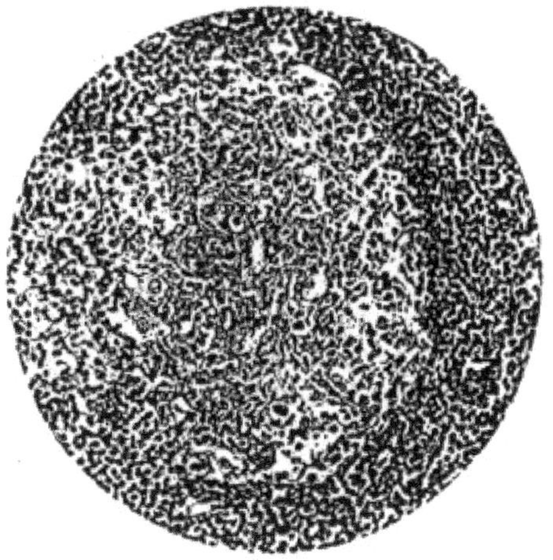

[redacted]

[redacted] 348 x200

([redacted] (

[redacted]

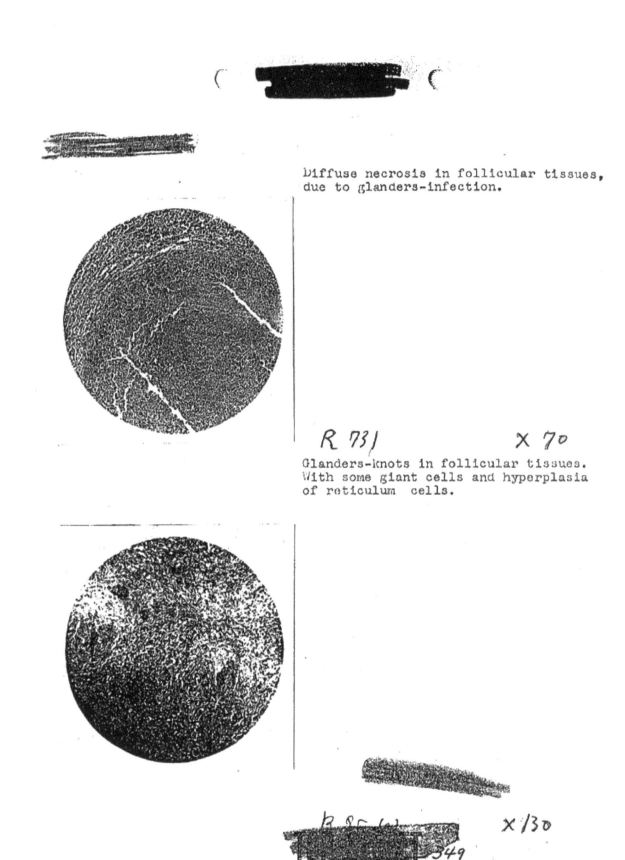

Diffuse necrosis in follicular tissues, due to glanders-infection.

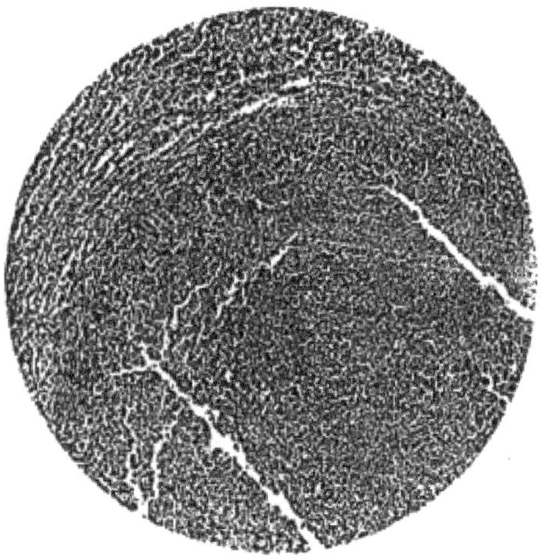

R 731 X 70

Glanders-knots in follicular tissues. With some giant cells and hyperplasia of reticulum cells.

[redacted]

[redacted] X 130

[redacted]

[redacted]

Glanders-knot with some giant cells, in high power.

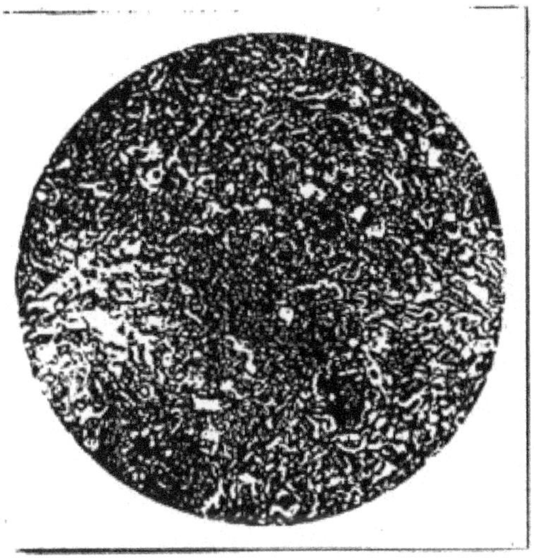

R. 85 (a)　　x 270

Intense edema in follicular tissues.

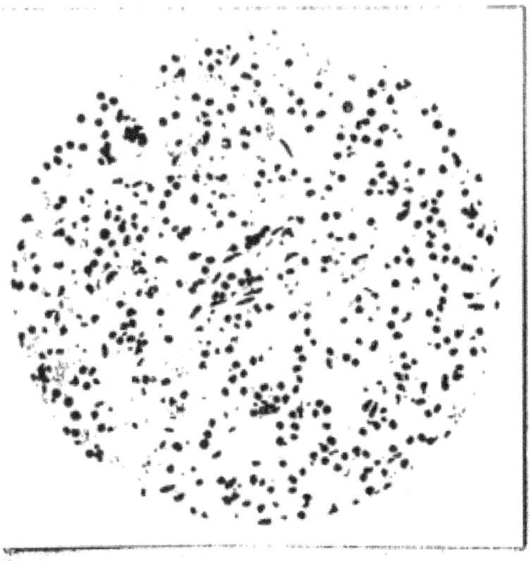

[redacted]

[redacted] 350　　X310

[redacted]

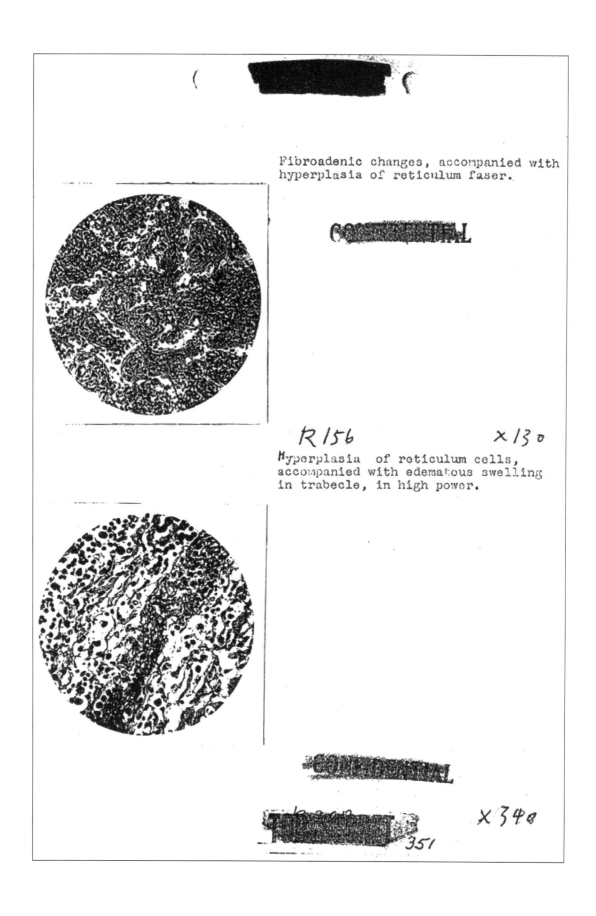

Fibroadenic changes, accompanied with hyperplasia of reticulum faser.

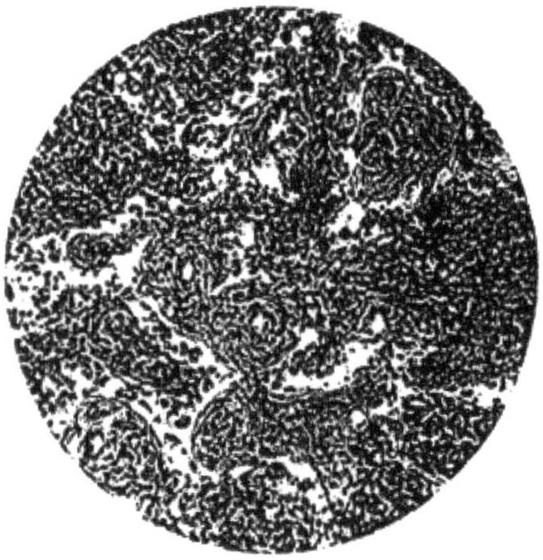

[redacted]

R156 x130

Hyperplasia of reticulum cells, accompanied with edematous swelling in trabecle, in high power.

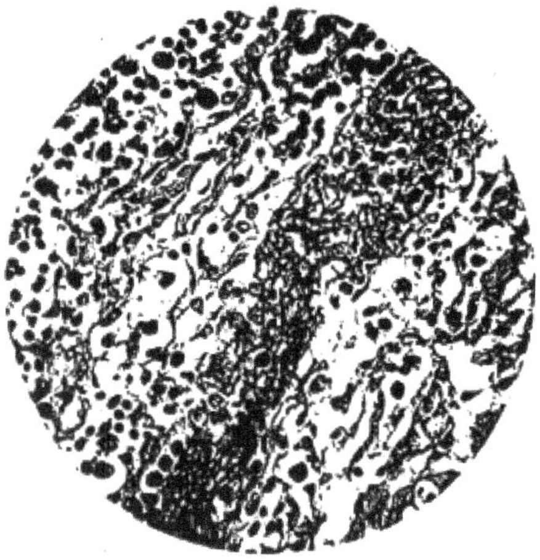

[redacted]

[redacted] 351 x340

[redacted]

Plasma cell reaction.

[redacted]

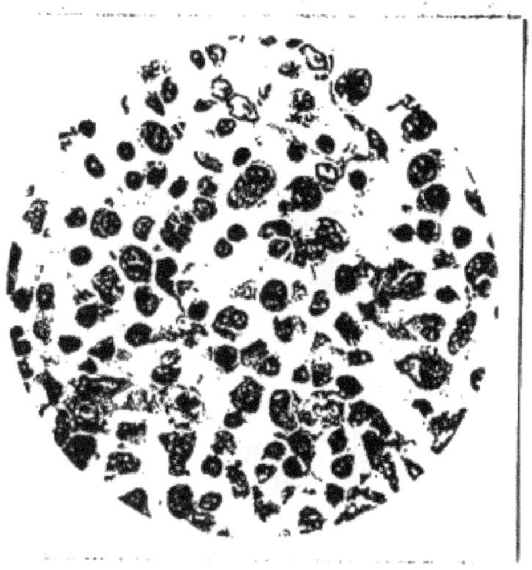

R 207 X730

Plasma cell reaction in capsule.

[redacted]

[redacted] 352 X620

[redacted]

[redacted]

Other Organs

[redacted]

[redacted]

353

([redacted] (

CONFIDENTIAL

MUSCLE.

(A) Microscopical Investigation.

I46. (I)

Multiple supermiliary or millet-corn large abscesses in muscular tissues. In abscess exist a large quantitiy of decayed masses (numerous leucocytes and their fragments, decayed masses of muscular tissues and some erythrocytes).

These abscesses spread to perifocal tissues intermusculously with more or less considerable reactive chagnes (hemorrhages and leucocytes-infiltration).

Muscular tissues at perifocal parts fall into waxy necrosis.

I46. (2)

Multiple miliary or millet-corn large abscesses with the same changes, as above mentioned.

I80. (I)

Multiple supermiliary or millet-corn large abscesses in muscular tissues. In abscess accumulate a large quantity of decayed masses (numerous leucocytes and their fragments, decayed masses of muscular tissues and some erythrocytes) with more or less hemorrhagic perifocal changes.

These hemorrhagic-leucocytic cell-infiltration propagate themselves to the neighbouring tissues intermusculously with somewhat hemorrhagic and leucocytic cell-infiltrations. Muscular tissues at perifocal parts fall into waxy necrosis and fragmentation.

CONFIDENTIAL TOP SECRET 354

([redacted] (

180. (2) [redacted]

Multiple supermiliary or millet-corn large abscesses in muscular tissues, with the same changes as above mentioned.

In the neighbouring tissues exist leucocytic and hemorrhagic proceases: severe edema, fibrinous separation, severe congestion and perivascular leucocytes infiltration.

These leucocytic cell-infiltration spread to the neighbouring tissues with more or less haemorrhagic and leucocytic cell infiltration (in intermuscular tissues exist severe edema, fibrinous separation, severe congestion and perivascular leucocytic cell infiltration).

180. (3)

Multiple millet-corn large abscesses with the same hemorrhagic and leucocytic cell-reactions.

At the margin-part of the abscess, slight increase of histiocytes, esp. at perivascular parts.

These inflammatory infiltration propagate themselves intermusculously with more or less hemorrhagic and leucocytic cell-reactions.

180. (4)

Multiple supermiliary abscesses with the same changes, as above mentioned. In the necrotic places exist yet remained nervous bundles. At the margin of more or less degenerated nervous bundles, slight increase of neuroplasts to form some cell groups.

[redacted] [redacted] 355

([redacted] (

I80. (5) [redacted]

Multiple miliary abscesses with the same changes, as above mentioned.

I80. (6)

Multiple rice-corn-large abscesses with the same changes, as above mentioned.

I80. (7)

Pea-large (I X 0.5 cm) abscess, bounded with thick walls of increased connective tissues more or less sharply.

The most places of abscess are rearranged with a large quantitiy of increased epithelial cells with frothy protoplasma (reparation or purification of abscess with myoblasts) and a little quantitiy of yet remained residual masses of ruined muscular cells and leucocytes.

At the perivascular parts in abscess accumulate some round-cells (lymphocytes and typical plasma-cells) and in the perifocal places of abscess exist a large quantity of increased connective tissuses to form the bounding walls, in which exist muscular cells in various types: some of them in degeneration and some of them in regeneration with increase of nucleus to form frequently giant cells (regeneration of muscle cells).

With perivascular round-cells-infiltration (lymphocytes and plasma-cells).

I80. (7)

0.8 X 0.4cm large abscess with the same changes, as above mentioned.

I80. (8)

0.6 X 0.3cm large abscess with the same changes.

[redacted] [redacted] 356

([redacted] (

254. [redacted]

Multiple poppy seed-large abscesses in muscular tissues.

Hematogenous metastatic abscess in which focal parts exist ruined arterioles with a large quantity of decayed masses of leucocytes as contents and ruined blood-vessel-walls.

Extremly severe leucocytic or necrotic processes at these peri-arteriolar parts with a large quantity of leucocytes and their various fragments, edematous swelling and hemorrhages to form the most parts of abscesses.

These inflammatory changes propagate themselves to the neighbouring tissues with more or less exudative and hemorrhagic reactions (severe edematous swelling, hemorrhages and leucocytes-emigration at perivascular tissues).

256.

Multiple supermiliary or millet-corn large abscesses in muscular tissues.

Hematogenous metastatic abscess with severe hemorrhagic and leucocytic cell-reactions.

In the focal places of abscess exist ruined arterioles with a large quantity of leucocytes and their fragments as contents and severely decayed blood-vessel-walls.

These inflammatory processes propagate themselves to the neighbouring tissues with severe hemorrhagic and leucocytic cell-reactions.

256. (2)

Multiple supermiliary or millet-corn large abscesses in muscular tissues.

[redacted]etastatic absc[redacted]emorrhagic or leucocytic

[redacted] 357

([redacted] (

[redacted]

or leucocytic cell-reactions. In the focal places of abscess exist decayed arterioles with a large quantity of leucocytes and their fragments as contenst and ruined vessel-walls.

Severe leucocytic and necrotic processes at the periarteriolar tissues to form the most parts of absecess.

These inflammatory processes spread to the heighbouring tissues with severe hemorrages and leucocytic cell-reactions.

In the intermuscular tissues: severe edematous swelling, congestion, hemorrhages and perivascular leucocytes-infiltrations.

[redacted] [redacted] 358

([redacted] (

[redacted]

(B) S U M M A R Y .

Miliary, supermiliary or millet-corn large abscesses in oval or irregular forms. These are formed mainly hematogenously from infected wounds.

In the focal places exist frequently decayed arterioles with a large quantity of leucocytes and their various fragments as contents and ruined blood-vessel-walls.

Severe leucocytic and hemorrhagic processes at the periarteriolar parts to form the most parts of abscesses: in abscesses exist extremly a large quantity of basophilic necrotic masses which originate from mainly leucocytes or their fragments in various forms and decayed muscular tissues.

These hemorrhagic and necrotic changes propagate themselves to the neighbouring tissues intermusculously with more or less remarkable exudative-hemorrhagic reactione (severe edema, severe congestion, hemorrhage and leucocytic infiltrations at the perivascular parts of intermuscular connective tissues).

Muscular cells at the perifocal parts fall into waxy necrosis (waxy swelling, disappearance of muscle-striations and fragmentation).

With the lapse of time, it inclines to get some reparative and regenerative processes:

At perifocal intermuscular tissues, slight increase of histiocytes, endothelial cells and adventitial cells. For example, in No. IO, shows it some cell-groups of slightly increased histiocytes at the margin-places of abscesses.

[redacted] [redacted] 359

([redacted] (

[redacted]

Nervous bundles in abscesses fall into also degeneration, but more resistible. At the margin-parts of more or less degenerated nervous bundles, accumulate some neuroplasts to form some cell-groups, so as in No. I0.

In No. I3, abscesses are bounded with the thick walls of increased connective tissues. In abscesses exist, instead of decayed masses, a large quantity of myoblasts which arranged densely cell by cell, to reparate and purify the necrotic places.

In the increased connective tissues, exist some perivascular round-cell-infiltration (lymphocytes and plasma-cells) and muscle cells in various forms: some of them in degeneration and some of them in regeneration with increased nuclear mitosis to form frequently giant cells.

[redacted] [redacted] 360

[redacted]

[redacted]

MUSCLE & ABSCESS

			146	-	180	-	-	-	-	-	-	-	-	254	256	[illegible]
Abscess	Elements	Leucocytic cells	++	++	÷	+	+	+	+	++	++	+÷	(++)	++	+++	++÷
		Lymphocytic cells	+	+	+	+	+	+	÷	÷	+++	+++	+++	÷	÷	÷
		Histiocytic cells	++	++	+	+	++	++	+	+	+	+	+	++	+	+
		Fragments of Nuclei	+++	+++	+++	+++	+++	+++	+++	+++	+	+	÷	+++	+++	+++
		Erythrocyte	++	++	++	++÷	++	++	++	++	+	+	÷	(++)	+	÷
		Giantcell	—	—	—	—	÷	—	—	—	+÷	+	÷	—	—	—
		Amorpheus Substance: acidophilic	÷	÷	+	+	+	+	÷	÷	÷	÷	÷	++	+	÷
		Amorpheus Substance: basophilic	+++	+++	++	++	++	+	+	++	÷	÷	÷	++	++	++
		Fibrin	—	—	—	+	+	+	—	—	—	—	—	+÷	+÷	—
		Rest of destroyed Muscle Fiber	÷	÷	+	+	++	++	—	÷	—	—	—	÷	÷	÷
		Production of Connectiv Tissue	—	—	—	—	—	—	—	—	+++	+++	+++	—	÷	—
Muscular Tissue around Abscess	Muscle Fiber	Disappearance of Striations	+	++	+++	++	+	++	+	+÷	+	+÷	+÷	++	++	++
		Couding	++	++	+++	++	++	++	+	++÷	÷	+÷	+÷	++	++	++
		Swelling	+	+	++	++	(++)	++	+	++	÷	(+÷)	+	÷	++	—
		Atrophia	÷	÷	÷	÷	(+)	÷	÷	÷	++	++	++	++÷	+	+++
		Hyaline Degeneration	÷	+	+	÷	÷	÷	—	+	—	—	—	—	+	÷
		Waxy Necrosis	÷	÷	÷	÷	—	—	—	÷	—	—	—	—	—	—
		Cloddy Decay	+	÷	÷	++÷	÷	÷	+	÷	—	—	—	—	÷	+
		Increase of Nuclei of Muscle Fiber	÷	÷	+	+	+	—	—	—	+	÷	÷	÷	—	+
	Interstitium	Edema	÷	÷	÷	+	+	÷	÷	+	+	+	++	+	+	++
		Hemorrhage	+÷	+÷	÷	+	+	+	÷	÷	—	—	÷	+++	+++	+++
		Contents of Blood vessels: Erythrocytes	++	++	+	+	+	+	+	+	÷	÷	+	++	÷	+
		Contents of Blood vessels: Leucocytes	÷	+	—	÷	÷	÷	÷	÷	—	÷	—	(++)	+	+++
		Contents of Blood vessels: Lymphocytes	÷	÷	÷	÷	÷	÷	+	÷	(+)	÷	—	÷	—	÷
		Contents of Blood vessels: Monocytes	÷	+	÷	(+÷)	++	÷	++	÷	(+)	÷	—	(÷)	—	+
		Endothelium of Bloodvessels: Swelling	+	+	—	(÷)	—	÷	—	÷	(÷)	÷	—	÷	—	+
		Endothelium of Bloodvessels: Desquamation	÷	—	—	—	—	—	—	—	—	—	—	—	÷	—
		Endothelium of Bloodvessels: Hyperplasia	÷	÷	÷	(÷)	—	—	÷	(÷)	÷	÷	—	÷	—	÷
		Infiltration of Small Round Cells	÷	+	÷	÷	÷	÷	÷	÷	+++	+++	+++	÷	÷	+
		Infiltration of Leucocytes	(++)	(++)	÷	÷	—	—	÷	÷	÷	—	÷	÷	÷	+
		Prlt. of Fibro-histiocytic Cells	(++)	(++)	÷	÷	÷	÷	+	÷	+	÷	+	+	+	++÷
		Prlf. of Adventitial Cells	+	+	÷	+	÷	÷	++	÷	+	÷	÷	+	÷	÷

[redacted] [redacted] 361

[redacted]

Muscular abscess with intense
leucocytic-necrotic changes at
perivascular portion.

[redacted]

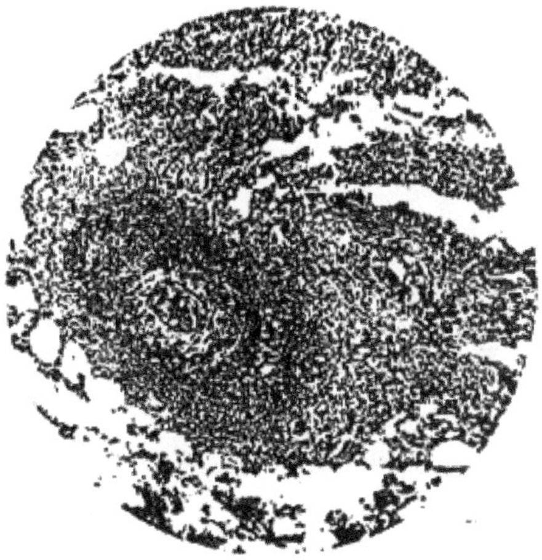

№ 180. (×100)

Diffuse muscular abscess.

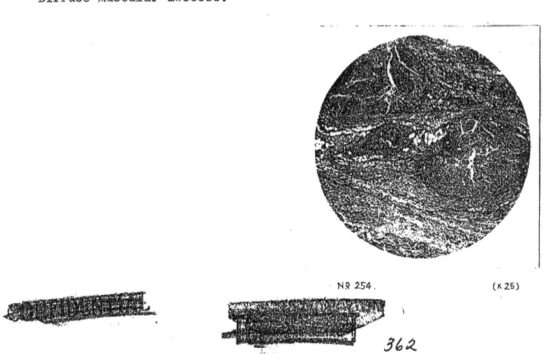

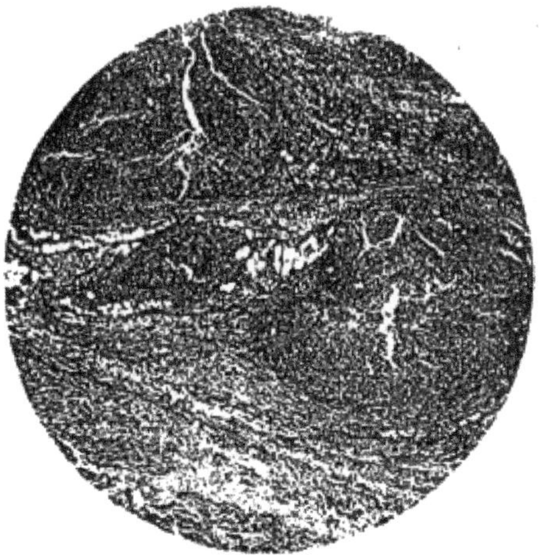

№ 254. (×25)

[redacted] [redacted]

362

([redacted])

Muscular abscess,accompanied with hemorrhages in degenerated nervous bundle.

[redacted]

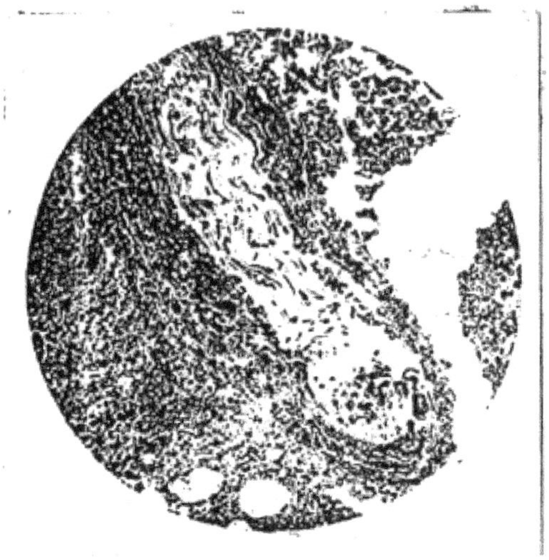

№ 180. (×160)

[redacted] [redacted] 363

[redacted]

[redacted]

Metastatic millet-corn large
muscular abscess.

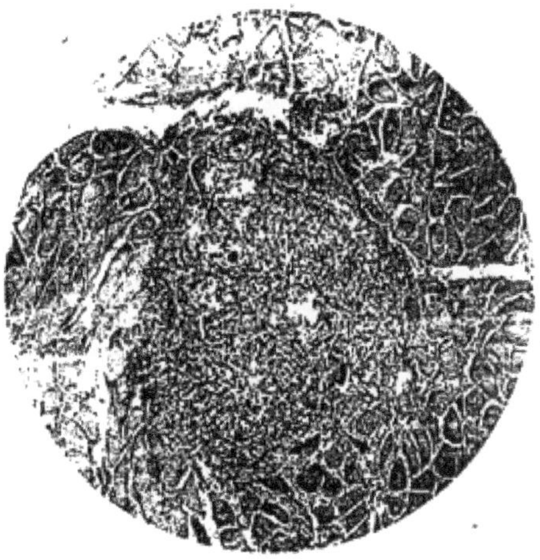

Nº 180 (×60)

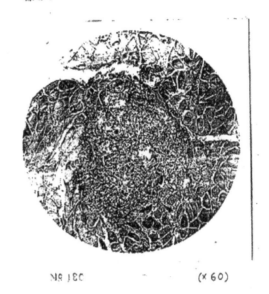

Increase of nuclei of muscular cells.

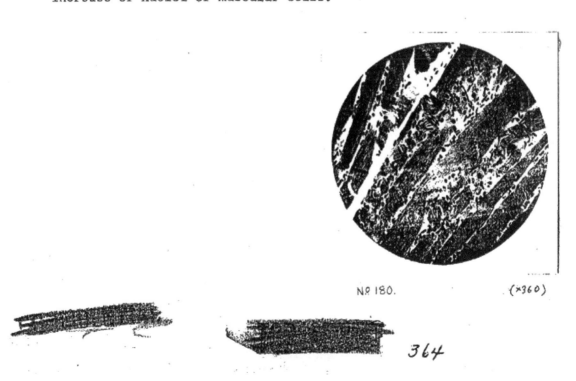

Nº 180. (×360)

[redacted] [redacted] 364

([redacted] (

[redacted]

Muscular abscess, accompanied with some increased myoblast and some plasma cells.

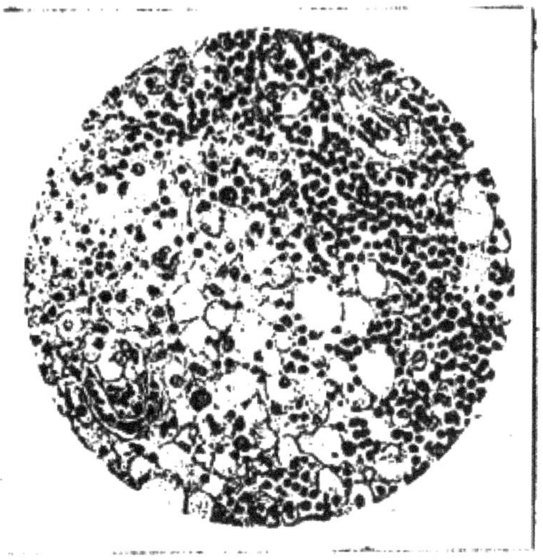

№ 180 (× 260)

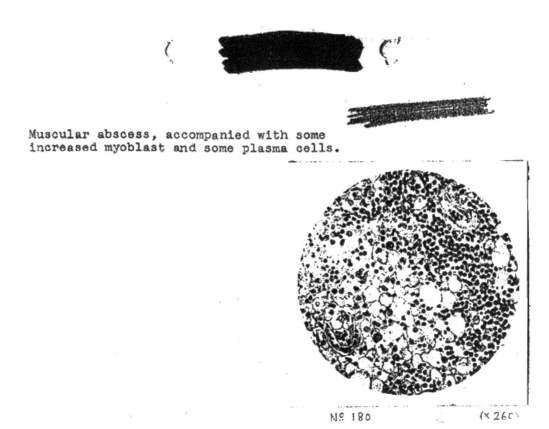

Muscular abscess at the margin portion, accompanied with some increased histiocytes andsome giant cells.(reparative process).

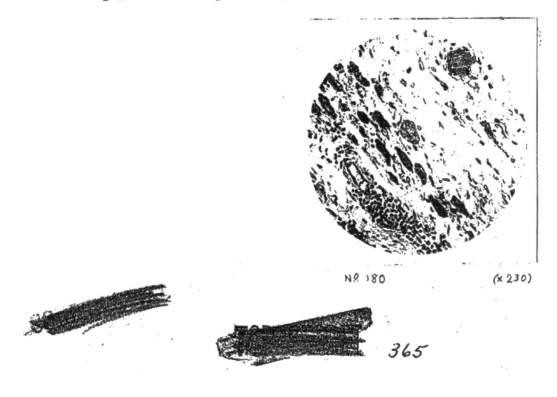

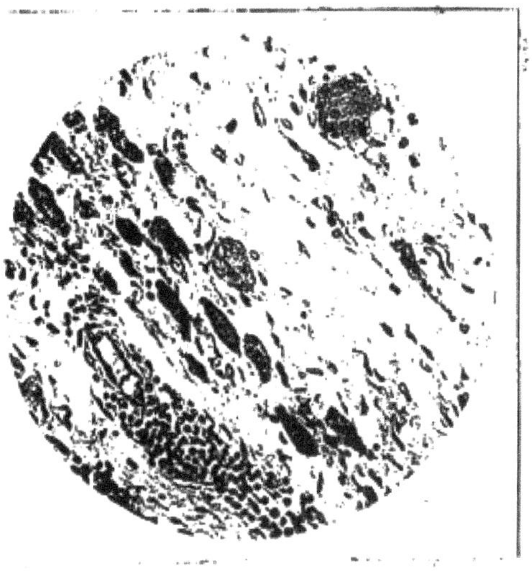

№ 180 (× 230)

[redacted] [redacted] 365

([redacted] (

[redacted]

B R A I N

(A) Microscop. Investigation.

I46.

Meniges : moderate congestion, edema and slight diffuse hemorrhages. Perivascular round-cell-infiltration.

Brain: Moderate congestion and edematous swelling of capillary-walls; slight perivascular edema, slight degeneration of ganglion cells and very slight hyperplasia of glia cells.

I52.

The same, but with more slighter changes than in No.I46-cases.

I67.

Meniges : moderate congestion, edema and slight hemorrhages. Perivascular round-celll-infiltration.

Brain : congestion and very slight hyperplasia of glia cells.

I78.

Meninges:Moderate congestion, edema and perivascular round-cell-infilt-ration.

Brain:moderate congestion, slight perivascular edema, slight degeneration of ganglion cells and very slight hyperplasia of glia cells.

I90.

Meninges : moderate congestion ,edema and slight hemorrhages. Considera-ble perivascular round-cell-infiltration.

[redacted] [redacted] 366

([redacted] (

[redacted]

Brain : moderate congestion and perivascular edema, slight degeneration of ganglion cells and very slight hyperplasia of glia cells.

I93. 22I. 222.

The same changes as above mentioned, but more slighter.

229. Almost normal. Slight stasis.

727. Almost normal. Slight stasis.

73I. Almost normal. Slight stasis.

Cerebellum 229. Almost normal. Slight stasis.

Summary :

[redacted]

[redacted] 367

([redacted] (

[redacted]

(B) S U M M A R Y.

Meninges : generally slight congestion, slight perivascular edema and sometimes slight hemorrhages.

Brain : generally slight congestion, slight perivascular edema and very slight hyperplasia of glia cells.

[redacted] [redacted] 368

[redacted]

[redacted]

UNCLASSIFIED

A O R T A.

152.

178.

221.

256.

No remarkable changes.

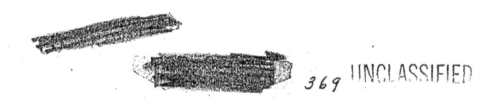

[redacted]

[redacted] 369 UNCLASSIFIED

([redacted] [redacted] (

[redacted]

UNCLASSIFIED

T H Y M U S.

(A) Microscop. Investigation.

I6.

Generally atrophic lobulus (physiological involution) with considerable decrease of lymphocytes in cortical tissues. Some reticulum-cells fall into pycnosis.

Generally Hassall's corpuscles are regressive · many caseous corpuscles and some of them in softening or lithiasis.

Intense edema in medullary and cortical tissues.

85.

Remarkable atrophia of lobulus, resulting in the trabecular arrangements.

Generally with some regressive Hassall's corpuscles (some of them in hyalinous corpuscles).

Some islet-likely regenerated medullat in parenchymatous tissues, consisted of some swollen reticulum-cells.

Thickening of blood-vessels-walls, with some perivascular edema and some epitheloid cells accumulations.

[redacted] [redacted] 370 UNCLASSIFIED

([redacted])

[redacted]

P H A R Y N X.

(A) Microscopical. Investigation.

UNCLASSIFIED

I52.

Slight round-cell-infiltration in mucous tissues and no remarkable changes else.

I78.

Swelling and roughness of all tissues layers, due to intense edema. Deciducous desquamation of epithel cells and some hyalinisation of T. muscularis.

I80.

Slight congestion and slight edema.

Slight round-cell-infiltration along the efferent ducts of glands.

No remarkable changes else.

I90.

Slight serous and cellular infiltration in mucous tissues, and roughness of connectine tissues.

Some increased lymph-nodulus with germinative centres, esp. along the effernt ducts of glands.

I93.

Some round-cell-infiltration in submucous tissues and invading of some lymphocytes into epitheliums of mucous membrane and glands.

[redacted]

[redacted] UNCLASSIFIED

371

[redacted]

[redacted]

UNCLASSIFIED

A P P E N D I X.

Prostate I76.

Slight round cell infiltration in interstitium with some corpora amylacea in acinuses. No changes else.

Urinary bladder 22I.

Slight submucous congestion, slight edema and slight proliferation of adventitial cells, No remarkable changes else.

Seminal vesicle I90.

No remarkable change, except slight edema in muscularis.

Spermatic cord 222.

Considerable congestion with slight haemorrhage in interstice, Slight edema and slight round-cell-infiltration.

Regraded ______ by
authority of ______
by ______, on ______

UNCLASSIFIED [redacted]

[redacted]

372